Taking Sides: Clashing Views in Crime and Criminology, 12/e
Thomas J. Hickey

http://create.mheducation.com

ISBN-10: 1259670627   ISBN-13: 9781259670626

Contents

Detailed Table of Contents

Unit 1: Explanations of Crime

Is Crime Beneficial to Society?
Yes: Emile Durkheim, from "The Normal and the Pathological," The Free Press (1938)
No: Daniel Patrick Moynihan, from "Defining Deviancy Down," *The American Scholar* (1993)

Classic sociologist Emile Durkheim (1858 – 1917) theorizes that crime reaffirms moral boundaries and helps bring about needed social changes. Former U.S. Senator Daniel Patrick Moynihan (D-New York) argues that modern crime has gone way beyond the point of being functional.

Is Criminal Behavior Determined Biologically?
Yes: Adrian Raine, from "The Biological Basis of Crime," Institute for Contemporary Studies Press (2002)
No: Sean Maddan, from "Criminological Explanations of Crime," Original Work (2016)

Adrian Raine argues that one of the principal reasons why we have been so unsuccessful in preventing adult crime is because crime control policies have systematically ignored the biological sides of human behavior. Professor Sean Maddan asserts that social forces create the conditions that become sources of crime in American society.

Does a "Warrior Gene" Make People More Prone to Violence?
Yes: Kevin M. Beaver and Joseph A. Schwartz, adapted from "MAOA Genotype Contributes to Violent and Criminal Behaviors," *Comprehensive Psychiatry* (2010)
No: Joshua W. Buckholtz, from "Neuroprediction and Crime," *NOVA ScienceNOW* (2012)

Professors Kevin M. Beaver and Joseph A. Schwartz argue that a "Warrior Gene" has been demonstrated to be related to aggressive and violent behavior. In fact, humans with a low-activity form of the MAOA gene are much more prevalent in populations with a history of warfare. These individuals are also more likely to join gangs and to use weapons in committing crimes than other persons. Professor Joshua W. Buckholtz, in contrast, asserts that the "Warrior Gene" theory has as much power to explain and predict the actions of an individual as a deck of tarot cards. Moreover, he believes that although genes may be able to influence our behavior, the environment in which we live influences our genes as well.

Unit 2: Contemporary Public Policy Issues in Criminology and Criminal Justice

Are "Stand Your Ground" Laws an Effective Way to Stop Violent Crime?
Yes: Jorge Amselle, from "Why We Need 'Stand Your Ground' Laws," *The Daily Caller* (2014)
No: James Beckman, from "The Problem with Stand Your Ground Laws: A Proven Detriment to Public Safety," Original Work (2016)

Writer and firearms instructor Jorge Amselle asserts that "stand your ground" laws are needed for self-defense in the United States. Such laws provide those who use weapons for self-defense and defense of personal property with an effective legal defense in these cases. Professor and author James A. Beckman, in contrast, argues that "stand your ground laws" are an anachronism in modern society. Moreover, Beckman believes that these laws encourage situations wherein individuals will choose to escalate potentially violent encounters rather than diffusing them.

Is Racial Profiling an Acceptable Law Enforcement Strategy?
Yes: Jared Taylor and Glayde Whitney, from "Racial Profiling: Is There an Empirical Basis?" *Mankind Quarterly* (2002)
No: Michael J. Lynch, from "Misleading 'Evidence' and the Misguided Attempt to Generate Racial Profiles of Criminals; Correcting Fallacies and Calculations Concerning Race and Crime in Taylor and Whitney's Analysis of Racial Profiling," *Mankind Quarterly* (2002)

Jared Taylor, president of the New Century Foundation, and Glayde Whitney argue that the disparity in crimes committed by members of different races justifies racial profiling by the police. Professor Michael J. Lynch, however, argues that a proper analysis of the crime data does not support Taylor and Whitney's conclusions. He finds racial profiling to be objectionable from a legal and moral perspective as well.

Should Juvenile Courts Be Abolished?
Yes: Barry C. Feld, from "Juvenile Justice in Minnesota: Framework for the Future," *Council on Crime and Justice* (2007)
No: Vincent Schiraldi and Jason Ziedenberg, from "The Florida Experiment: An Analysis of the Impact of Granting Prosecutors Discretion to Try Juveniles As Adults," The Justice Policy Institute (1999)

Law professor Barry C. Feld contends that creating a separate juvenile court system has resulted in unanticipated negative consequences for America's children and for justice. Vincent Schiraldi, director of the Justice Policy Institute, and researcher Jason Ziedenberg, maintain that moving thousands of kids into adult courts is unnecessary, harmful, and racist.

Is Exposure to Pornography Related to Increased Rates of Rape?
Yes: Diana E.H. Russell, from "Pornography as a Cause of Rape," *dianarussell.com* (2004)
No: Anthony D'Amato, from "Porn Up, Rape Down," *Northwestern Public Law Research Paper* No. 913013 (2006)

Diana E.H. Russell argues that the evidence is overwhelming that exposure to pornography is a major causal factor of rape. She utilizes the concept of "multiple causation" to explain the relationship between pornography and rape. Anthony D'Amato contends that the incidence of rape has declined 85 percent in the last 25 years while access to pornography via the Internet has become more widely available to teenagers and adults.

Does the United States Have a Right to Torture Suspected Terrorists?
Yes: Andrew A. Moher, from "The Lesser of Two Evils? An Argument for Judicially Sanctioned Torture in a Post–9/11 World," *Thomas Jefferson Law Review* (2004)
No: Elisa Massimino, from "Leading by Example? U.S. Interrogation of Prisoners in the War on Terror," *Criminal Justice Ethics* (2004)

Attorney Andrew A. Moher argues that judicially sanctioned torture of terrorists is appropriate for the purpose of preventing a greater evil. He further contends a judicially monitored system in the United States would be far superior to the current policy of practicing torture "under the radar screen" in other countries. Elisa Massimino believes that the use of torture is immoral and counterproductive for the United States. She asserts that if the United States wishes to rely on the protections of the Geneva Conventions, then it must comply with its provisions prohibiting the torture of prisoners.

Should It Be a Hate Crime to Display the Confederate Flag?
Yes: Ta-Nehisi Coates, from "Take Down the Confederate Flag—Now," *The Atlantic* (2015)
No: Alberto R. Gonzales, from "The Confederate Flag and Free Speech," *The Hill* (2015)

Noted author Ta-Nehisi Coates contends that even though the Confederate flag's defenders often claim it represents "heritage not hate," it is a heritage of white supremacy and cowardice and should be banned. Former U.S. Attorney General Alberto R. Gonzales, in contrast, argues that displaying a confederate flag is a form of expression protected by the First Amendment to the U.S. Constitution.

Unit 3: Punishment

Does the Use of Solitary Confinement or "Administrative Segregation" in U.S. Correctional Facilities Constitute Cruel and Unusual Punishment?
Yes: Alison Shames, Jessa Wilcox and Ram Subramanian, from "Solitary Confinement: Common Misconceptions and Emerging Safe Alternatives," Vera Institute of Justice (2015)
No: William Daly, from "Segregation: A Necessary Evil," *CorrectionsOne* (2013)

Alison Shames, Jessa Wilcox and Ram Subramanian from The Vera Institute of Justice contend that solitary confinement produces many unwanted and harmful outcomes—for the mental and physical health of those placed in isolation, for the public safety of the communities to which most will return, and for the corrections budgets of jurisdictions that rely on the practice for facility safety. William Daly, in contrast, argues that correctional administrators need to be proactive in controlling situations, rather than waiting to respond after their lives are endangered. This may include administrative segregation, which is used to isolate those who have been deemed to be disruptive and dangerous.

Unit 4: Trends in Criminology and Criminal Justice

being brought into jails. Associate Justice Stephen Breyer, in contrast, believes that because strip searches involve close observation of the private areas of the body, they constitute a serious invasion of personal privacy and may not be justified in cases involving minor offenses.

Does an Imprisoned Convict Who Claims Innocence Have a Constitutional Right to Access the State's Evidence for DNA Testing?
Yes: John Paul Stevens, from "Dissenting Opinion, *District Attorney's Office v. Osborne*," United States Supreme Court (2009)
No: John Roberts, from "Majority Opinion, *District Attorney's Office v. Osborne*," United States Supreme Court (2009)

Justice John Stevens, in a dissenting opinion in *District Attorney's Office for the Third Judicial District v. Osborne* (2009), contends that a fundamental responsibility to ensure that "justice" has been served requires a state to provide a defendant with postconviction access to DNA evidence. Because it could conclusively establish whether an accused had committed the crime in the first place, this right should be protected by the Fourteenth Amendment's Due Process Clause. Chief Justice John Roberts, writing for the majority opinion in *District Attorney's Office for the Third Judicial District v. Osborne* (2009), held that the U.S. Constitution's Due Process Clause provides no right to postconviction access to DNA evidence because it would take the development of rules and procedures in criminal cases out of the hands of state legislatures and courts.

Preface

But the peculiar evil of silencing the expression of an opinion is that it is robbing the human race, posterity as well as the existing generation—those who dissent from the opinion, still more than those who hold it. If the opinion is right, they are deprived of the opportunity of exchanging error for truth; if wrong, they lose, what is almost as great a benefit, the clearer perception and livelier impression of truth produced by its collision with error.

—(John Stuart Mill, *On Liberty,* 1859).

Discussion and debate are essential components of the learning process. To have confidence in our viewpoints, we must expose them to others and learn from their ideas in a constant process of reformulation and refinement. As J. S. Mill teaches, only rarely does any point of view present a complete version of the truth; however, we move closer to the truth when we are willing to exchange our opinions with others, defend our positions, and refine our ideas by what we learn from an intellectual opponent.

This book presents students and teachers with an opportunity to exchange viewpoints by focusing on a series of controversial issues in crime and criminology. Few issues in modern society generate more substantial disagreement in our morning newspapers or around the dinner table. They focus on an important aspect of modern life and were selected in an effort to engage students. Hopefully, they will also generate classroom discussion and debate and provide a vehicle for interactive learning.

Many of the topics presented in this volume are hotly contested. Few reflective people will find themselves adopting truly neutral positions on these issues and there may be a tendency to embrace one side of a debate without fully considering the opposing arguments. As you read these materials, try to resist that temptation and keep an open mind. For example, if you are a death penalty advocate, think about how you would develop an argument against capital punishment. Even though such an exercise may not change your views, it will provide you with greater insight into the capital punishment debate.

Book Organization

This book considers important issues in crime and criminology and includes articles presented in a pro and con format. The *Introduction* to each issue presents a synopsis

and sets the stage for the *Yes* and *No* debate between the authors. Learning outcomes are identified for each issue and questions are provided for critical thinking and reflection. All issues conclude with a section that asks whether there is common ground between the positions advocated by the authors and provides a listing of both traditional and online resources that may be used to pursue additional research on the topics considered in both selections.

Changes to this edition   This edition of *Taking Sides* continues the tradition of providing a detailed analysis of contemporary issues in Crime and Criminology. Because this field changes so rapidly, however, it is important to reevaluate prior editions to determine if there are issues that have taken on a greater importance. Thus, considerable changes have been made. There are a number of new issues and several of the selections in other issues have been updated to reflect recent developments in law and public policies.

Editor of This Volume

THOMAS J. HICKEY is a professor of Government at State University of New York. He teaches criminology, constitutional law, environmental law, and courses related to American government. He received his PhD from Sam Houston State University and his law degree from the University of Oregon, School of Law. He is a member of the Rhode Island and Pennsylvania Bar Associations. Thomas's current research interests include constitutional issues and civil liberties, governmental crime, and higher education legal issues.

Acknowledgments

I would like to thank several of my friends and colleagues for their help and support: Sue Titus Reid, Rolando del Carmen, Alisa Smith, John Matthews, Trey Williams, Marilyn McShane, and Alex Thomas.

Thomas J. Hickey
State University of New York
(SUNY Cobleskill)

Academic Advisory Board Members

Members of the Academic Advisory Board are instrumental in the final selection of articles for each edition of *Taking Sides*. Their review of articles for content, level, and appropriateness provides critical direction to the editor and staff. We think that you will find their careful consideration well reflected in this volume.

Introduction

The study of human behavior is a fascinating and complex enterprise. Throughout recorded history, people have speculated about the origins and causes of behavior. Early explanations focused on metaphysical forces, such as evil spirits or the devil, which were believed to somehow compel people to act. Later, the philosophers of the Enlightenment, including Jeremy Bentham and Jean Jacques Rosseau, who emphasized the rational nature of human behavior, believed that one's actions were freely chosen.

Based on this important idea, the early classical theorists maintained that crime could be controlled by making punishments associated with criminal behavior more painful than the pleasure that could be derived from the acts. Later, with the emergence of positivism, biological theories of human behavior became popular. Early biological positivists believed that a person's propensity for criminal behavior could be determined with simple measurements of physical features. For example, in the late nineteenth century, Cesare Lombroso, regarded by many as the father of modern criminology, believed that the length of a person's arms and the size of his teeth could indicate a criminal predisposition.

During the 1930s, sociological theories of criminal behavior became prominent in the United States. Theorists of the Chicago School of Sociology emphasized urban social conditions as the primary determinant of criminal behavior. The social policies that emerged from these theories became the driving force behind modern efforts to eradicate poverty, provide children with better educational opportunities, build stronger communities, and create better employment prospects for the poor. In fact, many of the crime control strategies that emerged from the Chicago School of Sociology have become cornerstones of American social policy in the twenty-first century. For example, even politically conservative social programs with attractive slogans such as "No child left behind" proceed directly from the assumption that adverse social conditions, such as those produced by bad schools, broken homes, single-parent families, a lack of parental attachment, and drug abuse, lead directly to antisocial behavior.

Although many U.S. social programs continued to assume a deterministic relationship between adverse social conditions and criminal behavior, a more conservative political climate began to emerge in the early 1970s. One influential criminologist, Robert Martinson, who had evaluated prison rehabilitation programs throughout the United States, concluded that they were largely ineffective. In the aftermath of these findings, as well as the realization that official measures of reported crime rates had increased during this period, conservative criminologists began to embrace a "new," more punitive approach to criminals and a return to the classical approach. This time, classical criminology was repackaged as rational choice theory.

James Q. Wilson, a UCLA political scientist, became one of the primary crusaders for the new classical movement. Wilson believed that regardless of the causes of criminal behavior, society must recognize the fact that "[w]icked people exist." Thus, the only solution is "to set them apart from innocent people."[1] The revised edition of his now-classic 1975 work, *Thinking About Crime*, outlined the foundations of the new classical philosophy:

> [T]he rate of crime is influenced by its costs. It is possible to lower the crime rate by increasing the certainty of sanctions . . . the wisest course of action for society is to try simultaneously to increase both the benefits of non-crime and the costs of crime.[2] . . .

Other prominent criminologists also embraced the new conservative approach to crime prevention. Legal philosopher and penal theorist Andrew von Hirsch developed a model of punishment termed "just deserts," which emphasizes that criminals should be punished simply because they have earned it. Moreover, von Hirsch believes that punishing criminals can have a utilitarian effect: It helps to return society to a condition of equilibrium that is disrupted by crime. In addition, imitating the philosophies of Cesare Beccaria and Jeremy Bentham of the late eighteenth century, von Hirsch asserts that principles of social justice require that all criminals who commit a particular offense should be punished in the same way.

Rational Choices, Irrational Policies?

Has rational choice theory produced irrational social policies? After three decades, the weight of the evidence suggests that it may have. According to some criminologists, the ideas of the new rational choice advocates were converted into draconian and regressive social policies by politicians eager to find reductionist, "sound bite" solutions to criminal behavior. The problem is that some of these policies have had disastrous consequences for the U.S. justice system. For example, during the early part of his presidency, Ronald Reagan, who had embraced James Q. Wilson's new classical criminology, declared a "war on drugs." Since it began, this initiative has emphasized stringent law enforcement, interdiction efforts, and increasing sanctions for drug law violations, including mandatory minimum sentencing policies. The results of these initiatives have been striking: From 1980 to 1997, the number of persons incarcerated for drug offenses has risen by approximately 1040 percent, an 11-fold increase.[3]

More recently, even very conservative social critics such as William F. Buckley, Jr., have questioned the wisdom of this so-called "war on drugs." Stated Buckley:

> What are the relative costs, on the one hand, of medical and psychological treatment for addicts and, on the other incarceration for drug offenses? [T]reatment is seven times more cost-effective. By this is meant that one dollar spent on the treatment of an addict reduces the probability of continued addiction seven times more than one dollar spent on incarceration. . . . [T]he cost of the drug war is many times more painful, in all its manifestations, than would be the licensing of drugs combined with intensive education of non-users and intensive education designed to warn those who experiment with drugs. . . . [I]t is outrageous to live in a society whose laws tolerate sending young people to life in prison because they grew, or distributed, a dozen ounces of marijuana.[4]

Data from a wide variety of sources, including the U.S. Department of Justice, appear to support Buckley's position. According to the Bureau of Justice Statistics, in 2000, 64.4 percent of the inmates confined in U.S. federal prisons and approximately 20.7 percent of those in state prisons were confined for drug law violations.[5] The costs of confining these individuals are a fiscal time bomb. At an average rate of $21,837.95 per inmate per year in the federal prison system, the annual cost to confine the 72,764 incarcerated drug offenders is approximately $1.6 billion.[6] At an average cost of $20,261.15, the price tag to the states for confining drug offenders exceeds $50 billion annually.[7]

A related policy trend has been the passage of "three strikes" sentencing laws, which provide generally that an offender will receive a mandatory life prison sentence upon conviction of a third felony. Such laws are rapidly turning U.S. prisons into expensive retirement homes for an aging inmate population. One study has projected that in 2010, U.S. prisons will confine approximately 200,000 elderly inmates, who will require special treatment and advanced medical care.[8] At an average cost of $75,000 for each elderly inmate, that amounts to a price tag in the neighborhood of $15 billion annually.[9]

Furthermore, the Bureau of Justice Statistics has found that in 2000, persons aged 45 years or older, who comprise approximately 33 percent of the U.S. population, accounted for less than 10 percent of the serious crime arrests.[10] This finding is consistent with virtually all of the credible research that points to a very strong inverse relationship between age and crime. Thus, it makes very little sense to confine elderly inmates in U.S. prisons. In view of these policies, perhaps the new mantra for U.S. corrections will become "Three strikes, we're out of money."

Moreover, the preceding discussion considered only the direct costs of imprisoning large numbers of nonviolent offenders. The indirect costs of confining these individuals may be substantially greater still. According to criminologist Todd Clear, "The removal of offenders who pose no risk to society can deplete valued resources, a particularly costly outcome for already disadvantaged neighborhoods." One must also question the wisdom of nonviolent offender confinement policies that produce single-parent households, financial instability, and social disorganization in many of our nation's poorest neighborhoods. As one of my students has cogently observed, "It's hard to coach your kid's basketball team from the inside of a prison."

Several important questions emerge logically from the preceding analysis: Are we utilizing justice system policies that simply do not work? Are governmental budgets so flush with cash that we can afford to fill our prisons with nonviolent inmates who present little genuine threat to society? Are we wasting our money on failed crime control policies when we could better spend it for providing shelter for homeless families, affordable health care for the poor, or a better education for our children? Are we as a society being sold a "bill of goods" by persons masquerading as experts who have a vested interest in keeping the current system the way it is?

Answers to the preceding questions must emerge from the systematic scientific study of crime and human behavior. Moreover, although there is much that we still have to learn, substantial progress has already been made.

Rational Justice System Policies That Work

Our thinking about crime has often been preoccupied with the idea of "causation." Voluminous research into crime and criminality demonstrates conclusively, however, that social scientists are on much more solid footing when they identify factors that correlate with higher crime rates. For example, while it would be inaccurate to state that "drinking alcohol causes crime" (because not all people who drink alcohol commit crimes), it would be quite accurate to suggest that alcohol consumption correlates with higher crime rates. Moreover, a great deal of solid research suggests that the relationship is a compelling one.

There are other things we know about crime as well, although once again, the relationships are best described as correlations, rather than causes. Although far from exhaustive, the following list of factors that appear to correlate with higher crime rates is instructive:

- Broken homes produce more criminals than two-parent families.
- People learn to commit crime; therefore, many children who are abused by their parents are more likely to become abusive adults.
- Children need a structured home environment in order to develop their full human potential.
- The ingestion of lead paint by children is strongly related to low intelligence and failure in school.
- Substance abuse (including alcohol and illegal drugs) is related to criminal behavior.
- Deteriorated urban areas have higher crime rates.
- African Americans and members of other minority groups are more often arrested and processed in our justice system.
- Women commit less crime than men, but the rate of female offending is increasing.
- Older people commit less crime than young persons.
- People tend to drift in and out of conventional and criminal behavior.
- Areas that have developed a sense of "community" have lower crime rates.
- Some human behavior may have a biological/genetic basis. Punishing such behaviors may be a waste of time and resources.

What we do know about crime and criminality should be used to develop effective social policies. For example, if poor nutrition is related to deficient school performance, policies that provide children from low-income homes with an adequate breakfast make a great deal of sense. Although spending on prisons skyrocketed under the Bush administration, nutritional programs have been gutted. It may be that such "liberal" policies are inconsistent with a conservative ideology stressing "just deserts" and social Darwinism. In the long run, however, providing children with a nutritious breakfast, better schools, and a stronger sense of community affiliation may be far cheaper than incarcerating them in prison for the rest of their lives.

Circularity in Our Study of Crime and Justice—Old Becomes New Once Again

To paraphrase George Santayana, "Those who cannot remember the lessons of history are condemned to repeat it." It is hard to study the history of crime and criminality and fail to notice a striking circularity in criminological theory. To illustrate, the Classical approach, which originated in the late eighteenth century, emphasized free will and a utilitarian approach to punishment. The early classicists also urged the elimination of judicial sentencing discretion, adoption of determinate sentencing laws, and the use of imprisonment as a form of punishment. Rational choice proponents also emphasize free will and a utilitarian approach to punishing criminals. Furthermore, the determinate sentencing laws that have been adopted by many states and the federal government virtually eliminate judicial sentencing discretion.

Just as classical criminology reemerged during the 1970s, biological positivism has reappeared more recently. Although the theories of the nineteenth- and twentieth-century positivists were interesting and novel in their time, their technical ability to measure and quantify their findings in a scientifically accurate way was very limited. At this point in time we may be witnessing the development of a new biological positivism in criminology, one that emphasizes the interaction of genetic and environmental forces to produce human behavior. This time, however, our scientific measurement capabilities may actually have evolved to the point we will be able to draw meaningful conclusions about how biological factors interact with environmental forces to produce human behavior. In fact, we may be at the cutting edge of the emergence of a truly "new criminology," which emphasizes a synthesis of biological and social forces that produce human behavior.

In any case, it is an exciting time to be engaged in the study of criminal behavior. Criminology in the twenty-first century may provide us with the opportunity to learn to creatively manage human behavior in a way that is more consistent with human value and dignity. In the years ahead, criminologists will be called upon to provide honest answers to important policy questions that will have a substantial impact on the quality of life in the United States. We can only hope that those entrusted to develop enlightened social policies based on the answers we provide will learn history's lessons and resist the temptation to embrace politically expedient solutions that will eventually be exposed as expensive policy failures.

Notes

1. James Q. Wilson, *Thinking About Crime,* rev. ed. (Vintage Books, 1983, p. 128).

2. *Ibid.,* p. 143.

3. Center on Juvenile and Criminal Justice Executive Summary, "Poor Prescription: The Costs of Imprisoning Drug Offenders in the United States," (July 2000).

4. William F. Buckley, Jr., "The War on Drugs Is Lost," *The National Review* (July 1, 1996).

5. Bureau of Justice Statistics, *Sourcebook of Criminal Justice Statistics 2001* (U.S. Department of Justice, 2002).

6. George M. Camp and Camille Graham Camp, *The Corrections Yearbook, 1998* (Criminal Justice Institute, 1999).

7. *Ibid.*

8. Herbert J. Hoelter, "Proceedings: Technologies for Successful Aging—Institutional Issues," *Journal of Rehabilitation Research and Development* (vol. 38, no. 1, 2001, p. S38).

9. *Ibid.*

10. *Ibid.,* note 5, at p. 345.

Unit 1

Explanations of Crime

*E*xactly what constitutes crime, what causes it, who commits it, and why crime rates often vary so significantly are core questions for criminologists and social policy makers alike. Even defining what constitutes crime can be a challenging issue. Moreover, is crime necessarily a bad thing for society, or does it provide benefits to everyone? To illustrate, the marijuana laws in many jurisdictions have changed significantly in recent years. Was it because many persons were willing to engage in criminal behavior by using marijuana that these laws were eventually changed? Is the fact that these laws have changed a positive thing for society? One of the authors in this unit contends that crime is both "normal" and "functional" in that it may create a climate wherein the law can evolve to better reflect the values of society. Other issues presented in this section include whether criminal behavior may have biological origins, or whether it is caused by social factors. These are compelling questions.

Selected, Edited, and with Issue Framing Material by:
Thomas J. Hickey, *State University of New York at Cobleskill*

ISSUE

Is Crime Beneficial to Society?

YES: Emile Durkheim, from "The Normal and the Pathological," The Free Press (1938)

NO: Daniel Patrick Moynihan, from "Defining Deviancy Down," *The American Scholar* (1993)

Learning Outcomes
After reading this issue, you will be able to:
• Discuss why crime is an integral part of a healthy society.
• Discuss why crime is "normal."
• Discuss why crime would exist even in a society of saints.
• Discuss why deviant persons provide needed services to society.
• Discuss how crime levels in society become "normalized."

ISSUE SUMMARY

YES: Classic sociologist Emile Durkheim (1858–1917) theorizes that crime reaffirms moral boundaries and helps bring about needed social changes.

NO: Former U.S. Senator Daniel Patrick Moynihan (D-New York) argues that modern crime has gone way beyond the point of being functional.

What is crime? Who commits it? And why? The importance given to these questions, and their answers, varies among different categories of people, although there is little certainty that any one group's meanings and interpretations are superior to those of another. For example, younger and older people have different perceptions of crime (older people are more likely to fear crime, even though younger people are far more likely to be victims of crime). Public officials also disagree about crime. During election years many politicians inflate the number of crimes committed and attribute crime to forces and influences that only the politicians, if elected, can combat.

Criminological and criminal justice scholars, although generally slightly less shrill and self-serving than politicians in their definitions and explanations of crime, are also very likely to disagree among themselves about what crime is and what its causes are. Unlike politicians, they do not follow 4-year cycles in their crime conceptualizations, but they do reflect trends. For example, 20 years

ago most criminologists probably reflected a liberal ideology in their crime explanations and suggested treatments. Today some are more likely to reflect an ideologically conservative scholarly bias. Radical or Marxist criminologists continue to have a marginal position within the discipline.

The seminal essay by Emile Durkheim, excerpted in the YES selection, argues that deviancy, including crime, is functional and exists in all societies because it is needed to establish moral boundaries and to distinguish between those who obey and those who disobey society's rules. Although it was written almost 100 years ago, Durkheim's original structural or sociological approach continues to be relied on by criminological and criminal justice scholars.

There are, of course, many variants of the sociological approach to crime, its definitions, and its causes. However, Durkheim's approach is central for many criminologists and especially *structural functionalists*. Structural functionalists attempt to determine what patterns of interaction or structures exist in various groups. They investigate what these patterns contribute to the maintenance of a group and of the society to which the group belongs. In the United States, for example, dating patterns and their relation to marriage are studied. Marriage patterns and their relation to the economy, to religion, and so on are traced. In addition, structural functionalists want to know about the consequences of patterns of behavior for groups, for members of groups, and for society as a whole. Such consequences can be both positive and negative, and intentional and unintentional.

Durkheim selects a pattern of behavior, in this case deviant acts, and attempts to determine what it contributes to the maintenance of society and what its consequences might be, including intended and unintended ones. Durkheim asserts that crime is functional (not necessarily good and certainly not to be encouraged) and helps to establish moral boundaries. Deviant acts also provide a sense of propriety and a feeling of righteousness for those who do not commit crimes, as they share sentiments of moral indignation about those who do violate society's norms. Durkheim says that crime also allows for a social change. It prevents a society from having too much rigidity and from becoming too slavish in its obedience to norms.

In the NO selection, politician and sociologist Daniel Patrick Moynihan acknowledges his debt to Durkheim and to sociologist Kai T. Erikson, a follower of some of Durkheim's ideas. But he questions the soundness of Durkheim's contention that crime is functional for societies, especially in the context of violence-ridden 1990s' America. Moynihan argues that on the one hand, certain classes of relatively harmless behavior are nowadays being defined as deviant, if not criminal (dysfunctional contraction of moral boundaries). On the other hand, and far more serious to Moynihan, moral boundaries are becoming too elastic as society expands its tolerance for serious crime. He asks, how can deviancy be said to be functional if citizens are no longer shocked by outrageous violence?

As you read the YES and NO selections by Durkheim and Moynihan, respectively, consider examples from your life in which a type of deviancy might be functional or an act that might have been viewed as criminal a generation ago is no longer viewed that way. In addition, what types of acts do you tolerate today that would have been morally outrageous to your grandparents? Have society's legal and ethical boundaries become "too elastic"?

YES ↵

Emile Durkheim

The Normal and the Pathological

Crime is present not only in the majority of societies of one particular species but in all societies of all types. There is no society that is not confronted with the problem of criminality. Its form changes; the acts thus characterized are not the same everywhere; but, everywhere and always, there have been men who have behaved in such a way as to draw upon themselves penal repression. If, in proportion as societies pass from the lower to the higher types, the rate of criminality, i.e., the relation between the yearly number of crimes and the population, tended to decline, it might be believed that crime, while still normal, is tending to lose this character of normality. But we have no reason to believe that such a regression is substantiated. Many facts would seem rather to indicate a movement in the opposite direction. From the beginning of the [nineteenth] century, statistics enable us to follow the course of criminality. It has everywhere increased. In France the increase is nearly 300 percent. There is, then, no phenomenon that presents more indisputably all the symptoms of normality, since it appears closely connected with the conditions of all collective life. To make of crime a form of social morbidity would be to admit that morbidity is not something accidental, but, on the contrary, that in certain cases it grows out of the fundamental constitution of the living organism; it would result in wiping out all distinction between the physiological and the pathological. No doubt it is possible that crime itself will have abnormal forms, as, for example, when its rate is unusually high. This excess is, indeed, undoubtedly morbid in nature. What is normal, simply, is the existence of criminality, provided that it attains and does not exceed, for each social type, a certain level, which it is perhaps not impossible to fix in conformity with the preceding rules.[1]

Here we are, then, in the presence of a conclusion in appearance quite paradoxical. Let us make no mistake. To classify crime among the phenomena of normal sociology is not to say merely that it is an inevitable, although regrettable phenomenon, due to the incorrigible wickedness of men; it is to affirm that it is a factor in public health, an integral part of all healthy societies. This result is, at first glance, surprising enough to have puzzled even ourselves for a long time. Once this first surprise has been overcome, however, it is not difficult to find reasons explaining this normality and at the same time confirming it.

In the first place crime is normal because a society exempt from it is utterly impossible. Crime, we have shown elsewhere, consists of an act that offends certain very strong collective sentiments. In a society in which criminal acts are no longer committed, the sentiments they offend would have to be found without exception in all individual consciousnesses, and they must be found to exist with the same degree as sentiments contrary to them. Assuming that this condition could actually be realized, crime would not thereby disappear; it would only change its form, for the very cause which would thus dry up the sources of criminality would immediately open up new ones.

Indeed, for the collective sentiments which are protected by the penal law of a people at a specified moment of its history to take possession of the public conscience or for them to acquire a stronger hold where they have an insufficient grip, they must acquire an intensity greater than that which they had hitherto had. The community as a whole must experience them more vividly, for it can acquire from no other source the greater force necessary to control these individuals who formerly were the most refractory. For murderers to disappear, the horror of bloodshed must become greater in those social strata from which murderers are recruited; but, first it must become greater throughout the entire society. Moreover, the very absence of crime would directly contribute to produce this horror; because any sentiment seems much more respectable when it is always and uniformly respected.

One easily overlooks the consideration that these strong states of the common consciousness cannot be thus reinforced without reinforcing at the same time the more feeble states, whose violation previously gave birth to mere infraction of convention—since the weaker ones are only the prolongation, the attenuated form, of the stronger. Thus robbery and simple bad taste injure the same single altruistic sentiment, the respect for that which is another's. However, this same sentiment is less grievously offended by bad taste than by robbery; and since, in addition, the average consciousness had not sufficient intensity to react keenly to the bad taste, it is treated with greater tolerance. That is why the person guilty of bad taste is merely blamed, whereas the thief is punished. But, if this sentiment grows stronger, to the point of silencing in all consciousnesses the inclination which disposes man to steal, he will become more sensitive to the offenses which, until then, touched him but lightly. He will react against them, then, with more energy; they will be the object of greater opprobrium, which will transform certain of them from the simple moral faults that they were and give them the quality of crimes. For example, improper contracts, or contracts improperly executed, which only incur public blame or civil damages, will become offenses in law.

Imagine a society of saints, a perfect cloister of exemplary individuals. Crimes, properly so called, will there be unknown; but faults which appear venial to the layman will create there the same scandal that the ordinary offense does in ordinary consciousnesses. If, then, this society has the power to judge and punish, it will define these acts as criminal and will treat them as such. For the same reason, the perfect and upright man judges his smallest failings with a severity that the majority reserve for acts more truly in the nature of an offense. Formerly, acts of violence against persons were more frequent than they are today, because respect for individual dignity was less strong. As this has increased, these crimes have become more rare; and also, many acts violating this sentiment have been introduced into the penal law which were not included there in primitive times.[2]

In order to exhaust all the hypotheses logically possible, it will perhaps be asked why this unanimity does not extend to all collective sentiments without exception. Why should not even the most feeble sentiment gather enough energy to prevent all dissent? The moral consciousness of the society would be present in its entirety in all the individuals, with a vitality sufficient to prevent all acts offending it—the purely conventional faults as well as the crimes. But a uniformity so universal and absolute is utterly impossible; for the immediate physical milieu in which each one of us is placed, the hereditary antecedents, and the social influences vary from one individual to the next, and consequently diversify consciousnesses. It is impossible for all to be alike, if only because each one has his own organism and that these organisms occupy different areas in space. That is why, even among the lower peoples, where individual originality is very little developed, it nevertheless does exist.

Thus, since there cannot be a society in which the individuals do not differ more or less from the collective type, it is also inevitable that, among these divergences, there are some with a criminal character. What confers this character upon them is not the intrinsic quality of a given act but that definition which the collective conscience lends them. If the collective conscience is stronger, if it has enough authority practically to suppress these divergences, it will also be more sensitive, more exacting; and, reacting against the slightest deviations with the energy it otherwise displays only against more considerable infractions, it will attribute to them the same gravity as formerly to crimes. In other words, it will designate them as criminal.

Crime is, then, necessary; it is bound up with fundamental conditions of all social life, and by that very fact it is useful, because these conditions of which it is a part are themselves indispensable to the normal evolution of morality and law.

Indeed, it is no longer possible today to dispute the fact that law and morality vary from one social type to the next, nor that they change within the same type if the conditions of life are modified. But, in order that these transformations may be possible, the collective sentiments at the basis of morality must not be hostile to change, and consequently must have but moderate energy. If they were too strong, they would no longer be plastic. Every pattern is an obstacle to new patterns, to the extent that the first pattern is inflexible. The better a structure is articulated, the more it offers a healthy resistance to all modification; and this is equally true of functional, as of anatomical, organization. If there were no crimes, this condition could not have been fulfilled; for such a hypothesis presupposes that collective sentiments have arrived at a degree of intensity unexampled in history. Nothing is good indefinitely and to an unlimited extent. The authority which the moral conscience enjoys must not be excessive; otherwise no one would dare criticize it, and it would too easily congeal into an immutable form. To make progress, individual originality must be able to express itself. In order that the originality of the idealist whose dreams transcend this century may find expression, it is necessary that the originality of the criminal, who is below the level of his time, shall also be possible. One does not occur without the other.

Nor is this all. Aside from this indirect utility, it happens that crime itself plays a useful role in this evolution. Crime implies not only that the way remains open to necessary changes but that in certain cases it directly prepares these changes. Where crime exists, collective sentiments are sufficiently flexible to take on a new form, and crime sometimes helps to determine the form they will take. How many times, indeed, it is only an anticipation of future morality—a step toward what will be! According to Athenian law, Socrates was a criminal, and his condemnation was no more than just. However, his crime, namely, the independence of this thought, rendered a service not only to humanity but to his country. It served to prepare a new morality and faith which the Athenians needed, since the traditions by which they had lived until then were no longer in harmony with the current conditions of life. Nor is the case of Socrates unique; it is reproduced periodically in history. It would never have been possible to establish the freedom of thought we now enjoy if the regulations prohibiting it had not been violated before being solemnly abrogated. At that time, however, the violation was a crime, since it was an offense against sentiments still very keen in the average conscience. And yet this crime was useful as a prelude to reforms which daily become more necessary. Liberal philosophy had as its precursors the heretics of all kinds who were justly punished by secular authorities during the entire course of the Middle Ages and until the eve of modern times.

From this point of view the fundamental facts of criminality present themselves to us in an entirely new light. Contrary to current ideas, the criminal no longer seems a totally unsociable being, a sort of parasitic element, a strange and unassimilable body, introduced into the midst of society.[3] On the contrary, he plays a definite role in social life. Crime, for its part, must no longer be conceived as an evil that cannot be too much suppressed. There is no occasion for self-congratulation when the crime rate drops noticeably below the average level, for we may be certain that this apparent progress is associated with some social disorder. Thus, the number of assault cases never falls so low as in times of want.[4] With the drop in the crime rate, and as a reaction to it, comes a revision,

or the need of a revision in the theory of punishment. If, indeed, crime is a disease, its punishment is its remedy and cannot be otherwise conceived; thus, all the discussions it arouses bear on the point of determining what the punishment must be in order to fulfil this role of remedy. If crime is not pathological at all, the object of punishment cannot be to cure it, and its true function must be sought elsewhere.

Notes

1. From the fact that crime is a phenomenon of normal sociology, it does not follow that the criminal is an individual normally constituted from the biological and psychological points of view. The two questions are independent of each other. This independence will be better understood when we have shown, later on, the difference between psychological and sociological facts.

2. Calumny, insults, slander, fraud, etc.

3. We have ourselves committed the error of speaking thus of the criminal, because of a failure to apply our rule (*Division du travail social*, pp. 395–96).

4. Although crime is a fact of normal sociology, it does not follow that we must not abhor it. Pain itself has nothing desirable about it; the individual dislikes it as society does crime, and yet it is a function of normal physiology. Not only is it necessarily derived from the very constitution of every living organism, but it plays a useful role in life, for which reason it cannot be replaced. It would, then, be a singular distortion of our thought to present it as an apology for crime. We would not even think of protesting against such an interpretation, did we not know to what strange accusations and misunderstandings one exposes oneself when one undertakes to study moral facts objectively and to speak of them in a different language from that of the layman.

Emile Durkheim (1858–1917) was a French sociologist and one of the founders and leading figures of modern sociology. He was a professor of philosophy at the University of Bordeaux.

Daniel Patrick Moynihan  **NO**

Defining Deviancy Down

In one of the founding texts of sociology, *The Rules of Sociological Method* (1895), Emile Durkheim set it down that "crime is normal." "It is," he wrote, "completely impossible for any society entirely free of it to exist." By defining what is deviant, we are enabled to know what is not, and hence to live by shared standards. . . . Durkheim writes:

> From this viewpoint the fundamental facts of criminology appear to us in an entirely new light. . . . [T]he criminal no longer appears as an utterly unsociable creature, a sort of parasitic element, a foreign, inassimilable body introduced into the bosom of society. He plays a normal role in social life. For its part, crime must no longer be conceived of as an evil which cannot be circumscribed closely enough. Far from there being cause for congratulation when it drops too noticeably below the normal level, this apparent progress assuredly coincides with and is linked to some social disturbance.

Durkheim suggests, for example, that "in times of scarcity" crimes of assault drop off. He does not imply that we ought to approve of crime—"[p]ain has likewise nothing desirable about it"—but we need to understand its function. He saw religion, in the sociologist Randall Collins's terms, as "fundamentally a set of ceremonial actions, assembling the group, heightening its emotions, and focusing its members on symbols of their common belongingness." In this context "a punishment ceremony creates social solidarity."

The matter was pretty much left at that until seventy years later when, in 1965, Kai T. Erikson published *Wayward Puritans,* a study of "crime rates" in the Massachusetts Bay Colony. The plan behind the book, as Erikson put it, was "to test [Durkheim's] notion that the number of deviant offenders a community can afford to recognize is likely to remain stable over time." The notion proved out very well indeed. Despite occasional crime waves, as when itinerant Quakers refused to take off their hats in the presence of magistrates, the amount of deviance in this corner of seventeenth-century New England fitted nicely with the supply of stocks and shipping posts. Erikson remarks:

> It is one of the arguments of the . . . study that the amount of deviation a community encounters is apt to remain fairly constant over time. To start at the beginning, it is a simple logistic fact that the number of deviancies which come to a community's attention are limited by the kinds of equipment it uses to detect and handle them, and to that extent the rate of deviation found in a community is at least in part a function of the size and complexity of its social control apparatus. A community's capacity for handling deviance, let us say, can be roughly estimated by counting its prison cells and hospital beds, its policemen and psychiatrists, its courts and clinics. Most communities, it would seem, operate with the expectation that a relatively constant number of control agents is necessary to cope with a relatively constant number of offenders. The amount of men, money, and material assigned by society to "do something" about deviant behavior does not vary appreciably over time, and the implicit logic which governs the community's efforts to man a police force or maintain suitable facilities for the mentally ill seems to be that there is a fairly stable quota of trouble which should be anticipated.
>
> In this sense, the agencies of control often seem to define their job as that of keeping deviance within bounds rather than that of obliterating it altogether. Many judges, for example, assume that severe punishments are a greater deterrent to crime than moderate ones, and so it is important to note that many of them are apt to impose harder penalties when crime seems to be on the increase and more lenient ones when it does not, almost as if the power of the bench were being used to keep the crime rate from getting out of hand.

Erikson was taking issue with what he described as "a dominant strain in sociological thinking" that took for granted that a well-structured society "is somehow designed to prevent deviant behavior from occurring." In both authors, Durkheim and Erikson, there is an undertone that suggests that, with deviancy, as with most social goods, there is the continuing problem of demand exceeding supply. Durkheim invites us to

> imagine a society of saints, a perfect cloister of exemplary individuals. Crimes, properly so called, will there be unknown; but faults which appear venial to the layman will create there the same scandal that the ordinary offense does in ordinary consciousness. If, then, this society has the power to judge and punish, it will define these acts as criminal and will treat them as such.

Recall Durkheim's comment that there need be no cause for congratulations should the amount of crime drop "too noticeably below the normal level." It would not appear that Durkheim anywhere contemplates the possibility of too much crime. Clearly his theory would have required him to deplore such a development, but the possibility seems never to have occurred to him.

Erikson, writing much later in the twentieth century, contemplates both possibilities. "Deviant persons can be said to supply needed services to society." There is no doubt a tendency for the supply of any needed thing to run short. But he is consistent. There can, he believes, be *too much* of a good thing. Hence "the number of deviant offenders a community can *afford* to recognize is likely to remain stable over time." [My emphasis]

Social scientists are said to be on the lookout for poor fellows getting a bum rap. But here is a theory that clearly implies that there are circumstances in which society will choose *not* to notice behavior that would be otherwise controlled, or disapproved, or even punished.

It appears to me that this is in fact what we in the United States have been doing of late. I proffer the thesis that, over the past generation, since the time Erikson wrote, the amount of deviant behavior in American society has increased beyond the levels the community can "afford to recognize" and that, accordingly, we have been re-defining deviancy so as to exempt much conduct previously stigmatized, and also quietly raising the "normal" level in categories where behavior is now abnormal by any earlier standard. This redefining has evoked fierce resistance from defenders of "old" standards, and accounts for much of the present "cultural war" such as proclaimed by many at the 1992 Republican National Convention.

Let me, then, offer three categories of redefinition in these regards: the *altruistic,* the *opportunistic,* and the *normalizing.*

The first category, the *altruistic,* may be illustrated by the deinstitutionalization movement within the mental health profession that appeared in the 1950s. The second category, the *opportunistic,* sees in the interest group rewards derived from the acceptance of "alternative" family structures. The third category, the *normalizing,* is to be observed in the growing acceptance of unprecedented levels of violent crime. . . .

Our *normalizing* category most directly corresponds to Erikson's proposition that "the number of deviant offenders a community can afford to recognize is likely to remain stable over time." Here we are dealing with the popular psychological notion of "denial." In 1965, having reached the conclusion that there would be a dramatic increase in single-parent families, I reached the further conclusion that this would in turn lead to a dramatic increase in crime. In an article in *America,* I wrote:

> From the wild Irish slums of the 19th century Eastern seaboard to the riot-torn suburbs of Los Angeles, there is one unmistakable lesson in American history: a community that allows a large number of young men to grow up in broken families, dominated by women, never acquiring any stable relationship to male authority, never acquiring any set of rational expectations about the future—that community asks for and gets chaos. Crime, violence, unrest, unrestrained lashing out at the whole social structure—that is not only to be expected; it is very near to inevitable.

The inevitable, as we now know, has come to pass, but here again our response is curiously passive. Crime is a more or less continuous subject of political pronouncement, and from time to time it will be at or near the top of opinion polls as a matter of public concern. But it never gets much further than that. In the words spoken from the bench, Judge Edwin Torres of the New York State Supreme Court, Twelfth Judicial District, described how "the slaughter of the innocent marches unabated: subway riders, bodega owners, cab drivers, babies; in laundromats, at cash machines, on elevators, in hallways." In personal communication, he writes: "This numbness, this near narcoleptic state can diminish the human condition to the level of combat infantrymen, who, in protracted campaigns, can eat their battlefield rations seated on the bodies of the fallen, friend and foe alike. A society that loses its sense of outrage is doomed to extinction." There is no expectation that this will change, nor any efficacious public insistence that it do so. The crime level has been *normalized.*

Consider the St. Valentine's Day Massacre. In 1929 in Chicago during Prohibition, four gangsters killed seven gangsters on February 14. The nation was shocked. The event became legend. It merits not one but two entries in the *World Book Encyclopedia.* I leave it to others to judge, but it would appear that the society in the 1920s was simply not willing to put up with this degree of deviancy. In the end, the Constitution was amended, and Prohibition, which lay behind so much gangster violence, ended.

In recent years, again in the context of illegal traffic in controlled substances, this form of murder has returned. But it has done so at a level that induces denial. James Q. Wilson comments that Los Angeles has the equivalent of a St. Valentine's Day Massacre every weekend. Even the most ghastly reenactments of such human slaughter produce only moderate responses. On the morning after the close of the Democratic National Convention in New York City in July, there was such an account in the second section of the *New York Times.* It was not a big story; bottom of the page, but with a headline that got your attention. "3 Slain in Bronx Apartment, but a Baby is Saved." A sub-head continued: "A mother's last act was to hide her little girl under the bed." The article described a drug execution; the now-routine blindfolds made from duct tape; a man and a woman and a teenager involved. "Each had been shot once in the head." The police had found them a day later. They also found, under a bed, a three-month-old baby, dehydrated but alive. A lieutenant remarked of the mother, "In her last dying act she protected her baby. She probably knew she was going to die, so she stuffed the baby where she knew it would be safe." But the matter was left there. The police would do their best. But the event passed quickly; forgotten by the next day, it will never make *World Book.*

Nor is it likely that any great heed will be paid to an uncanny reenactment of the Prohibition drama a few months later, also in the Bronx. The *Times* story, page B3, reported:

9 Men Posing as Police
Are Indicted in 3 Murders
Drug Dealers Were Kidnapped for Ransom

The *Daily News* story, same day, page 17, made it *four* murders, adding nice details about torture techniques. The gang members posed as federal Drug Enforcement Administration agents, real badges and all. The victims were drug dealers, whose families were uneasy about calling the police. Ransom seems generally to have been set in the $650,000 range. Some paid. Some got it in the back of the head. So it goes.

Yet, violent killings, often random, go on unabated. Peaks continue to attract some notice. But these are peaks

above "average" levels that thirty years ago would have been thought epidemic.

LOS ANGELES, AUG. 24. (Reuters) Twenty-two people were killed in Los Angeles over the weekend, the worst period of violence in the city since it was ravaged by riots earlier this year, the police said today.

Twenty-four others were wounded by gunfire or stabbings, including a 19-year old woman in a wheelchair who was shot in the back when she failed to respond to a motorist who asked for directions in south Los Angeles.

["The guy stuck a gun out of the window and just fired at her," said a police spokesman, Lieut. David Rock. The woman was later described as being in stable condition.

Among those who died was an off-duty officer, shot while investigating reports of a prowler in a neighbor's yard, and a Little League baseball coach who had argued with the father of a boy he was coaching.]

The police said at least nine of the deaths were gang-related, including that of a 14-year old girl killed in a fight between rival gangs.

Fifty-one people were killed in three days of rioting that started April 29 after the acquittal of four police officers in the beating of Rodney G. King.

Los Angeles usually has above-average violence during August, but the police were at a loss to explain the sudden rise. On an average weekend in August, 14 fatalities occur.

Not to be outdone, two days later the poor Bronx came up with a near record, as reported in *New York Newsday:*

Armed with 9-mm. pistols, shotguns and M-16 rifles, a group of masked men and women poured out of two vehicles in the South Bronx early yesterday and sprayed a stretch of Longwood Avenue with a fusillade of bullets, injuring 12 people.

A Kai Erikson of the future will surely need to know that the Department of Justice in 1990 found that Americans reported only about 38 percent of all crimes and 48 percent of violent crimes. This, too, can be seen as a means of *normalizing* crime. In much the same way, the vocabulary of crime reporting can be seen to move toward the normal-seeming. A teacher is shot on her way to class. The *Times* subhead reads: "Struck in the Shoulder in the Year's First Shooting Inside a School." First of the season.

It is too early, however, to know how to regard the arrival of the doctors on the scene declaring crime a "public health emergency." The June 10, 1992, issue of the *Journal of the American Medical Association* was devoted entirely to papers on the subject of violence, principally violence associated with firearms. An editorial in the issue signed by former Surgeon General C. Everett Koop and Dr. George D. Lundberg is entitled: "Violence in America: A Public Health Emergency." Their proposition is admirably succinct.

> Regarding violence in our society as purely a sociological matter, or one of law enforcement, has led to unmitigated failure. It is time to test further whether violence can be amenable to medical/public health interventions.
>
> We believe violence in America to be a public health emergency, largely unresponsive to methods thus far used in its control. The solutions are very complex, but possible.

The authors cited the relative success of epidemiologists in gaining some jurisdiction in the area of motor vehicle casualties by re-defining what had been seen as a law enforcement issue into a public health issue. Again, this process began during the Harriman administration in New York in the 1950s. In the 1960s the morbidity and mortality associated with automobile crashes was, it could be argued, a major public health problem; the public health strategy, it could also be argued, brought the problem under a measure of control. Not in "the 1970s and 1980s," as the *Journal of the American Medical Association* would have us think: the federal legislation involved was signed in 1965. Such a strategy would surely produce insights into the control of violence that elude law enforcement professionals, but whether it would change anything is another question.

For some years now I have had legislation in the Senate that would prohibit the manufacture of .25 and .32 caliber bullets. These are the two calibers most typically used with the guns known as Saturday Night Specials. "Guns don't kill people," I argue, "bullets do."

Moreover, we have a two-century supply of handguns but only a four-year supply of ammunition. A public health official would immediately see the logic of trying to control the supply of bullets rather than of guns.

Even so, now that the doctor has come, it is important that criminal violence not be defined down by epidemiologists. Doctors Koop and Lundberg note that in 1990 in the state of Texas "deaths from firearms, for the first time in many decades, surpassed deaths from motor vehicles, by 3,443 to 3,309." A good comparison. And yet keep in mind that the number of motor vehicle deaths, having leveled off since the 1960s, is now pretty well accepted as normal at somewhat less than 50,000 a year, which is somewhat less than the level of the 1960s—the "carnage," as it once was thought to be, is now accepted as normal. This is the price we pay for high-speed transportation: there is a benefit associated with it. But there is no benefit associated with homicide, and no good in getting used to it. Epidemiologists have powerful insights that can contribute to lessening the medical trauma, but they must be wary of normalizing the social pathology that leads to such trauma.

The hope—if there be such—of this essay has been twofold. It is, first, to suggest that the Durkheim constant, as I put it, is maintained by a dynamic process which adjusts upwards and *downwards*. Liberals have traditionally been alert for upward redefining that does injustice to individuals. Conservatives have been correspondingly sensitive to downward redefining that weakens societal standards. Might it not help if we could all agree that there is a dynamic at work here? It is not revealed truth, nor yet a scientifically derived formula. It is simply a pattern we observe in ourselves. Nor is it rigid. There may once have been an unchanging supply of jail cells which more or less determined the number of prisoners. No longer. We are building new prisons at a prodigious rate. Similarly, the executioner is back. There is something of a competition in Congress to think up new offenses for which the death penalty is deemed the only available deterrent. Possibly also modes of execution, as in "fry the kingpins." Even so, we are getting used to a lot of behavior that is not good for us.

As noted earlier, Durkheim states that there is "nothing desirable" about pain. Surely what he meant was that there is nothing pleasurable. Pain, even so, is an indispensable warning signal. But societies under stress, much like individuals, will turn to pain killers of various kinds that end up concealing real damage. There is surely nothing desirable about *this*. If our analysis wins general acceptance, if, for example, more of us came to share Judge Torres's genuine alarm at "the trivialization of the lunatic crime rate" in his city (and mine), we might surprise ourselves how well we respond to the manifest decline of the American civic order. Might.

Daniel Patrick Moynihan is a former senior U.S. senator (D) from New York (1976–2001). He has held academic appointments at Cornell University, Syracuse University, and Harvard University.

EXPLORING THE ISSUE

Is Crime Beneficial to Society?

Critical Thinking and Reflection

1. Having read the YES and NO selections by Durkheim and Moynihan, consider examples from your life in which a type of deviancy might be functional or an act that might have been viewed as criminal a generation ago is no longer viewed that way.
2. What types of acts do you tolerate today that would have been morally outrageous to your grandparents?
3. Have society's legal and ethical boundaries become "too elastic"?

Is There Common Ground?

One of the first American sociologists who attempted to use the insights of Durkheim was Robert Merton in his classic article "Social Structure and Anomie," *American Sociological Review* (1938). Merton attempted to show the bearing that culturally established goals and legitimate means for achieving them or their absence has upon criminogenic behavior. A significant revision of Durkheim's and Merton's thinking is *Crime and the American Dream*, 2nd ed., by S. Messner and R. Rosenfeld (Wadsworth, 1997). Also helpful is F. Hearn, *Moral Order and Social Disorder* (Aldine de Gruyter, 1998), especially Chapters 3 and 4 on anomie and Durkheim's sociology of morality. An analysis of communities' responses to crime in a culture outside of America is *Banana Justice: Field Notes on Philippine Crime and Customs* by W. T. Austin (Greenwood, 1999).

Note that Moynihan argues roughly from the same theoretic tradition as Durkheim: structural functionalism. Their disagreement centers around when deviancy becomes dysfunctional. A third argument would be that of some Marxists who see crime, including violent crime, as *functional* but only for the elite because it deflects society's concerns away from their own corporate crimes. For an outstanding presentation of this view, see J. Reiman's *The Rich Get Richer and the Poor Get Prison: Ideology, Class, and Criminal Justice*, 5th ed. (Allyn & Bacon, 1998). M. Lynch et al. identify linkages between economic cycles and criminal justice in "A Further Look at Long Cycles, Legislation and Crime," *Justice Quarterly* (June 1999).

Partial support of Moynihan's thinking can be found in *To Establish Justice, to Insure Domestic Tranquility* (Milton S. Eisenhower Foundation, 1999), a 30-year update of the 1969 violence report by the National Commission on the Causes and Prevention of Violence. A recent work by Moynihan is *Miles to Go: A Personal History of Social Policy* (Harvard University Press, 1997), and a discussion of Moynihan's ideas can be found in R. A. Katzmann, *Daniel Patrick Moynihan: The Intellectual in Public Life* (Johns Hopkins University Press, 1998).

There are many current analyses of crime and justice in terms of gender, including *Working With Women in the Criminal Justice System* by K. S. van Wormer and C. Bartollas (Allyn & Bacon, 1999) and part 1 of Sally Simpson, ed., *Of Crime and Criminality: The Use of Theory in Everyday Life* (Pine Forge Press, 2000). The neglected theoretical and research contributions of black criminologists are delineated by S. L. Gabbidon in "W. E. B. Du Bois on Crime," *The Criminologist* (January/February 1999). An interesting study on how U.S. scholars currently view crime is "Criminologists' Opinions About Causes and Theories of Crime," by L. Ellis and A. Walsh, *The Criminologist* (July/August 1999).

Additional Resources

David Emile Durkheim, http://edurkheim.tripod.com /id17.html

Internet References . . .

Emile Durkheim

www.emile-durkheim.com/

Paper by Andrew Karmen

www.albany.edu/scj/jcjpc/vol2is5/deviancy.html

American Spectator

http://spectator.org/archives/2011/06/22/defending-deviancy-down

Selected, Edited, and with Issue Framing Material by:
Thomas J. Hickey, *State University of New York at Cobleskill*

ISSUE

Is Criminal Behavior Determined Biologically?

YES: Adrian Raine, from "The Biological Basis of Crime," Institute for Contemporary Studies Press (2002)

NO: Sean Maddan, from "Criminological Explanations of Crime," Original Work (2016)

Learning Outcomes

After reading this issue, you will be able to:

- Discuss the classical legal reform movement.
- Discuss the principle of hedonism and the doctrine of social utilitarianism.
- Discuss the implications and logic of twin studies for the study of human behavior.
- Discuss factors that suggest a biological link to criminal behavior.
- Discuss how social factors correlate with crime.
- Discuss how social programs may reduce crime rates.
- Discuss how cultural factors may produce crime.

ISSUE SUMMARY

YES: Adrian Raine argues that one of the principal reasons why we have been so unsuccessful in preventing adult crime is because crime control policies have systematically ignored the biological side of human behavior.

NO: Professor Sean Maddan asserts that social forces create the conditions that become sources of crime in American society.

Is human behavior a product of our biological makeup, or is it socially determined? This question has confronted those who have studied human behavior throughout history. It is an extremely important question because the answer determines everything from the types of social policies used to control deviant behavior to philosophical questions including the nature of human morality.

The classical legal reform movement, a product of the Enlightenment, originated during the late eighteenth century in Europe. In reaction to the idea that metaphysical forces controlled all aspects of human existence, Classical theorists, including Cesare Beccaria and Jeremy Bentham, believed that people were motivated by hedonism—the pursuit of pleasure and avoidance of pain. They also embraced the notion of rationality and free will as guiding principles in human affairs. The classicists believed that people, as rational beings, would choose to obey the law if punishments were slightly more severe than the pleasure they would derive from committing unlawful acts. In addition, they embraced the doctrine of utilitarianism, a principle that holds that the guiding principle of all social policy, including criminal punishment, must be "the greatest good for the greatest number."

Modern Western legal systems are predicated on these ideals. For example, criminal responsibility is based on the principle that a criminal has the capacity to formulate *mens rea,* or criminal intent based on an evil mind. Thus, at common law, children under the age of seven years were presumed incapable of committing a crime because they were unable to foster criminal intent. Likewise, those who are proved to be mentally insane at the time they committed a crime are not held responsible for their actions.

Our legal system assumes that punishment is justified because a criminal has freely chosen to violate the law and embraces the proposition that it serves a utilitarian purpose and will deter others from committing similar offenses.

What would happen to these assumptions, however, if it were to be demonstrated that internal biological forces compel people to act? Would it then be morally acceptable for society to "punish" criminals for committing antisocial acts? What if criminologists were able to completely eradicate an offender's desire to commit crime? Would such a treatment also eliminate the moral aspect of human conduct? Anthony Burgess, in the introduction to his classic work, *A Clockwork Orange,* considered this dilemma. Stated Burgess:

> [B]y definition, a human being is endowed with free will. He can use this to choose between good and evil. If he can only perform good or only perform evil, then he is a clockwork orange—meaning that he has the appearance of an organism lovely with colour and juice but is in fact only a clockwork toy to be wound up by God or the Devil or (since this is increasingly replacing both) the Almighty State. (ix)

The issues contemplated in this passage may have important consequences for the study of criminology as well as justice system policy in the twenty-first century. In the first reading, Adrian Raine details many compelling examples of the emerging vitality of the biological approach to the study of human behavior. His extensive review of twin studies, human cortical arousal, and brain abnormalities in criminals presents compelling evidence of a biological component of human behavior.

Sean Maddan, however, asserts that social factors, including poverty and social disorganization, cultural forces, social policies, and learning generate circumstances in which people will violate the law. Maddan would posit that a variety of social programs can work to reduce crime, including family therapy and parent training for delinquent and at-risk youths, teaching of social competency skills, vocational training, extra police patrols in high crime areas, and effective drug and rehabilitation programs for offenders.

What are the arguments on both sides of the "nature or nurture" controversy? Perhaps criminal behavior is a complex combination of both types of factors. When you read these articles, try to develop your own sense of whether criminality is primarily determined by biological or social forces as well as the implications of this controversy for our notions of criminal responsibility and justice system policy.

YES ↵

Adrian Raine

The Biological Basis of Crime

Recognition is increasing that biological processes are at some level implicated in the development of criminal behavior. There is certainly debate about the precise contribution of such factors to crime outcome, and there is considerable debate about the precise mechanisms that these biological factors reflect. Yet few serious scientists in psychology and psychiatry would deny that biological factors are relevant to understanding crime, and public interest in and understanding of this perspective are increasing. The discipline of criminology, on the other hand, has been reluctant to embrace this new body of knowledge. Part of the reason may be interdisciplinary rivalries, part may simply be a lack of understanding, and part may be due to deep-seated historical and moral suspicions of a biological approach to crime causation. For whatever reason, these data have been largely ignored by criminologists and sociologists. . . .

Genetics

Twin Studies

The twin method for ascertaining whether a given trait is to any extent heritable makes use of the fact that monozygotic (MZ) or "identical" twins are genetically identical, having 100 percent of their genes in common with one another. Conversely, dizygotic (DZ) or "fraternal" twins are less genetically alike than MZ twins, and are in fact no more alike genetically than non-twin siblings. . . .

Are identical twins more concordant for criminality than fraternal twins? The answer from many reviews conducted on this expanding field is undoubtedly yes. As one example, a review of all the twin studies of crime conducted up to 1993 showed that although twin studies vary widely in terms of the age, sex, country of origin, sample size, determination of zygosity, and definition of crime, nevertheless all thirteen studies of crime show greater concordance rates for criminality in MZ as opposed to DZ twins. If one averages concordance rates across all studies (weighting for sample sizes), these thirteen studies result in concordances of 51.5 percent of MZ twins and 20.6 percent for DZ twins. Furthermore, the twin studies that have been conducted since 1993 have confirmed the hypothesis that there is greater concordance for antisocial and aggressive behavior in MZ relative to DZ twins. . . .

Adoption Studies

Adoption studies also overcome the problem with twin studies because they more cleanly separate out genetic and environmental influences. We can examine offspring who have been separated from their criminal, biological parents early in life and sent out to other families. If these offspring grow up to become criminal at greater rates than foster children whose biological parents were not criminal, this would indicate a genetic influence with its origin in the subject's biological parents. . . .

[A] review of fifteen other adoption studies conducted in Denmark, Sweden, and the United States shows that all but one find a genetic basis to criminal behavior. Importantly, evidence for this genetic predisposition has been found by several independent research groups in several different countries. . . .

Psychophysiology

Since the 1940s an extensive body of research has been built up on the psychophysiological basis of antisocial, delinquent, criminal, and psychopathic behavior. For example, there have been at least 150 studies on electrodermal (sweat rate) and cardiovascular (heart rate) activity in such populations, and in electroencephalographic (EEG) research alone there have been hundreds of studies on delinquency and crime. . . .

Definitions of psychophysiology vary, but one useful perspective outlined by Dawson is that it is "concerned with understanding the relationships between psychological states and processes on the one hand and

Raine, Adrian. From *Crime: Public Policies for Crime Control*, 2002, pp. 43–74. Copyright © 2002 by Institute for Contemporary Studies.

physiological measures on the other hand." Psychophysiology is uniquely placed to provide important insights into criminal behavior because it rests at the interface between clinical science, cognitive science, and neuroscience. . . .

There are many psychophysiological correlates of antisocial, criminal, and psychopathic behavior. The focus here will lie with one particular psychophysiological construct, low arousal, because—as will become clear—it is the strongest psychophysiological finding in the field of antisocial and criminal behavior.

EEG Underarousal

One influential psychophysiological theory of antisocial behavior is that antisocial individuals are chronically underaroused. Traditional psychophysiological measures of arousal include heart rate, skin conductance activity, and electroencephalogram (EEG) measured during a "resting" state. Low heart rate and skin conductance activity, and more excessive slow-wave EEG . . . indicate underarousal, that is, less than average levels of physiological arousal. Most studies tend to employ single measures of arousal, although studies that employ multiple measures are in a stronger position to test an arousal theory of antisocial behavior.

EEG is recorded from scalp electrodes that measure the electrical activity of the brain. Literally hundreds of studies assessing EEG in criminals, delinquents, psychopaths, and violent offenders have been done over the past sixty years, and it is clear that a large number of them implicate EEG abnormalities in violent recidivistic offending behavior. . . . Murderers have more recently been shown to have more EEG deficits in the right than the left hemisphere of the brain, with multiple abnormalities being especially present in the right temporal cortex. On the other hand, Pillmann et al. showed greater abnormalities in the *left* temporal region of repeat violent offenders.

Generally speaking, the prevalence of EEG abnormalities in violent individuals in this large literature ranges from 25 percent to 50 percent, with the rate of abnormalities in normals estimated as ranging from 5 percent to 20 percent. The bulk of this research implicated the more frontal regions of the brain, areas that regulate executive functions such as planning and decision making. . . .

Cardiovascular Underarousal

Data on resting heart rate provides striking support for underarousal in antisocials. Indeed, the findings for heart rate level (HRL) on non-institutionalized antisocials are believed to represent the strongest and best replicated biological correlate of antisocial behavior.

A low resting heart rate is the best-replicated biological marker of anti-social and aggressive behavior in childhood and adolescent community samples. Resting HRL was measured in a wide variety of ways, including polygraphs, pulse meters, and stopwatches. A wide number of definitions of antisocial behavior are used, ranging from legal criminality and delinquency to teacher ratings of antisocial behavior in school, self-report socialization measures, diagnostic criteria for conduct disorder, and genetically inferred law breaking (i.e. offspring of criminals). Subjects were also assessed in a wide variety of settings, including medical interview, study office, school, university laboratory, and hospital. In the light of such variability, it is surprising that consistency in findings have been obtained, attesting to the robustness of the observed effects. Importantly, there has also been good cross-laboratory replication of the finding, and it has also been found in six different countries—England, Germany, New Zealand, the United States, Mauritius, and Canada—illustrating invariance to cultural context.

The link between low heart rate and crime is not the result of such things as height, weight, body bulk, physical development, and muscle tone; scholastic ability and IQ; excess motor activity and inattention; drug and alcohol use; engagement in physical exercise and sports; or low social class, divorce, family size, teenage pregnancy, and other psychosocial adversity. Intriguingly, an unusual and important feature of the relationship is its diagnostic specificity. No other psychiatric condition has been linked to low resting heart rate. Other psychiatric conditions, including alcoholism, depression, schizophrenia, and anxiety disorder, have, if anything, been linked to *higher* (not lower) resting heart rate.

Low heart rate has been found to be an independent predictor of violence. . . . Indeed, low heart rate was more strongly related to both self-report and teacher measures of violence than having a criminal parent. These findings led Farrington to conclude that low heart rate may be one of the most important explanatory factors for violence. . . . Low heart rate characterizes female as well as male antisocial individuals. Several studies, including two that are prospective, have now established that, *within* females, low heart rate is linked to antisocial behavior. . . .

Interpretations of Low Arousal: Fearlessness and Stimulation-Seeking Theories

Why should low arousal and low heart rate predispose to antisocial and criminal behavior? There are two main theoretical interpretations. Fearlessness theory indicates that low levels of arousal are markers of low levels of fear. For example, particularly fearless individuals such as bomb disposal experts who have been decorated for their bravery have particularly low HRLs and reactivity, as do British paratroopers decorated in the Falklands War. A fearlessness interpretation of low arousal levels assumes that subjects are not actually at "rest," but that instead the rest periods of psychophysiological testing represent a mildly stressful paradigm and that low arousal during this period indicates lack of anxiety and fear. Lack of fear would predispose to antisocial and violent behavior because such behavior (for example, fights and assaults) requires a degree of fearlessness to execute, while lack of fear, especially in childhood, would help explain poor socialization since low fear of punishment would reduce the effectiveness of conditioning. Fearlessness theory receives support from the fact that autonomic underarousal also provides the underpinning for a fearless or uninhibited temperament in infancy and childhood.

A second theory explaining reduced arousal is stimulation-seeking theory. This theory argues that low arousal represents an unpleasant physiological state; antisocials seek stimulation in order to increase their arousal levels back to an optimal or normal level: Antisocial behavior is thus viewed as a form of stimulation-seeking, in that committing a burglary, assault, or robbery could be stimulating for some individuals. . . .

Psychophysiological Protective Factors against Crime Development

Until recently, there had been no research on biological factors that *protect* against crime development, but that is changing. We are discovering that *higher* autonomic activity during adolescence may act as a protective factor against crime development. . . . Findings suggest that boys who are antisocial during adolescence but who do not go on to adult criminal offending may be protected from such an outcome by their high arousal levels.

Overall, the initial profile that is being built up on the psychophysiological characteristics of the Desistor is one of heightened information processing (better orienting), greater responsivity to environmental stimuli in general (fast recovery), greater sensitivity to cues predicting punishment in particular (better classical conditioning), and higher fearfulness (high HRLs). The importance of research on psychophysiological protective factors such as these is that they offer suggestions for possible intervention and prevention strategies.

Brain Imaging

Advances in brain imaging techniques in the past fifteen years have provided the opportunity to gain dramatic new insights into the brain mechanisms that may be dysfunctional in violent, psychopathic offenders. In the past, the idea of peering into the mind of a murderer to gain insights into his or her acts was the province of pulp fiction or space-age movies. Yet now we can literally look at, and into, the brains of murderers using functional and structural imaging techniques that are currently revolutionizing our understanding of the causes of clinical disorders.

Brain imaging studies of violent and psychopathic populations . . . concur in indicating that violent offenders have structural and functional deficits to the frontal lobe (behind the forehead) and the temporal lobe (near the ears). . . . Despite some discrepancies, the first generation of brain imaging studies supports earlier contentions from animal and neurological studies implicating the frontal (and to some extent temporal) brain regions in the regulation and expression of aggression.

Prefrontal Dysfunction in Murderers

In the first published brain imaging study of murderers, we scanned the brains of twenty-two murderers pleading not guilty by reason of insanity (or otherwise found incompetent to stand trial) and compared them to the brains of twenty-two normal controls who were matched with the murderers on sex and age. The technique we used was positron emission tomography (PET), which allowed us to measure the metabolic activity of many different regions of the brain including the prefrontal cortex, the frontalmost part of the brain. We had subjects perform a task that required them to maintain focused attention and be vigilant for a continuous period of time, and it is the prefrontal region of the brain that in part subserves this vigilance function.

The key finding was that the murderers showed significantly poorer functioning of the prefrontal cortex, that part of the brain lying above the eyes and behind the forehead. . . . Prefrontal damage also encourages risk-taking, irresponsibility, rule breaking, emotional and aggressive outbursts, and argumentative behavior that can also predispose to violent criminal acts. Loss of self-control, immaturity, lack of tact, inability to modify and inhibit behavior appropriately, and poor social judgment could predispose to violence as well. This loss of intellectual flexibility and problem-solving skills, and reduced ability to use information provided by verbal cues can impair social skills essential for formulating nonaggressive solutions to fractious encounters. Poor reasoning ability and divergent thinking that results from prefrontal damage can lead to school failure, unemployment, and economic deprivation, thereby predisposing to a criminal and violent way of life. . . .

Other Biological Processes: Birth Complications, Minor Physical Anomalies, Nutrition, and Neurochemistry

Birth Complications

Several studies have shown that babies who suffer birth complications are more likely to develop conduct disorder, delinquency, and impulsive crime and violence in adulthood. Birth complications such as anoxia (getting too little oxygen), forceps delivery, and preeclampsia (hypertension leading to anoxia) are thought to contribute to brain damage, and this damage in turn may predispose to antisocial and criminal behavior. On the other hand, birth complications may not by themselves predispose to crime, but may require the presence of negative environmental circumstance to trigger later adult crime and violence.

One example of this "biosocial interaction" is a study of birth complications and maternal rejection in all 4,269 live male births that took place in one hospital in Copenhagen, Denmark. A highly significant interaction was found between birth complications and maternal rejection. Babies who only suffered birth complications or who only suffered maternal rejection were no more likely than normal controls to become violent in adulthood. On the other hand, those who had both risk factors were much more likely to become violent. . . .

Nutrition

Although deficiency in nutrition itself has been rarely studied in relation to childhood aggression, several studies have demonstrated the effects of related processes including food additives, hypoglycemia, and more recently cholesterol on human behavior. In addition, some studies have shown associations between overaggressive behavior and vitamin and mineral deficiency. Furthermore, one study claimed that nearly a third of a population of juvenile delinquents (mostly males) showed evidence of iron deficiency. Nevertheless, these findings remain both conflicting and controversial.

One intriguing study illustrates the potentially causal role of malnutrition as early as pregnancy in predisposing to antisocial behavior. Toward the end of World War II when Germany was withdrawing from Holland, they placed a food blockade on the country that led to major food shortages and near starvation in the cities and towns for several months. Women who were pregnant at this time were exposed to severe malnutrition at different stages of pregnancy. The male offspring of these women were followed up into adulthood to ascertain rates of Antisocial Personality Disorder and were compared to controls who were not exposed to malnutrition. Pregnant women starved during the blockade had 2.5 times the rates of Antisocial Personality Disorder in their adult offspring compared to controls.

Initial evidence also shows relationships between both protein and zinc deficiency and aggression in animals. Recent studies of humans support these animal findings. Protein and zinc deficiency may lead to aggression by negatively impacting brain functioning. . . . In humans, zinc deficiency in pregnancy has been linked to impaired DNA, RNA, and protein synthesis during brain development, and congenital brain abnormalities. . . . The amygdala, which also shows abnormal functioning in PET imaging of violent offenders, is densely innervated by zinc-containing neurons, and males with a history of assaultive behavior were found to have lower zinc relative to copper ratios in their blood compared to nonassaultive controls. Consequently, protein and zinc deficiency may contribute to the brain impairments shown in violent offenders which in turn are thought to predispose to violence.

Environmental Pollutants and Neurotoxicity

It has long been suspected that exposure to pollutants, particularly heavy metals that have neurotoxic effects, can lead to mild degrees of brain impairment which in turn predisposes to antisocial and aggressive behavior. One of the best studies to date is that of Needleman et al. who assessed lead levels in the bones of 301 eleven-year-old schoolboys. Boys with higher lead levels were found to have significantly higher teacher ratings of delinquent and aggressive behavior, higher parent ratings of delinquent and aggressive behavior, and higher self-report delinquency scores. These findings do not occur in isolation: Similar links between lead levels and antisocial, delinquent behavior and aggression have been found in at least six other studies in several different countries. . . .

Less strong to date, but nevertheless provocative, are findings with respect to manganese. At high levels, manganese has toxic effects on the brain and can damage the brain so much that it can even lead to Parkinson-like symptoms. Furthermore, it reduces levels of serotonin and dopamine, neurotransmitters that play a key role in brain communication. . . .

Hormones

Testosterone. Excellent reviews and discussions of the potential role played by testosterone in both animals and man can be found in Olweus, Brain, Archer, and Susman and Ponirakis. Animal research suggests that the steroid hormone testosterone plays an important role in the genesis and maintenance of some forms of aggressive behavior in rodents, and early exposure to testosterone had been found to increase aggression in a wide range of animal species. . . .

The critical question in this literature concerns whether testosterone-violence relationships are causal. Little doubt exists that castration decreases aggression in animals and administration of testosterone increases aggression. Few experimental studies have been conducted in humans, but there is nevertheless evidence of a causal relationship. Olweus et al. assessed their finding of higher testosterone in male adolescents with high levels of self-reported aggression using path analysis and concluded that testosterone had causal effects on both provoked and unprovoked aggressive behavior. One study that comes close to such an ideal experiment is that of Wille and Beier, who showed that ninety-nine castrated German sex offenders had a significantly lower recidivism rate eleven years postrelease (3 percent) compared to thirty-five noncastrated sex offenders (46 percent). . . .

Clearly, links between testosterone and aggression are complex, and simplistic explanations of this link are probably incorrect. By the same token, it would be equally erroneous to discount the evidence for the role of hormones in influencing aggression merely because hormones are influenced by the environment. . . .

Policy Implications

One of the biggest and widely held myths in criminology research is that biology is destiny. Instead, the reality is that the biological bases of crime and violence are amenable to change through benign interventions. In the past fifty years, intervention programs have not been as successful in reducing crime and violence as had been hoped, and it is possible that part of their failure has been due to the fact that they have systematically ignored the biological component of the biosocial equation.

Brain damage and poor brain functioning have been shown to predispose to violence, and one possible source of this brain damage could be birth complications. The implication is that providing better pre- and postbirth health care to poor mothers may help reduce birth complications and thus reduce violence. . . .

Another source of brain damage could be poor nutrition; and as has been seen earlier, there is evidence for a link between poor nutrition during pregnancy and later crime. Furthermore, cigarette and alcohol usage during pregnancy have been linked to later antisocial behavior. . . . These studies provide more support to the notion that nutrition plays a causal role in the development of childhood aggression, but future prevention trials that focus explicitly on the specific role of nutrition are required to further support the specific role of malnutrition.

It has been shown that low physiological arousal is the best-replicated biological correlate of antisocial behavior in child and adolescent samples. An important question from a prevention perspective concerns whether low arousal is amenable to change using noninvasive procedures. Recent findings from Mauritius suggest that it is. A nutritional, physical exercise, and educational enrichment from ages three to five resulted in increased psychophysiological arousal and orienting at age eleven compared to a matched control group. . . .

The policy implications of biological research on crime also extend to the criminal justice system. One question raised by these and other studies is whether any of us have freedom of will in the strict sense of the term. If brain deficits make it more likely that a person will commit violence, and if the cause of the brain deficits was not under the control of the individual, then the question becomes whether or not that person should be held fully responsible for the crimes. Of course we have to protect society, and unless we can treat this brain dysfunction, we may need to keep violent offenders in secure conditions for the rest of their lives; but do they deserve to be executed given the early constraints on their free will? It could be argued that if an individual possesses risk factors that make him disproportionately more likely to commit violence, then he has to take responsibility for these predispositions. Just like an alcoholic who knows he suffers from the disease of alcoholism, the person at risk for violence needs to recognize his risk factors and take preventive steps to ensure that he does not harm others. These persons have risk factors, but they still have responsibility and they have free will. . . .

Biological research is beginning to give us new insights into what makes a violent criminal offender. It is hoped that these early findings may lead us to rethink our approach to violence and goad us into obtaining new answers to the causes and cures of crime while we continue to protect society.

ADRIAN RAINE is the Robert Grandford Wright Professor in the Department of Psychology, University of Southern California. He received his bachelor's degree in experimental psychology from Oxford University in 1977, and his DPhil in psychology from York University in England in 1982. After working as a prison psychologist, he became a university professor. Dr. Raine's research has focused on the biosocial bases of violent behavior. He is a prolific writer who has published numerous books and over 100 professional journal articles.

Sean Maddan

 **NO**

Criminological Explanations of Crime

Since the mid-1800s, the link between nature and nurture as the cause of various forms of human behavior has been hotly debated. At various points over the twentieth century, both have claimed superiority as causal explanations for human actions. While each approach has its strengths and weakness in predicting human behavior, nowhere has this debate been more contested than in the area of criminology. Criminality represents one of the more serious threats to a society. As such, explaining this particular strain of human behavior is important, whether it be attributed to nature or nurture.

In the 1800s, explanations of crime were still in their infancy. One of the most cutting-edge theories of the day revolved around the biological genesis of crime. Cesare Lombroso attempted to link various biological and physiological characteristics of inmates in an Italian prison to crime. Lombroso surmised that criminals were evolutionary throwbacks to an earlier era of human development; this was termed atavism. Lombroso's research did not find a link between criminality and atavism. Indeed, his research suggested that criminals could be more likely termed criminaloids, individuals whose criminality is predicated by sociological causes, rather than biological correlates.

Even though Lombroso's work was groundbreaking at the time, it has subsequently been met with derision. The failure of Lomborso's Biological School was hastened by the advent of a new academic discipline: Sociology. Sociology focused on how social structure and social interaction influences human behavior within a society. The study of sociology quickly incorporated the study of crime under its aegis. Sociology, especially the School of Sociology at the University of Chicago, was aggressive in its assimilation and expansion of theories of criminality. Sociological explanations of crime argued that social structure and social interactions created the necessary conditions for criminal behavior; sociological theories discount the effect of biological impulses in addition to the role of

choice in criminality. Over the last hundred years, sociological explanations of crime have received a great deal of empirical support in explaining the incidence of crime.

The preceding chapter by Adrian Raine explored contemporary biological attempts to explain criminality. This selection focuses on the alternative sociological-based theories of criminality and research on these theories that have occurred over the course of the twentieth century to the present. In particular, the theories are separated by social interaction and social structure, which are the key forms of sociological-based crime explanations.

Social Interaction Theories

Social interaction theories evaluate the behavior of individuals via personal interaction in everyday situations. The interplay between individuals can lead to criminality via those people/peers individuals associate with (differential association), how individuals interact with other people (social control), and interplay between individuals and society at large. The primary social interaction theories in criminology are social learning, social control, and labeling theory. This section evaluates these theories and research supporting each.

Social Learning

The earliest social interaction theory was a precursor to social learning theory. Throughout the 1930s, Edwin Sutherland developed his theory of differential association. Differential association suggested that individuals associate with many people throughout the course of their lives. While the majority of the individuals people associate with are non-criminal, some of these individuals associated with are in fact criminals. Sutherland suggested that people will become criminal if they associate with too many criminals. The association with too many criminals can lead to individuals being exposed to pro-criminal beliefs and definitions. When the number of pro-criminal beliefs exceeds anti-criminal definitions, an individual will engage in crime. While differential association was a crucial first step in explaining learned criminality, it was greatly hampered by the fact that one could only learn criminal behavior from others.

Continued research on differential association led to refinement of this theory into social learning theory, which has largely been elaborated on by Ron Akers. Akers suggested that the process of social learning occurred via differential association, differential reinforcement, definitions, and imitation. Akers added differential reinforcement, which looked at learning via punishments, expanded on the concept of definitions conducive to violation of the law, and explored the imitation of others' behavior. Akers iteration of learning theory indicated that individuals can potentially learn criminal behavior from a myriad of sources, not just from other people.

There has been a great deal of research on both differential association and social learning theory. In fact, social learning theory is one of the most tested theories across criminology. The key independent variable in this line of research is the total number of criminals one associates with. The vast majority of research that utilizes this variable finds that criminality is linked to association with a greater number of peers. Differential reinforcement, usually measured as whether a particular punishment will deter an individual from engaging in crime, is also shown to be important in predicting criminality. The research findings on the concepts of definitions and imitation are rare across the research; when these indicators are present in empirical studies, the findings are often mixed (some support and some refutation). What is key about social learning theory is that the findings in relation to differential association is both a consistent and strong finding across all social learning studies.

Social Control

The next social interaction theory is a grouping of theories referred to as social control theories. Social control theories are contrary to most other criminological theories. Instead of asking why individuals commit crime, social control theories ask what keeps people from engaging in crime. While there are a host of social control theories (containment, self-control, etc.), the primary social control theory that has received the most attention is Travis Hirschi's social bond theory developed in the 1960s. Hirschi argued that four concepts kept individuals from engaging in crime: attachments, commitments, involvement, and beliefs. Attachments to others include parents, friends/peers, significant others, and children. Attachments to people indicate a social network; people generally do not want to let people in their social

network down due to feelings of shame. To avoid letting these people down (shame), most people will not engage in crime. Commitments involve a focus upon the future. If one is committed to their future education or career, they are unlikely to engage in crime as criminality can impede these commitments in the form of expulsion or job termination. Involvement in traditional conforming activities is a time management issue. If individuals are occupied with extracurricular activities like sports, band, chess club, or other positive group activities, there is literally less, or no, time that one can engage in criminal behavior. Belief in the moral authority of a law will likely keep individuals from breaking laws. A good example here is of underage drinking; many adults and adolescents do not necessarily believe in the utility of underage drinking statutes, thus many underage individuals every year consume alcohol despite the fact that it is illegal. When these four bonds are either weakened or broken entirely, criminality will ensue.

The social bond theory has received a great deal of empirical attention. The research in this area has largely substantiated social bond theory. Those with strong attachments, commitment to the future, involvement with pro-social activities, and a moral belief in the law are less likely to engage in criminal activities. Those with weak bonds are more likely to engage in crime. While the research history of social bond theory has been overwhelmingly supportive, the theory does suffer from a lack of conceptualization on how weak a bond has to be before it will lead to criminality. Despite this conceptual void, the theory indicates that strong bonds are equated with lesser criminal involvement.

Labeling

In the 1970s, a fully imagined labeling theory came to the forefront of criminology. More commonly considered a perspective, labeling has its roots in symbolic interaction, a sociological theory that suggests individuals act in the manner they believe others think they should act. Howard Becker, and other labeling theorists, believed that it was not enough to simply focus on criminal offenders; rather, a full explanation of criminality would require a focus on community and societal reactions to criminal behavior. When rules/laws are applied to individuals, those to whom the rules/laws have been applied are labeled. Labeled individuals are likely to internalize the label and behave according to the label. If one is labeled as a criminal, the individual is likely to behave according to that criminal label. The labeling perspective is an important theory as almost 70 percent of criminals are likely to recidivate (reengage in crime) every year.

While the labeling approach is actually a combination of social interaction and social structure theories, the bulk of the research in this area focuses on the social interaction angle of the perspective. While the labeling perspective does a poor job of explaining the originating criminal act, the bulk of the research seems to indicate that labeling has a profound impact on secondary criminality (recidivism). While the effect of labeling ranges from small to large effects, the majority of studies, especially in relation to juveniles and younger offenders, indicates that labeled individuals are more likely to engage in subsequent criminality.

Social Structure Theories

Theories that focus on social structure examine the composition of society and how that composition influences the behavior of people. Social structure includes an emphasis on how societies can be dissected via economics (poverty), demographics (majorities and minorities), and common beliefs about norms and goals shared by individuals within a society. The principle social structure theories are social disorganization, strain, subculture, and critical criminology. This section will provide overviews of each of these theories and a discussion of research that has been conducted in each of these areas.

Social Disorganization

Based on disparate studies completed dating back to the 1830s, human ecology and social disorganization would provide one of the most important explanations for crime. Social disorganization theory examined the role of neighborhoods in accounting for crime. It is a fact in most cities, and even small towns, that there is an area that is often considered undesirable to reside in by most within the community; this area is often impoverished and has a great deal of crime. While classical accounts of social disorganization theory explore the role of population turnover, population characteristics, economic forces within and without the community, and the physical nature of the neighborhood, modern interpretations of this theory evaluate the ability of a neighborhood to exert social control on its members (collective efficacy).

Unlike the research conducted for social interaction theories above, social disorganization theory research occurs at the macro-level. Rather than focus on individuals, social disorganization theorists focus on neighborhoods and block-level data. The data generally are a combination of U.S. Census data and police arrest reports. Findings in the social disorganization literature indicate some of the strongest findings across all of criminological thought. Neighborhoods characterized with high population turnover, population heterogeneity, physical deterioration, single-heads of household, low incomes, large percentage of rental properties, and a high level of overall poverty will have much greater crime rates. This is not to say that everyone in these areas is a criminal, only that there is more crime in areas with these structural impediments. Many individuals residing in these areas are law-abiding citizens, but the high level of community social disorganization has impeded the ability of the community to exert its own social control.

Strain/Anomie

In the 1930s, Robert Merton advanced the strain theory based on Emile Durkheim's work on anomie in the 1800s. Merton suggested that every society contains goals for its members. These goals are greatly desired by the vast majority of members in the society; these goals generally have a monetary basis. The means, or ability, to achieve these goals is not equally distributed to every member of society. When an individual experiences a disjuncture between societal goals and the means to achieve those goals, strain ensues. When an individual experiences strain, the individual has to adapt to the strain. Merton suggested that there were several modes of adaptation: conformity, innovation, ritualism, retreat, or rebellion. The mode of adaptation most likely to result in criminality is innovation. For example, if a person works at a grocery store 40 hours per week for an entire year is going to make less than $25,000 per year. An innovator might see that they can never achieve their dream of a large house, family, and career working at this grocery store for so little. Based on the strain created from this realization, the innovator might then decide to engage in robbery or selling drugs. Either option will yield more money but for a much lesser effort.

While Merton's theory has received a great deal of empirical support, most research efforts on strain theory focus on one of two theoretical elaborations: general strain theory and institutional anomie theory. General strain theory (GST) was developed by Robert Agnew in the 1990s. As can be seen above, strain theory can readily explain property and non-violent crime; it does a poor job of explaining crimes like murder or rape. Agnew suggested that the way strain theory could explain violent crime is through the negative affect, or the extreme anger that ensues when a person experiences strain. General strain theory has been tested extensively by many criminologists over the last 20 years. This research supports the impact of strain on producing all forms of criminality.

Steven Messner and Richard Rosenfeld extended strain theory to focus on the American Dream in their theory of Institutional Anomie. This dream is imbued with both cultural and social conditions that are prized by all Americans. The values associated with the American Dream necessarily create an anomic atmosphere; anomie is loosely translated as a degree of normlessness. This anomie leads to a degradation of non-economic social institutions, a lack of social control and an increase in crime. Research has largely supported Messner and Rosenfeld's Institutional Anomie theory.

Subculture

Based on the success of strain theory, subculture theory was developed to explain how individuals become involved in criminal groups. It is a fact that most criminals, serious and non-serious, tend to complete their crimes in groups rather than alone. Many crimes then have a group nature. Subculture theory suggested that individuals come together in criminal groups due to experiencing the same form of strain. This can then account for individuals who come together in drug subcultures, street gangs, and organized crime. Research in this area tends to be focused upon a single subculture, generally operating within a finite area. Research in this area tends to have few implications for other groups.

One area of subculture theory that has received a great deal of focus is in relation to the Southern Subculture of Violence. Marvin Wolfgang and colleagues first explored the concept of the subculture of violence; according to the theory, a subculture of violence is indicative of groups whose primary form of conflict resolution is violence. Primarily, Wolfgang was concerned with explaining murder that resulted from conflicts of members of the subculture of violence. This theory was quickly adopted to explain high murder rates in the southern United States. The south is characterized by high murder rates every year, more so than in any other region of the United States. Some have suggested that based on the south's history (the confederacy during the Civil War, child rearing practices, rural areas, and need for protection, etc.) is accountable for elevated homicide rates. Despite conceptual ambiguities and methodological problems, many studies seem to suggest that there is in fact a subculture unique to the south in relation to engaging in violence in general and the commission of homicide specifically.

Critical Criminology

In the 1960s, criminologists inspired by the works of Karl Marx in the 1800s began to look at the role of the economy in explaining crime. In particular, these "radical" criminologists suggested that capitalism was specifically geared to breed high levels of crime. In capitalist societies there are effectively two groups: haves and have nots. The haves are a very small group who control the modes of production within a society. The way in which the haves control the modes of production is via the creation of law, specifically criminal law. The criminal law is used as a weapon to control surplus labor. When there is too much surplus labor, the criminal justice system is utilized to control the excess labor supply. While this is the key to Marxist criminology, critical criminology is actually a block of theories that examine the impact of the social structure, the economy and the gendered nature of society to account for crime (feminist criminology, left realism, postmodernist criminology, etc.).

The research on critical criminology, especially the Marxist strain, is largely non-existent despite the fact that the theory has been around since the 1960s. The reason for this is that critical criminologists tend to eschew the research methods contained within positivism. As such, research on critical theories is difficult to come by and generally comes in the form of anecdotes or historical analyses. Two areas of research give us some light into the utility of critical theories. First, work on white-collar crime is very much linked to ideas contained in Marxist criminology. The work on white-collar crime suggests that these offenders are treated much more leniently by the criminal justice system than offenders who engage in street level crimes. Second, research on the link between crime and the economy has shown inconsistency due to multiple combinations of a variety of economic indicators that have been used as proxies of the economy, and the possibility of a time-lag effect in the data (i.e., high crime rates appear later, and not in conjunction with economic downturns).

Conclusion

As indicated in this chapter, non-biological explanations of crime have permeated the academic record. This is largely attributable to the rise of sociology and the wealth of sociologically based studies of crime. Despite the veracity of these theories it is clear that there are drawbacks to the sociological approach. Primarily, each theory seeks to explain a very important aspect of crime. The majority of theories do not account for all criminal actions and, in fact, most theories cannot account for every form of criminality. For instance, subculture theories evaluate group criminality. While a great deal of crime is committed within groups, there are many criminal acts that are perpetrated by a single offender (serial killers for instance).

As another example, labeling theory does an excellent job of explaining recidivism; unfortunately, the labeling perspective is a weak theory when it comes to explaining why an individual commits crime in the first place. As each theory explains an important aspect of crime, it might seem like a good idea to combine theories. All theories are based on assumptions, definitions, and research history. These assumptions, definitions, and empirical histories are often conflicting across studies. Thus, theoretical integration is difficult if not next to impossible.

Despite these drawbacks, sociological-based theories of criminology offer the strongest evidence of why individuals engage in criminal behavior. Is this wealth of empirical evidence enough to let us conclude that nurture is more important than nature in explaining criminal behavior? The answer to this is probably a mixed one. While sociological-based theories of criminality can account for a great deal of the explanation of crime, we cannot simply discount biological correlates of criminality. One of the more robust findings in criminology in the last 25 years has been the link of aggression and anti-social behavior to crime. Aggression and anti-social behavior are not traditional sociological constructs; rather, both of these concepts are more in line with biological explanations of crime. In fact, there are genetic markers for aggression. Any fully developed theory accounting for criminality should incorporate indicators of both nature (biology) and nurture (sociology/criminology). Based on over a hundred years of empirical research, it is likely that sociological/criminological indicators of crime are more important than biological factors, but both approaches are necessary if we are to ever paint a complete picture of the causes of crime.

Sean Maddan is an associate Professor in the Criminology Department at the University of Tampa. He has published numerous articles in academic and professional journals about the social origins of crime and criminal behavior. His research interests include social and biological correlates of crime and matters pertaining to the U.S. justice system.

EXPLORING THE ISSUE

Is Criminal Behavior Determined Biologically?

Critical Thinking and Reflection

1. What are the basic assumptions of the classical legal reform movement, including the principle of hedonism and the doctrine of utilitarianism?
2. Do "twin studies" provide evidence of a biological link to human behavior?
3. What factors seem to suggest a biological link to criminal behavior?
4. What are the social factors that appear to correlate with crime?
5. What types of social programs that appear to help to reduce crime rates?
6. How may cultural factors generate crime?
7. How may social learning contribute to crime?
8. How may social disorganization contribute to crime?

Is There Common Ground?

For much of the twentieth century, the biological perspective in criminology was regarded as an anachronism that conjured images of Cesare Lombroso slicing open cadavers and the early phrenologists measuring the contours of criminals' heads. As Adrian Raine demonstrates, however, the biological approach to the study of criminal behavior is making a strong comeback. For example, it is hard for modern criminologists to ignore identical twin studies, which indicate a significant amount of behavioral concordance, even when the individuals are separated shortly after birth and raised apart. In fact, as technology advances and our ability to identify the biological correlates of human behavior further improves, we may reach a point when behavioral scientists are more prepared to assign hard percentages to the nature–nurture controversy.

On the other hand, as Sean Maddan demonstrates, there is also a significant social component to human behavior. People are social beings. Just examine the interaction dynamics in your classroom and think about how we influence the behavior of others in virtually every social situation. Moreover, Maddan's theory has a great deal of intuitive appeal. Most people would agree about a number of the sources of crime in U.S. society. For example, although things appear to have started to change, we know that contemporary drug control policies have been largely ineffective; however, we appear to lack the political will to make the changes to our social policies that will have a lasting impact on drug crimes. It appears likely that the definitive answer to the mystery of human behavior may eventually determine that both biological factors and social forces combine in a complex interactive web. Thus, for future behavioral scientists it is quite possible that the "nature OR nurture" controversy will become the "nature AND nurture" issue.

Additional Resources

Edmund O. Wilson, *Sociobiology* (Harvard University Press, 1975).

Robert M. Sade's "Introduction: Evolution, Prevention, and Responses to Aggressive Behavior and Violence," *The Journal of Law, Medicine & Ethics* (vol. 32, no. 1, 2004).

Gene E. Robinson, "Beyond Nature and Nurture," *Science* (April 16, 2004).

Christiane Charlemaine, "What Might MZ Twin Research Teach Us about Race, Gender & Class Issues," *Race, Gender & Class* (October 31, 2002).

Michael Edmund O'Neill in "Stalking the Mark of Cain," *Harvard Journal of Law and Public Policy* (vol. 25, no. 1, Fall 2001).

Internet References . . .

Caitlin M. Jones, "Genetic and Environmental Influences on Criminal Behavior." (2005).

www.personalityresearch.org

National Public Radio (NPR), "Criminologist Believes Violent Behavior is Biological." April 30, 2013.

www.npr.org

Jeremy W. Wilson, "Debating Genetics as a Predictor of Criminal Offending and Sentencing." *Student Pulse,* 2011, vol. 3, no. 11.

www.studentpulse.com

Selected, Edited, and with Issue Framing Material by:
Thomas J. Hickey, *State University of New York at Cobleskill*

ISSUE

Does a "Warrior Gene" Make People More Prone to Violence?

YES: Kevin M. Beaver and Joseph A. Schwartz, from "MAOA Genotype Contributes to Violent and Criminal Behaviors," *Comprehensive Psychiatry* (2010)

NO: Joshua W. Buckholtz, from "Neuroprediction and Crime." *NOVA ScienceNOW* (2012)

Learning Outcomes

After reading this issue, you will be able to:

- Discuss the adequacy of theories that have traditionally tried to explain criminal behavior.
- Discuss the basic assumptions of biosocial criminology.
- Discuss the relationship between genetics and criminal behavior.
- Discuss the implications of the MAOA gene for the study of criminal behavior.
- Discuss whether there is a relationship between having the MAOA gene and gang membership and weapon use.
- Discuss the potential problems arising from the prediction of criminal behavior.

ISSUE SUMMARY

YES: Professors Kevin M. Beaver and Joseph A. Schwartz argue that a "Warrior Gene" has been demonstrated to be related to aggressive and violent behavior. In fact, humans with a low-activity form of the MAOA gene are much more prevalent in populations with a history of warfare. These individuals are also more likely to join gangs and to use weapons in committing crimes than other persons.

NO: Professor Joshua W. Buckholtz, in contrast, asserts that the "Warrior Gene" theory has as much power to explain and predict the actions of an individual as a deck of tarot cards. Moreover, he believes that although genes may be able to influence our behavior, the environment in which we live influences our genes as well.

The "nature or nurture" debate has been an enduring source of controversy for many years. Does a person's intrinsic biological makeup determine his or her behavior, or are environmental influences the more important factor? More precisely for purposes of the present inquiry, do biological factors influence an individual's propensity for criminal behavior, or is the environment in which he or she lives the crucial determinant?

In the late nineteenth and early twentieth centuries, biological theories of human behavior were popular and were used by governmental authorities to try to predict individual propensities for violent behavior. *Biological positivism* described the approach of some early criminologists who tried to apply the scientific method to the task of determining who was a criminal. For example, in the late eighteenth and early nineteenth centuries, Franz Joseph Gall and others popularized the "science of *phrenology*," the theory that the contours of a person's brain influenced human behavior. Gall believed that the human brain could be divided into discrete compartments, or "organs." These organs, in turn, were each associated with a distinct human capacity. Some of these included: the love of one's children, affection, memory, a sense of color, a sense of mechanics, and friendship. According to his theory, examining the shape of someone's skull could reveal his or her propensity for antisocial behavior.

More recently, in the early twentieth century, an Italian physician and early criminologist, Cesare Lombroso, believed that biological factors influenced human behavior. Based on Darwin's theory of evolution, Lombroso used a concept called *atavism* to explain his view that criminals were biological "throwbacks" to an earlier stage in the evolutionary process. Moreover, he believed that criminals displayed atavistic physical manifestations, including enlarged incisor teeth, longer arms, larger skulls, facial asymmetry, flattened noses, and other characteristics that served to support his belief that they were biologically inferior—closer to their primitive ancestors on an evolutionary scale than to modern people. Lombroso also used the term *born criminal* to describe individuals who manifested several of the characteristics listed above. His theory emphasized that approximately 30 percent of criminals fell within this category.

Professor Sue Titus Reid has recognized that the early biological explanations of criminal behavior were inadequate because they were riddled with exceptions. Reid uses the term *dualistic fallacy* to describe the failure of such theories to be able to explain why some individuals with a given physical characteristic actually commit crimes, whereas others do not. For example, how can we explain why one person with long arms becomes a criminal, whereas others with the same physical characteristics become law-abiding citizens? The dualistic fallacy problem is an excellent barometer for the adequacy of explanations of human behavior. As you read the various theories of criminal behavior presented in this work, ask yourself whether a particular theory would be subject to a dualistic fallacy. If so, it is at best an incomplete theory of human behavior.

Biological theories of human behavior have become much more sophisticated since the time of Lombroso. This should not be surprising when one considers the dramatic technological advances that we have made in the fields of biology and medicine in the years since these early theories were developed.

The issue presented in this section presents one such theory and raises the question of the role of human genetics in antisocial behavior. It asks whether there is a so-called "Warrior Gene" that predisposes some persons to become criminals. According to Professors Beaver and Schwartz, a warrior gene has been demonstrated to be related to aggressive and violent behavior. In fact, humans with a low-activity form of the MAOA gene are much more prevalent in groups with a history of warfare. Professor Buckholtz, in contrast, believes that this type of scientific evidence "has as much power to explain and predict the actions of an individual as a deck of tarot cards." He further asserts that nature and nurture are inextricably linked and that there is always an environmental component to human behavior.

Which argument do you find to be the more compelling one? Can the presence of the MAOA gene predict human behavior, or is such prediction dependent on the interaction between an individual's genetic structure and his or her environment? Moreover, is the "Warrior Gene" theory of criminal behavior susceptible to Professor Reid's dualistic fallacy criticism? Such questions are important and have highly significant implications for the study of human behavior.

YES ⤶

Kevin M. Beaver and Joseph A. Schwartz

MAOA Genotype Contributes to Violent and Criminal Behaviors

Introduction

The vast majority of criminological theories proposed within the past half-century have focused exclusively on environmental explanations of criminal and antisocial behavior (e.g., Akers, 1998; Hirschi, 1969; Sampson, Raudenbush, & Earls, 1997). While the resulting amount of literature stemming from these theories is quite impressive, how well they explain criminal and antisocial behaviors is questionable at best. In an effort to better understand how well criminologists explain crime and whether their efforts have improved over time, Weisburd and Piquero (2008) performed a systematic investigation of nearly 200 criminological studies published between 1968 and 2005. The two primary findings of the study were surprising to say the least. First, criminologists did not do a very good job explaining criminal behavior, with most studies leaving between 80–90% of differences in criminal behavior between individuals unexplained. Second, criminologists do not seem to have gotten any better at explaining crime over time. Despite the presence of a multitude of refinements and revisions suggested by studies testing the major theories of criminal behavior, the explanatory power of such theories has not increased over time.

A line of research within the field of criminology may provide an opportunity to increase the explanatory power of criminological theories that focus exclusively on environmental explanations of criminal and antisocial behavior. This alternative perspective, referred to as biosocial criminology, focuses on the manner in which biological *and* environmental factors influence criminal and antisocial behaviors (Beaver, 2009; Moffitt, 2005). Biosocial explanations of criminal behavior acknowledge the potentially powerful impact that environmental factors have on various behaviors, but these explanations also take into account the powerful effects that biological influences have on these same behaviors. The consideration of both biological and environmental influences on criminal behaviors results in greater explanatory power in two ways. First, biosocial explanations integrate theories, empirical findings, and methodological techniques from a wide variety of disciplines *outside* of criminology including evolutionary psychology, psychiatry, molecular genetics, and neuroscience. The integration of ideas and analytic techniques from these disciplines into criminology provides criminologists with a larger and more diverse set of tools that may be used to better explain why some people commit crime and others do not. This particular advantage of a biosocial approach not only benefits existing criminological theory, but also may benefit future theories.

Second, a biosocial approach directly integrates the role of biological influences on criminal behavior into criminological theories and research. One set of biological factors that has been found to significantly impact criminal and antisocial behaviors and has received a significant amount of attention is genetic influences. A long string of studies has provided irrefutable evidence that genetic factors significantly influence criminal and antisocial behaviors (Ferguson, 2010). More specifically, the results of over 100 empirical studies indicate that approximately 50% of the between-individual differences in criminal and antisocial behavior behaviors are explained by genetic influences (Moffitt, 2005). This finding indicates that the vast majority of criminological studies dramatically limit how well they explain criminal behavior by focusing exclusively on environmental factors and completely ignoring the important role that genetic factors play. Against this backdrop, it is not surprising that existing criminological theories and research do not sufficiently explain criminal behavior.

*Adapted from: Beaver, K. M., DeLisi, M., Vaughn, M.G., & Barnes, J.C. (2010). Monoamine Oxidase A Genotype Is Associated with Gang Membership and Weapon Use. *Comprehensive Psychiatry*, 51, 130–134.

Genetics and Criminal Behavior

A small handful of criminologists have recently recognized the importance of genetic influences when examining the development of criminal behavior (Beaver, 2009). Many studies examining the effect of genetic influences on criminal behavior employ behavior genetic research methodologies. These methodologies estimate the proportion of variance in a given behavior that can be explained by genetic (symbolized as h^2) and environmental influences. Behavior genetic studies also examine the amount of variance in the examined outcome that can be explained by two different types of environmental influences. Shared environmental influences (symbolized as c^2) refer to environmental influences that equally impact all children raised in the same household and make them more alike. For example, living in poverty is likely an influence that all siblings within a given household experience collectively, and may make them more similar. Nonshared environmental influences (symbolized as e^2) refer to environments that are different for siblings from the same household and ultimately result in differences between them. For example, siblings raised in the same household may have quite different peer groups which may result in differences in their behavior.

Behavior genetic methodologies are a powerful research tool, but even so, they also possess distinct limitations. Perhaps the most concerning limitation of these methodologies is directly related to the provided h^2 estimate. More specifically, the h^2 coefficient reported in such studies provides an estimation of additive genetic influences on criminal behaviors and it is expressed as a proportion (or percentage). In this way, it is not possible to use this information to determine which specific genes have a direct effect on the examined outcome. In other words, we can determine the extent to which genes significantly impact a specific behavior (e.g., criminal behavior), but these types of studies do not help to identify the specific individual genes that are involved.

There are, however, additional methods available to remedy this limitation of behavior genetic studies. Recent advances in molecular genetics and the mapping of the human genome allow for the examination of the association between specific genes and specific antisocial behaviors. Most of the specific genes that have been found to be associated with antisocial behaviors are directly involved with a process referred to as neurotransmission. During neurotransmission, signals are passed between brain cells (referred to as neurons) in the form of both electrical impulses and chemical messages (neurotransmitters). Both electrical and chemical messages are required due to

a small gap—referred to as a synapse—that separates the two neurons. Neurotransmitters bridge this gap and pass the signal on to the neuron receiving the signal. This process is repeated until the signal ultimately reaches its final destination and the desired behavior or function is performed. After the process of neurotransmission is completed some neurotransmitters remain in the synapse and have to be removed. One way that they are removed is via enzymes. With this process, enzymes are released into the synapse where they degrade excess neurotransmitters. Genes that code for the production of enzymes are thought to be among the most likely candidate genes for criminal behavior because they are partially responsible for determining levels of neurotransmitters in the brain.

MAOA and Criminal Behavior

One of the genes directly involved with neurotransmission and that has been found to be associated with antisocial behavior is the monamine oxidase A (MAOA) gene (Caspi et al., 2002). The MAOA gene is located on the X chromosome and is responsible for the production of the MAOA enzyme, which is involved in the degradation of various neurotransmitters such as serotonin, dopamine, and norepinephrine after neurotransmission. While all normal human beings have at least one copy of the MAOA gene (females have two since the gene is located on the X chromosome), there are at least five different variants of the MAOA gene in the general population. These variants are referred to as alleles and genes with more than two alleles in the general population are referred to as polymorphisms. Therefore, the MAOA gene is actually a polymorphism with at least five different copies or alleles. In this way, all normal humans have one copy (or two copies for females) of the MAOA gene, but the actual version (or allele) of the gene that a given individual possesses can be different from the version that another individual possesses. Importantly, research has revealed that different alleles produce enzymes with different activity levels (Sabol, Hu, & Hamer, 1998). Some alleles produce a more active enzyme that more efficiently clears neurotransmitters out of the synapse, while other alleles produce a less active enzyme that is less efficient in clearing neurotransmitters from the synapse. Based on these findings, studies have hypothesized that alleles which produce the less efficient enzyme should be associated with increased levels of antisocial behavior.

Studies have examined whether different alleles of the MAOA gene result in behavioral differences. One of the first studies to identify a direct association between MAOA and antisocial behavior was conducted by Brunner and his colleagues (1993). These researchers examined a Dutch family in which certain males engaged in a wide variety of antisocial and criminal behaviors including aggression, arson, and rape. The results of the study indicated that the observed behavioral problems were associated with a defective MAOA gene. More specifically, males within this family possessed a rare allele of the MAOA gene that resulted in a complete lack of production of the MAOA enzyme. While this finding may explain the concentration of antisocial behavior in the examined family, the allele possessed by each of the family members does not occur in the general population and does not explain other forms of antisocial behavior occurring outside of the examined family.

While individuals in the general population are not likely to possess the rare allele identified by Brunner et al. (1993), low-activity MAOA alleles present within the general population may result in a less effective version of the MAOA enzyme, significantly increasing the risk of antisocial behavior. A significant number of studies have examined the potential association between low-activity MAOA alleles and various antisocial behaviors. The results of these studies suggest that individuals who possess low-activity MAOA alleles are more likely to suffer from a range of psychopathologies, including antisocial outcomes (Caspi et al., 2002) and criminal behaviors (Guo et al., 2008).

MAOA, Gang Membership, and Weapon Use

Despite the significant amount of attention focusing on the association between low-activity MAOA alleles and various antisocial and criminal behaviors, only recently did a study examine whether MAOA genotype was related to the propensity to join a gang and the use of weapons in a fight. In this study, Beaver et al. (2010) examined data from a large and nationally representative sample of youth in the US known as the National Longitudinal Study of Adolescent Health (Add Health). The Add Health includes information on nearly 20,000 youths from adolescence to adulthood. A unique aspect of the Add Health is that DNA information was collected from more than 2,500 of the participants.

In order to examine whether MAOA was related to gang membership and to weapon use, a series of statistical models were estimated. The first set of statistical models examined the effect of MAOA on gang membership and weapon use for females only. The results of these models revealed that MAOA was unrelated to joining a gang and

it was also unrelated to using a weapon in a fight. The second set of models examined the effect of MAOA on gang membership and weapon use for males. The results of these models were quite different from the models only examining females. More specifically, males who had low-activity MAOA alleles were nearly 100% more likely to be a gang member and approximately 82% more likely to use a weapon in a fight than males with high-activity MAOA alleles.

The next set of statistical models examined the association between MAOA and weapon use among respondents who indicated that they were gang members. As in previous models, males and females were analyzed separately. Once again there was no association between MAOA and weapon use among female gang members. For male gang members, however, there was a significant association, wherein male gang members with low-activity MAOA alleles were over 4 times more likely to use a weapon in a fight than male gang members who carried high-activity alleles. Figure 1 displays a graphical depiction of the association between MAOA and weapon use for male gang members. As can be seen, there were 21 male gang members with the high-activity MAOA genotype. Of these gang members, 81% had not used a weapon in a fight, whereas 19% had used a weapon in a fight. In contrast, there were 33 male gang members with the low-activity MAOA genotype. Of these gang

Figure 1

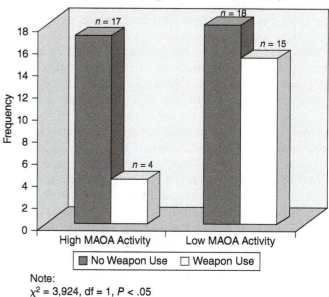

The Relationship between MAOA and Weapon Use among Male Gang Members (N = 54)

Note:
$\chi^2 = 3,924$, df = 1, $P < .05$

members, 55% had not used a weapon in a fight, whereas 45% had used a weapon in a fight.

Concluding Remarks

A significant amount of research has shown that genetic factors influence a wide range of antisocial behaviors, including criminal behavior (Ferguson, 2010; Moffitt, 2005). A related line of research indicates that individuals who carry low-activity MAOA genotypes are more likely to engage in various antisocial behaviors, including violent criminal behavior (Caspi et al., 2002; Guo et al., 2008). Recently, this line of research was extended to examine the association between MAOA and gang membership and between MAOA and weapon use. The results of the analyses revealed a pattern of findings that directly coincide with previous studies examining the association between MAOA and various violent criminal behaviors. More specifically, the results indicated that male carriers of low-activity MAOA alleles were more likely to join a gang than males who possessed high-activity MAOA alleles. In addition, males who carried low-activity alleles were more likely to use a weapon in a fight than males with high-activity alleles. Also of interest was that MAOA was able to distinguish between male gang members who used weapons in a fight and male gang members who did not use weapons in a fight. This finding is of particular interest because it indicates that differences in violence between gang members may be partially explained by differences in their genes.

Another important finding to emerge from the Beaver et al. study was that there was no association between MAOA and gang membership and MAOA and weapon use for females. This finding was expected since the MAOA gene is located on the X chromosome, and the criminogenic effects of the gene are thought to be strongest for males. This is likely due to the fact that males only possess a single X chromosome and therefore only on copy of the MAOA gene. Females, in contrast, possess two X chromosomes and therefore two copies of the MAOA gene. In this way, it remains possible for females to possess one low-activity allele and one high-activity allele (or two high-activity alleles). Since females possess more than one copy of the MAOA gene, it is much more difficult to isolate the effect of MAOA on antisocial behaviors for females than for males.

Despite the growing body of research tying MAOA to antisocial outcomes, more research is needed to elucidate the processes by which MAOA is ultimately tied to crime, gang membership, and even weapon use. As for now, however, the results of a body of rigorous

methodological research have shown that the underlying structure of criminal behaviors is highly complex, but most likely includes a genetic foundation. Criminologists must begin to integrate these findings into empirical research and theoretical perspectives if they want to remain consistent with the broader literature that is being produced in many other fields of study. Although there are certainly hundreds of genes that are associated with antisocial behaviors that can be studied, a focus on MAOA is justified given the amount of research showing its association with criminal, violent, and aggressive behaviors.

References

Akers, R. L. (1998). *Social learning and social structure: A general theory of crime and deviance.* Boston: Northeastern University Press.

Beaver, K. M. (2009). *Biosocial criminology: A primer.* Dubuque: Kendall/Hunt.

Beaver, K. M., DeLisi, M., Vaughn, M. G., & Barnes, J. C. (2010). Monoamine oxidase A genotype is associated with gang membership and weapon use. *Comprehensive Psychiatry, 51,* 130–134.

Brunner, H. G., Nelen, M., Breakefield, X. O., Ropers, H. H., & Van Oost, B. A. (1993). Abnormal behavior associated with a point mutation in the structural gene for monoamine oxidase A. *Science, 262,* 578–580.

Caspi, A., McClay, J., Moffitt, T. E., Mill, J., Martin, J., Craig, I. W., Taylor, A., et al. (2002). Role of genotype in the cycle of violence in maltreated children. *Science, 297,* 851–854.

Ferguson, C. J. (2010). Genetic contributions to antisocial personality and behavior: A meta-analytic review from an evolutionary perspective. *The Journal of Social Psychology, 150,* 160–180.

Guo, G., Ou, X. M., Roettger, M., & Shih, J. C. (2008). The VNTR 2 repeat in MAOA and delinquent behavior in adolescence and young adulthood: associations and MAOA promoter activity. *European Journal of Human Genetics, 16,* 626–634.

Hirschi, T. (1969). *Causes of delinquency.* Berkeley: University of California Press.

Moffitt, T. E. (2005). The new look of behavioral genetics in developmental psychopathology: Gene-environment interplay in antisocial behaviors. *Psychological Bulletin, 131,* 533–554.

Sabol, S. Z., Hu, S., & Hamer, D. (1998). A functional polymorphism in the monoamine oxidase A gene promoter. *Human Genetics, 103,* 273–279.

Sampson, R. J., Raudenbush, S. W., & Earls, F. (1997). Neighborhoods and violent crime: A multilevel study of collective efficacy. *Science, 277,* 918–924.

Weisburd, D., & Piquero, A. R. (2008). How well do criminologists explain crime? Statistical modeling in published studies. *Crime and Justice, 37,* 453–502.

KEVIN M. BEAVER is a professor and director of the Distance Learning Program at Florida State University, School of Criminology. His research examines the biosocial underpinnings to antisocial behaviors. He is the past recipient of the American Society of Criminology's Young Scholar Award and the National Institute of Justice's graduate research fellowship. Beaver has published more than 150 articles and is the author/editor of 10 books, including *Biosocial Criminology: A Primer.*

JOSEPH A. SCHWARTZ is an assistant professor in the School of Criminology and Criminal Justice at the University of Nebraska, Omaha. He received his PhD in Criminology and Criminal Justice at Florida State University. His research interests include biosocial criminology, behavioral genetics, intelligence and crime, and developmental and life-course criminology.

Joshua W. Buckholtz

 **NO**

Neuroprediction and Crime

Sixty minutes goes by in the blink of an eye. It's barely enough time to accomplish much of anything, really. But by the next tick of the long hand, two Americans will have lost their lives to acts of violence. In that same hour, 250 more will need medical treatment for a violence-related injury. As the hours pass, so mount the costs: on average $1.3 million for each violent fatality and $80,000 for each non-fatal assault. Each year, nearly 3% of our country's gross domestic product is lost due to violence.

As these staggering numbers make clear, violent crime is one of the most pressing public health problems of our age. Scientists have a duty to address large-scale social problems like violent crime, and scientific research aimed at preventing antisocial behavior would seem likely to provide a particularly good return on taxpayer investment. But to what extent can science actually help? I believe there is a considerable disconnect between the aims of science and the goals of criminal law, and that should lead us to be cautious.

There is broad support in both the U.S. and Europe for applying scientific methods and data to crime prevention. One potentially promising and exceptionally controversial zone of engagement is "prediction." The effort to predict "future dangerousness" is motivated by the belief that we can reduce antisocial behavior by identifying those people most likely to commit crimes. But clearly prediction is a double-edged sword: while we can use this information to more efficiently target costly social resources toward preventing violence in at-risk children, labeling any child a "future criminal" is likely to have serious adverse consequences all its own. Similarly, it's reasonable to think that scientific data could be a critical tool for evaluating the likelihood that an adult criminal will commit violent crime in the future. But if science is being used to make decisions about whether, or how long, to deprive someone of their freedom, it is imperative that we have confidence in the validity and reliability of our predictive tools.

Science Fact and Science Fiction

In the "old days," our predictive tools were blunt: the clinician's hunch with its obvious limitations—lack of objectivity and reliability to name two—served as a gold standard. Newer methods borrow from the language and statistics of actuaries, who compute insurance risks, overcoming objectivity and reliability problems with mathematical rigor. Actuarial prediction approaches are highly structured. They asses each individual according to the same set of specific variables—such as age at first offense, gender, or diagnosis of substance abuse—to assign that person to a high, medium, or low risk level. Though actuarial methods are unquestionably more reliable and valid than clinical assessment, judges and juries have been slow to warm to prediction by such "bean counting."

Enter the brain. Neuroscience has allowed us to peer into the black box of the human mind with a level of detail that would have been unthinkable twenty years ago. Advances in brain imaging and genomic science have begun to shed light on the biological origins of violence and antisocial behavior, spurring intense debate about their potential use as prediction tools. Some have embraced this potential with a particular eagerness, heralding the coming age of "neuroprediction."

This enthusiasm is grounded in two assumptions. First is the belief that individual measures of biology have an intrinsic reliability and validity that non-biological tools lack. Second is that we can make determinations about specific individuals, which is the aim of criminal law, based on what we know of a general phenomenon from averaging scientific data across many, many individuals, which is the goal and method of science. Unfortunately, when it comes to something as complex and messy as human behavior, both of these assumptions can fail badly. Brain images and DNA sequences may some day prove useful for forecasting individual behavior. But for today, the tools of neuroscience are still far too crude and our understanding of the brain too imperfect to tout unabashedly the promise of neuroprediction. As the genetics example below illustrates, such a future has not yet arrived.

It's misleading to talk about "having" or "not having" the "warrior gene."

Imagine a line of hushed grade-schoolers snaking down the scrupulously white halls of an overly bright clinic. A nurse sweeps briskly from child to child, each offering a single index finger, upturned and extended. As she passes, a handheld device lightly grazes the succession of outstretched digits, drawing an aliquot of blood so small that it can barely be seen with the naked eye. The machine noiselessly sifts through the liquid to isolate each child's genetic material; chromosome 5 is quickly scanned for a single letter at one specific position in the nucleotide sequence. The two options are "A" or "G." The A's will be free to leave. The G's, marked with the genetic signature of violence, must stay behind for further evaluation.

The scene described above is clearly science fiction, but the notion that an individual's DNA can be used to explain and predict their behavior is now taken quite seriously in many hallowed quarters. In several recent high-profile murder cases in the US and Europe, courts have permitted defendants to be tested for the so-called "warrior gene" and allowed positive results to be submitted as a mitigating factor. (The gene is called monamine oxidase A, or just "MAOA.") When presented to sitting judges in mock trials, warrior gene evidence exerts a powerful effect on their punishment decisions, affirming the unconscious deference paid to biological explanations of human behavior—even when those explanations are wrong. You see, MAOA is not a warrior gene. In fact, there is not now, nor could there ever really be any such thing as a warrior gene. Why not?

Enormous Variability

Our genome is a set of construction documents that dictates, among other things, how our brain cells are built, function, and get wired together. Everything that we are, we are because of our brains. Every consequential thought and every meaningless derailment, every blush of malice and every bite of conscience, every rush of joy and every slow bloom of sadness, every act of generation and every movement towards destruction, all of it, arises from coherent patterns of firing brain cells.

Across the entire population, one readily observes that there is enormous variability in human behavior of all kinds; this variability in behavior is driven by dramatic variability in the way that our brains work. In turn, individual differences in brains are determined, in large part, by individual

differences in genes. The "other part" is, of course, environment, which also shapes behavior by shaping brain fuction. So genes cause differences in behavior by causing differences in the way that each of our brains work. But the path from gene to behavior through the brain is a tortuous one indeed.

It takes more than one bad allele to produce a violent person.

MAOA gained notoriety as a warrior gene from the study of a Dutch family. The men in this family were very violent and antisocial, and it was found that they all carried a very rare mutation that "knocked out" their MAOA gene. This kind of circumstance is incredibly uncommon, though. Most of the time, genes vary between people in very small ways. We all have all of the same genes, but slight differences in the form that those genes take between people change the way that they work. This is why it's misleading to talk about "having" or "not having" the "warrior gene." Everyone has the MAOA gene, but it can come in at least two very slightly different versions, or "alleles." Early studies found that people who had one version—the Low version found in about one third of the population—were statistically more likely to be aggressive compared to folks who carried the other version—the High version.

But since these original studies, our understanding of genetics has advanced considerably. We now know that each of these small allele differences has an absolutely tiny effect on behavior when considered individually. There are millions of people who have the "bad" Low version of MAOA but who are not violent, and thousands of people who do not have the Low version but are violent. It takes more than one "bad" allele to produce a violent person; it takes hundreds, or even thousands. We also now understand that genetic differences rarely affect human behavior with the kind of selectivity or specificity desired and required by the law. While MAOA is thought of as a warrior gene, or as a violence gene, people with the Low version have been found to have such "un-warrior-like" syndromes as depression, schizophrenia, and panic disorder. Together, these two points highlight the idea that any test for a single genetic marker will likely be meaningless for either explaining or predicting human behavior.

Science and the Legal System

There is a final specter that haunts the entire enterprise of neuroprediotion: the group-to-individual, or G2I problem. This issue has its roots in a key difference between the aim and methods of science and the goals of the legal system. Science is focused on understanding universal phenomena; we do this by averaging data across groups of individuals. Law, on the other hand, only cares about specific individual people—the individual on trial. Neuroprediction is based largely on the assumption that you can individualize scientific data and inferences. If a study found that a certain allele in gene Y is statistically associated with violence risk, one might assume that finding out whether a person carries that allele would provide important information for determining whether he was likely to become violent. But this assumption is terminally flawed.

Recent work has shown that fMRI images have a "seductive allure."

The same is true for brain imaging. If a study found that on average people with relatively lower fMRI signal in a specific brain region during a specific task were more likely to commit crimes—relative to people with a higher fMRI signal in that region—it does not follow that any one individual's fMRI signal level will have any meaningful ability to predict crime. Because of these issues, I believe that it is extremely premature to talk about, much less submit as evidence, specific potential biomarkers for violence and antisocial behavior based on either brain imaging or genetic studies. At a bare minimum, we must carefully study the sensitivity and specificity of these potential biomarkers before we even consider permitting such evidence to influence judgments about individuals.

Human behavior is exquisitely complex and often counterintuitive. It would be folly to think that serious examination of the causes of behavior and its pathological variants would yield simple explanations. Unfortunately, the sophistication of our technologies can too often incite overconfidence in the explanatory power of a given bit of neuroscience datum. This is not merely an academic quibble, a bit of ivory-tower contrarianism. Indeed, recent work has shown that fMRI images can possess a "seductive allure" for jurors. Mere exposure to colorful neuroimaging evidence can enhance the credibility of otherwise implausible explanations of individual behavior. When presented to judges in mock trials, fMRI and DNA evidence has a powerful effect on punishment decisions, affirming the authority commanded by biology in the courts. Overly simplistic explanations of human behavior based in neuroscientific data are far too easily taken on face value; when applied to individuals, such explanations are fatally flawed.

Science, the great and final arbiter of truth, can and should be used to promote justice. However, we are starting to ask questions of neuroscience data that these data cannot reasonably answer. As a result, lives and freedom may be decided on the basis of scientific evidence, that, while cutting edge, has as much power to explain and predict the actions of an individual as a deck of tarot cards.

Joshua W. Buckholtz is currently an assistant professor of Psychology at Harvard University, where he directs the Systems Neuroscience of Psychopathology laboratory (SNPlab).

EXPLORING THE ISSUE

Does a "Warrior Gene" Make People More Prone to Violence?

Critical Thinking and Reflection

1. Discuss the limitations of neuroscience for predicting the behavior of specific individuals.
2. Discuss whether you agree with the following statement: "[T]here is not now, nor could there ever really be any such thing as a warrior gene."

Is There Common Ground?

This is an important issue with very significant implications for the study of human behavior. On one hand, Professors Beaver and Schwartz argue that "a long string of studies has provided irrefutable evidence that genetic factors significantly influence criminal and antisocial behaviors. Moreover, these authors contend that the results of over 100 empirical studies indicate that "approximately 50 percent of the individual differences in criminal and antisocial behaviors are explained by genetic influences." This indicates that most theories of criminal behavior drastically limit how well they explain crime by focusing exclusively on environmental factors and ignoring the important role that genetic factors play.

One compelling type of study that has provided a strong case for the role of biological/genetic factors in human behavior involve analyzing the behavioral similarity of twins. *Monozygotic (MZ)* or identical twins have identical genetic structures because they result from a single fertilized egg, or *zygote*, that has split during pregnancy. *Dizygotic (DJ)* or fraternal twins have developed from separate fertilized eggs during pregnancy. They therefore have no more genetic similarity than other siblings. A basic assumption of twin studies is that MZ twins should display greater behavioral similarity, or *behavioral concordance*, than DZ twins. Moreover, for purposes of behavioral research, it is best to study behavioral concordance for MZ and DZ twins that have been separated and or adopted at an early age, so-called *adoption studies,* thus varying their environmental influences. If behavioral concordance rates for separated MZ twins exceed those for separated DZ twins, we could therefore assert with confidence that the difference is due in some measure to genetic factors.

One of the problems with conducting this type of research, however, is that there are not that many pairs of MZ twins. How many sets of MZ twins do you know, especially sets of MZ twins, that are no longer living together? The answer is "probably not many." Therefore, research in this area has often focused on large groups of individual subjects, a so-called *macro-level* study, sometimes utilizing data on all such subjects from an entire region of the world.

As Professor Adrian Raine observes, almost all of these studies of adopted twins, which were conducted by different research groups in countries including Denmark, Sweden, and the United States indicate a genetic basis to criminal behavior. In all but one of the studies, MZ twins were found to display a high degree of behavioral concordance—if one MZ twin was found to have engaged in criminal behavior, there was a high probability that the other was involved in similar behavior. In fact, MZ twins displayed much higher behavioral concordance for aggressive and antisocial behavior than DZ twins. This leads Professor Raines to assert with confidence that there is a biological/genetic component to human behavior.

There seems to be little questioning, however, that the social environment also plays a role in human behavior. Biological factors may provide a foundation for a certain type of behavior, such as aggression, but do not alone provide a sufficient explanation for why one person with a predisposition for aggressive behavior becomes a criminal, whereas another with the same characteristics becomes a hard-charging corporate CEO, or an all-pro NFL linebacker. Some of the same aggressive tendencies may be needed for success in all three of these occupations.

In the reading accompanying this issue, Professors Beaver and Schwartz contend that another genetic factor, the presence of the monamine oxidase A (MAOA) gene has been found to be associated with antisocial behavior. To support their claim, they identify a number of studies that suggest that individuals who possess a low-activity form of the MAOA gene are more likely to suffer from a range of psychological maladies, including antisocial behavior. In addition, these authors conducted their own study on approximately 20,000 youths from adolescence to adulthood. They found that males who had a low-activity form of the MAOA gene were nearly 100 percent more likely to be a gang member and approximately 82 percent more likely to use a weapon in a fight than males with the high-activity MAOA gene. Moreover, it is significant that these researchers found no link between MAOA and gang membership and MAOA and weapon use for females. This provides further evidence of a genetic basis for these behaviors because the MAOA gene is located on the X chromosome, which females do not possess.

Professor Buckholtz, however, questions the assumption that such data will ever permit predictions about the behavior of particular individuals. He suggests the aim of our criminal justice system, by averaging scientific data across many individuals, should be the goal and method of science. He further states that the tools of neuroscience are still far too crude and our understanding of the brain too imperfect to tout the promise of neuroprediction. Thus, Buckholtz concludes:

> There is a final specter that haunts the entire enterprise of neuroprediction: the group-to-individual, or G2I problem. This issue has its roots in a key difference between the aim and methods of science and the goals of the legal system. Science is focused on understanding universal phenomena; we do this by averaging data across groups of individuals. Law, on the other hand, only cares about specific individual people—the individual on trial. Neuroprediction is based largely on the assumption that you can individualize scientific data and inferences. If a study found that a certain gene . . . is associated with violence risk, one might assume that finding out whether a person

carries that [gene] would provide important information for determining whether he was likely to become violent. But this assumption is terminally flawed.

What is your position on this important issue? Do you agree with Professors Beaver and Schultz that a "Warrior Gene" predisposes some persons to violent and antisocial behavior? Or, do you agree with Professor Buckholtz that our knowledge and understanding of neuroscience may never reach the point of being able to predict individual behavior? Moreover, is the "Warrior Gene" theory of criminal behavior subject to Professor Reid's dualistic fallacy criticism, considered earlier?

Additional Resources

Additional reading in this area is available. See Ronald L. Akers, *Social Learning and Social Structure: A General Theory of Crime and Deviance* (Northeastern University Press, 1998); Kevin M. Beaver, *Biosocial Criminology: A Primer* (Kendall/Hunt, 2009); Travis Hirschi, *Causes of Delinquency* (University of California Press, 1969); Sue Titus Reid, *Crime and Criminology* (13th ed.) (Oxford University Press, 2011); Frank P. Williams III and Marilyn D. McShane, *Criminological Theory* (6th ed.) (Pearson Higher Education, 2013); Michael Tonry (ed.), *Crime and Justice: A Review of Research*, vol. 27 (University of Chicago Press, 2001); Rolf Loeber and David P. Farrington (eds.), *Serious and Violent Juvenile Offenders: Risk Factors and Successful Interventions*, (Sage, 1998); See also: Kevin M. Beaver, M. DeLisi, M. G. Vaughn & J. C. Barnes, "Monoamine Oxidase A Genotype Is Associated with Gang Membership and Weapon Use," *Comprehensive Psychiatry* (2010, vol. 51); T. E. Moffit, "The New Look of Behavioral Genetics in Developmental Psychopathology: Gene-Environment Interplay in Antisocial Behaviors," *Psychological Bulletin* (2005, vol. 131); D. Weisburd & A. R. Piquero, " How Well Do Criminologists Explain Crime? Statistical Modeling in Published Studies," *Crime and Justice* (2008, vol. 37).

Internet References . . .

National Geographic Channel

http://natgeotv.com/ca/inside-the-warrior-gene

NOVA

www.pbs.org/wgbh/nova/body/neuroprediction-crime.html

Unit 2

UNIT

Contemporary Public Policy Issues in Criminology and Criminal Justice

*U*nderstanding society's reactions to crime, including why some behaviors are labeled criminal, while other potentially more harmful actions remain lawful can be a challenging enterprise. In some cases, our justice system has been accused of ignoring injustices committed against children, women, and minorities. At the same time the crimes of "white-collar" criminals are virtually ignored. This Unit analyzes modern justice system practices, including: whether "stand your ground" laws constitute a good social policy, racial profiling by law enforcement officers, the state of juvenile court systems, exposure to pornography and its relationship to crime, whether the United States has a right to torture suspected terrorists, and whether it should be a hate crime to display the Confederate Flag. These are cutting-edge issues in our justice system that should be explored by policy makers, criminologists, and students alike.

Selected, Edited, and with Issue Framing Material by:
Thomas J. Hickey, *State University of New York at Cobleskill*

ISSUE

Are "Stand Your Ground" Laws an Effective Way to Stop Violent Crime?

YES: Jorge Amselle, "Why We Need 'Stand Your Ground' Laws," *The Daily Caller* (2014)

NO: James Beckman, "The Problem with Stand Your Ground Laws: A Proven Detriment to Public Safety," Original Work (2016)

Learning Outcomes

After reading this issue, you will be able to:

- Discuss the role of the National Rifle Association (NRA) in supporting the passage of "stand your ground" laws in the United States.
- Discuss the early origins of "self-defense" laws and whether they are consistent with the adoption of "stand your ground" statutes.
- Discuss the "duty to retreat" doctrine.
- Present several arguments favoring the development of "stand your ground" laws in the United States.
- How do "stand your ground" laws increase the rate of justifiable homicide findings in criminal cases?
- Present several arguments opposing the development of "stand your ground" laws in the United States.
- Discuss how "stand your ground" laws increase the rate of justifiable homicide findings in criminal cases.
- Discuss whether "stand your ground" laws do more harm than good to public safety.

ISSUE SUMMARY

YES: Writer and firearms instructor Jorge Amselle asserts that "stand your ground" laws are needed for self-defense in the United States. Such laws provide those who use weapons for self-defense and defense of personal property with an effective legal defense in these cases.

NO: Professor and author James Beckman, in contrast, argues that "stand your ground" laws are an anachronism in modern society. Moreover, Beckman believes that these laws encourage situations wherein individuals will choose to escalate potentially violent encounters rather than diffusing them.

The self-defense doctrine has a long history in the Anglo-American legal tradition. Our courts have held consistently that a person has a right to use self-defense to prevent an impending attack on him/herself, in defense of personal property, or in defense of others. *Black's Law Dictionary* (1979), a classic legal treatise, defines self-defense as follows:

> An excuse for the use of force in resisting an attack on the person, and especially for killing an assailant. The right of a man to repel force by force even to the taking of life in defense of his person, property, or habitation, or of a member of his family, against anyone who manifests, intends, attempts or endeavors by violence of surprise, to commit a forcible felony.

To establish the traditional defense, a defendant must show that he/she did not provoke the incident and that there must be imminent peril. It also required the person using self-defense to demonstrate that there was no convenient or reasonable means of escape. Moreover, if an injury was done by a defendant in self-defense, he/she could not be held liable in a criminal case or a resulting civil action. (Id. 1220-1221). The case law also makes clear that it is never reasonable to use deadly force in a disproportionate manner—one is not justified to use deadly force to repel a non-deadly attack.

There are two forms of legal self-defense claims. *Imperfect self-defense* occurs when someone kills another person and he/she honestly believed that deadly force was needed to thwart the attack; however, it later turns out that the belief that deadly force was necessary was not a reasonable one. For example, suppose that you had recently received online death threats due to your political activism and someone walks toward you carrying a blue plastic sledge hammer that you honestly believe is a real one. Suppose further that he/she swings the hammer in your direction and you respond by shooting the individual with a .9 mm handgun that was concealed in your jacket and the assailant dies from the gunshot. If at trial you bring a self-defense claim, the question that will arise is whether your honest belief that the hammer swinging individual's conduct actually threatened your life was a reasonable one. If the court concludes that it was, the claim of self-defense would be a complete defense. If not, however, it could still mitigate your degree of criminal responsibility. In fact, in these circumstances it may well result in the reduction of charges from murder to a lesser degree of homicide, such as manslaughter.

A claim of perfect self-defense is established, in contrast, when a defendant's belief that his/her life is threatened by an attacker is an objectively reasonable one. For example, if someone confronts you with a real pistol and demands your wallet and threatens your life, responding with deadly force may well be determined to be an objectively reasonable course of action. In such circumstances, a self-defense claim may establish a complete defense and no criminal (or even civil) charges would arise.

An additional example may help to clarify the nature of self-defense claims in the real world. In a now-famous case that employed a self-defense claim to murder charges in the State of California, Erik and Lyle Menendez shot and killed their parents, Jose and Kitty Menendez, in the family's Beverly Hills home on August 20, 1989. The prosecution's theory supporting murder charges was that the killings were motivated by greed and the brothers' desire to acquire by early inheritance their parents' considerable wealth. However, after abandoning a story cooked up for police investigators that the Mafia had killed their parents, Erik and Lyle claimed at trial that the killings were the result of years of physical, sexual, and psychological abuse, and thus not murder, but only manslaughter. Their first trial resulted in a hung jury. The jury was unable to agree on a degree of homicide, landing all over the board with votes for first degree murder, second degree murder, voluntary manslaughter, and involuntary manslaughter. (*Menendez v. Ca Terhune,* 422 F.2d 1012).

At their second murder trial (double jeopardy does not apply if a first trial results in a hung jury mistrial), where they raised the same self-defense claim, the Menendez brothers were convicted of first degree premeditated murder and were sentenced to life imprisonment without the possibility of parole. Their convictions and sentences were later affirmed by the California Supreme Court and their petition for post-conviction relief was denied by the U.S. Court of Appeals (9th Cir.).

The Menendez case illustrates the difficulty of establishing a self-defense claim in a criminal trial. It also illustrates the highly subjective nature of these cases: The jury at the first trial could not agree on a verdict: Apparently while some jurors did not believe the brothers' self-defense claims, and voted to convict them of first degree murder, others accepted their claims and believed that voluntary or involuntary manslaughter were the more appropriate verdicts.

Self-defense cases, then, often present challenging factual issues. As noted earlier, in order to establish a self-defense case in some states a defendant must show that there was no convenient or reasonable means to avoid a confrontation, a so-called "duty to retreat." Other states, such as Florida, however, have eliminated the "duty to retreat." Florida's "Justifiable Use of Force" statute (Title XLVI, Chapter 776.013) provides:

> A person is presumed to have held a reasonable fear of imminent peril of death or great bodily harm to himself or herself or another when using or threatening to use defensive force that is intended or likely to cause death or great bodily harm to another if: . . . (b) The person who uses or threatens to use defensive force knew or had reason to believe . . . that an unlawful and forcible act was occurring or had occurred.

Thus, Florida law does not require a duty to retreat in order to establish self-defense. A highly controversial Florida case, which presented a self-defense claim, involved the 2012 shooting death of Trayvon Martin, a 17-year-old African American, by George Zimmerman, a self-declared neighborhood watch captain. At trial, the evidence showed that Martin was visiting his father, Tracy Martin, in the Twin Lakes gated community, in Sanford,

Florida. On February 26, Zimmerman called 911 to report a "suspicious person" in the neighborhood. The dispatcher instructed him not to get out of his SUV, or otherwise engage the person. Zimmerman disregarded this directive and moments later witnessed heard gunfire. When police arrived, Zimmerman acknowledged shooting Martin, who was found bleeding from the nose and back of head and later died from his injuries. The next day Zimmerman went to his family doctor, who testified that he had two black eyes, a fractured nose and two cuts on his head. Zimmerman was later charged in Florida court with second degree murder. A Florida jury accepted Zimmerman's self-defense claim and found him not guilty. In 2015, the U.S. Department of Justice declined to file civil rights charges against Zimmerman. Moreover, in a recent and somewhat macabre postscript to this case, George Zimmerman has offered publicly to sell online the gun he used to kill Trayvon Martin. The opening bid was set at $100,000. (Reuters, *World*, May 16, 2016).

Zimmerman's defense team decided tactically to use a traditional self-defense strategy in this case and forego a "stand your ground" (SYG) law pretrial hearing. Had he successfully established the "SYG" defense, he could have not been faced criminal or civil proceedings in this case. Is such a law a good social policy, however? The authors of the articles in this Chapter would have very different answers to this question.

Jorge Amselle contends that "SYG" law opponents are trying to make the case that these laws have turned lawful gun owners into a "shoot first ask questions later" people and that SYG has made this both acceptable and legal. He contends, in response, that SYG laws do not change the criteria for claiming legitimate self-defense or the use of deadly force. Moreover, the use of force must normally be proportionate to the existing threat.

James Beckman, in contrast, argues that modern "SYG" laws are a threat to public safety. They encourage individuals to escalate threating situations and have led to an increase in homicides in states where they have been adopted.

Which of these positions do you support? While reading the selections in this issue, think carefully about the purposes and objectives of self-defense claims and the goals of the U.S. justice system? Do SYG laws facilitate these goals?

YES ⤶

Jorge Amselle

Why We Need "Stand Your Ground" Laws

It is no surprise that the lefty media hates guns but ever since the Travon Martin shooting in Florida they have become especially apoplectic about Stand Your Ground (SYG) laws. In their continued criticism they have brought up two other Florida shooting incidents and one in Arizona. They conveniently ignore the fact that in all of these incidents, including the Travon Martin case SYG was either not a factor or most likely doesn't apply. . . .

Basically these laws make it clear that in a self-defense situation you do not have a duty to retreat before using lethal force. They are the law in 22 states. In the rest of the country, at least outside your home, you may have a duty to retreat.

The most recent anti-SYG rant comes from Dahlia Lithwick over at Slate.com. She is smart and an attorney (who should know better) and occasionally makes good points just not on guns. Using the aforementioned examples she tried to make the case that SYG has turned gun owners into a "shoot first ask questions later" type and that the law has actually made this both acceptable and legal.

Let's start with the obvious. SYG laws do not change the criteria for claiming legitimate self-defense or the use of lethal force. It is not enough to say you thought you saw a gun or that you were in fear for your life. The specifics have to be such that a reasonable person would feel the same way. Keep in mind that this reasonable person will be sitting in a comfortable chair, far away from danger, and dispassionately considering your argument. Absent clear physical evidence or witnesses it isn't as easy to prove self-defense as the media makes it out to be.

The use of force also has to be proportional in most cases. If someone is simply threatening you with their words and gestures, you can't shoot them no matter how scared you are. If you get in a fight with someone and are a participant in the altercation your ability to later claim self-defense if you use lethal force will be severely compromised. SYG changes none of this.

Lithwick also makes it seem that SYG is a new phenomenon, something states just started instituting in the last decade. It is true that legislatures started passing these laws in a very specific manner more recently but case law questioning the Duty to retreat (which is the basis for SYG) goes back well over 100 years. The best known example of this is *Brown v. United States* (1921) where the U.S. Supreme Court held that there was no duty to retreat in a legitimate self-defense case.

Here is an excerpt about this case from Wikipedia "if a man reasonably believes that he is in immediate danger of death or grievous bodily harm from his assailant he may stand his ground and that if he kills him he has not exceed the bounds of lawful self-defense." Wow, they were using the term "stand your ground" in 1921. Further, Justice Oliver Wendell Holmes wrote (also from Wikipedia), "Detached reflection cannot be demanded in the presence of an uplifted knife. Therefore, in this Court, at least, it is not a condition of immunity that one in that situation should pause to consider whether a reasonable man might not think it possible to fly with safety or to disable his assailant rather than to kill him." And there is that SOB the reasonable man again.

In simple terms we need SYG laws because too often prosecutors in self-defense cases ended up doing exactly what Justice Holmes warns against, using their own detached reflection outside the presence of that uplifted knife to judge the legitimacy of the actions of another. Grand juries go along and jurors are told how the state law says you have a duty to retreat if you can safely do so. Twelve people sitting in perfect safety get to decide if it was safe for you to retreat before they have to decide if it was OK for you to use lethal force to defend yourself.

Duty-to-retreat laws place an extra and unreasonable burden on those claiming legitimate self-defense. That is why so many states have enacted specific legislation to eliminate duty to retreat. Frankly, as an advocate of self-defense and a firearms instructor, I think it is a good idea to retreat if you can but I don't feel qualified to sit in judgment of another person's decisions when in mortal danger. Liberals seem to have no qualms about judging others, it seems.

JORGE AMSELLE is a certified firearms instructor and writer covering all aspects of the gun industry from military and law enforcement firearms and training to the shooting sports.

James Beckman

 **NO**

The Problem with Stand Your Ground Laws: A Proven Detriment to Public Safety

Introduction

The passage of the Florida "Stand Your Ground" (SYG) legislation in 2005 was truly like the proverbial gun shot heard round the world. Immediately upon passage of the law, visitors from around the globe were advised to be careful when visiting Florida because of this new law, and leaflets were even handed out at the Florida airports advising incoming tourists of this potentially life-threatening change to Florida's laws. The passage of this state law in 2005 was the result of very heavy lobbying by the influential National Rifle Association (NRA). Since that time, thirty-three additional states have revised their deadly use of self-defense laws to emulate Florida's 2005 legislation. As such, the NRA's successful campaign in this area can rightly be described as one of its more successful efforts in recent history at implementing laws relating to gun ownership (or more accurately, the protection of gun owners and right to carry laws) throughout the United States. Yet, the debate over the use of deadly force in self-defense has existed for centuries, and certainly long before Florida's 2005 alternations to the classical rules of the use of deadly force in self-defense in cases when one was in imminent fear of great bodily harm or death, or the protection of another in such legitimate imminent fear.

Thus, the often misunderstood and misquoted underlying history of SYG laws goes back well before Florida in 2005 and is relevant to understanding why such laws were initially passed, the current climate and status of SYG laws, and whether such laws are ultimately good or bad for public safety in the United States. In ultimately advocating that the SYG laws as currently formulated do not constitute wise public policy, I would like to divide and discuss my comments into three interrelated areas, namely: (1) the historical and classic rules pertaining to the use of deadly force and the proper rules of the so-called "duty to retreat" doctrine that existed in many states before 2005; (2) Florida's revisions to classic deadly force

self-defense rules through its promulgation of its famous/infamous SYG law of 2005—both as to what the revisions entail, why changes to the law were purportedly needed, and the alleged chief arguments in favor of these laws; and (3) the chief arguments today in opposition of SYG laws and this author's conclusions as to the efficacy and value of SYG laws (as currently formulated) in ultimately serving as a detriment to public safety in instances involve self-defense or in active shooter scenarios. To be clear, this author is not proposing that one may not use deadly force to repel attacks where one is imminent fear of grave harm or death. Rather, it will be argued that the recent SYG laws are actually superfluous to the state of the law for victims before 2005 (even in "duty to retreat" states) and that the laws since 2005 have been shown to do more harm than good to public safety.

Classic Rules Pertaining to Use of Deadly Force and the Duty to Retreat Rule

The concept of lawful self-defense permeates every aspect of human existence, from one-on-one interactions between two individuals on a street corner to interactions between nation-states under international law. In fact, Article 51 of the United Nations Charter speaks of a nation's "inherent right" of self-defense against the armed attacks of other countries, or even threats of such armed attacks. In English Common Law, there have been rules on the individual use of deadly force in self-defense for centuries, and certainly since the thirteenth century (Levin, 2010, p. 528). Interestingly, even in the early middle ages, the killing of another human being, even if in self-defense, was still considered homicide by the Crown. Phrased another way, early English Common Law did not permit one to "stand one's ground" and kill in self-defense, and only permitted the killing of another if one was attempting to apprehend a so-called "fleeing felon," if you need to kill to protect yourself from a robbery attempt or were acting under special permission (a writ) from the Crown (Mischke, 1981, pp. 1002–1003). The origins of the ability to kill in self-defense ironically initially developed as almost a post-trial mitigating factor in sentencing, by showing that one tried to retreat as far as possible and only killed as a last resort. If a defendant could prove that he or she attempted to flee and retreat and only killed as a last resort, the jury could enter a special finding of guilty. This enabled the Crown to intervene in the case and possibly commute or pardon the defendant's sentence, based upon any unique case circumstances (Brown, 1991, p. 3). Thus, ironically, for hundreds and hundreds of years before the United States became a separate country in 1783, English Common Law disfavored the so-called modern-day right to stand one's ground in self-defense. The requirement that a convicted defendant could have the Crown intercede on his or her behalf by showing that he or she retreated to the wall and did everything possible to avoid bloodshed was the legal requirement for hundreds of years and was the genesis of the "duty to retreat" rules that gain a prominent foothold in the United States centuries and centuries later. As one law scholar has written, for centuries at common law, the Crown made clear through its laws and "communicated to the citizens that the right to defend one's self against an attack was not an automatic license to kill" (Glinton, 2013, p. 1), arguably unlike the mentality of many in the United States today under modern SYG laws.

Yet, early on in the American experience, states (particularly those in the South and West) allowed for the use of deadly force to defend against deadly force and refused to impose the "duty to retreat" that had existed for centuries in England (Catafalmo, 2007, p. 507). These states become known as "no retreat" jurisdictions. These states constituted a majority of states well into the 1960s. Particularly after the drafting the influential Model Penal Code (MPC) in 1962 (which advocated for a "duty to retreat" before utilizing deadly force in self-defense), more and more states began imposing a "duty to retreat" requirement before using deadly force in self-defense (when outside of one's home). Simply put, in jurisdictions adopting this rule, the victim must retreat if outside the home (if he or she could do so safely) before utilizing deadly force. For those states that refused to adopt the "duty to retreat" rule (which MPC acknowledged was still a majority of states when the MPC was finalized in 1962), one could already stand one's ground, and utilize deadly force *if* one was in imminent fear of grave bodily harm or death. Phrased another way, at least in the 1960s, a majority of jurisdictions had laws that specified that "a person should not be required to resort to what some might deem cowardice

in order to spare the life of the one who precipitated the difficulty in the first place" (Loewy, 2003, p. 76). The idea behind this retreat rule (beyond its centuries old mooring in the law) is that one should not needlessly shed blood (even an alleged criminal's blood) "when a person can avoid danger by running away" (Loewy, 2003, p. 76).

The "duty to retreat" rule began to gain traction and was adopted by more and more jurisdictions between 1962 and 2005. Indeed, a variety of well accepted criminal law textbooks asserted that "duty to retreat" states actually outnumbered "no retreat" states for many years after the completion of the MPC and prior to the passage of Florida's SYG law in 2005 (see, for e.g., Schmalleger, 2002, p. 163; Loewy, 1987, p. 68). Indeed, as late as 2002, one prominent scholar (Dr. Frank Schmalleger, Professor Emeritus at the University of North Carolina) asserted that "most jurisdictions impose a retreat rule upon those who would claim self-defense" (Schmalleger, 2002, p. 163). Another prominent law professor similarly asserted several decades earlier that "the 'retreat' rule . . . is adopted by many jurisdictions and the M.P.C. [Model Penal Code] . . ." (Loewy, 1987, p. 68). While somewhat speculative, the reason why many states adopted this rule was because requiring victims of crime to retreat when they safely could do so clearly had the tendency to reduce the loss of life (and not increase it) and de-escalate violent situations (and not increase them). Further, as will be explained below, the "duty to retreat" rule, while much maligned by the NRA, actually did not actually preclude victims of potential crimes from utilizing deadly force if the victim had any subjective doubt whatsoever that he or she could not escape completely and safely without harm. If the potential victim had any doubts, he or she could utilize deadly force to defend themselves.

Thus, one of the most deliberately overlooked aspects of the "duty to retreat" rule during political debates was the fact that victims need not retreat at all unless that person subjectively believes and knows that he or she could retreat with *complete and utter safety* (Loewy, 2003, p. 77). Thus, as one law professor has written, "even though a reasonable person might have known that he could retreat in complete safety, if this [victim] did not know it, he would be under no duty to retreat rather than use deadly force" (Loewy, 2003, p. 77). Likewise Professor Emeritus Frank Schmalleger has acknowledged that a victim's retreat is only required "if [the] retreat can be accomplished with 'complete safety'" (Schmalleger, 2002, p. 163). Yet, this salient and important element of the "duty to retreat" requirement was conveniently left out (or unintentionally or deliberately downplayed) in the political discussions leading up to the promulgation of Florida's SYG law of 2005, and the passage of similar laws in other states thereafter. Thus, put simply, if a victim did not subjectively believe he or she could extract themselves out of the situation with complete safety, a potential victim could lawfully use deadly force to repel an attack when he or she was in imminent fear of grave bodily harm or death regardless of the jurisdiction wherein the potential attack took place.

The Florida SYG Revolution

On April 26, 2005, then-Florida Governor Jeb Bush signed Florida Senate Bill 436 into law, amending Florida's statutory laws on the use of deadly force in self-defense. What did these revisions do to the existing standards discussed above? First, the law eliminated entirely any duty to retreat for a potential victim in any place the potential victim was entitled to be (street corner, movie theatre, car, shopping mall, etc.)—basically making any public space a person's "castle" for self-defense laws, even though the potential victim could have escaped the situation with complete and utter safety. Second, the law eliminated civil liability for those who utilized their concealed weapons in self-defense. Third, the revised law created a presumption of reasonable fear for the individual claiming self-defense, meaning the potential victim no longer needed to claim and offer some evidence that he or she was in imminent fear of grave bodily harm or death (Cheng and Hoekstra, 2012, p. 1). These changes prompted one of the twenty Florida legislators (Dan Gerber) who voted against the law to state that "it legalizes fighting to the point of death, without anybody having a duty to retreat" (Weaver, 2008, p. 397).

Marion Hammer, a former president of the NRA, was one of the chief advocates and lobbyists for the ultimate passage of Florida's now famous/infamous SYG law in 2005. One of the most effective political arguments of proponents of this new law was that the law was needed so that innocent victims need not have to try to futilely escape before being able to defend themselves with deadly force—even if the potential victims had doubts about their ability to escape (something never required by the "duty to retreat" rule). As evidence of this type of argument in trying to convince the legislature in Florida (and the electorate in Florida, generally), Marion Hammer was quoted in 2005 as providing the following example as evidence for a need to change Florida's existing laws on self-defense:

> [I]f someone had tried to drag a woman into an alley to rape her, the women [sic]—even though she might be licensed to carry concealed and ready to protect herself, the law would not allow her to do it. It required her to try to get away and run and be chased down by the perpetrator before she could then use force to protect herself. (Center for Individual Freedom, 2005)

Roughly seven years later (in 2012), in the aftermath of the George Zimmerman shooting of Trayvon Martin, and when many were protesting Florida's SYG law, two other Florida politicians attempted to defend the law on the same erroneous arguments made by Hammer seven years prior by setting forth an equally erroneous application of what "duty to retreat" laws actually entailed. The politicians stated:

> Consider an elderly woman in a dimly lit parking lot or a college girl walking to her dorm at night. If either was attacked, her duty was to turn her back and try to flee, probably be overcome and raped or killed. Prior to 'Stand Your Ground,' that victim didn't have the choice to defend herself, to meet force with force. (Schorsch, Gaetz, and Gaetz, 2012; also, Franks, 2016, p. 145)

Thus, if the only premise for a revision to Florida's law to eliminate any duty to retreat was based upon the above type scenarios, the justification for such revisions were quite weak indeed—as one could always use deadly force (regardless of jurisdiction—whether it was a "retreat" or "no retreat" jurisdiction—if one did not subjectively believe one could flee completely and utterly successful from one's attackers). However, a critical analysis of concerns and motivations of gun owners reveal a concern that was a more pragmatic argument in favor of these laws (but not as viscerally emotional as the above two examples)—namely the protection and insulation of gun owners with "concealed carry permits" from civil and/or criminal investigation of when they utilized their weapons in self-defense.

John R. Lott, Jr., a famous scholar who has written extensively on his theory of "more guns, less crime," has postulated a number of reasons why he believes SYG laws make sense (summarized briefly below). However, at this point, it is relevant to note that Lott has suggested that SYG laws are needed to remove discretion from prosecutors and prosecuting attorneys, who arguable might be suspicious and paranoid of gun owners generally. That is, in order to protect and insulate gun owners who use a concealed firearm in self-defense against another, SYG laws (and the civil and criminal immunity provisions often contained within such laws) are needed to protect these law abiding gun owners from overreaching investigations by police or overzealous prosecutors who arguably might be anxious to indict the gun owners from killing the person who allegedly posed a threat in the first place (Lott, 2013). John Roman, an expert on crime and a Senior Fellow at the Urban Institute, testified to the United States Judiciary Committee that the primary motive behind the promulgation of SYG laws was really to protect and insulate gun owners from the avoidance of a criminal trial. If an investigation or trial did occur, then "the purpose of enacting SYG is to increase the rate of justifiable homicide findings" in those cases (Roman, 2013). Thus, according to another firearms expert Glenn H. Utter, the SYG laws really have their genesis in the NRA's desire to "avoid the financial cost of legal defense and the trauma of being tried in court for criminal conduct" and SYG laws "can most appropriately be understood as the result of a major increase in the number of citizens (estimated at more than 11 million) who have qualified for a concealed carry permit and who thus may face the legal entanglements resulting from the use of firearms in deadly confrontations" (Utter, 2016). As explained by Utter, "SYG laws negate the traditional duty to retreat from such confrontations and in several states provide for criminal and civil immunity" (Utter, 2016). Another scholar commented likewise stating that the rationale behind these laws "is to eliminate the fear of prosecution experienced by those who may act in self-defense" (Megale, 2010, p. 119). This makes 11 million (and growing) concealed gun owners more confident about their "right" to use their weapon in situations they deem merited, without fear of overzealous or overreaching prosecution, or in being sued in a civil action. Marion Hammer, one of the chief proponents of Florida's law, acknowledged as such when he stated that these laws were necessary to protect the victim of attacks (i.e., lawful gun owners) from prosecution (Weaver, 2008, p. 397). It was never really about little old ladies or college females in dark alleys who could not outrun their potential attackers or being lawfully precluded from legally utilizing a firearm that she might have been carrying in her purse for her self-defense to thwart a violent attack.

In order to fully understand the deficiencies in SYG laws, one first must have an appreciation of the other arguments put forth by advocates of SYG laws. That is, setting aside the above political and pragmatic considerations of providing civil and criminal immunity to those currently carrying concealed firearms, are there actual other benefits to these laws? Phrased another way, what other arguments have made publically in defense of SYG laws? Perhaps the most well-known advocate for the theory of "more guns equals less crimes" and also a defender of SYG laws is John R. Lott, Jr. Lott has argued that SYG laws remove any element of doubt in the minds of the victim as to the propriety of the use of deadly force in self-defense,

and this removal of the element of doubt may save the victim precious seconds needed to protect him or herself (Lott, 2013). Further, advocates claim that SYG laws will ultimately deter violent crimes, as (so the argument goes) criminals will be less likely to commit a crime if they know their targeted victim is armed. For instance, one of the Florida legislators voting in favor of Florida's law (Dennis Baxley) stated that a "requiring a duty to retreat was 'a good way to get shot in the back,' and the new law would deter criminals . . ." (Zbrzenj, 2012, p. 257). Gun rights advocates also claim that allowing for an armed citizenry through robust "concealed firearm carry laws" in conjunction with SYG laws will allow as an active early defense to active shooter scenarios as well, wherein a "good guy" can thwart the "bad guy" from committing unprovoked attacks (Utter, 2016).

Chief Arguments in Opposition of SYG Laws

Despite the very laudatory intentions that SYG laws would deter violent crime and reduce the number of homicides in the United States, unfortunately no convincing evidence has been put forth to date to support this thesis. In fact, the opposite appears to be true. In the empirical studies that have been conducted in the roughly eleven years since the passage of Florida's law in 2005, several very persuasive studies have emerged that cast serious doubt on the efficacy and effectiveness of SYG laws in decreasing violent confrontations or in decreasing the number of homicides in these states.

First, homicide rates have actually increased in states with SYG law (since passage of those laws) than in those states without SYG laws. By analyzing national data from the Center for Disease Control's National Vital Statistics System, economists Chandler McClellan and Erdal Tekin concluded that homicides significantly increased (especially among Caucasian shooters) in those states who had adopted Florida SYG type laws (McClellan and Tekin, 2012). On average, McClellan and Tekin also concluded that homicides increased 7.1% in states *after* those states adopted SYG laws. McClellan and Tekins' study was also replicated by two Texas A&M University professors, Cheng Cheng and Mark Hoekstra, who utilized the Federal Bureau of Investigation Uniform Crime Reports (through 2011) to analyze the impact (if any) of SYG laws on homicide rates and the potential deterrence of violent crimes. Consistent with McClellan and Tekin's study, Cheng and Hoekstra found that homicides increased after adoption of SYG laws. Also, comparing states the few remaining states without SYG laws with the great majority of states which now have SYG laws, the scholars additionally concluded that there was no evidence that SYG laws actually deterred crime and, quite the contrary, found that SYG laws is a significant factor which may logically lead all parties to a confrontation to escalation of violence (rather than defusing the situation) (Cheng and Hoekstra, 2013). Finally, a 2014 report by the American Bar Association concluded that "proponents of Stand Your Ground laws could point to no examples of cases wherein traditional self-defense law would not have protected a law-abiding individual operating in justified self-defense" (American Bar Association Report, 2014, p. 25).

Consistent with the above, Florida, the jurisdiction starting the SYG revolution within the United States, also has witnessed an increase (not decrease) in the number of homicides since Florida's SYG law was promulgated (Vendatam, 2013). Another very troubling statistical finding in Florida is that the SYG law, originally pitched to benefit the innocent law abiding citizens against hardened criminals, statistically appear to benefit criminal elements in society instead. For instance, in a ground breaking analysis by the *Tampa Bay Times* of over 100 SYG cases involving the fatal use of deadly force in self-defense since Florida's SYG law went into effect, the study found that almost half of those arrested (and claiming SYG and self-defense) were arrested at least three times before the fatal shooting, often for violent prior actions (Stanley and Humburg, 2012). Further, this same study found that a third of the shooters claiming self-defense under Florida's self-defense law had previously threatened to use a firearm against another, or at least were caught carrying firearms illegally.

Additionally, there is a growing body of evidence that has concluded that huge racial and gender disparities exist in SYG cases. For instance, the American Bar Association Task Force concluded that a fatal shooting by white individual (claiming self-defense under SYG laws) killing a black individual is 350 percent more likely to be found as justifiable homicide/shooting than if the a black shooter (claiming self-defense under SYG laws) were to kill a white individual (American Bar Association, 2014, p. 22). These disturbing racial and gender disparities have been extensively discussed by a number of scholars and studies in the recent past, including the American Bar Association (2014), Stanley and Humberg (2012), Franks (2016), Roman (2013), etc.

Occasionally advocates of SYG laws say that such laws are needed because it will prevent rampage shootings (if one of the targeted victims is armed). This argument is replete with fallacies and is an argument which assumes the person carrying the concealed weapon knows how to use the weapon very effectively. In fact, however, most states that allow individuals "concealed weapon permits" require very minimal training, including at least one state (Virginia) that allows this training to be completed entirely online. This is hardly the sort of training that would enable a concealed weapon holder to prevent a rampage shooting in an effective manner, without potential damage or injury to other innocent bystanders. Additionally, there are six states that do not even require a license to carry a concealed weapon, meaning no training whatsoever is required (Utter, 2016). These states currently include Alaska, Arizona, Kansas, Maine, Vermont, and Wyoming. While some states require minimal training, such training certainly falls woefully short of police officer training, which scholars have characterized as equally inadequate (Stoughton, 2014). If police officers are not being adequately trained in the proper use of deadly force to repeal deadly force, it is doubtful that the average citizen with a concealed weapon permit has superior training. Indeed, many law enforcement organizations focus on other ways to provide safe ways to de-escalate and subdue violent suspects. For instance, law enforcement has encouraged the use of such alternative methods such as the follows: use of stun guns and stun shields; use of mace, tear gas and other chemical sprays; pepper spray; and rubber bullets and other nonlethal projectiles (Gardner and Anderson, 2000, p. 123). According to a 2016 *New York Times* article, the Police Executive Research Forum stressed a list of 30 alternative options for police in de-escalating and resolving potential violent threats, without the officers using violence themselves in response (Baker, 2016, p. A10). As argued by Professor Glenn Utter, "these principles should also apply to private citizens who carry concealed weapons."

Finally, in the aftermath of every rampage shooting covered on national television (whether Columbine in 1999, Virginia Tech in 2007, or at Umpqua Community College in 2015), viewers see images of victims being rushed out of the buildings with hands held high in the air, in order for local law enforcement to quickly determine the active shooter from the scores of potential victims. If some of the potential victims to such an attack are seen to have firearms in their opposition, it does not take much imagination to envision the chaos and confusion such a visage might cause in the eyes of law enforcement quickly trying to determine "friend" from "foe" and to disable the identified "foe" as quickly as possible. There is no evidence that allowing people to actively arm themselves to combat these attacks has prevent even one attack, and it greatly increases the inability of responding law enforcement to respond in an effective matter in distinguishing the innocent victims from the active shooters.

Conclusions

For all of the foregoing reasons, the modern SYG laws are detrimental to public safety. They encourage a situation where individuals chose to escalate (and not de-escalate the situation), the laws have led to an increase in homicides wherein SYG laws have been adopted, they have not deterred crime they way initially proposed, the laws were passed on the incorrect assumption that "duty to retreat" rules were obsolete and not effective, and the SYG laws have been found to have been applied in both a discriminatory fashion as it has to do with both race and gender of the shooter and victim in a given case.

References

American Bar Association (2014), "Preliminary Report and Recommendations," *ABA National Taskforce on Stand Your Ground Laws Report* (August 8, 2014)

Baker, "Police Leaders Urge New Set of Standards," *New York Times* (January 30, 2016) at A10

Brown, Maxell Richard (1991), *No Duty to Retreat: Violence and Values in American History and Society*, New York: Oxford University Press

Catafalmo, Christine (2007), "Stand Your Ground: Florida's Castle Doctrine for the Twenty-First Century," *Rutgers Journal of Law and Public Policy*, Volume 4, pp. 505–539

Center for Individual Freedom (2005), "Interview with Marion Hammer," (November 3, 2005)

Cheng, Cheng and Hoekstra, Mark (2013), "Does Strengthening Self-Defense Law Deter Crime or Escalate Violence? Evidence from Expansions to Castle Doctrine," *Human Resources*, Volume 48 (summer): pp. 821–854, available at http://wwweconweb.tamu.edu/mhoekstra/castle_doctrine.pdf

Franks, Mary Ann (2016), "How Stand Your Ground Laws Hijacked Self-Defense," in *Guns and Contemporary Society: The Past, Present and Future of Firearm Policy*, Volume III, ed. Glenn H. Utter, 2016, Santa Barbara: Praegar (ABC-CLIO)

Gardner, Thomas J. and Anderson, Terry M. (2000), Belmont, CA: Wadsworth

Glinton, Vaughn G.S., Jr. (2013), "Southern Honor: An Analysis of Stand Your Ground Laws in Southern Jurisdictions," unpublished honors thesis, University of Central Florida, available at http://etd.fcla.edu/CF/CFH0004507/Glinton_Vaughn_G.S._201311_BA.pdf

Levin, Benjamin (2010), "A Defensible Defense? Reexamining Castle Doctrine Statutes," *Harvard Journal of Legislation*, Volume 47, pp. 523, 528, 530–531

Loewy, Arnold (1987), *Criminal Law in a Nutshell*, 2nd edition, St. Paul: West Publishing Company

Loewy, Arnold (2003), *Criminal Law in a Nutshell*, 4th edition, St. Paul: Thomson-West

Lott, John R. (2013), "Perspective: In Defense of Stand Your Ground Laws," *Chicago Tribune* (October 28, 2013)

Lott, John R. (2013), Testimony before the U.S Senate Judiciary Committee's Subcommittee on the Constitution, Civil Rights, and Human Rights, at http://www.judiciary.senate.gov/imo/media/doc/10-29-13LotTestimony.pdf (October 29, 2013) (last accessed on March 12, 2016)

McClellan, Chandler B. and Erdal Tekin (2012), "Stand Your Ground Laws, Homicides, and Injuries," in *National Bureau of Economic Working Paper No. 18187*, available at http://nber.org/papers/w18187

Megale, B. Elizabeth (2010), "Deadly Combinations: How Self-Defense Laws Pairing Immunity with Presumption of Fear Allows Criminals to Get Away with Murder," *American Journal of Trial Advocacy*, Volume 48, pp. 1000–1007

Mischke, Phillip (1981), "Recent Development: Criminal Law—Homicide—Self-Defense—Duty to Retreat: *State v. Kennamore*," *Tennessee Law Review*

Roman, John (2013), Testimony before the U.S Senate Judiciary Committee's Subcommittee on the Constitution, Civil Rights, and Human Rights, at http://www.urban.org/sites/default/files/alfresco/publications-pdfs/904607--Stand-Your-Ground-Laws-Civil-Rights-and-Public-Safety-Implications-of-the-Expanded-Use-of-Deadly-Force.PDF

Schmalleger, Frank (2002), *Criminal Law Today*, 2nd edition, New Jersey: Prentice Hall

Schorsch, Peter, Gaetz, Don, and Gaetz, Matt (2012), "Op-ed: Standing Up for 'Stand Your Ground'," *SaintPetersBlog* (May 2, 2012)

Stanley, Kameel and Connie Humburg (2012), "Many Killers Who go Free with Florida 'Stand Your Ground' Law Have History of Violence," *Tampa Bay Times*, July 20, 2012

Stoughton, Seth (2014), "How Police Training Contributes to Avoidable Deaths," *The Atlantic*, December 12, 2014.

Utter, Glenn H. (2016), "Stand your Ground Laws: Avoiding Prosecution," in ABC-CLIO *Enduring Issues* database, at http://issues2.abc-clio.com

Vendatam, Shankar (2013), "Stand Your Ground Linked to Increase in Homicides," *National Public Radio*, January 2, 2013, available at http://www.npr.org/2013/01/02/167984117/stand-your-ground-linked-to-increase-in-homicide

Weaver, L. Zachary (2008), "Florida's Stand Your Ground Law: The Actual Effects and The Need for Clarification," *The University of Miami Law Review*, Volume 68, pp. 395–417

Zbrzenj, Lydia (2012), "Florida's Controversial Gun Policy: Liberally Permitting Citizens to Arm Themselves and Broadly Recognizing the Right of Act in Self-Defense," *Florida Coastal Law Review*, Volume 13, pp. 231–266

JAMES BECKMAN is a professor of Legal Studies at the University of Central Florida (UCF) where he served as Chair from 2011 to 2015. He has also served as a law professor at the University of Tampa from 2000 to 2011 and is the author and/or editor of six books. Prior to teaching, Professor Beckman served as a litigation attorney for the U.S. government, including the Treasury Department and as an active duty Army judge advocate from 1994 to 1998.

EXPLORING THE ISSUE

Are "Stand Your Ground" Laws an Effective Way to Stop Violent Crime?

Critical Thinking and Reflection

1. Do the gun lobby, firearms industry, and National Rifle Association (NRA) have too much power in the United States?
2. How do "stand your ground" laws differ from traditional self-defense laws?
3. What is the "duty to retreat" doctrine?
4. What are several justifications for the adoption of "stand your ground" laws?
5. How do "stand your ground" laws increase the rate of justifiable homicide verdicts in criminal cases?

Is There Common Ground?

"Stand your ground" laws have generated substantial controversy in the U.S. legal system. Proponents of these laws argue that they are needed to support the Second Amendment's right to bear arms and contend that they are a necessary response to the problem of violent crime in society. "SYG" law opponents, in contrast, believe that these laws are a threat to public safety and contravene the principle of social utility, the idea that social policies should be geared to producing the greatest good for the greatest number of people. Moreover, those opposed to the adoption of "SYG" laws contend that they encourage vigilantism and have led to an increase in homicides in states where they have been adopted.

At the time of this writing, many states that have adopted "SYG" laws now include:

- Alabama
- Alaska
- Arizona
- Florida
- Georgia
- Indiana
- Kansas
- Kentucky
- Louisiana
- Michigan
- Mississippi
- Montana
- Nevada
- New Hampshire
- North Carolina
- Oklahoma
- Pennsylvania
- South Dakota
- Tennessee
- Texas
- Utah
- West Virginia

It is probably no accident that many of the states listed above would be considered to be political "red states." This indicates that they are generally conservative states that often vote for Republican candidates. In contrast, the states that have retained the more traditional approach to self-defense laws are more likely to be political "blue states." This indicates that they are more liberal or progressive states that are more likely to vote for democratic candidates in political elections.

Thus, the movement to adopt "SYG" laws may represent a mirror of larger political trends within our nation. The fact that it has been so difficult recently to find common ground in our political process may suggest that it will also prove challenging to develop a compromise position in the "SYG" law debate. In any case, it will be interesting to test this theory as time goes on: Will "SYG" laws lose traction, or will they become the rule rather than the exception throughout the United States? Only time will tell.

Additional Resources

The American Bar Association (ABA), "National Task Force on Stand Your Ground Laws: Report and Recommendations." (September 2015).

Adam Weinstein, "How the National Rifle Association and Its Allies Helped Spread a Radical Gun Law Nationwide," *Mother Jones* (June 7, 2012).

N. Ackerman, M. Goodman, K. Gilbert, C. Arroyo-Johnson, M. Pagano, "Race, Law, and Health: Examination of Stand Your Ground and Defendant Convictions in Florida," *Social Science & Medicine* (vol. 142, pp. 194–201, October 2015).

Internet References . . .

Santa Clara University, "Shot in the Dark: The Ethics of Stand Your Ground Laws." May, 2015.

www.scu.edu/ethics

Coca Currier, *Pro Publica,* "The 24 States That Have Sweeping Self-Defense Laws Just Like Florida's." March 22, 2012.

www.propublica.org

Marc Silver, "3 ½ Minutes. 10 Bullets." A Documentary. April, 2015.

www.1mdb.com

Selected, Edited, and with Issue Framing Material by:
Thomas J. Hickey, *State University of New York at Cobleskill*

ISSUE

Is Racial Profiling an Acceptable Law Enforcement Strategy?

YES: Jared Taylor and Glayde Whitney, from "Racial Profiling: Is There an Empirical Basis?" *Mankind Quarterly* (2002)

NO: Michael J. Lynch, from "Misleading 'Evidence' and the Misguided Attempt to Generate Racial Profiles of Criminals; Correcting Fallacies and Calculations Concerning Race and Crime in Taylor and Whitney's Analysis of Racial Profiling," *Mankind Quarterly* (2002)

Learning Outcomes

After reading this issue, you will be able to:

- Discuss the violent crime rate among African Americans, Hispanics, and whites in the United States.
- Discuss the violent crime rate among African Americans and whites in London.
- Discuss the National Crime Victimization Survey (NCVS).
- Discuss several different kinds of errors in different analyses of crime data sources that may have produced misleading results in studies of the relationship between race and crime.
- Present a philosophical and moral argument against the use of racial profiling by law enforcement officials.

ISSUE SUMMARY

YES: Jared Taylor, president of the New Century Foundation, and Glayde Whitney argue that the disparity in crimes committed by members of different races justifies racial profiling by the police.

NO: Professor Michael J. Lynch, however, argues that a proper analysis of the crime data does not support Taylor and Whitney's conclusions. He finds racial profiling to be objectionable from a legal and moral perspective as well.

One of the more controversial issues in American society is race relations. It has now been more than 50 years since the U.S. Supreme Court's seminal decision in *Brown v. Board of Education*, 347 U.S. 483 (1954), which ended the doctrine of "separate but equal" treatment of the races. This decision was grounded on the principle that separate treatment based on race can never truly be equal. Stated Chief Justice Earl Warren:

To separate [school children] from others of similar age and qualifications solely because of their race generates a feeling of inferiority as to their

status in the community that may affect their hearts and minds in a way unlikely ever to be undone. . . . (494)

Feelings of inferiority as to one's status in the community could be caused by many different things. Most of us have been stopped by the police for a traffic violation at one time or another. How did it make you feel? Did your heart rate increase? Did you begin to perspire slightly? Were you nervous, or did you become tongue-tied when you began to talk with the officer? Now, put yourself in the place of a 21-year-old African American male who is stopped by the police. Would the experience be any different? Would you be suspicious that the only reason you were stopped was because of your race? If you were a young Hispanic American male driving in an upscale neighborhood and were stopped by the police and were told "you don't belong here," would it produce the same feelings of inferiority? Is this the racial profiling Chief Justice Warren had described in *Brown v. Board of Education?*

In contrast, suppose that criminologists could show statistically that a disproportionate number of young minority group members were responsible for committing crimes such as burglary in the upscale neighborhood. Would the police be justified in questioning any young minority group member found in the area? Likewise, suppose it could be demonstrated that the individuals who carried out the September 11 bombings of the World Trade Center buildings were exclusively young males of Middle-Eastern descent. Would TSA officials at our nation's airports be justified in targeting such individuals for intensive pre-flight searches?

Jared Taylor and Glayde Whitney assert that the police are justified in using racial profiling strategies based on their analysis of macro-level crime data. These authors contend that African Americans commit violent crimes at four to eight times the white rate. Hispanics, they believe, commit violent crimes at approximately three times the white rate, and Asians at one-half to three-quarters the white rate. Taylor and Whitney assert that criminologists, in a spirit of political correctness, have succumbed to media and political pressure to avoid acknowledgment of the differences and their implications for public policy.

Criminologist Michael Lynch maintains that Taylor and Whitney have made errors in their analysis that produce misleading conclusions about racial profiling. While he agrees that African Americans are overrepresented in the crime data, he contends that this may be a measure of a bias that selects them more often for official processing within the justice system. Moreover, Lynch believes that Taylor and Whitney's views on the propriety of racial profiling by law enforcement officials either are purposely misleading or are completely naive analyses of crime and victimization data.

Suppose you accept Taylor and Whitney's view that the members of racial minorities do commit more crime in the United States. Does that mean that racial profiling by law enforcement officials is justified? Or, might there be a moral component to this debate, which says that it is wrong to target persons based on their race, no matter how effective the practice may potentially be? When you read these articles, try to develop your own sense of whether racial profiling is a legitimate law enforcement practice as well as its implications in a pluralistic nation.

YES ↩

Jared Taylor and Glayde Whitney

Racial Profiling: Is There an Empirical Basis?

The disparity between public sensibilities and empirical data has become so extreme that certain topics can no longer be investigated without bringing down cries of "racism." Nevertheless, blacks commit violent crimes at four to eight times the white rate. Hispanics commit violent crimes at about three times the white rate, and Asians at one half to three quarters the white rate. Blacks are as much more criminally violent than whites, as men are more violent than women. Therefore, just as police stop and question men more often than women, they should stop blacks more often than whites. Of the approximately 1,700,000 interracial crimes of violence involving blacks and whites, 90 percent are committed by blacks against whites. Blacks are 50 times more likely than whites to commit individual acts of interracial violence. They are up to 250 times more likely than whites to engage in multiple-offender or group interracial violence. There is more black-on-white than black-on-black violent crime. Fifty-six percent of violent crimes committed by blacks have white victims. Only two to three percent of violent crimes committed by whites have black victims. Violent crime and interracial violence are important, agonizing concerns in this country, and we cannot begin to formulate solutions until we understand the problems.

One of the strangest phenomena in contemporary criminology is the treatment of race and ethnicity. On the one hand there is a long history of academic attention to differences among racial and ethnic groups in involvement in various sorts of criminality (Hooton, 1939; Wilson & Herrnstein, 1985). On the other hand there appears to be media and political pressure to avoid acknowledgement of the differences and possible consequences of the differences. Recently the New Jersey State Police Superintendent Col. Carl Williams was fired by Gov. Christie Whitman after he said in an interview that some minority groups were more likely to be involved in certain crimes (AP, 1999). The Governor is quoted as having said that Williams' comments were "inconsistent with our efforts to enhance public confidence in the State Police." The same article reports that Williams said he did not condone racial profiling, and has never condoned racial profiling, but at the same time he said "it is naive to think race is not an issue" in some sorts of crime (AP, 1999). While Col. Williams claims not to condone racial profiling, the American Civil Liberties Union (ACLU) reported in June, 1999, that it was a widespread practice: "Citing police statistics, case studies from 23 states and media reports, the organization asserts that law-enforcement agencies have systematically targeted minority travelers for search . . . based on the belief that they are more likely than whites to commit crimes" (Drummond, 1999).

Although reports such as that of the ACLU which criticize the practice of racial profiling and criticize the "belief" that there may be race differences in criminality get wide media coverage, even being featured in national news magazines such as *Time* (Drummond, 1999), other reports that deal with the actual incidence of crimes as related to race get short shrift. The nationally syndicated columnist Samuel Francis recently wrote:

> Black Americans commit 90 percent of the 1.7 million interracial crimes that occur in the United States every year and are more than 50 times more likely to commit violent crimes against whites than whites are against blacks. These facts were the main findings of a study released earlier this month by the New Century Foundation, but they're not the really big news.
>
> The big news is that the report, despite having been made available to virtually all newspapers and news outlets in the United States as well as to most major columnists and opinion writers, has been almost totally ignored by the national news media. The study was released on June 2 of this year. To date, all of one single news story about it has appeared. (Francis, 1999)

It does indeed seem strange for there to be a great disparity between media reports and the subsequent public apperception, and the actual data concerning one of the more important issues in criminology today.

The inconsistency between media reports and criminological data concerning race is not a new phenomenon. About a decade ago we reviewed the literature dealing with race differences in criminal behavior. Taylor (1992) largely reviewed media reports, while Whitney (1990) reviewed the scientific literature. A main finding of the review of media accounts of race and crime was the existence of a double standard with regard to reports of crime that mentioned race of perpetrator or race of victim, with white victimization of blacks receiving considerably more prominent coverage than black victimization of whites (Taylor, 1992). The review of scientific literature was remarkable for both the quantity and consistency of prior literature (Whitney, 1990). Furthermore, the racial differences were accentuated when one considered more serious offenses and offenses that were variously described as victimful or predatory crimes. In a major review Ellis (1988) had reported that for serious victimful crimes, whenever comparisons had been made, blacks had always had higher rates than whites. Whenever blacks or whites had been compared with Orientals in roughly the same geographical areas, Orientals had always had the lowest serious victimful crime rates. The results were much less consistent for minor and/or victimless offenses. Overall, an order of blacks > whites > Orientals prevailed, with racial differences being larger the more serious and clearly victimful the offenses (Whitney, 1990).

In their classic *Crime and Human Nature,* Wilson and Herrnstein (1985:461) reviewed some literature on race and crime. They mentioned that blacks then constituted about one-eighth of the population of the United States and about one-half of arrestees for murder, rape, and robbery, and from one-fourth to one-third of arrestees for burglary, larceny, auto theft, and aggravated assault. Even with adjustments for other demographic variables, such as age and urban residence, in comparison to whites, blacks were overrepresented about four to one with regard to violent crimes and about three to one with regard to property crimes. Rushton (1985) pointed out that experience in England was consistent with that in the United States: blacks then constituted about 13 percent of the population of London and accounted for 50 percent of the crime. Indeed, violent crime by blacks had been mentioned as a factor contributing to the rearming of London's Metropolitan Police (Could & Waldren, 1986). Blacks were similarly overrepresented

with regard to white-collar crimes such as fraud and embezzlement. Blacks were underrepresented only with regard to offenses, such as securities violations, that usually required access to high-status occupations in which they were at that time underrepresented (Wilson & Herrnstein, 1985:462).

Whitney (1990) analyzed the race-specific arrest rates for various offenses that had been compiled for the years 1965 to 1986 (UCRP, 1988). For 19 categories listed in each of 22 years (418 comparisons), the rate for nonwhites always exceeded the rate for whites in the same year, typically by a factor of four to ten. For example, averaged across years, the nonwhite murder rate was nine times the white rate. Considerations of rate of crime combine prevalence (individuals who participate in crime) and incidence (recidivism, number of crimes by individuals who participate). Prevalence has been estimated through accumulation of first arrests across age (Blumstein & Graddy, 1981–1982; Blumstein & Cohen, 1987). Blumstein's results suggest that incidence is not strongly different among participants of different races. Rather, the race differences in crime rates are largely attributable to differences in the proportion of individuals of various races that participate in crime (Blumstein & Cohen, 1987). Among urban males the probability that by age 55 a black had been arrested for an FBI index crime was about 0.51; for whites it was 0.14 (Blumstein & Graddy, 1981–1982). Comparable age accumulated participation rates are not available for Orientals due primarily to their very low overall participation rates. Conversion of percentages to areas under a normal curve can be useful for comparing populations. These individual participation rates suggest about a one-standard-deviation difference between male urban blacks and whites for criminal liability (Whitney, 1990). The apologist argument that arrest data are inappropriate for documentation of race differences in crime rates due to bias in arrests was thoroughly considered, and essentially debunked in Wilbank's 1987 book *The Myth of a Racist Criminal Justice System.* More recently Dilulio (1996) has also presented data concerning crime disparities among races, and the suggestion that the disparities are real in that they do not reflect differential law enforcement.

For regions within the United States, Whitney (1995) pointed out that the best predictor of local murder rate was simply the percent of the population that was black. Across all of the 170 cities in the United States that had a 1980 population of at least 100,000, the correlation between murder rate and percent of the population that was black was r = +0.69. With data from 1980 aggregated for the 50 states of the United States, the simple correlation between murder rate and percent of the population that was black was r = +0.77. More recently Hama (1999) used data from 1995 to calculate the correlation across the 50 states between percent of the population that is black and violent crime rate, where violent crime rate was an aggregate of murder, non-negligent manslaughter, rape, robbery, and aggravated assault. Hama (1999) reported the correlation to be r = +0.76.

Clearly the existing data briefly reviewed above are quite consistent. They are also somewhat limited in scope. There are two areas of criminality related to race that are not considered above, but which have become of interest in recent years. One is the question of hate crime categorization, and the other is that of interracial crime. In crimes where the perpetrator and the victim are of different races, are there any patterns in incidence, and what amount of interracial crime gets included in hate crime statistics? The analyses reported in the present paper were conducted to obtain information concerning the questions of interracial crime and hate crimes, as well as to update the investigation of incidence of crime as related to race in the United States.

Sources and Methods

The primary sources of data for consideration were governmental compilations of statistical information having to do with crime. The major sources are described here. One of the most important sources is the National Crime Victimization Survey (NCVS). Every year since 1972, the U.S. Department of Justice has carried out what is called the NCVS to ascertain the frequency of certain kinds of crimes. The NCVS sample is large, upwards of 80,000 people from about 50,000 households, and carefully stratified on the basis of census data to be representative of the nation as a whole. The NCVS is unique as a record of criminal victimization as reported directly by Americans, not filtered through police reports. It is the only significant nationwide measure of interracial crime. The NCVS is carried out annually, but the Department of Justice does not issue full reports every year; 1994 is the most recent year for complete data.

Ever since passage of the Hate Crime Statistics act of 1990, the FBI has been charged with collecting national statistics on criminal acts "motivated, in whole or in part, by bias." The law does not compel local law enforcement agencies to supply the FBI with this information, but many do. In 1997, the most recent year for which data are available, the FBI received hate crime information from 11,211 local agencies serving more than 83 percent of the United States population.

Uniform Crime Reports (UCR), published annually by the FBI, is the standard reference work for crime and crime rates in the United States. The UCR is a nationwide compilation of criminal offenses and arrest data, reported voluntarily by local law enforcement agencies. In the most recent UCR, which covers 1997, the FBI included reports from 17,000 law enforcement agencies, covering 95 percent of the country's population. The UCR is unquestionably the most comprehensive and authoritative report on crimes brought to the attention of the police. News stories about rising or falling crime rates are almost always based on the UCR.

Our primary methodology throughout this study is to calculate rates of various offenses as a function of victim and offender characteristics. Such calculations are straightforward, but can appear arcane to investigators experienced with other analytical approaches. Therefore we here provide a detailed example.

The most recent complete NCVS data are for the year 1994 (USDJ, 1997). In that report Table 42 lists categories of single-offender interracial violent crimes. The various numbers at the top of the table represent totals calculated for single-offender violent crimes reported for that year. They are extrapolated from the actual crimes reported by the survey sample. We find that in 1994 6,830,360 whites were victims of violent crimes, and that 16.7 percent (1,140,670) reported that the perpetrator was black. Blacks were victims of 1,100,490 violent crimes, of which 12.3 percent (135,360) were committed by whites. Summing these figures for interracial crime (1,140,670 plus 135,360) we get a total of 1,276,030 interracial crimes, of which 1,140,670 or 89 percent were committed by blacks.

To get the rates at which blacks and whites commit interracial crime we divide the number of crimes by the population to get crimes per 100,000 population. The Census Bureau reports that the 1994 white and black populations were 216,413,000 and 32,653,000, respectively. Whites therefore committed acts of interracial violence at a rate of 62.55 per 100,000 while the black rate was 3,493.63 per 100,000, a figure that is 55.85 times the white rate. Put in the most straightforward terms, the average black was 56 times more likely to commit criminal violence against a white than was a white to commit criminal violence against a black. The multiple of 56 does not mean that blacks commit 56 times as much interracial violence as whites. What it means is that if whites commit interracial violence at a rate of 10 crimes per 100,000 whites, the rate for blacks is 560 per 100,000, or 56 times the white rate. This is the kind of calculation that is represented in most of the analyses in this report.

Results and Discussion

Calculations from the NCVS similar to those detailed above indicate that the black rate for interracial robbery, or "mugging," was 103 times the white rate. . . .

Again using the NCVS (USDJ, 1997), we calculate the total number of crimes committed by perpetrators of each race, and the percentage that is committed against the other race. The 1,140,670 acts of violence committed by blacks against whites constitute 56.3 percent of all violent crimes committed by blacks. That is to say that when blacks commit violent crimes they target whites more than half the time or, put differently, there is more black-on-white crime than black-on-black crime. Similar calculations for whites show that of the 5,114,696 acts of criminal violence committed by whites, only 2.6 percent were directed at blacks. Although homicide is a violent crime, the NCVS does not include it because victims cannot be interviewed. The number of interracial homicides is rather small and does not substantially affect the percentages and ratios presented here.

It may be suggested that blacks commit violence against whites because whites are more likely to have money and are therefore more promising robbery targets. However, of the 1,140,670 black-on-white acts of single-perpetrator violence reported in 1994, only 173,374 were robberies. The remaining 84.8 percent were aggravated assaults, rapes, and simple assaults, which presumably were not motivated by profit. Rape, in particular, has nothing to do with the presumed wealth of the victim. More than 30,000 white women were raped by black men in 1994, while about 5,400 black women were raped by white men. The black interracial rape rate was thus 38 times the white rate.

The NCVS (USDJ, 1997) Table 48 contains interracial crime data for acts of violence committed by multiple offenders. By doing calculations as before, we determine how much group or "gang" violence (not in the sense of organized gangs) is interracial and how much is committed by blacks and by whites. Of the total of 490,266 acts of multiple-offender interracial violence, no fewer than 93.9 percent were committed by blacks against whites. Robbery, for which there is a monetary motive, accounted for fewer than one-third of these crimes. The rest were gang assaults, including rapes, presumably for motives other than profit.

Rates of group violence for each race can be calculated as before, and the difference between the races is stark. The black rate of overall interracial gang violence is 101.75 times the white rate; for robbery it is 277.31 times the white rate. . . .

Race and Crime

Different racial groups in the United States commit crimes at different rates. Most Americans have a sense that non-white neighborhoods are more dangerous than white neighborhoods—and they are correct. However, it is very unusual to find reliable information on just how much more dangerous some groups are than others.

The Uniform Crime Reports (UCR) from the FBI is the standard reference for crime and crime rates in the United States. In trying to determine crime rates for different racial groups, it is important to be aware of the differences between the UCR and the NCVS referenced above. The NCVS contains only one kind of information: crimes Americans say they have suffered. The UCR includes two different kinds of data: crimes reported to the police and arrests of perpetrators. Even for the same year and for the same crime, these three sets of numbers are different. The largest numbers are in the NCVS, because they include crimes not reported to the police. Somewhat smaller are the UCR figures on offenses reported to authorities, and smaller still are arrest figures, which represent offenses for which a suspect is arrested.

For example, in the 1997 NCVS Americans say they suffered a total of 1,883,000 cases of aggravated assault (USDJ, 1998a), but according to the UCR, only 1,022,000 were reported to the police. During that same year, there were only 535,000 arrests for aggravated assault (UCR, 1998). Racial data enter the UCR numbers only when an arrest is made, so it can be argued that racial comparisons should not be based on UCR data. Different racial groups may report crime to the police at different rates, some groups may be more successful at escaping arrest, and the police may discriminate between racial groups in their arrest efforts. However, although racial bias in arrests is frequently discussed, when investigated the data suggest that arrest rates actually track perpetrator rates (Dilulio, 1996; Wilbanks, 1987). Furthermore, there is an advantage to using UCR data because its racial categories are more detailed. Unlike the NCVS, which reports only "black," "white," and "other," the UCR compiles arrest data on "black," "white," "American Indian/Eskimo," and "Asian/Pacific Islander." These are the only national crime data that make these distinctions. Also, as will be explicated below, UCR arrest data can be compared to other data sources in ways that make it possible to treat Hispanics as a separate ethnic category.

Another good reason to use UCR arrest data (race of persons arrested) is that the racial proportions are actually quite close to those from NCVS survey data (race of perpetrator as reported by victims). For example, according to the UCR, 57 percent of people arrested for robbery in 1997 were black, as were 37 percent of those arrested for aggravated assault (UCR, 1998). According to NCVS data on single-offender crimes, 51 percent of robbers were reported by their victims to be black as were 30 percent of those who committed aggravated assault (USDJ, 1997). Since there is a greater overrepresentation by blacks in NCVS-reported multiple-offender crimes, combining the two sets of figures brings the racial proportions in the NCVS figures extremely close to the racial proportions in UCR arrest numbers. Put differently, police are arresting criminals of different races in very close to the same proportions as Americans say they are victimized by people of those races.

By this measure, who is committing crime in America? . . .

The white rate is always set to one, so if the black rate is three, for example, it means that blacks are arrested at three times the white rate. Once again, it does not mean that three times as many blacks as whites were arrested; it means that if 100 of every 100,000 whites were arrested for a crime, 300 of every 100,000 blacks were arrested for the same crime. The data show a consistent pattern: Blacks are arrested at dramatically higher rates than other racial groups. American Indians and Eskimos (hereinafter "Indians") are arrested at slightly higher rates than whites, and Asians/Pacific Islanders (hereinafter "Asians") are arrested at consistently lower rates. The popular conception of crime in America is correct: rates are much higher among blacks than among whites or other groups.

To return to the view that arrest data reflect police bias rather than genuine group differences in crime rates, police actually have very little discretion in whom they arrest for violent crimes. Except for murder victims, most people can tell the police the race of an assailant. If a victim says she was mugged by a white man, the police cannot very well arrest a black man even if they want to. For this reason, many people accept that police have little discretion in whom they arrest for violent crime, but still believe drug laws are enforced unfairly against minorities. Drug offenses are beyond the scope of this investigation, but here, too, there is independent evidence that arrest rates reflect differences in criminal behavior, not selective law enforcement. The U.S. Department of Health and Human Services keeps records by race of drug-related emergency room admissions. It reports that blacks are admitted at 6.67 times the non-Hispanic white rate for heroin and morphine, and no less than 10.49 times the non-Hispanic white rate for cocaine (Rates for Hispanics are 2.82 and 2.35 times the

white rates; information is not reported for American Indians or Asians) (USDJ, 1998b). There is only one plausible explanation for these rates: Blacks are much more likely to be using drugs in the first place. Finally, if racist white police were unfairly arresting non-whites we would expect arrest rates for Asians to be higher than those for whites. Instead, they are lower for almost every kind of crime.

Measuring Hispanic Crime Rates

Any study of crime rates in America is complicated by the inconsistent treatment of Hispanics by different government agencies. For example, the Census Bureau's official estimate for the 1997 population of the United States divides all 268 million Americans into four racial groups: white, black, Indian and Eskimo, and Asian and Pacific Islander. The bureau then explains that among these 268 million people there are 29 million Hispanics who "can be of any race." However, it also counts non-Hispanic whites, non-Hispanic blacks, Indians, etc. Thus we find that although according to the strictly racial classification, there are 221 million whites in the United States, there are only 195 million non-Hispanic whites. When American Hispanics, approximately half of whom are Mexican, are apportioned to the four racial categories, the Census Bureau considers 91 percent to be white, six percent black, one percent American Indian, and two percent Asian.

The treatment of Hispanics can make for odd results. For example, according to the 1990 census, the 3,485,000 people of Los Angeles were 52.9 percent white, 13.9 percent black, 0.4 percent American Indian, and 22.9 percent Asian—which adds up to 100 percent. This makes the city appear to be majority white. However, Los Angeles was also 39.3 percent Hispanic, and if we subtract the 91 percent of them who are classified as whites, the non-Hispanic white population drops to only 16.6 percent.

What does this mean for crime statistics? Because the UCR figures do not treat Hispanics as a separate category, almost all the Hispanics arrested in the United States go into official records as "white." This is contrary to the usual cultural understanding of the term, which is not normally thought to include most Mexicans and Latinos.

If violent crime rates for Hispanics are different from those of non-Hispanic whites, putting Hispanics in the "white" category distorts the results. This is not as serious as in the case of hate crimes, in which the crime itself has to do with the very personal characteristics that are being omitted from the records, but there is no legitimate reason not to make ethnic and racial comparisons as accurate as possible. The UCR tabulates separate data on American

Indians and Eskimos—who are less than one percent of the population—but it ignores Hispanics, who are 12 percent of the population.

Some data-gathering agencies do treat Hispanic and non-Hispanic whites separately. The California Department of Justice, which records all arrests within the state, consistently makes this distinction (although it lumps Asians and American Indians into the "other" category) (Calif, 1998). In conjunction with Census Bureau population figures for Hispanics, non-Hispanic whites, and non-Hispanic blacks living in California in 1997, we can calculate the arrest rates for the different groups for various crimes. . . . As is the case with national UCR data, blacks are arrested at much higher rates than whites, but Hispanics are also arrested at considerably higher rates.

The different rates at which Hispanics and non-Hispanic whites are held in prisons and jails are another indicator of the differences in crime rates between the two groups. Although the UCR does not treat Hispanics as a separate category for arrest purposes, some government reports on the prison population do consider them separately. For example, the Department of Justice has calculated incarceration rates per 100,000 population for non-Hispanic whites (193), Hispanics (688), and non-Hispanic blacks (1,571) (USDJ, 1998b). Expressed as multiples of the white rate, the Hispanic rate is 3.56 and black rate is 8.14.

These multiples are close to those from the California arrest data, and justify the conclusion that Hispanics are roughly three times more likely than non-Hispanic whites to be arrested for various crimes. By accepting this assumption, we can use the following formula to incorporate this differential into the UCR racial data on white arrests so as to calculate more accurate arrest rates for non-Hispanic whites:

R(Number of non-Hispanic whites) + 3R(Number of white Hispanics) = Actual Number of Arrests.

Here, R is the arrest rate for non-Hispanic whites and 3R is the arrest rate for Hispanics who are categorized as white when they are arrested. Calculations of this sort show that if Hispanics are broken out as a separate ethnic category with an arrest rate three times the non-Hispanic rate, the rate for non-Hispanic whites decreases by 19.5 percent. . . . Due to lack of precise information, the multiple for Hispanics is set to three times the white rate for all crimes even though there is certain to be some variation in the multiples for different types of crimes. . . .

It should be noted here that the NCVS survey data on interracial crime also includes most Hispanics in the "white" category. It is therefore impossible to know how many of the "whites" who committed violent crimes against blacks were actually Hispanic or how many of the "whites" against whom blacks committed violent crimes were Hispanic. If Hispanics commit violent crimes against blacks at a higher rate than whites—and judging from their higher arrest and incarceration rates for violent offenses this seems likely—the NCVS report also inflates the crime rates of non-Hispanic whites.

Men vs. Women, Blacks vs. Whites

Many people resist the idea that different racial groups have substantially different rates of violent crime. However, there are several group differences in crime rates that virtually everyone accepts and, indeed, takes for granted. Men in their late teens and 20s, for example, are much more prone to violence than men beyond their 50s. When young men are arrested more frequently for violent offenses, no one doubts that it is because they commit more violent crime. Likewise, virtually no one disputes the reason for higher arrest rates for men than for women: Men commit more violent crime than women (Wilson & Herrnstein, 1985). This is the case for racial groups as well: Asians are arrested at lower rates than whites because they commit fewer crimes; blacks and Hispanics are arrested at higher rates because they commit more crimes (Levin, 1997; Rushton, 1995; Whitney, 1990).

When it comes to violent crime, blacks are approximately as much more likely to be arrested than whites, as men are more likely to be arrested than women. The multiples of black vs. white arrest rates are very close to the multiples of male vs. female arrest rates, suggesting that blacks are as much more dangerous than whites as men are more dangerous than women.

What does this mean? Although most people have no idea what the arrest rate multiples may be, they have an intuitive understanding that men are more violent and dangerous than women. If someone in unfamiliar circumstances is approached by a group of strange men she feels more uneasy than if she is approached by an otherwise similar group of strange women. No one would suggest that this differential uneasiness is "prejudice." It is common sense, born out by the objective reality that men are more dangerous than women.

In fact, it is just as reasonable to feel more uneasy when approached by blacks than by otherwise similar whites; the difference in danger as reflected by arrest rates is virtually the same. It is rational to fear blacks more than whites, just as it is rational to fear men more than women. Whatever additional precautions a person would take are justified because a potential assailant was male rather than female are, from a statistical point of view, equally justified if a potential assailant is black rather than white. . . .

Likewise, there is now much controversy about so-called "racial profiling" by the police, that is, the practice of questioning blacks in disproportionate numbers in the expectation that they are more likely than people of other races to be criminals. The philosophical, legal and rational case for racial profiling has been elaborated by the philosopher Michael Levin (Levin, 1997). "Racial" profiling is just as rational and productive as "age" or "sex" profiling. Police would be wasting their time if they stopped and questioned as many little old ladies as they do young black men. It is the job of the police to catch criminals, and they know from experience who is likely to be an offender. Americans who do not question the wisdom of police officers who notice a possible suspect's age and sex should not be surprised to learn those officers also notice race.

Conclusions

Two things can be said about most of the information in this investigation: It is easily discovered but little known. Every year, the FBI issues its report on hate crimes, and distributes thousands of copies to scholars and the media. Why does no one find it odd that hundreds of whites are reportedly committing hate crimes against whites? And why does no one question the wisdom of calling someone white when he is a perpetrator but Hispanic when he is a victim?

For some years there has been an extended national discussion about the prevalence of black-on-black crime—and for good reason. Blacks suffer from considerably more violent crime than do Americans of other races. And yet, amid this national outcry over the extent of black-on-black crime, there appears to be little concern about the fact that there is actually more black-on-white crime. Nor does there seem to be much interest in the fact that blacks are 50 to 200 times more likely than whites to commit interracial crimes of violence. Differences as great as this are seldom found in comparative studies of group behavior, and they cry out for causal investigation and explanation. It is probably safe to say that if the races were reversed, and gangs of whites were attacking blacks at merely four or five times the rate at which blacks were attacking whites the country would consider this a national crisis that required urgent attention.

Everyone knows that young people are more dangerous than old people, and that men are more dangerous than women. We adjust our behavior accordingly and do not apologize for doing so. Why then must we pretend that blacks are no more dangerous than whites or Asians? But of course it is no more than pretense. Everyone knows that blacks are dangerous, and everyone—black and white—takes greater precautions in black neighborhoods or even avoids such neighborhoods entirely.

The answers to these questions lie in the current intellectual climate. Americans are extremely hesitant to "perpetuate stereotypes," and generally take care not to draw or publicize conclusions that may reflect badly on racial minorities. This is understandable, but has reached the point that certain subjects can no longer be investigated without bringing down cries of "racism." Needless to say, research that reflects badly on the majority population is not constrained by the same fears. However, our willingness to ignore sensibilities should not be selective. Violent crime and interracial violence are important, agonizing concerns in this country, and we cannot begin to formulate solutions unless we understand the problems.

References

AP, 1999, Whitman fires State Police superintendent over remarks to newspaper. Trenton NJ: Associated Press, March 1, 1999.

Blumstein, A., and J. Cohen, 1987, Characterizing criminal careers. *Science,* 237: 985–991.

Blumstein, A., and E. Graddy, 1981–82, Prevalence and recidivism in index arrests: A feedback model. *Law and Society Review,* 16: 265–290.

Calif, 1998, Adult and juvenile arrests reported, 1997. Race/ethnic group by specific offense statewide, January through December 1997. California Department of Justice Division of Criminal Justice, Criminal Justice Statistics Center: p. 5939, printed 04/15/98 (unpublished).

Could, R.W., and M.J. Waldren, 1986, *London's Armed Police: 1829 to the present.* London: Arms and Armour Press.

Dilulio, John J., Jr., 1996, My black crime problem and ours. *City Journal,* Spring: 14ff.

Drummond, Tammerlin, 1999, It's not just in New Jersey. *Time* 153 (23), June 14, 1999: 61.

Ellis, Lee, 1987, The victimful–victimless crime distinction, and seven universal demographic correlates of victimful criminal behavior. *Personality and Individual Differences,* 91: 525–548.

Francis, Samuel, 1999, Media blackout on black-on-white crime. *Conservative Chronicle,* June 30, 1999: 23.

Hama, Aldric, 1999, Demographic changes and social breakdown: The role of intelligence. (manuscript under review).

Hooton, Earnest Albert, 1939, *Crime and the Man.* Cambridge MA: Harvard University Press.

Levin, Michael, 1997, *Why Race Matters: Race differences and what they mean.* Westport, CT: Praeger.

Rushton, J. Philippe, 1985, Differential K theory: The sociobiology of individual and group differences. *Personality and Individual Differences,* 6: 441–452.

Rushton, J. Philippe, 1995, *Race, Evolution, and Behavior. A life history perspective.* New Brunswick, NJ: Transaction.

Taylor, Jared, 1992, *Paved with Good Intentions: The failure of race relations in contemporary America.* New York: Carroll & Graf.

UCR, 1998, Crime in the United States, 1997. Washington DC: U.S. Department of Justice, Federal Bureau of Investigation, USGPO.

USDJ, 1997, Criminal Victimization in the United States, 1994. Washington DC: U.S. Department of Justice, Bureau of Justice Statistics, USGPO.

USDJ, 1998a, Criminal Victimization in the United States, 1997. Washington DC: U.S. Department of Justice, Bureau of Justice Statistics, USGPO.

USDJ, 1998b, Sourcebook of Criminal Justice Statistics, 1997. Washington DC: U.S. Department of Justice, Bureau of Justice Statistics, USGPO.

Whitney, Glayde, 1990, On possible genetic bases of race differences in criminality. In: Ellis, Lee and Harry Hoffman (Eds.), *Crime in Biological, Social, and Moral Contexts.* Westport CT: Praeger, 134–149.

Whitney, Glayde, 1995, Ideology and censorship in behavior genetics. *The Mankind Quarterly,* 35: 327–342.

Wilbanks, William, 1986, *The Myth of a Racist Criminal Justice System.* Monterey CA: Brooks/Cole.

Wilson, James Q., and Richard J. Herrnstein, 1985, *Crime and Human Nature.* New York: Simon & Schuster.

JARED TAYLOR is the president of the New Century Foundation and is an author and commentator on race in U.S. politics. He is also the editor of *American Renaissance* magazine. His works include *Paved with Good Intentions: The Failure of Race Relations in Contemporary America* (Carol & Graf, 1992).

GLAYDE WHITNEY is a behavioral geneticist and psychology professor at Florida State University.

Michael J. Lynch  **NO**

Misleading "Evidence" and the Misguided Attempt to Generate Racial Profiles of Criminals; Correcting Fallacies and Calculations Concerning Race and Crime in Taylor and Whitney's Analysis of Racial Profiling

In 1999, *The Journal of Social, Political and Economic Studies* published an article written by Taylor and Whitney that endeavored to demonstrate the efficacy of racial profiling of criminals. In that article, Taylor and Whitney made two significant general errors that influenced their conclusions concerning the utility of racial profiling. Their first error threatens the validity of their theoretical position. The second invalidates their statistical results and conclusions. Taken together, these general errors invalidate their position on race and crime.

To be more specific about these errors, Taylor and Whitney ground their argument concerning race and crime on a rather restricted review of extant literature. Excluding their own prior research from considerations, Taylor and Whitney refer approvingly to studies by Hooton, Wilson and Herrnstein, Wilbanks and Rushton, and appear to hold them out as exposing sound criminological explanations of the relationship between race and crime. In truth, the views on race and crime expressed by these authors have been refuted and rejected by the majority of criminologists (for criticism of these researchers and their general views on race see: Cernovsky and Litman, 1993; Gabor and Roberts, 1990; Lynch, 1990, 2000; Neopolitan, 1998; Shipman, 1994; Yee et al., 1993; Zuckerman, 1990).

Taylor and Whitney also make several methodological errors in their analyses of criminological data sources that generate misleading results and conclusions concerning the appropriateness of racial profiling. Specifically, these errors include: the use of prevalence rates rather than incidence rates; the failure to use race-based population-adjusted comparisons for offender and victimization data; focusing on rare forms of inter-racial crime and generalizing to the entire populations of criminals; and using data useful for addressing racial biases in criminal justice processes (Uniform Crime Report and imprisonment data) to calculate racial differences in offending.

To be sure, Blacks are over-represented in criminal justice data. But, Black over-representation in the criminal justice system (measured against the size of the Black population) cannot be employed as evidence that Blacks are responsible for more crime than Whites because over-representation may be a measure of processing biases (Mann, 1993). In short, observations concerning Black over-representation in criminal justice data do not directly translate into claims related to racial differences in offending. Taylor and Whitney, however, use criminal justice data as evidence of differences in offending by race. They are not the first to make this error and the researchers they site approvingly (Rushton, Wilbanks, Wilson and Herrnstein) have also misinterpreted criminal justice data as indicating race differences in offending.[1] Taylor and Whitney's argument begins with literature based on a misinterpretation of criminal justice data, and justifies this view with what can be described either as purposefully misleading or completely naive analyses of crime and victimization data. In either case, their conclusions are incorrect.

Taylor and Whitney's specific focus centers on the fact that "society" seems to express greater concern over Black-on-Black crime when, in fact, Taylor and Whitney believe that Black-on-White crime is the larger social problem. Had their argument been limited to this minor issue, their point would have some validity (though, as we

Lynch, Michael J. From *Mankind Quarterly,* vol. 42, no. 3, Spring 2002, pp. 313–329. Copyright © 2002 by Michael J. Lynch. Reprinted by permission.

demonstrate, even this contention turns out to be incorrect). But, this turns out not to be their point at all. Rather, as they conclude "it is certainly understandable that police should take these statistics into account when searching for suspects, and that they may wish to take more precautions when entering some neighborhoods than others."[2] This conclusion, as we demonstrate below, is the result of the inappropriate use, analysis of and generalizations made from criminal justice data.

Taylor and Whitney make numerous errors in their analysis and use of criminal justice data. It is not our intention to review each of these errors here because these errors are repeated across different sources of data and our comments would become unnecessarily lengthy. Thus, to simplify our analysis, we focus only on one aspect of Taylor and Whitney's analysis: their use of National Crime Victimization Survey (NCVS). To further reduce unnecessary repetition, we have restricted this reanalysis of NCVS data to violent crimes where victims report a single offender.

The NCVS

According to the Bureau of Justice Statistics, The National Crime Victimization Survey is the Nation's primary source of information on criminal victimization. Each year, data are obtained from a nationally representative sample of roughly 50,000 households comprising nearly 100,000 persons on the frequency, characteristics, and consequences of criminal victimization in the United States. The survey enables BJS to estimate the likelihood of victimization by rape, sexual assault, robbery, assault, theft, household burglary, and motor vehicle theft for the population as a whole as well as for segments of the population such as women, the elderly, members of various racial groups, city dwellers, or other groups. The NCVS provides the largest national forum for victims to describe the impact of crime and characteristics of violent offenders. . . .

Taylor and Whitney report on data from the 1994 NCVS, while this reanalysis reports on 1999 NCVS data. Employing a different year for NCVS should not be problematic or invalidate our reanalysis. NCVS data do not change dramatically from year to year, and are especially consistent with respect to reports of offender's race. Further, since Taylor and Whitney's goal is to validate racial profiling of criminals, evidence that this profile is stable across time would need to be produced. Consequently, it makes sense to repeat their analysis with several different years of NCVS data.

For the present discussion, we employ 1999 victim reports of offender's race for three violent or personal offenses where victims reported a single or lone offender: rape, robbery and assault. These three crimes are the only ones for which victim reports of offender race are available. . . . The next section provides an overview of these data.

Overview of the 1999 NCVS

In 1999, the NCVS indicated 5,620,080 lone offender victimizations for the crimes of rape, robbery, and assault reported by Black and White victims.[3] Approximately eighty-five percent of these victimizations were reported by White victims (N = 4,760,930). The remaining 867,150 victimizations were reported by Blacks.

Taylor and Whitney direct our attention to the inter-racial offenses reported in these data—that is, cases involving Black offenders and White victims, and cases involving White offenders and Black victims. In 1999, there were 748,058 inter-racial victimizations (91,050 + 657,008). This figure, which appears to indicate an abundance of Black-on-White crime is misleading on two accounts. First, inter-racial violent crimes are rare events with respect to all crimes, comprising less than 2 percent of all reported criminal victimizations in any given year. Second, inter-racial violence is only one dimension of crime and thus generalizations from these data alone may lead to invalid conclusions.

Of these 748,058 inter-racial acts of violence, 657,008 involved a Black offender-White victim, while 91,050 involved a White offender-Black victim pairing. Taylor and Whitney make much of this finding, claiming that these data illustrate the extensively disproportionate nature of interracial victimizations involving White victims-Black offenders. That fact that nearly 88 percent of violent interracial victimizations involve Black offender-White victim dyads is interesting, but, as we demonstrate below, not unexpected given the claims of opportunity theory, which would predict this outcome based upon knowing the racial distribution of the U.S. population.

Employing less than 2 percent of crimes—that is, by focusing on data depicting the extent of inter-racial crimes of violence—Taylor and Whitney conclude that Black-on-White crimes are serious enough to justify the use of racial profiling. As we have already noted, this conclusion is likely to be misleading because it is generalized from a non-representative sub-sample of all crimes. To get a better understanding of the relationship between race and violent criminal victimizations, it is necessary to analyze a broader portion of NCVS cases for which offender race is reported. The next section begins to address the basis for a reanalysis of NCVS data that presents the "big picture" of crime.

The Bigger Picture of Crime

In 1999, White victims of personal violence reported that 74.5 percent of lone attackers in rape, robbery and assault cases were White (N = 3,546,893), while only 13.3 percent were Black. In other words, the majority of crimes committed against Whites were by White offenders. This is not the conclusion drawn from reading Taylor and Whitney's research.

A similar picture of crime and victimization emerges when we examine Black responses to the NCVS: Blacks report that 80 percent of lone attackers are Black, while 10.5 percent are White. Taken together, these data clearly indicate that for the majority of offenses, crime is an intra-racial phenomenon, involving a victim and offender of the same race. From a crime profiling perspective, these data indicate that racial profiling, if we accept this idea as legitimate, should be performed on the basis of the victim's race because of the high correlation between race of victim and offender. It should be noted, however, that this form of profiling, while legitimate statistically, is hardly practical, since it fails in its mission of reducing the pool of potential suspects sufficiently.

The basic data provided by the NCVS makes it clear that the "crime problem" for each racial group consists of other members of the racial group to which one belongs. This conclusion is not apparent in Taylor and Whitney's research, which consistently points to the threat Black offenders present to Whites. How is it that Taylor and Whitney derive and justify this result? Answering this question requires investigating the proper use of rate standardized crime data that focuses on racial comparisons.

Misleading with Rate Comparisons

Taylor and Whitney mislead readers when they engage in a common criminological practice by using rate standardized data as a basis for comparing crime across racial groups. While it is commonplace for criminologists to standardize crime data and transform them into rates per 100,000 for comparison, racial comparisons based on rate standardization lead to erroneous conclusions. Rate standardization is useful for specific kinds of comparisons. One appropriate use would be to compare the prevalence of crime across locations known to have different sized populations. Doing so, we might address questions of relative safety. Second, we can use a rate comparison when we are able to assume that the populations in question may be present in equal proportions. In the United States, this latter assumption is violated when race is the basis of the comparison. Black-White racial

compositions vary from place to place. Whites, however, comprise a higher percentage of the U.S. population than Blacks. Locations where the population is represented by an equal number of Blacks and Whites would be rare or unusual (Massey and Denton, 1993). Thus, there would be relatively few places to which racially specific standardized rates of victimization (or offending) would be applicable.[4]

Taylor and Whitney further compound the prediction error they make by relying on rate standardized race comparisons when they transform these standardized rates into ratios or odds of victimization and offending. For example, Taylor and Whitney calculate the ratio of Black to White rates of inter-racial offending by dividing the rate of White victim-Black offenders per 100,000 population by the Black victim-White offender rate per 100,000 population. Constructing ratios from standardized rates that depict unequal populations as existing in equal proportions inflates the level of crime attributable to one group, while deflating the level of crime attributed to the other. This procedure, in other words, contains two opposing errors that compound the original error and inflate the ratio substantially. In this case, the ratio is inflated in a way that favors the interpretation that Black-on-White crime is more serious than White-on-Black crime.

Rate standardized data cannot be directly employed to reach conclusions concerning levels of offending by race. Rather, rate data need to be adjusted properly before comparisons across races are made, and before we can draw conclusions concerning the contribution of each race to crime. To do so, race specific rates need to be adjusted to reflect race-based population compositions. A corrected example of how race specific rates of offending should be used is provided below.

Turning Race-Specific Rates into Meaningful Data: An Example

The U.S. population is approximately 12 percent Black and 80 percent White. These figures have been rounded to make the calculations which follow simpler. Each calculation is an approximation, and the results reported are valid though not exact.

In 1999, 4,760,930 single offender violent crime victimizations were reported by Whites. Translated into a rate per 100,000, Whites report approximately 2204 victimizations per 100,000 Whites in the populations (Number of victimizations reported by Whites/White Population for the U.S. × 100,000). The comparable victimization rate for Blacks is 2710 victimizations per 100,000 Blacks in the population. These figures tell us that in a population composed of an equal number of Black and Whites (100,000), Blacks are more likely to be the victim of crimes than Whites (2710/2204 = 1.23).

The problem with this comparison is that in most locales the population is not composed of an equal number of Blacks and Whites, and the practice of standardization misrepresents the real victimization ratio. To address this problem of unequivalent populations, we could either rely on raw numbers of victims if available, or adjust the standardized race specific victimization (or offering) rate by the population's racial composition. We will illustrate this procedure by applying victimization data to a fictitious city (City X) with a population of 100,000 and a racial composition that reflects the national average for the US: 80 percent White and 12 percent Black. In City X there will be 80,000 Whites and 12,000 Blacks.

Our first step is to calculate the number of White victims from the race-specific standardized victimization rate data and City X population data cited above. We know that the standardized White victimization rate was 2204/100,000. Thus, we can multiply the victimization rate by the White population parameter in City X—80% or .80—to derive the number of White victims (2204 × .80). Doing so, we discover that there are 1763 White victims of interpersonal violence in City X. We then follow the same procedure to calculate the number of Black victims of interpersonal crime in City X. Thus, we take the Black rate of interpersonal victimization (2710/100,000) and multiply this figure by the Black population parameter, 12% or .12, yielding 325. Black victims of interpersonal violence in City X is 325.

Before going any further, let us be clear about the meaning of the figures that were just derived. In City X there are 2088 Black and White victims of violent, interpersonal crimes. Eighty-four percent of these victims are White. The ratio of White to Black victims in City X is 5.4; that is, there are 5.4 White victims for every 1 Black victim of interpersonal violence.

Now that we have derived the total number of victims of each race from population and victimization rate data, we can employ the number of victims we have derived to calculate the number of offenders by race. We do so by multiplying NCVS perceived race of offender data by City X victimization figures. . . .

In total, there are 1850 interpersonal victimizations involving only Black and White victims-offenders (while Black and Whites report a total of 2088 victimizations, 238 of these are committed by members of a racial group other than Black or White). Seventy-one percent of these victimizations were committed against Whites by White offenders (1313/1850). In contrast, 14.5 percent of victimizations (260/1850) are committed by Blacks against Blacks; 13.3 percent are committed by Blacks versus Whites (243/1850); and 1.8 percent are by Whites versus Blacks (34/1850). Overall, Whites commit 73 percent of interpersonal crimes of violence in City X (1313 + 34/1850), which represents an average American city in terms of racial composition and interpersonal victimization and perceived offending by race as described in the NCVS.

What implications do these population adjusted victimization and offending data have for efforts at criminal profiling? They indicate that the offender is White in nearly three out of four crimes of interpersonal violence involving Black or White crime victims. Further, they illustrate that numerically, Black-on-White crimes of interpersonal violence (N = 243) are less likely than Black-on-Black crimes of interpersonal violence (N = 260). This finding from population adjusted rates is important because it directly disproves one of Taylor and Whitney's contentions; namely, that Black-on-White crime is more frequent than Black-on-Black crime. As we argued earlier, Taylor and Whitney's conclusion was generated by making inappropriate use of criminological data. The use of standardized rates of victimization and offending makes it appear that Whites are more likely to be victimized by violent Black offenders than Blacks are when, in reality, the situation is reversed. This occurs because the standardized rate comparison assumes equivalent sized Black and White populations. When we adjust these rates to reflect the real world, the conclusion is reversed.

Taylor and Whitney also employed the use of odds or ratio calculations to reach conclusions concerning Black-on-White and White-on-Black crime. The odds they present are inaccurate and invalid because they are derived from rate standardized data and are not adjusted for real racial population proportions. Below we describe a more valid approach to deriving the ratio of White-on-Black to Black-on-White crimes of violence.

Calculating the Odds of Victimization

Throughout their article, Taylor and Whitney assert that the odds of Black-on-White crime are between 50–200 times greater than the odds of White-on-Black crimes. As Taylor and Whitney admit early on, the figures they represent as odds are not actually odds because of the manner in which they are calculated. Consistent with our earlier argument, we contend that the odds they calculated provide inaccurate estimates because they are based on prevalence rates (rates per 100,000) rather than incidence data.

Taylor and Whitney hinge their argument here on the statement that the odds of a White being victimized by a Black is disproportionate. But, disproportionate to what? Taylor and Whitney fail to define what they mean by the word disproportionate, and we are left to ponder the significance of this idea.

As we have already shown using population adjusted victimization rates, Black-on-White crime is not disproportionate to Black-on-Black crime. This finding fails to support an essential aspect of Taylor and Whitney's argument. Thus, the only remaining means for interpreting this idea of disproportionate racial offending is to compare real victim-offender ratios to expected victim-offender ratios. The justification for doing so is easily derived from the popular criminological position called "opportunity theory" (Cohen and Felson, 1980a, 1980b; Felson and Cohen). Recent evidence supports the utility of opportunity theory for making predictions concerning violent victimizations (Lee, 2000).

Opportunity theory predicts that crime results from an intersection of motivated offenders with suitable targets. The opportunities for crime vary by numerous situational characteristics, but are defined or limited in the absolute sense by the availability of potential targets. The nature of targets varies by the type of crime. For crimes of violence, this opportunity is measured by the availability of potential victims. The first parameter of opportunity, in this case, is defined by the size of a population.

In the specific case under examination, the opportunity dimension for crime is being defined by racial composition of the population. In other words, if opportunity arguments are correct, and there are no other forces in operation, the opportunity for inter-racial violent crime ought to be a product of the White/Black population ratio. This is easily calculated. In our hypothetical city—City X—we can divide the White population by the Black population. Doing so, we derive a White/Black population ratio of 6.7 (80,000/12,000). This figure indicates that we would expect Whites to be the victims of more crime more often than Blacks solely on the basis of opportunity for violence. This assumption can be easily assessed as follows.

First, we derive the ratio of victimization by race by creating a ratio of White to Black victimizations. We use the population data derived for our hypothetical city for these calculations which represented an average US city of 100,000 in terms of racial composition, crime and victimization patterns. Total White victimizations in City X was 1556 (1313 + 243); total Black victimization was 294 (260 + 34). The overall race victimization ratio

is 1556/294, or 5.3—much lower—20 percent lower—than the expected ratio of 6.7. This figure indicates that in general, White victimizations are below the level predicted simply on the basis of opportunity or availability.

As noted, Taylor and Whitney's arguments specifically and consistently focused only on interracial crimes. The same opportunity ratios can be calculated for interracial crimes of violence. Though these ratios may be misleading because of the relative rare nature of the behavior in question, we estimate these ratios to illustrate the extent to which Taylor and Whitney's odds calculations are inflated by relying on prevalence (rate per 100,000) rather than incidence data.

To calculate the interracial opportunity ratio, we simply take the number of cases involving White victims and Black offenders (243) and dividing by the number of cases where there are Black victims and White offenders (34). The opportunity ratio in this case is 7.2, slightly higher (7%) than the interracial ratio predicted by opportunity theory alone (6.7).[5]

In sum, the disproportionate ratio or odds of Black-on-White violent crime victimization that appear to "shock" Taylor and Whitney are actually a function of their method for calculating odds. Using incidence data and appropriate populations for comparison, we estimated that Black victimizations of Whites are not disproportionate to Black/White population ratios. Indeed, our calculations confirmed the idea that victimization ratios could be explained by opportunity theory as a function of the US population's racial composition.

Conclusion

Taylor and Whitney conclude their article with the following:

> Everyone knows that young people are more dangerous than old people, and that men are more dangerous than women. We adjust our behavior accordingly and do not apologize for doing so. Why then must we pretend that statistics regarding race differences in violent crime are to be ignored?

If Taylor and Whitney's analysis was valid, used appropriate methods for comparing racially-linked criminal justice data, and did not mislead readers by generalizing from a fraction of violent crime to either all violent crimes or all crimes, then we might have to take their question seriously. However, because they either purposefully or unintentionally deceived readers due to their ignorance of the proper use of criminal justice data and specific issues that emerge when making comparisons of standardized race-based crime data, their question can be dismissed as nonsense. Their conclusion, in other words, is as misleading as their analysis and interpretation of victimization, crime, and criminal justice data.

As I have shown, proper use of NCVS data does not support Taylor and Whitney's contentions. Using NCVS data appropriately—focusing on all crimes of violence as the appropriate basis for generalization rather than Taylor and Whitney's focus on a fraction of violent crime—we can clearly see that the majority of victims of violent crime report that their offender was White. This is not a statistical fallacy; there are more White than Black victims of crimes; the majority of Whites—nearly three-quarters—report that their offenders are White, not Black. Further, when we use the NCVS appropriately, one of the lessons we learn is that crime is primarily an intra-racial phenomenon. Whites are more likely to victimize Whites; Blacks are more likely to victimize Blacks. Further, the incidence of inter-racial crime is a function of opportunities for victimization as determined by the racial composition of the US population.

One of Taylor and Whitney's primary concerns is that society concentrates too much attention on Black-on-Black crime while neglecting Black-on-White crime. Their argument seems, then, to express concern for the safety of Whites. Their focus on Black-on-White crimes, however, creates a misleading conclusion concerning the threat Whites face. As we have demonstrated employing NCVS data, the majority of White crime victims are victimized by White offenders. In short, the safety of Whites is more greatly threatened by Whites rather than by Blacks.

Further, if Taylor and Whitney had actually been concerned that society concentrates too strongly on Black-on-Black crime, the correct comparison group for analysis should be White-on-White crime. By using this comparison group we could indeed argue that society's emphasis on Black-on-Black crime is misdirected, and that, instead, society's focus ought to be on White-on-White crimes, which are much more numerous. But, pointing out that the majority of crimes are committed by Whites, and that White victimization frequently comes at the hands of a White offender would not fit the broader research agenda established by these investigators.

Taylor and Whitney's claim that Black-on-White crime is extensive enough to justify racial profiling is based on the misuse of data and inappropriate comparisons and generalizations. As we have argued, the conclusion that racial profiling is acceptable is based on generalizing from less than 2 percent of crime—this 2 percent being the approximate percent of crime that is comprised of inter-racial crimes of violence. No criminologists would find such a procedure legitimate.

Taylor and Whitney also legitimize racial profiling by using prevalence rather than incidence data. Incidence data indicates that most crimes are committed by Whites; indeed the ratio of White-to-Black crimes of violence in the NCVS is 2.69 White offenders per every Black offender. Thus, despite the prevalence of crime among Black communities and populations, and despite the fact that Blacks are over-represented in criminal justice data, Whites are the problematic crime population. Consequently, if we favored the use of racial profiling—and we do not—correct calculations of offender incidence indicate that police ought to concentrate their efforts on Whites: as potential offenders Whites far outnumber Blacks. Further, if the police were to use racial profiling, it should be based on the race of the victim. NCVS data makes it clear that the race of the victim and offender are the same more than seventy-five percent of the time. Thus, if a Black victim reports a crime, the police would do well to look for a Black offender based upon odds alone. Likewise, if a White victim reports a crime to police, the police would do well to look for a White offender, based on odds alone.

When people speak of racial profiling, what they mean is the creation of criminal profiles that target Black offenders. As our analysis indicates, the legitimacy of racial profiling—of targeting Black offenders over White offenders—is misleading at best, and at worst, a form of institutionalized racism. Our data indicate that it is high time that the notion of racial profiling be put to rest.

Throughout this article, we have demonstrated that racial profiling is objectionable from a statistical perspective. In closing, it should also be noted that racial profiling is objectionable to criminologists from both a legal and philosophical perspective. Our nation's criminal laws are based on the premise that guilt is determined on a case-by-case basis as a result of specific evidence. The inquiry that examines this evidence should be carried out without prejudice. Further, crime suspects are to be assumed innocent until proven guilty. Our Constitution, Courts, and legal scholars speak to principles including: probable cause, which requires direct evidence rather than a suspicion or hunch based on someone's race or other status; due process of law and the rule of law; and the right to be judged by a juror of peers rather than by police or other actors in the criminal justice system. The idea of racial profiling reverses the important legal and philosophical ideas upon which the American system of democratic justice rests. Taylor and Whitney's support of racial profiling is not only misleading and inaccurate, it strikes at the heart of the American justice system and American democracy.

Notes

1. It bears mention that among Rushton, Wilbanks, Wilson and Herrnstein, only Wilbanks was trained as a criminologist.

2. What police may want to take into account when deciding the dangerousness of a situation is the data on police killings and assaults. Taylor and Whitney's conclusions concerning police safety and race would be considered misleading and inaccurate based on even a cursory reading of these data. For example, between 1988 and 1997, the Sourcebook of Criminal Justice Statistics notes that White offenders (49%) are responsible for killing more police officers than Black offenders (42%). While Black killings may be disproportionate to their population composition, this does not eliminate the fact that police are more likely to be killed by Whites than by Blacks. Further, these data do not take into account the differential treatment Blacks receive that may escalate their reactions to police such as heightened use of force and a greater likelihood of being killed by police than White suspects (Mann 1993).

3. We have excluded other racial groups from consideration to simplify the results and discussion. Including other races would not significantly alter the results reported here.

4. While it may sometimes be useful to employ rate standardized data to compare the prevalence of a behavior among race-groups, a reliance on rate standardized data would still produce misleading results when we employ them to make generalizations concerning the amount of crime each racial group produced. An example of this situation is illustrated in the text of this article.

5. This minor difference in estimation could be due in part to the exclusion of other races from the analysis, and to rounding of population figures used to generate these outcomes. It is also possible that White-on-Black and Black-on-White crime are the product of factors other than opportunity.

References

Cernovsky, Z., and L. Litman. 1993. Reanalysis of Rushton's Crime Data. *Canadian Journal of Criminology.* 35, 1: 31–36.

Cohen, Lawrence, and Marcus Felson, 1980a. The Property Crime Rate in the United States: A Macro-Dynamic Analysis, 1947–1977, With Ex-Ante Forecasts for the Mid-1980s. *American Journal of Sociology.* 86, 1: 90–118.

Gabor, T., and J. Roberts. 1990 Rushton on Race and Crime: The Evidence Remains Unconvincing. *Canadian Journal of Criminology.* 32: 335–343.

Lee, Matthew. 2000. Community cohesion and violent predatory victimization: A theoretical extension and cross-national test of opportunity theory. *Social Forces.* 79, 2: 683–706.

Lynch, M.J. 2000. J. Phillippe Rushton on Crime: An Examination and Critique of the Explanation of Crime and Race. *Social Pathology.* 6, 3: 228–244.

Lynch, M.J. 1990. "Racial Bias and Criminal Justice: Methodological and Definitional Issues." In B. MacLean and D. Milovanovic's (eds.), *Racism, Empiricism and Criminal Justice.* Vancouver: Collective Press.

Mann, Coramae Richey. 1993. *Unequal Justice.* Bloomington, IN: University of Indiana Press.

Massey, Douglas, and Nancy Nenton. 1993. *American Apartheid.* Cambridge, MA: Harvard University Press.

Neopolitan, J. 1998. Cross-National Variation in Homicide: Is Race a Factor? *Criminology.* 36, 1: 139–155.

Shipman, Pat. 1994. *The Evolution of Racism: Human Differences and the Use and Abuse of Science.* NY: Simon and Schuster.

Taylor, Jared, and Glayde Whitney. 1999. Crime and Racial Profiling by U.S. Police: Is There any Empirical Evidence? *The Journal of Social, Political and Economic Studies.* 24, 4: 485–510.

Yee, A., H. Fairchild, F. Weizmann, and G. Wyatt. 1993. Addressing Psychology's Problems with Race. *The American Psychologist.* 48: 1132–1140.

Zuckerman, M. 1990. Some Dubious Premises in Research and Theory on Racial Differences. *The American Psychologist.* 45: 1297–1303.

MICHAEL J. LYNCH is a professor in the Department of Criminology at the University of South Florida. He has published extensively in the area of environmental crime, race and justice, and criminological theory. His most recent book, coauthored with Ronald G. Burns, is titled *The Sourcebook on Environmental Crime* (LFB Publishers, 2004). Professor Lynch has also served as division chair for the Critical Criminology section of the American Society of Criminology.

EXPLORING THE ISSUE

Is Racial Profiling an Acceptable Law Enforcement Strategy?

Critical Thinking and Reflection

1. Which author presents the most compelling arguments? Remember that to justify racial profiling, the government must be able to support these practices on an empirical, legal, and moral basis as well.
2. Based on the available evidence, why would it seem that supporters of these practices will face an uphill battle on all levels?

Is There Common Ground?

Racial issues have a way of generating substantial controversy. One of the more contentious issues in the U.S. justice system in recent years has been whether members of minority groups commit more crime, or if the disparity in official crime statistics among different races reflects a systemic selection bias. In other words, are the members of minority groups selected for arrest and official processing in the U.S. justice system more often than whites?

Taylor and Whitney assert that there is a true difference in the number of crimes committed by different races. In fact, these authors believe that racial profiling is just as rational and productive as age or gender profiling. Because "it is the job of the police to catch criminals, and they know from experience who is likely to be an offender," they are justified in following policies that emphasize race as a predictor of criminal behavior.

Michael J. Lynch believes that racial profiling is not justified by the crime data. Moreover, he contends that racial profiling may be a thinly veiled form of institutional racism and that it is objectionable from a legal and philosophical perspective as well.

The legal problems with racial profiling by law enforcement officials are indeed compelling. In *United States v. Brignoni-Ponce*, 422 U.S. 873 (1975), the U.S. Supreme Court held that stopping subjects because they "appear[ed] to be of Mexican ancestry," violated the Fourth Amendment to the U.S. Constitution. Following this principle, law enforcement practices that target minority group members for investigation due solely to their appearance seem likely to be held unconstitutional by reviewing courts.

Moreover, as Professor Lynch observes, racial profiling by law enforcement officials may be challenged from a philosophical and moral perspective as well. Is it morally permissible to stereotype people based on a group characteristic such as their race or religion? We must remember too that when law enforcement personnel as agents of our government use racial profiling strategies, it lends an official stamp of approval to the practices. Does this not conjure images of governmentally enforced school segregation and institutionalized racism during the Civil Rights era?

Additional Resources

There is a wealth of additional information available on this topic. Please see: David A. Harris, *Profiles in Injustice: Why Racial Profiling Cannot Work* (The New Press, 2002); Avram Bornstein, "Antiterrorist Policing in New York City after 9/11: Comparing Perspectives on a Complex Process," *Human Organization* (Spring 2005); P. A. J. Waddington, Kevin Stenson, and David Don, "In Proportion: Race and Police Stop and Search," *The British Journal of Criminology* (November 2004); Bernard E. Harcourt, "Rethinking Racial Profiling: A Critique of the Economics, Civil Liberties, and Constitutional Literature, and of Criminal Profiling More Generally," *The University of Chicago Law Review* (Fall 2004); Thomas Gabor, "Inflammatory Rhetoric on Racial Profiling Can Undermine Police Services," *Canadian Journal of Criminology and Criminal Justice* (July 2004); and Bernard E. Harcourt, "Unconstitutional Police Searches and Collective Responsibility," *Criminology & Public Policy* (July 2004).

Internet References . . .

American Civil Liberties Union

www.aclu.org/blog/tag/racial-profiling

Racial Profiling Data Collection Resource Center

www.racialprofilinganalysis.neu.edu/

Selected, Edited, and with Issue Framing Material by:
Thomas J. Hickey, *State University of New York at Cobleskill*

ISSUE

Should Juvenile Courts Be Abolished?

YES: Barry C. Feld, from "Juvenile Justice in Minnesota: Framework for the Future," Council on Crime and Justice (2007)

NO: Vincent Schiraldi and Jason Ziedenberg, from *The Florida Experiment: An Analysis of the Impact of Granting Prosecutors Discretion to Try Juveniles as Adults*, The Justice Policy Institute (1999)

Learning Outcomes
After reading this issue, you will be able to: • Discuss the *parens patriae* model of juvenile justice.   • Discuss the differences between a "rehabilitative" juvenile court, a juvenile version of a criminal court, and an integrated criminal court.   • Discuss whether U.S. juvenile courts have been characterized by a failure of implementation and/ or conception.   • Discuss the characteristics of juvenile offenders who are transferred to adult criminal court.   • Discuss the risks that young offenders face in adult jails.

ISSUE SUMMARY

YES: Law professor Barry C. Feld contends that creating a separate juvenile court system has resulted in unanticipated negative consequences for America's children and for justice.

NO: Vincent Schiraldi, director of the Justice Policy Institute, and researcher Jason Ziedenberg maintain that moving thousands of kids into adult courts is unnecessary, harmful, and racist.

In the 1890s Judge Ben Lindsey, with the help of socially prominent and active citizens and their wives, helped to establish the juvenile court movement. His work was hailed as innovative and compassionate. Horror tales and news exposés of the dreadful treatment of America's youngsters in adult prisons, as well as in the adult courts, which often processed them as if they were common criminals, were well-known. Progressive elements among the rich and the intellectuals maintained something had to be done. They felt that child criminals and criminal children needed help, guidance, love, an opportunity for a second chance, and education, not punishment, humiliation, degradation, additional undeserved pain, and torment.

Soon states around the country had separate facilities for treating juvenile offenders as well as separate facilities for incarcerating them. In some areas judges were called "Masters" and were encouraged to be kind and sympathetic, not gruff, procedural, and legalistic. *Parens patriae* (state as parents) became the role of the juvenile court procedures. Guilt or innocence was not the issue, nor was "punishment." The goal was to determine through case studies what the needs of referred youngsters were, and then, if necessary, to provide for these needs through a juvenile facility. Such needs could include food, shelter, education, separation from terrible families or neighborhoods, separation from peers who smoked, and so on.

Since the function of the proceedings was to ascertain and provide needs, legalities such as determining guilt or innocence or even a specific sentence were ignored. Often youngsters who were not initially charged with criminal offenses but were status offenders were sentenced to juvenile facilities. Status offenses included truancy, running away from home, hanging out on the street, and sassing teachers or social workers. Some more progressive states had a classification system distinguishing such offenders. These terms included *CINS* (children in need of supervision) and *PINS* (persons in need of supervision). However, often they were housed under the same administrative roof as youngsters who were charged with more serious offenses.

The age range for juveniles varied from state to state; some classified juveniles as anyone who is 19 or younger, and most demarcated children from adults at age 18 or 16. Many juvenile facilities, though, would keep offenders until they were 21 "for their own good." Since the purpose of the juvenile system was to "help" youngsters, a 12-year-old who had been truant could be held in custody until he was 18 or even 21. Until Supreme Court decisions in the 1960s provided some basic constitutional rights, children were not entitled to an attorney, could not appeal their sentences, and could be held incommunicado indefinitely.

Yet the juvenile courts were almost universally considered progressive. Eventually, some had second thoughts. It was theorized that the real function of the courts and juvenile system was to "Americanize" the children of immigrants and to more smoothly pipe marginal American children (poor white ethnics and blacks) into mainstream industrial society. According to this perspective, the juvenile court system, along with required public school education, functioned as socializing agencies more than as helping ones. Meanwhile, word slowly leaked out that many juvenile reformatories were quite different from what many people thought. Treatment was often nonexistent, and a variety of cruelties were typical.

As we enter the twenty-first century still carrying the weight of a very conservative, get-tough-with-all-delinquent-kids mode, to some the question becomes, which is the lesser of two evils, juvenile courts or adult courts for criminal children? The issue is in many ways a very sad one for the protagonists. Barry C. Feld, who has worked to help troubled youth for many years, reluctantly advocates abolishing juvenile courts. He is convinced that trying to salvage the existing system will only enable the get-tough side to do even worse things to delinquents. Vincent Schiraldi, who is arguably America's top advocate for the compassionate treatment of children, is convinced that additional transfers of juveniles into adult courts will be a disaster. He and coauthor Jason Ziedenberg draw from empirical research to document their concerns.

YES ↵

Barry C. Feld

Juvenile Justice in Minnesota: Framework for the Future

Over the past four decades, judicial, legislative, and administrative changes have transformed the juvenile court from a nominally rehabilitative social welfare agency into a scaled-down, second-class criminal court for youths that provides neither therapy nor justice. The Supreme Court in *Kent v. United States*, 383 U.S. 541, 556 (1966), observed that "juvenile justice" is an oxymoron: "the child receives the worst of both worlds: he gets neither the protections accorded to adults nor the solicitous care and regenerative treatment postulated for children." Since the Supreme Court in *In re Gault*, 387 U.S. 1 (1967) mandated some procedural safeguards in delinquency adjudications, there has been a substantive and procedural convergence between juvenile and criminal courts. But even as delinquency sanctions have become more punitive, juvenile courts provide a procedural regime under which few adults charged with a serious crime would consent to be tried.

At the beginning of the twentieth century, economic modernization fostered rapid industrialization, immigration, and urbanization. Social changes altered family structure and function and promoted a newer cultural construction of childhood as a period of innocence and vulnerability. The Progressive movement emerged to address the host of problems associated with social change, combined their belief in state power with the newer conception of childhood, and enacted a number of child-centered reforms—juvenile courts, child labor laws, welfare laws, and compulsory school attendance laws (Feld, 1999). During this period, positive criminology supplanted classical explanation of crime as the product of free-will choices. Reformers attributed criminal behavior to deterministic forces, deemphasized individual responsibility, employed medical analogies to treat offenders, and focused on efforts to reform rather than to punish them. Juvenile courts melded the new vision of childhood with new theories of social control, introduced a judicial-welfare alternative to the criminal justice system, and enabled the state, as *parens patriae*, to monitor ineffective child-rearing. Juvenile courts emphasized reform and rehabilitation, used informal procedures, excluded lawyers and juries, conducted confidential hearings, and adopted a euphemistic vocabulary. Judges imposed indeterminate and non-proportional sentences to secure juveniles' "best interests" and future welfare rather than to punish them for their past offenses.

Minnesota joined the nationwide movement and enacted its first juvenile court legislation effective June 1, 1905. Initially, the law to "regulate the treatment and control of dependent, neglected, and delinquent children" applied only to children under the age of 17 years. Reflecting the breadth of legislative concerns, the original act defined a "delinquent child" as any child who

> violates any law of this state or any city or village ordinance; or who is incorrigible; or who knowingly associates with thieves, vicious or immoral persons; or who without just cause and without the consent of its parents or custodian absents itself from its home or place of abode; or who is growing up in idleness or crime; or who knowingly frequents a house of ill fame; or who knowingly patronizes any policy shop or place where any gaming device is or shall be operated; or who frequents any saloon or dram shop where intoxicating liquors are sold, or who patronizes or visits any public pool room or bucket shop; or who wanders about the streets in the night time without being in any lawful business or occupation; or who habitually wanders about any railroad yards or tracks or jumps or hooks on to any moving train or enters any care or engine without lawful authority; or who habitually uses vile, obscene, vulgar, profane or indecent language; or who is

Feld, Barry C., "Juvenile Justice in Minnesota: Framework for the Future" from *Justice Where Art Thou? A Framework for the Future*. October 2007, Council on Crime and Justice. Used with permission of the author.

guilty of immoral conduct in any public place or about any school house.

The legislation's purpose clause further provided that it should be "liberally construed" to ensure "That the care, custody and discipline of a child shall approximate as nearly as may be that which should be given by its parents, and in all cases where it can properly be done, the child to be placed in an approved family home and become a member of the family by legal adoption or otherwise." Amendments to the Juvenile Code effective January 1, 1918, raised the age of delinquency jurisdiction to children under 18 years of age, closed delinquency proceedings to the public, provided confidentiality for court records, and expanded juvenile courts' purpose to ensure that they "act upon the principle that to the child concerned there is due from the state the protection and correction which he needs under the circumstances disclosed in the case. . . ."

In 1967, the Supreme Court in *In re Gault* concluded that most states' juvenile court procedures violated the Constitution and required a substantial overhaul. *Gault* identified two crucial disjunctions between juvenile justice rhetoric and reality: the theory versus the practice of rehabilitation and the differences between the procedural safeguards available to criminal defendants and to delinquents. The Court required juvenile courts to use "fundamentally fair" procedures which included advance notice of charges, a fair and impartial hearing, the assistance of counsel, an opportunity to confront and cross-examine witnesses, and the privilege against self-incrimination. Although the Court based delinquents' rights to notice, counsel, and confrontation on generic notions of due process and "fundamental fairness" under the Fourteenth Amendment rather than the specific requirements of the Sixth Amendment, it explicitly relied on the Fifth Amendment to grant delinquents the privilege against self-incrimination. As a result, juvenile courts' proponents no longer could characterize delinquency adjudications as either "non-criminal" or "non-adversarial." In subsequent decisions, the Court further equated criminal and delinquency proceedings. In *In re Winship*, 397 U.S. 358 (1970), the Court required states to prove delinquency "beyond a reasonable doubt," rather than by the lower, civil "preponderance of the evidence" standard of proof. The Court reasoned that while *parens patriae* intervention may be a laudable goal to deal with miscreant youths, "that intervention cannot take the form of subjecting the child to the stigma of a finding that he violated a criminal law and to the possibility of institutional confinement on proof insufficient to convict him were

he an adult." 397 U.S. at 367. However, in a plurality decision that produced five separate opinions, the Court in *McKeiver v. Pennsylvania*, 403 U.S. 528 (1971), declined to grant delinquents all of the procedural safeguards of adult criminal trials. Although the Court in *Duncan v. Louisiana*, 391 U.S. 145 (1968), previously had held that the Sixth Amendment right to a jury trial applied to state criminal proceedings, *McKeiver* insisted that "the juvenile court proceeding has not yet been held to be a 'criminal prosecution,' within the meaning and reach of the Sixth Amendment, and also has not yet been regarded as devoid of criminal aspects merely because it usually has been given the civil label." 403 U.S. at 541. *McKeiver* held that the constitution did not require jury trials in state delinquency trials because "due process" required only "accurate fact-finding," which a judge could do as well as a jury. The *McKeiver* plurality denied that delinquents required protection from the State, invoked the imagery of the paternalistic juvenile court judge, ignored the jury's crucial role in upholding *Winship*'s standard of "proof beyond a reasonable doubt," and rejected concerns that juvenile courts' closed hearings could prejudice the accuracy of fact finding. *McKeiver* emphasized the adverse impact that jury trials could have on the informality, flexibility, and confidentiality of juvenile court proceedings.

Gault and its progeny transformed the Progressives' conception of the juvenile court as a social welfare agency into a second-class criminal court for juveniles. Progressive reformers intervened on the basis of a child's "real needs" and viewed proof of a crime as secondary. Although *McKeiver* denied delinquents the right to a jury trial, *Gault* and *Winship* imported the adversarial model, attorneys, the privilege against self-incrimination, and the criminal standard of proof. By adopting some criminal procedures, the Court shifted the focus of the juvenile court from "real needs" to proof of criminal acts and formalized the connection between criminal conduct and coercive intervention. Although the Court did not intend to preclude juvenile courts' rehabilitative agenda, judicial and legislative changes have fostered a procedural and substantive convergence with criminal courts. Constitutional theory, states' delinquency laws, and actual practices continue to provide juveniles with "the worst of both worlds." Youths receive fewer and less adequate procedural safeguards than do adult criminal defendants, especially the right to a jury and access to effective assistance of counsel. Despite these deficiencies, once states provided delinquents with even a semblance of procedural justice, they more readily departed from a rehabilitative model and adopted "get tough" policies. Although racial inequality provided the initial impetus for the Court's focus on juveniles' procedural safeguards, granting delinquents some rights legitimized the increasingly punitive, "get tough" penalties that now fall most heavily on minority offenders (Feld, 2003).

Since 1980, the Minnesota legislature and Supreme Court have adopted laws and rules of procedure that have fostered a criminalizing of juvenile justice. On the one hand, the explicit endorsement of punishment as an element of juvenile sentencing policy in Minnesota repudiates juvenile courts' original postulates that children should be treated differently than adults and contradicts *McKeiver*'s assumptions that delinquents require fewer procedural safeguards than do adult criminal defendants. At the same time, many juveniles do not receive even the limited procedural safeguards that *Gault* envisioned (Feld, 1989; 1993). Although juvenile courts increasingly converge with criminal courts, Minnesota does not provide youths with either procedural safeguards equivalent to those of adult criminal defendants, or with special procedures that more adequately protect them from their own immaturity. Instead, state laws and judicial opinions place juveniles on an equal footing with adult criminal defendants when formal equality acts to their detriment, and employ less effective juvenile court procedures when they provide the state with an advantage (Feld, 1984; 1989; 1995). . . .

In 1983, the Minnesota Supreme Court replaced an urban- and rural-county patchwork of rules with one set of statewide rules to govern juvenile court proceedings (Feld, 1984). The new rules responded to *Gault*'s requirements for greater procedural formality and marked a further criminalizing of juvenile courts. However, the Court made a number of policy decisions to provide delinquents with less adequate safeguards than those afforded criminal defendants. In every instance in which the Court had an opportunity to recognize youths' immaturity and vulnerability and to provide them with more effective procedural safeguards than those afforded criminal defendants, the Court treated juveniles just like adults. Conversely, in every instance in which the court had an opportunity to treat delinquents at least as well procedurally as criminal defendants, it adopted juvenile court procedures that provided less effective safeguards (Feld, 1984). As a result, juveniles in Minnesota continued to receive "the worst of both worlds." For example, when *Gault* granted delinquents the privilege against self-incrimination, the procedural safeguards developed in *Miranda v. Arizona*, 384 U.S. 436 (1966) also became available to juveniles. Allowing juveniles to waive their *Miranda* rights and their right to counsel under the adult standard of "knowing, intelligent, and voluntary" under the "totality of the circumstances"

is an example of formal equality producing practical inequality. Developmental psychologists long have recognized that juveniles—especially those younger than 16 years of age—lack the understanding, maturity, judgment, experience and competence to exercise legal rights on a par with adults (Feld, 2006). Despite youths' limitations, the Minnesota Court repeatedly has rejected appeals for additional procedural safeguards, such as the presence of a parent during interrogation, and instead endorsed the adult waiver standard (Feld, 1984; 2006). On the other hand, the legislature and Court adhere to *McKeiver* and continue to deny delinquents the right to a jury trial that adult criminal defendants enjoy. The denial of a jury right affects many other aspects of juvenile justice administration as well (Feld, 1984; 2003). Trial judges and juries apply *Winship*'s standard of proof "beyond a reasonable doubt" differently and, as a result, it is easier for the state to convict delinquents in juvenile courts than it is to convict adults in criminal courts (Feld, 2003). Despite that, the Minnesota Supreme Court allows the state to include those procedurally deficient delinquency convictions in the criminal history score to enhance the sentences of adult offenders. *State v. McFee*, 721 N.W.2d 607 (MN. 2006). The *McKeiver* plurality denied delinquents a jury trial because it feared that juries would bring to the juvenile system "the traditional delay, the formality, and the clamor of the adversary system and, *possibly, the public trial.*" 403 U.S. 528 (1971). Illustrating the punitiveness and procedural schizophrenia of juvenile justice, the 1986 legislature opened delinquency hearings to the public of juveniles 16 years of age or older and charged with a felony level offense while simultaneously denying them the right to a jury trial. Minn. Stat. § 260.155 Subd. 1(c) (1986).

Although *Gault* likened the seriousness of a delinquency proceeding to a felony prosecution, Minnesota's use of the adult waiver standard—"knowing, intelligent, and voluntary" under the "totality of the circumstances"—to gauge juveniles' waivers of the right to counsel has denied many juveniles effective assistance of counsel (Feld, 1989; 1993). Research conducted in the late-1980s reported that a majority of juveniles who appeared in juvenile courts lacked the assistance of counsel. One-third of juveniles removed from their homes and nearly a quarter of delinquents confined in institutions were not represented by counsel at their delinquency adjudications (Feld, 1989; 1993). Moreover, despite statewide laws and procedural rules, juvenile justice administration varied widely throughout the state. Judges in different locales appointed counsel, detained, and sentenced youths very differently and provided "justice by geography" (Feld,

1991; 1993). Judges in urban counties appointed counsel for delinquents more than twice as often as did rural judges; the majority of youths in rural counties charged with felony offenses lacked representation (Feld, 1991; 1993).

In addition to geographic disparities, research reports substantial racial disparities in juvenile justice administration (Feld, 1989; 1993). Both nationally and in Minnesota, studies consistently report racial disparities in detention, sentencing, and waiver decisions by juvenile court judges (Feld, 2003). After controlling for the seriousness of the present offense and prior record, juvenile court judges are more likely to transfer minority youths than similarly situated white youths to criminal court (Feld, 2003). Empirical evaluations of juvenile court delinquency sentencing practices report two consistent findings. First, the ordinary principles of the criminal law—present offense and prior record—explain most of the variance in how juvenile court judges sentence delinquents. Because the state defines delinquency jurisdiction based on a child committing a criminal act, judges' sentencing practices focus primarily on the seriousness of the present offense and prior record. Secondly, after controlling for offense variables, juvenile courts consistently produce racial disparities in pre-trial detention and sentencing (Feld, 1999; 2003). Black youths engage in higher rates of violent offenses and use of firearms than do white juveniles and this accounts for some of the racial differentials in sentencing (Feld, 1999). Part of the differences in rates of offending by race is attributable to differential exposure to risk factors associated with crime and violence—poverty, segregation and cultural isolation in impoverished neighborhoods, lack of access to health care, and the like—and a "culture of the street" within some urban settings which exacerbates youth violence (Feld, 1999; 2003). Regardless of the causes of crime, no society and, especially the law-abiding victims within the affected communities, can tolerate youth violence. But, justice system responses may aggravate the cumulative disadvantage of minority youths. Research consistently reports that even after controlling for variables such as the seriousness of the offense and prior record, judges detain and sentence minority youths at higher rates than they do white youths (Feld, 1999; 2003). In a society marked by economic and racial inequality, minority youths are most "in need" and therefore most "at risk" for juvenile court intervention. The structural context of juvenile justice places minority youths at a dispositional disadvantage. Urban juvenile courts are procedurally more formal and sentence all delinquents more severely. Urban courts have greater access to detention facilities and juvenile

court judges sentence detained youths more severely than those who remain at liberty. Because proportionally more minority youths live in urban counties, the geographic and structural context of juvenile justice administration interacts with race to produce minority over-representation in detention facilities and correctional institutions (Feld, 1989; 2003). The Minnesota Council on Crime and Justice (2006) reported that the Hennepin County Juvenile Detention Center detained disproportionately more black juveniles for all forms of violations—new offenses, warrants, and arrest and detention orders—and for longer periods than their white counterparts. The Minnesota Supreme Court Task Force on Racial Bias in the Judicial System (1993) reported substantial disparities in Minnesota's juvenile justice system in rates of detention and out-of-home placement of minority youths compared with white juveniles charged with similar offenses and prior records. The Race Bias Task Force also reported substantial geographic disparities in detention and sentencing that compounded racial disparities.

In 1995, the Minnesota legislature enacted a comprehensive package of law reforms that fostered even greater substantive and procedural convergence between juvenile and criminal courts (Feld, 1995). In the early-1990s, increases in youth violence and homicide, especially within the urban black male population, provided impetus nationwide and in Minnesota to "get tough" and "crack down" on juvenile crime (Feld, 1999; 2003). The 1995 amendments used the offense criteria of the adult sentencing guidelines to make it easier to waive juveniles to criminal court and excluded from juvenile court jurisdiction youths 16 years of age and older charged with first-degree murder (Feld, 1995). Once the state tries youths in criminal court, judges sentence them as if they were adults and impose mandatory sentences of life imprisonment on youths as young as 14 or 15 years of age without any recognition of youthfulness as a mitigating factor. *State v. Mitchell*, 577 N.W.2d 481 (MN. 1998). Most significantly, the legislature enacted a blended sentencing law—Extended Jurisdiction Juvenile (EJJ) prosecution—through which the state tried youths in juvenile court with adult criminal procedural safeguards including the right to a jury trial and imposed both juvenile dispositions that continued until age twenty-one and a stayed adult criminal sentence (Feld, 1995). Although the legislature intended EJJ to provide judges with a stronger juvenile treatment alternative to waiver, the law instead had a substantial "net-widening" effect; judges continued to waive the same numbers and type of youths that they had transferred previously *and* revoked the probation and executed the adult sentences of nearly one-third of EJJ youths, many of whom were younger and first-offenders (Podkopacz and Feld, 2001). Most of those youths, judges previously had decided should *not* be waived and many of them had their probation revoked for technical violations rather than new offenses. In addition, the legislation expanded and extended the use of delinquency convictions in the criminal history score to enhance the sentences of adults. As a result, waived juveniles and young adult offenders may receive substantially longer sentences based on delinquency convictions obtained without the right to a jury trial (Feld, 1995; 2003). In addition to increasing juvenile courts' sentencing powers, the new legislation also strengthened provision for appointment of counsel (Feld, 1995). Although the Minnesota legislature and Supreme Court long had recognized that only half of juveniles received assistance of counsel, earlier proposals to expand delivery of legal services foundered. The 1995 code required judges to appoint counsel for all youths charged with a felony or gross-misdemeanor offense or in which out-of-home placement is contemplated (Feld, 1995). Despite these changes, rates of representation of juveniles remain lower than those of adults charged with comparable offenses. And, the legislature again declined to provide delinquents charged with crimes the right to a jury trial.

The juvenile court in Minnesota today is a very different one from that envisioned a century ago. There has been a substantial convergence between the sentencing policies and procedures of the juvenile and criminal justice systems. And, in the contemporary juvenile court, youths *continue* to receive "the worst of both worlds . . . neither the protections accorded to adults nor the solicitous care and regenerative treatment postulated for children." A study conducted by the Legislative Auditor of Minnesota's state-run institutions and largest private programs reported very high rates of recidivism and concluded that "Minnesota's most-used residential programs have shown a limited ability change entrenched criminal values and behavior patterns among juveniles" (Feld, 1995). Minnesota's legislation, judicial opinions, and juvenile justice practices emphasize the greater role of punishment. This is reflected in the juvenile code purpose clause, judges sentencing practices of ordinary delinquents, the greater use of the adult sentencing guidelines to structure prosecutorial decision-making, waiver and EJJ decisions, and the expanded role of delinquency convictions in the adult criminal history score (Feld, 1995). Notwithstanding *McKeiver*'s fond hopes, juvenile courts' trials simply replicate those of criminal courts, albeit with fewer, less adequate procedural protections. The denial of a right to a jury trial affects every other aspect of juvenile justice administration—adherence to the criminal standard of "proof beyond a reasonable doubt," access to

and the performance of counsel, the timing of evidentiary hearings, and the like. Minnesota denies delinquents jury trials in an increasingly punitive juvenile justice system and then compounds that inequity when it uses those nominally rehabilitative sentences to extend terms of adult imprisonment. Finally, criminal courts sentence youths tried as adults without any formal recognition of youthfulness as a mitigating factor in sentencing. And all of these consequences fall disproportionately heavily on minority youth (Feld, 1999; 2003).

Confronted with Minnesota juvenile courts' punitive sentencing practices, Judge Gary Crippen, in *In re D.S.F.*, 416 N.W.2d 772 (Mn. Ct. App. 1987), posed three plausible policy options:

1. [T]he juvenile delinquency systems could be "restructured to fit their original [rehabilitative] purpose."

2. [W]e can . . . embrac[e] punitive dispositions as an acceptable and inherent part of delinquency proceedings, but call[] upon the Minnesota Legislature and the Minnesota Supreme Court to extend to accused juveniles all procedural safeguards guaranteed for adults in criminal cases. Most critically, we could assert the demonstrated need for jury trials in accusatory proceedings where juveniles may be incarcerated, and the additional need for representation by competent counsel in every case where a juvenile is faced with incarceration.

3. [W]e could call for dismantling a system that openly exacts from our younger citizens a sacrifice of liberties and gives in return a false promise to serve the best interests of those who come before it. The federal and state constitutions do not permit a criminal justice system without criminal procedural safeguards.

Two decades later, we face the same issues of procedure and substance against the backdrop of an even more punitive juvenile justice system in which youths continue "to receive the worst of both worlds." As long as juvenile courts operate in a societal context that does not provide adequate support and services for children in general, intervention in the lives of those who commit crimes inevitably will be for purposes of crime control, rather than for social welfare. Addressing the "real needs" of young people—social welfare, family assistance, health, housing, nutrition, education, segregation, and poverty—requires a public and political commitment to the welfare of children that extends far beyond the resources or competencies of any juvenile justice system.

References

Council on Crime and Justice, "An Analysis of Racial Disproportionality in Juvenile Confinement: An Analysis of Disproportionate Minority Confinement in the Hennepin County Juvenile Detention Center" (2006).

Barry C. Feld, "Criminalizing Juvenile Justice: Rules of Procedure for the Juvenile Court," 69 *Minnesota Law Review* 141 (1984).

Barry C. Feld, "The Right to Counsel in Juvenile Court: An Empirical Study of When Lawyers Appear and the Difference They Make," 79 *Journal of Criminal Law & Criminology* 1185 (1989).

Barry C. Feld, "Justice by Geography: Urban, Suburban, and Rural Variations in Juvenile Justice Administration," 82 Journal of Criminal Law & Criminology 156 (1991).

Barry C. Feld, *Justice for Children: The Right to Counsel and the Juvenile Courts* (Boston: Northeastern University Press 1993).

Barry C. Feld, "Violent Youth and Public Policy: A Case Study of Juvenile Justice Law Reform," 79 *Minnesota Law Review* 965 (1995).

Barry C. Feld, *Bad Kids: Race and the Transformation of the Juvenile Court* (New York: Oxford University Press 1999).

Barry C. Feld, "The Constitutional Tension Between *Apprendi* and *McKeiver*: Sentence Enhancements Based on Delinquency Convictions and the Quality of Justice in Juvenile Courts," 38 Wake Forest Law Review 1111 (2003a).

Barry C. Feld, "Race, Politics, and Juvenile Justice: The Warren Court and the Conservative 'Backlash'," 87 *Minnesota Law Review* 1447 (2003b).

Barry C. Feld, "Juveniles' Competence to Exercise *Miranda* Rights: An Empirical Study of Policy and Practice," 91 *Minnesota Law Review* 26 (2006).

Marcy Rasmussen Podkopacz and Barry C. Feld, "The Back-Door to Prison: Waiver Reform, 'Blended Sentencing', and the Law of Unintended Consequences," 91 *Journal of Criminal Law and Criminology* 997 (2001).

BARRY C. FELD is the Centennial Professor of Law at the Minnesota Law School, where he has been teaching since 1972, and the author of *Readings in Juvenile Justice Administration* (1999).

Vincent Schiraldi and
Jason Ziedenberg

The Florida Experiment

"Anthony Laster is the kind of kid who has never been a danger to anyone. A 15-year-old, eighth grader with an IQ of 58, Anthony is described by relatives as having the mind of a five-year-old. Late last year, a few days after his mother died, Anthony asked another boy in his class at a Florida middle school to give him lunch money, claiming he was hungry. When the boy refused, Anthony reached into his pocket and took $2. That's when Anthony ran smack into Palm Beach County prosecutor Barry Kirscher's brand of compassionless conservatism. Rather than handling the case in the principal's office, where it belonged, Mr. Kirscher decided to prosecute Anthony as an adult for this, his first arrest. Anthony spent the next seven weeks—including his first Christmas since his mother died—in custody, much of it in an adult jail."[1]

Introduction

Anthony Laster was one of 4,660 youth who Florida prosecutors sent to adult court last year under the wide ranging powers they enjoy with the state's direct file provisions. Florida is one of 15 states that allow prosecutors—not a judge—to decide whether children arrested for crimes ranging from shoplifting to robbery should be dealt with in the juvenile justice or criminal justice system.[2] While 43 states have changed their laws to make it easier for judges to send children into the adult criminal system since 1993, Florida is leading the nation in using prosecutors to make the decision to try children as adults. In 1995 alone (Figure 1), Florida prosecutors sent 7,000 cases to adult court nearly matching the number of cases judges sent to the criminal justice system nationwide that year.[3]

Figure 1

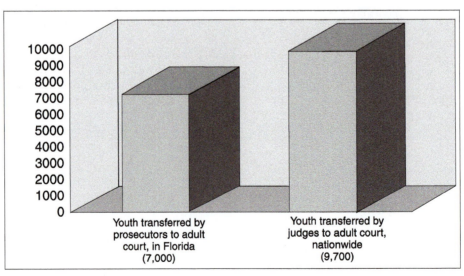

In 1995, Florida Prosecutors Rival Judges in the Rest of U.S. in Sending Youth to Adult Court

Youth transferred by prosecutors to adult court, in Florida (7,000)

Youth transferred by judges to adult court, nationwide (9,700)

Source: The Urban Institute, 1998.

Figure 2

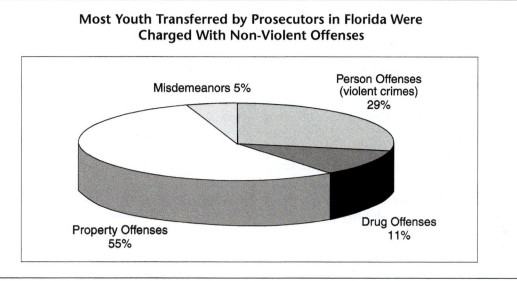

Most Youth Transferred by Prosecutors in Florida Were Charged With Non-Violent Offenses

Misdemeanors 5%

Person Offenses (violent crimes) 29%

Property Offenses 55%

Drug Offenses 11%

Source: Notre Dame Journal of Law, Ethics, and Public Policy (1996).

A juvenile crime bill currently being considered by the U.S. Congress (House-Senate Conference Committee) would give U.S. Attorneys even greater powers than those enjoyed by prosecutors in Florida.

The change in federal law would remove judges from the process of deciding which justice system would serve young people, and transfer that power to the sole discretion of prosecutors. The Justice Department also appears to support giving prosecutors expanded powers to try youth as adults in federal court.[4] Given the current legislative drive, it is worthwhile to examine the Florida experience to see what the future will hold for the nation.

Profile: Who Are Prosecutors Sending to Adult Court in Florida?

I. Offense Category

When prosecutorial waiver was introduced in 1981, the percentage of delinquency cases transferred to adult court in Florida soared from 1.2% to nearly 9% by 1987.[5] In fiscal year 1997–98, 6,425 of the 94,693 cases disposed of by judicial processing in Florida resulted in transfer to adult court. While these waiver provisions were originally designed to ensure that violent juvenile offenders were being detained, a 1991 study of two representative Florida counties showed that only 28% of the youths prosecutors waived to adult court were for violent crimes.[6] More than half (55%) of the youths prosecutors sent to adult court were charged with

property offenses that involved no violence, and fully 5% were tried as adults for misdemeanors (Figure 2). Almost a quarter of the cases waived were first-time, low-level offenders.[7]

II. Disproportionate Minority Confinement

The most striking feature of Florida's transferred youth population profile is the extent to which minority youth are overrepresented in the ranks of the youth being referred to adult court. One study conducted by the Florida Department of Juvenile Justice found that black youths were 2.3 times more likely than white youth to be transferred in Florida.[8] Even though non-whites account for 24% of the 10–17 age bracket in Florida, they currently represent 74% of those 10–17 held in the Florida prison system.[9] "I think the way the system sets up programs shows some institutional bias," is the way one candid Florida prosecutor describes it.[10]

Policy Impact in Florida

I. Sentencing: Longer Terms for Youths in Adult Court?

While some have suggested that huge numbers of children are being held in adult facilities across the state, it is not clear that youth going to adult court via prosecutorial waiver are serving long sentences. A study published in the *Notre Dame Journal of Law, Ethics and Public Policy* found that, of the youth who were incarcerated after disposition, half received short sentences, some shorter than they would have received in the juvenile justice system. The majority (54%) of those sentenced to prison were released within three years.[11] A 1998 survey of the Florida transferred population shows that a majority of youth prosecutors sent to adult court for property, drug and weapons offenses received jail sentences or probation terms well within the range of what could have been prescribed to them in the juvenile court.[12] The same study showed that in 1995, 61% of the youth found guilty in adult court were incarcerated, but only 31% were served prison terms.[13]

II. More Youths to Adult Jail and to Juvenile Detention

While it might be expected that prosecutorial waiver would reduce the number of youths being funneled into Florida's juvenile justice system, the opposite has been true. Between 1993 and 1998, the number of annual commitments to Florida's juvenile justice system increased by 85% despite its liberal use of waiver to adult court. Florida has the sixth highest incarceration rate for youth per 100,000 in the nation, and detains young people at a rate 25% greater than the national average.[14] This happened during a time when the number of waiver cases was increasing, and the number of felony referrals to the juvenile justice system was decreasing. This is happening, despite the fact that youths waived to adult court are held before trial in adult jails, further slackening the numbers that would need to be held in juvenile detention. Rather than the happy prospect of devoting more resources in the juvenile justice system to fewer youths, the system has widened its "net of control" by committing youth for lower level offenses.[15]

Crime Control Impact

I. Recidivism: Adult Court Prosecution Increases Propensity for Crime

Quantitative: Studies and Data
A number of studies have shown that youth sent to adult court generally recidivate at a higher rate than they do if they are sent to the juvenile justice system. A series of studies in Florida have analyzed what happens to youth referred to adult court—90% of whom are referred there directly by a prosecutor. A study published in the journal *Crime and Delinquency* showed that youth transferred to adult court in Florida were a third more likely to reoffend

than those sent to the juvenile justice system.[16] The transferred youths reoffended almost twice as fast as those who were sent to juvenile detention.[17] Of those who committed new crimes, the youth who had previously been tried as adults committed serious crimes at double the rate of those sent to juvenile court.[18] While a 1997 study by the same authors showed that property offenders were slightly less likely to recidivate when transferred to adult court, the authors note: "Once the effect of offense type was controlled, the logistic regression analysis indicated that transfer led to more recidivism. Moreover, the transferred youths who subsequently reoffended were rearrested more times and more quickly than were the non-transferee youth who reoffended regardless of the offense for which they were prosecuted . . . although property felons who were transferred may have been less likely to reoffend, when they did reoffend they reoffended more often and more quickly."[19]

JUVENILE OFFENDERS GENERALLY FOLLOW ONE OF THREE PATHS TO ADULT COURT

Judicial Waiver: *A juvenile court judge waives jurisdiction over the case after considering the merits of transfer for the individual youth.*

Legislative Exclusion: *A state legislature determines that an entire class of juvenile crimes should be sent to adult court automatically, usually serious and violent offenses.*

Prosecutorial Discretion: *A state or local prosecutor has the authority to file charges against some juveniles directly in adult court.*

Source: The Urban Institute, 1998

Qualitative: Interviews With Youths in Deep End Juvenile Programs
The same authors recently conducted in-depth interviews with fifty youths sent to prison by Florida prosecutors, versus fifty who were sent to a state "maximum risk" juvenile detention facility.[20] This study found that the youth themselves recognized the rehabilitative strengths of the juvenile justice system in contrast to the adult prison system.

Sixty percent of the sample sent to juvenile detention said they expect they would not reoffend, 30% said they were uncertain whether they would reoffend, while 3% said they would likely reoffend. Of those expected not to reoffend, 90% said good juvenile justice programming and services were the reason for their rehabilitation. Only one of the youths in juvenile detention said they were learning new ways to commit crimes. Most reported at least one favorable contact with a staff person that helped them. As such, the juvenile justice system responses were overwhelmingly positive:

A: "This place is all about rehabilitation and counseling.... This place here, we have people to listen to when you have something on your mind . . . and need to talk. They understand you and help you."

B: "They helped me know how to act. I never knew any of this stuff. That really helped me, cause I ain't had too good a life."[21]

By contrast, 40% of the transferred youth said they were learning new ways to commit crimes in prison. Most reported that the guards and staff in prisons were indifferent, hostile, and showed little care for them. Only 1/3 of the youths in prison said they expected not to reoffend. Not surprisingly, the youths sent to prison by prosecutors responded in an overwhelmingly despondent and negative way:

C: "When I was in juvenile programs, they were telling me that I am somebody and that I can change my ways,

and get back on the right tracks. In here, they tell me I am nobody and I never will be anybody."

D: "In the juvenile systems, the staff and I were real close. They wanted to help me. They were hopeful for me here. They think I am nothing but a convict now."

II. Crime Control Impact: Crime Rate

Despite having prosecutorial waiver on the books since 1981, Florida has the second highest overall violent crime rate of any state in the country, and that status has remained virtually unchanged throughout the 1990s.[22] Florida's violent juvenile crime rate is fully 48% higher than the national average (Figure 3).[23]

Though Florida leads the nation in using prosecutorial waiver, the other 14 states which allow states attorneys discretion to send youth to criminal court do not fare much better. Of the 15 states that currently employ prosecutorial waiver provisions, five (Florida, Arizona, Massachusetts, the District of Columbia and Louisiana) are among the ten states with the highest violent crime arrest rate (age 10–17). While the rest of the nation enjoyed a decline in juvenile crime between 1992 and 1996, five states that employ prosecutorial waiver—Arkansas, Nebraska, Arizona, Virginia, and New Hampshire—actually experienced an increase in their violent juvenile crime rates.[24]

Figure 3

Florida Has the Second Highest Violent Crime Rate in the Country, 48% Higher Than the National Average

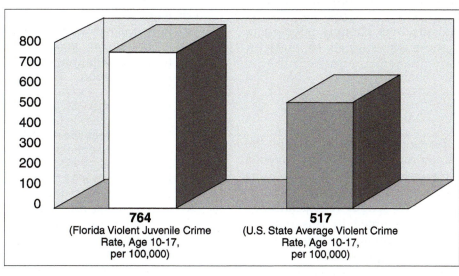

Source: Office of Juvenile Justice and Delinquency Prevention, 1997.

The Risks Youth Face in Adult Jails

The children who prosecutors are sending to adult court in Florida face greater threats to their life, limb and future when they enter Florida's adult jail and prison systems. These well-documented risks affect both the youth who are convicted in adult court, and those (like Anthony Laster) who are merely being held in pre-trial detention in jail, on crimes of which they may be exonerated.

One study has shown that youths are five times more likely to report being a victim of rape when they are held in an adult facility versus juvenile detention.[25] Youth in adult jails are also twice as likely to report being beaten by staff and 50% more likely to be attacked with a weapon. A Justice Department study done in 1981 showed that the suicide rate of juveniles in adult jails is 7.7 times higher than that of youth in juvenile detention centers.[26]

The Will of the People?: Public Opinion and Prosecutorial Waiver

A survey published in the journal *Crime and Delinquency* found that a majority of Americans oppose changing federal law to allow for prosecutorial waiver of youth to adult court.[27] When asked, "Would you agree strongly, agree somewhat, disagree somewhat, or disagree strongly that federal prosecutors should have total discretion to try juveniles as adults for all felonies?," 56% of a nationally representative sample of Americans disagreed or disagreed strongly with the idea (41% agreed, and 3% said they had no opinion). Nearly twice as many respondents were strongly opposed to the idea compared to those who strongly supported it (29% vs. 16%).[28]

Conclusion

As the United States Congress and states around the country weigh various approaches to curbing juvenile crime, the "Florida Experiment" of giving prosecutors broad discretion to decide whether juveniles should be tried as adults has come under serious consideration.[29] On almost every measure examined in this report—statewide crime control, individual recidivism, racial equity, and the youth's own perception of future offense behavior—the Florida system of prosecutorial discretion waiver was found wanting.

Notes

1. Schiraldi, Vincent. "Prosecutorial Zeal vs. America's Kids." *The Christian Science Monitor,* March 22, 1999.
2. The 15 states or jurisdictions which employ Direct File (prosecutorial discretion waiver) include Arkansas, Colorado, Florida, Georgia, Louisiana, Michigan, Nebraska, New Hampshire, Vermont, Arizona, Massachusetts, Montana, Oklahoma, Virginia, and the District of Columbia. Griffin, P., Torbet, P., and Szymanski, L. 1998. "Trying Juveniles as Adults in Criminal Court: Analysis of State Transfer Provisions." Washington, D.C.: U.S. Department of Justice, Office of Justice Programs, Office of Juvenile Justice and Delinquency Prevention.
3. Butts, Jeffrey A. and Adele V. Harrell. "Delinquents or Criminals: Policy Options for Young Offenders." Washington, D.C.: The Urban Institute, 1998, p. 6.
4. "In our view, the system should be fundamentally altered so that, in appropriate circumstances, the prosecutor alone determines whether to prosecute the juvenile as an adult." Gregory, Kevin V., Deputy Assistant Attorney General, in Testimony before the Subcommittee on Crime, Committee on the Judiciary, U.S. House of Representatives, March 10, 1999.
5. 1999 Annual Report and Juvenile Justice Fact Book, Florida Juvenile Justice Accountability Board, February, 1999.
6. Bishop, Donna M. and Charles E. Frazier. "Transfer of Juveniles to Criminal Court: A Case Study and Analysis of Prosecutorial Discretion." *The Notre Dame Journal of Law, Ethics and Public Policy,* Vol. 5: pp. 281–302, 1991.
7. Ibid.
8. Department of Juvenile Justice-Management Report, No. 42. March 24, 1996.
9. Inmate Population: Current Inmate Age. Agency Annual Report, Department of Corrections, 1998.
10. Bishop, Donna M. and Charles E. Frazier, "Race Effects in Juvenile Justice Decision Making: Findings of a Statewide Analysis." *The Journal of Criminal Law and Criminology,* Vol. 86, 1996.
11. Bishop, et al., 1991.
12. Bishop, Donna M. and Charles E. Frazier, "The Consequences of Transfer" in *The Changing Borders of Juvenile Justice: Transfer of Adolescents to the Criminal Court.* Chicago: University of Chicago Press [in press].
13. Bishop, Donna M., Charles E. Frazier, Lonn Lanza-Kaduce and Henry George White. "Juvenile Transfers to Criminal Court Study: Phase I

Final Report." Washington, D.C.: Office of Juvenile Justice and Delinquency Prevention, 1998.

14. Snyder, Howard N. and Melissa Sickmund. "Juvenile Offenders and Victims: Update on Violence." Washington, DC: Office of Juvenile Justice and Delinquency Prevention, 1998.
15. Bishop and Frazier [in press].
16. Bishop, Donna M. et al. "The Transfer of Juveniles to Criminal Court: Does It Make a Difference?" *Crime & Delinquency,* Vol. 42, No. 2, April 1996.
17. Ibid.
18. Ibid.
19. Bishop, Donna M., Charles E. Frazier, Lonn Lanza-Kaduce and Lawrence Winner. "The Transfer of Juveniles to Criminal Court: Reexamining Recidivism Over the Long Term." *Crime and Delinquency,* Vol. 43, No. 4, October 1997.
20. Bishop and Frazier, Office of Juvenile Justice and Delinquency Prevention, 1998.
21. Ibid, and keynote address, National Association of Sentencing Advocates Conference, Miami, Florida, April 15, 1999.
22. Snyder, p. 22.
23. Ibid.
24. Kathleen Maguire and Ann L. Pastore, eds., *Sourcebook of Criminal Justice Statistics 1997.* U.S. Department of Justice, Bureau of Justice Statistics, 1997; (1996); (1995). U.S. Department of Justice, Bureau of Justice Statistics. Washington, D.C., USGPO, 1998 (1997); (1996).
25. Fagan, Jeffrey, Martin Forst, and T. Scott Vivona. "Youth in Prisons and Training Schools: Perceptions and the Consequences of the Treatment Custody Dichotomy." *Juvenile and Family Court,* No. 2, 1989, p. 10.
26. Flaherty, Michael G. "An Assessment of the National Incidences of Juvenile Suicides in Adult Jails, Lockups and Juvenile Detention Centers." The University of Illinois, Urbana, Champaign, 1980.
27. Schiraldi, Vincent and Mark Soler. "The Will of the People: The Public's Opinion of the Violent and Repeat Juvenile Offender Act of 1997." *Crime and Delinquency,* Vol. 44., No. 4, October, 1998.
28. Ibid.
29. For example, in March, 2000, Californians will be voting on the "Gang Violence and Juvenile Crime Prevention Act of 1998" initiative, which will give prosecutors discretion to try certain juveniles as adults at the age of 14.

VINCENT SCHIRALDI was one of the nation's foremost advocates for the compassionate treatment of children. He was a prolific scholar who published many influential books and articles focusing on justice system policies. He served most recently as a senior research fellow at Harvard's Kennedy School of Government. He passed away in 2016.

JASON ZIEDENBERG is currently the Director of Research and Policy at the Justice Policy Institute where he has strategic and operational responsibility for generating and coordinating JPI's research and policy initiatives.

EXPLORING THE ISSUE

Should Juvenile Courts Be Abolished?

Critical Thinking and Reflection

1. Do violent youth deserve capital punishment?
2. Are the arguments to abolish juvenile courts valid?

Is There Common Ground?

As the public and politicians increasingly reflect intolerance toward criminals, especially violent ones, might Feld's proposal be viewed as an extreme one rising from desperation? That is, if we lived in different times, needed monies and staffing for juvenile courts, facilities, and services in the community would be provided. Is Feld's "sliding scale" fair for youngsters in adult courts? Can it be argued that because it is impossible to tell precisely how emotionally "developed" a youth is, it is ethically and legally unacceptable to sentence one youngster to a longer term than another youngster who did the same crime? Is Feld correct when he asserts that the juvenile court concept itself is untenable because it is impossible to have both the goal of crime control and treatment simultaneously? For instance, Schiraldi and Ziedenberg could argue that if courts were sympathetic toward and knowledgeable of youth, programs could be developed to treat children and consequently to reduce their involvement in crime.

For the most part, Schiraldi and Ziedenberg base their arguments on a Florida study. Is that a good basis for suggesting national policy, especially since Florida is an extreme case? Are the authors confusing the issues of waivering kids to adult courts and incarcerating kids in adult jails and prisons? Does their drawing from tear-jerking testimonies of selected child cases really serve to clarify the issue? For instance, might one just as easily juxtapose their reports with sad statements from victims of juvenile violence?

Can the two positions be synthesized? If federal monies were provided for randomly selected states to experiment with abolishing juvenile courts for, say, 20 years, would that be a better basis for deciding what is best for society and for child criminals? Meanwhile, should juvenile courts be abolished, as Feld says, or should the traditional system be maintained, as Schiraldi and Ziedenberg suggest?

Additional Resources

Among the many works by Feld pertaining to the issue is his *Readings in Juvenile Justice Administration* (Oxford University Press, 1999). Among the many publications of the Justice Policy Institute, which is directed by Schiraldi, is *Second Chances: One Hundred Years of the Children's Court* (1999).

A positive, though balanced, overview is "Juvenile Justice: A Century of Experience," by S. Drizin, *Current* (November 1999). Several highly favorable articles on juvenile courts can be found in the special issue of *Juvenile Justice* entitled "100th Anniversary of the Juvenile Court, 1899–1999" (December 1999), published by the Office of Juvenile Justice and Delinquency Prevention (OJJDP). Several other relevant reports are available from the OJJDP, including *From the Courthouse to the Schoolhouse: Making Successful Transitions* (March 2000), *Focus on Accountability: Best Practices for Juvenile Court and Probation* (1999), and *Offenders in Juvenile Court, 1996* (1999). Two helpful overviews of female offenders and the system are *Women Offenders* by L. Greenfeld and T. Snell (December 1999), published by the Bureau of Justice Statistics, and *Juvenile Justice Journal*, vol. VI, no. 1 (Investing in Girls: A Twenty-First Century Strategy) (October 1999), published by the OJJDP. An alternative system that neither of the protagonists address is teen courts, which are explored in J. Butts, D. Hoffman, and J. Buck, *Teen Courts in the United States: A Profile of Current Programs* (1999), also available from the OJJDP.

An excellent source from the federal level is S. G. Mezey's *Children in Court: Public Policymaking and Federal Court Decisions* (State University of New York Press, 1996). A brief discussion of a judge's analysis is "Judge Recommends Over-haul of Juvenile Supervision System," *Criminal Justice Weekly* (August 3, 1999). Two news articles that outline problems and prospects of the juvenile court system are "Regrettable Regression in the Way We

Treat Young Criminals," by L. Dodge, *The Washington Post* (August 29, 1999) and "Juvenile Court Comes of Age," by C. Wetzstein, *The Washington Times* (August 29, 1999). An analysis of gender differences can be found in "Explaining the Gender Difference in Adolescent Delinquent Behavior: A Longitudinal Test of Mediating Mechanisms," by X. Liu and H. B. Kaplan, *Criminology* (February 1999).

Internet References . . .

The Heartland Institute

http://heartland.org/policy-documents/abolish
-juvenile-justice-system

Urban Institute

www.urban.org/publications/1000232.html

Selected, Edited, and with Issue Framing Material by:
Thomas J. Hickey, *State University of New York at Cobleskill*

ISSUE

Is Exposure to Pornography Related to Increased Rates of Rape?

YES: **Diana E. H. Russell**, from "Pornography as a Cause of Rape," dianarussell.com (2004)

NO: **Anthony D'Amato**, from "Porn Up, Rape Down," *Northwestern Public Law Research Paper* No. 913013 (2006)

Learning Outcomes
After reading this issue, you will be able to: • Discuss *Miller v. California*, 413 U.S. 15 (1972), and its impact on the law of pornography. • Discuss the implications of the following statement: "Pornography is somebody's life before it becomes the pornographer's free speech." • Discuss college and high school students' attitudes about rape and sexual assault. • Discuss the relationship between exposure to pornography and rape. • Discuss whether Internet pornography has "de-mystified" sex.

ISSUE SUMMARY

YES: Diana E. H. Russell argues that the evidence is overwhelming that exposure to pornography is a major causal factor of rape. She utilizes the concept of "multiple causation" to explain the relationship between pornography and rape.

NO: Anthony D'Amato contends that the incidence of rape has declined 85 percent in the last 25 years while access to pornography via the Internet has become more widely available to teenagers and adults.

T he role of pornography in rape and sexual assault cases is a highly controversial issue. While many persons believe that the availability of pornography is directly or indirectly related to increasing rates of aberrant forms of sexual behavior, others believe that access to pornographic materials may be a healthy form of sexual expression. In some countries, pornography is readily available to virtually everyone. In the United States, serious efforts have been made through the legal system to control its distribution and availability, although there appears to be an ambivalent attitude toward pornography throughout society. This ambivalence is reflected in the decisions of U.S. court systems as they have struggled to define precisely what constitutes pornography.

For example, one of the U.S. Supreme Court's most important decisions on pornography was *Miller v. California*, 413 U.S. 15 (1972). The Court had previously held that pornography, as a form of expression, is not protected by the First Amendment. In reaffirming that principle, the Court developed the contemporary legal standard for lower courts to use to determine whether a specific depiction of sexual behavior is pornographic. Chief Justice Warren Burger described this standard as whether:

(a) the average person, 'applying contemporary community standards' would find that the work, taken as a whole, appeals to the prurient interest (b) whether the work depicts or describes, in a patently offensive way, sexual conduct specifically defined by the applicable state law, and (c) whether the work, taken as a whole, lacks serious literary, artistic, political, or scientific value.

As a practical matter, the *Miller* standard has led to very few restrictions on the publication of sexually explicit materials in the United States. Attorneys arguing that state pornography laws should be upheld have often struggled to convince the courts that particular depictions lack serious literary, artistic, political, or scientific value. The result has been that even representations that most people would find to be highly offensive are protected by the First Amendment.

But what is the impact of exposure to pornography on the Internet, and elsewhere, on increased rates of rape? Diana E. H. Russell argues that the evidence is overwhelming: Exposure to pornography is a major causal factor in rape cases. She takes issue with the idea that pornography should not be viewed as a "cause" of rape because there are a number of other factors that are also contributing factors in rape cases. States Russell:

> Because all viewers of pornography are not equally affected by it, many people conclude that pornography cannot be playing a causative role in rape and other forms of violence against women. This is similar to the tobacco industry's defense of cigarette smoking. They maintain that because many smokers do not die of lung cancer, and because some nonsmokers *do* die of this disease, it is incorrect to believe that smoking causes lung cancer. But the tobacco industry's reasoning here is faulty. They have no grounds for assuming that the proponents of smoking as a cause of lung cancer believe that smoking is the *only* cause.

Anthony D'Amato, in contrast, argues that the incidence of rape has actually declined 85 percent in the last 25 years while access to pornography via the Internet has become more freely available to teenagers and adults. States D'Amato:

> From data compiled by the National Telecommunications and Information Administration in 2001, the four states with the *lowest* per capita access to the internet were Arkansas, Kentucky, Minnesota, and West Virginia. The four states with the *highest* internet access were Alaska, Colorado, New Jersey, and Washington. . . . While the nationwide incidence of rape was showing a drastic decline, the incidence of rape in the four states having the *least* access to the internet showed an actual *increase* in rape over the same time period.

Moreover, in the states with the *most* access to the Internet, three of the four states showed declines in the incidence of rape during the same time period. D'Amato concludes that "[I]nternet porn has thoroughly demystified sex," and has resulted in substantial decreases in rape and sexual assault.

Before reading these articles in their entirety, which of the positions embraced by these authors appears to be the more intuitively compelling one? Do you believe that exposure to pornography is directly related to increased or decreased rates of rape and other forms of sexual violence? The answer to this question has very significant implications for the future development of law and social policy in this country and will have a profound impact on our cultural conversation about appropriate sexual behavior in the twenty-first century.

YES ⤶

Diana E.H. Russell

Pornography as a Cause of Rape

Introduction: What Is Pornography?

Proponents of the antipornography-equals-censorship school deliberately obfuscate any distinction between erotica and pornography, using the term erotica for all sexually explicit materials. In contrast, antipornography feminists consider it vitally important to distinguish between pornography and erotica, and support or even advocate erotica.

Although women's bodies are the staple of adult pornography, it is important to have a gender neutral definition that encompasses gay pornography, as well as child pornography. Animals are also targets of pornographic depictions. Hence, I define *pornography* as *material that combines sex and/or the exposure of genitals with abuse or degradation in a manner that appears to endorse, condone, or encourage such behavior.*

This article will focus on adult male heterosexual pornography because most pornography is produced for this market and because males are the predominant abusers of women. I define *heterosexual pornography* as *material created for heterosexual males that combines sex and/or the exposure of genitals with the abuse or degradation of females in a manner that appears to endorse, condone, or encourage such behavior.*

Erotica refers to *sexually suggestive or arousing material that is free of sexism, racism, and homophobia, and respectful of all human beings and animals portrayed.* This definition takes into account that humans are not the only subject matter of erotica. For example, I remember seeing a short award-winning erotic movie depicting the peeling of an orange. The shapes and coloring of flowers or hills can make them appear erotic. Many people find Georgia O'Keeffe's paintings erotic. But erotica can also include overtly or explicitly sexual images.

The definition's requirement of non-sexism means that the following types of material qualify as pornography rather than erotica: sexually arousing images in which women are consistently shown naked while men are clothed or in which women's genitals are displayed but

men's are not; or in which men are always portrayed in the initiating, dominant role. An example of sexualized racism which pervades pornography entails depictions of women that are confined to young, white bodies fitting many white men's narrow concept of beauty, i.e., very thin, large-breasted, and blonde.

Canadian psychologists Charlene Senn and Lorraine Radtke found the distinction between pornography and erotica to be significant and meaningful to female subjects in an experiment which they conducted. After slides had been categorized as violent pornography, nonviolent pornography (sexist and dehumanizing), or erotica (nonsexist and nonviolent), these researchers found that the violent and nonviolent images had a negative effect on the mood states of their women subjects, whereas the erotic images had a positive effect (1986, pp. 15–16; also see Senn, 1993). Furthermore, the violent images had a greater negative impact than the nonviolent pornographic images. This shows that a conceptual distinction between pornography and erotica is both meaningful and operational.

The term *abusive* sexual behavior in my definition refers to sexual conduct that ranges from derogatory, demeaning, contemptuous, or damaging to brutal, cruel, exploitative, painful, or violent. *Degrading* sexual behavior refers to sexual conduct that is humiliating, insulting, and/or disrespectful; for example, urinating or defecating on a woman, ejaculating in her face, treating her as sexually dirty or inferior, depicting her as slavishly taking orders from men and eager to engage in whatever sex acts men want, or calling her insulting names while engaging in sex, such as bitch, cunt, nigger, whore.

Note the abuse and degradation in the portrayal of female sexuality in Helen Longino's description of typical pornographic books, magazines, and films:

> **Women are represented as passive and as slavishly dependent upon men. The role of female characters is limited to the provision of sexual services to men. To the extent that women's sexual pleasure is represented at all, it is subordinated**

to that of men and is never an end in itself as is the sexual pleasure of men. What pleases women is the use of their bodies to satisfy male desires. While the sexual objectification of women is common to all pornography, women are the recipients of even worse treatment in violent pornography, in which women characters are killed, tortured, gang-raped, mutilated, bound, and otherwise abused, as a means of providing sexual stimulation or pleasure to the male characters.

(Longino, 1980, p. 42)

What is objectionable about pornography, then, is its abusive and degrading portrayal of females and female sexuality, not its sexual content or explicitness. A particularly important feature of my definition of pornography is the requirement that *it appears to endorse, condone, or encourage abusive sexual desires or behaviors.* These attributes differentiate pornography from materials that include abusive or degrading sexual behavior for educational purposes. Movies such as "The Accused," and "The Rape of Love," for example, present realistic representations of rape with the apparent intention of helping viewers to understand the reprehensible nature of rape, and the agony experienced by rape victims. I have used the expression *"it appears"* instead of *"it is intended"* to endorse, condone, or encourage sexually abusive desires or behavior to avoid the difficult, if not impossible, task of establishing the intentions of producers. My definition differs from most definitions which focus instead on terms like "obscenity" and "sexually explicit materials...." Members of *WAVPM (Women Against Violence in Pornography and Media),* for example, used to refer to record covers, jokes, ads, and billboards as pornography when they were sexually degrading to women, even when nudity or displays of women's genitals were not portrayed (Lederer, 1980).

Some people may object that feminist definitions of pornography that go beyond sexually explicit materials differ so substantially from common usage that they make discussion between feminists and nonfeminists confusing. First of all, however, there is no consensus on definitions among nonfeminists or feminists. Some feminists, for example, do include the concept of sexual explicitness as a defining feature of pornography. Andrea Dworkin and Catharine MacKinnon define pornography as "the graphic sexually explicit subordination of women through pictures and/or words" (1988, p. 36). They go on to spell out nine ways in which this overall definition can be met, for example, "women are presented dehumanized as sexual objects, things, or commodities." James Check (1985) uses the term sexually explicit materials instead of pornography, presumably in the hope of bypassing the many controversies associated with the term pornography. But

these scholars have not, to my knowledge, defined what they mean by sexually explicit materials.

Sometimes there can be a good reason for feminists to employ the same definition as nonfeminists. For example, in my study of the prevalence of rape, I used a very narrow, legal definition of rape because I wanted to be able to compare the rape rates obtained in my study with those obtained in government studies. Had I used a broader definition that included oral and anal penetration, for example, my study could not have been used to show how grossly flawed the methodology of the government's national surveys are in determining meaningful rape rates.

But if there is no compelling reason to use the same definition as that used by those with whom one disagrees, then it makes sense to define a phenomenon in a way that best fits feminist principles. As my objection to pornography is not that it shows nudity or different methods of sexual engagement, I see no reason to limit my definition to sexually explicit material. Unlike MacKinnon and Dworkin, who sought to formulate a definition that would be the basis for developing a new law on pornography, I have not been constrained by the requirements of law in constructing mine.

My definition of pornography does not include all the features that commonly characterize such material since I believe that concise definitions are preferable to complex or lengthy definitions. Pornography, for example, frequently depicts females, particularly female sexuality, inaccurately. "Pornography Tells Lies About Women" declared a bold red and black sticker designed by *Women Against Violence in Pornography and Media* to deface pornography. It has been shown, for example, that pornography consumers are more likely to believe that unusual sexual practices are more common than they really are (Zillmann, 1989). These distortions often have serious consequences. Some viewers act on the assumption that the depictions are accurate, and presume that there is something wrong with females who do not behave like those portrayed in pornography. This can result in verbal abuse or physical abuse, including rape, by males who consider that they are entitled to the sexual goodies that they want or that they believe other men enjoy.

Sexual objectification is another common characteristic of pornography. It refers to the portrayal of *human beings—usually women—as depersonalized sexual things, such as "tits, cunt, and ass," not as multi-faceted human beings deserving equal rights with men.* As Susan Brownmiller so eloquently noted,

(In pornography) our bodies are being stripped, exposed, and contorted for the purpose of ridicule to bolster that "masculine esteem" which gets its kick and sense of power from viewing females as anonymous, panting playthings, adult toys,

dehumanized objects to be used, abused, broken and discarded.

(1975, p. 394)

However, the sexual objectification of females is not confined to pornography. It is also a staple of mainstream movies, ads, record covers, songs, magazines, television, art, cartoons, literature, pin-ups, and so on, and influences the way that many males learn to see women and even children. This is why I have not included it as a defining feature of pornography. . . .

Pornography as Violence Against Women

"I don't need studies and statistics to tell me that there is a relationship between pornography and real violence against women. My body remembers."
—*Woman's testimony, 1983*

"The relationship between particularly sexually violent images in the media and subsequent aggression . . . is much stronger statistically than the relationship between smoking and lung cancer."
—*Edward Donnerstein, 1983*

When addressing the question of whether or not pornography causes rape, as well as other forms of sexual assault and violence, many people fail to acknowledge that the actual *making* of pornography sometimes involves, or even requires, violence and sexual assault. Testimony by women and men involved in such activity provide numerous examples of this (*Public Hearings*, 1983; *Attorney General's Commission*, 1986).

In one case, a man who said he had participated in over a hundred pornographic movies testified at the *Commission* hearings in Los Angeles as follows: "I, myself, have been on a couple of sets where the young ladies have been forced to do even anal sex scenes with a guy which [sic] is rather large and I have seen them crying in pain" (1986, p. 773).

Another witness testified at the Los Angeles hearings as follows:

"Women and young girls were tortured and suffered permanent physical injuries to answer publisher demands for photographs depicting sadomasochistic abuse. When the torturer/ photographer inquired of the publisher as to the types of depictions that would sell, the torturer/ photographer was instructed to get similar existing publications and use the depictions therein

for instruction. The torturer/photographer followed the publisher's instructions, tortured women and girls accordingly, and then sold the photographs to the publisher. The photographs were included in magazines sold nationally in pornographic outlets."

(1986, pp. 787–788)

. . . . It should not be assumed that violence occurs only in the making of violent pornography. For example, although many people would classify the movie *Deep Throat* as nonviolent pornography because it does not portray rape or other violence, we now know from Linda (Lovelace) Marchiano's two books (*Ordeal*, 1980, and *Out of Bondage*, 1986), as well as from her public testimony (for example, *Public Hearings*, 1983), that this film is in fact a documentary of her rape from beginning to end.

Many people, including some of the best researchers on pornography in this country, ignore the violence used by pornographers in the manufacturing of these misogynist materials (for example, see Malamuth and Donnerstein, 1984). Catharine MacKinnon points out the frequently forgotten fact that "before pornography became the pornographer's speech it was somebody's life" (1987, p. 179). Testimony presented at the hearings held on the antipornography civil rights ordinance in Minneapolis, Minnesota in 1983, provides powerful evidence for the truth of this statement (*Public Hearings*, 1983; Russell, 1993a).

Because it is important to know the proclivities and the state of mind of those who read and view pornography, I will start by discussing some of the data on males' propensity to rape.

Males' Propensity to Rape

"Why do I want to rape women? Because I am basically, as a male, a predator and all women look to men like prey. I fantasize about the expression on a woman's face when I 'capture' her and she realizes she cannot escape. It's like I won, I own her."
—*Male respondent, Shere Hite, 1981, p. 718*

Research indicates that 25 to 30 percent of male college students in the United States and Canada admit that there is some likelihood they would rape a woman if they could get away with it. In the first study of males' self-reported likelihood to rape that was conducted at the University of California at Los Angeles, the word rape was not used; instead, an account of rape (described below) was read to the male subjects, of whom 53 percent said there was some likelihood that they would behave in the same fashion as the man described in the story, if they could be sure of getting away with it (Malamuth, Haber, and Feshbach, 1980). Without this assurance, only 17 percent said they might emulate the rapist's behavior. It is helpful to know exactly what behavior these students said they might emulate:

> *Bill soon caught up with Susan and offered to escort her to her car. Susan politely refused him. Bill was enraged by the rejection. "Who the hell does this bitch think she is, turning me down," Bill thought to himself as he reached into his pocket and took out a Swiss army knife. With his left hand he placed the knife at her throat. "If you try to get away, I'll cut you," said Bill. Susan nodded her head, her eyes wild with terror.*

The story then depicted the rape. There was a description of sexual acts with the victim continuously portrayed as clearly opposing the assault (Malamuth, Haber, and Feshbach, 1980, p. 124).

In another study, 356 male students were asked: "If you could be assured that no one would know and that you could in no way be punished for engaging in the following acts, how likely, if at all, would you be to commit such acts?" (Briere and Malamuth, 1983). Among the sexual acts listed were the two of interest to these researchers: "forcing a female to do something she really didn't want to do" and "rape" (Briere and Malamuth, 1983). Sixty percent of the sample indicated that under the right circumstances, there was some likelihood that they would rape, use force, or do both.

In a study of high school males, 50 percent of those interviewed believed it is acceptable "for a guy to hold a girl down and force her to have sexual intercourse in instances such as when 'she gets him sexually excited' or 'she says she's going to have sex with him and then changes her mind'" (Goodchilds and Zellman, 1984). . . .

Looking at sexual arousal data alone (as measured by penile tumescence), not its correlation with self-reported likelihood to rape, Malamuth reports that:

- About 10 percent of the population of male students are sexually aroused by *very extreme violence* with *a great deal of blood and gore* that *has very little of the sexual element* (1985, p. 95)
- About 20 to 30 percent show substantial sexual arousal by depictions of rape in which the woman never shows signs of arousal, only abhorrence (1985, p. 95)
- About 50 to 60 percent show some degree of sexual arousal by a rape depiction in which the victim is portrayed as becoming sexually aroused at the end (personal communication, August 18, 1986).

Given these findings, it is hardly surprising that after reviewing a whole series of related experiments, Neil Malamuth concluded that "the overall pattern of the data is . . . consistent with contentions that many men have a proclivity to rape" (1981b, p. 139).

Shere Hite (1981, p. 1123) provides data on men's self-reported desire to rape women from the general population outside the university laboratory. Distinguishing between those men who answered the question anonymously and those who revealed their identities, Hite reports the following answers by the anonymous group to her question "Have you ever wanted to rape a woman?": 46 percent answered "yes" or "sometimes," 47 percent answered "no," and 7 percent said they had fantasies of rape, but presumably had not acted them out—yet (1981, p. 1123).

Surprisingly, the non-anonymous group of men reported slightly more interest in rape; 52 percent answered "yes" or "sometimes," 36 percent answered "no," and 11 percent reported having rape fantasies. (Could it be that many men don't think there is anything wrong with wanting to rape women?) Although Hite's survey was not based on a random sample, and therefore, like the experimental work cited above, cannot be generalized to the population at large, her finding that roughly half of the more than 7,000 men she surveyed admitted to having wanted to rape a woman on one of more occasions suggests that men's propensity to rape is probably very widespread indeed. . . .

The studies reviewed here suggest that at this time in the history of our culture, a substantial percentage of the male population has some desire or proclivity to rape females. Indeed, some males in this culture consider themselves deviant for not wanting to rape a woman. For example, the answer of one of Hite's male respondents was: "I have never raped a woman, or wanted to. In this I guess I am somewhat odd. Many of my friends talk about rape a lot and fantasize about it. The whole idea leaves me cold" (1981, p. 719; emphasis added). Another replied: "I must admit a certain part of me would receive some sort of thrill at ripping the clothes from a woman and ravishing her. But I would probably collapse into tears of pity and weep with my victim, unlike the traditional man" (1981, p. 719; emphasis added). . . .

A Theory About the Causative Role of Pornography

. . . In *Sexual Exploitation* (1984) I suggest many factors that may predispose a large number of males in the United States to want to rape or assault women sexually. Some examples discussed in this book are (1) biological factors, (2) childhood experiences of sexual abuse, (3) male sex-role socialization, (4) exposure to mass media that encourage rape, and (5) exposure to pornography. Here I will discuss only the role of pornography.

Although women have been known to rape both males and females, males are by far the predominant perpetrators of sexual assault as well as the biggest consumers of pornography. Hence, my theory will focus on male perpetrators. . . .

As previously noted, in order for rape to occur, a man must not only be predisposed to rape, but his internal and social inhibitions against acting out his rape desires must be undermined. My theory, in a nutshell, is that pornography (1) predisposes some males to want to rape women and intensifies the predisposition in other males already so predisposed; (2) undermines some males' internal inhibitions against acting out their desire to rape; and (3) undermines some males' social inhibitions against acting out their desire to rape.

The Meaning of Cause

Given the intense debate about whether or not pornography plays a causal role in rape, it is surprising that so few of those engaged in it ever state what they mean by "cause." A definition of the concept of *simple causation* follows:

> *An event (or events) that precedes and results in the occurrence of another event. Whenever the first event (the cause) occurs, the second event (the effect) necessarily or inevitably follows. Moreover, in simple causation the second event does not occur unless the first event has occurred. Thus the cause is both the **sufficient condition** and the **necessary condition** for the occurrence of the effect.*
> *(Theodorson and Theodorson, 1979)*

By this definition, pornography clearly does not cause rape, as it seems safe to assume that some pornography consumers do not rape women, and that many rapes are unrelated to pornography. However, the concept of *multiple causation* is applicable to the relationship between pornography and rape.

> *With the concept of **multiple causation**, various possible causes may be seen for a given event, any one of which may be a sufficient but not necessary condition for the occurrence of the effect, or a necessary but not sufficient condition. In the case of multiple causation, then, the given effect may occur in the absence of all but one of the possible sufficient but not necessary causes; and, conversely, the given effect would not follow*

> *the occurrence of some but not all of the various necessary but not sufficient causes.*
> *(Theodorson and Theodorson, 1979)*

As I have already presented the research on males' proclivity to rape, I will next discuss some of the evidence that pornography can be a sufficient (though not necessary) condition for males to desire to rape. I will mention when the research findings I describe apply to violent pornography and when to pornography that appears to the viewer to be nonviolent.

I. The Role of Pornography in Predisposing Some Males to Want to Rape

> *"I went to a porno bookstore, put a quarter in a slot, and saw this porn movie. It was just a guy coming up from behind a girl and attacking her and raping her. That's when I started having rape fantasies. When I saw that movie, it was like somebody lit a fuse from my childhood on up . . . I just went for it, went out and raped."*
> *Rapist interviewed by Beneke, 1982, pp. 73–74*

According to Factor I in my theoretical model, pornography can induce a desire to rape women in males who previously had no such desire, and it can increase or intensify the desire to rape in males who already have felt this desire. This section will provide the evidence for the four different ways in which pornography can induce this predisposition that are listed alongside Factor I.

(I) Pairing Sexually Arousing/Gratifying Stimuli with Rape

The laws of social learning (for example, classical conditioning, instrumental conditioning, and social modeling), about which there is now considerable consensus among psychologists, apply to all the mass media, including pornography. As Donnerstein testified at the Hearings in Minneapolis: "If you assume that your child can learn from Sesame Street how to count one, two, three, four, five, believe me, they can learn how to pick up a gun" (Donnerstein, 1983, p. 11). Presumably, males can learn equally well how to rape, beat, sexually abuse, and degrade females.

A simple application of the laws of social learning suggests that viewers of pornography can develop arousal responses to depictions of rape, murder, child sexual abuse, or other assaultive behavior. Researcher S. Rachman of the Institute of Psychiatry, Maudsley Hospital, London, has demonstrated that male subjects can learn to become sexually aroused by seeing a picture of a woman's boot after repeatedly seeing women's boots in association with sexually arousing slides of nude females (Rachman and Hodgson, 1968). The laws of learning that operated in the acquisition of the boot fetish can also teach males who were not previously aroused by depictions of rape to become so. All it may take is the repeated association of rape with arousing portrayals of female nudity (or clothed females in provocative poses).

Even for males who are not sexually excited during movie portrayals of rape, masturbation subsequent to the movie reinforces the association. This constitutes what R.J. McGuire, J.M. Carlisle, and B.G. Young refer to as "masturbatory conditioning" (Cline, 1974, p. 210). The pleasurable experience of orgasm—an expected and planned—for activity in many pornography parlors—is an exceptionally potent reinforcer. The fact that pornography is widely used by males as ejaculation material is a major factor that differentiates it from other mass media, intensifying the lessons that male consumers learn from it.

(II) Increasing Males' Self-Generated Rape Fantasies

Further evidence that exposure to pornography can create in males a predisposition to rape where none existed before is provided by an experiment conducted by Malamuth. Malamuth classified 29 male students as sexually force-oriented or non-force-oriented on the basis of their responses to a questionnaire (1981a). These students were then randomly assigned to view either a rape version or a mutually consenting version of a slide-audio presentation. The account of rape and accompanying pictures were based on a story in a popular pornographic magazine, which Malamuth describes as follows:

> *The man in this story finds an attractive woman on a deserted road. When he approaches her, she faints with fear. In the rape version, the man ties her up and forcibly undresses her. The accompanying narrative is as follows: "You take her into the car. Though this experience is new to you, there is a temptation too powerful to resist. When she awakens, you tell her she had better do exactly as you say or she'll be sorry. With terrified eyes she agrees. She is undressed and she is willing to succumb to whatever you want. You kiss her and she returns the kiss." Portrayal of the man and woman in sexual acts follows; intercourse is implied rather than explicit.*
>
> *(1981a, p. 38)*

In the mutually consenting version of the story the victim was not tied up or threatened. Instead, on her awakening in the car, the man told her that "she is safe and that no one will do her any harm. She seems to like

you and you begin to kiss." The rest of the story is identical to the rape version (Malamuth, 1981a, p. 38).

All subjects were then exposed to the same audio description of a rape read by a female. This rape involved threats with a knife, beatings, and physical restraint. The victim was portrayed as pleading, crying, screaming, and fighting against the rapist (Abel, Barlow, Blanchard, and Guild, 1977, p. 898). Malamuth reports that measures of penile tumescence as well as self-reported arousal "indicated that relatively high levels of sexual arousal were generated by all the experimental stimuli" (1981a, p. 33).

After the 29 male students had been exposed to the rape audio tape, they were asked to try to reach as high a level of sexual arousal as possible by fantasizing about whatever they wanted but without any direct stimulation of the penis (1981a, p. 40). Self-reported sexual arousal during the fantasy period indicated that those students who had been exposed to the rape version of the first slide-audio presentation, created more violent sexual fantasies than those exposed to the mutually consenting version *irrespective of whether they had been classified as force-oriented or non-force-oriented* (1981a, p. 33).

As the rape version of the slide-audio presentation is typical of what is seen in pornography, the results of this experiment suggests that similar pornographic depictions are likely to generate rape fantasies even in previously non-force-oriented consumers. As Edna Einsiedel points out (1986, p. 60):

> *Current evidence suggests a high correlation between deviant fantasies and deviant behaviors ... Some treatment methods are also predicated on the link between fantasies and behavior by attempting to alter fantasy patterns in order to change the deviant behaviors.*

. . . . When children do what they see in pornography, it is even more improbable than in the case of adults to attribute their behavior entirely to their predispositions. . . .

Almost all the research on pornography to date has been conducted on men and women who were at least 18 years old. But as Malamuth points out, there is "a research basis for expecting that children would be more susceptible to the influences of mass media, including violent pornography if they are exposed to it" than adults (1985, p. 107). Bryant's telephone interviews show that very large numbers of children now have access to both hard-core and soft-core materials. For example:

- The average age at which male respondents saw their first issue of *Playboy* or a similar magazine was 11 years (1985, p. 135).

- All of the high school age males surveyed reported having read or looked at *Playboy, Playgirl,* or some other soft-core magazine (1985, p. 134).
- High school males reported having seen an average of 16.1 issues, and junior high school males said they had seen an average of 2.5 issues.
- In spite of being legally under age, junior high students reported having seen an average of 16.3 "unedited sexy R-rated films" (1985, p. 135). (Although R-rated movies are not usually considered pornographic, many of them meet my definition of pornography.)
- The average age of first exposure to sexually oriented R-rated films for all respondents was 12.5 years (1985, p. 135).
- Nearly 70 percent of the junior high students surveyed reported that they had seen their first R-rated film before they were 13 (1985, p. 135).
- The vast majority of all the respondents reported exposure to hard-core, X-rated, sexually explicit material (1985, p. 135). Furthermore, "a larger proportion of high school students had seen X-rated films than any other age group, including adults": 84 percent, with the average age of first exposure being 16 years, 11 months (1985, p. 136).

. . . . Clearly, more research is needed on the effects of pornography on young male viewers, particularly in view of the fact that recent studies suggest that "over 50 percent of various categories of paraphiliacs (sex offenders) had developed their deviant arousal patterns prior to age 18" (Einsiedel, 1986, p. 53). Einsiedel goes on to say that "it is clear that the age-of-first-exposure variable and the nature of that exposure needs to be examined more carefully. There is also evidence that the longer the duration of the paraphilia, the more significant the association with use of pornography" (Abel, Mittleman, and Becker, 1985).

The first two items listed under Factor I in my theoretical model both relate to the viewing of *violent* pornography. But sexualizing dominance and submission is a way in which nonviolent pornography can also predispose some males to want to rape women.

. . .(IV) Creating an Appetite for Increasingly Stronger Material

Dolf Zillmann and Jennings Bryant have studied the effects of what they refer to as "massive exposure" to pornography (1984). (In fact, it was not particularly massive: 4 hours and 48 minutes per week over a period of six weeks.) These researchers, unlike Malamuth and Donnerstein, focus on trying to ascertain the effects of *nonviolent* pornography and, in the study to be described, they use a sample drawn from a non-student adult population.

Male subjects in the *massive exposure* condition saw 36 nonviolent pornographic films, six per session per week; male subjects in the intermediate condition saw 18 such movies, three per session per week. Male subjects in the control group saw 36 nonpornographic movies. Various measures were taken after one week, two weeks, and three weeks or exposure, including the kind of materials that the subjects were most interested in viewing.

Zillmann and Bryant found that a desire for stronger material was fostered in their subjects. "Consumers graduate from common to less common forms of pornography," Zillman maintains, that is, to more violent and more degrading materials (1984, p. 127). Zillmann suggests this may be "because familiar material becomes unexciting as a result of habituation" (1984, p. 127).

According to Zillmann and Bryant's research, then, pornography can transform a male who was not previously interested in the more abusive types of pornography, into one who is turned on by such material. This is consistent with Malamuth's findings (described on p. 53) that males who did not previously find rape sexually arousing, generate such fantasies after being exposed to a typical example of violent pornography.

II. The Role of Pornography in Undermining Some Males' Internal Inhibitions Against Acting Out the Desire to Rape

> *"The movie was just like a big picture stand with words on it saying 'go out and do it, everybody's doin' it, even the movies'."*
> *(Rapist interviewed by Beneke, 1982, p. 74.)*

Evidence has been cited showing that many males would like to rape a woman, but that an unknown percentage of these males have internal inhibitions against doing so. Some males' internal inhibitions are likely to be weak, others' very strong. Presumably, the strength of internal inhibitions also varies in the same individual from time to time. . . .

(I) Objectifying Women

The first way in which pornography undermines some males' internal inhibitions against acting out their desires to rape is by objectifying women. Feminists have been emphasizing the role of objectification in the occurrence of rape for years (e.g., Medea and Thompson, 1974; Russell, 1975). Objectification makes it easier to rape them. "It was difficult for me to admit that I was dealing with a human being when I was talking to a woman," one rapist reported, "because, if you read men's magazines, you hear about your stereo, your car, your chick" (Russell, 1975, pp. 249–250). After this rapist had hit his victim several times in her face, she stopped resisting and begged, "All right, just don't hurt me." "When she said that," he reported, "all of a sudden it came into my head, 'My God, this is a human being!' I came to my senses and saw that I was hurting this person." Another rapist said of his victim, "I wanted this beautiful fine thing and I got it" (Russell, 1975, p. 245).

Dehumanizing oppressed groups or enemy nations in times of war is an important mechanism for facilitating brutal behavior toward members of those groups. Ms. U, for example, testified that: "A society that sells books, movies, and video games like 'Custer's Last Stand' ['Custer's Revenge'] on its street corners, gives white men permission to do what they did to me. Like they [her rapists] said, I'm scum. It is a game to track me down, rape and torture me" (Russell, 1993a). However, the dehumanization of women that occurs in pornography is often not recognized because of its sexual guise and its pervasiveness. It is important to note that the objectification of women is as common in nonviolent pornography as it is in violent pornography. . . .

(II) Rape Myths

If males believe that women enjoy rape and find it sexually exciting, this belief is likely to undermine the inhibitions of some of those who would like to rape women. Sociologists Diana Scully and Martha Burt have reported that rapists are particularly apt to believe rape myths (Burt, 1980; Scully, 1985). Scully, for example, found that 65 percent of the rapists in her study believed that "women cause their own rape by the way they act and the clothes they wear"; and 69 percent agreed that "most men accused of rape are really innocent." However, as Scully points out, it is not possible to know if their beliefs preceded their behavior or constitute an attempt to rationalize it. Hence, findings from the experimental data are more telling for our purposes than these interviews with rapists.

As the myth that women enjoy rape is widely held, the argument that consumers of pornography realize that such portrayals are false, is totally unconvincing (Brownmiller, 1975; Burt, 1980; Russell, 1975). Indeed, several studies have shown that portrayals of women enjoying rape and other kinds of sexual violence can lead to increased acceptance of rape myths in both males and females. In an experiment conducted by Neil Malamuth and James Check, for example, one group of college students saw a pornographic depiction in which a woman was portrayed as sexually aroused by sexual violence, and a second group was exposed to control materials. Subsequently, all subjects were shown a second rape portrayal. The students who had been exposed to the pornographic depiction of rape were significantly more likely than the students in the control group (1) to perceive the second rape victim as suffering less trauma; (2) to believe that she actually enjoyed it; and (3) to believe that women in general enjoy rape and forced sexual acts (Check and Malamuth, 1985, p. 419).

Other examples of the rape myths that male subjects in these studies are more apt to believe after viewing pornography are as follows: "A woman who goes to the home or the apartment of a man on their first date implies that she is willing to have sex"; "Any healthy woman can successfully resist a rapist if she really wants to"; "Many women have an unconscious wish to be raped, and many then unconsciously set up a situation in which they are likely to be attacked"; "If a girl engages in necking or petting and she lets things get out of hand, it is her own fault if her partner forces sex on her" (Briere Malamuth, and Check, 1985, p. 400).

In Maxwell and Check's 1992 study of 247 high school students described above, they found very high rates of what they called "rape supportive beliefs," that is, acceptance of rape myths and violence against women. The boys who were the most frequent consumers of pornography and/or who reported learning a lot from it, were more accepting of rape supportive beliefs than their peers who were less frequent consumers and/or who said they had not learned as much from it.

A full 25% of girls and 57% of boys indicated belief that in one or more situations, it was at least "maybe okay" for a boy to hold a girl down and force her to have intercourse. Further, only 21% of the boys and 57% of the girls believed that forced intercourse was "definitely not okay" in any of the situations. The situation in which forced intercourse was most accepted was that in which the girl had sexually excited her date. In this case 43% of the boys and 16% of the girls stated that if was at least "maybe okay" for the boy to force intercourse.

(1992, abstract)

According to Donnerstein, "After only 10 minutes of exposure to aggressive pornography, particularly material in which women are shown being aggressed against, you find male subjects are much more willing to accept these particular myths" (1983, p. 6). These males are also more inclined to believe that 25% of the women they know would enjoy being raped (1983, p. 6).

(III) Acceptance of Interpersonal Violence

Males' internal inhibitions against acting out their desire to rape can also be undermined if they consider male violence against women to be acceptable behavior. Studies have shown that viewing portrayals of sexual violence as having positive consequences increases male subjects' acceptance of violence against women. Examples of some of the attitudes used to measure acceptance of interpersonal violence include "Being roughed up is sexually stimulating to many women"; "Sometimes the only way a man can get a cold woman turned on is to use force"; "Many times a woman will pretend she doesn't want to have intercourse because she doesn't want to seem loose, but she's really hoping the man will force her" (Briere, Malamuth, and Check, 1985, p. 401). . . .

(IV) Trivializing Rape

According to Donnerstein, in most studies on the effects of pornography, "subjects have been exposed to only a few minutes of pornographic material" (1985, p. 341). In contrast, Zillman and Bryant examined the impact on male subjects of what they refer to as "massive exposure" to non-violent pornography (4 hours and 48 minutes per week over a period of six weeks; for further details about the experimental design, see page 27). After three weeks the subjects were told that they were participating in an American Bar Association study that required them to evaluate a trial in which a man was prosecuted for the rape of a female hitchhiker. At the end of this mock trial various measures were taken of the subjects' opinions about the trial and about rape in general. For example, they were asked to recommend the prison term they thought most fair.

Zillmann and Bryant found that the male subjects who were exposed to the massive amounts of pornography considered rape a less serious crime than they did before they were exposed to it; they thought that prison sentences for rape should be shorter; and they perceived sexual aggression and abuse as causing less suffering for the victims, even in the case of an adult male having sexual intercourse with a 12-year-old girl (1984, p. 132). They concluded that "heavy exposure to common non-violent pornography trivialized rape as a criminal offense" (1984, p. 117). . . .

(V) Desensitizing Males to Rape

In an experiment specifically designed to study desensitization, Linz, Donnerstein, and Penrod showed ten hours of R-rated or X-rated movies over a period of five days to male subjects (Donnerstein and Linz, 1985,

p. 34A). Some students saw X-rated movies depicting sexual assault; others saw X-rated movies depicting only consenting sex; and a third group saw R-rated sexually violent movies—for example, "I Spit on Your Grave," "Toolbox Murders," and "Texas Chainsaw Massacre." Donnerstein (1983) describes "Toolbox Murders" as follows: There is an erotic bathtub scene in which a woman massages herself. A beautiful song is played. Then a psychotic killer enters with a nail gun. The music stops. He chases the woman around the room, then shoots her through the stomach with the nail gun. She falls across a chair. The song comes back on as he puts the nail gun to her forehead and blows her brains out. According to Donnerstein, many young males become sexually aroused by this movie (1983, p. 10).

Donnerstein and Linz point out that, "It has always been suggested by critics of media violence research that only those who are already predisposed toward violence are influenced by exposure to media violence" (1985, p. 34F). These experimenters, however, actually preselected their subjects to ensure that they were not psychotic, hostile, or anxious.

Donnerstein and Linz described the impact of the R-rated movies on their subjects as follows:

> *Initially, after the first day of viewing, the men rated themselves as significantly above the norm for depression, anxiety, and annoyance on a mood adjective checklist. After each subsequent day of viewing, these scores dropped until, on the fourth day of viewing, the males' levels of anxiety, depression, and annoyance were indistinguishable from baseline norms.*
>
> *(1985, p. 34F)*

III. The Role of Pornography in Undermining Some Males' Social Inhibitions Against Acting Out Their Desire to Rape

> *"I have often thought about it [rape], fantasized about it. I might like it because of having a feeling of power over a woman. But I never actually wanted to through fear of being caught and publicly ruined."*
>
> *(Male respondent, Hite, 1981, p. 715)*

A man may want to rape a woman *and* his internal inhibitions against rape may be undermined by his hostility to women or by his belief in the myths that women really enjoy being raped and/or that they deserve it, but he may still not act out his desire to rape because of his social inhibitions. Fear of being caught and convicted for the crime is the most obvious example of a social inhibition. In addition to Hite's respondent quoted above, a second man's answer to her question on whether he had ever wanted to rape a woman illustrates this form of inhibition:

I have never raped a woman, but have at times felt a desire to—for the struggle and final victory. I'm a person, though, who always thinks before he acts, and *the consequences wouldn't be worth it. Besides I don't want to be known as a pervert.* (1981, p. 715). . . .

If there were more effective social sanctions against pornography, this would almost certainly increase the reluctance of some people to participate in the pornography industry. There are many reasons why progressive people are strenuously opposed to government efforts to censor pornography. There are, however, many alternative kinds of sanctions that need to be explored. For example, many women have been forced to participate in pornography against their will. I would have thought that pornographic publications that publish photos of these women would be accessories after the fact to false imprisonment, rape, assault, and sometimes, possibly, murder.

(I) Diminishing Fear of Disapproval by Peers

Fear of disapproval from one's peers is another social inhibition that may be undermined by pornography. Zillman, for example, found that "massive" exposure to nonviolent pornography caused subjects to overestimate the number of people who engage in uncommon sexual practices, such as anal intercourse, group sexual activities, sadomashochism, and bestiality (1985, p. 118). Rape is portrayed as a very common male practice in much violent pornography, and the actors themselves may serve as a kind of pseudo-peer group and/or role models for consumers. Further research is needed to evaluate these hypotheses.

In general, I hypothesize the following disinhibiting effects of viewing violent pornography, particularly in "massive" amounts: (a) Viewers' estimates of the percentage of other males who have raped women would probably increase; (b) viewers would be likely to consider rape a much easier crime to commit than they had previously believed; (c) viewers would be less likely to believe that rape victims would report their rapes to the police; (d) viewers would be more likely to expect that rapists would avoid arrest, prosecution and conviction in those cases that are reported; (e) viewers would become less disapproving of rapists, and less likely to expect disapproval from others if they decided to rape. . .

. . . . The exposure of sex offenders to pornography is another area of research that is relevant to the causal connections between pornography and rape. It is well known that many sex offenders claim that viewing pornography affects their criminal behavior. Ted Bundy is perhaps the most notorious of these males. For example, in one study of 89 nonincarcerated sex offenders conducted by William Marshall, "slightly more than one-third of the child molesters and rapists reported at least occasionally being incited to commit an offense by exposure to forced or consenting pornography" (Einsiedel, 1986, p. 62). Exactly a third of the rapists who reported being incited by pornography to commit an offense said that they deliberately used pornography in their preparation for committing the rape. The comparable figure for child molesters was much higher—53 percent versus 33 percent (Einsiedel, 1986, p. 62).

However, as these sex offenders appear to have used the pornography to arouse themselves after they had already decided to commit an offense, it could be argued that it was not the pornography that incited them. To what extent they actually required the pornography in order to commit their offenses, like some perpetrators require alcohol, we do not know. Even if these perpetrators were eliminated from the data analysis, however, that still leaves 66 percent of the rapists and 47 percent of the child molesters who claimed that they were at least sometimes incited by pornography to commit an offense.

Gene Abel, Mary Mittleman, and Judith Becker (1985) evaluated the use of pornography by 256 perpetrators of sexual offenses, all of whom were undergoing assessment and treatment. Like Marshall's sample, these males were outpatients, not incarcerated offenders. This is important because there is evidence that the data provided by incarcerated and non-incarcerated offenders differ (Einsiedel, 1986, p. 47). Abel and his colleagues reported that 56 percent of the rapists and 42 percent of the child molesters implicated pornography in the commission of their offenses. Edna Einsiedel, in her review of the social science research for the 1985 *Attorney General's Commission of Pornography,* concluded that these studies "are suggestive of the implication of pornography in the commission of sex crimes among *some* rapists and child molesters" (p. 63, emphasis in original).

In another study, Michael Goldstein and Harold Kant found that incarcerated rapists had been exposed to hard-core pornography at an earlier age than males presumed to be non-rapists. Specifically, 30 percent of the rapists in their sexual offender sample said that they had encountered hard-core pornographic photos in their preadolescence (i.e., before the age of 11; 1973, p. 55). This 30 percent figure compares with only 2 percent of the control group subjects exposed to hard-core pornography as preadolescents. (The control group was obtained by a random household sample that was matched with the offender group for age, race, religion, and educational level; 1973, p. 50.) Could it be that this early exposure of the offenders to hard-core pornography played a role in making them rapists? Hopefully, future research will address this question.

Conclusion

. . . I have described my theory that pornography—both violent and nonviolent—can cause rape, citing the findings of recent research that support this theory. I believe that my theory can also be adapted to apply to other forms of sexual assault and abuse, as well as to woman battering and femicide (the misogyny—motivated killing of women). I have done the preliminary work on such an adaptation to the causal relationship between pornography and child sexual abuse and plan to publish this work in the future.

In conclusion, I believe that the right and varied data now available to support us from all kinds of sources, when considered together, strongly support my theory:

- A high percentage of nonincarcerated rapists and child molesters have said that they have been incited by pornography to commit crimes;
- Pre-selected normal healthy male students say they are more likely to rape a woman after just one exposure to violent pornography;
- A high percentage of male junior high students, high school students, and adults in a non-laboratory survey report imitating X-rated movies within a few days of exposure;
- Hundreds of women have testified in public about how they have been victimized by pornography;
- Ten percent of a probability sample of 930 women in San Francisco and 25 percent of female subjects in an experiment on pornography in Canada report having been upset by requests to enact pornography (Russell, 1980; and Senn and Radtke, 1986);
- Many prostitutes report that they have experienced pornography-related sexual assault (Silbert and Pines, 1984; Everywoman, 1988; and Russell, 1993a);
- The laws of social learning must surely apply to pornography at least as much as they do to the mass media and general. Indeed, I—and others—have argued that sexual arousal and orgasm are likely to serve as unusually potent reinforcers of the messages conveyed by pornography;
- A large body of experimental research has shown that the viewing of violent pornography results in higher rates of aggression against women by male subjects.

It is no wonder that Donnerstein stated that the relationship between pornography and violence against women is stronger than the relationship between smoking and lung cancer.

One of the effects of viewing nonviolent pornography discovered by Zillmann is that "the more extensive the exposure, the more accepting of pornography subjects became" (Zillmann and Bryant, 1984, p. 133). Although females expressed significantly less acceptance than males, this effect also applied to females. Pornography has expanded into a multi-billion dollar-a-year industry, and I believe we are seeing on a massive scale some of the very effects so brilliantly and carefully documented in some of the experiments by Malamuth, Donnerstein, Zillmann, and their colleagues. Donnerstein's description of the desensitization that occurred in healthy pre-selected male students after only five days of viewing woman-slashing films may apply to ever-growing segments of our society (Donnerstin, Linz, and Penrod, 1987).

Van White, the Chairperson of the *Hearing on Pornography* in Minnesota in 1983, commented as follows on the impact of the testimony by the survivors of pornography-related abuse: "These horror stories made me think of the history of slavery in this country—how Black women were at the bottom of the pile, treated like animals instead of human beings. As I listened to these victims of pornography, I heard young women describe how they felt about . . . the way women's breasts and genitals are displayed and women's bodies are shown in compromising postures. I thought about the time of slavery, when Black women had their bodies invaded, their teeth and limbs examined, their bodies checked out for breeding, checked out as you would an animal, and I said to myself, 'We've come a long way, haven't we.'"

Today we have an industry . . . showing women in the same kind of submissive and animalistic roles" (1984).

United States' culture appears to have been affected by the very effects the research shows. The massive propaganda campaign is working; people now actually *see* differently. Pornography has to become increasingly extreme before people are disturbed by, or even notice, the violence and degradation portrayed in it. Very few see the real abuse that is happening to some of the women who are photographed. As Zillmann and

Bryant show, "heavy consumption of common forms of pornography fosters an appetite for stronger materials" (1984, p. 127). What was considered hardcore in the past has become soft-core in the present. Where will this all end? Will we as a culture forever refuse to read the writing on the wall?

DIANA E.H. RUSSELL is a feminist writer and social activist. She was born in Cape Town, South Africa, moved to England in 1957, and then to the United States in 1961. She has been involved in research on sexual violence against women for many years.

Anthony D'Amato

Porn Up, Rape Down

The headlines are shouting RAPE IN DECLINE![1]

Official figures just released show a plunge in the number of rapes per capita in the United States since the 1970s. Even when measured in different ways, including police reports and survey interviews, the results are in agreement: there has been an 85% reduction in sexual violence in the past 25 years. The decline, steeper than the stock market crash that led to the Great Depression, is depicted in this chart prepared by the United States Department of Justice:

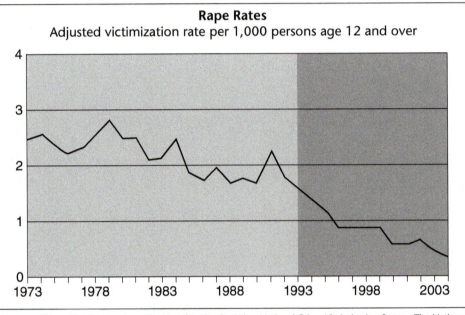

Rape Rates
Adjusted victimization rate per 1,000 persons age 12 and over

Source: U.S. Department of Justice • Office of Justice Programs, Bureau of Justice Statistics, National Crime Victimization Survey. The National Crime Victimization Survey. Includes both attempted and completed rapes.

As the chart shows, there were 2.7 rapes for every 1,000 people in 1980; by 2004, the same survey found the rate had decreased to 0.4 per 1,000 people, a decline of 85%.

Official explanations for the unexpected decline include:

- less lawlessness associated with crack cocaine;
- women have been taught to avoid unsafe situations;
- more would-be rapists already in prison for other crimes;
- sex education classes telling boys that "no means no."

But these minor factors cannot begin to explain such a sharp decline in the incidence of rape.

There is, however, one social factor that correlates almost exactly with the rape statistics. The American public is probably not ready to believe it. My theory is that the sharp rise in access to pornography accounts for the decline in rape. The correlation is inverse: the more pornography, the less rape. It is like the inverse correlation: the more police officers on the street, the less crime.

The pornographic movie *Deep Throat* which started the flood of X-rated VHS and later DVD films, was released in 1972. Movie rental shops at first catered primarily to the adult film trade. Pornographic magazines also sharply increased in numbers in the 1970s and 1980s. Then came a seismic change: pornography became available on the new internet. Today, purveyors of internet porn earn a combined annual income exceeding the total of the major networks ABC, CBS, and NBC.

Deep Throat has moved from the adult theatre to a laptop near you.

National trends are one thing; what do the figures for the states show? From data compiled by the National Telecommunications and Information Administration in 2001, the four states with the *lowest* per capita access to the internet were Arkansas, Kentucky, Minnesota, and West Virginia. The four states with the *highest* internet access were Alaska, Colorado, New Jersey, and Washington. (I would not have guessed this.)

Next I took the figures for forcible rape compiled by police reports by the Disaster Center for the years 1980 and 2000. The following two charts display the results:

Table 1

States with Lowest Internet Access[2]

STATE	Internet 2001	Rape 1980	Rape 2000
Arkansas	36.9	26.7	31.7
Kentucky	40.2	19.2	27.4
Minnesota	36.1	23.2	45.5
W. Virginia	40.7	15.8	18.3

All figures are per capita.

Table 2

States with Highest Internet Access[3]

STATE	Internet 2001	Rape 1980	Rape 2000
Alaska	64.1	56.8	70.3
Colorado	58.5	52.5	41.2
New Jersey	61.6	30.7	16.1
Washington	60.4	52.7	46.4

All figures are per capita.

While the nationwide incidence of rape was showing a drastic decline, the incidence of rape in the four states having the *least* access to the internet showed an actual *increase* in rape over the same time period. This result was almost too clear and convincing, so to check it I compiled figures for the four states having the *most* access to the internet. Three out of four of these states showed declines (in New Jersey, an almost 50% decline). Alaska was an anomaly: it increased both in internet access and incidence of rape. However, the population of Alaska is less than one-tenth that of the other three states in its category. To adjust for the disparity in population, I took the combined population of the four states in each table and calculated the percentage change in the rape statistics:

Table 3

Combined Per Capita Percentage Change in Incidence of Rape

Aggregate per capita increase or decline in rape	
Four states with lowest internet access	Increase in rape of 53%
Four states with highest internet access	Decrease in rape of 27%

I find these results to be statistically significant beyond the .95 confidence interval.

Yet proof of correlation is not the same thing as causation. If autumn regularly precedes winter, that doesn't mean that autumn causes winter. When six years ago my former Northwestern colleague John Donohue, together with Steven Levitt,[4] found that legalized abortion correlated with a reduction in crime, theirs would have only been an academically curious thesis if they had not identified a causal factor. But they did identify one: that prior to legalization there were many unwanted babies born due to the lack of a legal abortion alternative. Those unwanted children became the most likely group to turn to crime.

My own interest in the rape-pornography question began in 1970 when I served as a consultant to President Nixon's Commission on Obscenity and Pornography. The Commission concluded that there was no causal relationship between exposure to sexually explicit materials and delinquent or criminal behavior. The President was furious when he learned of the conclusion.

Later President Reagan tried the same thing, except unlike his predecessor he packed the Commission with persons who passed his ideological litmus test. (Small wonder that I was not asked to participate.) This time, Reagan's Commission on Pornography reached the approved result: that there does exist a causal relationship between pornography and violent sex crimes.

The drafter of the Commission's report was Frederich Schauer, a prominent law professor. In a separate statement, he assured readers that neither he nor the other Commissioners were at all influenced by their personal moral values.[5]

Professor Schauer's disclaimer aroused my skepticism. If the commissioners were unbiased, how could the social facts have changed so drastically in the decade between the Nixon and Reagan reports as to turn non-causality into causality? My examination of the Commission's evidence resulted in an article published by the *William and Mary Law Review*.[6]

Although the Reagan Commission had at its disposal all the evidence gathered by psychology and social-science departments throughout the world on the question whether a student's exposure to pornography increased his tendency to commit antisocial acts, I found that the Commission was unable to adduce a shred of evidence to support its affirmative conclusion. No scientist had ever found that pornography raised the probability of rape. However, the Commission was not seeking truth; rather, as I said in the title to my article, it sought political truth.

Neither Professor Schauer nor the other Commissioners ever responded to my *William & Mary* article. Now they can forget it. For if they had been right that exposure to pornography leads to an increase in social violence, then the vast exposure to pornography furnished by the internet would by now have resulted in scores of rapes per day on university campuses, hundreds of rapes daily in every town, and thousands of rapes per day in every city. Instead, the Commissioners were so incredibly wrong that the incidence of rape has actually declined by the astounding rate of 85%.

Correlations aside, could access to pornography actually cause a decline in rape? In my article I mentioned one possibility: that some people watching pornography may "get it out of their system" and thus have no further desire to go out and actually try it. Another possibility might be labeled the "Victorian effect": the more that people covered up their bodies with clothes in those days, the greater the mystery of what they looked like in the nude. The sight of a woman's ankle was considered shocking and erotic. But today, internet porn has thoroughly de-mystified sex. Times have changed so much that some high school teachers of sex education are beginning to show triple-X porn movies to their students in order to depict techniques of satisfactory intercourse.

I am sure there will be other explanations forthcoming as to why access to pornography is the most important causal factor in the decline of rape. Once one accepts the observation that there is a precise negative correlation between the two, the rest can safely be left to the imagination.

Notes

1. SE.G., *Washington Post,* June 19, 2006; *Chicago Tribune,* June 21, 2006.
2. Statistics on Internet Access compiled from National Telecommunications and Information Administration, at . . .
3. Statistics on forcible rape compiled from . . .
4. Author of *Freakonomics* (2005).
5. U.S. Dept. of Justice, *Final Report: Attorney General's Commission on Pornography* 176–79 (1986) (personal statement of Commissioner Schauer).
6. Anthony D'Amato, "A New Political Truth: Exposure to Sexually Violent Materials Causes Sexual Violence," 31 *Wm. & Mary L. Rev.* 575 (1990), downloadable at . . .

Anthony D'amato is the Leighton Professor of Law at Northwestern University. He received his law degree from Harvard Law School. In 1968 he became a Social Science Council Fellow in Advanced Statistics at the University of Michigan.

EXPLORING THE ISSUE

Is Exposure to Pornography Related to Increased Rates of Rape?

Critical Thinking and Reflection

1. What is the significance of *Miller v. California* for the law of pornography in the United States?
2. What are the implications of the following statement: "Pornography is somebody's life before it becomes the pornographer's free speech"?
3. What are college and high school students' attitudes about rape and sexual assault?
4. What is the relationship between exposure to pornography and rape and sexual assault?

Is There Common Ground?

This very interesting question has intrigued researchers for years. On an intuitive level, it may seem more likely that exposure to pornography would lead some susceptible individuals to commit rape and sexual assault. As the articles in this issue illustrate, however, arguments that seem to make sense on an intuitive level may lead to conclusions that are not accurate when tested empirically and legally. Moreover, while it may be difficult legally to prevent depictions of sexual relations between consenting adults, there seems to be little debate that states may prohibit depictions of sexual behavior involving children. U.S. courts have adopted a much less tolerant stance in these cases and have held consistently that depictions of sexual activity involving children is not a form of expression protected by the First Amendment.

In *New York v. Ferber*, 458 U.S. 747 (1982), a New York law prohibited knowingly promoting a sexual performance by a child under the age of 16 by distributing materials that illustrated such acts. The law defined "sexual performance" as any one that included sexual conduct by a child, which was described as actual or simulated sexual intercourse, deviant sexual intercourse, sexual bestiality, masturbation, sadomasochistic abuse, or lewd exhibition of the genitals. A New York City bookstore operator was convicted under the law for selling films of young boys masturbating. The New York Court of Appeals reversed the conviction, holding that the law violated the First Amendment. The State of New York appealed the case to the U.S. Supreme Court.

Writing for a unanimous Supreme Court, Associate Justice Byron White upheld the New York law. Stated Justice White:

> It is evident beyond the need for elaboration that a State's interest in 'safeguarding the physical and psychological well-being of a minor' is compelling. 'A democratic society rests, for its continuance, upon the healthy, well-rounded growth of young people into full maturity as citizens.' Accordingly, we have sustained legislation aimed at protecting the physical and emotional well-being of youth even when the laws have operated in the sensitive area of constitutionally protected rights. . . . The prevention of sexual exploitation and abuse of children constitutes a government objective of surpassing importance. . . .We shall not second-guess this legislative judgment. (757–758) [Citations omitted].

In addition to state laws prohibiting child pornography, the U.S. Congress has made it a felony to possess or distribute pornographic depictions of sexual activities involving children. In the Internet age, given the ease with which virtually any material may be "forwarded" to others, this is an important law. Title 18, U.S.C. Section 2252, is titled "Certain Activities Relating to Material Involving the Sexual Exploitation of Minors." This statute prohibits the possession or distribution of materials or a visual depiction that "involves the use of a minor engaging in sexually explicit conduct." The law further provides that persons violating these provisions may be fined and imprisoned for "not less than 5 years and not more than 20 years." If, however, a defendant has a prior conviction for a sexual offense under applicable state or federal law, he or she may be fined and imprisoned "for not less than 15 years or more than 40 years."

It is important to know as well that the law states that it is a defense to these charges if a recipient "promptly and in good faith," and without providing access to the materials to others, "took reasonable steps to destroy each such visual depiction, or reported the matter to a law enforcement agency and afforded that agency access to each such visual depiction." The rule that emerges from this law is an easy and important one to remember: If you receive an email message or other material that you believe may depict children engaging in sexually explicit conduct, take immediate steps to destroy it or report it to law enforcement authorities. Under no circumstances should you print or convey it to anyone other than law enforcement authorities.

The preceding discussion has focused on the legal issues regarding pornographic materials. The authors of the articles in this section focused more closely on what is perhaps the most compelling empirical question in the pornography debate: What is the impact of exposure to pornography on rape and sexual assault?

Diana Russell argues that the evidence is overwhelming that exposure to pornography is a major causal factor of rape and sexual assault. Russell's position is compelling intuitively. Excessive exposure to pornographic materials has long been associated with aberrant sexual behavior. Moreover, her contention that exposure to pornographic materials may exert a desensitization effect on susceptible males seems to be an accurate one. Further, as Russell suggests, the actors and actresses involved in the production of pornography should be considered victims as well.

Russell's contention that exposure to pornography is a central "cause" of rape is more problematic, however. Like the relationship between body type and crime, perhaps it may be more accurate to describe the relationship between exposure to pornography and rape as one that demonstrates a correlation, rather than a causal one.

It is also difficult to dismiss Anthony D'Amato's analysis of the relationship between exposure to pornography on the Internet and declining rates of rape and sexual assault. If, in fact, the incidence of rape has declined 85 percent in the last 25 years while access to pornography via the Internet has become more freely available to teenagers and adults, it may suggest that exposure to this medium is a healthy and positive thing. While this data does not constitute conclusive proof of a cause-and-effect inverse relationship between Internet usage and the incidence of rape, it is certainly compelling evidence.

Additional Resources

Catherine A. MacKinnon, *Women's Lives, Men's Laws* (Belknap Press, 2005).

Philipe Bensimon, "The Role of Pornography in Sexual Offending," *Sexual Addiction & Compulsivity* (vol. 14, no. 2, 2007).

Janis Wolak, Kimberly Mitchell, and David Finkelhor, "Unwanted and Wanted Exposure to Online Pornography in a National Sample of Youth Internet Users," *Pediatrics* (vol. 119, no. 2, 2007).

Chiara Sabina, Janis Wolak, and David Finkelhor, "The Nature and Dynamics of Pornography Exposure for Youth," *CyberPsychology & Behavior* (vol. 11, no. 6, 2008).

Alan McKee, "The Relationship Between Attitudes Towards Women, Consumption of Pornography, and Other Demographic Variables in a Survey of 1,023 Consumers of Pornography," *International Journal of Sexual Health* (vol. 19, no. 1, 2007).

Internet References . . .

California Coalition Against Sexual Assault (CALCASE), "What is the Influence of Pornography on Rape?" March 19, 2010.

www.calcase.org

Milton Diamond, "Pornography: Good For Us?" March 19, 2010.

www.thescientist.com

Mary Anne Layden, "Pornography and Violence: A New Look at Research." 2009.

www.socialcostsofpornography.com

Selected, Edited, and with Issue Framing Material by:
Thomas J. Hickey, *State University of New York at Cobleskill*

ISSUE

Does the United States Have a Right to Torture Suspected Terrorists?

YES: Andrew A. Moher, from "The Lesser of Two Evils? An Argument for Judicially Sanctioned Torture in a Post–9/11 World," *Thomas Jefferson Law Review* (2004)

NO: Elisa Massimino, from "Leading by Example? U.S. Interrogation of Prisoners in the War on Terror," *Criminal Justice Ethics* (2004)

Learning Outcomes

After reading this issue, you will be able to:

- Identify a potential deficiency in the doctrine of utilitarianism in cases involving the use of torture.
- Distinguish between "punishment-based" torture and torture for the purpose of preventing a greater evil.
- Identify several U.S. constitutional prohibitions on the use of torture.
- Identify several international prohibitions against the use of torture.
- Discuss the potential for developing a "torture warrant."
- Identify and discuss several arguments against the use of torture in all circumstances.

ISSUE SUMMARY

YES: Attorney Andrew A. Moher argues that judicially sanctioned torture of terrorists is appropriate for the purpose of preventing a greater evil. He further contends a judicially monitored system in the United States would be far superior to the current policy of practicing torture "under the radar screen" in other countries.

NO: Elisa Massimino believes that the use of torture is immoral and counterproductive for the United States. She asserts that if the United States wishes to rely on the protections of the Geneva Conventions, then it must comply with its provisions prohibiting the torture of prisoners.

Torture is an insidious practice, which conjures sadistic images of medieval dungeons, the rack, and thumbscrews. Consider the following hypothetical situation: A suspected terrorist has planted a nuclear bomb somewhere in a large U.S. city of 2 million people. Based on information from an informant, who has proven to be completely reliable on many past occasions, government authorities have reason to believe that it is set to explode in three hours. It would be impossible to evacuate the city within this time frame. Moreover, the informant has given the authorities the name and description of the suspected terrorist, and he is taken into custody. If the suspect refuses to talk, is torture justified?

The Introduction of this book discussed the doctrine of utilitarianism, which asserts that a social policy should be assessed according to whether it produces the greatest benefit for public good. In our hypothetical situation, the greatest public benefit would be served by locating the bomb and defusing it. Do you believe that the greatest public good would be served by using whatever means were necessary to extract the information from the suspect? This situation illustrates a potential deficiency in the doctrine of utilitarianism—perhaps there are absolute principles that should never be compromised, regardless of whether an action will serve the greatest public good. The use of torture to extract information *may* be one of these principles.

U.S. courts have consistently condemned the use of torture by government authorities to gain information from criminal suspects because it violates due process of law, a "principle of justice so rooted in the traditions and conscience of our people as to be ranked as fundamental." For example, in *Brown v. Mississippi,* 297 U.S. 278 (1936), sheriff's deputies obtained the confessions of three African American suspects in a murder case by whipping and hanging them. And they were convicted of murder in state court. The U.S. Supreme Court held, however: "[T]he freedom of the State in establishing its policy is the freedom of constitutional government. . . . The rack and torture chamber may not be substituted for the witness stand. . . ."

The authors of the articles in this section have different viewpoints on the use of torture to extract information from suspected terrorists. Andrew Moher argues that judicially sanctioned torture of terrorists is appropriate for the purpose of preventing a greater evil. He further contends a judicially monitored system in the United States would be far superior to the current policy of practicing torture "under the radar screen" in other countries. Moher's position is fundamentally a statement of a utilitarian approach to the use of torture to extract information from terrorists.

Elisa Massimino, in contrast, believes that the use of torture is immoral and counterproductive for the United States. She asserts that if the United States wishes to rely on the protections of the Geneva Conventions, then it must comply with its provisions regarding torture of prisoners. Massimino's position is consistent with an absolutist position regarding the use of torture—it is contrary to human dignity and always wrong.

What is your position regarding the use of torture to extract information from suspected terrorists? Are your views influenced by the bombing of the World Trade Center in New York City on 9/11/2001? As you read the articles in this section, try to develop a sense of whether you support the utilitarian or absolutist positions regarding the use of torture.

YES ↵

Andrew A. Moher

The Lesser of Two Evils? An Argument for Judicially Sanctioned Torture in a Post–9/11 World

I. Introduction

Torture is illegal under both United States and international law. It is considered among the most heinous practices in human history, and its use is publicly condemned by nearly every government in existence today. However, it is also considered an effective method of gathering information, and to that end it is habitually employed "under the radar screen" in desperate situations by these same governments. Since the catastrophic attacks of September 11, 2001, several noted scholars and politicians have advocated the use of torture in extreme scenarios, while others have expressed fear that legitimizing torture would spawn a dangerous slippery slope of morally reprehensible state actions. Specifically, the use of torture to extract information from terrorists with knowledge of impending attacks has been the subject of intense debate.

Before surveying the landscape of state sponsored torture, it is essential to distinguish between two categories of torture. The more notorious form of torture is punishment-based. It is inextricably intertwined with medieval images of diabolical torture devices found in movies and museums around the world. Such methods have historically been used in violent tyrannies and dictatorships, and exist in "rogue" states today. This type of torture is morally indefensible and is not at issue here. Rather, this discussion deals with torture for the purpose of preventing a greater evil, as part of the interrogation process. Such methods have been used in the past, with some success.

An interesting dialogue might be fashioned on whether the United States should adhere to international restrictions on torture under the shadow of post-9/11 threats of terrorism. After all, many potential subjects of torture are "part of the conspiracy [to destroy] . . . innocent Americans." Conversely, there is a danger that condoning torture of suspects might harm innocents unnecessarily, or that American captives would be subjected to inhumane treatment in response to United States policy. These contentions are largely beyond the scope of this discussion, and serve as background to the present debate.

This Note will argue that judicially sanctioned torture is appropriate, but only under certain, well-defined circumstances. Part II will discuss the current status of domestic and international law as it applies to torture. Part III will analyze the pattern of United States noncompliance with these laws, and the general ineffectiveness of the current policy on torture. Finally, Part IV will illustrate why a balanced approach allowing judicially sanctioned torture would be a more effective and humane alternative to the current practice of using torture "under the radar screen."

II. The Legality of Torture Under Current United States Law

The United States is compelled by both domestic and international law not to practice torture. Torture is banned by several amendments to the Constitution, and implicitly barred by the sentiment of the Constitution itself. Furthermore, the practice of torture conflicts with United States obligations under international law, including signed and ratified treaties. Over the years, the prohibition against torture has become a fixture of international law, and has been routinely condemned by the vast plurality of nations. Today, the torturer is considered "hostis humani generis," an enemy of all mankind.

A. Constitutional Prohibitions on Torture

The practice of torture runs directly counter to the Fifth, Eighth, and Fourteenth Amendments of the Constitution. Some advocates of legalizing torture have argued that loopholes exist in each of these amendments, and suggest torture could be rationalized under existing law. Upon closer examination, it is clear the use of torture is wholly incompatible

Moher, Andrew A. From *Thomas Jefferson Law Review*, vol. 26, issue 2, Spring 2004, pp. 469–489. Copyright © 2004 by Thomas Jefferson Law Review. Reprinted by permission.

with the Constitution. This contention is further borne out by important court decisions emphasizing the protections of personal liberty from governmental intrusion.

The Eighth Amendment bans all cruel and unusual punishment. This prohibition would ostensibly include torture, as the drafters of the amendment were "primarily concerned . . . with proscribing 'tortures' and other barbarous forms of punishment." On the other hand, the Eighth Amendment has been construed by the Supreme Court to protect only those convicted of crimes. Thus, it stands to reason that although convicted criminals are protected under the Eighth Amendment, others (such as prisoners of war, or so-called "enemy combatants") are not protected. Through this loophole created under the guise of the Supreme Court's interpretation, the Eighth Amendment would most likely be deemed ineffectual in cases involving suspected terrorists that have not yet been convicted in the criminal justice system.

Even if the practice of torture were to effectively circumvent the Eighth Amendment, it would almost certainly be found unconstitutional under the due process protections of the Fifth and Fourteenth Amendments. These protections grant all persons the substantive rights not to be deprived of life, liberty, and property, without due process of law. Although substantive due process is admittedly a very subjective and malleable standard, it has been utilized in the past to overturn practices less odious than torture. In recent years, the Supreme Court has adopted the rationale that state conduct that "shocks the conscience" will violate due process protections.

In *Brown v. Mississippi*, the police severely whipped a subject while hanging him from a tree to coerce a confession. The Supreme Court of the United States declared, "[I]t would be difficult to conceive of methods more revolting to the sense of justice than those taken to procure [these] confessions." The Court later lowered the bar when it found less violent conduct to meet the "shock the conscience" benchmark. In *Rochin v. United States*, the Supreme Court found a violation of due process when authorities pumped the stomach of a man suspected of swallowing morphine capsules. Speaking for the court in *Rochin*, Justice Frankfurter defined the objective of substantive due process as "respect for those personal immunities which . . . are 'so rooted in the traditions and conscience of our people as to be ranked as fundamental.'"

Brown and its progeny illustrate the scope of substantive due process, and its incompatibility with the practice of torture. Indeed, the atrocious whipping in *Brown* could easily be analogized to torture, and that conduct was found to violate due process. The broader standard put forth in *Rochin* further strengthens the case against torture. If the

right to be free from torture was not egregious enough to meet justice Frankfurter's standard of fundamental rights, it would be hard to imagine what conduct would be. Based on these cases, and the Court's obvious desire to protect bodily integrity, the intentional infliction of pain by torture would sufficiently "shock the conscience" to violate due process.

B. International Prohibitions Against Torture

The United States is further bound by several international treaties that prohibit the practice of torture. International treaties have authority so long as they do not offend the Constitution. The United States is obligated to provide humane treatment to prisoners of war under the 1949 incarnation of the Geneva Convention. The United States is also bound by the International Covenant on Civil and Political Rights, or ICCPR, which contains express prohibitions against torture. Article 7 of the ICCPR states, inter alia, "No one shall be subjected to torture or to cruel, inhuman, or degrading treatment or punishment." Under the Convention, the right to be protected from torture is non-derogable, meaning that it applies at all times, including wartime. The ICCPR, like the Geneva Convention, bars torture under any and all circumstances.

The United States is also party to the Convention against Torture (CAT), a subsidiary to the ICCPR that was ratified by the United States in 1994. Under UUU Article 4, the CAT demands that "each state party . . . ensure that all acts of torture are offences under its criminal law," and that the offences are "punishable by appropriate penalties which take into account their grave nature." The State Department recently confirmed the full implementation of the CAT into United States law, averring, "every act constituting torture under the [CAT] constitutes a criminal offense under the law of the United States."

Finally, the United States must adhere to jus cogens. According to the Vienna Convention on the Law of Treaties, jus cogens are international legal standards that are "accepted and recognized by the international community of States as a whole as a norm from which no derogation is permitted and which can be modified only by a subsequent norm of general international law having the same character." In other words, universally abhorred practices such as genocide, slavery, and summary executions qualify as jus cogens and are illegal at all times and all places, regardless of existing laws. Torture has long been considered an immutable violation of jus cogens, and declared as such in Federal court. The United States is therefore bound by jus cogens not to practice torture under any conceivable scenario.

III. The Reality of Torture Under Current United States Law

Few writers would be naive enough to suggest torture has been completely eradicated from all societies today. Yet many would underestimate its prevalence as a tool of interrogation, particularly in "civilized" countries such as the United States. There has been a plethora of evidence since the September 11 attacks suggesting United States complicity in interrogational torture and yet no tangible ramifications have been encountered to date. Often, a nation can avoid responsibility by exploiting the amorphous definition of torture under various laws. It has become evident that the implementation mechanisms of the international system are not compatible with the security concerns of the post-9/11 world.

A. United States Evasion of International Law

As arguably the world's lone remaining superpower, the United States is in a unique position with regards to its participation in international law, most notably in its ability to avoid repercussions for its legal offenses. International law has long been criticized as ineffective because of its weak enforcement mechanisms. For example, Iraq has been a party to the ICCPR since before the United States' ratification, yet has managed to avoid responsibility for its government's blatantly illegal mass murder of the Kurds in the north of the country. Indeed, the most damaging punishment for a nation's violation of international law is often the so-called "mobilization of shame," whereby the publication of the offending nation's transgressions can damage its perception among the other nations of the world. The sheer power and influence of the United States at the present time renders it all but immune from this attempt at deterrence, and in this light the consequences of offending the international law system appear obsolete.

To that end, the United States has acted evasively in carrying out its obligations under international treaties. For example, the United States recently rebuffed claims that it was in violation of the Geneva Convention regarding its treatment of suspected former Taliban fighters at Camp X-Ray in Guantanamo Bay, Cuba. The United States government escaped liability under the provisions of the Convention by refusing to label the captives 'prisoners of war.' By repudiating any classification of the Guantanamo inmates, the government was successful in employing an obvious labeling loophole in the Geneva Convention, thereby allowing the United States to interrogate the prisoners in a manner unrestricted by the Convention. The United States Supreme Court will decide this year whether the Guantanamo inmates can appeal their detentions to the Government, or whether they will continue to be held in a prison that operates entirely outside of the law. In the interim, the United States and similarly situated nations continue to exploit the inefficacies of the international law system.

B. Torture Under a Different Name

The Convention Against Torture (CAT) defines torture as:

> [A]ny act by which severe pain or suffering, whether physical or mental, is intentionally inflicted on a person for such purposes as obtaining from him or a third person information or a confession, punishing him for an act he or a third person has committed or is suspected of having committed, or for any reason based on discrimination of any kind, when such pain or suffering is inflicted by or at the instigation of, or with the consent or acquiescence of a public official or other person acting in an official capacity.

This definition, while not dispositive, is certainly illustrative of the general conception of torture and its legal boundaries. Many nations, however, sidestep admissions of the practice of torture simply by redefining the word. Recently, academics and politicians have analyzed the distinction between "torture" and "torture lite." The latter, it is reasoned, is tantamount to aggressive but legal interrogation and is distinguishable from the traditional concept of torture in several important ways.

Torture is intended, it would seem, to encompass activities that bring about severe pain and suffering. Understandably, the question of what is severe has never been definitively resolved. Traditional methods of torture, such as mutilation, amputation, mock executions, rape, and stoning are presumably intended to cause severe pain. By contrast, torture lite is commonly understood as referring to interrogation methods such as sleep deprivation, exposure to extreme temperatures, mild physical abuse, use of drugs to cause confusion, or psychological coercion. Arguably, these types of methods do not cause severe pain, and are therefore beyond the dominion of torture, at least as defined by the CAT.

The result of this exercise in semantics is increased confusion about what exactly is allowed under international law and what is prohibited. The Geneva Convention, for instance, bans all mistreatment of prisoners during wartime, which probably prohibits both torture and torture lite. In contrast, the International Covenant on Civil and Political Rights may leave the door open to torture lite practices with its subjective "cruel, inhuman, or degrading standard." Under this paradigm, a nation acting from purely selfish interests would likely argue that practices such as mind games and sleep deprivation do not meet the threshold of cruel, inhuman, or degrading punishment. Similarly, the CAT definition of torture presents the aforementioned uncertainty of what is severe. A ruling by the United Nations High Commissioner for Human Rights under the CAT underscores the ambiguity of the law: "[W]hen employed for the purpose of breaking a prisoner's will, sleep deprivation may in some cases constitute torture." Such deviation in the definition of torture leads to a classic slippery slope scenario, where the lines may be loosely drawn to serve the interests of the interrogating nation.

Not surprisingly, there remains a lack of consensus among international courts regarding the point at which interrogation becomes torture. In 1976, the European Commission of Human Rights found that a British combination of five tactics used against Northern Irish prisoners collectively constituted torture under the European Convention of Human Rights. The tactics used included subjecting the prisoners to hooding, extended wall standing in painful postures, loud noises, sleep deprivation, and deprivation of food and drink. Two years later, the European Court for Human Rights reversed this ruling, declaring the conduct had risen to the level of "inhuman and degrading treatment," but not torture. This TT decision influenced one official inquiry by the state of Israel, defining moderate physical pressure against a suspected Palestinian terrorist as compatible with international laws on interrogation. The Israeli High Court of justice later declared this treatment illegal. These inconsistent interpretations of the law allow countries to practice torture under a different name, which cannot be an acceptable solution to the problem of torture.

C. Evidence of United States Practice of Torture

Whether the United States uses torture as a method of interrogation is an open question, subject to both the interpretation of testimony and the definition of torture itself. It would not be inaccurate to conclude the questioning methods of the United States often transcend the lines of humane interrogation. Representatives of the United States have repeatedly implied that torture-like methods are utilized to prevent future terrorist attacks. Cofer Black, then-head of the CIA Counterterrorist Center joint hearing of the House and Senate Intelligence Committees, acknowledged, "[T]here was a before 9/11, and there

was an after 9/11. After 9/11 the gloves come off." An unnamed official, interviewed by the *Washington Post,* added: "[I]f you don't violate someone's human rights some of the time, you probably aren't doing your job."

Third party accounts by respected non-governmental organizations also tend to support the notion that the United States uses torturous techniques in its interrogations. Amnesty International reported that prisoners under United States control at the Bagram Air Base in Afghanistan were deprived of sleep with a 24-hour bombardment of lights, held in awkward, painful positions, and constantly subjected to stress and duress techniques. Indeed, many prisoners have attempted suicide at Camp X-Ray in Guantanamo Bay. Human Rights Watch added in their report that prisoners were "subjected to electric shocks . . . and beaten throughout the night." In an open letter to President George W. Bush, Human Rights Watch Executive Director Kenneth Roth relayed his concern that the United States might be "in violation of some of the most fundamental prohibitions of international human rights law."

The Central Intelligence Agency ("CIA"), though understandably reluctant to admit such practices, is fully cognizant of the effectiveness of torture in investigation. CIA officials sometimes refer to the Kubark Manual, a journal of interrogative techniques, which includes physical and psychological tactics that could easily be classified as torture. A representative from the CIA described the questioning methods used against a typical high-level terrorist suspect:

> He would most likely have been locked naked in a cell with no trace of daylight. The space would be filled day and night with light and noise, and would be so small that he would be unable to stand upright, to sit comfortably, or to recline fully. He would be kept awake, cold, and probably wet. If he managed to doze, he would be roughly awakened. He would be fed infrequently and irregularly, and then only with thin, tasteless meals. . . . On occasion he might be given a drug to elevate his mood prior to interrogation; marijuana, heroin, and sodium pentothal have been shown to overcome a reluctance to speak, and methamphetamine can unleash a torrent of talk in even the most stubborn subjects.

It is interesting to note that all of these techniques, individually, might be classified as torture lite. Taken together, however, they seem to epitomize a routine of torture so devious that it cannot reasonably be described any other way. It becomes impractical to make legal exceptions for torture lite practices when they will add up to extreme torture in the aggregate.

D. The Question of Rendition

The most obvious example of United States complicity in torture is the practice of irregular rendition. Rendition, a system of sending captives to other countries with less progressive human rights standards in order to interrogate them more aggressively, often results in torture. Since September 11, the United States has sent prisoners to Pakistan, Saudi Arabia, Egypt, Morocco, and Uzbekistan, as well as other countries with documented histories of torturing suspects. Through this process, the United States can gain valuable information with impunity, while claiming that they have "no direct knowledge" of the host country's interrogation methods. Fred Hitz, the former CIA Inspector General, commented on the practice of rendition: "We don't do torture, and we can't countenance torture in terms of we can't know of it. But if a country offers information gleaned from interrogations, we can use the fruits of it."

There is no accountability in rendition, and some nations have accused the United States of rendering suspects for immoral or political reasons. The case of Maher Arar is illustrative. Arar, a longtime Canadian citizen, was captured by United States authorities and rendered to Syria. He was tortured at the hands of Syrian and Jordanian authorities, which ceased the treatment only when he "confessed" to being associated with another Canadian citizen who had been arrested. The rendition of Mr. Arar has sparked criticism from various human rights groups.

Renditions are also considered dangerous because the interrogation methods of the receiving countries are often ghastly in nature. The case of Abdul Hakim Murad sheds light on the procedures used during some renditions. Murad was rendered to the Philippines in 1995. According to the *Washington Post,* Philippine authority agents beat Murad, "with a chair and a long piece of wood [breaking most of his ribs], forced water into his mouth, and crushed lighted cigarettes into his private parts." After 63 days of this "tactical interrogation," Murad disclosed a plan to assassinate the pope, and to crash eleven commercial airliners carrying approximately four thousand passengers into the Pacific Ocean, as well as to fly a private plane packed with explosives into CIA headquarters. Although the veracity of Murad's confessions has recently come into dispute, his experience remains an informative example of the techniques utilized during rendition.

The consequence of rendition is the manipulation of the international law system, as well as the circumnavigation of domestic law prohibitions against torture. Again, mobilization of shame appears the most effective international remedy against nations suspected of irregular rendition, and again, some nations are influenced far more than others. Human Rights Watch utilized a mobilization of shame tactic when they publicly announced: "The United States . . . has a duty to refrain from sending persons to countries with a history of torture without explicit, verifiable guarantees that they will not be tortured or otherwise mistreated." The United States' response was evasive, insisting that the renditions occur for the purpose of cultural affinities, as opposed to illegal interrogations. Although this might conceivably be a factor in the renditions, the totality of the evidence yields the conclusion that torture has become a frequent by-product of these renditions.

E. The Two Choices

The stark reality that torture is practiced today leaves a responsible society with two choices. The first is the implementation of an effective international body to regulate torture. In order to address the many problems of today's system, the body would first need a controlling definition of torture. This would effectively limit a nation's ability to practice torture under the guise of torture lite. An effective body would also have implementation powers beyond that of the current mobilization of shame. Without such "teeth," the system would not be effective against powerful nations. Finally, the body would have to make rendition explicitly illegal, and punish countries accordingly. Unfortunately, without drastic and unprecedented cooperation among the myriad nations of the world, this model is not realistic under today's international system.

The other choice is to legalize torture.

IV. Should Torture Be Legalized?

In his farewell address from the presidency, Ronald Reagan spoke of America as a "shining city upon the hill." Reagan's Utopian vision included a principled commitment to human rights and freedoms, similar to that espoused by the current United States administration. In the 2002 State of the Union Address, President George W. Bush proclaimed, "America will always stand firm for the non-negotiable rights of human dignity." This self-imposed higher standard of morality may prove to be both a blessing and a curse. On one hand, this approach has traditionally given the United States a powerful and respected voice in the world community. On the other, the legalization of torture might be considered irreconcilable with President Reagan's "shining city." Although it may be difficult to conceive of a moral society practicing torture, there is an argument to be made that legalizing torture would actually enhance the moral stature of the United States when juxtaposed against the current policy of underground torture.

A. History of State-Sponsored Torture

The concept of state-sponsored torture is not without precedent. The English overtly incorporated torture into their legal system in the seventeenth century. The English employed torture warrants against people that were thought to have information necessary to prevent attacks on the state. The torture warrant served several beneficial purposes, such as making the practice more visible and thus "more subject to public accountability." However, the English torture policy was conducted at a time quite different than our own, and by a government structured quite different than our own.

Perhaps a more germane comparison to this debate is the Israeli experience. Few, if any, countries in the history of the world have been under the constant shadow of terrorism as much as modern-day Israel. The Israelis face threats from both hostile neighboring countries and international terrorist organizations such as Hamas, Hizbollah, and Islamic Jihad. In order to cope with the threat of homicide bombings, the Israelis have traditionally employed torture lite tactics. In 1987, a commission led by former Israeli Supreme Court President Moshe Landau investigated the interrogation practices of the Israeli General Security Service. The commission found that, under the rule of necessity, the use of force in interrogation was authorized if the interrogator reasonably believed the lesser evil of force was necessary to get information that would prevent the greater evil of loss of innocent lives. This ruling temporarily established the foundation for legalized torture in Israel.

Predictably, there were both significant benefits and significant problems associated with the Israeli legalization of torture. Like the English model, the use of torture was publicized and became more visible. However, witnesses claim that Israeli interrogators were loathe to stop at the proscribed limits of questioning. In fact, some authors suggest that up to 85% of Palestinian inmates were tortured by Israeli authorities. Moreover, at least 10 Palestinians died as a result of torture prior to 1994. The publication of these abuses alarmed the United Nations, and their involvement led to a landmark 1999 decision in which the High Court of justice in Israel found the use of moderate physical pressure in interrogation

to "[infringe] on both the suspect's dignity and his privacy." The Israeli government subsequently scaled back physical force during interrogations, although some suggest the ruling merely moved the torture movement underground.

B. The Dershowitz Torture Warrant

In his book *Why Terrorism Works: Understanding the Threat, Responding to the Challenge,* Professor Alan Dershowitz analyzes the applicability of judicially sanctioned torture to modernday American jurisprudence. Specifically, Professor Dershowitz addresses the problem of the ticking-bomb terrorist, who possesses crucial information of an imminent disastrous attack, but refuses to give information to his captors. In this situation, one writer emphasizes, society "pay[s] for his silence in blood."

To obtain this critical information, Professor Dershowitz introduces the concept of a torture warrant: a process whereby a neutral magistrate would decide whether there was sufficient evidence to compel a suspect to be subjected to torture. Unlike the current policy, the torture would be medically supervised and designed not to cause any permanent physical damage. One possibility anticipated in the book is the insertion of a long needle under the fingernail, intended to cause excruciating pain but no lasting damage. Professor Dershowitz's proposal is largely based on a cost-benefit framework, reminiscent of philosopher Jeremy Bentham's moral calculus of utility. In the end, Professor Dershowitz theorizes, "absolute opposition to torture—even nonlethal torture in the ticking bomb case—may rest more on historical and aesthetic considerations than on moral or logical ones."

Professor Dershowitz's support of torture is not without its critics. Theorists have unleashed a parade of horribles that could result from the legalization of torture. Foremost among these events are the violation of human dignity, the potential for abusing the law, and the fear of instigating a domino effect and creating a world of legalized torture. Although these arguments are meritorious in their own respects, they are all easily answered from Professor Dershowitz's perspective. With regards to human dignity, the legalization of torture would promote respect for human dignity, insofar as torture would be changed from an inhumane tool of oppression to a last-resort tool for saving lives. The potential for abusing the law is another legitimate concern, but this can be addressed by instituting the necessary and appropriate safeguards. Finally, worldwide legalization of torture is not a negative event in Professor Dershowitz's eyes, if it can be regulated effectively. The legalization of torture is not a perfect solution, and it doubtless would have its downfalls. As Professor Dershowitz observes, "[S]uch is the nature of tragic choices in a complex world."

C. "Degrees" of Torture and the Balancing Test

When weighing the benefits of legalizing torture against preserving the status quo, it is essential to understand the difference in "degrees" of torture. Torture in a legalized system would consist of a nonpermanent act meant to maximize the possibility of gaining crucial information, while minimizing necessary pain. By contrast, torture in rendition might utilize the mind-numbing tactics used against Abdul Hakim Murad in the Philippines, if not worse. The torturers in these situations are not accountable to any authority, and seemingly would not hesitate to take the lives of uncooperative subjects. The degree of torture used in the legalization proposal is, therefore, inherently more humane than the degree of torture practiced today.

Courts often use balancing tests to influence the direction of the law. For instance, in a classic decision on due process, the Supreme Court explained that whether an individual's constitutional rights have been violated "must be determined by balancing [the individual's] liberty interest against the relevant state interests." Here, this logic would probably support the use of torture in a dire situation. Assume, for example, that a known terrorist announced the presence of a nuclear bomb in a major U.S. city that would kill thousands of people. The terrorist further stated that he knew the location and time assigned for the detonation of the bomb, but refused to disclose these crucial details. The terrorist's liberty interest in not being tortured is, no doubt, significant. However, the state interest in saving thousands of lives is far more compelling. Applying constitutional due process analysis, the use of torture would seemingly be upheld.

There are additional benefits that may be gained from the system without resorting to torture. According to the Kubark Manual, "the threat of coercion usually weakens or destroys resistance more effectively than coercion itself." For example, it is an effective practice to stage mock executions in neighboring cells while a prisoner is interrogated. The CIA's finding that the threat of coercion often leads to compliance, without the actual use of coercion (i.e. torture), is promising. If such a system were implemented, it is possible that important information might be gleaned from a suspect without having to ever resort to torture. Similarly, a transparent regulation of torture practice would encourage dialogue among prisoners such as Maher Arar, without fear of deportation or forced

confessions. Both of these factors weigh heavily in favor of a regulated torture system.

There are negative factors that must be considered as well. Legalizing torture would set a dangerous precedent for other countries who might abuse their newfound ability to practice torture. United States officials might abuse their discretion in validating torture warrants. The truth of the statements made under duress of torture might be questioned. Furthermore, some writers have made the argument that legalizing torture would do little to curb the existence of underground torture. For instance, writer Jean Maria Arrigo hypothesized, "[A] regulated program cannot eliminate use of rogue torture interrogation services, because they still serve to circumvent moral and procedural constraints on the official program." Although there is undoubtedly some truth in this theory, there is still hope that a regulated system would curb underground torture to a very significant degree.

Furthermore, these dangers pale in comparison to the dangers in today's system. Currently, the United States participates in underground rendition, which leads to undocumented torture and manipulation. This practice involves a more severe and brutal form of torture, and likely contributes to many undocumented fatalities. Moreover, the information gained from this process is probably less reliable than information extrapolated from a judicially monitored system. The documentation of rendition activities is sparse, and the penalties for offending international laws on torture are virtually nonexistent. On balance, there is much more to lose by embracing the status quo. The balancing test in this analysis yields the conclusion that legalizing torture provides an overall benefit for humankind.

D. Towards a More Humane System

Assuming the requisite support in principle for legalizing torture, the creation and implementation of the torture policy would be both complicated and controversial. Every ambit of these new laws would be duly scrutinized on such an unstable world stage. Who would make the decision of granting or denying the torture warrant? Would there be an adequate appeals system? How would the safety of the torture subjects be ensured? How could the United States condone a policy that offends its Constitution and flagrantly violates the peremptory norms of international law?

Many of these questions are directed towards the intricacies of the torture system itself, and are thus beyond the scope of this Note. However, there are some policy concerns worth discussing. Time constraints would likely pose the biggest roadblock to an effective policy. If a terrorist threatens a bomb strike within hours, it becomes a formidable task to employ a traditional appeals process before initiating torture. The protocol would necessarily be more elaborate than the search warrant process, which demands only an objectively reasonable action by a police officer to obtain a search warrant. The former Israeli standard (reasonable belief that force is necessary to prevent a greater evil) is probably not exacting enough to justify torture. Perhaps the standard should mirror that of the public necessity defense under American tort law, which is limited to actions necessary to avert an impending public disaster. Whatever the solution, it is of the utmost importance that torture be used as a last resort in only the most desperate of scenarios.

An interesting blueprint for a torture warrant procedure might be drawn from the Foreign Intelligence Surveillance Act (FISA) and its implementation. "FISA was created by the United States government as a corollary to the public legal system in order to discreetly process search warrants against suspected terrorists and spies. As initially enacted, FISA allowed specially designated judges to authorize surveillance to acquire foreign intelligence information under certain circumstances, on a court known as the Foreign Intelligence Surveillance Committee (FISC). The seven-judge FISC court was expanded to eleven judges under the 2001 USA Patriot Act. This model is adaptable to the torture warrant proposal, insofar as an eleven-judge panel might be effective at quickly expediting decisions on torture warrants, and making tough decisions regarding ticking-bomb terrorists.

Unfortunately, the FISC model (as amended by the Patriot Act and other legislation) has also proved an embodiment of the critics' worst fears. The records and files of cases involving FISC search warrants are sealed and may only be revealed to an extremely limited degree. Furthermore, the annual reports to Congress for the calendar year 2002 showed that 1,226 of 1,228 applications for search warrants had been approved by the FISC. The remaining two were approved by the supplementary appeals council to the FISC, the FISCR. A system that always approves torture warrant applications would bluntly defeat the purpose of the system. Moreover, the sealing of the documents would defeat the goals of transparency and accountability. Only an arrangement that accounted for these inherent flaws in government-run judgment panels would be able to legitimize torture and bring an appropriate warrant system to fruition.

V. Conclusion

It is incumbent upon us to engage in an open and truthful debate about the state of torture in the world today. Even if there is no perfect solution, the creation of a transparent and judicially monitored system on torture would mark a dramatic improvement over the current policy of ignorance. The dangers for abuse in the current system are truly boundless, and the practice of rendition often leaves the fate of suspects in the dangerous hands of acknowledged torturers. The practice of torture should not be denied simply because it is concealed and hidden half a world away. Legalizing torture certainly presents imposing obstacles, both in its challenging implementation and in its visceral dissonance. Compared to the current policy of practicing torture "under the radar screen," however, it may indeed be the lesser of two evils.

ANDREW A. MOHER received his BA from the University of Michigan (2002) and his JD from the Thomas Jefferson School of Law (2005). He is now a practicing attorney.

Elisa Massimino

Leading by Example? U.S. Interrogation of Prisoners in the War on Terror

When "trophy photos" taken by soldiers involved in the abuse of Iraqi prisoners at Abu Ghraib prison—one of the most notorious under Saddam Hussein's regime—were made public in late April 2004, the Pentagon had already completed two investigations into allegations of abuse at the prison. The graphic and disturbing photographs, some aired on prime-time American television, show naked Iraqi prisoners in humiliating poses, many with smiling uniformed soldiers looking on and pointing or giving a "thumbs up" sign. In one of the photographs, two naked prisoners are posed to make it look as though one is performing oral sex on another. Another shows a hooded prisoner standing on a box with wires attached to his wrists; the army says the prisoner was told that if he fell off the box, he would be electrocuted. Two pictures show dead prisoners—one with a battered and bruised face, the other whose bloodied body was wrapped in cellophane and packed in ice. One shows an empty room, splattered with blood. Reportedly, there is video as well.

These gruesome photographs were splashed across the front pages of newspapers in the Middle East and around the world, the headlines screaming "TORTURE." But the abuse was not news to the Pentagon. According to news accounts, a scathing 53-page report by Major General Antonio M. Taguba, completed in February, concluded that there was ongoing systematic and criminal abuse of detainees at the Abu Ghraib prison. As Seymour Hersh reported in the *New Yorker* magazine in May, General Taguba's report confirmed that abuses were taking place at the prison, including: threatening male detainees with rape, sodomizing a male detainee with a broomstick or chemical light, threatening detainees with dogs, and pouring chemicals from broken light bulbs onto detainees. As a result of this investigation, six soldiers are facing court-martial on charges that include cruelty toward prisoners, dereliction of duty, and indecent acts.

Are the soldiers who engaged in these acts just "sick bastards," as their commanding officer recently said, or is there something more profoundly disturbing going on here? Why did the soldiers feel free to document their crimes on camera? Some answers to these questions will likely emerge in the prosecution of the soldiers involved. But it appears from the information already available that this was abuse with a particular purpose—to "create conditions favorable for successful interrogation"—that is, to break down a prisoner's will.

The Descent to Lawlessness

As shocking as these abuses are, to anyone who has followed closely the Bush Administration's descent into lawlessness in its prosecution of the "war on terrorism," they are not surprising. Three factors contribute to an environment in which such torture and cruelty can proliferate.

First is the Administration's persistent degradation of the Geneva Conventions and other international standards governing its conduct toward prisoners. Beginning with the initial transfer of prisoners from Afghanistan to Guantanamo, White House officials argued that the Geneva Conventions were not relevant to the war on terrorism. Later, under pressure from secretary of State Colin Powell and other current and former military officers who revere the Geneva Conventions as a source of protection in case of capture, the Administration announced that it "believes in the principles" of the Geneva Conventions, but neither Taliban fighters nor al Qaeda suspects were eligible for their protections. Thus, as we continue to learn from Guantanamo, Bagram, and now Abu Ghraib, believing in the principles of the Geneva Conventions and actually complying with them are two different things—and there is no in-between. Complying with the Geneva Conventions requires that all of the detainees on Guantanamo and elsewhere have a recognized legal status. This, the Administration has steadfastly refused to do. But if the United States wants to be able to rely on the protections in the Geneva Conventions, then it must comply with them—not just in word, but in deed. Failing to do so

Massimino, Elisa, "Leading by Example? U.S. Interrogation of Prisoners in the War on Terror" *Criminal Justice Ethics*, vol. 23, issue 1, Winter 2004, pp. 2–5. Copyright © 2004 John Jay College of Criminal Justice of The city University of New York, reprinted by permission of Taylor & Francis Ltd, www.tandfonline.com on behalf of John Jay College of Criminal Justice of The City University of New York.

not only places U.S. soldiers at greater risk, but contributes to a situation in which the details and importance of the Geneva Conventions are completely unrecognized by soldiers, like those at Abu Ghraib, charged with guarding and interrogating prisoners.

Second is the way in which the United States has played fast and loose with the prohibition on torture and cruel, inhuman, or degrading treatment. For example, one government official described the interrogation of an alleged high-ranking al Qaeda operative as "not quite torture, but about as close as you can get." Various administration officials—as well as some detainees who have been released—report that prisoners in U.S. custody have been beaten; thrown into walls; subjected to loud noises and extreme heat and cold; deprived of sleep, light, food, and water; bound or forced to stand in painful positions for long periods of time; kept naked; hooded; and shackled to the ceiling. Euphemistically called "stress and duress" techniques, U.S. officials who admit to these practices seem to think they are permissible so long as they don't cross the line into "outright torture." They are mistaken. When President Bush's father pushed the Convention Against Torture through the Senate, he committed to interpret the phrase "cruel, inhuman or degrading treatment or punishment" in ways consistent with the Eighth Amendment's prohibition on cruel and unusual punishment. To put these "stress and duress" techniques into constitutional context, the U.S. Supreme Court ruled in 2002 that handcuffing a prisoner to a hitching post in a painful position for eight hours clearly violated the protection against cruel and unusual punishment. While there are certainly some interrogation methods that are unpleasant but not illegal, "stress and duress" interrogation techniques are clearly illegal. Pentagon General Counsel William J. Haynes III asserts that U.S. policy is "to treat all detainees and conduct all interrogations wherever they may occur, in a manner consistent with" the prohibition on cruel treatment. But because many detainees are interrogated without the presence of lawyers or even the confidentiality-bound International Committee of the Red Cross (ICRC), it is difficult to know if that policy is known to interrogators, let alone whether they comply with it.

The third factor contributing to the kinds of interrogation abuses that are now coming to light is the Administration's focus on using interrogation almost exclusively for the purpose of obtaining information, rather than to obtain a confession or other evidence admissible in court. When the goal of interrogation is prosecution, the rules are familiar: Miranda, lawyers, a day in court. But what are the rules when there is no day in court in a detainee's

future? Almost immediately after September 11, 2001, Attorney General Ashcroft and other senior officials at the Justice Department began talking about a fundamental shift in approach when dealing with terrorist suspects, from prosecution to prevention. Facilitated by an "enemy combatant" policy that so far has allowed the government to keep even U.S. citizens in incommunicado detention for prolonged periods, the Administration argues that detainees have no rights—to counsel, to appear before a judge, to speak to anyone at all—that might interfere with the sense of dependency and lack of control designed to make a detainee "lose hope."

Justifying Torture

Most discussions of interrogation and torture begin with the so-called "ticking time bomb" scenario, which posits a situation in which a detainee has information that, if revealed, could spare those about to be slaughtered. Is torture permissible if it would save those lives? People who focus on this hypothetical often do so in order to expose as "soft" those wide-eyed moralists unwilling to "do what is necessary" for the greater good. Since September 11, some lawyers and even judges have argued that if the taboo against torture has not already been broken, it should be now. Harvard law professor Alan Dershowitz proposed "torture warrants" for the ticking time bomb scenario, so that the abuses could be undertaken with judicial and societal sanction. Federal Judge Richard Posner has said that anyone who doubts torture is permissible when the stakes are high enough should not be in a position of responsibility. The end—saving innocent lives—justifies the means.

This is tough talk. But those who advocate for torture in these circumstances are the ones who are out of touch with reality. Many experienced interrogators have pointed out that the "ticking time bomb" scenario, with its factual (if not moral) clarity, is a fantasy, a situation that simply never presents itself in the real world. Abu Ghraib prison, on the other hand, is reality, and it is a reality where the means—torture and humiliation—quite likely will help to undermine the ends that the U.S. government is pursuing—Iraqi acceptance of a U.S. military presence in a free and democratic Iraq.

Outlawing Torture

Just before the beating deaths of two Afghan prisoners who died under interrogation at Bagram Air Force Base were made public, I told a friend of mine—a senior military officer at the Pentagon—how disturbed I was by the fact that so many Americans with whom I talked casually believed, without distress or the slightest bit of cognitive dissonance, that the United States was torturing suspects for information. I asked my friend whether he believed that prisoners being held by the United States were being tortured. "I can't believe that," he said. "I could never be involved in a mission that relied on torture and abuse. It's a betrayal of everything we stand for."

Not only that, it's also illegal. When the U.S. Senate gave its advice and consent to ratification of the United Nations Convention Against Torture and Other Cruel, Inhuman or Degrading Treatment or Punishment, it recognized that ratification would have to await the passage and implementation of legislation, required by the treaty, making torture a crime. Congress did so in 1994. Title 18, Section 2340 of the United States Code defines torture as "an act committed by a person acting under the color of law specifically intended to inflict severe physical or mental pain or suffering (other than pain or suffering incidental to lawful sanctions) upon another person within his custody or physical control." Section 2340A makes torture, attempted torture, and conspiracy to commit torture a federal crime, punishable by up to 20 years in prison; if the victim dies as a result of torture, the punishment could be death. The law applies only to torture committed outside the United States, but includes acts by U.S. citizens. While the conduct of U.S. soldiers is governed by the Uniform Code of Military Justice (hence the charges of "cruelty" and "indecent acts" in the Abu Ghraib prison abuse case), it appears that other U.S. personnel—private contractors and intelligence officials—may also have been involved in the abuse. In the 10 years that the anti-torture law has been on the books, not a single person has been charged under its provisions. That may now change.

No Exceptions

Regardless of the words used to prohibit it, the ban on the use of torture is absolute. Unlike other provisions of international human rights law—such as the right to be free from arbitrary arrest or detention—that can be suspended during a declared emergency that "threatens the life of the nation," no exigency can justify torture.

This prohibition applies to the outsourcing option as well. International law prohibits the United States, as a signatory of the Convention Against Torture, from sending a person to a country where there is a substantial likelihood that he will be tortured. Congress reiterated this obligation in legislation in 1998, requiring regulations from all relevant executive agencies detailing how this obligation would be implemented. The Departments of Justice and State both issued regulations; the Pentagon and the CIA

never complied. Over the last 18 months, a number of Administration officials have confirmed that the United States is handing some al Qaeda suspects in military or CIA custody over to other governments for interrogation. These transfers are known as "extraordinary rendition"—a highly legalistic term for a completely extra-legal arrangement. Some of the countries where the detainees are sent—Egypt, Syria, Morocco—are places where, according to the State Department's annual country reports on human rights practices, torture and other prisoner abuse is routine. Some detainees have been transferred with a list of questions that their American interrogators want answered; in other cases, U.S. officials maintain more of a distance, simply receiving the fruits of the interrogation. It is unclear whether U.S. officials are ever present at these sessions. But even if they are not, it is a fiction that "extraordinary rendition" allows the United States to preserve clean hands, despite one U.S. official's claim that "We don't kick the [expletive] out of them. We send them to other countries so they can kick the [expletive] out of them." Interestingly, when those countries comply, they may get a free pass from the State Department. In 2002, new instructions were issued to U.S. embassy personnel who draft the human rights reports: "Actions by governments taken at the request of the United States or with the expressed support of the United States should not be included in the report."

When pressed to explain how its policy of "extraordinary rendition" to countries known to practice torture comports with its obligations under both the Convention Against Torture and domestic law, the Administration's response is either disingenuous or rather naïve. In a letter to Senator Patrick Leahy responding to just this question, Pentagon General Counsel Haynes said that when it transfers a detainee to a third country, U.S. policy is "to obtain specific assurances from the receiving country that it will not torture the individual being transferred to that country." In other words, we just take Syria's word for it. As Senator Leahy responded, "mere assurances from countries that are known to practice torture systematically are not sufficient." Though Haynes has said that the United States will follow up on any evidence that these "diplomatic assurances" were not being honored, it seems that it would be awfully rare that such evidence would ever emerge, since the detention is likely to be incommunicado.

However, though rare, such evidence is not impossible. In September of 2002, U.S. officials arrested Maher Arar, a dual citizen of Canada and Syria, as he was changing planes at JFK airport in New York, en route home to Canada. Although he was traveling on his Canadian passport, U.S. officials—apparently CIA and Justice Department working together—secretly transferred Arar first to Jordan then to Syria, a move that evoked strong protest in Canada. Arar arrived in Syria after being interrogated for 11 days at a CIA interrogation center in Jordan. He then spent 10 months in a Syrian jail, during which time he alleges he was repeatedly tortured. Under increasing public pressure from Canadians and human rights groups, Syria finally released Arar, claiming they never had any interest in him anyway, but had only jailed and interrogated him to curry favor with the United States. This case provides an opportunity to test whether the United States is serious about the safeguards it says it employs when it transfers detainees to the custody of other governments. Did the United States government seek "diplomatic assurances" from Syria before handing Arar over? It hasn't said. If it did, has it complained to Syria that its treatment of Arar violates those assurances? It appears not. Perhaps that is because, as Arar alleges, the transfer to Syria was for the purpose of interrogation under torture. While in Syrian custody, Arar confessed to being a terrorist and having trained in an al Qaeda camp, all of which he now denies. With the Syrian government's later dismissal of Arar's importance, it appears even the Syrians did not believe his confessions.

Credibility

If another country is willing to torture a prisoner in whom it has no independent interest just to appease the United States, imagine what effect we are having on repressive governments anxious to legitimize their own abusive conduct towards political dissidents and others they wish to silence. As the world stares in horror at pictures of grinning American soldiers engaging in war crimes, it is becoming increasingly deaf to the President's proclamation that "America will always stand firm for the non-negotiable demands of human dignity." Last summer, the President issued a clear and forceful statement reaffirming the "inalienable human right" to be free from torture. "The United States is committed to the world-wide elimination of torture and we are leading this fight by example," President Bush said in a statement commemorating the U.N. International Day in Support of Victims of Torture. Now, nearly a year later, the world has good reason to doubt the integrity of the President's pledge.

ELISA MASSIMINO is Washington director of Human Rights First. She is the organization's chief advocacy strategist, an expert on a range of international human rights issues, and a national authority on U.S. compliance with human rights law. She holds philosophy degrees from Trinity University (BA, 1982) and Johns Hophins (MA, 1984), and a JD from the University of Michigan School of Law. She has taught international human rights law at the University of Virginia School of Law and teaches refugee and asylum law at the George Washington University School of Law.

EXPLORING THE ISSUE

Does the United States Have a Right to Torture Suspected Terrorists?

Critical Thinking and Reflection

1. Are interrogation techniques that focus on "stress and duress" torture?
2. Could you make a case for the practice of rendition? Think about the evidence from the selections by Moher and Massimino and how they might support your argument.

Is There Common Ground?

U.S. Supreme Court Associate Justice Hugo Black once stated that in times of social crisis "the fog of public excitement obscures the ancient landmarks set up in our Bill of Rights. Yet then, of all times, should this Court adhere more closely to the course they mark." The Bill of Rights, the first ten amendments to the U.S. Constitution, establishes the framework for protection of basic liberties by our government. The rights provided therein include some of the most fundamental values of American society: Freedom of the Press, Speech, and Religion, the right to be free from unreasonable searches and seizures, the right to be free from double jeopardy, the privilege against self-incrimination, the right to counsel, the right to a trial by jury, the right not to be subjected to cruel and unusual punishment, and the right to due process of law.

Do you agree with Justice Black's statement that at times of social crisis public sentiment may tempt us to compromise our most important social values? What are the implications of Justice Black's position for the development of laws in the wake of the war on terrorism?

In the articles presented in this section, attorney Andrew Moher argues for laws permitting judicially sanctioned torture of terrorists when it is necessary to prevent a greater evil. Moreover, Moher asserts that a judicially monitored system in the United States is far preferable to the Bush administration's current policy of practicing torture "under the radar screen." Elisa Massimino, in contrast, believes that the use of torture is immoral and counterproductive. She asserts that if the United States wishes to rely on the protections of the Geneva Conventions, then it must comply with its provisions prohibiting the torture of prisoners.

After reading the articles in this section and considering Justice Black's statement, what is your position on the use of torture of suspected terrorists? Is there any middle ground in this debate?

Additional Resources

There is a good deal of compelling and recent literature relevant to the issue considered in this section. For an excellent analysis of the philosophical problems associated with using torture, see David Sussman, "What's Wrong with Torture?" *Philosophy and Public Affairs* (vol. 33, no. 1, 2005). Anthony Lewis, the author of *Gideon's Trumpet,* has also written a very interesting article discussing the state of civil liberties in the aftermath of the war on terrorism, "One Liberty at a Time," *Mother Jones* (vol. 29, no. 3, 2004); see also, Harvey Silverglate, "Civil Liberties and Enemy Combatants," *Reason* (vol. 36, no. 8, 2005); Mark Bowden, "The Dark Art of Interrogation," *The Atlantic Monthly* (vol. 292, no. 3, 2003); Christopher Tindale, "The Logic of Torture: A Critical Examination," *Social Theory and Practice* (vol. 22, no. 3, 1996); George J. Annas, "Unspeakably Cruel—Torture, Medical Ethics, and the Law," *The New England Journal of Medicine* (May 19, 2005); Stuart Taylor, "The Perils of Torturing Suspected Terrorists," *National Journal* (May 8, 2004); and Laura M. Kelly, "Big Brother Inc: Surveillance, Security and the U.S. Citizen," *Analog Science Fiction & Fact* (vol. 125, no. 5, 2005).

Internet References . . .

Debate.org

www.debate.org/opinions/is-the-use-of-torture
-against-terrorist-suspects-ever-justified

The Torture Debate by Rumney

www.academia.edu/644187/The_torture_debate

Debatewise

http://debatewise.org/debates/807-torture-should-be
-allowed-against-terror-suspects/

Selected, Edited, and with Issue Framing Material by:
Thomas J. Hickey, *State University of New York at Cobleskill*

ISSUE

Should It Be a Hate Crime to Display the Confederate Flag?

YES: Ta-Nehisi Coates, "Take Down the Confederate Flag—Now," *The Atlantic* (2015)

NO: Alberto R. Gonzales, "The Confederate Flag and Free Speech," *The Hill* (2015)

Learning Outcomes
After reading this issue, you will be able to:
• Identify the fundamental rights protected by the First Amendment.
• Discuss the "clear and present danger test" for speech.
• Discuss the idea that the cure for speech that people find objectionable is simply more speech.
• Distinguish between verbal and symbolic speech and discuss why "fighting words" do not merit First Amendment protection.
• Discuss the U.S. Supreme Court's historic decision in *Tinker v. DesMoines*.
• Discuss the U.S. Supreme Court's historic decision in *Brandenburg v. Ohio*.
• Discuss the U.S. Supreme Court's historic decision in *Texas v. Johnson* and its relevance to the current controversy.
• Present your opinion about whether the Supreme Court would uphold a statute making it a crime to display a Confederate flag.

ISSUE SUMMARY

YES: Noted author Ta-Nehisi Coates contends that even though the Confederate flag's defenders often claim it represents "heritage not hate," it is a heritage of white supremacy and cowardice and should be banned.

NO: Former U.S. Attorney General Alberto R. Gonzales, in contrast, argues that displaying the Confederate flag is a form of expression protected by the First Amendment to the U.S. Constitution.

The First Amendment to the U.S. Constitution is a cornerstone of our Republic. It provides: "Congress shall make no law respecting an establishment of religion, or prohibiting the free exercise thereof; or abridging the freedom of speech, or of the press; or the right of the people peacefully to assemble, and to petition the Government for a redress of grievances." Throughout our history, the U.S. Supreme Court has been highly protective of these fundamental constitutional rights. In fact, a number of cases in this area have become classic precedents.

For example, in *Schenck v. United States*, 249 U.S. 47 (1919), the great Justice Oliver Wendell Holmes developed what has become known as the "Clear and Present Danger Test" to assess laws passed by the government that restrict free speech. Stated Holmes: "The question in every case is whether the words used are used in such circumstances and are of such a nature as to create a clear and present danger that they will bring about the substantive evils that Congress has a right to prevent."

The "clear and present danger test" was later expounded by Louis Brandeis, another great Supreme

Court Justice in *Whitney v. California*, 274 U.S. 357 (1927). Stated Brandeis:

> Those who won our independence by revolution were not cowards. They did not fear political change. They did not exalt order at the cost of liberty. To courageous, self-reliant men, with confidence in the power of free and fearless reasoning applied to the process of popular government, no danger flowing from speech can be deemed clear and present unless the incidence of evil apprehended is so imminent that it may befall before there is opportunity for full discussion. If there be time to expose through discussion the falsehoods and fallacies, to avert the evil by the process of education, the remedy to be applied is more speech. . . . Such must be the rule if authority is to be reconciled with freedom. (377).

Justice Brandeis thus identified a principle that has become a modern cornerstone of First Amendment law: The cure for speech that a government or majority of the people dislike is simply more speech. As Americans, we are encouraged to debate vigorously all social policies. Free speech and thought within the "marketplace of ideas" are essential to the American governmental system. That is why all laws passed by the states or the U.S. Congress that attempt to restrict expression bear such a heavy burden under the First Amendment.

An exception to this general rule was identified by the Supreme Court, however, in *Chaplinsky v. New Hampshire*, 315 U.S. 568 (1942). In that case a Jehovah's Witness who was involved in an argument with a police officer called him a "God-damned racketeer" and a "damned facist." The Supreme Court held that such words were "likely to provoke an average person to retaliation." It therefore established that "fighting words" are not protected by the First Amendment because they are not "part of any exposition of ideas and are of such slight social value as a step to truth that any benefit that may be derived from them is clearly outweighed by the social interest in order and morality."

Another case that presented the issue of the legality of state action to restrict free expression, occurred in *Tinker v. Des Moines Independent Community School District*, 393 U.S. 503 (1968). In this famous case three public high school students in Des Moines, Iowa, were suspended from school for wearing black armbands to protest the Government's Vietnam War policies. The school district had adopted a rule that any student wearing an armband to school would be asked to remove it, and, if he refused, would be suspended until he or she was willing to return to school without an armband. The students, who were aware of the policy, wore their black armbands to school and were sent home and suspended. At trial in the U.S. District Court, the attorneys representing the students requested an injunction preventing school officials from disciplining the students and sought nominal damages. The U.S. District Court judge dismissed the case, upheld the constitutionality of the school's actions, and held that it was reasonable in order to prevent disturbance of school discipline. On appeal, the Court of Appeals (5th Cir.) affirmed and the U.S. Supreme Court granted certiorari.

Associate Justice Abe Fortas observed that the wearing of armbands by the students in these circumstances was closely akin to "pure speech," which is entitled to "comprehensive protection under the First Amendment. Stated Fortas:

> First Amendment rights, applied in light of the special characteristics of the school environment, are available to teachers and students. It can hardly be argued that either students or teachers shed their constitutional rights to freedom of speech or expression at the schoolhouse gate. . . . That they are educating the young for citizenship is reason for scrupulous protection of Constitutional freedoms of the individual, if we are not to strangle the free mind at its source and teach youth to discount important principles of our government as mere platitudes. (636).

Justice Fortas further emphasized that the students did not cause any disruption of school activities and wore the armbands to exhibit their disapproval of the War in Vietnam. He therefore concluded that because wearing the armbands were a form of pure expression, the students' conduct was protected by the First Amendment.

Tinker v. Des Moines, then, teaches us a few different First Amendment lessons: First, students and teachers retain First Amendment rights to express themselves as long as the expression does not disrupt a school's educational mission. Second, it demonstrates that "speech" may include symbolic demonstrations intended to convey a particular message as well as verbal expressions. Or, as the Supreme Court has stated in *United States v. O'Brien*, 391 U.S. 367 (1968), "conduct may be sufficiently imbued with elements of communication to fall within the scope of the First and Fourteenth Amendments." Third, it shows that governmental policies that attempt to suppress disfavored or unpopular messages will be carefully scrutinized by the courts. Later precedents have interpreted this principle to include messages or speech that many people would find highly offensive, or even hateful.

Such a case was presented to the Supreme Court shortly after *Tinker* was decided. In *Brandenburg v. Ohio*, 395 U.S. 444 (1969), the Court was called upon to decide the constitutionality of a state law that made it a crime to "advocate the duty, necessity, or propriety of crime, sabotage, violence, or unlawful methods of terrorism as a means of accomplishing political reform," and to "voluntarily assemble with any group formed to teach or advocate doctrines of criminal syndicalism." The case arose from a videotape of a Ku Klux Klan (KKK) rally at which a robed and hooded Klan leader gave a speech in which he stated: "We have hundreds of members throughout the State of Ohio.... We're not a revengent (sic) organization, but if our President, our Congress, our Supreme Court, continues to suppress the white Caucasian race, it's possible that there might have to be some revengence (sic) taken."

Brandenburg was arrested and convicted under the Ohio Criminal Syndicalism statute, fined $1,000, and sentenced to one to ten years' imprisonment. Appellate courts in Ohio affirmed his conviction and the U.S. Supreme Court granted certiorari. The Supreme Court held:

> [T]he constitutional guarantees of free speech and free press do not permit a State to forbid or proscribe advocacy of the use of force or of law violation except where such advocacy is directed to inciting or producing imminent lawless action and is likely to incite or produce such action (447).... [T]he mere abstract teaching . . . of the moral propriety or even moral necessity for a resort to force and violence is not the same as preparing a group for violent action and steeling it to such action . . . (448). Accordingly, . . . a statute, which purports to punish mere advocacy and to forbid . . . assembly with others merely to advocate the described type of action [violates the First and Fourteenth Amendments.] (449).

As a result of *Brandenburg*, it is extremely difficult for a government to restrict or prosecute speech in the United States. In order to do so, the prosecution must demonstrate that the speech is "directed to inciting or producing imminent lawless action" in circumstances where it is likely to produce the violent result. We must always keep in mind, however, the great Justice Oliver Wendell Holmes's famous aphorism that one does not have a right "to yell fire in a crowded theatre." What he means is that free speech rights are not absolute if they are likely to cause harm to others. Despite this noteworthy caveat, however, the *Brandenburg* standard presents an extremely difficult challenge to any government attempting to prosecute someone for delivering an objectionable message.

What implications then, do these precedents have for the debate presented in this chapter? Should displaying a Confederate flag be a crime? The authors of the selections in this section would answer this question in very different ways. Ta-Nehisi Coates believes that crimes such as the murders of nine church members in Charleston, South Carolina, by Dylann Roof, who embraced the Confederate battle flag, "cannot be divorced from the ideology of white supremacy which long animated his state." Coates concludes: "Drive out this cult of death and chains. Save your lovely souls. Move forward. Do it now." Former U.S. Attorney General Alberto R. Gonzales, in contrast, believes that "[w]hile it may appear obvious to some that racist hate speech undermines the constitutional principle of equality, as a general matter, such expressions are protected speech."

As you review the selections in this section consider whether displaying the Confederate battle flag bears important similarities to the practice of wearing black armbands in *Tinker v. DesMoines*. Do both types of conduct convey a message that would be subject to protection by the First and Fourteenth Amendments? Moreover, think about whether a state law to prevent the display of the Confederate flag would violate *Brandenburg's* principle that in order to ban an expression, the prosecution must demonstrate that it is directed to produce "imminent" violent action in circumstances where it is likely to occur. These are intriguing issues that are highly relevant in modern society and will continue to generate substantial controversy throughout the United States in the coming years.

YES ↵

Ta-Nehisi Coates

Take Down the Confederate Flag—Now

The flag that Dylann Roof embraced, which many South Carolinians embrace, endorses the violence he committed.

Last night, Dylann Roof walked into a Charleston church, sat for an hour, and then killed nine people. Roof's crime cannot be divorced from the ideology of white supremacy which long animated his state nor from its potent symbol—the Confederate flag. Visitors to Charleston have long been treated to South Carolina's attempt to clean its history and depict its secession as something other than a war to guarantee the enslavement of the majority of its residents. This notion is belied by any serious interrogation of the Civil War and the primary documents of its instigators. Yet the Confederate battle flag—the flag of Dylann Roof—still flies on the Capitol grounds in Columbia.

The Confederate flag's defenders often claim it represents "heritage not hate." I agree—the heritage of white supremacy was not so much birthed by hate as by the impulse toward plunder. Dylann Roof plundered nine different bodies last night, plundered nine different families of an original member, plundered nine different communities of a singular member. An entire people are poorer for his action. The flag that Roof embraced, which many South Carolinians embrace, does not stand in opposition to this act—it endorses it. That the Confederate flag is the symbol of white supremacists is evidenced by the very words of those who birthed it:

> Our new government is founded upon exactly the opposite idea; its foundations are laid, its corner-stone rests, upon the great truth that the negro is not equal to the white man; that slavery subordination to the superior race is his natural and normal condition. This, our new government, is the first, in the history of the world, based upon this great physical, philosophical, and moral truth. . . .

This moral truth—"that the negro is not equal to the white man"—is exactly what animated Dylann Roof. More than any individual actor, in recent history, Roof honored his flag in exactly the manner it always demanded—with human sacrifice.

Surely the flag's defenders will proffer other, muddier interpretations which allow them the luxury of looking away. In this way they honor their ancestors. Cowardice, too, is heritage. When the white supremacist John Wilkes Booth assassinated Abraham Lincoln 150 years ago, Booth's fellow travelers did all they could to disassociate themselves. "Our disgust for the dastardly wretch can scarcely be uttered," fumed a former governor of South Carolina, the state where secession began. Robert E. Lee's armies took special care to enslave free blacks during their Northern campaign. But Lee claimed the assassination of the Great Emancipator was "deplorable." Jefferson Davis believed that "it could not be regarded otherwise than as a great misfortune to the South," and angrily denied rumors that he had greeted the news with exultation.

Villain though he was, Booth was a man who understood the logical conclusion of Confederate rhetoric:

> "TO WHOM IT MAY CONCERN":
> Right or wrong. God judge me, not man. For be my motive good or bad, of one thing I am sure, the lasting condemnation of the North.
> I love peace more than life. Have loved the Union beyond expression. For four years have I waited, hoped and prayed for the dark clouds to break, and for a restoration of our former sunshine. To wait longer would be a crime. All hope for peace is dead. My prayers have proved as idle as my hopes. God's will be done. I go to see and share the bitter end. . . .

I have ever held the South were right. The very nomination of ABRAHAM LINCOLN, four years ago, spoke plainly, war—war upon Southern rights and institutions. . . .

This country was formed for the white, not for the black man. And looking upon African Slavery from the same stand-point held by the noble framers of our constitution. I for one, have ever considered if one of the greatest blessings (both for themselves and us,) that God has ever bestowed upon a favored nation. Witness heretofore our wealth and power; witness their elevation and enlightenment above their race elsewhere. I have lived among it most of my life, and have seen less harsh treatment from master to man than I have beheld in the North from father to son. Yet, Heaven knows, no one would be willing to do more for the negro race than I, could I but see a way to still better their condition.

By 1865, the Civil War had morphed into a war against slavery—the "cornerstone" of Confederate society. Booth absorbed his lesson too well. He did not violate some implicit rule of Confederate chivalry or politesse. He accurately interpreted the cause of Jefferson Davis and Robert E. Lee, men who were too weak to truthfully address that cause's natural end.

Moral cowardice requires choice and action. It demands that its adherents repeatedly look away, that they favor the fanciful over the plain, myth over history, the dream over the real. Here is another choice.

Take down the flag. Take it down now.

Put it in a museum. Inscribe beneath it the years 1861–2015. Move forward. Abandon this charlatanism. Drive out this cult of death and chains. Save your lovely souls. Move forward. Do it now.

Ta-Nehisi Coates is an American writer, journalist, and educator. He is a national correspondent for *The Atlantic*, where he writes about cultural, social, and political issues, particularly as they concern African Americans.

Alberto R. Gonzales   ➡ **NO**

The Confederate Flag and Free Speech

The tragic shootings in a church in Charleston, S.C., by an apparent Confederate disciple have intensified debate over the meaning of the Confederate battle flag. Many Americans believe this flag is a symbol of hate and a reminder of the evils of slavery. Others say it is merely a symbol of our heritage and a way of life gone by. Either way the Confederate flag is a symbol that conveys a message—therefore, it is speech. In fact, the stronger the reaction to the Confederate flag, the stronger the argument that the flag conveys a message that ordinarily is protected under the First Amendment.

Many Nashville commuters who live to the South travel on Interstate 65 and pass a monument dedicated to Nathan Bedford Forrest, a Confederate general. The odd-looking statute is surrounded by Confederate battle flags and sits on a small parcel of private property adjacent to the highway. Some Tennesseans have urged that steps be taken to either remove, conceal, or regulate in some way the Forrest monument. If the monument sat on public grounds it would be a relatively straight-forward matter to have it removed, assuming that was the will of government leaders. Unfortunately for monument opponents, the monument sits on private property, and its owner has refused to remove it.

Some readers may be wondering why local or state authorities don't just regulate or restrict the monument in some manner. While the right to speak under the First Amendment is not absolute, government officials who seek to restrict it rightfully face a heavy burden.

The government could claim that the monument, in particular the Confederate flags around it, is nothing more than racist hate speech, and that such speech falls outside the protection of the First Amendment. Government restrictions on hate speech, however, often fail to survive First Amendment scrutiny because of the difficulties in applying a definition of racist speech that is not unconstitutionally vague and overbroad. While it may appear obvious to some that racist hate speech undermines the constitutional principle of equality, as a general matter, such expressions are protected speech. Under the First Amendment the government simply may not outlaw symbols of hate or bigotry, such as the swastika or the Confederate battle flag.

Advocates of government action could argue that the message of the Confederate flag equates to fighting words that arouse passion and others to breach the peace. A regulation intended to regulate such speech would not violate the First Amendment. The U.S. Supreme Court disagrees, finding that government restrictions based on the fighting words doctrine are usually vague and overbroad. Furthermore, the Forrest monument has sat relatively quiet along I-65 for many years now, and anyone offended by the image can merely avert their eyes as they pass by.

Finally, proponents of government regulation could assert that, like cross burnings, displaying the Confederate flag is intended to intimidate, and thus can be prohibited. However, even cross burning enjoys protection under the First Amendment and cannot be completely outlawed. The government may only prohibit similar public displays that constitute speech when the speech is conveyed in a manner that constitutes a true threat—a burden not likely to be met in the case of the Forrest monument.

The importance and value of the First Amendment is that it protects speech from government censorship, no matter how racist, hateful, or inflammatory. Efforts to limit such speech are not only unconstitutional but unwise, as experience demonstrates such government regulation is eventually most likely to be used against minorities.

The Confederate battle flag is a reminder of a dark period in our past, and there are painful lessons to learn from those mistakes so that we avoid repeating them. Any symbol that causes so much pain and anger should be relegated to a footnote in history. It deserves no place of prominence in our future.

Today we are a stronger country because of our diversity, yet we are still a people divided by race. Who can say whether the prejudices that feed the fear, distrust, and hatred of others we perceive to be different can be overcome through understanding and tolerance. Hopefully so, but achieving it will surely not be possible without the robust dialogue in the "marketplace of ideas" envisioned in the protections of the First Amendment.

Alberto R. Gonzales was the 80th U.S. Attorney General, appointed in 2005 by President George W. Bush. He is a graduate of Harvard Law School and Harvard University.

EXPLORING THE ISSUE

Should It Be a Hate Crime to Display the Confederate Flag?

Critical Thinking and Reflection

1. What are the fundamental rights protected by the First Amendment?
2. What are your thoughts regarding the idea that the cure for speech that people find objectionable is simply more speech?
3. What were the results of the U.S. Supreme Court's decisions in *Brandenburg v. Ohio* and *Texas v. Johnson*? Do you agree with the Supreme Court's opinion? Why or why not?
4. What are the distinctions between verbal and symbolic speech? Why don't "fighting words" merit First Amendment protection?
5. Do you think that the U.S. Supreme Court would uphold a law making it a crime to display a Confederate flag? Explain your answer.

Is There Common Ground?

It was no accident that the founding fathers protected those rights we cherish most in the First Amendment: Freedom of speech, press, religion, assembly, and the right to petition our government for redress of grievances. Our commitment to these important principles is sometimes tested most vigorously in those instances where the expression of an unpopular minority viewpoint conflicts with closely held values of a majority of society.

If a state legislature or the federal government were to pass a law restricting the display of the Confederate flag it is very likely that a reviewing court would look to the U.S. Supreme Court's decision in *Texas v. Johnson,* 491 U.S. 397 (1989) as an important precedent. During the 1984 Republican National Convention, Johnson participated in a political demonstration to pretest the policies of the Reagan administration and some Dallas-based corporations. After a march through city streets, Johnson burned an American flag while protesters chanted. No one was physically injured or threatened with injury, although several witnesses were seriously offended by the flag burning. Johnson was convicted of desecration of a venerated object in violation of a Texas law and the state appeals court affirmed. The Texas Court of Criminal Appeals reversed, however, holding that Johnson's actions were expressive conduct under the First Amendment. The State of Texas appealed and the U.S. Supreme Court granted certiorari.

In striking down the Texas statute Associate Justice William Brennan reiterated a fundamental principle

of First Amendment law: "If there is a bedrock principle underlying the First Amendment, it is that the government may not prohibit the expression of an idea simply because society finds the idea offensive or disagreeable." Justice Brennan further stated:

> To conclude that the government may permit designated symbols to be used to communicate only a limited set of messages would be to enter territory having no discernable or defensible boundaries. Could the government on this theory prohibit the burning of state flags? Of copies of the presidential seal? Of the Constitution? In evaluating these choices under the First Amendment, how would we decide which symbols were sufficiently special to warrant this unique status? To do so, we would be forced to consult our own political preferences, and impose them on the citizenry, in the very way that the First Amendment forbids us to do. (417).

Also relevant to our discussion of governmental efforts to make it a hate crime to display the Confederate flag were Justice Brennan's comments about racial discrimination. He asserted: "The First Amendment does not guarantee that other concepts virtually sacred to our Nation as a whole—such as the principle that discrimination on the basis of race is odious and destructive—will go unquestioned in the marketplace of ideas." (418).

Does displaying the Confederate flag raise the issue of white supremacy and racial dominance? Or, is it a symbol of southern heritage and history? Moreover, even assuming for the sake of argument that flag does promote racism and white supremacy, should its message be suppressed by the government through a law banning its display, or, to paraphrase Justice Brandeis's prescription, is the solution simply more speech to counteract the racist message? In addition, could it be argued credibly that displaying the Confederate Flag is analogous to uttering "fighting words," which do not merit First Amendment protection?

After reviewing the Supreme Court precedents considered in this section, however, do you believe that it would uphold a statute making it a hate crime to display a Confederate flag? And, if the Court were to uphold such a statute would that be a positive development for our society and the free exchange of ideas that is a cornerstone of the American experience?

Additional Resources

Fred W. Friendly, *The Good Guys, The Bad Guys and the First Amendment: Free Speech vs. Fairness in Broadcasting* (Random House, 2013).

Alpheus Thomas Mason and Donald Grier Stephenson, Jr., *American Constitutional Law.* (Pearson-Prentice Hall, 2009).

Kathleen Sullivan and Noah Feldman, *Constitutional Law.* (Foundation Press, 2013).

Laurence H. Tribe, *Constitutional Choices* (Harvard University Press, 1986).

Internet References . . .

Nick Bromell, "Let's Make the Confederate Flag a Hate Crime: It is the American Swastika and We Should Recoil in Horror from It." July 10, 2015

www.salon.com

Wendy Kaminer, "Confederate Flag: Who's Free to Fly It and Why the Distinction Matters." June 25, 2015

www.cognoscenti.wbur.org

Alex Thomas, "Leftist Professor Wants Citizens Put in Jail for Displaying Flag." July 11, 2015

www.intellihub.com

Unit 3

UNIT

Punishment

*S*ince the 1950s, scholars have supported the idea that imprisonment, especially for youthful offenders, should be avoided. If incarceration was unavoidable in a particular case, its central focus should be rehabilitation, not retribution, deterrence, or incapacitation. In the early 1970s, however, crime rates spiked in some of our nation's communities and a more punitive approach to correctional policy began to take hold. This has resulted in extremely high incarceration rates in this country that has generated a ripple effect throughout U.S. justice systems. Prison crowding, fragmented communities, unjust convictions, and the wholesale abandonment of the rehabilitative ideal are just some of the consequences. This Unit considers U.S. penal policies, including the use of solitary confinement, three-strikes sentencing laws, whether "for-profit" corporations should run U.S. prisons, and whether the death penalty is a bad public policy. We also assess whether these policies satisfy the principle of social utility—the idea that all social policies should constitute the greatest good for the greatest number of people.

Selected, Edited, and with Issue Framing Material by:
Thomas J. Hickey, *State University of New York at Cobleskill*

ISSUE

Does the Use of Solitary Confinement or "Administrative Segregation" in U.S. Correctional Facilities Constitute Cruel and Unusual Punishment?

YES: Alison Shames, Jessa Wilcox, and Ram Subramanian, from "Solitary Confinement: Common Misconceptions and Emerging Safe Alternatives," Vera Institute of Justice (2015)

NO: William Daly, "Segregation: A Necessary Evil," *CorrectionsOne* (2013)

Learning Outcomes

After reading this issue, you will be able to:

- Discuss the "hands-off" doctrine used by U.S. courts until the 1960s and 1970s.
- Discuss the U.S. Supreme Court's decisions in *Estelle v. Gamble,* and *Hutto v. Finney.*
- Discuss the concept of "cruel and unusual punishment" in the United States.
- Present several possible reasons for the increased use of solitary confinement in U.S correctional facilities in recent years.
- Present and discuss several common misconceptions about the use of solitary confinement in U.S. prisons.
- Discuss whether you believe that solitary confinement is a "necessary evil" in U.S. correctional facilities.
- Discuss Amnesty International's position on the use of solitary confinement in U.S federal prisons.
- Discuss the early use of solitary confinement in the *Pennsylvania System* of corrections.
- Compare the financial cost of confining inmates in solitary confinement as opposed to traditional corrections alternatives.

ISSUE SUMMARY

YES: Alison Shames, Jessa Wilcox and Ram Subramanian from The Vera Institute of Justice contend that solitary confinement produces many unwanted and harmful outcomes—for the mental and physical health of those placed in isolation, for the public safety of the communities to which most will return, and for the corrections budgets of jurisdictions that rely on the practice for facility safety.

NO: William Daly, in contrast, argues that correctional administrators need to be proactive in controlling situations, rather than waiting to respond after their lives are endangered. This may include administrative segregation, which is used to isolate those who have been deemed to be disruptive and dangerous.

Inmates in solitary confinement or administrative segregation are often some of the most difficult individuals that correctional systems must confine. The reasons that a convict may be placed in solitary confinement vary, but often include violent behavior in other types of facilities, confrontation with correctional officers, severe behavioral problems, or the inability to live in the general prison population. In addition, several studies have documented that many inmates in solitary confinement have serious mental health problems including psychosis, severe depression, and antisocial personality disorder. Strict regulations and policies in these units regulate virtually every aspect of an inmate's life. It is not uncommon for inmates in solitary confinement units to spend 23 hours of every day locked in a very small six by eight foot cell with fluorescent lighting that is never turned off and no windows. Their communication with other inmates and staff is highly restricted and reading materials and other "privileges" must be earned through good behavior. It should not be surprising then that the regimentation and sensory deprivation associated with these units appears to produce a substantially higher rate of mental illness among inmates.

As corrections scholar Hans Toch has observed, such penal techniques are nothing new. The conditions prevalent in solitary confinement units have been adopted at various times in the past but were abandoned because they produced high rates of mental illness among inmates. Another corrections scholar, Sasha Abramsky has stated that the conditions in these units may have become the high-tech equivalent of the nineteenth-century snake pit.

Throughout much of the Twentieth Century, U.S. courts had accorded great deference to prison authorities' decisions regarding the conditions of confinement in our nation's prison systems. This approach to corrections law, which the courts followed closely until the 1960s, has been termed the "hands-off" doctrine. It assumed that because correctional officials were the "experts" in penal policy, the courts should defer to their judgments.

You may recall a now classic movie starring Paul Newman and George Kennedy titled *Cool Hand Luke*, which illustrated just how bad the conditions were in some 1950s-era correctional facilities. Due in large part to the inhumane conditions existing in many prison systems, the courts gradually started to scrutinize the decisions of correctional administrators. In fact, during 1960s and 1970s, the conditions of confinement in several state prison systems were held to violate the Eighth Amendment's prohibition against cruel and unusual punishment and significant correctional reforms were instituted.

For example, in *Estelle v. Gamble*, 429 U.S. 97 (1976), the U.S. Supreme Court expounded on the types of penal measures that will violate the Cruel and Unusual Punishment Clause. Justice Thurgood Marshall asserted that these include "punishments which are incompatible with 'the evolving standards of decency that mark the progress of a maturing society,' or which 'involve the unnecessary and wanton infliction of pain.'"

A later case considered specifically examined whether a prison system's solitary confinement practices violated the Eighth Amendment. In *Hutto v. Finney*, 437 U.S. 678 (1978), the U.S. Supreme Court upheld a U.S. District Court ruling that conditions in the Arkansas penal system constituted cruel and unusual punishment in violation of the Eighth and Fourteenth Amendments. The State of Arkansas had appealed the lower court's order that placed a maximum limit of 30 days on confinement in punitive isolation, or solitary confinement. Justice John Paul Stevens described the conditions in punitive isolation as follows:

> Confinement in punitive isolation was for an indeterminate period of time. An average of 4, and sometimes as many as 10 or 11, prisoners were crowded into windowless 8' X 10' cells containing no furniture other than a source of water and a toilet that could only be flushed from outside the cell. At night, the prisoners were given mattresses to spread on the floor. Although some prisoners suffered from infectious diseases such as hepatitis and venereal disease, mattresses were removed and jumbled together each morning and then returned to the cells at random in the evening. Prisoners in isolation received fewer than 1,000 calories a day; their meals consisted primarily of 4-inch squares of "grue," a substance created by mashing meat, potatoes, oleo, syrup, vegetables, eggs, and seasoning into a paste and baking the mixture in a pan. (682).

Justice Stevens then discussed the meaning of the Eighth Amendment's Cruel and Unusual Punishment Clause: It "proscribes more than physically barbarous punishments. . . . It prohibits penalties that are grossly disproportionate to the offense, as well as those that transgress today's 'broad and idealistic concepts of dignity, civilized standards, humanity and decency.'" [Citations omitted]. The Court then upheld the District Court's order that prohibited the Arkansas prison system from confining inmates in punitive isolation for more than 30 days. It did not, however, fashion a blanket rule that holding an inmate in punitive isolation or solitary confinement was cruel and unusual punishment per se; rather, it is the responsibility of a reviewing court to examine the circumstances in each individual case to determine whether they violate the Eighth Amendment.

The 1970s and 1980s witnessed an increasing conservatism in the United States. At least partially in response to rising crime rates, the "war on drugs," and the pervasive belief that rehabilitation programs were ineffective, some scholars and politicians began to advocate a "get tough" approach to crime control. The policies that resulted from this movement included mandatory sentencing laws and a correctional philosophy that emphasized incapacitation and punishment, rather than rehabilitation. The increased use of solitary confinement in our nation's prison systems was directly related to the adoption of mandatory sentencing laws, which increased prison populations dramatically throughout the United States. In fact, in 2015, the Vera Institute estimated that the use of this practice increased as much as by 42 percent between 1995 and 2005.

In its 2015 Report, The Vera Institute of Justice asserts that solitary confinement produces many unwanted and harmful outcomes—for the mental and physical health of those placed in solitary confinement, for the public safety of the communities to which most will eventually return, and for the corrections budgets of jurisdictions that rely on the practice for facility safety. In recent years the tide appears to have turned against this controversial practice, however. In 2014, 10 states announced or implemented policy changes to reduce the number of adults or juveniles held in segregation, improve the conditions in segregation unit, or facilitate the return of inmates held in solitary confinement to a prison's general population. The Report then identifies and discusses 10 common misconceptions about solitary confinement as a corrections practice and concludes that although some U.S. jurisdictions are making progress and are reforming their solitary confinement policies, much more remains to be done.

William Daly, in contrast, believes that solitary confinement is a necessary evil in U.S. correctional facilities. He asserts that current research is "a bit austere and premature" to argue against the use of such practices. He cites a study by the National Institute of Justice (NIJ) that examined the psychological effects of solitary confinement and demonstrated that the mental health of most inmates in isolation did not decline during the course of the year. He believes that although social research on the impact of solitary confinement on inmates is useful, it sometimes falls short in identifying solutions for correctional administrators trying to control violent, unruly and, disruptive inmates.

In the Introduction to this volume we considered the doctrine of social utility. Basically, this concept asserts that the guiding principle for all social policies should be the well-being of the majority of people. Does the use of solitary confinement in our nation's prisons satisfy this principle? Is it an appropriate way to punish hardened criminals? The authors of the YES and NO selections in this section would answer these questions in different ways.

YES ⤶

**Alison Shames, Jessa Wilcox,
and Ram Subramanian**

Solitary Confinement: Common Misconceptions and Emerging Safe Alternatives

Introduction

What is commonly known as solitary confinement is a practice still widely used by corrections officials in the United States today, largely as a means to fulfill a prison's or jail's top priority: the safety of its staff and the incarcerated people under its care. While it is most often deployed when incarcerated people break rules or engage in violent or disruptive behavior, it is also used as a preventative measure in an effort to protect those at high risk of sexual assault and physical abuse in a prison's or jail's general population (for example, incarcerated people who are transgender or former law enforcement officers). The term solitary confinement, however, is often not used by corrections officials, who prefer labels such as restricted housing, segregated housing, and special or intensive management.

Naming the Practice

Corrections officials in the United States refer to solitary confinement by many names, and placement policies also vary by jurisdiction and facility type. The terms in most frequent use today include:

- **Disciplinary or punitive segregation** is used to punish incarcerated people for violating facility rules. As in the larger criminal justice process, charges are written, a hearing is held, evidence is presented, and, if found guilty, a term in segregated housing is imposed.
- **Administrative segregation** is used to remove incarcerated people from the general prison or jail population who are thought to pose a risk to facility safety or security. It may be used for those believed to be members of gangs or active in other restricted activities, even if no violation has been identified. Administrative segregation is not technically a sanction or a punishment, and can be indefinite.

- **Protective custody** is a form of administrative segregation that is used to remove incarcerated people from a facility's general population who are thought be at risk of harm or abuse, such as incarcerated people who are mentally ill, intellectually disabled, gay, transgender, or former law enforcement officers. While some people who fear for their safety in the general population may request protective custody, this status is often conferred involuntarily.
- **Temporary confinement** in segregated housing is used when a reported incident is being investigated or related paperwork is being completed, or when no beds are available for transfers.

Some incarcerated people are held in solitary confinement in prisons or jails, while others are held in disciplinary and administrative segregation in supermax facilities, which are freestanding prisons or distinct units in prisons where the entire incarcerated population is housed in solitary confinement.

All prisons and many jails in the United States use some form of solitary confinement. Whatever the label, the experience for the person is the same—confinement in an isolated cell (alone or with a cellmate) for an average of 23 hours a day with limited human interaction, little constructive activity, and in an environment that ensures maximum control over the individual. When sources cited in this report refer to the practice as solitary confinement, the authors do as well. Otherwise, consistent with American Bar Association standards, "segregated housing" is used as the generic term for the practice.

There are indications that the use of segregated housing has grown substantially in recent years (perhaps as much as by 42 percent between 1995 and 2005), yet the precise number of people held in segregated housing on any given day is not known with any certainty.[1] Estimates range from 25,000 (which includes only those held in supermax facilities) to 80,000 (which includes those held in some form of segregated housing in all state and federal prisons).[2] None of these estimates include people held in segregated housing in jails, military facilities, immigration detention centers, or juvenile justice facilities in the United States. Based on research conducted by the Vera Institute of Justice (Vera) and others, the percentage of a state's prison system's daily population that is held in segregated housing ranges from five to eight percent, while more recent research found that, in November 2013, the Federal Bureau of Prisons—the largest prison system within the United States—held five percent of its prisoners in segregated housing units.[3] Moreover, because these estimates are only one-day snapshots, they most likely underestimate the total number of people subjected to one or more periods in segregated housing over the course of their incarceration.

Against this backdrop, evidence mounts that segregated housing produces many unwanted and harmful outcomes—for the mental and physical health of those placed in isolation, for the public safety of the communities to which most will return, and for the corrections budgets of jurisdictions that rely on the practice for facility safety. As these negative impacts have come to light, concern about its overuse has grown. The severe conditions to which people in segregated housing are subjected are now regularly exposed by mainstream journalists.[4] Incarcerated people who participate in hunger strikes against its use, such as those at Pelican Bay state prison in California in 2013, receive sympathetic national attention.[5] And in response to the shift in public opinion, local, state, and federal policymakers are turning their attention to the overuse of segregated housing by the nation's prisons and jails. A subcommittee of the U.S. Senate Judiciary Committee held a series of hearings in 2012 and 2014 focused on reassessing the use of solitary confinement.[6] In 2014, 10 states announced or implemented policy changes to reduce the number of adults or juveniles held in segregated housing, improve the conditions in segregation units, or facilitate the return of segregated people to a prison's general population.[7] Some, like Colorado, passed legislation that removed entire classes of people—for example, those with serious mental illnesses—from being housed in long-term segregation.[8] And, most recently, New York City's Department of Correction made the historic decision to ban the use of segregated housing for all those in its custody 21 years old and younger.[9]

Despite increased attention to the issue, many people—policymakers, corrections officials, and members of the public—still hold misconceptions about and misguided justifications for the use of segregated housing. This report aims to dispel the most common of these misconceptions and highlight some of the promising alternatives that are resulting in fewer people in segregated housing.

Misconception #1: Conditions in Segregated Housing Are Stark But Not Inhumane

". . . [I]t's anything but quiet. You're immersed in a drone of garbled noise—other inmates' blaring TVs, distant conversations, shouted arguments. I couldn't make sense of any of it, and was left feeling twitchy and paranoid. I kept waiting for the lights to turn off, to signal the end of the day. But the lights did not shut off. I began to count the small holes carved in the walls. Tiny grooves made by inmates who'd chipped away at the cell as the cell chipped away at them."[10]

This is solitary confinement, described not by an incarcerated person or an advocate but by Rick Raemisch, director of the Colorado Department of Corrections. Charged by the governor with reforming the use of segregated housing by the state's prison system, Director Raemisch decided he needed to experience it firsthand.

When an incarcerated person is placed in segregated housing, he or she is confined to a cell (either alone or with a cellmate) for 22 to 24 hours a day.[11] The cell is typically six by eight feet, smaller than a standard parking space. It is furnished with a metal toilet, sink, and bed platform. Reading materials are either strictly limited or prohibited altogether. Natural sunlight in the cell is limited to a very small window or does not exist at all, and fluorescent bulbs light the cell, often throughout the night.[12] Recreation is limited to one hour a day, five days per week, which is taken alone in a cage outdoors or an indoor area (sometimes with a barred top).[13] Every time the incarcerated person is taken out of solitary confinement and returned to it, he or she is strip-searched.[14] Interactions with people (other than a cellmate, if double celled) are brief and infrequent. Officers deliver meal trays through a slot in the door; there are only occasional meetings with healthcare practitioners, counselors, or attorneys; and visitation with family may be restricted or prohibited. Any meetings or visits, when they do occur, are almost always conducted through the cell door or conducted by video, speaker, or telephone through a thick glass window.[15] When an in-person visitation is permitted, the incarcerated person is placed in restraints and separated from the visitor by a partition.

Although this is how most incarcerated people experience segregated housing, it need not be this restrictive. Some jurisdictions are experimenting with making conditions more humane and less solitary. For example, Colorado now requires that incarcerated people held in its Management Control Unit receive four hours of time outside their cell each day.[16] New York State, as part of a legal settlement, gives 16- and 17-year-olds in segregated housing at least five hours of exercise and programming outside of their cells five days per week.[17] Maine requires that incarcerated people in segregated housing receive group recreation, counseling sessions, and opportunities to increase privileges through good behavior, as well as greater access to radios, televisions, and reading materials.[18]

Some jurisdictions have developed different levels of segregated housing, including "step-down" incentive programs that are structured in progressive phases that provide increasing privileges—such as more time out of the cell, the opportunity to participate in group activities, television in the cell, and additional reading materials—for sustained compliance to facility rules. Pennsylvania, Washington, and New Mexico have all created step-down programs for gang members held in segregated housing.[19] Washington has an Intensive Transition Program for incarcerated people with chronic behavior problems who are frequently placed in segregated housing, in which they move through a curriculum in stages, progressively learning self-control and gradually engaging in opportunities to socialize until they are ready to return to the prison's general population.[20] Michigan operates an Incentives in Segregation pilot project, in which incarcerated people work through six stages (each stage requiring different tasks and bestowing additional privileges) over several months.[21] The Virginia Department of Corrections has developed a successful step-down program for incarcerated people in administrative segregation that uses evidence-based practices first developed in the community corrections setting. Since 2011, the program has reduced the number of incarcerated people in administrative segregation by 53 percent and the number of prison incidents by 56 percent.[22]

Misconception #2: Segregated Housing Is Reserved Only for the Most Violent

It is still widely believed that the incarcerated people who end up in segregated housing are the worst of the worst, the most feared, the incorrigibly dangerous. However, several studies have revealed that a significant proportion of the segregated population is placed there for being neither violent nor dangerous. Many are there not as punishment for actually engaging in violence; rather they are there because they have been categorized as potentially dangerous or violent—often because prison officials have

identified them as gang members.[23] This type of segregation, based on identification rather than individual activity, is referred to as administrative segregation.[24]

Segregated housing is not only used to anticipate or react to dangerous or disruptive behavior, it is also used for incarcerated people in protective custody who prison officials believe will be unsafe in the general population. They may be at risk for reasons of mental illness (or other special needs, such as developmental disability), age (such as young people under the age of 18 tried, convicted, and sentenced as adults), former gang or law enforcement affiliation, sexual vulnerability or gender nonconformity, or other reasons, including temporary confinement of someone who has been victimized in general population pending an investigation of the incident.[25] Individuals may even request to be removed from the general population. Although these incarcerated people are separated for their own safety, they are subject to the same restrictive conditions as others in segregation.

The most commonly understood justification for segregation is as punishment for a violation of a prison rule. While this practice, known as disciplinary segregation, is used as a response to behavior that is violent or dangerous, Vera's experience in the field has shown that disruptive behavior—such as talking back, being out of place, failure to obey an order, failing to report to work or school, or refusing to change housing units or cells—frequently lands incarcerated people in disciplinary segregation.[26] In some jurisdictions, these "nuisance prisoners" constitute the majority of the people in disciplinary segregation.[27] Before collaborating with Vera, Illinois found that more than 85 percent of the people released from disciplinary segregation during a one-year period had been sent there for relatively minor infractions, such as not standing for a count and using abusive language.[28] In Pennsylvania, the most common violation associated with a sentence to segregated housing was "failure to obey an order," with 85 percent of those written up for this type of violation sent there.[29] In 2013, an incarcerated person in South Carolina received a penalty of more than 37 years in solitary confinement for posting on Facebook on 38 different days.[30] Piper Kerman, who was incarcerated in a federal prison and is the author of the memoir *Orange is the New Black*, reported to the United States Senate Judiciary Committee in 2014 that she saw many women sent to solitary confinement for at least 30 days for minor infractions such as moving around a housing unit during a count, refusing an order from a corrections officer, and possession of low-level contraband such as small amounts of cash or underwear other than that issued by the prison.[31]

Misconception #3: Segregated Housing Is Used Only as a Last Resort

Although many jurisdictions have a list of alternative sanctions that can be used to discipline incarcerated people who are unruly or difficult to manage, the reality is that far too many turn to segregated housing as the first response to bad behavior. This is in stark contrast to the system used in certain European countries, where corrections officers are trained to impose disciplinary measures that are relative and proportionate to the disruptive behavior. Dutch and German prison officials use sanctions such as reprimands, restrictions on money and property, and restrictions on movement or leisure activities. Care is taken to relate the sanction to the alleged infraction.[32] In these countries, solitary confinement is used rarely and only for very brief periods of time. For example, an adult male prison in Germany reported using segregation just two or three times in 2012, and another German prison for young adults had utilized its segregation cell twice between 2008 and 2012, and only for a few hours each time.[33]

One of the most basic measures that a prison can take to ensure that disciplinary segregation is reserved for those who truly pose a risk to the safety of staff and other incarcerated people is to prohibit its use as a punishment for less serious violations. For instance, Pennsylvania no longer sends anyone to segregated housing as a sanction for the least serious violations, such as taking unauthorized food from the dining hall and unexcused absences from work, school, or mandatory programs.[34] The Illinois Department of Corrections also prohibits the use of segregated housing as a response to certain disciplinary violations.[35] And corrections officials in Maine use a range of less severe restrictions, such as limiting work opportunities, in response to minor infractions.[36]

Some states use structured sanction grids to provide corrections officers with guidance on the appropriate and proportionate punishment for particular behaviors. The sanction grids articulate when less restrictive sanctions (such as mediation or anger management classes, withholding access to the commissary, removing TV privileges, restricting visitation rights, making the prisoner responsible for the costs of damaged property, and assigning the prisoner to an undesirable work shift) may be used, and when more serious sanctions, such as revocation of good time credit and segregation, are appropriate.[37]

Misconception #4: Segregated Housing Is Used Only for Brief Periods of Time

As a matter of policy within the federal prison system and in at least 19 states, corrections officials are permitted to hold people in segregated housing indefinitely.[38] While placement in administrative segregation can, with some level of periodic review, be open-ended, a term in disciplinary segregation is almost always a defined period of time.[39] Notably, if a term in disciplinary segregation is thought to be too brief, corrections officials can easily "move" incarcerated people from "short-term" disciplinary segregation to long-term administrative segregation by the simple process of reclassification.[40]

After Colorado Department of Corrections Director Rick Raemisch spent 20 hours in a cell in segregated housing, he reported that it was "practically a blink" in comparison to the experience of incarcerated people in Colorado who, at the time, spent an average of 23 months in segregation, with many spending multiple years.[41] In 2009, the average length of stay at the Illinois supermax facility, since closed, was more than 6 years; in 2011, the average length of stay in Washington's intensive management unit was 11 months; and in Texas, the average amount of time in administrative segregation is almost four years.[42]

Vera begins its work with a jurisdiction by conducting a comprehensive analysis of administrative data in order to understand how the jurisdiction is actually using segregated housing. Vera's inquiry encompasses areas that, due to the data limitations addressed above (see "Research and Data Limitations" on page 7), are not typically examined by corrections systems. The findings from these analyses often surprise corrections officials, who overwhelmingly agree that no one should stay in segregation any longer than necessary to achieve the original safety and disciplinary goals underlying the placement. However, Vera's review of the data regularly shows that incarcerated people who are not violent or overly disruptive stay in segregated housing for long periods of time, ranging from months to years and even decades. These findings have led some jurisdictions to implement reforms designed to reduce the likelihood of a person staying in segregated housing for periods of time incongruent with the behavior leading to the placement. For example, the Washington Department of Corrections reduced the amount of time an incarcerated person can be held in administrative segregation from 60 to 47 days, absent direct approval from the Deputy Director.[43]

To ensure that no one remains in segregated housing for indefinite or very long periods of time, some states mandate frequent reviews and assessments.[44] Those who are reclassified or are no longer deemed dangerous can be transferred to less restrictive housing units. In Colorado and Pennsylvania, for example, multi-disciplinary committees review segregated housing placements, making it more likely that they are appropriate and objective.[45] In Pennsylvania, those sentenced to disciplinary segregation may be released upon completion of one-half of the imposed sanction and a review of the Program Review Committee.[46] In California, after changing its segregated housing placement criteria, the state conducted case-by-case reviews of all people held in segregation that resulted in many being transferred to less restricted housing.[47]

Another method of reducing the amount of time someone spends in segregated housing is to implement a system of incentives that allows an incarcerated person to earn his or her way out earlier than the imposed term. This strategy is informed by research that has demonstrated that positive reinforcement of pro-social behavior increases the chances of that behavior being repeated in the future.[48] To this end, several states have devised programs designed to target behavior issues.[49] Some states provide programming for certain incarcerated people, such as gang members with histories of violence, who would otherwise face long-term administrative segregation. Washington instituted the Motivating Offender Change program, which focuses on gang-affiliated people in its maximum custody units. It provides opportunities to learn and practice cognitive-behavioral skills to help reduce violent behavior. Successful graduates of the program are transferred to a lower custody environment within the general prison population.[50]

Misconception #5: The Harmful Effects of Segregated Housing Are Overstated and Not Well Understood

Despite the long-established consensus among researchers that solitary confinement damages, often irreparably, those who experience it for even brief periods of time, its continued use in prisons and jails in the United States implies that many jurisdictions and correctional officials are unaware of or minimize the importance of this body of evidence. According to one report, "[n]early every scientific inquiry into the effects of solitary confinement over the past 150 years has concluded that subjecting an individual to more than 10 days of involuntary segregation results in a distinct set of emotional, cognitive, social, and physical pathologies."[51] The characteristics that define segregated housing—social isolation, reduced environmental stimulation, and loss of control over all aspects of daily life—create a "potent mix" that produces a litany of negative impacts, including: hypersensitivity to stimuli, distortions and hallucinations, increased anxiety and nervousness, diminished impulse control, severe and chronic depression, appetite loss and weight loss, heart

palpitations, talking to oneself, problems sleeping, nightmares, self-mutilation, difficulties with thinking, concentration, and memory, and lower levels of brain function, including a decline in EEG activity after only seven days in segregation.[52] Upon release from segregated housing, these psychological effects have the potential to undermine significantly an incarcerated person's adjustment back in the prison's general population or the community to which he or she returns.[53]

The harmful effects are compounded for people with mental illness, who make up one-third to one-half of all incarcerated people in segregated housing.[54] The conditions of segregated housing can exacerbate a preexisting condition or prompt a reoccurrence. As one psychiatric expert explained, "Prisoners who are prone to depression and have had past depressive episodes will be come very depressed in isolated confinement. People who are prone to suicide ideation and attempts will become more suicidal in that setting. People who are prone to disorders of mood . . . will become that and will have a breakdown in that direction. And people who are psychotic in any way . . .will have another breakdown."[55]

Suicide rates and incidents of self-harm (such as banging one's head against the cell wall) are much higher for people in segregation than those in the general prison population.[56] For example, in California, where an estimated five percent of the prisoners are placed in segregated housing, 69 percent of the suicides in 2006 occurred in those units.[57] In Texas, incarcerated people in segregation are five times more likely to commit suicide than those in the general population.[58] In New York, between 1993 and 2003, suicide rates were five times higher among incarcerated people in segregation than among those in the general prison population.[59]

Several states are revising their segregation policies in light of the harm it poses to vulnerable populations, especially those with mental illness. To settle a lawsuit that charged Pennsylvania with violating the constitutional rights of incarcerated people with serious mental illnesses by keeping them in solitary confinement without access to treatment, the state agreed in January 2015 to keep them out of non-therapeutic segregated housing and to improve their care.[60] In Colorado, a law enacted in 2014 requires the removal from long-term segregated housing of all incarcerated people with serious mental illness.[61] Washington created a Reintegration and Progression Program that targets incarcerated people with mental health issues, especially those who engage in chronic self-injurious behavior. The program addresses maladaptive thought and behavior patterns and teaches enhanced coping skills to gradually integrate them into a lower level of custody.[62]

Misconception #6: Segregated Housing Helps Keep Prisons and Jails Safer

The most widely accepted and cited reason for using segregated housing is to ensure safety, order, and control within a prison.[63] Some prison officials believe that the mere existence of segregated housing controls the amount and seriousness of violence within their facilities (both among prisoners and between officers and prisoners).[64] However, there is little evidence to support the claim that segregated housing increases facility safety or that its absence would increase in-prison violence.[65] One study found no relationship between the opening of supermax prisons and the aggregate levels of prisoner-on-prisoner assaults in three prison systems (Illinois, Arizona, and Minnesota).[66] With respect to the impact on the number of prisoner-on-staff assaults after the opening of supermax facilities, although the number of staff assaults dropped in Illinois, staff injuries from prisoner assaults temporarily increased in Arizona, and there was no effect in Minnesota on the incidents of violence directed toward staff.[67]

While corrections administrators and officers remain concerned that a decrease in the use of segregated housing will endanger both incarcerated people and staff, the fear may be unsubstantiated. Colorado has decreased its use of segregated housing by 85 percent and prisoner-on staff assaults are the lowest they have been since 2006.[68] Colorado decreased its use of segregated housing by narrowing the criteria for placement and reducing the length of stay, which included a step-down program that allows those with compliant behavior to be released to the general population.[69] Other states (for example, Illinois, Maine, New Mexico, and Washington) have also reduced their use of segregated housing and increased the use of alternative strategies.[70] Although it is too soon to fully assess outcomes in these states, evidence to date suggests there has been little or no increase in violence.[71]

Misconception #7: Segregated Housing Deters Misbehavior and Violence

Many prison officials support the use of segregated housing for managing disruptive and violent behavior because they believe that it has both a general and individual deterrent effect on misbehavior.[72] However, empirical and anecdotal evidence suggests that segregated housing may have little influence on improving the behavior of incarcerated people.

Studies have contrasted "control-oriented" prisons, which rely on formal sanctions like segregated housing, with others that are "responsibility-based," which provide incarcerated people with self-governance opportunities, or "consensual," which incorporate features of both the control-oriented and responsibility-based models of prison management.[73] Researchers tested the relationship between these approaches and prison order and found that prisons that employed a responsibility-based or consensual management model experienced lower levels of minor and serious disorder than prisons that were more control oriented.[74] Moreover, there is no evidence that confinement in a supermax facility produces a deterrent effect on the individual.[75] A recent study found that exposure to short-term disciplinary segregation as a punishment for initial violence did not deter incarcerated people from committing further violence in prison.[76]

Some theoretical models describe the behavior of incarcerated people as a reaction to the strains, frustrations, and pains of imprisonment combined with little access to mitigating factors.[77] Subjecting incarcerated people to the severe conditions of segregated housing and treating them as the "worst of the worst" can lead them to become more, not less, violent.[78]

Rather than rely on segregated housing to deter misbehavior, some prison systems are providing incarcerated people who are most likely to misbehave with special programming. For example, Washington has an Intensive Transition Program for incarcerated people with chronic behavior problems who are frequently placed in segregated housing, in which they move through a curriculum in stages, progressively learning self-control and gradually engaging in opportunities to socialize until they are ready to return to the prison's general population.[79] Pennsylvania is in the process of implementing Behavior Modification Units with a similar focus.[80]

Misconception #8: Segregated Housing Is the Only Way to Protect the Vulnerable

Some people in segregated housing are not violent and do not misbehave but require or request protection from the general population. These include incarcerated people who suffer from mental illness, have developmental or intellectual disabilities, are vulnerable because of their sexuality (e.g., they are lesbian, gay, bisexual, or transgender), may be retaliated against by other prisoners (e.g., they are former gang members or have testified against someone in the facility), committed sex offenses against children, or are former law enforcement officers or public officials. Many prison officials believe these vulnerable incarcerated people can only be kept safe by placing them in segregated housing with conditions as restrictive as those imposed on people who commit the most violent and dangerous acts.

Some jurisdictions are taking a different approach. Rather than isolating those at risk of victimization, they are creating specialized units, which house vulnerable incarcerated people together and provide privileges and programs that are similar to those available in the general population units.[81] In Washington state, for example, the Skill Building Unit houses incarcerated people with developmental and intellectual disabilities in a general population setting that is dedicated to meeting their needs.[82] The unit provides out-of-cell programming, including daily opportunities to interact with each other and staff during meals and recreation in the dayroom. Unit residents also participate in supported work and other activities to help them function more independently while in prison and upon release. Corrections officers assigned to the unit are trained how to respond appropriately to people with special needs and help them live healthy and safe lives.[83] The Washington Department of Corrections reports that the unit has resulted in safer living conditions for these incarcerated people and safer working conditions for corrections staff.[84]

Still other jurisdictions have reformed or are in the process of reforming their use of segregated housing for certain types of vulnerable incarcerated people: Pennsylvania now sends those with significant mental illness, who formerly would have been placed in disciplinary or administrative segregation, to therapeutic units; New York State banned the use of segregated housing to discipline pregnant women or any incarcerated person under the age of 18; in California, a federal judge has ordered the state to find more suitable housing for physically disabled prisoners; and New York City has pledged to eliminate the use of segregated housing for all incarcerated people aged 21 years old and younger.[85] Alaska and Maine have also enacted laws that ban the use of segregated housing for juveniles for punitive reasons.[86]

Misconception #9: Safe Alternatives to Segregated Housing Are Expensive

A common objection among corrections officials to reducing the use of segregation is that few safe alternatives exist and they are too costly to implement. However, growing concern among policymakers and the public about over-incarceration in the United States has put the use of segregated housing under particular scrutiny, and for good reason: segregated housing harms those subject to it, produces little, if any, improvement in public and prison safety, and is much more expensive than less restrictive housing. The significant fiscal costs associated with building and operating segregated housing units and facilities are due

to the reliance on single-cell confinement, enhanced surveillance and security technology, and the need for more corrections staff (to handle escorts, increased searches, and individualized services).[87] For example, in 2013, the estimated daily cost per inmate at the federal administrative maximum (supermax) facility was $216.12 compared to $85.74 to house people in the general prison population.[88] In 2003, the daily per capita costs of operating a supermax prison in Ohio were estimated at two-to-three times that of regular security units—$149 per day compared to $63 per day, with one corrections officer for every 1.7 prisoners in supermax compared to one for every 2.5 in less restricted housing.[89]

Many of the policy and practice changes undertaken by jurisdictions to reduce their reliance on segregated housing described in this report cost little to implement. Time and patience are required, but not necessarily an enhanced budget. In addition, many of the alternative programs, such as reentry programming and integrated housing units, may only require extending programs that already exist, which would save on start-up costs. Finally, by safely decreasing the number of incarcerated people held in segregated housing, jurisdictions may be able not only to close expensive segregation units and supermax prisons, but free up the staff and other resources needed to pursue evidence-based programming that will help many more incarcerated people return successfully to their communities.

Misconception #10: Incarcerated People Are Rarely Released Directly to the Community from Segregated Housing

While national data are not available, jurisdictions often hold people in segregated housing until they complete their sentences, releasing them directly to the community. Between 1987 and 2007, California released an estimated 900 incarcerated people each year directly to the community from its secure housing units; in 2013, Texas released more than 1,200 incarcerated people in this way.[90] Releasing people directly from segregated housing into the community sets them up for failure—and endangers the safety and well-being of the communities to which they return-because in segregated housing, people more often than not receive no reentry planning services or rehabilitative programming, such as substance abuse counseling or classes related to life skills or anger management.

Moreover, data from some states suggest that recidivism rates for incarcerated people who have been held in segregated housing, regardless of whether they are released directly to the community, is significantly higher than for those who have not spent time in segregated housing while in prison. A 2001 review of recidivism data in Connecticut found that 92 percent of those who had been held in administrative segregation were rearrested within three years, compared to 66 percent of incarcerated people who had not been held in administrative segregation.[91] Another study found that confinement in supermax housing is associated with an increased risk of violent reoffending.[92] In Colorado, the recidivism rate for those who had been held in administrative segregation was between 60 and 66 percent, while the recidivism rate for those in general population was 50 percent.[93]

While the research is mixed, there is at least one study that shows the likelihood of reoffending by those who have been held in segregated housing may be reduced by returning them to the general prison population for as brief a period as three months before they are released to the community.[94] In Colorado, all people leaving restrictive housing (formerly called administrative segregation) spend up to 180 days in a transition unit where they receive cognitive behavioral programming and spend six hours a day outside of their cell before they return to the general prison population or to their communities.[95] Other jurisdictions have introduced reentry programming to those in segregated housing, primarily aimed at helping them re-socialize and get accustomed to interacting with other people. New Mexico created a Re-Entry and Release Unit for people in segregated housing who are within 180 days of release where they participate in education and behavioral health programming, are not in restraints during group education activities, and move freely amongst other incarcerated people in recreation areas.[96]

Conclusion

Segregated housing remains a mainstay of prison management and control in U.S. prisons and jails largely because many jurisdictions still subscribe to some or all of the common misconceptions laid out in this report. Few in American corrections would dispute that its use may be unavoidable from time to time and for very brief periods to manage incarcerated people who have committed especially violent or dangerous acts. However, increasingly, policymakers, corrections officials, and the general public are justifiably questioning the human and societal toll of its widespread use. A large body of evidence has now well established that the typical circumstances and conditions of segregated housing—the deprivation of regular social intercourse and interaction, the removal of the rudimentary sights and sounds of life, and the severe restrictions on such basic human activities as eating, showering, or

recreating—damage, sometimes irreparably, the people thus confined and the communities to which they return. And they fail to make prisons and jails any safer for those incarcerated or for the people who work in them.

Much of this research affirms the objections expressed by the United States Supreme Court 125 years ago in its landmark case of *In re Medley*. The court declared that solitary confinement is not "a mere unimportant regulation as to the safe-keeping of the prisoner. . . . [A] considerable number of the prisoners . . . f[a]ll, after even a short confinement, into a semi-fatuous condition . . . [while] others bec[o]me violently insane; others still, [commit] suicide; while those who st[an]d the ordeal better [are] not generally reformed, and in most cases d[o] not recover sufficient mental activity to be of any subsequent service to the community."[97]

Whether prompted by the public's growing appetite for broad criminal justice reform or compelled by court orders, some jurisdictions are making progress. But much more remains to be done. Every effort must involve the implementation of policies and practices that effectively ban the use of segregated housing as an emergency response to minor rule infractions and as the default placement for those in need of protection—such as incarcerated people with serious mental illness, physical disabilities, or who are at risk of sexual victimization or violent retaliation. Not only will safe alternatives to segregated housing improve overall conditions in prisons and jails, but they will help build the foundation all incarcerated people need to return successfully to their communities.

Notes

1. Percent increase calculation done by Vera Institute of Justice researchers as part of its Segregation Reduction Project, based on data from the 1995 and 2005 *Census of State and Federal Adult Correctional Facifities*. For an estimate of the number of people in segregated housing in 1995, see U.S. Department of Justice, Bureau of Justice Statistics, *Census of State and Federal Adult Correctional Facilities, 1995* [Computer file]. Conducted by the U.S. Department of Commerce, Bureau of the Census. ICPSR ed. Ann Arbor, Ml: Inter-university Consortium for Political and Social Research [producer and distributor], 1998. Doi:10.3886/ICPSR06953. v1. For an estimate of the number of people in segregated housing in 2005, see United States Department of Justice, Office of Justice Programs, Bureau of Justice Statistics, *Census of State and Federal Adult Correctional Facilities,*

2005. ICPSR24642-v2. Ann Arbor, Ml: Inter-university Consortium for Political and Social Research [distributor], 2010-10-05. http://doi.org/10.3886/ICPSR24642.v2.

2. For the estimate of 25,000 incarcerated people in segregated housing, see Daniel P. Mears, *Evaluating the Effectiveness of Supermax Prisons* (Washington, DC: Urban Institute, 2006), 4. For the estimate of approximately 80,000 incarcerated people in segregated housing, see United States Department of Justice, Office of Justice Programs, Bureau of Justice Statistics, *Census of State and Federal Adult Correctional Facilities, 2005*. ICPSR24642-v2. Ann Arbor, Ml: Inter university Consortium for Political and Social Research [distributor], 2010-10-05. http://doi.org/10.3886/ICPSR24642.v2.

3. In 2002, 40 states responded to a National Institute of Corrections survey with respondents having an average of 5 percent of prisoners in administrative and disciplinary custody. See James Austin and Kenneth McGinnis, *Classification of High-Risk and Special Management Prisoners: A National Assessment of Current Practices,* (Washington, DC: US Department of Justice, National Institute of Corrections, 2004), 29-30. https://s3.amazonaws.com/static.nicic.gov/Library/019468.pdf. This mirrors more recent calculations. For example, in 2010, 5.3 percent of Washington state's prison population was in segregated housing. This included 2.1 percent held in administrative or disciplinary segregation and 3.2 percent in the highest custody level of maximum. See Bernie Warner, secretary, Washington Department of Corrections, e-mail exchange with Vera, Washington, DC, March 12, 2015. In 2011, seven percent of Colorado's prison population was held in administrative segregation. See James Austin and Emmitt Sparkman, *Colorado Department of Corrections Administrative Segregation and Classification Review,* (Washington, DC: National Institute of Corrections, 2011, Technical Assistance # 11P1022) https://www.aclu.org/files/assets/final_ad_seg.pdf. In 2014, 5.1 percent of Pennsylvania's prison population was held in segregated housing. See Shirley Moore Smeal, executive deputy secretary, Pennsylvania Department of Corrections, e-mail exchange with Vera, Washington, DC, February 27, 2015. For information on the percentage of incarcerated people in segregation in the custody of the Federal Bureau of Prisons, see CNA, *Federal Bureau of Prisons: Special Housing Unit Review and Assessment* (Washington, DC: CNA, December, 2014). A report from the U.S. Government Accountability Office (GAO) found seven percent of the prison population housed in segregated housing as of February, 2013. U.S. Government Accountability Office (GAO), *Bureau of Prisons: Improvements Needed in Bureau of Prisons' Monitoring and Evaluation of Impact of Segregated Housing* (Washington, DC: GAO, 2013).

4. Ted Conover, "From Gitmo to an American Supermax, the Horrors of Solitary Confinement," *Vanity Fair,* January 16, 2015; Laura Dimon, "How Solitary Confinement Hurts the Teenage Brain," *The Atlantic,* June 30, 2014; and Atul Gawande, "Hellhole," *The New Yorker,* March 30, 2009.

5. See Benjamin Wallace-Wells, "The Plot From Solitary," *New York Magazine,* February 26, 2014.

6. United States Senate Committee on the Judiciary, Subcommittee on the Constitution, Civil Rights and Human Rights, *Reassessing Solitary Confinement: The Human Rights, Fiscal, and Public Safety Consequences,* June 19, 2012, http://www.judiciary.senate.gov/imo/media/doc/CHRG-112shrg87630.pdf; United States Senate Committee on the Judiciary, Subcommittee on the Constitution, Civil Rights, and Consequences, *Reassessing Solitary Confinement II: The Human Rights, Fiscal, and Public Safety Consequences,* February 25, 2014, http://www.judiciary.senate.gov/meetings/reassessing-solitary-confinement-ii-the-human-rights-fiscal-and-public-safety-consequences.

7. Eli Hager and Gerald Rich, "Shifting Away from Solitary," *The Marshall Project,* December 23, 2014. Also, South Dakota repealed a law that allowed a county prisoner to be kept in solitary confinement on bread and water for refusal to labor or obey necessary orders, see 2014 S.D. Laws 118 repealed S.D. Codified Laws § 24-11-34 (2014).

8. "The department shall not place a person with serious mental illness in long-term isolated confinement except when exigent circumstances are present," Colorado Revised Statute, 17-1-113.8 (2014).

9. In September 2014, the New York City Department of Correction ordered the end of solitary confinement for 16- and 17-year-olds by the end of the year. See Michael Shwirtz, "Solitary Confinement to End for Youngest at Rikers Island," *New York Times,* September 28, 2014. In January 2015, the New York City Board of Correction adopted rules relating to enhanced supervision housing and punitive segregation, which stated that sufficient resources are made available for staffing and implementing necessary alternative programming; as of January 1, 2016,

inmates ages 18 through 21 will no longer be placed in enhanced supervision housing. Rules of the City of New York, Chapter 1, Title 40, §1-16 (c)(1)(ii).

10. Rick Raemisch, "My Night in Solitary," *New York Times,* February 20, 2014, p. A25, http://www.nytimes.com/2014/02/21/opinion/my-nightin-solitary.html. For several personalized accounts of life in segregated housing, see American Civil Liberties Union of Texas, Texas Civil Rights Project-Houston, *A Solitary Failure: The Waste, Cost and Harm of Solitary Confinement in Texas* (Houston: ACLU, 2015).

11. For more information on double celling, see Scarlet Kim, Taylor Pendergrass, and Helen Zelon, *Boxed In: The True Cost of Extreme Isolation in New York's Prisons* (New York: NYCLU, 2012), 34: "Doublecelled prisoners experience the same isolation and idleness, withdrawal and anxiety, anger and depression as do prisoners living alone in the SHU. But double-celled, they must also endure the constant, unabating presence of another man in their personal physical and mental space."

12. Caroline Isaacs and Matthew Lowen, *Buried Alive: Solitary Confinement in Arizona's Prisons and Jails* (Arizona: American Friends Service Committee: 2007), 10-11.

13. Craig Haney, "Mental Health Issues in Long-Term Solitary and 'Supermax' Confinement," *Crime & Delinquency* 49, no. 1 (2003): 126.

14. Isaacs and Lowen, 2007, p. 11.

15. Haney, 2003, p. 126; Eric Lanes, "The Association of Administrative Segregation Placement and Other Risk Factors with the Self-Injury-Free Time of Male Prisoners," *Journal of Offender Rehabilitation* 48 (2009): 532; Fred Cohen, "Isolation in Penal Settings: The Isolation-Restraint Paradigm," *Washington University Journal of Law & Policy,* 22 (2006): 297-299.

16. Kellie Wasco, deputy director, Colorado Department of Corrections, e-mail exchange with Vera, Washington, DC, April 17, 2015.

17. Benjamin Weiser, "New York State in Deal to Limit Solitary Confinement," *The New York Times,* February 19, 2014.

18. American Civil Liberties Union of Maine, *Change is Possible: A Case Study of Solitary Confinement Reform in Maine* (Portland, ME: ACLU of ME, 2013), 13. http://www.aclumaine.org/sites/default/files/uploads/users/admin/ACLU_Solitary_Report_webversion.pdf.

19. For information on Washington state, see Bernie Warner, secretary, Washington Department of Corrections, e-mail exchange with Vera, Washington, DC, March 12, 2015. For additional information on Washington, see Jonathan Martin, "State Prisons Rethink Solitary Confinement," *Seattle Times* (January 7, 2013). For information on New Mexico, see Gregg Marcantel, secretary, New Mexico Corrections Department, e-mail exchange with Vera, Washington, DC, March 25, 2015. For information on Pennsylvania, see Shirley Moore Smeal, executive deputy secretary, Pennsylvania Department of Corrections, e-mail exchange with Vera, Washington, DC, February 27, 2015; Pennsylvania Department of Corrections, "STGMU Program" (unpublished memorandum, Pennsylvania Department of Corrections, 2014).

20. Carlyne Kujath, manager, Strategic Operations, Washington Department of Corrections, e-mail exchange with Vera, Washington, DC, April 15, 2015.

21. For information on Michigan, see Daniel Heyns, "Incentives in Segregation Program," Director's Office Memorandum (December 23, 2014) http://www.michigan.gov/documents/corrections/DOM_2015-5_478829_7.pdf.

22. "Virginia Step Down Program for Administrative Segregation," *Southern Legislative Conference* (2013), http://www.slcatlanta.org/STAR/2013documents/VA_Step_Down.pdf. Mississippi also uses a step down unit for prisoners with significant mental illness, see Terry A. Kupers et al., "Beyond Supermax Administrative Segregation: Mississippi's Experience Rethinking Prison Classification and Creating Alternative Mental Health Programs," *Criminal Justice and Behavior* 36 (2009):1037-50. Maine conducts risk assessments for each prisoner in administrative segregation and uses this information to develop individualized behavioral programs, which can include in cell as well as group counseling. See American Civil Liberties Union of Maine, 2013.

23. Haney, 2003, p. 127. In a survey of supermax admission characteristics, Butler and Griffin found 36 percent of states responded that gang membership or participation in a security threat group was an adequate reason for inmate supermax placement. See H. Daniel Butler, O. Hayden Griffin III, and W. Wesley Johnson, "What Makes You the 'Worst of the Worst?': An Examination of State Policies Defining Supermax Confinement," *Criminal Justice Policy Review* 24, no. 6 (2012): 687.

24. At least 46 states have specific criteria that govern who is placed in long-term administrative segregations. See Hope Metcalf et al., "Administrative Segregation, Degrees of Isolation, and Incarceration:

A National Overview of State and Federal Correction Policies," *Public Law Working Paper* (New Haven: Yale Law School, 2013), 2, http://papers.ssrn.com/sol3/papers.cfm?abstract_id=2286861; and Haney, 2003, p. 127.

25. For information on incarcerated people in segregation due to mental instability, see Craig Haney, 2003, pp. 124-156. For information on children in segregated housing, see American Civil Liberties Union and Human Rights Watch, *Growing Up Locked Down: Youth in Solitary Confinement in Jails and Prisons Across the United States* (New York: ACLU & HRW, 2012) https://www.aclu.org/files/assets/us1012webwcover.pdf. Additional reasons to place someone in protective custody include advanced age, former affiliation as a law enforcement officer, the crime committed (e.g., a particularly heinous act or sex offenders), owe debts to others in the facility, and testified against someone in the facility.

26. Angela Browne, Alissa Cambier, and Suzanne Agha, "Prisons Within Prisons: The Use of Segregation in the United States," *Federal Sentencing Reporter* 24, no. 1 (2011): 46-49.

27. Leena Kurki and Norval Morris, "The Purposes, Practices, and Problems of Supermax Prisons," *Crime and Justice,* 28 (2001): 385-424, 389; David Lovell, Kristin Cloyes, David Allen, and Lorna Rhodes, "Who Lives in Super-Maximum Custody? A Washington State Study," *Federal Probation Journal* 64, no. 2 (2000): 33-38; and Jean Casella and James Ridgeway, "New York's Black Sites," *The Nation* (July 30-August 6, 2012).

28. Bryan Gleckler, chief of staff, Illinois Department of Corrections, e-mail exchange with Vera, Washington, DC, April 3, 2015.

29. Shirley Moore Smeal, executive deputy secretary, Pennsylvania Department of Corrections, e-mail exchange with Vera, Washington, DC, February 27, 2015.

30. An investigation revealed that South Carolina was sending incarcerated people caught posting on social media sites to segregated housing for an average of 512 days. See Emily Bazelon, "The Shame of Solitary Confinement," *New York Times,* February 19, 2015.

31. Testimony of Piper Kerman, Senate Committee on the Judiciary, Subcommittee on the Constitution, Civil Rights and Human Rights, "Reassessing Solitary Confinement II: The Human Rights, Fiscal, and Public Safety Consequences," (February 24, 2014), http://www.judiciary.senate.gov/imo/media/doc/02-25-14KermanTestimony.pdf.

32. Ram Subramanian and Alison Shames, *Sentencing and Prison Practices in Germany and the Netherlands: Implications for the United States* (New York: Vera Institute of Justice, 2013), 13. The corrections systems in Germany and the Netherlands embrace two principles that the National Research Council finds particularly missing from current criminal justice policies and practices in the United States: proportionality—i.e., offenses should be punished in proportion to their seriousness—and parsimony—i.e., the period of confinement should be sufficient but not greater than necessary to achieve the goals of the disciplinary policy. See National Research Council, Committee on Causes and Consequences of High Rates of Incarceration, Jeremy Travis, Bruce Western, and Steve Redburn, eds., *The Growth of Incarceration in the United States: Exploring Causes and Consequences* (Washington, DC: The National Academies Press, 2014).

33. Subramanian and Shames, 2013, p. 13.

34. These violations are eligible for informal resolution, which does not permit segregated housing as a sanction. Should these violations be referred for formal resolution, the only sanctions levied are those sanctions other than segregated housing.

35. Bryan Gleckler, chief of staff, Illinois Department of Corrections, e-mail exchange with Vera, Washington, DC, April 3, 2015.

36. American Civil Liberties Union of Maine, 2013, p. 15.

37. Washington Department of Corrections, *Prison Sanctioning Guidelines* (DOC 320.150 Attachment 2), on file with Vera.

38. Ryan Jacobs and Jaeah Lee, "Maps: Solitary Confinement, State by State," *Mother Jones,* November/December 2012.

39. See American Correctional Association, Standards for Adult Correctional Institutions (4th edition, 2003), § 4-4249. For information on review while in administrative segregation, see Hope Metcalf et al., 2013, pp. 15-17, http://papers.ssrn.com/sol3/papers.cfm?abstract_id 2286861.

40. Cohen, 2006, p. 300.

41. Raemisch, 2014, p. A25.

42. For information on length of stay in Illinois, see Illinois Department of Corrections, *Tamms Closed Maximum Security Unit: Overview and Ten-Point Plan* (Springfield, IL: Illinois Department of Corrections, September 3, 2009), p. 39, Table 4; in Washington, Carlyne Kujath, manager of strategic operations, Washington Department of Corrections, e-mail exchange with Vera, Washington, DC, April 17, 2015; and in Texas, see American

Civil Liberties Union of Texas, 2015, 2. This report does not specify the year(s) for which data was analyzed. According to the report's author, the average length of stay in Texas was calculated using data available as of August 13, 2013. Burke Butler, Arthur Liman Fellow, the Texas Civil Rights Project, e-mail exchange with Vera, Washington, DC, April 18, 2015.

43. Bernie Warner, secretary, Washington Department of Corrections, e-mail exchange with Vera, Washington, DC, March 12, 2015.

44. In a review of the policies of 47 jurisdictions, Metcalf et al. found that every jurisdiction required some form of review of prisoners in administrative segregation. The majority of jurisdictions required an initial review within seven days with subsequent reviews ranging from weekly to yearly. The decision makers for the review can include facility staff, warden, a specially designated committee, and high-level administrators. Additional research is needed on whether and how the frequency of reviews correlates with the length of time spent in segregation. Metcalf et al., 2013, pp. 15-16.

45. Shirley Moore Smeal, executive deputy secretary, Pennsylvania Department of Corrections, e-mail exchange with Vera, Washington, DC, February 27, 2015. Kellie Wasco, deputy director, Colorado Department of Corrections, e-mail exchange with Vera, Washington, DC, April 17, 2015.

46. Shirley Moore Smeal, executive deputy secretary, Pennsylvania Department of Corrections, e-mail exchange with Vera, Washington, DC, February 27, 2015.

47. Data obtained from the California Department of Corrections and Rehabilitation reveals that 69 percent of Security Housing Unit case reviews led to release to a step down program or a general population setting and 63 percent of administrative segregation unit case reviews led to a return to the general population. See Sal Rodriguez, "In California Prisons, Hundreds Have Been Removed from Solitary Confinement—and Thousands Remain," *Solitary Watch*, January 27, 2015.

48. Paul Gendreau, Sheila A. French, and Angela Gionet, "What Works (What Doesn't Work): The Principles of Effective Correctional Treatment," *Journal of Community Corrections* 13 (Spring 2004): 5.

49. Metcalf et al. specify Connecticut, Massachusetts, Mississippi, New Jersey, New Mexico, and Virginia as states that have structured programs that target behavior issues. Metcalf et al., 2013, p. 18.

50. Bernie Warner, secretary, Washington Department of Corrections, e-mail exchange with Vera, Washington, DC, March 12, 2015. The Washington State Department of Corrections uses the Risk-Need-Responsivity Model as a foundation of the Washington State Department of Corrections Offender Change Model. For more information on the Risk-Need-Responsivity model, see James Bonta and D. A. Andrews, *Risk-Need-Responsivity Model for Offender Assessment and Rehabilitation* (Ottawa: Public Safety Canada, 2007), http://www.publicsafety.gc.ca/cnt/rsrcs/pblctns/rsk-nd-rspnsvty/index-eng.aspx.

51. David H. Cloud, Ernest Drucker, Angela Browne, and Jim Parsons, "Public Health and Solitary Confinement in the United States," *American Journal of Public Health*, 105, no.1 (2015): 18-26. For a comprehensive summary of the published studies documenting this statement see Haney, 2003, pp. 124-156. On historical research on the "sizable and impressively sophisticated literature, now largely forgotten," that documented significant damage to incarcerated people held in segregated housing, see Peter Scharff Smith, "The Effects of Solitary Confinement on Prison Inmates: A Brief History and Review of the Literature," *Crime and Justice*, 34, no. 1 (2006): 441. One contrasting study of incarcerated people in administrative segregated housing in Colorado found no mental deterioration while in segregation, see Maureen L. O'Keefe et al., "One Year Longitudinal Study of the Psychological Effects of Administrative Segregation." (National Institute of Justice Document 232973, October 2010). However, experts with long professional track records in correctional mental health have taken issue with the design of that study and caution not to draw any conclusions from the study. See Kirsten Weir, "Alone in the Hole: Psychologists Probe the Mental Health Effects of Solitary Confinement," *American Psychological Association* 43, no. 5 (May 2012): 54, http://www.apa.org/monitor/2012/05/solitary.aspx; and Stuart Grassian and Terry Kupers, "The Colorado Study vs. the Reality of Supermax Confinement," *Correctional Mental Health Report*, 13, no.1 (May/June 2011): 1-4.

52. For information on the "potent mix," see Sharon Shalev, *A Sourcebook on Solitary Confinement* (London: Mannheim Centre for Criminology, London School of Economics, 2008). For information on negative effects of solitary confinement, see Haney, 2003, pp. 130-136; Paul Gendreau, et al. "Changes in EEG Alpha Frequency and Evoked Response Latency During

Solitary Confinement," *Journal of Abnormal Psychology* 79 (1972), 57-58; Stuart Grassian, "Psychiatric Effects of Solitary Confinement," *Washington University Journal of Law & Policy,* 22 (January 2006): 325-383; Stuart Grassian, "Psychopathological Effects of Solitary Confinement," *American Journal of Psychiatry* 140, no.11 (1983): 1450-1454.

53. See Craig Haney and Mona Lynch, "Regulating Prisons of the Future: A Psychological Analysis of Supermax and Solitary Confinement," *New York University Review of Law and Social Change* 23 (1997): 568.

54. While precise estimates are difficult, Professor Haney writes that the number of prisoners in segregated housing with mental illness may be twice as high as in the general prison population. See Haney, 2003, pp. 124-156; Sasha Abramsky and Jamie Fellner *Ill-Equipped: US Prisons and Offenders With Mental Illness* (New York: Human Rights Watch, 2003); David Lovell, "Patterns of Disturbed Behavior in a Supermax Prison," *Criminal Justice and Behavior* 3, no. 8 (2008): 985-1004.

55. Abramsky and Fellner, 2003, available at http://www.hrw.org/reports/2003/usa1003/18.htm, citing an e-mail from Dr. Terry A. Kupers, who testified in *Jones 'EI v. Berge,* 164 F. Supp 2d 1096 (W.D. Wisconsin, 2001), which challenged the conditions in a Wisconsin supermax.

56. Fatos Kaba et al., "Solitary Confinement and Risk of Self-Harm Among Jail Inmates," *American Journal of Public Health* 104, no. 3, (2014): 442-447; Eric Charles Lanes, "Are the 'Worst of the Worst' Self-Injurious Prisoners More Likely to End Up in Long-Term Maximum-Security Administrative Segregation?" *International Journal of Offender Therapy and Comparative Criminology* 55, no. 7 (2011):1034-1050.

57. Kevin Johnson, "Inmate Suicides Linked to Solitary," *USA Today,* December 27, 2006.

58. American Civil Liberties Union of Texas, 2015, p. 10. Rates for suicide and self-harm calculated using data from fiscal year 2013 per Burke Butler, Arthur Limas Fellow, Texas Civil Rights Project, email exchange with Vera, Washington, DC, April 18, 2015.

59. For an examination of suicides from 1993-2003, see Bruce Way et al., "Inmate Suicide and Time Spent in Special Disciplinary Housing in New York State Prison," *Psychiatric Services* 58, no. 4 (2007): 558-560.

60. Samantha Melamed, "Deal Aims to End Solitary Confinement For Seriously Mentally Ill Prisoners in Pa." *Philadelphia Inquirer,* January 8, 2015.

61. Colorado Revised Statute, 17-1-113.8 (2014).

62. Bernie Warner, secretary, Washington Department of Corrections, e-mail exchange with Vera, Washington, DC, March 12, 2015.

63. See Mears, 2006, p. 41; Chad S. Briggs, Jody L. Sundt, and Thomas C. Castellano, "The Effect of Supermaximum Security Prisons on Aggregate Levels of Institutional Violence," *Criminology* 41, issue 4 (2003): 1342.

64. Mears, 2006, p. 42. Interestingly, the physical conditions of a prison—some of which are present in segregated housing units—have been found to relate to misconduct, with worse levels of noise, clutter, dilapidation, and lack of privacy predicting higher levels of violence. D.M. Bierie, "Is Tougher Better? The Impact of Physical Prison Conditions on Inmate Violence," *International Journal of Offender Therapy and Comparative Criminology* 56, no. 3 (2012): 338-355.

65. There are few, if any, credible studies on the impact of administrative segregation on facility safety, see Daniel P. Mears, "Supermax Prisons: The Policy and the Evidence," *Criminology & Public Policy* 12, no. 4 (2013): 681-720. The authors of a report on the use of segregated housing in federal prisons said that the literature does not make it "clear if there is a causal relationship between segregation policies and institutional safety," see CNA, 2014. Moreover, the federal Bureau of Prison's has never assessed whether the use of segregated housing has any effect on prison safety, see U.S Government Accountability Office (GAO), 2013, p. 33.

66. Briggs, Sundt, and Castellano, 2003, p. 1367.

67. Ibid, pp. 1365-1367.

68. In October 2009, Colorado Department of Corrections housed 1,166 incarcerated people in long-term administrative segregation. In April 2014, 215 incarcerated people were housed in long-term administrative segregation. Office of Planning and Analysis Prison Operations, Colorado Department of Corrections (CDOC), *SB 11-176 Annual Report: Administrative Segregation For Colorado Inmates* (Colorado: CDOC, 2015), 3; Rick Raemisch, director, Colorado Department of Corrections, e-mail exchange with Vera, Washington, DC, February 27, 2015.

69. CNA, 2014, p. 48; and Office of Planning and Analysis Prison Operations, Colorado Department of Corrections (CDOC), 2015, pp. 3-4.

70. Colorado, Kansas, Maine, Mississippi, and Ohio greatly reduced their use of segregated housing and officials reported little or no adverse impact on facility safety, see U.S. Government

Accountability Office (GAO), 2013, 34. Washington has reduced the number of prisoners assigned to maximum custody by 47 percent from January 2011 to December 2014, see Bernie Warner, secretary, Washington Department of Corrections, e-mail exchange with Vera, Washington, DC, March 12, 2015; Gregg Marcantel, secretary, New Mexico Corrections Department, e-mail exchange with Vera, Washington DC, March 25, 2015.

71. When Maine cut its population in segregated housing, incidents of prison violence dropped. See American Civil Liberties Union of Maine, 2013, pp. 30-31.

72. Jesenia M. Pizarro and Raymund E. Narag, "Supermax Prisons: What We Know, What We Do Not Know, and Where We Are Going," *The Prison Journal* 88, no. 1 (2008): 29; Mears, 2006.

73. John J. Dilulio, *Governing Prisons: A Comparative Study of Correctional Management* (New York: Free Press, 1987); and Michael D. Reisig, "Rates of Disorder in Higher-Custody State Prisons: A Comparative Analysis of Managerial Practices," Crime and Delinquency, 44, no. 2 (1998), 230.

74. Michael D. Reisig, 1998, p. 239.

75. Chad S. Briggs, Jody L. Sundt, and Thomas C. Castellano, 2003, p. 1370.

76. Robert G. Morris, "Exploring the Effect of Exposure to Short-Term Solitary Confinement Among Violent Prison Inmates," *Journal of Quantitative Criminology* DOI 10.1007/s10940-015-9250-0 (2015): 1-24.

77. See Kristie R. Blevins et al., "A General Strain Theory of Prison Violence and Misconduct: An Integrated Model of Inmate Behavior," *Journal of Contemporary Criminal Justice* 26, no. 2 (2010): 148-166; Gresham M. Sykes, *The Society of Captives* (Princeton, New Jersey: Princeton University Press, 1958); Hans Toch, *Living in Prison: The Ecology of Survival* (New York: Free Press,1977); and Burt Useem and Anne Piehl, "Prison Buildup and Disorder," *Punishment and Society* 8, no. 1 (2006): 87-115.

78. Kate King, Benjamin Steiner, and Stephanie Ritchie Breach, "Violence in the Supermax: A Self-Fulfilling Prophecy," *The Prison Journal,* 88, no. 1 (2008): 161-62.

79. Carlyne Kujath, manager, Strategic Operations, Washington Department of Corrections, e-mail exchange with Vera, Washington, DC, April 15, 2015.

80. See Shirley Moore Smeal, executive deputy secretary, Pennsylvania Department of Corrections, e-mail exchange with Vera, Washington, DC, April 10, 2015.

81. Pennsylvania houses prisoners with special needs in a specialized unit, which provides privileges and programming similar to those offered in the general population. See Shirley Moore Smeal, executive deputy secretary, Pennsylvania Department of Corrections, e-mail exchange with Vera, Washington, DC, April 10, 2015.

82. Bernie Warner, secretary, Washington Department of Corrections, e-mail exchange with Vera, Washington, DC, March 12, 2015; Washington State Department of Corrections, "Skill Building Unit – Cedar Hall, WCC for Offenders with Cognitive Disabilities," (unpublished memorandum, Washington State Department of Corrections) on file with Vera. More information is available at http://www.doc.wa.gov/facilities/prison/wcc/.

83. Ibid.

84. Bernie Warner, secretary, Washington Department of Corrections, e-mail exchange with Vera, Washington, DC, March 12, 2015.

85. For information on Pennsylvania, see Samantha Melamed, January 8, 2015, http:/articles.philly.com/2015-01-08/news/57797425_1_solitary-confinement-illness-inmates. For information on New York State, see Benjamin Weiser, February 19, 2014, http://www.nytimes. com/2014/02/20/nyregion/new-york-state-agrees-to-big-changes-in-how-prisons-discipline-inmates.html?ref=solitaryconfinement. Despite California's agreement in 2012, the state continues to house disabled prisoners in segregation units. A federal judge ordered the state to suspend this practice in February 2015. Paige St. John, "Federal Judge Orders California to Stop Isolation Housing of Disabled Inmates," *Los Angeles Times,* February 3, 2015. For New York City's new policy, see endnote 9.

86. Alaska Delinquency Rule 13 (Oct. 15, 2012); Me. Rev. Stat. tit. 34-A § 3032 (5) (2006).

87. Daniel P. Mears and William D. Bales, "Supermax Incarceration and Recidivism," *Criminology* 47, no. 4, 2009:1135.

88. U.S. Government Accountability Office (GAO), 2013, p. 32.

89. Calculating costs from 2003, see Mears, 2006, p. 26.

90. For information on California, see Keramet A. Reiter, "Parole, Snitch, or Die: California's Supermax Prisons & Prisoners, 1987–2007," *Punishment and Society,* 14 (2012): 552-553. For information on Texas, see American Civil Liberties Union of Texas, 2015, p. 2.

91. Legislative Program Review and Investigations Committee, *Recidivism in Connecticut* (2001), http://www.ct.gov/opm/lib/opm/cjppd/cjresearch/recidivismstudy/2001recidivisminconnecticut.pdf.

92. Mears and Bales, 2009, p. 1151. The study found no effect of supermax incarceration on recidivism in general, but did find that supermax incarceration was associated with an increase in violent recidivism. Ibid, p. 1154.

93. Maureen L. O'Keefe, Analysis of Colorado's *Administrative Segregation* (Colorado Springs, Colorado: Colorado Department of Corrections, 2005), iii, 25. This study of incarcerated people held in segregated housing between 1995 and 2003 did not match incarcerated people (for example on past offending record, current offense, behavior while incarcerated) held in segregated housing with incarcerated people held in the general population.

94. One study shows that incarcerated people who are released from segregated housing directly to the community reoffend more quickly and at higher rates than those who spent at least three months back in the general prison population before their return to the community. See David Lovell, L. Clark Johnson, and Kevin C. Cain, "Recidivism of Supermax Prisoners in Washington State," *Crime and Delinquency* 53 no. 4 (2007): 649-650. However, a different study found no evidence that the timing of the supermax experience influenced recidivism, see Mears and Bales, 2009, p. 1154.

95. Kellie Wasco, deputy director, Colorado Department of Corrections, e-mail exchange with Vera, Washington, DC, April 17, 2015. Colorado Department of Corrections has not released any incarcerated person from administrative segregation or restrictive housing maximum security status directly to the community since May 2014. See Office of Planning and Analysis Prison Operations, Colorado Department of Corrections (CDOC), 2015, p. 8.

96. Gregg Marcantel, secretary, New Mexico Corrections Department, e-mail exchange with Vera, Washington, DC, March 25, 2015.

97. See *In re Medley,* 134 US 160, 168 (1890), per Mr. Justice Miller.

The Vera Institute of Justice's essential purpose is to help to change social policies and improve justice systems that ensure fairness, promote safety, and strengthen communities. In an effort to promote this vision, the Institute studies the problems that impede dignity and justice; attempts solutions that are transformative and achievable and harness the power of evidence to drive effective policy and practice.

William Daly

 **NO**

Segregation: A Necessary Evil

Though research is still needed on the topic of segregation, meeting present needs takes precedence

In recent years, due to the extensive construction and use of maximum security facilities, the topics of solitary confinement and segregation, both long- and short-term, have been brought front and center not only by those in the field of corrections but increasingly among professions such as behavioral health, academic scholars, and researchers. Such confinement has been described as a "necessary evil" of correctional administrators. Current research by academics and researchers may be a bit austere and premature to argue against the use of such confinement.

What Is "Super Max"?

"Over the last two decades, super-maximum custody (or 'super max') prisons have become increasingly common throughout the American correctional landscape."[1] By many standards, the United States has become the Mecca of maximum security prisons, with approximately 60 such classified facilities. It is important to note that such solitary confinement is not unusual and has been around since the early years of prisons. The practice's roots date back to the first forms of American incarceration, Eastern State Penitentiary in Pennsylvania being one of the first.[2]

It's evident that there is no accurate representation of what occurs behind the walls of our nation's jails and prisons. Most public perceptions of super max prisons, jails, and local lockups are illustrated on television and in movies. Nearly all of these secure facilities are run by the individual states in the union.

An appropriate definition of those in need of super max, segregation, and/or isolation today are those who are recalcitrant: those who require a single, high-security facility to create greater levels of order throughout the systems in which they are housed.[3] It can be further defined as a free-standing facility, or a distinct unit within a facility, that provides control of inmates who are designated as violent and disruptive, a threat to safety and security, and/or whose behavior needs to be controlled by separation, restricted movement, and limited access to staff and inmates.[4]

Some additional requirements may also include 23-hour lockdown, single-cell housing, no contact, in-cell feeding, tight and restricted movement, limited or no opportunities for educational or vocational training, and constant video surveillance. These requirements may also apply to individual facility punitive segregation units within a facility, not necessarily classified as super max, but which operate under the same premise. These are typically referred to as the SHU (special housing unit), SMU (special management unit), and other comparable names often found at many facilities in this country.

Segregation and isolation have been around for years; the extended use is just the next evolution of adjudicating punishment for those deviants who cannot and/or will not comply with prison regulations, the "end of the line" for the "worst of the worst."[5]

For those not in the field of corrections, the bleak and disturbing images described above may pale in comparison to the research of academic scholars and behavioral health professionals who go much deeper into effects that segregated isolation may have on inmates, specifically from the psychological vantage point. Although the staunchest opponents of jails and prisons generally would not object to the main theory of controlling those in custody, what appears to differentiate practitioners and those "outside looking in" is the methods correctional administrators employ to determine who should or should not be classified in such segregation/isolation units. Questions have been raised about retribution, rehabilitation, incapacitation, and deterrence having lost their effectiveness and may instead create inadvertent consequences.

Why It's Used

Correctional administrators manage such facilities and methods of confinement to address their immediate management obligations of institution security and that which hampers the systematic operations of their respective facilities. They are living in the immediate present, using their knowledge, skills, and abilities to navigate not only their own worlds but responding to political calls for action by those external to their venue.

The use and necessity of such methods of confinement may be considered subjective to each individual jurisdiction and institution. However, those looking in from the outside are arguably concerned with the effectiveness, costs, and unintended consequences of these conditions.

In the last several years, concerns regarding isolation tactics have been raised by correctional professionals. One of the unintended consequences regarding segregation and long- and short-term isolation can lead to social withdrawal. Long-term stays in isolation have the potential for ominous destructive precipitation of various forms of psychopathology.[6] These conditions often result in exacerbated feelings of rage and resentment, which then exacerbates the already tough situation faced by corrections personnel.

However, a more recent study by the National Institute of Justice (NIJ) examined the psychological effects of solitary confinement in corrections and showed that the mental health of most inmates in isolation did not decline during the course of the year, contrary to the findings of previous reports and studies.[7]

So what is the correctional administrator to do? How do they resolve the dilemma of controlling violent, unruly, and disruptive inmates in the best interest of the facility? Research often outlines deficiencies but falls short in identifying solutions, which is what's needed by correctional administrators.

Working Together

Jails and prisons are the custodial part of the judicial system, relatively limited in resources and yet burdened with the responsibility of controlling a commonly violent environment inhabited with society's deviants. They are expected to resolve the social ills of those who come through its doors. Society and the judicial system cannot be dependent upon jails and prisons to be "de facto" mental hospitals, education systems, and social service departments for those criminal and deviant.

Yet administrators are confronted with such challenges both internally and externally each and every day.

There is remarkably little research that exists for how system-wide order and segregation/isolation is related or codependent upon each other.[8] Those who have only devoted a "minute of time" inside our nation's jails, using very small samples of inmates, not only contest but ridicule the work done by correctional administrators instead of working with them. This is important since critics often disbelieve and/or question the validity of practitioner claims.

The often whimsical and broad descriptions of the use of these segregation units and facilities fail to resolve what could contain legitimate cooperation and concerns on both sides. But let us not dismiss the correctional administrator's necessity for flexibility and autonomy to expeditiously and instantaneously manage an explosive backdrop.

Administrators need to be proactive in controlling situations, rather than waiting to respond after lives are in danger. This may include segregation and isolation methods. The use of the dispersion model, which dictates inmates being dispersed across several locations within a department, is a preferred method used by correctional facilities to control problem inmates. Others may use single locations within a building to isolate those who are disruptive.

As a whole, segregation is used to isolate those that have been deemed disruptive and behavior which is egregious. Is there misuse? Surely. But for opponents to cherry pick a few instances and broadly paint the use of segregation units in negative light is not wise either.

The authority of classification, discipline, and due process is that of correctional administrators. Work undoubtedly needs to be done for a more consistent use of segregation and isolation, but for some to suggest that it is based upon "flimsy" evidence, weak justifications, and lack of due process is a flawed argument.

This does not imply there should be a discounting of scholarly or professional behavioral research. But there may be some disconnect between research and practical theory, as there is with all professions and academia. What needs to be understood is correctional administrators are faced with an ever-growing population of violent deviants, mentally ill, and various other social issues that are transported from society's communities to inside the walls of jails, prisons and local lockups.

Increasing pressure to manage budgets and reduce fiscal spending, all while maintaining a safe and secure environment for staff and inmates alike, should not be a vindication, but is reality. Because super max and segregation facilities are by nature restrictive, there is no doubt they will be subject to scrutiny, challenges, and lawsuits by external groups and organizations as well as inmates.

There is a need to encourage research and collaboration between those in the field of corrections and those outside to ensure the decision-making process is sound, applicable, lawful, and does not cause further damage or result in the corrections profession moving backward. Practitioners require relevant research and should be open to new theories, while researchers need to be open to solving relevant and practical issues that are easily accessible and understandable to correctional administrators.

The ability to precipitously manage a disruptive, volatile, and violent environment is not executed flippantly and cannot be controlled by those who do not walk in the shoes of the men and women in this profession. The jail and/or prison setting will never be a picturesque place and those of us in this field will persevere, scrutinize, and observe ways to perfect upon our current state of operations.

It is clear, a difference in opinion is present on the use of super max, segregation, and isolation facilities; however, since little research is available and daily operational needs are ever present, the utilization of such facilities will be the "necessary evil" until more studies and alternatives can be flushed out.

References

1. Daniel P. Mears and Michael D. Reisig, The theory and practice of supermax prisons Punishment & Society. January 2006, 8: 33-57, doi:10.1177/1462474506059139

2. Daniel P. Mears and Michael D. Reisig, The theory and practice of supermax prisons Punishment & Society. January 2006, 8: 33-57, doi:10.1177/1462474506059139

3. Daniel P. Mears and Michael D. Reisig, The theory and practice of supermax prisons Punishment & Society. January 2006, 8: 33-57, doi:10.1177/1462474506059139

4. Henningsen, R. J., Corrections Management. Quarterly Volume 3, Issue 2, Spring 1999, pp. 53 to 59.

5. Daniel P. Mears and Michael D. Reisig, The theory and practice of supermax prisons Punishment & Society. January 2006, 8: 33-57, doi:10.1177/1462474506059139

6. Haney, C., "Infamous Punishment: The psychological Consequences of Isolation," in Latessa, Edward and Holsinger, Alexander *Correctional Contexts: Contemporary and Classical Readings*, 2011

7. Phillip Bulman, *Corrections Today magazine*, American Correctional Association, June/July 2012 p. 58.

8. Daniel P. Mears and Michael D. Reisig, The theory and practice of supermax prisons Punishment & Society. January 2006, 8: 33-57, doi:10.1177/1462474506059139

WILLIAM DALY has worked in U.S. corrections for over 25 years. He is currently the Director at the Salt River Department of Corrections in Scottsdale, Arizona. He advocates for the continuation of solitary confinement and contends that it is needed for correctional officers to do their jobs and keep their facilities safe.

EXPLORING THE ISSUE

Does the Use of Solitary Confinement or "Administrative Segregation" in U.S. Correctional Facilities Constitute Cruel and Unusual Punishment?

Critical Thinking and Reflection

1. What was the "hands off" doctrine used by U.S. Courts until the 1960s and 1970s?
2. How did the U.S. Supreme Court's decisions in *Estelle v. Gamble* and *Hutto v. Finney* affect the medical treatment of inmates?
3. What are the several possible reasons for the increased use of solitary confinement in U.S. correctional facilities in recent years?
4. Is solitary confinement a "necessary evil" in U.S. correctional facilities?
5. What is Amnesty International's position on the use of solitary confinement in U.S. federal prisons?
6. What are the differences between the financial costs of confining inmates in solitary confinement as opposed to traditional corrections alternatives?

Is There Common Ground?

The Eighth Amendment's Cruel and Unusual Punishment Clause has a long history. After reviewing the U.S. Supreme Court's precedents in this area, several important principles begin to emerge. First, punishments that are physically barbarous will not be tolerated by U.S. courts. For example, whipping prison inmates, as illustrated in the movie *Cool Hand Luke*, discussed earlier in this issue would no longer be tolerated in American correctional institutions. That is because the Eighth Amendment embraces "broad and idealistic concepts of dignity, civilized standards, humanity, and decency." Moreover, torture and other such barbaric practices are inconsistent with "the evolving standards of decency that mark the progress of a maturing society," and "involve the unnecessary and wanton infliction of pain." *Estelle v. Gamble*, 429 U.S. 97, 103 (1976).

Do you believe that the use of solitary confinement in U.S. correctional facilities violates the principles outlined above? Amnesty International, an organization with a global movement of more than three million supporters, members, and activists in more than 150 countries, who campaign to end grave abuses of human rights, believes that solitary confinement does violate these principles. In

its 2014 report titled, *Entombed: Isolation in the U.S. Federal Prison System*, it states:

> The USA stands virtually alone in the world in incarcerating thousands of prisoners in long-term or indefinite solitary confinement defined by the UN Special Rapporteur on Torture and other Cruel, Inhuman or Degrading Treatment or Punishment as the 'the physical and social isolation of individuals who are confined to their cells for 22 to 24 hours a day. More than 40 US states are believed to operate 'super-maximum security" units or prisons, collectively housing at least 25,000 prisoners. This number does not include the many thousands of other prisoners serving shorter periods in punishment or administrative segregation cells—estimated to be 80,000 on any given day.(2) [Citations omitted].

Moreover, the report asserts that the USA has ratified and approved the United Nations (UN) Convention against Torture and other Cruel, Inhuman or Degrading treatment or Punishment and the International Covenant on Civil and Political Rights, both of which affirm the absolute prohibition of torture and other cruel, inhuman or degrading treatment or punishment (34). The Report concludes with the following recommendations, among others, for the use of isolated confinement:

- All institutions should ensure that solitary or isolated confinement, whether imposed for administrative or disciplinary purposes, is imposed only as a last resort and for the minimum period possible.
- No prisoner should be held in prolonged or indefinite isolation.
- All prisoners in segregated confinement should have access to meaningful therapeutic, educational and rehabilitation programs.
- Conditional in all segregation facilities should provide minimum standards for a humane environment so that prisoners even in the most restrictive settings have adequate facilities for outdoor exercise, access to natural light, and meaningful human contact both within the facility and with the outside world.
- Children—that is those under 18—should never be held in solitary confinement. All youthful offenders should receive treatment appropriate to their age and developmental needs with the primary goal of rehabilitation as required under international standards.
- No prisoner with mental illness, mental disabilities or severe behavioral disorders or who is identified as being at risk of developing these conditions should be held in solitary or isolated cellular confinement.
- There should be regular, external review of conditions in segregation facilities and of the procedures and operation of such facilities. (38).

Do you agree that U.S. correctional facilities should follow these recommendations? It is not surprising that these standards and recommendations are consistent with the Vera Institute's positions, outlined in the first selection in this section. Perhaps somewhat more interesting, however, would be the reactions of correctional officials and other practitioners who have to work in our nation's prison systems on a daily basis. In the second selection, William Daly, himself a correctional administrator, asserts that administrative segregation is a reasonable response to inmates who cannot be controlled effectively in other ways. Prisoners who are violent or otherwise dangerous need to be incapacitated until they are capable of functioning in a less highly controlled environment.

Which, in your opinion, should be the priority: The humane treatment of inmates, or institutional control of potentially dangerous individuals? This controversy has confronted American correctional systems for most of our history.

In 1829, one of the earliest prisons in the United States was constructed in Cherry Hill, Pennsylvania. The Eastern Pennsylvania prison was sponsored by American Quakers. The *Pennsylvania System* as it came to be known utilized a system of solitary confinement and labor for all prisoners. The Quakers believed that such a system would best contribute to the rehabilitation of all prisoners, without utilizing the draconian forms of physical punishment that were prevalent at the time. Not unlike many modern correctional facilities using solitary confinement, prisoners spent approximately 23 hours per day in their cell and their opportunities to communicate with other inmates was closely restricted. One of the central problems with this approach was that it required individual cells and was therefore expensive. It was also widely regarded as a cause of mental illness among the prisoners so confined. Is it surprising, then, that the same criticisms of this practice have resurfaced today?

In these times of fiscal austerity and budgetary constraints the most significant factor that may ultimately lead to a decline in the use of solitary confinement in U.S. correctional systems may be the cost of this practice. As the Vera Institute of Justice has observed, in 2013, the daily cost of confining an inmate in a federal solitary confinement facility was $216.12 compared to $85.74 to house inmates in a traditional federal penitentiary. Can we as a society really afford to continue this practice when our nation's infrastructure is crumbling? In any case it will be interesting to watch what happens to solitary confinement as a corrections practice in the future.

Additional Resources

Marilyn D. McShane and Franklin P. Williams III, *The Encyclopedia of American Prisons* (Garland, 1996).

Sue Titus Reid, *Crime & Criminology* (McGraw-Hill, 2006).

Mikel-Meredith Weidman, "The Culture of Judicial Deference and the Problem of Supermax Prisons," *UCLA Law Review*. (vol. 51, no. 5, 2004).

Laurence H. Tribe, *Constitutional Choices* (Harvard University Press, 1986).

Internet References . . .

American Friends Services Committee
(AFSC), "Solitary Confinement Facts."

www.afsc.org/resource/solitaryconfinement
-facts.com

Erica Goode, "Solitary Confinement:
Punished for Life." *New York Times—
Health*, August 3, 2015.

www.nytimes.com/2015/08/04

Public Broadcasting System (PBS), "What
Does Solitary Confinement Do to Your
Mind?" April 22, 2015.

www.pbs.org/wgbh/frontline

Selected, Edited, and with Issue Framing Material by:
Thomas J. Hickey, *State University of New York at Cobleskill*

ISSUE

Do "Three-Strikes" Sentencing Laws and Other "Get Tough" Approaches to Crime Really Work?

YES: William B. Mateja, "Sentencing Reform, the Federal Criminal Justice System, and Judicial and Prosecutorial Discretion," *Notre Dame Journal of Law, Ethics & Public Policy* (2004)

NO: American Civil Liberties Union (ACLU), "10 Reasons to Oppose '3 Strikes, You're Out,'" American Civil Liberties Union (2015)

Learning Outcomes

After reading this issue, you will be able to:

- Discuss whether increasing the severity of criminal sentences is likely to reduce crime in the United States.
- Discuss the incapacitation and deterrence rationales for sentencing.
- Discuss the retribution and rehabilitation rationales for sentencing.
- Discuss the financial costs of keeping persons incarcerated in state and federal prisons.
- Discuss whether "three-strikes sentencing laws" have worked in the United States.
- Discuss the "proportionality" principle as it relates to sentencing practices.
- Discuss whether the principle of "social utility" is served by contemporary U.S. sentencing policies.
- Discuss the U.S. Supreme Court's holding in *Johnson v. United States*.
- Discuss whether the United States has become a safer place because of stringent sentencing policies.

ISSUE SUMMARY

YES: Former U.S. Deputy Attorney General William B. Majeta contends that the current 30-year low in violent crime is not an accident. Reducing crime means reducing the number of criminals on the streets, which requires consistent, tough penalties that incapacitate the dangerous and deter those considering the commission of a crime.

NO: The American Civil Liberties Union (ACLU) argues that our nation's crime control policies for the past 20 years have been based on the belief that harsh sentences deter people from committing crimes. But today, with more than one million people behind bars, and state budgets depleted by the huge costs of prison construction, we are no safer than before. New approaches to the problem of crime are needed, but instead, our political leaders keep serving up the same old punitive strategies.

What are the reasons for punishing those who break society's rules? This question has had a number of sometimes contrasting answers at different times in our history. Traditional rationales have included: retribution (sometimes termed vengeance, or revenge), deterrence, incapacitation,

and at times, rehabilitation of the offender. The influence of any single rationale has largely reflected our society's dominant political climate at any given time.

For example, at times during the twentieth century criminologists and liberal politicians emphasized rehabilitation. For a number of reasons, including increasing violent and property crime rates, a shrinking economy, and the election in 1980 of a conservative president, Ronald Reagan, there was a decisive paradigmatic shift.

"Lock them up, and throw away the key," is a common mantra, because criminals deserve to be punished, to deter others from committing similar crimes, and to get bad people off the streets. The environmental correlates of crime and social programs to address these issues have largely been ignored by some of these new classical criminologists. Factors such as racism, social inequality, blocked opportunities to succeed, lack of education, poverty, and other social correlates of crime, which imply a need for rehabilitation (such as "head start" or job training programs), were largely abandoned in favor of the more punitive approach that "three-strikes" sentencing laws embrace.

Proponents of "three-strikes" sentencing laws contend that if an offender has already committed two felonies, what can be more rational than making sure that he gets a *sentencing enhancement*—perhaps even a life sentence for his third crime. Some research has shown that a small group of hardened offenders, if removed from society, would save taxpayers hundreds of thousands of dollars per year. A life sentence would clearly incapacitate such individuals. To continue the logic, would-be criminals are deterred from committing a third offense, and general deterrence would result from others being afraid of being imprisoned for life under such laws.

There are a few different problems with these arguments, however. First, they presume that crime is "rational." Scores of research studies have demonstrated that many crimes, such as domestic assaults and other types of violent crime, are largely impulsive and are not generally a product of a rational thought process.

Second, in some jurisdictions an offender's third "strike" could result from a conviction for a nonviolent property crime, such as shoplifting. Basic principles of fairness and *proportionality* should require that, consistent with the theories of the early Classical criminologists in the late 1700s, such as Cesare Beccaria and Jeremy Bentham, "the punishment should fit the crime." Is it fair to impose a long term of incarceration on an offender for a relatively minor offense? The U.S. Supreme Court has upheld California's three-strikes law against a challenge that it was grossly disproportionate to the severity of the crime committed in *Ewing v. California,* 538 U.S. 11 (2003). It held that because these statutes may serve a state's legitimate goal of deterring and incapacitating recidivist offenders they do not violate the Eighth Amendment's Cruel and Unusual Punishment Clause. In 2015, however, the Supreme Court considered a challenge to a federal three-strikes law, the Armed Career Criminal Act (ACCA).

In *Johnson v. United States*, 576 U.S.___(2015), Justice Scalia held that the statute was unconstitutionally vague and overturned Johnson's enhanced sentence for possession of a sawed-off shotgun.

Johnson may indicate that U.S. Courts are becoming more skeptical about the impact of three-strikes laws on criminal defendants and on society. It seems plausible to speculate that they are effectively asking whether these laws satisfy the principle of *social utility* considered in the Introduction to this volume. This doctrine requires that all social policies must represent "the greatest good for the greatest number" of people. Does it make sense to warehouse nonviolent criminals in our nation's prisons at a cost that may exceed $60,000 per year in some states when initiatives such as proper funding for "Head Start" educational programs, or community-based correctional alternatives are far more effective at reducing crime and costs? These are important philosophical and pragmatic issues that social policymakers must consider, especially in challenging financial times amid budgetary constraints.

The authors of the YES and NO selections in this issue would provide very different answers to the questions posed above. Former U.S. Deputy Attorney General William B. Majeta contends that the current 30-year low in violent crime is not an accident. Reducing crime means reducing the number of criminals on the streets, which requires consistent, tough penalties that incapacitate the dangerous and deter those considering the commission of a crime. States Majeta:

> The American people, through their elected representatives, through initiatives, and other means, are speaking clearly on the sentencing and corrections policy and rejecting maximum [judicial] sentencing discretion. They are doing so to further two important principles. The first is that similar crimes should be punished similarly. The second is that it is better to protect the innocent by imposing long imprisonment terms on the guilty than to risk public safety by gambling too soon on a "rehabilitated" offender. (528).

The American Civil Liberties Union (ACLU) argues that our nation's crime control policies for the past 20 years have been based on the belief that harsh sentences deter people from committing crimes. But today, with no less than one million people behind bars, and state budgets depleted by the huge costs of prison construction, we are no safer than before. New approaches to the problem of crime are needed, but instead, our political leaders keep serving up the same old punitive strategies. They assert:

The "3 Strikes" proposals are based on the mistaken belief that focusing on an offender after the crime has been committed, which harsh sentencing schemes do, will lead to a reduction in the crime rate. But if 34 million serious crimes are committed each year in the U.S., and only three million result in arrest, something must be done to prevent those crimes from happening in the first place. Today, the U.S. has the dubious distinction of leading the industrialized world in per capita prison population, with more than one million men and women behind bars. . . . Only when we begin to deal with the conditions that cause so many of our young people to turn to crime and violence will we begin to realize a less crime ridden society. (7).

Do you agree initially with Deputy Attorney General Majeta, or with the American Civil Liberties Union? Do you believe that "three-strikes" laws and other "get tough" approaches to crime really work? Or, are there better and less costly alternatives to incarceration? These are intriguing questions that will have a highly significant impact on corrections policy and state's budgets in the future.

YES ⤶

William B. Mateja

Sentencing Reform, the Federal Criminal Justice System, and Judicial and Prosecutorial Discretion[1]

Introduction

The United States is experiencing a thirty-year low in crime. After years of rising and unprecedented levels of violent and non-violent crime, sweeping and historic change took place in our nation's sentencing and corrections policy beginning in the 1970s. The sentencing system in place before these changes was marked by three key elements. First, the primary goal underlying sentencing and corrections was that a defendant's sentence should foster the defendant's own rehabilitation. Second, determining the correct sentence to fulfill this rehabilitative purpose was left almost entirely to the discretion of an individual sentencing judge. And third, the sentence meted out by that judge and announced to the public was subject to being undermined at some later point by an administrative parole authority, if and when that authority determined the defendant was rehabilitated. All three of these elements have now been rejected at the federal level and by many states, and we are now reaping the benefits of that change.

The current thirty-year low in violent crime is not an accident. Reducing crime means reducing the number of criminals on the streets. Reducing the number of criminals on the streets in turn requires consistent, tough penalties that incapacitate the dangerous and deter those considering the commission of a crime. The nation's sentencing and corrections policy now, more than at any time in the last century, has resulted in consistent and tough penalties and, as such, has not only helped to reduce crime but has also made our nation's criminal justice system far less arbitrary and much more fair.

The Bureau of Justice Statistics (BJS) reported that the rate of every major violent and property crime measured by BJS declined from 1993 through 2002. Rape and sexual assault were down 56%; robbery down 63%; aggravated assault down 64%; simple assault down 47%;

household burglary down 52%; motor vehicle theft down 53%; and property theft down 49%. The decline in violent victimization has been experienced by persons in every demographic category considered—gender, race, national origin, and household income. If 1993 rates of crime had occurred in each year since that time, in the last decade, 68,000 more Americans would have murdered, 1.4 million more Americans would have been raped or sexually assaulted, 3.8 million more Americans would have been robbed, and 22 million more Americans would have been physically assaulted. Nearly 27½ million violent crimes were not committed in the last decade because of the reduction in crime. The Department of Justice welcomes the chance to speak for all those who would have been victimized, but for these sweeping changes in our nation's sentencing and corrections policy.

Although most prisoners are held in state prison facilities, when we examine combined federal and state prison populations nationwide, we find that about eight in ten prisoners have a prior conviction history and about two in three prisoners have a current or past history of convictions for a violent offense. Combining these two sentencing criteria—repeat offending and violence—accounts for 93% of the prison population nationwide. In other words, the present system is working. It is incapacitating those offenders who need to be incapacitated.

Tonight I'd like to examine the changes in the nation's sentencing policy over the last two decades, showing why sentencing reform at the federal level is a model to be replicated. I want to address how the key elements of federal sentencing reform—mandatory minimum sentences, truth-in-sentencing, limited judicial discretion, and overall consistency-in-sentencing—are critical to crime reduction and to fundamental fairness. I also want to take a special look at mandatory minimum sentencing statutes to rebut the myths that they are somehow ineffective and unjust.

Mateja, William B., "Sentencing Reform, The Federal Criminal Justice System, and Judicial and Prosecutorial Discreation," *Notre Dame Journal of Law, Ethics and Public Policy,* 18(2) January 1, 2004. Copyright © 2004 William B. Mateja. Used with permission of the author.

In sum, the Department of Justice believes tough penalties demonstrate that there are real consequences for predatory and lawless behavior. We are now in an era where revolving-door injustice is largely over and real consequences for crime are the order of the day. We are committed to treating every crime seriously, every criminal justly, and every victim compassionately, and we believe the nation's sentencing and corrections policy should embody these values.

I. Sentencing Reform, the Federal Criminal Justice System, and Judicial and Prosecutorial Discretion

A. The Advent of Sentencing Reform

For many years, beginning in the 1960s, this country has been struggling with the profound problem of crime. The available statistics show that while crime rates fluctuate over time, a historic increase in crime began in the 1960s. Since that time, federal, state, and local governments, in order to fulfill their first responsibility to protect the well-being of their citizens, have been working hard to develop and implement various strategies to combat crime. For most of this country's history, effective crime policy meant strong and ample criminal laws, powerful investigative agencies, and vigorous prosecutions. In the late 1970s and early 1980s, however, policymakers began to realize that this strategy was not enough; that there was a gaping hole in the nation's criminal justice system, namely sentencing policy, that was standing in the way of effective anti-crime policy. Many legislators saw the need to close this gap; to put in place a more effective sentencing policy so that all parts of the criminal justice system—legislation, investigation, prosecution, sentencing, and corrections—would work together in order to achieve, through a more effective national strategy of crime control, a safer and more secure society for all citizens.

The system of sentencing in place before the sentencing reform of the 1980s and 90s was almost entirely discretionary. Choosing a sentence for those convicted of most felony offenses was left to the unfettered discretion of judges and essentially was ungoverned by law. Beyond a statutory direction limiting the maximum sentence, judges had the discretion to decide what factors in a case were relevant to sentencing and how such factors should be weighed.

Moreover, the undergirding principle of that sentencing system was rehabilitation. While it was acknowledged that there were four purposes of sentencing—rehabilitation, deterrence, incapacitation, and just punishment—the agreed-upon primary purpose of sentencing for many decades was rehabilitation. The hope was that an offender would go to a penitentiary to do penance, and to contemplate his crime and to take advantage of available services for a period of time, sometimes determined in advance and sometimes not. The hope was that when the offender was rehabilitated—ready to reenter the community—the offender would be paroled back into the community.

By the 1970s, however, serious questions were being raised about whether rehabilitation was working and whether a wholly discretionary sentencing system was fair. Research conducted in the mid-1960s through the early 1970s showed no link between rehabilitation program involvement and any decrease in recidivism, a conclusion that eviscerated the premise that parole boards could effectively assess the rehabilitative potential of inmates. This research led to most states significantly reducing discretionary sentencing and the role of parole boards.

At the federal level, in 1984, Congress found the discretionary sentencing system too often resulted in unacceptable outcomes. Studies showed that judges used their largely unlimited discretion in sentencing decisions to reach inconsistent results. The legislative history leading up to the passage of federal sentencing reform documents clearly show that similar offenders were being treated in dramatically different ways depending on the presiding judge. Such disparity was not surprising given varying judicial backgrounds and philosophies and the strong disagreement among judges on the purposes of sentencing. The problem was exacerbated by the existence of the parole system, under which some incarcerated offenders served all of their sentences and others as little as one-third. With sentencing authority divided between the judge and the parole authority, some judges attempted to craft sentences to anticipate the decisions of the parole commission, while others did not. And, of course, a substantial percentage of offenders were never subject to parole because they were not sentenced to prison at all. The net result of the entire process was that, with disturbing regularity, similar offenders who committed similar offenses received and served substantially *different* sentences. And on many occasions, the sentences simply were not sufficiently punitive to serve the purposes of just punishment of the offender and deterrence of others.

Congress, recognizing that the inconsistency and uncertainty in federal sentencing practices were incompatible with effective crime control, declared that "the existing Federal system lacks the sureness that criminal justice must provide if it is to retain the confidence of

American society and if it is to be an effective deterrent against crime." Congress further concluded that the evidence that rehabilitation was working was sketchy, at best.

A body of research was also emerging that suggested that a very small number of criminals was responsible for a huge proportion of crimes committed. The pioneering work of Marvin Wolfgang and others began to document this phenomenon, which led many in Congress and across the country to consider new crime fighting strategies; strategies aimed at incapacitating that small number of criminals for long periods of time to promote greater public safety.

B. Sentencing Reform in the Federal Criminal Justice System

In 1984, in an attempt to address the shortcomings in the criminal justice system created by the then-existing sentencing policy, Congress passed the Sentencing Reform Act as part of the Comprehensive Crime Control Act of 1984. The Act created the United States Sentencing Commission and mandated that the Commission design sentencing guidelines to bring consistency and certainty to federal sentencing law. It rejected rehabilitation as a purpose of sentencing. The Sentencing Reform Act was intended, in the words of the Senate Report, to bring about "sweeping" reform. Both the statute creating the Commission and its legislative history made clear that the guidelines Congress envisioned were to be detailed and comprehensive.

At around this same time, Congress also created mandatory minimum sentencing statutes to work in conjunction with federal sentencing guidelines. These statutes were reserved for repeat offenders or for particularly heinous or dangerous crimes—first degree murder would carry a mandatory life sentence; high level narcotics trafficking would carry a mandatory ten-year sentence; and using a gun in the commission of a violent crime would carry a mandatory five-year sentence.

The result of these congressional enactments is that today's federal sentencing system—involving both congressionally mandated mandatory minimum statutes and sentencing guidelines promulgated by a sentencing commission—is very different from the inconsistent and uncertain system in place before the Sentencing Reform Act. It is a model system, structured and tough. Under the existing statutes and guidelines, sentencing courts are directed to evaluate specific enumerated factors grounded in experience and reason and to engage in appropriate fact-finding to determine whether these factors are present in each case. If they are, the statutes and guidelines provide the court with directions as to how these factors

ordinarily should contribute to the sentence. As Justice Stephen Breyer, one of the architects of federal sentencing reform, has said, this structure provides fairness, predictability, and appropriate uniformity. In addition, the structure allows for the targeting of longer sentences to espe cially dangerous or recidivist criminals.

The structure, though, is only part of the story. Federal statutes and guidelines substantively are tough, providing in most cases appropriately punitive sentences for violent, predatory, and other dangerous offenders, sentences substantially longer than those meted out before sentencing reform. Studies have shown, for example, that since sentencing reform at the federal level, sentences for drug and violent offenders have increased substantially. In addition, penalties have increased for white collar offenses and civil rights crimes.

Importantly, this new sentencing system also brings the critical element of honesty to the sentencing process by abolishing early release through parole. Now, the sentence meted out by the court is what the defendant must serve with only a very small percentage of the sentence available for "good time" credit. We believe this system of sentencing is a vast improvement over the system that existed prior to the Sentencing Reform Act.

C. Judicial and Prosecutorial Discretion

Within this structured federal system, however, there remains significant and appropriate judicial discretion. For example, judges are relied upon to determine whether a defendant has played an aggravating or mitigating role in a crime, the extent to which accomplice liability will attach, and whether, in certain circumstances, to depart, or in other words, move away from the narrow parameters of uniformity, either up or down, in unusual cases. In the latter circumstance, the reason for the departure must be stated clearly and the sentence and departure are subject to appellate review. To conform with the Sentencing Reform Act, departures are to be rare so that defendants with similar criminal histories who commit similar acts are treated the same way in all but the most extraordinary cases.

Moreover, once a sentencing range is determined under the sentencing guidelines, the sentencing judge is given a significant range within which to select a final sentence. In most circumstances, the top of the range provides for imprisonment that is 25% higher than the bottom of the range. The current sentencing law thus ensures a general rule of firm, fair, uniform sentences, while permitting case-specific adjustments by the sentencing judge to account for the nuances of the individual offense and to account for the truly exceptional case. We think this system provides the right balance between appropriate uniformity in sentencing and sufficient judicial discretion to account for case-specific factors and the unusual case.

Just as we believe the sentence for a particular crime should not hinge on the sentencing judge, we also think it should not hinge on the individual prosecutor involved in his case. It is for this reason that the Attorney General recently issued new guidance to federal prosecutors. Like federal judges, federal prosecutors nationwide have an obligation to be fair, consistent, and tough. Federal prosecutors now have guidance to ensure that they charge and pursue the most serious, readily provable offenses supported by the facts in each case. Except in limited, narrow circumstances, victims, as well as their criminal perpetrators, will see the ideal of equal justice under the law made a reality. The new guidelines also require federal prosecutors to pursue hard-hitting sentencing enhancements against hard-core criminals. Repeat offenders, child predators, criminal bosses, drug kingpins, and violent gun criminals will face the toughest charges and spend the most time behind bars.

II. Mandatory Minimum Penalty

A. Generally

Because there has been significant criticism of mandatory minimum statutes—especially at the federal level—we believe it appropriate to address this issue separately here. As stated above, at the federal level, mandatory minimum statutes are generally reserved for the most serious offenses and offenders. The majority of crimes prosecuted in the federal system are not subject to mandatory minimum sentencing statutes; rather, mandatory minimums typically involve the use of a gun in the commission of a crime or the trafficking of significant amounts of illegal drugs. We strongly believe the existing mandatory minimum statutes are both appropriate and good policy. At the same time, we believe the current mandatory minimum laws strike the right balance by allowing nonviolent offenders to escape the statutorily mandated sentences in appropriate circumstances. We take this position for several reasons.

First, in a way sentencing guidelines can't and don't, mandatory minimum statutes provide a level of uniformity and predictability determined by Congress to deter certain types of criminal behavior by clearly forewarning the potential offender and the public at large of the potential consequences of the offense. Second, mandatory

minimum sentences incapacitate dangerous offenders for long periods of time, thereby increasing public safety. And third, mandatory minimum sentences provide an indispensable tool for prosecutors, because they allow, through the use of cooperation agreements, relief for specific defendants who assist in the prosecution of another individual, further enhancing public safety.

B. Drug Cases

In drug cases, mandatory minimum statutes are especially significant. Unlike a bank robbery, for which a witness could be a bank teller or an ordinary citizen, typically in drug cases, especially serious narcotics cases, the only witnesses are other drug traffickers. Drug dealers take pains to do their work away from the prying eyes of law enforcement, and the more sophisticated the drug dealer, the more cautious he is about dealing with those who might be assisting law enforcement. The offer of relief from a mandatory minimum sentence in exchange for truthful testimony and other forms of substantial assistance allows the government to move up the chain of supply, offering the sentence against the lesser dealers to effectively prosecute the more serious drug traffickers—the organizers and the source of supply.

Cooperation agreements also allow for the gathering of the best evidence concerning a trafficking organization—evidence from the inside of the organization. It allows the Government to strip away the secrecy in which narcotics traffickers conduct their business and to obtain the truth. Such cooperation is essential, and our prosecutors use it every day. It is no exaggeration to say that it would be impossible to prosecute drug organizations effectively without cooperation agreements largely made possible by the threat of mandatory minimum sentences.

Nevertheless, while we view mandatory minimums as effective law enforcement tools, we also recognize the need to apply the provisions appropriately and to provide for appropriate exceptions. In 1994, Congress added the so-called "safety valve provision" to federal law to provide for just such exceptions. The safety valve allows the courts to impose a sentence without regard to any mandatory minimum sentence in certain cases. Specifically, the safety valve permits an offender who did not use a fire arm or violence, who is not a leader, manager, organizer, and who does not have a serious criminal history, to be sentenced below the otherwise applicable mandatory minimum. The defendant, in exchange, must truthfully disclose to the prosecutor all of the facts he knows about the case. The safety valve provision is applied thousands of times each year.

C. Gun Cases

Two years ago, President Bush made a commitment, through Project Safe Neighborhoods, to reduce gun crime by getting gun criminals off the streets. In FY 2002 compared to FY 2000, federal gun prosecutions increased by approximately 36%. In FY 2002 compared to FY 2001, the number of persons charged with federal gun offenses rose by over 20%, the largest single-year increase ever recorded. And as prosecutions have risen, the incidence of gun crimes has gone down substantially. There were approximately 130,000 fewer victims of gun crime in 2001–02 than there were in 1999–2000, marking the first two-year period with fewer than a million gun crime victims since 1993. Gun crime has been reduced so dramatically that last year just 7% of violent crimes were committed with a firearm—the lowest number of violent crimes committed with a firearm ever recorded.

Project Safe Neighborhoods—with its emphasis on partnerships between all levels of law enforcement—has contributed significantly to this success. As part of Project Safe Neighborhoods, federal and state prosecutors meet to determine the most appropriate jurisdiction for the prosecution of gun offenses. Particularly for violent crimes involving firearms, the federal system has numerous advantages—mandatory minimum statutes, federal sentencing guidelines, and no parole. The stringent federal gun laws have allowed federal prosecutors to work with their state and local counterparts to attack the problem of violent crime and take violent offenders off the street.

Conclusion

Sentencing and corrections policy reflects moral judgments about the heinousness of crime and those who commit it. Much of the criticism about current sentencing and correction policy, we believe, has stemmed simply from the fact that sentences under mandatory minimum statutes and sentencing guidelines are more consistent and longer than sentences under the fully discretionary pre-guidelines system of sentencing. Those who criticize the current trend in sentencing policy cling to an outdated and largely refuted notion that maximum sentencing discretion will achieve greater justice and at the same time yield lower crime rates.

The American people, through their elected representatives, through initiatives, and other means, are speaking clearly on sentencing and corrections policy and rejecting maximum sentencing discretion. They are doing so to further two important principles. The first is that similar crimes should be punished similarly. The second is that it is better to protect the innocent by imposing long imprisonment terms on the guilty than to risk public safety by gambling too soon on a "rehabilitated" offender. Mandatory minimum statutes, three-strikes laws, and sentencing guidelines are the manifestations of these principles, as is a prison and jail population that has risen above two million people. Most importantly, the falling crime rates are the most obvious manifestation of these principles. People are safer today because of them. And violent crime is down for all racial and ethnic groups measured and for all ages across all income levels in every region of the country. It would be folly and would risk the lives of countless Americans to ignore the experience of the last thirty years.

I want to thank the University of Notre Dame, its Law School, and the *Notre Dame journal of Law, Ethics & Public Policy* for the opportunity to join in this symposium and to address this critically important issue.

Note

1. William B. Mateja was the second speaker at the Symposium on Mandatory Minimums and the Curtailment of Judicial Discretion: Does the Time Fit the Crime?, hosted by the *Notre Dame journal of Law, Ethics & Public Policy* on April 1, 2004. *See also* John S. Martin, Jr., Why Mandatory Minimums Make No Sense, Speech at the Notre Dame Journal of Law, Ethics & Public Policy Symposium on Mandatory Minimums and the Curtailment of Judicial Discretion: Does the Time Fit the Crime? (April 1, 2004), *in* 18 Notre Dame J.L. Ethics & Pub. Pol'y 303, 311 (2004); G. Robert Blakey, Mandatory Minimums: Fine in Principle, Inexcusable When Mindless, Speech at the Notre Dame Journal of Law, Ethics & Public Policy Symposium on Mandatory Minimums and the Curtailment of Judicial Discretion: Does the Time Fit the Crime? (April 1, 2004), *in* 18 Notre Dame J.L. Ethics & Pub. Pol'y 303, 329 (2004).

William J. Mateja is a principal in the Dallas Office of Fish & Richardson, P.C. He has served as Senior Counsel to two U.S. Deputy Attorneys General in Washington, D.C., and has also served as the point person for the President's Corporate Fraud Task Force. He also formerly served as well for the U.S. Justice Department's white collar health care fraud and corporate fraud efforts.

American Civil Liberties Union (ACLU)

 **NO**

10 Reasons to Oppose "3 Strikes, You're Out"

The American public is alarmed about crime, and with good reason. Our crime rate is unacceptably high, and many Americans feel like prisoners in their own homes, afraid to venture out for fear of becoming another statistic.

For more than past 20 years, state and federal crime control policies have been based on the belief that harsh sentencing laws will deter people from committing crimes. But today, with more than one million people behind bars, and state budgets depleted by the huge costs of prison construction, we are no safer than before. New approaches to the problem of crime are needed, but instead, our political leaders keep serving up the same old strategies.

Take the so-called "3 Strikes, You're Out" law, for example. Embraced by state legislators, Congress, and the President himself, this law imposes a mandatory life sentence without parole on offenders convicted of certain crimes. Despite its catchy baseball metaphor, this law is a loser, for the following reasons.

1. "3 Strikes" Is an Old Law Dressed Up in New Clothes

Although its supporters act as if it is something new, "3 Strikes" is really just a variation of an old theme. States have had habitual offender laws and recidivist statutes for years. All of these laws impose stiff penalties, up to and including life sentences, on repeat offenders. The 1987 Federal Sentencing Guidelines and mandatory minimum sentencing laws in most states are also very tough on repeaters. The government may be justified in punishing a repeat offender more severely than a first offender, but "3 Strikes" laws are overkill.

2. "3 Strikes" Laws Won't Deter Most Violent Crimes

Its supporters claim that "3 Strikes" laws will have a deterrent effect on violent crime. But these laws will probably not stop many criminals from committing violent acts. For one thing, most violent crimes are not premeditated. They are committed in anger, in the heat of passion, or under the influence of alcohol. The prospect of a life sentence is not going to stop people who are acting impulsively, without thought to the likely consequences of their actions.

Another reason why repeat offenders do not consider the penalties they face before acting is because they do not anticipate being caught, and they are right. According to the American Bar Association, out of the approximately 34 million serious crimes committed each year in the United States, only 3 million result in arrests.

3. "3 Strikes" Laws Could Lead to an Increase in Violence

Many law enforcement professionals oppose the "3 Strikes" law out of fear that such laws would spur a dramatic increase in violence against police, corrections officers, and the public. A criminal facing the prospect of a mandatory life sentence will be far more likely to resist arrest, to kill witnesses, or to attempt a prison escape. Dave Paul, a corrections officer from Milwaukee, Oregon, wrote in a newspaper article: "Imagine a law enforcement officer trying to arrest a twice-convicted felon who has nothing to lose by using any means necessary to escape. Expect assaults on police and correctional officers to rise precipitously." (*Portland Oregonian,* 3/94). Ironically, these laws may cause more, not less, loss of life.

4. "3 Strikes" Laws Will Clog the Courts

The criminal courts already suffer from serious backlogs. The extraordinarily high arrest rates resulting from the "war on drugs" have placed enormous burdens on prosecutors, defense lawyers and judges, whose caseloads have grown exponentially over the past decade. "Three-strikes" laws will make a bad situation even worse. Faced with a mandatory life sentence, repeat offenders will demand costly and time-consuming trials rather than submit to plea bargaining. Normal felonies resolved by a plea bargain cost $600 to defend, while a full blown criminal trial costs as much as $50,000. Since most of the defendants will be indigent and require public defenders, the expense of their defense will be borne by taxpayers.

5. "3 Strikes" Laws Will Take All Sentencing Discretion Away from Judges

The "3 Strikes" proposals differ from most habitual offender laws in that they make life sentences without parole mandatory. Thus, they tie the hands of judges who have traditionally been responsible for weighing both mitigating and aggravating circumstances before imposing sentence. Judicial discretion in sentencing, which is admired all over the world for treating people as individuals, is one of the hallmarks of our justice system. But the rigid formula imposed by "3 Strikes" renders the role of sentencing judges almost superfluous.

Eliminating the possibility of parole ignores the fact that even the most incorrigible offenders can be transformed while in prison. Countless examples are on record of convicts who have reformed themselves through study, good works, religious conversion, or other efforts during years spent behind bars. Such people ought to deserve a second chance that "3 Strikes" laws make impossible.

6. The Cost of Imprisoning 3-Time Losers for Life Will Be Prohibitively High

The passage of "3 Strikes" laws will lead to a significant increase in the nation's already swollen prison population, at enormous cost to taxpayers. Today, it costs about $20,000 per year to confine a young, physically fit offender. But "3 Strikes" laws would create a huge, geriatric prison population that would be far more expensive to care for. The estimated cost of maintaining an older prisoner is three times more than required for a younger prisoner—about $60,000 per year.

The cost might be worth it if older prisoners represented a danger to society. But experts tell us that age is the most powerful crime reducer. Most crimes are committed by men between the ages of 15 and 24. Only one percent of all serious crimes are committed by people over age 60.

7. "3 Strikes" Will Have a Disproportionate Impact on Minority Offenders

Racial bias in the criminal justice system is rampant. African American men, in particular, are overrepresented in all criminal justice statistics: arrests, victimizations, incarceration, and executions.

This imbalance is largely the result of the "war on drugs." Although studies show that drug use among blacks and whites is comparable, many more blacks than whites are arrested on drug charges. Why? Because the police find it easier to concentrate their forces in inner-city neighborhoods, where drug dealing tends to take place on the streets, than to mount more costly and demanding investigations in the suburbs, where drug dealing generally occurs behind closed doors. Today, one in four young black men is under some form of criminal sanction, be it incarceration, probation, or parole.

Because many of these laws include drug offenses as prior "strikes," more black than white offenders will be subject to life sentences under a "3 Strikes" law.

8. "3 Strikes" Laws Will Impose Life Sentences on Offenders Whose Crimes Don't Warrant Such Harsh Punishment

Although "3 Strikes" sponsors claim that their purpose is to protect society from only the most dangerous felons, many of the "3 Strikes" proposals encompass a broad range of criminal conduct, from rape to minor assaults. In an open letter to the Washington State voters, more than 20 current and former prosecutors urged the public to vote against the "3 Strikes" proposal. To explain why they opposed the law's passage, they described the following scenario:

> An 18-year old high school senior pushes a classmate down to steal his Michael Jordan $150 sneakers—Strike One; he gets out of jail and shoplifts a jacket from the Bon Marche, pushing aside the clerk as he runs out of the store—Strike Two; he gets out of jail, straightens out, and nine years later gets in a fight in a bar and intentionally hits someone, breaking his nose—criminal behavior, to be sure, but hardly the crime of the century, yet it is Strike Three. He is sent to prison for the rest of his life.

9. Let the Punishment Fit the Crime—A Constitutional Principle

Under our system of criminal justice, the punishment must fit the crime. Individuals should not be executed for burglarizing a house nor incarcerated for life for committing relatively minor offenses, even when they commit several of them. This principle, known as "proportionality," is expressed in the Eighth Amendment to the Bill of Rights:

> "Excessive bail shall not be required, nor excessive fines imposed, nor cruel and unusual punishments inflicted."

Many of the "3 Strikes" proposals depart sharply from the proportionality rule by failing to take into consideration the gravity of the offense. Pennsylvania's proposed law treats prostitution and burglary as "strikes" for purposes of imposing a life sentence without parole. Several California proposals provide that the first two felonies must be "violent," but that the third offense can be any felony, even a non-violent crime like petty theft. Such laws offend our constitutional traditions.

10. "3 Strikes" Laws Are Not a Serious Response to Crime

The "3 Strikes" proposals are based on the mistaken belief that focusing on an offender after the crime has been committed, which harsh sentencing schemes do, will lead to a reduction in the crime rate. But if 34 million serious crimes are committed each year in the United States, and only 3 million result in arrest, something must be done to prevent those crimes from happening in the first place.

Today, the United States has the dubious distinction of leading the industrialized world in per capita prison population, with more than one million men and women behind bars. The typical inmate in our prisons is minority, male, young, and uneducated. More than 40 percent of inmates are illiterate; one-third were unemployed when arrested. This profile should tell us something important about the link between crime and lack of opportunity, between crime and lack of hope.

Only when we begin to deal with the conditions that cause so many of our young people to turn to crime and violence will we begin to realize a less crime ridden society.

THE AMERICAN CIVIL LIBERTIES UNION (ACLU) has served, for nearly 100 years as the nation's guarding of liberty, working in courts, legislatures, and communities to defend and preserve the individual rights and liberties that the Constitution and laws of the U.S. guarantee to everyone.

EXPLORING THE ISSUE

Do "Three-Strikes" Sentencing Laws and Other "Get Tough" Approaches to Crime Really Work?

Critical Thinking and Reflection

1. Does increasing the severity of criminal sentences reduce crime in the United States?
2. What are the incapacitation, deterrence, retribution, and rehabilitation rationales for sentencing?
3. What are the financial costs of keeping persons incarcerated in state and federal prisons?
4. Have "three-strikes" sentencing laws been successful the United States?
5. What is the "proportionality" principle as it relates to sentencing practices?
6. What do you think about the Supreme Court's holding in *Johnson v. United States*?
7. Has the United States become a safer place because of stringent sentencing policies?

Is There Common Ground?

Before three-strikes sentencing laws, most states already had provisions for enhancing sentences for those with prior serious convictions. With the passage of three-strikes laws, however, life or lengthy sentences after a third violent felony conviction became mandatory. Moreover, several significant problems with these laws have developed in recent years.

First, the issue of precisely which felonies may constitute a third "strike" has generated substantial controversy. Should only violent crimes qualify as a third strike, or should less-serious felonies, such as forging checks satisfy the statutory requirement? Moreover, if the latter type of offense can be considered a third strike does it make moral and practical sense to sentence someone to a lifetime in prison? Are such policies consistent with the principle of social utility?

Second, the number of persons incarcerated in our federal and state prisons has exploded in the era of three-strikes laws. In 2013, it cost approximately $85.74 per day ($31,295.10 annually) to house an inmate in the general prison population and an astounding $216.12 ($78,883.80 annually) to confine someone in a federal super max prison facility. Similarly, in some states it can cost as much as $65,000 per year to confine an inmate in a state prison. Can we as a society really afford to dedicate such staggering sums to our prison systems when the money is needed to repair our aging infrastructure such as water pipes, bridges, and highways throughout our nation?

Third, our nation's crowded court systems have suffered due to the adoption of three-strikes and other mandatory sentencing laws. Such laws have reduced or eliminated the incentive to enter a negotiated plea arrangement. In fact, many offenders have been choosing to forego plea bargaining altogether and go to trial when faced with a mandatory penalty of life in prison under a three-strikes law.

Finally, a number of our nation's prosecutors have expressed reluctance to charge offenders who may face a life prison term for a relatively minor felony offense under a three-strikes statute. Because prosecutors have great discretion in our justice system, some have chosen to pursue a more appropriate disposition in certain cases by circumventing three-strikes laws.

Two states that adopted three-strikes laws original, Washington and California, have had radically different experiences. Washington has had only 86 inmates under its three-strikes law, while California has incarcerated over 26,000 individuals. The issue of fairness in the application and use of these laws is certainly called into question by this data. Moreover, the U.S. Supreme Court has upheld California's three-strikes sentencing law in California; those who were convicted under a three-strikes statute were convicted of nonviolent felonies. Moreover, in contrast to William Majeta's position, a fair reading of the data suggests potential alternative explanations for a reduction in crime rates beginning in the 1990s. Voluminous research has demonstrated rather conclusively that as people get older they "age out" of crime. Thus, isn't it plausible that the decline in crime rates are a result of demographic trends (a reduction in the population of the most crime-prone age group, 15–25 years) and an overall aging of the general population?

Individual cases may be identified, however, that would seem to provide a ringing endorsement for three-strikes laws. In 1994, 7-year-old Megan Kanga was murdered by two-time convicted felon Jesse Timmendequas. In 1978, violent felon Lawrence Singleton chopped off a 15-year-old California girl's arms after raping her. He served less than 10 years in prison and was later convicted of first-degree murder in Florida. These are difficult cases that seem to highlight an important legal aphorism that "hard cases make bad law."

Additional Resources

Lorna A. Rhodes, *Total Confinement: Madness and Reason in the Maximum Security Prison* (University of California Press, 2004).

Michael Tonry (Ed.), *The Future of Imprisonment* (Oxford University Press, 2004).

Angelo Zhao, "Three Strikes and You're In: The Unconstitutionality of Three-Strikes Law," *Center for Community Change* (July 13, 2015).

Vincent Schiraldi, Jason Colburn, and Eric Lotke, "Three Strikes and You're Out: An Examination of 3-Strike Laws 10 Years After Their Enactment," *Justice Policy Institute* (2009).

Internet References . . .

The Atlantic. "The Aftermath of Reversing California's Severe Three Strikes Law." May 23, 2016.

www.theatlantic.com/video

Prison Policy Organization, "'Three Strikes Laws': Five Years Later." (2004).

www.prisonpolicy.org

The Stanford Justice Advocacy Project.

https://law.stanford.edu/stanford-justice-advocacy -project/

Three Strikes Organization, "15 Years of 'Three Strikes,' 1994 to 2008 and Still Working."

www.threestrikes.org/pdf/

Selected, Edited, and with Issue Framing Material by:
Thomas J. Hickey, *State University of New York at Cobleskill*

ISSUE

Should Private "For-Profit" Corporations Be Allowed to Run U.S. Prisons?

YES: Wayne H. Calabrese, from "Low Cost, High Quality, Good Fit: Why Not Privatization?" Transaction Publishers (1996)

NO: Jeff Sinden, from "The Problem of Prison Privatization: The U.S. Experience," Clarity Press (2003)

Learning Outcomes

After reading this issue, you will be able to:

- Compare the financial costs to society of permitting private corporations to run prisons.
- Discuss the potential negative effects of cost-cutting in prisons run by private corporations.
- Discuss why the states and federal governments became involved in operating prison systems during the early twentieth century.
- Present a compelling legal argument against privatizing America's prisons.

ISSUE SUMMARY

YES: Wayne H. Calabrese, vice president of the Wackenhut Corporation, argues that the privatization of U.S. prisons saves money and provides quality services.

NO: Jeff Sinden, managing editor of *Human Rights Tribune*, contends that the private prison industry has failed to achieve substantial cost savings and that there have been systemic human rights abuses in for-profit correctional institutions.

Should private corporations be allowed to profit from the punishment of prison inmates? Is there something wrong morally with allowing a corporation's stockholders to make a profit from human misery? These are difficult questions that will become increasingly relevant as governmental administrators try to squeeze limited financial resources from tight state budgets. Moreover, the movement to privatize corrections in the United States appears to be consistent with conservative political principles sweeping our nation that emphasize a more restrictive view of government services. For example, in the last several years the federal government has privatized some services at our national parks. Local privatization initiatives have included basic social services, educational programs, water treatment, and trash collection.

Private prisons are not a new development. As Jeff Sinden observes, privately run jails operated in England centuries ago. In the United States, early prisons in California and Texas were privately owned. The operation of U.S. prisons became a governmental responsibility during the twentieth century as a direct result of the squalid conditions existing in the privately owned penal facilities.

The contemporary privatization movement in American corrections has focused on providing a number of different types of services: inmate health care, psychological services, food services, educational programs, maintenance, as well as traditional confinement and security. It is also noteworthy that many college students may have something in common with some of our nation's prison inmates: Sodexho Marriott Services provides food services for a number of state correctional systems as well as many colleges and universities.

On a theoretical level, an offender is sentenced to prison for committing an act that has somehow harmed society. Most persons would have little trouble with the proposition that society has a right to punish the person and that the government, as society's representative, should administer the appropriate sanctions. Privatization of correctional facilities, however, appears to be somewhat inconsistent with this basic proposition.

The Introduction to this volume discussed the contemporary state of American corrections. According to recent studies, the United States has the highest imprisonment rates in the world. The total number of people housed in American prisons has reached 2.1 million and is continuing to grow at an alarming rate. This has occurred at a time when the crime rate in this country is actually falling! A large number of these individuals are confined to prisons for nonviolent offenses, such as possession of illegal drugs, and the cost to house them is staggering—perhaps as much as $15 billion for drug offenders alone.

Given the amount of money involved, is it surprising that private industry would become interested in providing correctional services? Is it an accident that conservative politicians, who receive campaign contributions from the private corrections corporations, would develop ever

more draconian laws that will result in the incarceration of increasing numbers of nonviolent offenders? These are interesting questions that the authors of the articles in this issue would be likely to answer in a very different way.

Wayne H. Calabrese, of the Wackenhut Corporation, asserts that in a time of dwindling public sector budgets, privatizing corrections services has one great advantage over governmental programs: highly significant cost savings. He believes that money is saved because "no one has yet developed a better pencil sharpener than free market competition."

Jeff Sinden, in contrast, maintains that the promised cost savings have not materialized. He cites a 2001 U.S. Department of Justice study concluding that "rather than the projected 20% savings, the average savings from privatization was only about one percent, and most of that was achieved through lower labor costs."

What are the arguments on both sides of the private prison debate? Do you believe that saving money is a good enough reason to privatize U.S. prisons? Moreover, does the move toward the privatization of our correctional institutions distract us from addressing more fundamental questions about the morality of our contemporary penal system? Should American corrections focus on alternatives to incarceration, such as drug rehabilitation and job training programs for nonviolent offenders? As you read the articles in this issue, try to develop a sense of whether privatization is likely to become the dominant model for U.S. corrections in the twenty-first century.

YES ↩

Wayne H. Calabrese

Low Cost, High Quality, Good Fit: Why Not Privatization?

As the privatization of corrections has taken root and grown, initial questions of propriety—"Should this be done?"—have given way to secondary questions of efficacy—"Does this work?" Perhaps inevitably in a time of dwindling public sector budgets and rising public service demands, those who seek a definitive answer to the question of privatization's value look to cost comparisons between public and private corrections. While the evidence thus far clearly establishes the economic advantages of privatized corrections, a careful analysis of the reasons for such advantages reveals a number of complex and subtle factors which contribute to cost savings. . . .

Of course, the inquiry into the relative worth of privatized corrections does not end with a chart of purported cost savings. Indeed, those who are critical of privatized corrections often cite reluctantly admitted cost savings as direct evidence of failed service delivery. To these critics, a dollar saved is a service shorted. The record indicates otherwise. The quality of services delivered by privatized corrections has, in the main, been equal or superior to the quality of correctional services delivered by the public sector. The second part of this chapter explores the ways public sector administrators can ensure adherence to quality standards by private providers of correctional services.

Finally, the third part of this chapter addresses a proper role for privatization in our criminal justice system, a role which can complement existing prison systems without unduly threatening the continued central role of public sector corrections departments.

Cost Comparisons

Add to the list of life's great imponderables the question of how much we are paying for our prisons. Political and religious discourse appear deliberate and calm compared to the sparks raised by those who grind their axes on the stone of public/private corrections cost comparisons. The

pitfalls are legion: aging public facilities compared to newly designed and constructed private facilities; security level, average length of stay, and offense category of compared incarcerated populations; required offender programming for public vs. private providers and degree of adherence to required standards; indirect and hidden public sector costs; to name only a few. . . .

Nevertheless, cost comparisons have been made that clearly indicate that privatization of correctional facilities leads to significant cost savings. In an article first published in the September/October 1989 issue of *NIJ Reports*, Charles Logan and Bill W. McGriff (1989) exhaustively examined the cost savings that Hamilton County, Tennessee, realized through the privatization of its 350-bed Hamilton County Penal Farm. The authors state,

> Hamilton County found that contracting out prison management generated annual savings of at least 4 to 8 percent—and more likely in the range of 5 to 15 percent—compared to the estimated cost of direct county management. (Logan and McGriff 1989, 2)

In a report of the University of Florida at Gainesville, Center for Studies in Criminology and Law, Charles W. Thomas (1990) examined available data on forty-five privately managed correctional facilities. Of the ten facilities readily capable of cost comparison with a public counterpart, all ten evidenced cost savings ranging from 10.71 percent to 52.23 percent. . . .

Construction Costs

While design-build and construction management models of new construction have made some inroads into public sector construction, the traditional three-party "pyramid" format, with the government/owner independently contracting with an architect-engineer firm to design the facility and with a general contractor to construct the facility,

Calabrese, Wayne H. From *Privatizing Correctional Institutions* by Gary W. Bowman et al., eds. (Transaction 1996), pp. 175–182, 189–191 (excerpts). Copyright © 1996 by Transaction Publishers. Reprinted by permission.

still prevails in most jurisdictions. The reasons for this continuing adherence to the traditional format include statutory/regulatory impediments or prohibitions, lack of public sector expertise or experience with relatively newer models, comfort with established methods, and so on.

The traditional public sector approach to constructing a new correctional facility has within its seemingly elegant three-sided design a built-in paradigm for cost overruns and missed schedules. First, the design phase must generally be completed before the construction begins. This lineal format adds months and consequential costs to the construction process. Second, the general contractor is generally selected through competitive bidding which requires an award to the "lowest and best bid." While the low bidder is not always selected, experienced contractors know that the "bottom line" receives significantly more scrutiny than the experience and creditworthiness of the subcontractors contributing to the total. Accordingly, subcontractors are frequently selected for the wrong reason—low cost—without regard to the level of experience or expertise they may bring to the project.

Third, the contractor may intentionally underbid the project, relying upon anticipated change-orders to regain the temporarily lost profit margin. No construction contract yet devised can eliminate all "gray areas." The traditional public sector construction model requires the architect-engineer firm to approve and certify all change orders and then pays the architect-engineer firm a percentage of the cost of any such changes. This feature alone virtually guarantees cost overruns. . . .

This system has many advantages. First, the design and construction processes are begun in coordinated tandem, saving months in the construction timetable. These time savings result in substantial cost savings based upon reduced project capitalized interest. Second, the general contractor is selected, as in turn are his subcontractors, based upon demonstrated expertise, experience, and reliability. The experienced private provider is therefore confident that the general contractor's bottom line is not a bottomless well. A bond of trust in this essential relationship can develop due, in part, to the contractor's desire to become part of the private provider's established team for future projects. . . .

Inasmuch as the project is delivered to the public sector client on a "turnkey" basis, the need for public sector participation in the day-to-day construction process is greatly reduced. Construction is monitored, rather than managed by the client. Only projects completed in accordance with project specifications and standards are accepted and paid for; incentive enough to generally guarantee completion of private design-build projects on time and within budget.

Operational Costs

Many of those who readily accept and agree with the premise that private providers can construct the same correctional facility in less time and at lower cost than the public sector, nevertheless have difficulty accepting the premise that the same private provider can manage and operate the facility at less cost with equivalent quality of service. Again, an examination of the factors contributing to operating costs reveals an almost inevitable cost advantage in privatizing corrections without any sacrifice of service quality.

Operational costs may be understood as consisting of three main categories: direct, indirect, and hidden. Direct costs, in turn, include costs associated with labor, supplies and services. Labor costs are comprised of wages and benefits. Private providers can, and generally will, pay wages equivalent to their public sector counterparts. Contrary to what some critics suggest, non-competitive wages result in disproportionately higher costs due to unacceptable levels of employee attrition. This results in increased employee training costs and other losses generally attributable to organizational upheaval.

The provision of employee benefits does, in fact, differ substantially between the public sector and the private provider. Public sector benefits include a retirement benefit known as a defined benefit plan which essentially guarantees the covered employee a specified benefit level upon retirement. This is generally expressed as a percentage of highest earnings formula. Private providers tend to either eliminate direct employer contribution retirement benefits, or if provided, the benefit is of the type known as a defined contribution plan. The defined contribution plan guarantees a level of contribution to a tax-deferred employee retirement account. . . .

The savings resulting from this single benefit are enormous. Public employee retirement contributions currently hover between 20 percent to 25 percent of the employee's wages in most public sector systems. Privatization offers the public sector client the flexibility to eliminate or modify the cost of such benefits without demonstrably affecting the quality of provided service.

Private providers also save money with respect to the procurement of facility supplies. Bulk purchasing through established national accounts, together with less bureaucratic purchasing systems, reduces costs through competitive pricing and reduced administrative overhead. The procurement of facility services such as medical, food, program instructors, counselors, and so on also benefit from competitive private sector pricing and lower administrative overhead. In short, the direct costs of operating a facility will almost always be lower for the private provider than the public sector, for reasons inherent in the respective systems of each. To recognize this advantage of the private provider is not to indict the public sector employee as less capable or motivated; rather, it is a recognition that public sector protections and systemic redundancies are purchased at a cost and eliminated or modified at a savings. . . .

No discussion of private/public cost comparisons would be complete without mention of the "hidden costs" of public sector corrections. These hidden costs are endemic to the public sector system. Private providers are sometimes criticized for operating on a for-profit basis, almost as though profitability is incompatible with the public good. The private providers have shareholder investors; the public sector has taxpayer investors. Both sets of investors expect a reasonable return on their investments. It is the means by which these expectations are measured that distinguish the private and public sectors from one another. The private sector marketplace regulates cost efficiency and quality of service by rewarding success and punishing failure. The public sector is not subject to the same rigors of the marketplace, and therefore is insulated in its "investor accountability." Public "profits" are seldom, if ever, returned to the investor. Budgets are exceeded and expanded, service quality suffers, and the hidden costs skyrocket until, as now, new and creative private market solutions are demanded by taxpayer investors in search of accountability. . . .

Resource Allocation

. . . [Public] sector corrections departments often perceive privatization as a threat or potential embarrassment. Yet, properly viewed, privatization can be presented as an integral part of a comprehensive correctional system with potential benefits to taxpayers and public sector departments alike.

Nearly every level of government responsible for incarcerating arrested or sentenced individuals is experiencing dramatic overcrowding and underfunding. Incarceration rates in the United States are at an all-time high and continue to spiral upward in response to social pressures to remove offenders from our streets, neighborhoods and communities. From Willie Horton presidential politics to worried local elected officials scanning the morning headlines for news of heinous crimes committed by felons released after serving as little as one-fifth of their sentence, prisons and prison costs remain the number one domestic issue facing America today.

There are hardened criminals in our society who require hard time behind bars. Maximum security prison beds are expensive to build and costly to operate. Too often, however, these maximum security beds are home to medium and minimum security inmates, inmates who require neither the level of security nor the allocation of cost attendant to the level of security built into the design of their cells.

Rather than spend scarce tax dollars on the construction and operation of more maximum security prisons, the public sector should, whenever possible, reallocate its resources to the construction and operation of lower security diversionary or pre-release detention facilities designed to concentrate on the specific security, programmatic, and rehabilitative needs of the intended incarcerated population.

When viewed as a continuum, the correctional system offers many opportunities for maximizing limited public resources. First-time offenders, nonviolent offenders, parole violators, sentenced offenders within one or two years of release, geriatric offenders, offenders suffering from mental illness, and so on, all represent "niche" populations capable of being incarcerated in facilities that cost less to build, and operate than the maximum security prisons in which they are currently housed. Privatization is perfectly suited to meet the needs of such populations. Private providers can design, finance, build and operate efficient facilities dedicated to the specific correctional needs of a specified population group. Based upon consistent average-lengths-of-stay, type of offense, security level, and so on, appropriate programmatic and rehabilitative services can be tailored to meet the needs of the incarcerated population.

By removing and allocating minimum/medium security inmates from maximum security beds, at least two important goals are met. First, the number of available maximum security beds within a system is increased at a lower cost than through the construction of new high security prisons; and second, targeted offender populations can be dealt with in a manner consistent with their level of security and classification, hopefully with better rehabilitative results. Public sector corrections officials should therefore regard privatized corrections as less threatening to their continued core function as keeper of our most hardened cases.

This is not to say that private providers cannot effectively manage and operate maximum security facilities. Obviously, nothing in the nature of maximum security prisons, in and of itself, mitigates against the use of private providers. The suggestion to concentrate on the privatization of the many "niche" offender populations is merely a recognition of deeply felt institutional resistance and acknowledgment of a cost-effective, less threatening, direction for embracing privatization as a meaningful part of a larger whole.

Conclusion

While advocates and opponents continue to make their closing arguments with respect to the advantages and disadvantages of privatized corrections, the jury has returned its verdict: privatization saves money, provides quality services and fulfills a need. Money is saved because no one has yet developed a better pencil sharpener than free market competition. Quality services can be ensured through careful attention to sound drafting of competitive procurement solicitations and resulting operating contracts. When properly utilized, privatization can become a cost-effective tool for fashioning specific correctional solutions within the context of the larger correctional system continuum.

References

Logan, Charles H. and Bill McGriff. (1989) *Comparing Costs of Public and Private Prisons: A Case Study.* NU Reports (September/October).

Thomas, Charles W. (1990) *Private Corrections Adult Secure Facility Census.* Correction Studies in Criminology and Law. Gainesville, Florida: University of Florida, May.

WAYNE H. CALABRESE has served as consultant of The GEO Group, Inc. since January 3, 2011. Calabrese served as the president of The GEO Group, Inc. (formerly, Wackenhut Corrections Corp.) from January 1997 to December 31, 2010 and served as its Chief Operating Officer from January 1996 to December 31, 2010.

Jeff Sinden    **NO**

The Problem of Prison Privatization: The U.S. Experience

The past two decades have witnessed a disturbing trend in the American criminal justice system. From immigration detention centers and work farms to county jails and state prisons, private corporations have entered the incarceration 'business' en masse. In fact, there are currently more than 100,000 people incarcerated in private prisons in the United States.[1] Privatization of the criminal justice system has been driven largely by the currently dominant ethos of a neoliberal agenda in which a wide variety of traditionally public goods have been transferred to the supposedly more efficient and less corrupt private sector. However, correctional services are fundamentally different from other goods, such as garbage collection, which have been transferred into private hands. Providing correctional services is a vastly complex and difficult task. Institutions are charged with the task not only of protecting society but also caring for the physical, psychological, and emotional needs of inmates so that they may one day successfully return to the community. Unfortunately, private corrections firms have failed miserably in the task they were so eager to take on, as systematic human rights abuses have become the rule and not the exception.

Various forms of private sector involvement in the corrections industry exist in the United States, some more problematic than others. The most common and least controversial involves the private delivery of goods and services in publicly run prisons. According to a report by the US Bureau of Justice Assistance, during the past twenty years, "the practice of state and local correctional agencies contracting with private entities for medical, mental health, educational, food services, maintenance, and administrative office security functions has risen sharply."[2] For example, Sodexho Marriott Services provides food services for public correctional institutions (and college and university campuses) across North America.[3] Generally, this practice is not incompatible with a healthy respect for prisoners' rights.

. . . [H]owever, many aspects of privatization have been much more problematic. For example, the private delivery of medical services in correctional institutions, both public and private, has caused significant problems as every dollar of a fixed annual stipend not spent on health services for prisoners benefits the company's bottom line, encouraging an unacceptable incentive to skimp on critical care.[4] In fact, a 1998 independent prison health care audit found that "more than twenty inmates died as a result of negligence, indifference, under-staffing, inadequate training or overzealous cost-cutting."[5]

The use of prisoner labor by the private sector to produce goods and services has also been controversial. There has been a long tradition of exploiting prison labor in the United States and throughout the world by governments and corporations alike.[6] For example, during the 19th century, inmates at the Kingston, Ontario penitentiary in Canada "were either leased out to farmers, or their work was contracted to provide industry with cheap labor."[7] While this practice was largely abolished during the early twentieth century, it has returned as of late. In 1986, former US Supreme Court Justice Warren Burger called for prisons in the United States to be transformed into "factories with fences" in order to reduce the costs of incarceration.[8] Prison administrators have taken his advice to heart as many states have allowed corporations to purchase convict labor at cut-rate prices. For example, in California, prisoners who make clothing for export make between 35 cents and $1 an hour.[9] Similarly, in Ohio, prisoners are paid approximately 50 cents an hour for data entry work.[10]

The most controversial form of private sector involvement in correctional services is the management and operation of entire correctional facilities by for-profit corporations. In some cases, private firms have taken over the operation of public facilities; in others, corporations have constructed and then managed entire sites. This type of involvement has fostered situations in which a myriad of human rights abuses have occurred.

In many cases, the corporation's desire for cost-effectiveness has led to simple corner-cutting, which in turn fosters abuses. For example, low pay and a subsequently high turnover rate has led to a grossly underqualified and inexperienced staff at many institutions.[11] Far too often, this has resulted in the flagrant abuse of prisoners. In 1997, a videotape surfaced in the media that showed guards at a private facility in Texas shooting unresisting prisoners with stun guns and kicking them to the ground. One of the guards involved had recently been fired from a government-run prison for similar conduct.[12]

Rehabilitation costs have also been systematically slashed by the prison firms. In many of the institutions, opportunities for meaningful education, exercise and rehabilitation are virtually non-existent. For example, in 1995 a private jail in Texas was investigated for diverting $700,000 intended for drug treatment when it was found that inmates with dependency problems were receiving absolutely no treatment.[13] This type of flagrant neglect amounts to abuse and almost certain recidivism as job training and education programs, drug and alcohol rehabilitation services, as well as social and psychological counseling, are absolutely critical if the transition back into society is to be successful.

Neoliberalism, Increased Criminalization, and the Drive to Privatize

Privately operated prisons are not a new phenomenon in the United States or in the Western world. In fact, privately run jails were in operation centuries ago in medieval England.[14] In the US, the seventeenth and eighteenth centuries witnessed the private ownership and operation of prisons in several states.[15] During this period, the Texas state penitentiary was leased out to a private business, which in turn subleased inmate labor to farms and industry. Similarly, the California state penitentiary at San Quentin was constructed and operated by private business.[16] "Conditions were so horrid" in these facilities, states John Dilulio, "that some inmates were driven to suicide while others maimed themselves to get out of work or as a pathetic form of protest."[17]

Partly as a result of poor conditions and systematic abuse, the ownership and operation of private correctional facilities were transferred to the state in the early 20th century and thereafter "the operations and administrative functions in correctional facilitates were delegated to governmental agencies, authorized by statute, staffed by government employees, and funded solely by the government."[18] During the ensuing period, there was virtually no private sector involvement in correctional services. This changed rapidly in the 1980s.

The 1980s saw the return of neoliberal, market-driven policies championed by President Reagan in the United States and Prime Minister Thatcher in the United Kingdom. In 1980, Ronald Reagan roared into the White House, riding a wave of popular anti-government sentiment and Cold War fear. His promise to get the government "off the backs" of the American people was welcomed by many in the US who were tired of the deep economic recession and growing public debt. Reagan's neoliberal mantra included deregulation, free trade, a hostility towards taxes and the labor unions and an almost maniacal desire for defense spending.[19] However, the central value of Reagan's doctrine and of neoliberalism itself is the notion of free-market competition. . . .

The American criminal justice system was seen as ripe for privatization by Reagan's supporters largely as a result of the rapid and steady increase in the cost of correctional services over the previous several years. According to the US General Accounting Office (GAO), total prison operating costs (for both federal and state) grew from about US $3.1 billion in 1980 to more than $17 billion in 1994, an increase of nearly 550 percent based on inflation-adjusted dollars.[20]

These increasing costs were a direct result of a similar rise in the prison population as the past twenty years has seen an explosion in the number of individuals incarcerated in America. The number of prisoners—with 2 million currently behind bars—has increased threefold since 1980.[21] This scale of imprisonment is unmatched throughout the world (with the possible exception of Russia); in 1998, the US incarcerated 690 residents per 100,000, compared with 123 per 100,000 in Canada and 60 per 100,000 in Sweden.[22]

How can this huge increase in the prison population be explained? Rising crime and arrests are clearly not the cause. Douglas McDonald documents that "the annual number of arrests nationwide rose only slightly during this period."[23] The increase is due mainly to sentencing policies. According to a 1996 report by the US GAO, "inmate population growth in recent years can be traced in large part to major legislation intended to get tough on criminals, particularly drug offenders. Examples of this new "get tough" policy include mandatory minimum sentences and repeat offender provisions."[24]

The War on Drugs, Mandatory Minimums, and Three Strikes Legislation

In the early 1980s, President Reagan began a concerted 'war on drugs', which he and First Lady Nancy Reagan

Notes

1. J. Austin and G. Coventry, *Emerging Issues on Privatized Prisons* (2001): x.
2. *Id.*, 2.
3. [. . .]
4. W. Allen and K. Bell, "Death, Neglect and the Bottom Line: Push to Cut Costs Poses Risks," *St. Louis Post-Dispatch,* 27 September 1998.
5. *Id.*
6. D. Shicor, *Punishment for Profit: Private Prisons/ Public Concerns* (1995): 31.
7. J. Gandy and L. Hurl, "Private sector involvement in prison industries" (1987): 186.
8. P. Wright, "Slaves of the State," *Prison Legal News,* May 1994.
9. *Id.*
10. D. Cahill, "The Global Economy Behind Ohio Prison Walls," *Prison Legal News,* March 1995 / April 1996.
11. J. Greene, "Prison Privatization: Recent Developments in the United States," Presented at the International Conference on Penal Abolition, 12 May 2000.
12. S. Smalley, "For-profit prisons offer privatization lessons," *National Journal,* 3 May 1999.
13. K. Silverstein, "America's Private Gulag," *Prison Legal News,* June 1997.
14. R. Pugh, *Imprisonment in Medieval England* (1968).
15. J. Dilulio, "The duty to govern" (1990): 158.
16. J. Austin and G. Coventry, *Emerging Issues on Privatized Prisons, supra* note 1 at 10.
17. J. Dilulio, "The duty to govern," *supra* note 15 at 159.
18. J. Austin and G. Coventry, *Emerging Issues on Privatized Prisons, supra* note 1 at 11.
19. J. Karaagac, *Between promise and policy* (2000).
20. *Id.*, 1.
21. "US Jails Two Millionth Inmate," *Manchester Guardian Weekly,* 17 February 2000: 1.
22. R. Walmsley, *World Prison Population List* (2000).
23. D. McDonald, ed., *Private Prisons and the Public Interest* (1990): 5.
24. United States General Accounting Office, "Private and public prisons—studies comparing operational costs and/or quality of service," (1996).
25. C. Parenti (1999): 17.
26. *Id.*
27. *Id.*, 50.
28. Office of National Drug Control Policy [. . .]
29. Federal Bureau of Investigation, Uniform Crime Reports . . .
30. Sentencing Project, *supra* note 31.
31. *Id.*
32. *Id.*
33. *Id.*
34. J. Austin and G. Coventry, *Emerging Issues on Privatized Prisons, supra* note 1 at 22.
35. Public choice theorists argue that the self-interest of public bureaucrats leads them to maximize their bureau's budget because larger budgets are a source of power, prestige and higher salaries. Please see Iain McLean, *Public Choice: An Introduction* (Oxford: Basil Blackwell, 1987).
36. C. Thomas, *Corrections in America* (1987).
37. C. Parenti, *supra* note 27 at 213.
38. J. Austin and G. Coventry, *Emerging Issues on Privatized Prisons,* supra note at 15.
39. A. Press, "The Good, the Bad and the Ugly" (1990): 25.
40. *Id.*, 25.
41. D. McDonald, *Private Prisons and the Public Interest, supra* note 25 at 1.
42. J. Austin and G. Coventry, *Emerging Issues on Privatized Prisons, supra* note 1.
43. *Id.*, ix.
44. A. Press, "The Good, the Bad and the Ugly," *supra* note 46 at 28.
45. C. Parenti, *supra* note 27 at 218.
46. *Id.*
47. *Id.*
48. *Id.*, 212.
49. *Id.*
50. S. Smalley, "For-profit prisons offer privatization lessons"; *supra* note 12.
51. *Id.*
52. C. Parenti, *supra* note 27 at 219.
53. J. Austin and G. Coventry, *Emerging Issues on Privatized Prisons, supra* note 1 at ix.
54. J. Dilulio, "The duty to govern," *supra* note 15 at 159.
55. D. Shicor, *Punishment for Profit, supra* note 6 at 52.
56. A. Press, "The Good, the Bad and the Ugly," *supra* note 46 at 25.
57. J. Austin and G. Coventry, *Emerging Issues on Privatized Prisons, supra* note 1 at iii.
58. *Id.*

JEFF SINDEN, managing editor of the *Human Rights Tribune,* is a staunch opponent of prison privatization and was formerly a research associate at *Human Rights Internet.*

EXPLORING THE ISSUE

Should Private "For-Profit" Corporations Be Allowed to Run U.S. Prisons?

Critical Thinking and Reflection

1. What are the advantages and disadvantages of allowing private corporations to run prisons?
2. Discuss the impact of the "war on drugs" on the movement to privatize prisons.

Is There Common Ground?

The Introduction to this volume discussed George Santayana's often-repeated observation that those who fail to learn from history are doomed to repeat it. It is interesting to consider whether this principle applies compellingly to the contemporary privatization movement in U.S. corrections.

Privatized correctional institutions are nothing new. As Jeff Sinden observes, privately owned jails operated in England centuries ago. In the United States, early prisons in California and Texas were privately owned. Corrections became a governmental responsibility as a direct consequence of the problems with these privately owned facilities.

Privately held corporations have one basic responsibility: to generate a profit for their investors. Suppose you were the director of a privately owned prison or jail that houses 2,000 detainees per year. Your contract with the corporation provides that you are to receive an annual performance bonus based on the profit generated at your facility. Assume further that it costs $12 per day to feed each inmate. If you could reduce the cost to $10 per day, your institution would save $1,460,000 in the following year. Would you be tempted to do so to improve the facility's bottom line and the prospects for your annual bonus? The same principle would apply to reducing the costs of medical care, clothing, security, education, drug and alcohol treatment, and job training.

The point is that the philosophy of correctional privatization may be fundamentally incompatible with what the ultimate goal of "corrections" should be: rehabilitating a person and enabling him or her to return to the community as a productive member of society. Privatizing corrections may distract us as well from attempting to find more effective alternatives to confinement for non-violent offenders. In addition, if private industry has invested huge sums of money in corrections facilities, is it likely that unscrupulous politicians, who have been known to benefit from corporate campaign contributions, will simply continue to pass draconian measures that will generate more unwilling "clients"?

Additional Resources

There are many additional resources that will shed additional light on the issues presented in this section. See Martha Minow, "Public and Private Partnerships: Accounting for the New Religion," *Harvard Law Review* (vol. 116, no. 5, March 2003); Gerald G. Gaes, "Prison Privatization in Florida: Promise, Premise, and Performance," *Criminology & Public Policy* (vol. 4, no. 1, February 2005); William D. Bales, Laura E. Beddard, Susan T. Quinn, David Ensley, and Glen P. Holley, "Recidivism of Public and Private State Prison Inmates in Florida," *Criminology & Public Policy* (Vol. 4, no. 1, February 2005); Colin Fenwick, "Private Use of Prisoners' Labor: Paradoxes of International Human Rights Law," *Human Rights Quarterly* (vol. 27, no. 1, February 2005); Sasha Abramsky, "Incarceration, Inc.," *The Nation* (vol. 279, no. 3, July 19–26, 2004); Mark Wilson, "Capitalist Punishment: Prison Privatization & Human Rights," *Prison Legal News* (vol. 15, no. 6, June 2004); Sean Nicholson-Crotty, "The Politics of Privatization: Contracting Out for Corrections Management in the United States," *Policy Studies Journal* (vol. 32, no. 1, February 2004); Patricia Lefevere, "Mixing Prisons and the Profit Motive," *National Catholic Reporter* (Vol. 39, no. 38, September 5, 2003); Gilbert Geis, Alan Mobeley, and David Shichor, "Private Prisons, Criminological Research, and Conflict of Interest: A Case Study," *Crime and Delinquency* (vol. 45, no. 3, 1999); Lanza-Kaduce, L., K. F. Parker, and C. W. Thomas, "Comparative Recidivism Analysis of Releasees from Private and Public Prisons," *Crime and Delinquency* (vol. 45, no. 1, 1999); Charles H. Logan, "Well Kept: Comparing Quality of Confinement in Private and Public Prisons," *Journal of Criminal Law and Criminology* (vol. 83, no. 3, 1992).

Additional resources that provide competing viewpoints on these issues include Gary W. Bowman, Simon Hakim, and Paul Seidenstat (eds.), *Privatizing Correctional Institutions* (Transaction Publishers, 1993); Andrew Coyle, Allison Campbell, and Rodney Neufeld (eds.), *Capitalist Punishment: Prison Privatization & Human Rights* (Clarity Press, 2003); C. W. Thomas, M. A. Frank, and S. L. Martin, *Privatization of American Corrections: A Selected Bibliography* (University of Florida Center for Studies in Criminology and Law, 1994).

Internet References . . .

American Civil Liberties Union

www.aclu.org/blog/prisoners-rights/two-weeks
-protests-start-tomorrow-30-years-profit-prisons
-nothing-celebrate

Public Broadcasting Corporation

www.pbs.org/now/shows/419/video.html

Selected, Edited, and with Issue Framing Material by:
Thomas J. Hickey, *State University of New York at Cobleskill*

ISSUE

Is Capital Punishment a Bad Public Policy?

YES: David Von Drehle, from "Miscarriage of Justice: Why the Death Penalty Doesn't Work," *The Washington Post* (1995)

NO: Ernest van den Haag, from "The Ultimate Punishment: A Defense," *Harvard Law Review* (1986)

Learning Outcomes
After reading this issue, you will be able to:
• Discuss the U.S. Supreme Court's rulings in *Furman v. Georgia* (1972) and *Gregg v. Georgia* (1976).
• Present several reasonable arguments against capital punishment.
• Present several reasonable arguments supporting capital punishment.

ISSUE SUMMARY

YES: David Von Drehle, a writer and the arts editor for *The Washington Post,* examines specific capital punishment cases and data and concludes that capital punishment is a bad social policy.

NO: Ernest van den Haag, a professor of jurisprudence and public policy (now retired), maintains that the death penalty is just retribution for heinous crime.

In 1968, only 38 percent of all Americans supported the death penalty for certain crimes. In 1972, when the U.S. Supreme Court handed down its decision in *Furman v. Georgia* stating that capital punishment violated the Eighth Amendment, which prohibits cruel and unusual punishment, many Americans were convinced that capital punishment was permanently abolished. After all, even though there were 500 inmates on death row at the time, there had been a steady decline in the number of executions in the United States: In the 1930s there were on average 152 executions per year; in 1962 there were 47 executions; and in 1966 there was 1. Polls in the late 1960s showed that most Americans opposed the death penalty, and virtually every other Western industrial nation had long since eliminated the death sentence or severely modified its use.

Polls taken in the 1990s showed that 75–80 percent of all Americans support capital punishment. In 1990,

23 people were executed, but in 1999, this number increased to 98. Since 1976, when capital punishment was restored, over 600 people have been executed. Currently, there are approximately 3500 people on death row. Eighteen states allow executions of defendants who are as young as 16, and there are currently over 60 juveniles on death row. Texas leads the nation in executions: 36 percent of all executions in 1999 were held in that state. Of the 1999 executions, 94 were by lethal injection, and 3 were by electrocution.

What has happened since the 1960s? We will probably never know the full answer to this question, but there are some clues. To begin with, in *Furman v. Georgia,* the Supreme Court did not really ban capital punishment because it was cruel and unusual in itself. It simply argued that it was unconstitutional for juries to be given the right to decide arbitrarily and discriminatorily on capital punishment. Thus, if states can show that capital punishment is not arbitrary or discriminatory and that the sentencing process is performed in two separate stages—first guilt or innocence is established, and *then* the determination of the sentence occurs—then some offenses are legally punishable by death. This was the Supreme Court's ruling in 1976 in *Gregg v. Georgia,* which effectively restored the death penalty.

Since the late 1960s, Americans have become more conservative. Fear of crime has greatly increased, although the number of crimes may not have changed. Moreover, many of the measures taken under the Omnibus Safe Streets Act to reduce crime, speed up judicial processes, and rehabilitate criminals are now viewed by professionals and laypeople alike as failures. The national mood is now solidly behind "getting tough" on criminals, especially drug dealers and murderers. Support and utilization of capital punishment make sense within the logic of the present cultural and political situation.

There is a movement among criminologists to reassess studies done before the 1960s that indicated that states in which capital punishment prevailed had homicide rates that were just as high as those in which it was not a penalty and that executions did not deter others from committing crimes. Isaac Ehrlich, for instance, in an extensive statistical analysis of executions between 1933 and 1967 reached very different conclusions. He contends not only that the executions reduced the murder rate but also that one additional execution per year between 1933 and 1967 would have resulted in seven or eight fewer murders per year!

Many scholars have bitterly attacked Ehrlich's empirical findings. Most attempt to fault his methods, but others assert that even if he is empirically correct, the trade-off is not worth it. The state should not have the right to extract such a primitive "justice" as the murder of a human being, even a convicted killer. Other scholars emphasize the fact that there have been a disproportionate number of blacks executed (between 1930 and 1967, 2066 blacks were executed as opposed to 1751 whites, even though blacks constituted only 10 percent of the total population then). Some counter that this simply indicates that more whites need to be executed as well!

Is capital punishment bad policy? If not, what crimes should it be reserved for? Murder? Rape? Espionage? Drug dealing? Kidnapping? How should it be carried out?

YES ↵

David Von Drehle

Miscarriage of Justice: Why the Death Penalty Doesn't Work

As a boy of 8, the son of good, poor parents, James Curtis "Doug" McCray had limitless dreams; he told everyone he met that someday he would be president of the United States. Soon enough, he realized that poor black children did not grow up to be president, but still he was a striver. At Dunbar High School in Fort Myers, Fla., he was an all-state receiver on the football team, an all-conference guard in basketball and the state champion in the 440-yard dash. He made the honor roll, and became the first and only of the eight McCray kids to attend college.

His was a success story, but for one flaw. McCray had a drinking problem. He washed out of college and joined the Army. A year and a half later, the Army gave him a medical discharge because he had been found to suffer from epilepsy. McCray married, fathered a son, tried college again; nothing took. He wound up back home, a tarnished golden boy.

On an October evening in 1973, an elderly woman named Margaret Mears was at home in her apartment, picking no trouble, harming no one, when someone burst in, stripped and raped her, then beat her to death. A bloody handprint was matched to Doug McCray's. He insisted that he had no memory of the night in question, and his jury unanimously recommended a life sentence. But McCray had the bad fortune to be tried by Judge William Lamar Rose.

. . . To him, the murder of Margaret Mears was precisely the type of savagery the law was intended to punish: committed in the course of another felony, and surely heinous, surely atrocious, surely cruel. Rose overruled the jury and banged the gavel on death.

⋘◉⋙

When McCray arrived at Florida State Prison in 1974, nine men awaited execution and he made 10. His case entered the appeals process, and as the years went by, McCray wept for his best friend on death row, John Spenkelink, who became the first man in America executed against his will under modern death penalty laws. He watched as a young man named Bob Graham became governor of Florida and led the nation in executing criminals. Eight years later, he watched Gov. Bob Martinez take Graham's place and sign 139 death warrants in four years. McCray saw the infamous serial killer Ted Bundy come to the row, and almost 10 years later saw him go quietly to Old Sparky.

Living on death row, McCray saw men cut, saw men burned, even saw a man killed. He saw inmates carried from their cells after committing suicide, and others taken away after going insane. He saw wardens and presidents come and go. Death row got bigger and bigger. By the time Spenkelink was executed in May 1979, Jacksonville police officers printed T-shirts proclaiming "One down, 133 to go!" . . .

Doug McCray watched as death row doubled in size, and grew still more until it was not a row but a small town, Death Town, home to more than 300 killers. Nationwide, the condemned population climbed toward 3,000. The seasons passed through a sliver of dirty glass beyond two sets of bars outside McCray's tiny cell on the row, which was very cold in the winter and very hot in the summer, noisy at all times and stinking with the odor of smoking, sweating, dirty, defecating men. Four seasons made a year, and the years piled up: 5, 10, 15, 16, 17 . . .

All this time, Doug McCray was sentenced to death but he did not die. Which makes him the perfect symbol of the modern death penalty.

People talk a great deal these days about getting rid of government programs that cost too much and produce scant results. So it's curious that one of the least efficient government programs in America is also among the most popular. Capital punishment is favored by more than three-quarters of American voters. And yet, in 1994, the death row population nationwide exceeded 3,000 for the first time ever; out of all those condemned prisoners, only 31 were executed. There are hundreds of prisoners in America who have been on death row more than a decade, and at least one—Thomas Knight of Florida—has been awaiting execution for 20 years. Every cost study undertaken has found that it is far more expensive, because of added legal safeguards, to carry out a death sentence than it is to jail a killer for life. Capital punishment is the principal burden on the state and federal appellate courts in every jurisdiction where it is routinely practiced. The most efficient death penalty state, Texas, has a backlog of more than 300 people on its death row. It manages to execute only about one killer for every four newly sentenced to die—and the number of executions may drop now that the U.S. Supreme Court has ordered Texas to provide lawyers for death row inmate appeals. Overall, America has executed approximately one in every 20 inmates sentenced to die under modern death penalty laws.

This poor record of delivering the punishments authorized by legislatures and imposed by courts has persisted despite a broad shift to the right in the federal courts. It has resisted legislative and judicial efforts to streamline the process. It has outlasted William J. Brennan Jr. and Thurgood Marshall, the Supreme Court's strongest anti-death penalty justices. It has endured countless campaigns by state legislators and governors and U.S. representatives and senators and even presidents who have promised to get things moving. If New York reinstates the death penalty this year, as Gov. George Pataki has promised, there is no reason to believe things will change; New York is unlikely to see another execution in this century. Congress extended the death penalty to cover more than 50 new crimes last year, but that bill will be long forgotten before Uncle Sam executes more than a handful of prisoners.

Most people like the death penalty in theory; virtually no one familiar with it likes the slow, costly, and inefficient reality. But after 20 years of trying to make the death penalty work, it is becoming clear that we are stuck with the reality, and not the ideal.

⋅⟨⊙⟩⋅

To understand why this is, you have to understand the basic mechanics of the modern death penalty. The story begins in 1972.

For most of American history, capital punishment was a state or even a local issue. Criminals were tried, convicted, and sentenced according to local rules and customs, and their executions were generally carried out by town sheriffs in courthouse squares. Federal judges took almost no interest in the death penalty, and even state appeals courts tended to give the matter little consideration.

Not surprisingly, a disproportionate number of the people executed under these customs were black, and the execution rate was most dramatically skewed for the crime of rape. As sensibilities became more refined, however, decent folks began to object to the spectacle of local executions. In Florida in the 1920s, for example, a coalition of women's clubs lobbied the legislature to ban the practice, arguing that the sight of bodies swinging in town squares had a brutalizing effect on their communities. Similar efforts around the country led to the centralizing of executions at state prisons, where they took place outside the public view, often at midnight or dawn.

Still, the death penalty remained a state matter, with the federal government extremely reluctant to exert its authority. Washington kept its nose out of the death chambers, just as it steered clear of the schools, courtrooms, prisons, and voting booths. All that changed, and changed dramatically, in the 1950s and '60s, when the Supreme Court, in the era of Chief Justice Earl Warren, asserted more vigorously than ever that the protections of the U.S. Constitution applied to actions in the states. For the first time, federal standards of equality were used to strike down such state and local practices as school segregation, segregation of buses and trains, poll taxes, and voter tests. The lengthened arm of the federal government reached into police stations: For example, in *Miranda v. Arizona,* the Supreme Court required that suspects be advised to their constitutional rights when arrested. The long arm reached into the courtrooms: In *Gideon v. Wainwright,* the high court declared that the federal guarantee of due process required that felony defendants in state trials be provided with lawyers.

Opponents of capital punishment urged the courts to reach into death rows as well. Anthony Amsterdam, at the time a Stanford University law professor, crafted arguments to convince the federal courts that the death penalty violated the Eighth Amendment (which bars "cruel and unusual punishments") and the 14th Amendment (which guarantees "equal protection of the laws"). Amsterdam's arguments won serious consideration in the newly aggressive federal courts, and on January 17, 1972, the greatest of Amsterdam's lawsuits, *Furman v. Georgia,* was heard in the Supreme Court.

Amsterdam delivered a brilliant four-pronged attack on capital punishment. He began by presenting statistical proof that the death penalty in America was overwhelmingly used against the poor and minorities. Next, Amsterdam argued that the death penalty was imposed arbitrarily, almost randomly. Judges and juries meted out their sentences without clear standards to guide them, and as a result men were on death row for armed robbery, while nearby, murderers served life, or less. Discretion in death sentencing was virtually unfettered. Amsterdam's third point was his most audacious, but it turned out to be crucial: The death penalty was so rarely carried out in contemporary America that it could no longer be justified as a deterrent to crime. In the years leading up to Amsterdam's argument, use of the death penalty had steeply declined. What made this argument so daring was that the sharp drop in executions was partly a result of Amsterdam's own legal campaign to abolish the death penalty. He was, in effect, challenging a state of affairs he had helped to create.

In closing, Amsterdam argued that the death penalty had become "unacceptable in contemporary society," that the "evolving standards" of decent behavior had moved beyond the point of legal killing. This was the weakest of his arguments, because nearly 40 states still had death penalty laws on the books, but previous Supreme Court decisions suggested that the shortest route to abolishing the death penalty would be to convince a majority of the justices that "standards of decency" had changed. Amsterdam had to try.

Behind closed doors, the nine justices of the court revealed a wide range of reactions to Amsterdam's case—from Brennan and Marshall, the court's liberal stalwarts, who voted to abolish capital punishment outright, to Justice William H. Rehnquist, the new conservative beacon, who rejected all of the arguments. Justice William O. Douglas was unpersuaded by the notion that standards of decency had evolved to the point that capital punishment was cruel and unusual punishment, but he agreed the death penalty was unconstitutionally arbitrary. Chief Justice Warren E. Burger and Justice Harry A. Blackmun both expressed personal opposition to capital punishment—if they were legislators, they would vote against it—but they believed that the language of the Constitution clearly left the matter to the states. That made three votes to strike down the death penalty, and three to sustain it.

Justice Lewis F. Powell Jr. also strongly objected to the court taking the question of the death penalty out of the hands of elected legislatures. This would be an egregious example of the sort of judicial activism he had always opposed. Though moved by Amsterdam's showing of racial discrimination, Powell believed this was a vestige of the past, and could be rectified without a sweeping decision in Furman. Powell's vote made four to sustain the death penalty. Justice Potter Stewart, painfully aware of the more than 600 prisoners whose lives were dangling on his vote,

moved toward Douglas's view that the death penalty had become unconstitutionally arbitrary. Stewart's vote made four to strike down the death penalty as it existed.

That left Justice Byron R. White, known to observers of the court as a strict law-and-order man. In his brusque opinions, White backed prosecutors and police at almost every turn. But he was deeply impressed by Amsterdam's presentation; he told his law clerks that it was "possibly the best" oral argument he had ever heard. The point that had won White was Amsterdam's boldest: that the death penalty was applied too infrequently to serve any purpose. White cast the deciding vote to strike down the death penalty not because he wanted to see an end to capital punishment, but because he wanted to see more of it.

The product of these deliberations was one of the most difficult decisions in the history of the U.S. Supreme Court. The broad impact of *Furman v. Georgia*, striking down hundreds of separate laws in nearly 40 separate jurisdictions, was unprecedented. Rambling and inchoate—nine separate opinions totaling some 50,000 words—it remains easily the longest decision ever published by the court. But for all its wordy impact, Furman was almost useless as a precedent for future cases. It set out no clear legal standards. As Powell noted in his stinging dissent:

"Mr. Justice Douglas concludes that capital punishment is incompatible with notions of 'equal protection' that he finds 'implicit' in the Eighth Amendment . . . Mr. Justice Brennan bases his judgment primarily on the thesis that the penalty 'does not comport with human dignity' . . . Mr. Justice Stewart concludes that the penalty is applied in a 'wanton' and 'freakish' manner . . . For Mr. Justice White it is the 'infrequency' with which the penalty is imposed that renders its use unconstitutional . . . Mr. Justice Marshall finds that capital punishment is an impermissible form of punishment because it is 'morally unacceptable' and 'excessive' . . .

"I [will not] attempt to predict what forms of capital statutes, if any, may avoid condemnation in the future under the variety of views expressed by the collective majority today."

In other words, totally missing from the longest Supreme Court decision in history was any clear notion of how the death penalty might be fixed.

❧

That painfully splintered 5-to-4 vote turned out to be a high-water mark of the Supreme Court's willingness to intervene in the business of the states. In *Furman*, the justices were willing to abolish the death penalty as it existed. But the justices were not willing to forbid executions forever. They kicked the question of whether the death penalty was "cruel and unusual" back to the state legislatures. For nearly 20 years, the states—especially the Southern states—had felt pounded by the Supreme Court. Rarely did they get the chance to answer. The court did not ask what they thought about school desegregation, or voting rights, or the right to counsel. But *Furman v. Georgia* invited the states to respond to a hostile Supreme Court decision.

Florida was the first state to craft an answer, after calling its legislature into special session. Blue-ribbon panels appointed by the governor and legislature struggled to make sense of Furman—but how? On the governor's commission, legal advisers unanimously predicted that no capital punishment law would ever satisfy the high court, but the membership turned instead to a nugget from Justice Douglas's opinion. Douglas wrote that the problem with the pre-*Furman* laws was that "under these laws no standards govern the selection of the penalty." Douglas seemed to be saying that judges and juries needed rules to guide their sentencing.

The legislative commission reached a different conclusion, simply by seizing on a different snippet from the Furman ruling. Figuring that Byron White was the most likely justice to change his position, commission members combed his opinion for clues. White had complained that "the legislature authorizes [but] does not mandate the penalty in any particular class or kind of case. . . ." That phrase seemed crucial: "Authorizes but does not mandate." Apparently, White would prefer to see death made mandatory for certain crimes.

Furman was as cryptic as the Gnostic gospels. Robert Shevin, Florida's attorney general at the time, was just as confused. He summoned George Georgieff and Ray Marky, his two top death penalty aides, to explain the ruling. "I've been reading it since it came out," Marky told his boss, "and I still have no idea what it means."

Gov. Reubin Askew refused to go along with mandatory sentences—he considered them barbaric. And so it was that while rank-and-file lawmakers made interminable tough-on-crime speeches, in the last month of 1972 Florida's power brokers hashed out a deal behind closed doors. Their new law spelled out "aggravating" circumstances—such as a defendant's criminal record and the degree of violence involved in the crime—which, if proven, would make a guilty man eligible for the death penalty. The law also spelled out "mitigating" circumstances, such as a defendant's age or mental state, that might suggest a life sentence instead. After a defendant was found guilty of a capital offense, the jury would hear evidence of aggravating and mitigating factors. By majority vote, the jurors would recommend either life in prison or the death penalty. Then the judge would be required to reweigh the aggravating and mitigating factors and impose the sentence, justifying it in writing. As a final safeguard, the sentence would be reviewed by the state's highest court. In this way, perhaps, they could thread the *Furman* needle: setting standards, limiting discretion, erasing caprice—all while avoiding mandatory sentences.

They were a few men in a back room, trading power and guessing over an incoherent Supreme Court document. It was not a particularly promising effort. Nevertheless, their compromise passed overwhelmingly, giving America its first legislative answer to *Furman*. Immediately, officials from states across the country began calling Florida for advice and guidance. And very soon, lawyers and judges began to discover that the law drafted in confusion and passed in haste was going to be hell to administer.

⁕

The problem was that underneath the tidy, legalistic, polysyllabic, etched-in-marble tone of the new law was a lot of slippery mishmash. The aggravating and mitigating factors sounded specific and empirical, but many of them were matters of judgment rather than fact. A murderer was more deserving of the death penalty, for example, if his actions involved "a great risk of death to many persons"—but where one judge might feel that phrase applied to a drive-by killer who sprays a whole street with gunfire, another might apply it to a burglar who stabs a man to death while the victim's wife slumbers nearby. How much risk makes a "great" risk, and what number of persons constitutes "many"?

Another aggravating circumstance was even harder to interpret—"especially heinous, atrocious or cruel." The idea was to identify only the worst of the hundreds of murders each year in Florida. But wasn't the act of murder itself "heinous, atrocious or cruel"? Again, this aggravating circumstance was very much in the eye of the beholder: To one judge, stabbing might seem more cruel than shooting, because it involved such close contact between killer and victim. Another judge, however, might think it crueler to place a cold gun barrel to a victim's head before squeezing the trigger. One jury might find it especially heinous for a victim to be killed by a stranger, while the next set of jurors might find it more atrocious for a victim to die at the hands of a trusted friend. And so forth. It was an attempt to define the undefinable.

The imprecision was even more obvious on the side of mitigation, where it weighed in a defendant's favor if he had no "significant history" of past criminal behavior. How much history was that? "The age of the defendant" was supposed to be considered under the new law—but where one jury might think 15 was old enough to face the death penalty, another might have qualms about executing a man who was "only" 20. What about elderly criminals? Was there an age beyond which a man should qualify for mercy—and if so, what was it?

Clearly, a lot of discretion was left to the judge and jury. Even more discretion was allowed in tallying the aggravating versus the mitigating circumstances, and still more in deciding what weight to give each factor. The jury was supposed to render an "advisory" opinion on the proper sentence, death or life in prison, but how much deference did the judge have to pay to that advice? The law said nothing. After the judge imposed a death sentence, the state supreme court was required to review it. But what standards was the court supposed to apply? The law said nothing.

These questions might have seemed tendentious and picayune, except for the fact that Doug McCray and dozens of others were quickly sent to death row, and these seemingly trivial questions became the cruxes of life-and-death litigation. The law, shot through with question marks, became a lawyer's playground. After all, laws were supposed to be clear and fixed; they were supposed to mean the same thing from day to day, courtroom to courtroom, town to town. And given that their clients were going to be killed for breaking the law, it seemed only fair for defense lawyers to demand that simple degree of reliability.

In 1976, when the U.S. Supreme Court returned to the question of capital punishment, the justices agreed that the laws must be reliable. By then some 35 states had passed new death penalty laws, many of them modeled on Florida's. In a string of rulings the high court outlawed mandatory death sentences and affirmed the complex systems for weighing specified factors in favor of and against a death sentence.

But in striking down mandatory sentences, the court made consistency a constitutional requirement for the death penalty; the law must treat "same" cases the same and "different" cases differently. The thousands of capital crimes committed each year in America raised a mountain of peculiarities—each criminal and crime was subtly unique. Somehow the law must penetrate this mountain to discern some conceptual key that would consistently identify cases that were the "same" and cull ones that were

"different." Furthermore, the court decided, the Constitution requires extraordinary consistency from capital punishment laws. "The penalty of death is qualitatively different from a sentence of imprisonment, however long," Justice Potter Stewart wrote. "Because of that qualitative difference, there is a corresponding difference in the need for reliability. . . ."

Each year, some 20,000 homicides are committed in America, and the swing justices expected the death penalty laws to steer precisely and consistently through this carnage to find the relatively few criminals deserving execution. Somehow, using the black-and-white of the criminal code, the system must determine the very nature of evil. King Solomon himself might demur.

"The main legal battle is over," declared the *New York Times* in an editorial following the 1976 decisions. In fact, the battles were only beginning.

❦

After Doug McCray was sentenced to die in 1974, his case went to the Florida Supreme Court for the required review. . . . In October 1980, the Florida Supreme Court agreed that Doug McCray should die. The following year the U.S. Supreme Court declined to review the state court's decision.

Through all this, McCray continued to insist that he had no memory of murdering Margaret Mears. He passed a lie detector test, and though such tests are not admissible in court, there was another reason to believe what he said. It was possible that McCray's epilepsy, which had first emerged in several powerful seizures during his Army basic training, was the type known as "temporal lobe seizure disorder." This disease often emerges in late adolescence; it is known to cause violent blackouts; and it can be triggered by alcohol. The possibility had not come out at McCray's trial, nor was it properly researched in preparation for his hearing on executive clemency. The hearing, held on December 16, 1981, went badly for McCray. An attorney, Jesse James Wolbert, had been appointed to represent him, but Wolbert did not bother to read the trial record, let alone prepare a compelling case for mercy. Perhaps he had other things on his mind: By the time McCray's death warrant was signed three months later, Wolbert had drained another client's trust fund and become a federal fugitive.

Wolbert's disappearance turned out to be a blessing for McCray, because an anti-death penalty activist named Scharlette Holdman persuaded Bob Dillinger of St. Petersburg to take the case, and Dillinger was a damn good lawyer. He filed a hasty appeal in the Florida Supreme Court asking for a stay of execution. The result was amazing: Having affirmed McCray's death sentence 18 months earlier, the justices now ordered a new trial. The sentence, they ruled, had been based on the theory that the murder had been committed in conjunction with a rape. "Felony murder," this is called—murder coupled with another felony. In 1982, the Florida Supreme Court, by a vote of 4 to 3, declared that the underlying felony, rape, had not been proven beyond a reasonable doubt. Eight years after the original sentence, Doug McCray was going back to trial.

Except that something even more amazing happened a few weeks later. The state supreme court granted the prosecution's request for a rehearing, and Justice Ray Ehrlich abruptly changed his mind. His vote made it 4 to 3 in favor of upholding McCray's death sentence. In the course of six months, Ehrlich had gone from believing McCray's sentence was so flawed that he should have a new trial to believing that his sentence was sound enough to warrant his death. The court contacted the company that publishes all its decisions and asked that the first half of this flip-flop—the order for a new trial—be erased from history.

Gov. Bob Graham signed a second death warrant on May 27, 1983. By this time, Bob Dillinger had located his client's ex-wife in California, where she lived with her son by Doug McCray. The son was what his father had once been: bright as a whip, interested in current events, a devourer of books, good at games. The ex-wife, Myra Starks, was mystified by the course her husband's life had taken. They had been high school sweethearts, and she had married him certain that he was upward bound. When McCray had left school to join the Army, Starks had clung to that vision, picturing a steady string of promotions leading to a comfortable pension. Then came the seizures and the medical discharge, and her husband's behavior changed horribly. He drank heavily, and sometimes when he was drunk he struck out at her violently—though after each of these outbursts, he insisted he remembered nothing. Myra Starks did not make a connection between the medical discharge and the change in her man; instead, she packed up their baby boy and moved out. Within a year, McCray was on trial for murder.

In addition to locating Starks, Bob Dillinger also arranged for a full-scale medical evaluation of his client, and the doctor concluded that McCray indeed suffered from temporal lobe seizure disorder. It all came together: the violent blackouts, triggered by drink. In prison, after a number of seizures, McCray was put on a drug regimen

to control his disease: Dilantin, a standard epilepsy treatment, in the mornings, and phenobarbital, a sedative, at night. When Dillinger arranged for Myra Starks to see her ex-husband, after a decade apart, she exclaimed, "He's just like the old Doug!"

But he was scheduled to die. Following established procedure, Dillinger returned to the Florida Supreme Court. It was the fifth time the court had considered McCray's case. This time, the justices concluded that the new medical evidence might be important in weighing whether death was the appropriate sentence. They ordered the trial court to hold a hearing and stayed the execution while this was done.

Doug McCray had lived on death row nine years. . . .

In all that time, though, his case had not moved past the first level of appeals. The Florida Supreme Court had weighed and reweighed his case, and with each weighing the justices had reached a different conclusion.

❦

McCray's case was far from unusual. Every death penalty case winds up on spongy ground, even the most outrageous. It took nearly a decade for Florida to execute serial killer Ted Bundy, and even longer for John Wayne Gacy to reach the end in Illinois. The courts routinely reverse themselves, then double back again. The same case can look different with each fresh examination or new group of judges. Defenders have learned to exploit every possible advantage from the tiniest detail to the loftiest constitutional principle. A conscientious defense attorney has no choice—especially if any question remains as to whether the condemned man actually committed the crime for which he was sentenced. The effort involves huge expenditures of time and resources, and results are notoriously uncertain. . . .

❦

By the time Doug McCray's case returned to the trial court for a new sentence in 1986, the hanging judge, William Lamar Rose, was gone. So many years had passed. But in his place was another stern man who was no less outraged at the enormity of McCray's crime. . . .

McCray had, over the years, become a favorite of death penalty opponents, because he seemed so gentle and redeemable. Frequently, they argued that not all death row prisoners are "like Ted Bundy," and McCray was the sort of prisoner they were talking about. The harshest word in his vocabulary was "shucks." He read every book he could get his hands on. There was a poignant vulnerability to him.

But the new judge focused, as the old one had done, on the crime: A defenseless, innocent, helpless woman alone, terrorized, apparently raped, then killed. He sentenced McCray to death once more. And the case returned to the Florida Supreme Court for a sixth time. In June 1987, after a U.S. Supreme Court decision in favor of another Florida inmate, the justices sent McCray's case back because the judge had overruled the jury's advisory sentence. What was his justification? The judge's justification was an elderly woman savagely murdered. Once again, he imposed the death sentence.

So the case of Doug McCray returned for the seventh time to the Florida Supreme Court. Did he deserve to die? Four times, a trial judge insisted that he did. Twice, the state's high court agreed. And four times, the same court expressed doubts. A single case, considered and reconsidered, strained and restrained, weighed and reweighed. A prism, a kaleidoscope, a rune of unknown meaning. The life of a man, viewed through the lens of a complex, uncertain, demanding law. Should he live or die?

In May 1991, after weighing his case for the seventh time in 17 years, the Florida Supreme Court reversed McCray's death sentence and imposed a sentence of life in prison. For 17 years, two courts had debated—the trial court and the state supreme court. No liberal outsiders stalled the process, no bleeding hearts intervened. Even the lawyers added little to the essential conundrum, which was in the beginning as it was in the end: Doug McCray, bad guy, versus Doug McCray, not-quite-so-bad guy. The case was far from aberrant. It was one of hundreds of such cases.

❧

Some politicians and pundits still talk as if the confusion over the death penalty can be eliminated by a healthy dose of conservative toughness, but among the people who know the system best that explanation is losing steam. More than 20 years have passed since *Furman v. Georgia;* courts and legislatures have gotten tougher and tougher on the issue—but the results have remained negligible. The execution rate hovers at around 25 or 30 per year, while America's death row population has swelled past 3,000. It makes no real difference who controls the courts, as California voters learned after they dumped their liberal chief justice in 1986. The court turned rightward, but 7½ years later, California had executed just two of the

more than 300 prisoners on its death row. (One of the two had voluntarily surrendered his appeals.) No matter how strongly judges and politicians favor capital punishment, the law has remained a mishmash.

It is hard to see a way out. The idea that the death penalty should not be imposed arbitrarily—that each case should be analyzed by a rational set of standards—has been so deeply woven into so many federal and state court rulings that there is little chance of it being reversed. Courts have softened that requirement, but softening has not solved the problem. Proposals to limit access to appeals for death row inmates have become staples of America's political campaigns, and many limits have been set. But it can take up to a decade for a prisoner to complete just one trip through the courts, and no one has proposed denying condemned inmates one trip.

. . . [E]ven the most vicious killers . . . cannot be executed quickly. Gerald Stano, who in the early 1980s confessed to killing more than two dozen women, is alive. Thomas Knight, who in 1980 murdered a prison guard while awaiting execution for two other murders, is alive. Jesus Scull, who in 1983 robbed and murdered two victims and burned their house around them, is alive. Howard Douglas, who in 1973 forced his wife to have sex with her boyfriend as he watched, then smashed the man's head in, is alive. Robert Buford, who in 1977 raped and beat a 7-year-old girl to death, is alive. Eddie Lee Freeman, who in 1976 strangled a former nun and dumped her in a river to drown, is alive. Jesse Hall, who in 1975 raped and murdered a teenage girl and killed her boyfriend, is alive. James Rose, who in 1976 raped and murdered an 8-year-old girl in Fort Lauderdale, is alive. Larry Mann, who in 1980 cut a little girl's throat and clubbed her to death as she crawled away, is alive.

And that's just in Florida. The story is the same across the country.

In 1972, Justice Harry Blackmun cast one of the four votes in favor of preserving the death penalty in *Furman v. Georgia,* and he voted with the majority to approve the new laws four years later. For two decades, he stuck to the belief that the death penalty could meet the constitutional test of reliability. But last year Blackmun threw up his hands. "Twenty years have passed since this Court declared that the death penalty must be imposed fairly and with reasonable consistency or not all," he wrote. ". . . In the years following Furman, serious efforts were made to comply with its mandate. State legislatures and appellate courts struggled to provide judges and juries with sensible and objective guidelines for determining who should live and who should die. . . . Unfortunately, all this experimentation and ingenuity yielded little of what Furman demanded . . . It seems that the decision whether a human being should live or die is so inherently subjective, rife with all of life's understandings, experiences, prejudices and passions, that it inevitably defies the rationality and consistency required by the Constitution . . . I feel morally and intellectually obligated simply to concede that the death penalty experiment has failed."

Also last year, an admiring biography of retired Justice Lewis Powell was published. Powell was one of the architects of the modern death penalty. As a swing vote in 1976, he had helped to define the intricate weighing system that restored capital punishment in America. Later, as the deciding vote in a 1987 case, *McCleskey v. Kemp,* Powell had saved the death penalty from the assertion that racial disparities proved the system was still arbitrary. Now Powell was quoted as telling his biographer, "I have come to think that capital punishment should be abolished." The death penalty "brings discredit on the whole legal system," Powell said, because the vast majority of death sentences are never carried out. Biographer John C. Jeffries Jr. had asked Powell if he would like to undo any decisions from his long career. "Yes," the justice answered. "McCleskey v. Kemp."

No one has done more than Ray Marky to make a success of the death penalty. As a top aide in the Florida attorney general's office, he worked himself into an early heart attack prosecuting capital appeals. Eventually, he took a less stressful job at the local prosecutor's office, where he watched, dispirited, as the modern death penalty—the law he had helped write and had struggled to enforce—reached its convoluted maturity. One day a potential death penalty case came across his new desk, and instead of pushing as he had in the old days, he advised the victim's mother to accept a life sentence for her son's killer. "Ma'am, bury your son and get on with your life, or over the next dozen years, this defendant will destroy you, as well as your son," Marky told her. Why put the woman through all the waiting, the hearings and the stays, when the odds were heavy that the death sentence would never be carried out? "I never would have said that 15 years ago," Marky reflected. "But now I will, because I'm not going to put someone through the nightmare. If we had deliberately set out to create a chaotic system, we couldn't have come up with anything worse. It's a merry-go-round, it's ridiculous; it's so clogged up only an arbitrary few ever get it.

"I don't get any damn pleasure out of the death penalty and I never have," the prosecutor said. "And frankly, if they abolished it tomorrow, I'd go get drunk in celebration."

DAVID VON DREHLE is an art editor for *The Washington Post.* His publications include *Among the Lowest of the Dead* (Times Books, 1995).

Ernest van den Haag   ➔ **NO**

The Ultimate Punishment: A Defense

In an average year about 20,000 homicides occur in the United States. Fewer than 300 convicted murderers are sentenced to death. But because no more than thirty murderers have been executed in any recent year, most convicts sentenced to death are likely to die of old age.[1] Nonetheless, the death penalty looms large in discussions: it raises important moral questions independent of the number of executions.

The death penalty is our harshest punishment. It is irrevocable: it ends the existence of those punished, instead of temporarily imprisoning them. Further, although not intended to cause physical pain, execution is the only corporal punishment still applied to adults. These singular characteristics contribute to the perennial, impassioned controversy about capital punishment.

I. Distribution

Consideration of the justice, morality, or usefulness, of capital punishment is often conflated with objections to its alleged discriminatory or capricious distribution among the guilty. Wrongly so. If capital punishment is immoral *in se,* no distribution among the guilty could make it moral. If capital punishment is moral, no distribution would make it immoral. Improper distribution cannot affect the quality of what is distributed, be it punishments or rewards. Discriminatory or capricious distribution thus could not justify abolition of the death penalty. Further, maldistribution inheres no more in capital punishment than in any other punishment.

Maldistribution between the guilty and the innocent is, by definition, unjust. But the injustice does not lie in the nature of the punishment. Because of the finality of the death penalty, the most grievous maldistribution occurs when it is imposed upon the innocent. However, the frequent allegations of discrimination and capriciousness refer to maldistribution among the guilty and not to the punishment of the innocent.

Maldistribution of any punishment among those who deserve it is irrelevant to its justice or morality. Even if poor or black convicts guilty of capital offenses suffer capital punishment, and other convicts equally guilty of the same crimes do not, a more equal distribution, however desirable, would merely be more equal. It would not be more just to the convicts under sentence of death.

Punishments are imposed on persons, not on racial or economic groups. Guilt is personal. The only relevant question is: does the person to be executed deserve the punishment? Whether or not others who deserved the same punishment, whatever their economic or racial group, have avoided execution is irrelevant. If they have, the guilt of the executed convicts would not be diminished, nor would their punishment be less deserved. To put the issue starkly, if the death penalty were imposed on guilty blacks, but not on guilty whites, or, if it were imposed by a lottery among the guilty, this irrationally discriminatory or capricious distribution would neither make the penalty unjust, nor cause anyone to be unjustly punished, despite the undue impunity bestowed on others.

Equality, in short, seems morally less important than justice. And justice is independent of distributional inequalities. The ideal of equal justice demands that justice be equally distributed, not that it be replaced by equality. Justice requires that as many of the guilty as possible be punished, regardless of whether others have avoided punishment. To let these others escape the deserved punishment does not do justice to them, or to society. But it is not unjust to those who could not escape.

These moral considerations are not meant to deny that irrational discrimination, or capriciousness, would be inconsistent with constitutional requirements. But I am satisfied that the Supreme Court has in fact provided for adherence to the constitutional requirement of equality as much as possible. Some inequality is indeed unavoidable as a practical matter in any system.[2] But, *ultra posse neo obligatur.* (Nobody is bound beyond ability.)

Recent data reveal little direct racial discrimination in the sentencing of those arrested and convicted of murder. The abrogation of the death penalty for rape has eliminated a major source of racial discrimination. Concededly, some discrimination based on the race of murder victims may exist; yet, this discrimination affects criminal victimizers in an unexpected way. Murderers of whites are thought more likely to be executed than murderers of blacks. Black victims, then, are less fully vindicated than white ones. However, because most black murderers kill blacks, black murderers are spared the death penalty more often than are white murderers. They fare better than most white murderers. The motivation behind unequal distribution of the death penalty may well have been to discriminate against blacks, but the result has favored them. Maldistribution is thus a straw man for empirical as well as analytical reasons.

II. Miscarriages of Justice

In a recent survey Professors Hugo Adam Bedau and Michael Radelet found that 7000 persons were executed in the United States between 1900 and 1985 and that 25 were innocent of capital crimes. Among the innocents they list Sacco and Vanzetti as well as Ethel and Julius Rosenberg. Although their data may be questionable, I do not doubt that, over a long enough period, miscarriages of justice will occur even in capital cases.

Despite precautions, nearly all human activities, such as trucking, lighting, or construction, cost the lives of some innocent bystanders. We do not give up these activities, because the advantages, moral or material, outweigh the unintended losses. Analogously, for those who think the death penalty just, miscarriages of justice are offset by the moral benefits and the usefulness of doing justice. For those who think the death penalty unjust even when it does not miscarry, miscarriages can hardly be decisive.

III. Deterrence

Despite much recent work, there has been no conclusive statistical demonstration that the death penalty is a better deterrent than are alternative punishments. However, deterrence is less than decisive for either side. Most abolitionists acknowledge that they would continue to favor abolition even if the death penalty were shown to deter more murders than alternatives could deter. Abolitionists appear to value the life of a convicted murderer or, at least, his nonexecution, more highly than they value the lives of the innocent victims who might be spared by deterring prospective murderers.

Deterrence is not altogether decisive for me either. I would favor retention of the death penalty as retribution even if it were shown that the threat of execution could not deter prospective murderers not already deterred by the threat of imprisonment.[3] Still, I believe the death penalty, because of its finality, is more feared than imprisonment, and deters some prospective murderers not deterred by the threat of imprisonment. Sparing the lives of even a few prospective victims by deterring their murderers is more important than preserving the lives of convicted murderers because of the possibility, or even the probability, that executing them would not deter others. Whereas the lives of the victims who might be saved are valuable, that of the murderer has only negative value, because of his crime. Surely the criminal law is meant to protect the lives of potential victims in preference to those of actual murderers.

Murder rates are determined by many factors; neither the severity nor the probability of the threatened sanction is always decisive. However, for the long run, I share the view of Sir James Fitzjames Stephen: "Some men, probably, abstain from murder because they fear that if they committed murder they would be hanged. Hundreds of thousands abstain from it because they regard it with horror. One great reason why they regard it with horror is that murderers are hanged." Penal sanctions are useful in the long run for the formation of the internal restraints so necessary to control crime. The severity and finality of the death penalty is appropriate to the seriousness and the finality of murder.

IV. Incidental Issues: Cost, Relative Suffering, Brutalization

Many nondecisive issues are associated with capital punishment. Some believe that the monetary cost of appealing a capital sentence is excessive. Yet most comparisons of the cost of life imprisonment with the cost of execution, apart from their dubious relevance, are flawed at least by the implied assumption that life prisoners will generate no judicial costs during their imprisonment. At any rate, the actual monetary costs are trumped by the importance of doing justice.

Others insist that a person sentenced to death suffers more than his victim suffered, and that this (excess) suffering is undue according to the *lex talionis* (rule of retaliation). We cannot know whether the murderer on death row suffers more than his victim suffered; however, unlike the murderer, the victim deserved none of the suffering inflicted. Further, the limitations of the *lex talionis* were meant to restrain private vengeance, not the social retribution that has taken its place. Punishment—regardless of the motivation—is not intended to revenge, offset, or compensate for the victim's suffering, or to be measured by it. Punishment is to vindicate the law and the social order undermined by the crime. This is why a kidnapper's penal confinement is not limited to the period for which he imprisoned his victim; nor is a burglar's confinement meant merely to offset the suffering or the harm he caused his victim; nor is it meant only to offset the advantage he gained.[4]

Another argument heard at least since Beccaria is that, by killing a murderer, we encourage, endorse, or legitimize unlawful killing. Yet, although all punishments are meant to be unpleasant, it is seldom argued that they legitimize the unlawful imposition of identical unpleasantness. Imprisonment is not thought to legitimize kidnapping; neither are fines thought to legitimize robbery. The difference between murder and execution, or between kidnapping and imprisonment, is that the first is unlawful and undeserved, the second a lawful and deserved punishment for an unlawful act. The physical similarities of the punishment to the crime are irrelevant. The relevant difference is not physical, but social.[5]

V. Justice, Excess, Degradation

We threaten punishments in order to deter crime. We impose them not only to make the threats credible but also as retribution (justice) for the crimes that were not deterred. Threats and punishments are necessary to deter and deterrence is a sufficient practical justification for them. Retribution is an independent moral justification. Although penalties can be unwise, repulsive, or inappropriate, and those punished can be pitiable, in a sense the infliction of legal punishment on a guilty person cannot be unjust. By committing the crime, the criminal volunteered to assume the risk of receiving a legal punishment that he could have avoided by not committing the crime. The punishment he suffers is the punishment he voluntarily risked suffering and, therefore, it is no more unjust to him than any other event for which one knowingly volunteers to assume the risk. Thus, the death penalty cannot be unjust to the guilty criminal.

There remain, however, two moral objections. The penalty may be regarded as always excessive as retribution and always morally degrading. To regard the death penalty as always excessive, one must believe that no crime—no matter how heinous—could possibly justify capital punishment. Such a belief can be neither corroborated nor refuted; it is an article of faith.

Alternatively, or concurrently, one may believe that everybody, the murderer no less than the victim, has an imprescriptible (natural?) right to life. The law therefore should not deprive anyone of life. I share Jeremy Bentham's view that any such "natural and imprescriptible rights" are "nonsense upon stilts."

Justice Brennan has insisted that the death penalty is "uncivilized," "inhuman," inconsistent with "human dignity" and with "the sanctity of life," that it "treats members of the human race as nonhumans, as objects to be toyed with and discarded," that it is "uniquely degrading to human dignity" and "by its very nature, [involves] a denial of the executed person's humanity." Justice Brennan does not say why he thinks execution "uncivilized." Hitherto most civilizations have had the death penalty, although it has been discarded in Western Europe, where it is currently unfashionable probably because of its abuse by totalitarian regimes.

By "degrading," Justice Brennan seems to mean that execution degrades the executed convicts. Yet philosophers, such as Immanuel Kant and G. F. W. Hegel, have insisted that, when deserved, execution, far from degrading the executed convict, affirms his humanity by affirming his rationality and his responsibility for his actions. They thought that execution, when deserved, is required for the sake of the convict's dignity. (Does not life imprisonment violate human dignity more than execution, by keeping alive a prisoner deprived of all autonomy?)

Common sense indicates that it cannot be death—or common fate—that is inhuman. Therefore, Justice Brennan must mean that death degrades when it comes not as a natural or accidental event, but as a deliberate social imposition. The murderer learns through his punishment that his fellow men have found him unworthy of living; that because he has murdered, he is being expelled from the community of the living. This degradation is self-inflicted. By murdering, the murderer has so dehumanized himself that he cannot remain among the living. The social recognition of his self-degradation is the punitive essence of execution. To believe, as Justice Brennan appears to, that the degradation is inflicted by the execution reverses the direction of causality.

Execution of those who have committed heinous murders may deter only one murder per year. If it does, it seems quite warranted. It is also the only fitting retribution for murder I can think of.

Notes

1. Death row as a semipermanent residence is cruel, because convicts are denied the normal amenities of prison life. Thus, unless death row residents are integrated into the prison population, the continuing accumulation of convicts on death row should lead us to accelerate either the rate of executions or the rate of commutations. I find little objection to integration.

2. The ideal of equality, unlike the ideal of retributive justice (which can be approximated separately in each instance), is clearly unattainable unless all guilty persons are apprehended, and thereafter tried, convicted, and sentenced by the same court, at the same time. Unequal justice is the best we can do; it is still better than the injustice, equal or unequal, which occurs if, for the sake of equality, we deliberately allow some who could be punished to escape.

3. If executions were shown to increase the murder rate in the long run, I would favor abolition. Sparing the innocent victims who would be spared, *ex hypothesi,* by the nonexecution of murderers would be more important to me than the execution, however just, of murderers. But although there is a lively discussion of the subject, no serious evidence exists to support the hypothesis that executions produce a higher murder rate. *Cf.* Phillips, *The Deterrent Effect of Capital Punishment: New Evidence on an Old Controversy,* 86 AM. J. Soc. 139 (1980) (arguing that murder rates drop immediately after executions of criminals).

4. Thus restitution (a civil liability) cannot satisfy the punitive purpose of penal sanctions, whether the purpose be retributive or deterrent.

5. Some abolitionists challenge: if the death penalty is just and serves as a deterrent, why not televise executions? The answer is simple. The death even of a murderer, however well-deserved, should not serve as public entertainment. It so served in earlier centuries. But in this respect our sensibility has changed for the better, I believe. Further, television unavoidably would trivialize executions, wedged in, as they would be, between game shows, situation comedies and the like. Finally, because televised executions would focus on the physical aspects of the punishment, rather than the nature of the crime and the suffering of the victim, a televised execution would present the murderer as the victim of the state. Far from communicating the moral significance of the execution, television would shift the focus to the pitiable fear of the murderer. We no longer place in cages those sentenced to imprisonment to expose them to public view. Why should we so expose those sentenced to execution?

Ernest van den Haag is a retired professor of jurisprudence and public policy. He has contributed more than 200 articles to magazines and sociology journals in the United States, England, France, and Italy, and he is the author of *Punishing Criminals: Concerning a Very Old and Painful Question* (Basic Books, 1978).

EXPLORING THE ISSUE

Is Capital Punishment a Bad Public Policy?

Critical Thinking and Reflection

1. Is capital punishment an "efficient" penal sanction?
2. Is the death penalty an "uncivilized" form of punishment? Explain your answer.

Is There Common Ground?

One of the most striking elements about the issue of capital punishment is that most of the public, the politicians, and even many criminological scholars do not seem to be fazed by empirical evidence. Each side marshalls empirical evidence to support its respective position. Opponents of capital punishment often draw from Thorsten Sellin's classic study *The Penalty of Death* (Sage Publications) to "prove" that the number of capital offenses is no lower in states that have the death penalty as compared to states that have abolished executions.

Almost all of the major presidential candidates in early 2000 supported the death penalty. In fact, most political candidates seem to support capital punishment nowadays. Supporters of capital punishment draw from numerous studies, including I. Ehrlich's "The Deterrent Effect of Capital Punishment," *American Economic Review* (vol. 65, 1975), pp. 397–417, and his "Capital Punishment and Deterrence: Some Further Thoughts and Additional Evidence," *Journal of Political Economy* (vol. 85, 1977), pp. 741–788. They also draw from W. Berns's *For Capital Punishment: Crime and the Morality of the Death Penalty* (Basic Books, 1979).

Generally, the empirical research indicates that the death penalty cannot conclusively be proven to deter others from committing homicides and other serious crimes. Entire scientific commissions have been charged with the responsibility of determining the deterrent effects of the death penalty (for example, the National Academy of Sciences in 1975). The gist of their conclusions was that the value of the death penalty as a deterrent "is not a settled matter."

As is typical with most aspects of human behavior, including crime and crime control, the issue is filled with much irony, paradox, and contradiction. First, clashing views over capital punishment rely largely on emotion.

The public's attitudes, politicians' attitudes, and even scholarly attitudes are frequently shaped more by sentiment and preconceived notions than by rational discourse. As F. Zimring and G. Hawkins indicate in *Capital Punishment and the American Agenda* (Cambridge University Press, 1986), very few scholars have ever changed their opinions about capital punishment.

However, a remarkable transformation occurred in February 2000: Governor George Ryan (R-Illinois) stopped executions in his state after 13 condemned criminals were exonerated while on death row. Twelve inmates had been executed in Illinois since 1976. Ryan and others now wonder if perhaps some of them had been innocent as well.

As we enter the twenty-first century, capital punishment remains a divisive issue. And despite dramatic opposition, such as Governor Ryan's, it probably has growing support. One useful, recent work in strong opposition to the practice is A. Sarat, ed., *The Killing State: Capital Punishment in Law, Politics, and Culture* (Oxford University Press, 1998). Also see "The Cruel and Ever More Unusual Punishment," *The Economist* (May 15, 1999).

Additional Resources

An interesting book that looks at both sides of the issue is *The Death Penalty: For and Against* (Rowman & Littlefield, 1997), with J. Reiman attacking and coauthor L. Pojman defending executions as retribution. An empirical study of a neglected aspect of the issue is "An Empirical Examination of Commutations and Executions in Post-*Furman* Capital Cases," by W. Pridemore, *Justice Quarterly* (March 2000). Another series of research articles can be found in the issue of *Criminal Justice Policy Review* entitled "Special Issue on the Death Penalty" (vol. 10, no. 1, 1999). A recent work by a longtime critic of capital punishment is R. M. Bohn's

Deathquest: An Introduction to the Theory and Practice of Capital Punishment in the United States (Anderson, 1999).

For a take on Hollywood's many films on executions, see "Death Row, Aisle Seat," by A. Sarat, *The American Prospect* (February 14, 2000). A good overview dealing with women and the death penalty is K. A. O'Shea's *Women and the Death Penalty in the United States, 1900–1998* (Greenwood, 1999). In addition to the many studies by Victor Streib on executing children, see *A Review of Juvenile Executions in America* by R. L. Hale (Edwin Mellen Press, 1997). A concise overview of relevant statistics through December 1999 is *Capital Punishment 1998,* a Bureau of Justice Statistics Bulletin (December 1999).

Two studies of the deterrence issue are "Capital Punishment and the Deterrence of Violent Crime in Comparable Countries," by D. Cheatwood, *Criminal Justice Review* (August 1993) and "Deterrence or Brutalization?" by J. Cochran et al., *Criminology* (February 1994). For a survey of the attitudes toward capital punishment among politicians, see M. Sandys and E. McGarrell, "Attitudes Toward Capital Punishment Among Indiana Legislators," *Justice Quarterly* (December 1994). A popular media account of a death penalty sentence given to a mentally impaired individual is "Untrue Confessions," by

J. Smolowe, *Time* (May 22, 1995). An interesting comparison of the effects of publicized executions on whites and blacks is "The Impact of Publicized Executions on Homicide," by S. Stack, *Criminal Justice and Behavior* (June 1995). The *Bureau of Justice Statistics Bulletin* routinely updates death penalty statistics. For an outstanding description of death row, see Von Drehle's *Among the Lowest of the Dead: The Culture of Death Row* (Times Books, 1995).

L. K. Gillespie's *Dancehall Ladies: The Crimes and Executions of America's Condemned Women* (University Press of America, 1997) is a solid historical discussion. D. A. Cabana's *Death at Midnight: The Confessions of an Executioner* (Northeast University Press, 1996) is an insightful insider's account. A helpful legal overview is *Death Penalty Cases: Leading U.S. Supreme Court Cases on Capital Punishment* by B. Latzer (Butterworth-Heinemann, 1998). Finally, two outstanding articles that provide both historical and theoretical background for understanding violence and capital punishment as an extension of inequalities maintenance are Roberta Senechal de la Roche, "Collective Violence as Social Control," *Sociological Forum* (March 1996) and "The Sociogenesis of Lynching," in W. F. Brundae, ed., *Under Penalty of Death: Essays on Lynching in the South* (University of North Carolina Press, 1997).

Internet References . . .

Death Penalty Information Center

www.deathpenaltyinfo.org/

National Geographic

http://news.nationalgeographic.com /news/2013/13/130412-death-penalty-capital -punishment-culture-amnesty-international/

Unit 4

UNIT

Trends in Criminology and Criminal Justice

Social research can sometimes be controversial; however, it remains a core task for criminologists and criminal justice scholars. Among the more important criminological research findings of the past 25 years is that a relatively small core of criminals commit a disproportionate amount of crime. Also important to criminal justice is the development and utilization of high technology, such as DNA testing, computer units and video cameras in patrol cars, and other innovations in investigatory techniques. Questions addressed in this section ask whether the United States should pass strict gun control laws, whether the police should enforce zero tolerance laws, whether marijuana should be legalized, whether the police should be required to wear body cameras, and whether Apple should be required to assist the government's efforts to crack cell phones needed for criminal investigations. Conducting high-quality research into crime and criminality, and then incorporating the results into effective social policies, is one of the biggest challenges facing modern criminologists.

Selected, Edited, and with Issue Framing Material by:
Thomas J. Hickey, *State University of New York at Cobleskill*

ISSUE

Should the United States Pass Strict Gun Control Laws?

YES: Morris M., "10 Arguments for Gun Control," *Listverse* (2013)

NO: FlameHorse, "10 Arguments Against Gun Control," *Listverse* (2013)

Learning Outcomes

After reading this issue, you will be able to:

- Present the U.S. Supreme Court's decisions in *United States v. Miller* (1937) and *District of Columbia v. Heller* (2008).
- Discuss the relationship between gun usage and violent crimes.
- Discuss the relationship between gun ownership and suicide rates.
- Discuss whether the wording of the Second Amendment actually prohibits the government from passing strict gun control laws.
- Present 10 arguments for against gun control laws.
- Discuss whether you believe the government can be trusted to be beneficent and just and, if not, whether we should have strict gun control laws.
- Discuss what the research data show about whether armed civilian interventions are likely to stop mass shootings.

ISSUE SUMMARY

YES: Writer "Morris M." argues that strict gun control laws will help to reduce the rates of carnage committed with firearms in the United States. Moreover, he states that the United States has 88.9 firearms for every 100 people. That's more than Yemen, Mexico, Pakistan, and the West Bank/Gaza combined. Yet there is a considerable amount of research to indicate that more gun control would keep us safer, and potentially even save our lives.

NO: Writer "FlameHorse" argues that "to debate gun control is a futile exercise. They cannot be controlled—not anymore. The continuation of buying and selling them cannot make the situation any worse because criminals will never again have to go far to find one."

Do strict gun control laws help to reduce violent crime? Or, do gun control laws fail to stem violent behavior and help social predators to victimize law-abiding citizens? Does the Second Amendment to the U.S. Constitution give people an absolute right to bear arms? These are interesting questions that have important implications for violence control in U.S. society.

Because the issue of a constitutional right to bear arms has been so controversial, perhaps it is best to begin our analysis here. The Second Amendment states: "A well-regulated Militia being necessary to the security of a free State, the right of the people to keep and bear Arms shall not be infringed." Throughout our history, the U.S. Supreme Court has held that most of the protections in the U.S. Constitution's Bill of Rights—"fundamental rights"—apply to state proceedings. In 2008, the Court held that the Second Amendment's "right to bear arms" is a fundamental right. Prior to this important case, the Court's main decision interpreting the Second Amendment was *United States v. Miller,* 307 U.S. 174 (1939), which upheld the National Firearms Act of 1934, the law that required the registration of sawed-off shotguns. The Court stated:

> [Without] any evidence tending to show that possession or use of a "shotgun having a barrel of less than 18 inches in length" at this time has some reasonable relationship to the preservation or efficiency of a well regulated militia, we cannot say that the Second Amendment guarantees the right to keep and bear such an instrument.

As *Miller* illustrates, the Supreme Court and most lower courts for most of our nation's history had tied the right to bear arms to the maintenance of a "well-regulated militia." They did not construe the Second Amendment to convey a more generalized right of the citizenry to own all types of firearms.

In 2008, however, the U.S. Supreme Court in *District of Columbia v. Heller,* 554 U.S. 570, recognized a personal right to own firearms based on the Second Amendment to the U.S. Constitution, independent of an individual's participation in a state militia. (This important precedent is considered in much greater detail in Issue 19 of this work). Under the *Heller* rationale it would seem inevitable that many state and local gun control laws throughout the United States will be invalidated.

Another important issue, however, is the impact that strict gun control laws would have on the United States. The authors of the YES and NO selections in this section have very different views on this controversy. Writer "Morris M." argues that there is a strong relationship between the prevalence of guns in society and the incidence of homicide and suicide. Moreover, he observes that the United States has 88.9 firearms for every one hundred people. That's more than Yemen, Mexico, Pakistan, and the West Bank/Gaza combined. Yet there is a considerable amount of research to indicate that more gun control would keep us safer, and potentially even save our lives.

Writer "FlameHorse" argues that "to debate gun control is a futile exercise. They cannot be controlled—not anymore. The continuation of buying and selling them cannot make the situation any worse because criminals will never again have to go far to find one." What is your position regarding the ownership of firearms? Should the right to own a firearm be a fundamental right of citizenship in the United States? Should states and their municipal subdivisions have the authority to regulate gun ownership? Should and can Americans trust the government to protect them against violent crime? Is taking guns from the population an effective measure to reduce homicide rates in the United States? These are important questions that directly impact our quality of life. As you read the selections in this section, try to develop a sense of whether gun ownership should be freely permitted, restricted, or banned altogether.

YES ↵

Morris M.

10 Arguments for Gun Control

There's no doubt about it—we sure do love our guns. Last year, the small arms survey concluded that the United States has 88.9 firearms for every one hundred people. That's more than Yemen, Mexico, Pakistan, and the West Bank/Gaza combined. Yet there's a heck-load of research out there indicating that a pinch of gun control would keep us safer, and potentially even save our lives. After all:

10. More Guns Equal More Homicides

If you compared gun ownership levels with homicide rates, what would you expect to see? Fewer people willing to start a fight when everyone is armed? No correlation at all? Well, not exactly: according to decades of data analyzed by the Harvard School of Public Health, guns and homicides go together like Nicholas Cage and terrible movies.

Put simply, if your fellow citizens have easy access to guns, they're more likely to kill you than if they don't have access. Interestingly, this turned out to be true not just for the 26 developed countries analyzed, but on a State-to-State level too.

Of course, this doesn't mean that you definitely won't get shot in Massachusetts—just as it's entirely possible that you'll live 90 years in Arizona and never experience the slightest harassment. But statistically, the trend holds true. And on the subject of statistics. . . .

9. More Guns Also Equal More Suicides

There's a widespread perception that committing suicide is like planning a wedding or something; you sit down, give it a lot of thought, set a date, and get on with it. But study after study indicates that suicide is not so much a rational decision, but something people do on the spur of the moment—meaning that a lack of access to a death-shooting murder-stick at that critical moment could be the difference between life and death.

It might sound far-fetched, but look at the evidence: according to this report in the Boston Globe, states with high levels of gun ownership have a suicide rate almost twice as high as those with low ownership levels. Even more worrying, people who committed suicide were found to be 17 times more likely to live with guns at home than not. Now, you might assume that gun owners or gun owning states are more likely to have mental health issues (for whatever reason), but research shows this isn't true. So you have a bunch of people exactly as miserable as people in other states, but anywhere between two and ten times more likely to end up "going the Heming-way."

8. The Public Supports (Some) Gun Control

For all the claims of politicians that they represent the public, the truth is that they basically don't. For every "Mr. Smith Goes to Washington" type sticking up for the little guy, there are about two hundred others doing their best to trample him into the ground.

Case in point: at least 44 percent of Americans support very strict gun laws, with that number rising to a whopping 91 percent (LINK 6) when it comes to common-sense stuff like required background checks. You may recognize this as the same common-sense policy Congress recently shot down in what can only be assumed was an effort to become even more unpopular.

This support for gun control, by the way, is pretty bipartisan: even with controversial stuff like reinstating the assault weapons ban, roughly half of Republicans are in favor, along with a majority of Democrats and Independents. In other words, people are largely pro-gun control—it's the politicians who aren't.

7. Most Massacres Utilize Legal Weapons

Between 1982 and 2012, the United States had roughly 62 mass shootings. That's an astonishing number—but it's not what I'm driving at. Instead, this research by Mother Jones (scroll down halfway) shows that, of those 62 shootings, 49 were perpetrated using legal weapons.

And guess what? Half of all mass shooters used assault weapons or high-capacity magazines—meaning that a few sensible restrictions could have saved a heck-load of lives. While someone really determined to pull off a massacre could do it using a handgun, shotgun, or even a musket if they had to, they'd be pretty unlikely to kill anywhere near as many people as they would with, say, an AR-15 assault rifle. So putting controls on the assault rifle has to be a good thing, right?

6. Banning Them Saves Lives

Unlike Congress, the Australian Parliament likes action. In 1996, a mass shooter killed 35 people in Port Arthur in a massacre so pointlessly depressing I'm not going to mention a single other detail. Two weeks later, the conservative Prime Minister, John Howard, launched perhaps the most aggressive clamp-down on gun ownership in history.

Around 650,000 automatic and semi-automatic weapons were destroyed and a whole raft of checks and controls brought in. The end result? The first decade of the law alone saw a 59 percent drop in Australian gun-homicides, while non-firearm-related homicides stayed level. In other words, people didn't switch to machetes or poison so much as they stopped killing altogether. As for mass shootings: well, Australia's gone all the way from 11 a decade (1986–1996) to zero.

5. The Second Amendment

No other passage in the U.S. Constitution is as hotly debated as the Second Amendment. In full, this controversial sentence reads:

> "A well-regulated militia, being necessary to the security of a free state, the right of the people to keep and bear arms, shall not be infringed."

Although most people focus on the "bear arms" part, the real key word is "militia." The thing is, in 1791, no one really knew if this whole "Union" thing was going to work out. Many of the States distrusted each other, and everyone distrusted big government. The possibility of

invasion was frighteningly real, and the Second Amendment was put in place to make sure that a citizen's militia could defend the principles of the constitution.

What the Second Amendment *didn't* do was grant any drunken asshole the right to stagger into a gun shop and buy an assault rifle without a single background check. In 1939, the Supreme Court even ruled that:

> "The Second Amendment must be interpreted and applied with the view of its purpose of rendering effective Militia."

By 2008, they'd extended that to cover self-defense in the home—something else that doesn't require a high-capacity magazine and the ability to kill everything within a three block radius. But that's all they'd extended it to: there's no constitutional "right" to carry a concealed weapon, no "right" to use armor-piercing bullets—just the right to defend yourself against intruders. And as Stephen King famously said: "if you can't kill an intruder with ten rounds, you need to go back to the shooting range."

4. Assault Weapons Aren't "Sport"

Let's be frank: very few of those who support gun control guys want an absolute, total ban on weapons. Personally, I think that if someone wants to buy a rifle and go hunting in the weekend, it's their business and has nothing to do with me. Equally, if you simply feel safer knowing that you have a shotgun in the house to defend your kids, fair enough.

But there's no conceivable reason to own an AR-15, a pump action shotgun, armor-piercing bullets or a high-capacity magazine. Firing a semi-auto at a piece of cardboard is no more "sport" than using a bazooka to play pool is "leisure." It simply appeals to the fraction of the population who dream of re-enacting Scarface's last stand, every time they get a letter from the IRS.

3. We Have Too Many Already

I mentioned in the introduction that the United States has more guns per capita than Yemen—but that doesn't even begin to describe our love of guns. According to data published in the *Guardian*, gun ownership in the United States is literally the highest in the world. Not in the "developed world," or the West; in the *whole* world. That makes Americans more heavily armed than Russians, Pakistanis, and people from Afghanistan.

Even Latin American countries overrun by drug cartels, with murder rates comparable to war zones—such as Colombia, Mexico, and Guatemala—have fewer guns per capita. Even literal war zones, like Somalia and D.R. Congo, have less heavy weaponry. When you feel more inclined to arm yourself than guys who live in a failed nation state where the average life expectancy is less than 50 years, it might be time to think about slowing down.

2. Arming Everyone Won't Help

Of course, we could just as easily go in the opposite direction. If everyone was armed, no mass shooter would stand a chance, right? Not exactly. When Mother Jones crunched the numbers, they found that successful interventions by armed civilians had occurred in only 1.6 percent of all mass shootings since 1980. In other words, it happened a single time in 30 years.

In two other cases, armed civilians managed to subdue a killer after the shooting had already happened, which you could argue is still a good thing. But plenty of less-fortunate people who tried to get involved have only wound up adding to the casualty list. In 2005, for example, Brendan McKown and Mark Wilson both tried separately to confront an armed shooter. McKown was blasted into a coma, while Wilson was instantly killed.

The trouble is, you might be an ace down the range—but when you're in the middle of utter carnage, it's another thing altogether. That's why one of the few possibly successful interventions—at the end of the 2002 Appalachian School of Law shooting—came from an ex-cop. Training makes a hell of a difference.

1. Assault Weapons Won't Save You

The last big myth about owning enough firepower to rival Pablo Escobar is that it'll protect you when the government comes. It won't. A psychopathic Federal Government would have the entire U.S. Army at its disposal, along with enough firepower to destroy the planet several times over. The best anyone making a "last stand" could hope for is to get out alive, instead of re-enacting the finale of the Waco Siege.

All that security assault weapons and their ilk might offer anyone is security of mind—which honestly doesn't seem worth it, stacked up against everything else on this list.

MORRIS M. is a freelance writer and newly qualified teacher. He hopes to make a difference in his students' lives. His articles have appeared on a wide variety of sites across the Internet.

FlameHorse

NO

10 Arguments Against Gun Control

This list is not intended to incite controversy, but to foster an even-sided debate. The issue of gun control is global, but since it is most controversial in the United States of America, that nation is referred to most in the following entries.

The US Constitution's Second Amendment reads: "A well regulated Militia, being necessary to the security of a free State, the right of the people to keep and bear Arms, shall not be infringed."

10 There Is Murder in the UK

Almost all handguns are banned from civilian possession, ownership, purchase, or sale in the United Kingdom as a result of the Second Firearms Act of 1997. This was in response to the Dunblane Massacre, in which 43-year-old Thomas Hamilton walked into an elementary school and shot dead 16 children, aged six or younger, and one teacher before killing himself. He used four handguns.

Now that modern handguns are no longer legal to have in the UK, let us take a look at some murder rates. The rate for intentional homicide in the UK in 1996—the year of the Dunblane Massacre—was 1.12 per 100,000. It was 1.24 in 1997, when the Firearms Act went into effect, and 1.43 in 1998. The rate rose to a peak of 2.1 in 2002 and has fallen since to 1.23 as of 2010. These numbers have, however, been called into question due to possible under-reporting of violent crimes in the UK.

It cannot be denied that the rate of homicides via guns has fallen dramatically since Dunblane, but the rate of murders has gone up. To say these higher numbers are the result of fewer people able to arm themselves for defense is drastically jumping to a conclusion, but the fact does remain that more people are killing each other in the UK today than when guns were legal to have. Even the police are almost all armed with tasers instead, so handguns are very hard to come by. All the numbers are higher in the US, of course, where there are more people, and there have been no more school shootings in the UK since Dunblane.

But in 2005, there were 765 intentional murders in the UK and most of these were committed with knives. Blunt objects follow, then strangulation, fire, and poison. Banning guns has halted rampage shootings, but it does not address the issue of people killing each other. In the US, the number of intentional homicides in 2004 was 10,654—a number that would have been much lower without access to guns, but still terribly high. Opponents of gun control are always quick to question how many victims of knives, clubs, and strangulation would be alive if they had had a gun.

9 Literary Infallibility

Thomas Jefferson once wrote "Our liberty depends on the freedom of the press, and that cannot be limited without being lost." Gun enthusiasts often couple this with a quote from Ben Franklin, "Democracy is two wolves and a lamb voting on what to have for lunch. Liberty is a well-armed lamb contesting the vote."

Unfortunately, Franklin never said that. It was probably written by someone on the Internet, who then tacked his name onto it. But Jefferson's premise of not limiting the freedom of the press can extend to any freedom. Right now, American legislators are up in arms, if you'll pardon the pun, over the question of whether to limit some firearms' ammunition capacities. Proponents cite the only obvious use for an assault rifle—killing people—and defend ammunition limitations as a compromise that will save lives. Opponents maintain that a single life lost due to some maniac with a gun is just as excessive as 30.

The issue of fully automatic firearms has been a hotbed for a long time. In some states, they are legal for civilians, provided that an extra fee is paid. In North Carolina, a fully automatic M2HB .50 Browning heavy machine gun is perfectly legal to use as a home defense weapon or for hunting. This is because that state considers any limitation of guns to be unconstitutional. California does not agree. In that state, no semiautomatic firearm may contain more than 10 rounds at any time. Assault rifles are completely banned. There are some federal limits: no caliber is permissible larger than .50 unless a special and expensive license is obtained and cannons are legal to own but not to fire with real ammunition.

The debates will go on for a very long time, and most of them center on the Constitution's wording of the Second Amendment. How should we define "a well-regulated militia"? Proponents of gun control claim this should entail proper training. Opponents claim that almost all gun owners train themselves in their free time. They further claim that, should any affront be made to the Second Amendment, those who want to control guns will no longer have any line to cross. They will interpret as they see fit any word or phrase of any Amendment in order to limit more and more rights until, in this case, all guns are banned from civilian use.

8 The Civilian Need for Assault Rifles

An assault rifle is any weapon which fires high-powered rifle rounds rather than pistol rounds, semi or fully automatically. The weapon reloads each round on its own—all you have to do is pull the trigger again and again. It is true that these weapons were invented for the purpose of warfare, not hunting, though they can be used for either. Proponents of even limited gun control maintain that, if nothing else is done, assault rifles should have magazines of no more than 10 rounds at a time. The argument typically brought out in defense of this position claims that in any self-defense scenario, assault rifles are overkill.

Gun control opponents, however, have long argued that the Second Amendment was put in place not just for ordinary home defense against burglars but specifically to guarantee that the nation could never be overcome by any military power foreign or domestic. If the five branches of the US military were beaten by, say, a nuclear holocaust, the only national defense left would be the civilians themselves. Any subsequent military invasion—probably armed with AK-47 variants—would find it very easy to overrun civilians armed only with lever, bolt, and pump action weapons.

7 Welcome to Texas

The first modern school shooting occurred on August 1, 1966 and deservedly made national headlines because no one had ever heard of such diabolical insanity. If you have a problem with your boss, you might get mad and shoot him, but sniping innocent random strangers from up to 400 yards for 90 minutes somehow makes even less sense. Whitman's tower rampage on the University of Austin

was not the first school shooting in the sense of a single maniac killing indiscriminately, but it was possibly the first to push the notion into the public eye. It was a direct cause of the institution of SWAT teams among city police forces around the nation. There were none before this incident, and the Austin police found themselves woefully outgunned at the outset.

They were considerably aided, in Ramiro Martinez's opinion, by several dozen students and passersby who did not take cover, but instead ran to their vehicles and brought back hunting rifles. They then took cover alongside police officers and opened fire on the observation deck, forcing Whitman to take cover and fire less often and less accurately. Martinez was one of the three officers who entered the tower and killed Whitman, and he thanked the civilians for their assistance. Whitman would certainly have killed many more than 12 from the 28th story observation deck had he not been harried by the civilians' return fire.

6 It Didn't Work for Germany

On March 10, 2009, 28-year-old Michael McClendon shot 10 people dead in a spree that covered three counties of Alabama. Gun control was immediately revived in national debates, primarily because he used two assault rifles for most of the rampage. He also had a shotgun and a pistol. McClendon had left a suicide note in which he made it clear that he despondent and enraged over his dead-end life. He began the spree by shooting his own mother, all three of her dogs, and burning down her house. He then drove down the highway shooting random people from his vehicle.

The gun control debate did not reach fever pitch, however, until a German high school student initiated a very similar rampage the next day in Winnenden, Baden-Wurttemberg, in southwestern Germany. Seventeen-year-old Timothy Kretschmer began at Albertville-Realschule, where he murdered 12 people, most of them women, then carjacked Igor Wolf and forced him to drive Kretschmer to the town of Wendlingen. While in the backseat, Kretschmer reloaded his magazines and answered Wolf's question of why he had done it. "For fun. Because it's fun." He ordered Wolf off the road near a car dealership and ran inside, murdered two more people, and then shot it out with the police, wounding two and being wounded in both legs. He opened fire on every random person he could see, then shot himself.

He killed 15 and wounded nine, all with a single 9mm pistol. This was his father's gun, since he was too young to own one, and it was the only gun his father had not locked in a safe. He had illegally kept it out and loaded in case of burglary. This is not illegal in the US. Here, we see that a child, who should not have been able to acquire a gun, did so in a nation with extremely strict laws on gun control.

5 Gun Control Equals Absolute Despotism

Of all arguments against controlling guns, this one crystallizes everything the ravenous pro-gun crowd has had to say over the years. Most Americans do not trust their government, or more properly, the people who hold the highest positions in it. This was the feeling long before Edward Snowden leaked proof of the government spying illegally on its own citizens and nations around the world. Snowden deemed this too similar to "Big Brother," as Orwell calls it, but the US government not only disagreed with him, it even defended what it was doing as not in any way criminal, though its own law books clearly differ. Snowden is not without supporters. Twitter has erected security firewalls to guard against NSA spying, and Google, Facebook, and Tumblr have followed suit.

Pro-gun citizens consider their guns the same protection. They arm themselves for the possibility of government agents taking away their rights one by one until they live in a police state in which the government is able to do anything it wants because the civilian populace is unarmed and cannot resist. In these terms, any gun control is viewed as a threat to liberty, and though the Constitution guarantees rights, it does not enforce anything. Guns do.

The Snowden fiasco in particular brought the rampant and frighteningly amoral dishonesty of the federal government back once again to the front of global debate, since America had been spying on China, France, Germany, and even Great Britain against their wishes. The pro-gun American citizens have seized on this embarrassment as yet more proof that the government is out to take away its citizens' rights, as many as possible until democracy is gone and tyranny is in place. The only truly effective protection of American citizens' rights to freedom of speech, press, religion, and others are their guns.

4 Rampage Shooters Like Soft Targets

If rampage killers are so depressed that they intend to kill themselves afterward, then why hasn't anyone whipped out an assault rifle and attempted to kill people inside the US Bullion Depository near Fort Knox? Because breaking into the White House would be a lot easier. Do these shooters fear the firepower lurking around the gold? Not if they want to die, but what they do fear is not killing a lot of people beforehand. They have a rage in them, and it appears to be always the same. Motive or not, they want to exact revenge. The more dead, the merrier. The media, of course, is largely to blame for turning any shooting incident into a circus. Presently, a lovers' spat that boils over in public will make brief national headlines as a possible rampage scene.

The James Holmeses, the Cho Seung-huis, and Adam Lanzas are the sort who want to one-up the last massacre, and this can't be done in a bank. The police are on the lookout for the banks and there aren't enough people anyway. It can't be done at the White House or a police station, but malls, schools, ordinary workplaces, and churches are all soft and rich targets because they contain many people and few of them are armed.

Suppose there were a guarantee that everyone in a church on Sunday morning were armed to the teeth— pistols, shotguns, and assault rifles, and more importantly, that they were all trained to fight back. Even the most desperately depressed rage-a-holic would pick a different target. The Amarillo school district in the good ol' state of Texas has gone to the extreme of arming its entire faculty and staff as a warning to would-be maniacs. This means the teachers, janitors, groundskeepers, and secretaries all have guns on their person.

3 The Eighteenth Amendment

This amendment prohibited the production, transport, and sale of alcohol within the United States of America. It was a result of the Temperance Movement. Most of the politicians in Washington, DC strongly supported the imposition of the ban, but when it went into effect on January 17, 1920, the public responded in a way that neither the temperance movement nor the politicians had expected—few people heeded the criminalization, and those who had been manufacturing alcohol continued doing so regardless of the law. Everyone seemed haughtily recalcitrant and alcohol use flourished even more than before. The police around the country were woefully ineffective in curbing its production, sale, or consumption.

Career criminals like Al Capone became extremely rich by gaining control over the importation to entire cities. Those too afraid of the police resorted to making their own booze at home, and this resulted in many deaths from poisoning.

Replace every reference to alcohol above with a reference to guns and you have the most assured aftermath of a similar prohibition on guns—except in this scenario, the crimes involved are much deadlier. The Al Capones who rise up will attempt to gain control over a city's illegal importation of guns, and there will be street violence worse than that of the most dangerous areas of Chicago today.

The public outcry leading up to the national ban might not cause a nationwide uprising. Such a disaster can only be conjectured as alternate history fiction, but if the government enforced the ban by raiding homes and businesses, there would certainly be small-scale uprisings that easily spread. Martial law would have to be imposed in some large cities, especially in Texas. Texas might actually make good on its common threat to secede, since it does retain a provision in its state constitution which permits this. There would be civil war, but with much deadlier weapons. The war would probably not be fought in as open a form as the previous Civil War, but those who refuse to relinquish their firearms would engage in guerrilla warfare and splinter cell terrorism. None of this is to say that the US military, if loyal to the ban, could not put down such rebellion to it, but the consequences would be horrific and long-lasting.

2 Laws Do Not Apply to Criminals

We've all heard this one many times, but a point of contention that just won't go away must be quite convincing to some. Gun laws are all founded on the principle of making a nation safer by limiting its civilian population's access to guns, but laws against murder and violence do not apply to those who have given up on life and intend to die while killing as many people as they can. Laws against theft do not apply to a person who intends to steal something. The sole thing the criminally-minded care about is not getting caught. Some are reformed in prison, but in large part, those who want to break a law are not going to feel remorse when they are caught. Give them a chance and they will do it again.

From this perspective, it is difficult to fathom the logic of enacting newer, stricter gun laws on an already lawful society. Most of us obey such laws. Sale of guns is forbidden within the city limits of Chicago, an ordinance that went into effect in 2010. For the year 2013, the city's murder count is 374. There were 432 in 2010 and 500 in 2012. The FBI has named Chicago the nation's murder capital. Thus, the city ordinance did nothing to reduce its murder rate.

None of this is to imply that in areas of well-armed civilians, the violent crime rate must go down. That is not true. The highest crime rates in 2012 were in the South, where gun ownership is at its highest. But this fact as well corroborates that any imposition of gun control does not address the issue of gun-related crime.

1 Maybe in a Perfect World . . .

Let us disentangle ourselves from the trees and take a look at the forest. Because there is no national gun registry, the exact number of guns in civilian hands in the US cannot be determined, but a conservative estimate places it—as of 2010, when the gun-buying craze was just reaching its peak—at 270 million weapons. This was about 89 guns per 100 people, the most heavily armed civilian population in the world. Yemen was second with 55 per 100, and Switzerland third. As of 2013, Serbia is second.

Another estimate, conducted by Congressional Research in 2012, places the total number of weapons in US civilian hands at 310 million as of 2009. By today, that means almost 1 gun for every single citizen, including infants. What would gun control even mean at this point? Assume this federal law: from 2014 on, no more assault rifles. Those who already own one may keep theirs, but such weapons will disappear from gun stores and pawn shops. Have we controlled much of anything? There are still at least 3 million assault rifles out there.

In a perfect world, gun control would mean going house to house throughout the nation and taking away every single firearm, including muzzle loaders. That would be impossible. Regardless of its constitutionality, gun owners would either fight back until there were a nationwide civil war or simply hide their weapons and claim they have none. Since most of those in the US are unregistered, no one knows who has what. Owners could always claim they destroyed those that are registered.

Thus, to debate gun control is a futile exercise. They cannot be controlled—not anymore. The continuation of buying and selling them cannot make the situation any worse because criminals will never again have to go far to find one.

FLAME**HORSE** is a writer for Listverse.

EXPLORING THE ISSUE

Should the United States Pass Strict Gun Control Laws?

Critical Thinking and Reflection

1. What do you think about the U.S. Supreme Court's decisions in *United States v. Miller (1937)* and *District of Columbia v. Heller* (2008)?
2. What is the relationship between gun usage and violent crimes?
3. What is the relationship between gun ownership and suicide rates?
4. Does the wording of the Second Amendment actually prohibit the government from passing strict gun control laws?
5. What are the 10 arguments for strict gun control laws? What are the 10 arguments against strict gun control laws?
6. Can our government be trusted to be beneficent and just and if not, should we have strict gun control laws?
7. What do the research data show about whether armed civilian interventions are likely to stop mass shootings?

Is There Common Ground?

Violent crime is an unfortunate fact of life in the United States. According to a study published in June 2005 by the U.S. Bureau of Justice Statistics (BJS), 16,204 murders were committed in the United States in 2002. The study also included information about the types of weapons used in these crimes. For all murders in 2002 in which the type of weapon used was known, 64.0 percent were committed with firearms. Interestingly, 51.7 percent of the murders were committed with handguns, 4.3 percent with rifles, 4.3 percent with shotguns, and 3.6 percent were not specified. Moreover, knives were used in 16.5 percent of the cases and blunt objects were used 5.7 percent of the time.

Similar patterns were observed in family violence cases. In the 1,958 murder cases involving family members, 50.1 percent used firearms: 36.8 percent involved handguns, 4.4 percent used rifles, 6.1 percent used shotguns, and 2.9 percent were not specified.

What then, do these statistics tell us about murder in the United States? First, a majority of murders and suicides are committed with firearms. Moreover, a large percentage of all murder cases involved handguns. In 2002, murder cases involving family members were somewhat less likely to involve firearms; however, a large number of these murders involved guns as well.

Based on these findings, do you believe that states should pass laws to remove firearms from the population? The authors of the both selections in this section would be likely to answer this question in very different ways.

Writer Morris M. would be likely to assert that the number of murders, mass murders, and suicides committed with firearms would support gun ownership restrictions. Conversely, professors Gordon Barnes and Robert Hadley believe that because the general populace cannot trust the government to be beneficent and just, the citizenry should be encouraged to own firearms.

After reading the selections in this section are you more or less likely to support restrictions on firearms ownership in the United States? Is there a middle ground in this debate that you would support, such as a ban on assault weapons, multi-shot magazines, or handguns?

References

Bureau of Justice Statistics, *Family Violence Statistics* (U.S. Department of Justice, 2005).

Additional Resources

Robert J. Spitzer, *The Politics of Gun Control* (Chatham House, 1995).

Lisa D. Brush, "Blown Away: American Women and Guns," *Violence Against Women* (vol. 11, no. 9, September 2005).

Linda A. Teplin, Gary M. McClelland, Karen M. Abram, and Darinka Miluesnic, "Early Violent Death Among Delinquent Youth: A Prospective Longitudinal Study," *Pediatrics* (vol. 115, no. 6, June 2005).

Jeffrey B. Bingenheimer, Robert T. Brennan, and Felton J. Earls, "Firearm Violence Exposure and Serious Violent Behavior," *Science* (vol. 308, no. 5726, May 27, 2005).

Janice Hopkins Tanne, "U.S. Workers Who Carry Guns Are More Likely to Be Killed on the Job," *British Medical Journal* (International Edition) (vol. 330, no. 7499, May 7, 2005).

Internet References . . .

The Atlantic, "The Aftermath of Reversing California's Severe Three Strikes Law." May 23, 2016.

www.theatlantic.com/video

Prison Policy Organization, "'Three Strikes Laws': Five Years Later." 2004.

www.prisonpolicy.org

The Stanford Justice Advocacy Project

https://law.stanford.edu/stanford-justice -advocacy-project/

Three Strikes Organization, "15 Years of 'Three Strikes,' 1994 to 2008 and Still Working."

www.threestrikes.org/pdf/

Selected, Edited, and with Issue Framing Material by:
Thomas J. Hickey, *State University of New York at Cobleskill*

ISSUE

Should Marijuana Be Legalized?

YES: Ethan A. Nadelmann, from "An End to Marijuana Prohibition: The Drive to Legalize Picks Up," *National Review* (2004)

NO: Charles D. Stimson, from "Legalizing Marijuana: Why Citizens Should Just Say No," *The Heritage Foundation* (2010)

Learning Outcomes

After reading this issue, you will be able to:

- Discuss the number of persons arrested and imprisoned for marijuana violations in the United States.
- Discuss the annual costs of enforcing marijuana laws in the United States.
- Discuss J. S. Mill's position on the nature and limits of power that can be legitimately exercised by society over an individual.
- Discuss whether marijuana is a "gateway" drug.
- Discuss the present legal status of "medical marijuana."
- Discuss the potential benefits of keeping marijuana illegal.
- Discuss the following statement: "Public support for the 'drug war' is more about moral values or fears than rational public safety measures."

ISSUE SUMMARY

YES: Ethan A. Nadelmann, founder and director of the Drug Policy Alliance, contends that contemporary marijuana laws are unique among American criminal laws because no other law is both enforced so widely and yet deemed unnecessary by such a substantial portion of the public. Enforcing marijuana laws also wastes tens of billions of taxpayer dollars annually.

NO: Charles D. Stimson, a senior legal fellow in the Center for Legal & Judicial Studies at the Heritage Foundation, argues that marijuana legalization will increase crime, drug use, and social dislocation—the exact opposite of what pro-legalization advocates promise. Moreover, he believes that there is substantial evidence to suggest that legalizing marijuana would lead to greater problems of addiction, violence, disorder, and death.

Should people be free to smoke marijuana without fear of criminal sanctions? Or, does smoking marijuana harm society as a whole as well as the drug user? A recent study by the Sentencing Project, a Washington-based think tank, has concluded that the drug war in the United States has shifted significantly in the past decade from a focus on hard drugs to marijuana law enforcement. Is this focus on marijuana suppression an effective or efficient way to spend our tax dollars? Moreover, is

it good social policy to use criminal punishment to try to prevent people from using marijuana? The answers to these questions defy an easy resolution; however, some things are very clear about marijuana usage in the United States.

First, large numbers of people are affected by the stringent enforcement of our nation's marijuana laws. A recent study found that approximately 700,000 people are arrested on marijuana charges each year, and 60,000 are confined to jails and prisons. Moreover, approximately

87 percent of marijuana arrests are for nothing more than simple possession of small quantities (Drug Policy Alliance, "Warning: Marijuana Causes Drug Czar to Behave Irrationally, Act Paranoid and Waste Billions of Dollars," May 4, 2005, http://drugpolicy.org). Second, the costs to taxpayers to enforce marijuana laws are considerable. The annual price tag for enforcing marijuana laws is approximately $10–15 billion.

Moreover, recent studies suggest that a large number of Americans appear to favor decriminalization of marijuana. One poll suggests that 72 percent of Americans believe that fines, not imprisonment, are appropriate sanctions for violating marijuana laws. Moreover, approximately 80 percent of the people surveyed supported medical marijuana use.

In his classic essay "On Liberty," nineteenth-century philosopher John Stuart Mill discussed the nature and limits of power that can be legitimately exercised by society over an individual. Stated Mill:

> [T]he sole end for which mankind are warranted, individually or collectively, in interfering with the liberty of action of any of their number is self-protection. That the only purpose for which power can rightfully be exercised over any member of a civilized community, against his will, is to prevent harm to others. His own good, either physical or moral, is not a sufficient warrant. He cannot rightfully be compelled to do so or forebear because it will be better for him to do so, because it will make him happier, because, in the opinions of others, to do so would be wise or even right.

Is the decision to use marijuana properly left to the realm of individual conscience? Or, is society merely trying to protect itself? The authors of the YES and NO selections have very different viewpoints on this issue.

Ethan A. Nadelmann, founder and director of the Drug Policy Alliance, believes that "the criminalization of marijuana is costly, foolish, and destructive." For example, Alabama currently imprisons people convicted three times of simple marijuana possession for 15 years to life. Moreover, foreign-born residents can be deported, and a parent's marijuana use may be the basis for taking away his or her children or placing them in foster care. Observes Nadelmann: "No one has ever died from a marijuana overdose, which cannot be said of most other drugs."

Charles D. Stimson, of the Heritage Foundation, disputes Nadelmann's contentions and believes that legalizing marijuana will increase crime, drug use, and social dislocation. Moreover, he believes that there is substantial evidence to suggest that legalizing marijuana would lead to greater problems of drug addiction, violence, disorder, and death.

So, which position is the correct one? Would the legalization of marijuana have dire consequences for society? Should society interfere with an individual's decision to smoke a joint in his or her living room at 10:00 PM on a Saturday night while eating a pepperoni pizza and watching a movie on television? What about persons undergoing medical treatment who believe that their conditions are somehow improved by smoking marijuana: Should they have access to legal marijuana without any fear of criminal prosecution?

YES ⤶

Ethan A. Nadelmann

An End to Marijuana Prohibition: The Drive to Legalize Picks Up

Never before have so many Americans supported decriminalizing and even legalizing marijuana. Seventy-two percent say that for simple marijuana possession, people should not be incarcerated but fined: the generally accepted definition of "decriminalization." Even more Americans support making marijuana legal for medical purposes. Support for broader legalization ranges between 25 and 42 percent, depending on how one asks the question. Two of every five Americans—according to a 2003 Zogby poll—say "the government should treat marijuana more or less the same way it treats alcohol: It should regulate it, control it, tax it, and only make it illegal for children."

Close to 100 million Americans—including more than half of those between the ages of 18 and 50—have tried marijuana at least once. Military and police recruiters often have no choice but to ignore past marijuana use by job seekers. The public apparently feels the same way about presidential and other political candidates. Al Gore, Bill Bradley, and John Kerry all say they smoked pot in days past. So did Bill Clinton, with his notorious caveat. George W. Bush won't deny he did. And ever more political, business, religious, intellectual, and other leaders plead guilty as well.

The debate over ending marijuana prohibition simmers just below the surface of mainstream politics, crossing ideological and partisan boundaries. Marijuana is no longer the symbol of Sixties rebellion and Seventies permissiveness, and it's not just liberals and libertarians who say it should be legal, as William F. Buckley Jr. has demonstrated better than anyone. As director of the country's leading drug-policy-reform organization, I've had countless conversations with police and prosecutors, judges and politicians, and hundreds of others who quietly agree that the criminalization of marijuana is costly, foolish, and destructive. What's most needed now is principled conservative leadership. Buckley has led the way, and New Mexico's former governor, Gary Johnson, spoke out courageously while in office. How about others?

A Systemic Overreaction

Marijuana prohibition is unique among American criminal laws. No other law is both enforced so widely and harshly and yet deemed unnecessary by such a substantial portion of the populace.

Police make about 700,000 arrests per year for marijuana offenses. That's almost the same number as are arrested each year for cocaine, heroin, methamphetamine, Ecstasy, and all other illicit drugs combined. Roughly 600,000, or 87 percent, of marijuana arrests are for nothing more than possession of small amounts. Millions of Americans have never been arrested or convicted of any criminal offense except this. Enforcing marijuana laws costs an estimated $10–15 billion in direct costs alone.

Punishments range widely across the country, from modest fines to a few days in jail to many years in prison. Prosecutors often contend that no one goes to prison for simple possession—but tens, perhaps hundreds, of thousands of people on probation and parole are locked up each year because their urine tested positive for marijuana or because they were picked up in possession of a joint. Alabama currently locks up people convicted three times of marijuana *possession* for 15 years to life. There are probably—no firm estimates exist—100,000 Americans behind bars tonight for one marijuana offense or another. And even for those who don't lose their freedom, simply being arrested can be traumatic and costly. A parent's marijuana use can be the basis for taking away her children and putting them in foster care. Foreign-born residents of the U.S. can be deported for a marijuana offense no matter how long they have lived in this country, no matter if their children are U.S. citizens, and no matter how long they have been legally employed. More than half the states revoke or suspend driver's licenses of people arrested for marijuana possession even though they were not driving at the time of arrest. The federal Higher Education Act prohibits student loans to young people convicted of any drug offense; all other criminal offenders remain eligible.

This is clearly an overreaction on the part of government. No drug is perfectly safe, and every psychoactive drug can be used in ways that are problematic. The federal government has spent billions of dollars on advertisements and anti-drug programs that preach the dangers of marijuana—that it's a gateway drug, and addictive in its own right, and dramatically more potent than it used to be, and responsible for all sorts of physical and social diseases as well as international terrorism. But the government has yet to repudiate the 1988 finding of the Drug Enforcement Administration's own administrative law judge, Francis Young, who concluded after extensive testimony that "marijuana in its natural form is one of the safest therapeutically active substances known to man."

Is marijuana a gateway drug? Yes, insofar as most Americans try marijuana before they try other illicit drugs. But no, insofar as the vast majority of Americans who have tried marijuana have never gone on to try other illegal drugs, much less get in trouble with them, and most have never even gone on to become regular or problem marijuana users. Trying to reduce heroin addiction by preventing marijuana use, it's been said, is like trying to reduce motorcycle fatalities by cracking down on bicycle riding. If marijuana did not exist, there's little reason to believe that there would be less drug abuse in the U.S.; indeed, its role would most likely be filled by a more dangerous substance.

Is marijuana dramatically more potent today? There's certainly a greater variety of high-quality marijuana available today than 30 years ago. But anyone who smoked marijuana in the 1970s and 1980s can recall smoking pot that was just as strong as anything available today. What's more, one needs to take only a few puffs of higher-potency pot to get the desired effect, so there's less wear and tear on the lungs.

Is marijuana addictive? Yes, it can be, in that some people use it to excess, in ways that are problematic for themselves and those around them, and find it hard to stop. But marijuana may well be the least addictive and least damaging of all commonly used psychoactive drugs, including many that are now legal. Most people who smoke marijuana never become dependent. Withdrawal symptoms pale compared with those from other drugs. No one has ever died from a marijuana overdose, which cannot be said of most other drugs. Marijuana is not associated with violent behavior and only minimally with reckless sexual behavior. And even heavy marijuana smokers smoke only a fraction of what cigarette addicts smoke. Lung cancers involving only marijuana are rare.

The government's most recent claim is that marijuana abuse accounts for more people entering treatment than any other illegal drug. That shouldn't be surprising, given that tens of millions of Americans smoke marijuana while only a few million use all other illicit drugs. But the claim is spurious nonetheless. Few Americans who enter "treatment" for marijuana are addicted. Fewer than one in five people entering drug treatment for marijuana do so voluntarily. More than half were referred by the criminal-justice system. They go because they got caught with a joint or failed a drug test at school or work (typically for having smoked marijuana days ago, not for being impaired), or because they were caught by a law-enforcement officer—and attending a marijuana "treatment" program is what's required to avoid expulsion, dismissal, or incarceration. Many traditional drug-treatment programs shamelessly participate in this charade to preserve a profitable and captive client stream.

Even those who recoil at the "nanny state" telling adults what they can or cannot sell to one another often make an exception when it comes to marijuana—to "protect the kids." This is a bad joke, as any teenager will attest. The criminalization of marijuana for adults has not prevented young people from having better access to marijuana than anyone else. Even as marijuana's popularity has waxed and waned since the 1970s, one statistic has remained constant: More than 80 percent of high-school students report it's easy to get. Meanwhile, the government's exaggerations and outright dishonesty easily backfire. For every teen who refrains from trying marijuana because it's illegal (for adults), another is tempted by its status as "forbidden fruit." Many respond to the lies about marijuana by disbelieving warnings about more dangerous drugs. So much for protecting the kids by criminalizing the adults.

The Medical Dimension

The debate over medical marijuana obviously colors the broader debate over marijuana prohibition. Marijuana's medical efficacy is no longer in serious dispute. Its use as a medicine dates back thousands of years. Pharmaceuticals products containing marijuana's central ingredient, THC, are legally sold in the U.S., and more are emerging. Some people find the pill form satisfactory, and others consume it in teas or baked products. Most find smoking the easiest and most effective way to consume this unusual medicine, but non-smoking consumption methods, notably vaporizers, are emerging.

Federal law still prohibits medical marijuana. But every state ballot initiative to legalize medical marijuana has been approved, often by wide margins—in California,

Washington, Oregon, Alaska, Colorado, Nevada, Maine, and Washington, D.C. State legislatures in Vermont, Hawaii, and Maryland have followed suit, and many others are now considering their own medical-marijuana bills—including New York, Connecticut, Rhode Island, and Illinois. Support is often bipartisan, with Republican governors like Gary Johnson and Maryland's Bob Ehrlich taking the lead. In New York's 2002 gubernatorial campaign, the conservative candidate of the Independence party, Tom Golisano, surprised everyone by campaigning heavily on this issue. The medical-marijuana bill now before the New York legislature is backed not just by leading Republicans but even by some Conservative party leaders.

The political battleground increasingly pits the White House—first under Clinton and now Bush—against everyone else. Majorities in virtually every state in the country would vote, if given the chance, to legalize medical marijuana. Even Congress is beginning to turn; last summer about two-thirds of House Democrats and a dozen Republicans voted in favor of an amendment co-sponsored by Republican Dana Rohrabacher to prohibit federal funding of any Justice Department crackdowns on medical marijuana in the states that had legalized it. (Many more Republicans privately expressed support, but were directed to vote against.) And federal courts have imposed limits on federal aggression: first in *Conant* v. *Walters*, which now protects the First Amendment rights of doctors and patients to discuss medical marijuana, and more recently in *Raich* v. *Ashcroft* and *Santa Cruz* v. *Ashcroft*, which determined that the federal government's power to regulate interstate commerce does not provide a basis for prohibiting medical-marijuana operations that are entirely local and non-commercial. (The Supreme Court let the *Conant* decision stand, but has yet to consider the others.)

State and local governments are increasingly involved in trying to regulate medical marijuana, notwithstanding the federal prohibition. California, Oregon, Hawaii, Alaska, Colorado, and Nevada have created confidential medical-marijuana patient registries, which protect bona fide patients and caregivers from arrest or prosecution. Some municipal governments are now trying to figure out how to regulate production and distribution. In California, where dozens of medical-marijuana programs now operate openly, with tacit approval by local authorities, some program directors are asking to be licensed and regulated. Many state and local authorities, including law enforcement, favor this but are intimidated by federal threats to arrest and prosecute them for violating federal law.

The drug czar and DEA spokespersons recite the mantra that "there is no such thing as medical marijuana," but the claim is so specious on its face that it clearly undermines federal credibility. The federal government currently provides marijuana—from its own production site in Mississippi—to a few patients who years ago were recognized by the courts as bona fide patients. No one wants to debate those who have used marijuana for medical purposes, be it Santa Cruz medical-marijuana hospice founder Valerie Corral or National Review's Richard Brookhiser. Even many federal officials quietly regret the assault on medical marijuana. When the DEA raided Corral's hospice in September 2002, one agent was heard to say, "Maybe I'm going to think about getting another job sometime soon."

The Broader Movement

The bigger battle, of course, concerns whether marijuana prohibition will ultimately go the way of alcohol Prohibition, replaced by a variety of state and local tax and regulatory policies with modest federal involvement. Dedicated prohibitionists see medical marijuana as the first step down a slippery slope to full legalization. The voters who approved the medical-marijuana ballot initiatives (as well as the wealthy men who helped fund the campaigns) were roughly divided between those who support broader legalization and those who don't, but united in seeing the criminalization and persecution of medical-marijuana patients as the most distasteful aspect of the war on marijuana. (This was a point that Buckley made forcefully in his columns about the plight of Peter McWilliams, who likely died because federal authorities effectively forbade him to use marijuana as medicine.)

The medical-marijuana effort has probably aided the broader anti-prohibitionist campaign in three ways. It helped transform the face of marijuana in the media, from the stereotypical rebel with long hair and tie-dyed shirt to an ordinary middle-aged American struggling with MS or cancer or AIDS. By winning first Proposition 215, the 1996 medical-marijuana ballot initiative in California, and then a string of similar victories in other states, the nascent drug-policy-reform movement demonstrated that it could win in the big leagues of American politics. And the emergence of successful models of medical-marijuana control is likely to boost public confidence in the possibilities and virtue of regulating non-medical use as well.

In this regard, the history of Dutch policy on cannabis (i.e., marijuana and hashish) is instructive. The "coffee shop" model in the Netherlands, where retail (but not wholesale) sale of cannabis is defacto legal, was not legislated into existence. It evolved in fits and starts following the decriminalization of cannabis by Parliament in 1976, as consumers, growers, and entrepreneurs negotiated and collaborated with local police, prosecutors, and other authorities to find an acceptable middle-ground policy. "Coffee shops" now operate throughout the country, subject to local regulations. Troublesome shops are shut down, and most are well integrated into local city cultures. Cannabis is no more popular than in the U.S. and other Western countries, notwithstanding the effective absence of criminal sanctions and controls. Parallel developments are now underway in other countries.

Like the Dutch decriminalization law in 1976, California's Prop 215 in 1996 initiated a dialogue over how best to implement the new law. The variety of outlets that have emerged—ranging from pharmacy-like stores to medical "coffee shops" to hospices, all of which provide marijuana only to people with a patient ID card or doctor's recommendation—play a key role as the most public symbol and manifestation of this dialogue. More such outlets will likely pop up around the country as other states legalize marijuana for medical purposes and then seek ways to regulate distribution and access. And the question will inevitably arise: If the emerging system is successful in controlling production and distribution of marijuana for those with a medical need, can it not also expand to provide for those without medical need?

Millions of Americans use marijuana not just "for fun" but because they find it useful for many of the same reasons that people drink alcohol or take pharmaceutical drugs. It's akin to the beer, glass of wine, or cocktail at the end of the workday, or the prescribed drug to alleviate depression or anxiety, or the sleeping pill, or the aid to sexual function and pleasure. More and more Americans are apt to describe some or all of their marijuana use as "medical" as the definition of that term evolves and broadens. Their anecdotal experiences are increasingly backed by new scientific research into marijuana's essential ingredients, the cannabinoids. Last year a subsidiary of *The Lancet*, Britain's leading medical journal, speculated whether marijuana might soon emerge as the "aspirin of the 21st century," providing a wide array of medical benefits at low cost to diverse populations.

Perhaps the expansion of the medical-control model provides the best answer—at least in the U.S.—to the question of how best to reduce the substantial costs and harms of marijuana prohibition without inviting significant increases in real drug abuse. It's analogous to the evolution of many pharmaceutical drugs from prescription to over-the-counter, but with stricter controls still in place.

It's also an incrementalist approach to reform that can provide both the control and the reassurance that cautious politicians and voters desire.

In 1931, with public support for alcohol Prohibition rapidly waning, President Hoover released the report of the Wickersham Commission. The report included a devastating critique of Prohibition's failures and costly consequences, but the commissioners, apparently fearful of getting out too far ahead of public opinion, opposed repeal. Franklin P. Adams of the *New World* neatly summed up their findings:

> Prohibition is an awful flop.
>   We like it.
> It can't stop what it's meant to stop.
>   We like it.
> It's left a trail of graft and slime
> It don't prohibit worth a dime
> It's filled our land with vice and crime.
>   Nevertheless, we're for it.

Two years later, federal alcohol Prohibition was history.

What support there is for marijuana prohibition would likely end quickly absent the billions of dollars spent annually by federal and other governments to prop it up. All those anti-marijuana ads pretend to be about reducing drug abuse, but in fact their basic purpose is sustaining popular support for the war on marijuana. What's needed now are conservative politicians willing to say enough is enough: Tens of billions of taxpayer dollars down the drain each year. People losing their jobs, their property, and their freedom for nothing more than possessing a joint or growing a few marijuana plants. And all for what? To send a message? To keep pretending that we're protecting our children? Alcohol Prohibition made a lot more sense than marijuana prohibition does today—and it, too, was a disaster.

Ethan A. Nadelmann is a highly respected critic of U.S. and international drug control policies. He received his BA, JD, and PhD degrees in political science from Harvard University as well as a masters degree in international relations from the London School of Economics. In 1994, with the support of George Soros, he founded the Lindesmith Center, a leading drug policy institute. He serves presently as director of the Lindesmith Center—Drug Policy Foundation. Nadelmann's works have been published in *Science, Rolling Stone, National Review, The Public Interest, Daedalus,* and various other publications.

Charles D. Stimson  **NO**

Legalizing Marijuana: Why Citizens Should Just Say No

The scientific literature is clear that marijuana is addictive and that its use significantly impairs bodily and mental functions. Marijuana use is associated with memory loss, cancer, immune system deficiencies, heart disease, and birth defects, among other conditions. Even where decriminalized, marijuana trafficking remains a source of violence, crime, and social disintegration. . . .

The . . . campaign, [to legalize marijuana] like previous efforts, downplays the well-documented harms of marijuana trafficking and use while promising benefits ranging from reduced crime to additional tax revenue. In particular, supporters of the initiative make five bold claims:

1. "Marijuana is safe and non-addictive."
2. "Marijuana prohibition makes no more sense than alcohol prohibition did in the early 1900s."
3. "The government's efforts to combat illegal drugs have been a total failure."
4. "The money spent on government efforts to combat the illegal drug trade can be better spent on substance abuse and treatment for the allegedly few marijuana users who abuse the drug."
5. "Tax revenue collected from marijuana sales would substantially outweigh the social costs of legalization."

As this paper details, all five claims are demonstrably false or, based on the best evidence, highly dubious.

Further, supporters of [legalization] simply ignore the mechanics of decriminalization—that is, how it would directly affect law enforcement, crime, and communities. Among the important questions left unanswered are:

- How would the state law fit into a federal regime that prohibits marijuana production, distribution, and possession?
- Would decriminalization, especially if combined with taxation, expand market opportunities for the gangs and cartels that currently dominate drug distribution?
- Would existing zoning laws prohibit marijuana cultivation in residential neighborhoods, and if not, what measures would growers have to undertake to keep children from the plants?
- Would transportation providers be prohibited from firing bus drivers because they smoke marijuana?

No one knows the specifics of how marijuana decriminalization would work in practice or what measures would be necessary to prevent children, teenagers, criminals, and addicts from obtaining the drug.

The federal government shares these concerns. Gil Kerlikowske, Director of the White House Office of National Drug Control Policy (ONDCP), recently stated, "Marijuana legalization, for any purpose, is a non-starter in the Obama Administration." The Administration—widely viewed as more liberal than any other in recent memory and, for a time, as embodying the hopes of pro-legalization activists—has weighed the costs and benefits and concluded that marijuana legalization would compromise public health and safety.

[V]oters, if they take a fair-minded look at the evidence and the practical problems of legalization, should reach the same conclusion: Marijuana is a dangerous substance that should remain illegal under state law. . . .

Unsafe in Any Amount: How Marijuana Is Not Like Alcohol

Marijuana advocates have had some success peddling the notion that marijuana is a "soft" drug, similar to alcohol, and fundamentally different from "hard" drugs like cocaine or heroin. It is true that marijuana is not the most dangerous of the commonly abused drugs, but that is not to say that it is safe. Indeed, marijuana shares more in common with the "hard" drugs than it does with alcohol.

A common argument for legalization is that smoking marijuana is no more dangerous than drinking alcohol and that prohibiting the use of marijuana is therefore no more justified than the prohibition of alcohol. As Jacob Sullum, author of *Saying Yes: In Defense of Drug Use*, writes:

> Americans understood the problems associated with alcohol abuse, but they also understood the problems associated with Prohibition, which included violence, organized crime, official corruption, the erosion of civil liberties, disrespect for the law, and injuries and deaths caused by tainted black-market booze. They decided that these unintended side effects far out-weighed whatever harms Prohibition prevented by discouraging drinking. The same sort of analysis today would show that the harm caused by drug prohibition far out-weighs the harm it prevents, even without taking into account the value to each individual of being sovereign over his own body and mind.

At first blush, this argument is appealing, especially to those wary of over-regulation by government. But it overlooks the enormous difference between alcohol and marijuana.

Legalization advocates claim that marijuana and alcohol are mild intoxicants and so should be regulated similarly; but as the experience of nearly every culture, over the thousands of years of human history, demonstrates, alcohol is different. Nearly every culture has its own alcoholic preparations, and nearly all have successfully regulated alcohol consumption through cultural norms. The same cannot be said of marijuana. There are several possible explanations for alcohol's unique status: For most people, it is not addictive; it is rarely consumed to the point of intoxication; low-level consumption is consistent with most manual and intellectual tasks; it has several positive health benefits; and it is formed by the fermentation of many common substances and easily metabolized by the body.

To be sure, there are costs associated with alcohol abuse, such as drunk driving and disease associated with excessive consumption. A few cultures—and this nation for a short while during Prohibition—have concluded that the benefits of alcohol consumption are not worth the costs. But they are the exception; most cultures have concluded that it is acceptable in moderation. No other intoxicant shares that status.

Alcohol differs from marijuana in several crucial respects. First, marijuana is far more likely to cause addiction. Second, it is usually consumed to the point of intoxication. Third, it has no known general healthful properties, though it may have some palliative effects.

Fourth, it is toxic and deleterious to health. Thus, while it is true that both alcohol and marijuana are less intoxicating than other mood-altering drugs, that is not to say that marijuana is especially similar to alcohol or that its use is healthy or even safe.

In fact, compared to alcohol, marijuana is not safe. Long-term, moderate consumption of alcohol carries few health risks and even offers some significant benefits. For example, a glass of wine (or other alcoholic drink) with dinner actually improves health. Dozens of peer-reviewed medical studies suggest that drinking moderate amounts of alcohol reduces the risk of heart disease, strokes, gallstones, diabetes, and death from a heart attack. According to the Mayo Clinic, among many others, moderate use of alcohol (defined as two drinks a day) "seems to offer some health benefits, particularly for the heart." Countless articles in medical journals and other scientific literature confirm the positive health effects of moderate alcohol consumption.

The effects of regular marijuana consumption are quite different. For example, the National Institute on Drug Abuse (a division of the National Institutes of Health) has released studies showing that use of marijuana has wide-ranging negative health effects. Long-term marijuana consumption "impairs the ability of T-cells in the lungs' immune system to fight off some infections." These studies have also found that marijuana consumption impairs short-term memory, making it difficult to learn and retain information or perform complex tasks; slows reaction time and impairs motor coordination; increases heart rate by 20 percent to 100 percent, thus elevating the risk of heart attack; and alters moods, resulting in artificial euphoria, calmness, or (in high doses) anxiety or paranoia. And it gets worse: Marijuana has toxic properties that can result in birth defects, pain, respiratory system damage, brain damage, and stroke.

Further, prolonged use of marijuana may cause cognitive degradation and is "associated with lower test scores and lower educational attainment because during periods of intoxication the drug affects the ability to learn and process information, thus influencing attention, concentration, and short-term memory." Unlike alcohol, marijuana has been shown to have a residual effect on cognitive ability that persists beyond the period of intoxication. According to the National Institute on Drug Abuse, whereas alcohol is broken down relatively quickly in the human body, THC (tetrahydrocannabinol, the main active chemical in marijuana) is stored in organs and fatty tissues, allowing it to remain in a user's body for days or even weeks after consumption. Research has shown that marijuana consumption may also cause "psychotic symptoms."

Marijuana's effects on the body are profound. According to the British Lung Foundation, "smoking three or four marijuana joints is as bad for your lungs as smoking twenty tobacco cigarettes." Researchers in Canada found that marijuana smoke contains significantly higher levels of numerous toxic compounds, like ammonia and hydrogen cyanide, than regular tobacco smoke. In fact, the study determined that ammonia was found in marijuana smoke at levels of up to 20 times the levels found in tobacco. Similarly, hydrogen cyanide was found in marijuana smoke at concentrations three to five times greater than those found in tobacco smoke.

Marijuana, like tobacco, is addictive. One study found that more than 30 percent of adults who used marijuana in the course of a year were dependent on the drug. These individuals often show signs of withdrawal and compulsive behavior. Marijuana dependence is also responsible for a large proportion of calls to drug abuse help lines and treatment centers.

To equate marijuana use with alcohol consumption is, at best, uninformed and, at worst, actively misleading. Only in the most superficial ways are the two substances alike, and they differ in every way that counts: addictiveness, toxicity, health effects, and risk of intoxication.

Unintended Consequences

Today, marijuana trafficking is linked to a variety of crimes, from assault and murder to money laundering and smuggling. Legalization of marijuana would increase demand for the drug and almost certainly exacerbate drug-related crime, as well as cause a myriad of unintended but predictable consequences.

To begin with, an astonishingly high percentage of criminals are marijuana users. According to a study by the RAND Corporation, approximately 60 percent of arrestees test positive for marijuana use in the United States, England, and Australia. Further, marijuana metabolites are found in arrestees' urine more frequently than those of any other drug.

Although some studies have shown marijuana to inhibit aggressive behavior and violence, the National Research Council concluded that the "long-term use of marijuana may alter the nervous system in ways that do promote violence." No place serves as a better example than Amsterdam.

Marijuana advocates often point to the Netherlands as a well-functioning society with a relaxed attitude toward drugs, but they rarely mention that Amsterdam is one of Europe's most violent cities. In Amsterdam, officials are in the process of closing marijuana dispensaries, or "coffee shops," because of the crime associated with their operation. Furthermore, the Dutch Ministry of Health, Welfare and Sport has expressed "concern about drug and alcohol use among young people and the social consequences, which range from poor school performance and truancy to serious impairment, including brain damage."

Amsterdam's experience is already being duplicated in California under the current medical marijuana statute. In Los Angeles, police report that areas surrounding cannabis clubs have experienced a 200 percent increase in robberies, a 52.2 percent increase in burglaries, a 57.1 percent increase in aggravated assault, and a 130.8 percent increase in burglaries from automobiles. Current law requires a doctor's prescription to procure marijuana; full legalization would likely spark an even more acute increase in crime.

Legalization of marijuana would also inflict a series of negative consequences on neighborhoods and communities. The nuisance caused by the powerful odor of mature marijuana plants is already striking California municipalities. The City Council of Chico, California, has released a report detailing the situation and describing how citizens living near marijuana cultivators are disturbed by the incredible stink emanating from the plants.

Perhaps worse than the smell, crime near growers is increasing, associated with "the theft of marijuana from yards where it is being grown." As a result, housing prices near growers are sinking.

Theoretical arguments in favor of marijuana legalization usually overlook the practical matter of how the drug would be regulated and sold. It is the details of implementation, of course, that will determine the effect of legalization on families, schools, and communities. Most basically, how and where would marijuana be sold?

- Would neighborhoods become neon red-light districts like Amsterdam's, accompanied by the same crime and social disorder?
- If so, who decides what neighborhoods will be so afflicted—residents and landowners or far-off government officials?
- Or would marijuana sales be so widespread that users could add it to their grocery lists?
- If so, how would stores sell it, how would they store it, and how would they prevent it from being diverted into the gray market?
- Would stores dealing in marijuana have to fortify their facilities to reduce the risk of theft and assault?

The most likely result is that the drug will not be sold in legitimate stores at all, because while the federal government is currently tolerating medical marijuana dispensaries, it will not tolerate wide-scale sales under general legalizational statutes. So marijuana will continue to be sold on the gray or black market.

The [movement to legalize marijuana] does not answer these or other practical questions regarding implementation. Rather, it leaves those issues to localities. No doubt, those entities will pass a variety of laws in an attempt to deal with the many problems caused by legalization, unless the local laws are struck down by California courts as inconsistent with the underlying initiative, which would be even worse. At best, that patchwork of laws, differing from one locality to another, will be yet another unintended and predictable problem arising from legalization as envisioned under this act.

Citizens also should not overlook what may be the greatest harms of marijuana legalization: increased addiction to and use of harder drugs. In addition to marijuana's harmful effects on the body and relationship to criminal conduct, it is a gateway drug that can lead users to more dangerous drugs. Prosecutors, judges, police officers, detectives, parole or probation officers, and even defense attorneys know that the vast majority of defendants arrested for violent crimes test positive for illegal drugs, including marijuana. They also know that marijuana is the starter drug of choice for most criminals. Whereas millions of Americans consume moderate amounts of alcohol without ever "moving on" to dangerous drugs, marijuana use and cocaine use are strongly correlated.

While correlation does not necessarily reflect causation, and while the science is admittedly mixed as to whether it is the drug itself or the people the new user associates with who cause the move on to cocaine, heroin, LSD, or other drugs, the RAND Corporation reports that marijuana prices and cocaine use are directly linked, suggesting a substitution effect between the two drugs. Moreover, according to RAND, legalization will cause marijuana prices to fall as much as 80 percent. That can lead to significant consequences because "a 10-percent decrease in the price of marijuana would increase the prevalence of cocaine use by 4.4 to 4.9 percent." As cheap marijuana floods the market both in and outside of California, use of many different types of drugs will increase, as will marijuana use.

It is impossible to predict the precise consequences of legalization, but the experiences of places that have eased restrictions on marijuana are not positive. Already, California is suffering crime, dislocation, and increased drug use under its current regulatory scheme. Further liberalizing the law will only make matters worse.

Flouting Federal Law

Another area of great uncertainty is how a state law legalizing marijuana would fit in with federal law to the contrary. Congress has enacted a comprehensive regulatory scheme for restricting access to illicit drugs and other controlled substances. The Controlled Substances Act of 1970 prohibits the manufacture, distribution, and possession of all substances deemed to be Schedule I drugs—drugs like heroin, PCP, and cocaine. Because marijuana has no "currently accepted medical use in treatment in the United States," it is a Schedule I drug that cannot be bought, sold, possessed, or used without violating federal law.

Under the Supremacy Clause of the Constitution of the United States, the Controlled Substances Act is the supreme law of the land and cannot be superseded by state laws that purport to contradict or abrogate its terms. The RCTCA proposes to "reform California's cannabis laws in a way that will benefit our state" and "[r]egulate cannabis like we do alcohol." But the act does not even purport to address the fundamental constitutional infirmity that it would be in direct conflict with federal law. If enacted and unchallenged by the federal government, it would call into question the government's ability to regulate all controlled substances, including drugs such as Oxycontin, methamphetamine, heroin, and powder and crack cocaine. More likely, however, the feds would challenge the law in court, and the courts would have no choice but to strike it down.

Congress has the power to change the Controlled Substances Act and remove marijuana from Schedule I. Yet after decades of lobbying, it has not, largely because of the paucity of scientific evidence in support of a delisting.

California, in fact, is already in direct violation of federal law. Today, its laws allow the use of marijuana as a treatment for a range of vaguely defined conditions, including chronic pain, nausea, and lack of appetite, depression, anxiety, and glaucoma. "Marijuana doctors" are listed in the classified advertising sections of newspapers, and many are conveniently located adjacent to "dispensaries." At least one "doctor" writes prescriptions from a tiny hut beside the Venice Beach Boardwalk.

This "medical marijuana" law and similar ones in other states are premised on circumvention of the Food and Drug Administration (FDA) approval process. "FDA's drug approval process requires well-controlled clinical trials that provide the necessary scientific data upon which FDA makes its approval and labeling decisions." Marijuana, even that supposedly used for medicinal purposes, has been rejected by the FDA because, among other reasons, it "has no currently accepted or proven medical use."

The lack of FDA approval means that marijuana may come from unknown sources, may be adulterated with foreign substances, or may not even be marijuana at all. Pot buyers have no way to know what they are getting, and there is no regulatory authority with the ability to go after bogus manufacturers and dealers. Even if one overlooks its inherently harmful properties, marijuana that is commonly sold is likely to be far less safe than that studied in the lab or elsewhere.

Marijuana advocates claim that federal enforcement of drug laws, particularly in jurisdictions that allow the use of medical marijuana, violates states' rights. The Supreme Court, however, has held otherwise. In 2002, California resident Angel Raich produced and consumed marijuana, purportedly for medical purposes. Her actions, while in accordance with California's "medical marijuana" law, clearly violated the Controlled Substances Act, and the local sheriff's department destroyed Raich's plants. Raich claimed that she needed to use marijuana, prescribed by her doctor, for medical purposes. She sued the federal government, asking the court to stop the government from interfering with her right to produce and use marijuana.

In 2006, the Supreme Court held in *Gonzales vs. Raich* that the Commerce Clause confers on Congress the authority to ban the use of marijuana, even when a state approves it for "medical purposes" and it is produced in small quantities for personal consumption. Many legal scholars criticize the Court's extremely broad reading of the Commerce Clause as inconsistent with its original meaning, but the Court's decision nonetheless stands. . . .

Bogus Economics

An innovation of the campaign in support of [legalization] is its touting of the potential benefit of legalization to the government, in terms of additional revenues from taxing marijuana and savings from backing down in the "war on drugs." The National Organization for the Reform of Marijuana Laws (NORML), for example, claims that legalization "could yield California taxpayers over $1.2 billion per year" in tax benefits. According to a California NORML Report updated in October 2009, an excise tax of $50 per ounce would raise about $770 million to $900 million per year and save over $200 million in law enforcement costs per year. It is worth noting that $900 million equates to 18 million ounces—enough marijuana for Californians to smoke one billion marijuana cigarettes each year.

But these projections are highly speculative and riddled with unfounded assumptions. Dr. Rosalie Liccardo Pacula, an expert with the RAND Corporation who has studied the economics of drug policy for over 15 years, has explained that the California "Board of Equalization's estimate of $1.4 billion [in] potential revenue for the state is based on a series of assumptions that are in some instances subject to tremendous uncertainty and in other cases not validated." She urged the California Committee on Public Safety to conduct an honest and thorough cost-benefit analysis of the potential revenues and costs associated with legalizing marijuana. To date, no such realistic cost-benefit analysis has been done.

In her testimony before the committee, Dr. Pacula stated that prohibition raises the cost of production by at least 400 percent and that legalizing marijuana would cause the price of marijuana to fall considerably—much more than the 50 percent price reduction incorporated into the state's revenue model. Furthermore, she noted that a $50-per-ounce marijuana tax was not realistic, because it would represent a 100 percent tax on the cost of the product. . . .

Other Negative Social Costs

In addition to its direct effects on individual health, even moderate marijuana use imposes significant long-term costs through the ways that it affects individual users. Marijuana use is associated with cognitive difficulties and influences attention, concentration, and short-term memory. This damage affects drug users' ability to work and can put others at risk. Even if critical workers—for example, police officers, airline pilots, and machine operators—used marijuana recreationally but remained sober on the job, the long-term cognitive deficiency that remained from regular drug use would sap productivity and place countless people in danger. Increased use would also send health care costs skyrocketing—costs borne not just by individual users, but also by the entire society.

For that reason, among others, the Obama Administration also rejects supporters' economic arguments. In his speech, Kerlikowske explained that tax revenue from cigarettes is far outweighed by their social costs: "Tobacco also does not carry its economic weight when we tax it; each year we spend more than $200 billion and collect only about $25 billion in taxes." If the heavy taxation of cigarettes is unable even to come close to making up for the health and other costs associated with their use, it seems doubtful at best that marijuana taxes would be sufficient to cover the costs of legalized marijuana—especially considering that, in addition to the other dangers of smoking marijuana, the physical health effects of just three to four joints are equivalent to those of an entire pack of cigarettes.

Other claims also do not measure up. One of the express purposes of [legalizing] initiative[s] is to "put dangerous, underground street dealers out of business, so their influence in our communities will fade." But as explained above, many black-market dealers would rationally choose to remain in the black market to avoid taxation and regulation. Vibrant gray markets have developed throughout the world for many products that are legal, regulated, and heavily taxed. Cigarettes in Eastern Europe, alcohol in Scandinavia, luxury automobiles in Russia, and DVDs in the Middle East are all legal goods traded in gray markets that are wracked with violence. In Canada, an attempt at a $3 per pack tax on cigarettes was greeted with the creation of a black market that "accounted for perhaps 30 percent of sales." . . .

In sum, legalization would put additional strain on an already faltering economy. In 2008, marijuana alone was involved in 375,000 emergency room visits. Drug overdoses already outnumber gunshot deaths in America and are approaching motor vehicle crashes as the nation's leading cause of accidental death. It is true that taxing marijuana sales would generate some tax revenue, but the cost of handling the influx of problems resulting from increased use would far outweigh any gain made by marijuana's taxation. Legalizing marijuana would serve only to compound the problems already associated with drug use.

Social Dislocation and Organized Crime

The final two arguments of those favoring legalization are intertwined. According to advocates of legalization, the government's efforts to combat the illegal drug trade have been an expensive failure. Consequently, they argue, focusing on substance abuse and treatment would be a more effective means of combating drug abuse while reducing the violence and social ills stemming from anti-drug enforcement efforts.

There is no doubt that if marijuana were legalized, more people, including juveniles, would consume it. Consider cigarettes: While their purchase by people under 18 is illegal, 20 percent of high school students admit to having smoked cigarettes in the past 30 days. Marijuana's illegal status "keeps potential drug users from using" marijuana in a way that no legalization scheme can replicate "by

virtue of the fear of arrest and the embarrassment of being caught." With increased use comes increased abuse, as the fear of arrest and embarrassment will decrease. . . .

Keeping marijuana illegal will undoubtedly keep many young people from using it. Eliminate that criminal sanction (and moral disapprobation), and more youth will use the drug, harming their potential and ratcheting up treatment costs.

Educators know that students using marijuana underperform when compared to their non-using peers. Teachers, coaches, guidance counselors, and school principals have seen the negative effect of marijuana on their students. The Rev. Dr. D. Stuart Dunnan, Headmaster of Saint James School in St. James, Maryland, says of marijuana use by students:

> The chemical effect of marijuana is to take away ambition. The social effect is to provide an escape from challenges and responsibilities with a like-minded group of teenagers who are doing the same thing. Using marijuana creates losers. At a time when we're concerned about our lack of academic achievement relative to other countries, legalizing marijuana will be disastrous.

Additionally, making marijuana legal . . . will fuel drug cartels and violence, particularly because the drug will still be illegal at the national level. The local demand will increase . . . but reputable growers, manufacturers, and retailers will still be unwilling—as they should be—to produce and distribute marijuana. Even without the federal prohibition, most reputable producers would not survive the tort liability from such a dangerous product. Thus, the vacuum will be filled by illegal drug cartels.

According to the Department of Justice's National Drug Threat Assessment for 2010, Mexican drug trafficking organizations (DTOs) "have expanded their cultivation operations in the United States, an ongoing trend for the past decade. . . . Well-organized criminal groups and DTOs that produce domestic marijuana do so because of the high profitability of and demand for marijuana in the United States."

Legalize marijuana, and the demand for marijuana goes up substantially as the deterrence effect of law enforcement disappears. Yet not many suppliers will operate legally, refusing to subject themselves to the established state regulatory scheme—not to mention taxation—while still risking federal prosecution, conviction, and prison time. So who will fill the void?

Violent, brutal, and ruthless, Mexican DTOs will work to maintain their black-market profits at the expense of American citizens' safety. Every week, there are news articles cataloguing the murders, kidnappings, robberies, and other thuggish brutality employed by Mexican drug gangs along the border. . . . Thus, marijuana legalization will increase crime, drug use, and social dislocation across the state of California—the exact opposite of what pro-legalization advocates promise.

Conclusion

Pro-marijuana advocates promoting [legalization] invite Californians to imagine a hypothetical and idyllic "pot market," but America's national approach to drug use, addiction, and crime must be serious, based on sound policy and solid evidence.

In 1982, President Ronald Reagan adopted a national drug strategy that took a comprehensive approach consisting of five components: international cooperation, research, strengthened law enforcement, treatment and rehabilitation, and prevention and education. It was remarkably successful: Illegal drug use by young adults dropped more than 50 percent.

Reagan was right to make drug control a major issue of his presidency. Illegal drugs such as marijuana are responsible for a disproportionate share of violence and social decline in America. Accordingly, federal law, representing the considered judgment of medical science and the nation's two political branches of government, takes the unequivocal position that marijuana is dangerous and has no significant beneficial uses.

[States] cannot repeal that law or somehow allow its citizens to contravene it. Thus, [they have] two options. By far the best option is to commit itself seriously to the federal approach and pursue a strategy that attempts to prevent illegal drug use in the first place and reduce the number of drug users. This may require changes in drug policy, and perhaps in sentencing guidelines for marijuana users charged with simple possession, but simply legalizing a harmful drug—that is, giving up—is not a responsible option.

The other option is to follow the above path in the short term while conducting further research and possibly working with other states in Congress to consider changes in federal law. Although those who oppose the legalization of marijuana have every reason to believe that further, legitimate scientific research will confirm the dangers of its use, no side should try to thwart the sober judgment of the national legislature and sister states.

In short, no state will likely be allowed to legalize marijuana on its own, with such serious, negative cross-state spillover effects. Yet even if [a state] could act as if it were an island, the legalization route would still end very badly. There is strong evidence to suggest that legalizing marijuana would serve little purpose other than to worsen the state's drug problems—addiction, violence, disorder, and death. While long on rhetoric, the legalization movement, by contrast, is short on facts.

Note

For references and supporting documentation accompanying this article go to www.heritage.org.

Charles D. Stimson is a senior legal fellow in the Center for Legal & Judicial Studies at The Heritage Foundation. Before joining The Heritage Foundation, he served as deputy assistant secretary of defense; as a local, state, federal, and military prosecutor; and as a defense attorney and law professor.

EXPLORING THE ISSUE

Should Marijuana Be Legalized?

Critical Thinking and Reflection

1. Is marijuana is a "gateway" drug? Explain your answer.
2. Do you agree with following statement: "Public support for the 'drug war' is more about moral values or fears than rational public safety measures." Why or why not?

Is There Common Ground?

Marijuana has been around for a long time. It was not until 1937 that the Marijuana Tax Act banned most recreational and medicinal uses of this popular drug in the United States. Since that time, there has been significant controversy about whether our marijuana laws are effective, or whether they are a bad social policy that should be abandoned in favor of a more enlightened approach to drug abuse.

According to a 1998 study by the Harvard School of Public Health, 78 percent of Americans believe that U.S. anti-drug efforts have failed. In addition, 94 percent believe that the United States has lost control of the illegal drug problem, and 58 percent maintain that the problem is getting worse. At the same time, only 14 percent favored drug legalization, while a majority favored more severe prison sentences. (See Robert J. Blendon and John T. Young, "The Public and the War on Illicit Drugs," *Journal of the American Medical Association* (March 18, 1998, p. 827). Please note that a more recent survey has found that 34 percent of Americans support making "the use of marijuana legal." See Colleen McMurray, "Medicinal Marijuana: Is It What the Doctor Ordered?" *The Gallup Poll Tuesday Briefing* (December 2003, p. 89). These statistics are interesting for a number of reasons.

At first glance, the percentages seem somewhat schizophrenic—even though the vast majority of Americans believe that U.S. drug control policies have failed and that the problem of drug abuse is getting worse, only a small minority of respondents believe that drugs should be legalized. One source asserts that this apparent contradiction may suggest that:

> [P]ublic support for the "drug war" is more about moral values or fears than rational public safety measures. The bureaucracies and businesses engaged in the "drug war" have been successful in creating support that is independent of failure to achieve objectives and rational analysis and evaluation. (PUBLIC OPINION, "News Briefs," March–April 1998)

Could the previous statement actually be true? Is it possible that bureaucracies, such as U.S. law enforcement agencies, and businesses with ties to drug law enforcement may have an interest in continuing the war on drugs regardless of whether it is good for society? For a classic discussion of these issues, see Howard S. Becker, *Outsiders: Studies in the Sociology of Deviance* (The Free Press, 1963); for a more recent treatment of these issues, see Jeffrey Reiman, *The Rich Get Richer and the Poor Get Prison: Ideology, Class and Criminal Justice*, 7th ed. (Allyn & Bacon, 2004); Robert J. MacCoun and Peter Reuter, Jr., *Drug War Heresies: Learning from Other Vices, Times and Places* (Cambridge University Press, 2001).

Additional Resources

Additional informative resources include: Clare Wilson, "Miracle Weed," *New Scientist* (February 5–11, 2005); David T. Courtwright, "Drug Wars: Policy Hots and Historical Cools," *Bulletin of the History of Medicine* (Johns Hopkins University Press, Summer 2004); Bruce Bullington, "Drug Policy Reform and Its Detractors: The United States as the Elephant in the Closet," *Journal of Drug Issues* (Summer 2004); Michael M. O'Hear, "Federalism and Drug Control," *Vanderbilt Law Review* (April 2004); Sasha Abramsky, "The Drug War Goes Up in Smoke," *The Nation* (August 18–25, 2003); David Boyum and Mark A. R. Kleiman, "Breaking the Drug-Crime Link," *Public Interest* (Summer 2003); Alex Kreit, "The Future of Medical Marijuana: Should the States Grow Their Own?" *University of Pennsylvania Law Review* (May 2003); Vanessa Grigoriadis, "The Most Stoned Kids on the Most Stoned Day on the Most Stoned Campus on Earth," *Rolling Stone* (September 16, 2004).

Internet References . . .

Alternet

www.alternet.org/drugs
/legalize-marijuana-now-here-are-10-reasons-why

NORML.org

http://norml.org/

Selected, Edited, and with Issue Framing Material by:
Thomas J. Hickey, *State University of New York at Cobleskill*

ISSUE

Should the Police Be Required to Wear Body Cameras?

YES: Jay Stanley, "Police Body-Mounted Cameras: With Right Policies in Place, a Win for All," American Civil Liberties Union (2015)

NO: Harvard Law Review, from "Considering Police Body Cameras: Developments in the Law," *Harvard Law Review* (2015)

Learning Outcomes

After reading this issue, you will be able to:

- Discuss the Founding Fathers' rationale for the Fourth Amendment.
- Discuss generally the legal status of the use of high technology surveillance by government agents.
- Discuss the significance of the Supreme Court's decision in *Dow Chemical Corporation v. United States.*
- Present and discuss several arguments for and against requiring police officers to wear body cameras.
- Discuss the privacy implications of requiring the police to wear body cameras.
- Discuss the significance of the Supreme Court's decision in *Tennessee v. Garner.*
- Present and discuss the significance of the "Rialto Study" on the use of body cameras by the police.

ISSUE SUMMARY

YES: American Civil Liberties Union (ACLU) Senior Policy Analyst Jay Stanley contends that if U.S. police departments develop proper policies for the use of police body cams they will be a "win for all." These devices will enhance police accountability and protect officers against false accusations of abuse.

NO: The Harvard Law Review argues that body cameras are a powerful—and indiscriminate—technology and their proliferation over the next decade will inevitably change the nature of policing in unexpected ways, quite possibly to the detriment of the citizens the cameras are intended to protect. Moreover, even when high-quality, graphic video footage is available, police officers may still not be indicted, let alone convicted.

Technological advances can be a wonderful thing. They have the potential to encourage creativity, innovation, and achievement and make life more satisfying and efficient in countless ways. It seems likely that 40 years ago this manuscript would have been prepared in handwritten form or on a standard typewriter, involving a much greater expenditure of time, effort, and scrap paper. Clearly, technology can make our lives easier; however, are there any downsides to technical advancement? Is it

possible to become so technologically advanced that we are held hostage by what we have created?

Think about what has happened with regard to surveillance technology recently. A few years ago, former National Security Agency (NSA) analyst Edward Snowden revealed that the agency had been tracking the Internet activity and cell phone calls of a large number of Americans as well as those of persons in various other countries. Moreover, during the last few years it has become possible for cameras mounted in police patrol cars to record the license plates of oncoming vehicles to check for active warrants, registration defects, or other problems. Likewise, highly sensitive surveillance cameras that may record all activity in a particular area have been deployed in some cities. Coupled with sophisticated facial recognition software, such surveillance has Orwellian implications for personal privacy in our nation.

The U.S. legal system and the courts in particular seem to have struggled to keep pace with some of these modern surveillance practices. The Fourth Amendment to the U.S. Constitution was adopted in 1786. It provides:

> The right of the people to be secure in their persons, houses, papers, and effects against unreasonable searches and seizures shall not be violated, and no Warrants shall issue, but upon probable cause, supported by oath or affirmation, and particularly describing the place to be searched, and the person or things to be seized.

At the time of its adoption, the Founding Fathers were chiefly concerned with abusive practices by the British government, such as the issuance of "general warrants" and "writs of assistance," which gave governmental authorities virtually unlimited power to search whomever they wished, even without any cause. The Fourth Amendment was a direct reaction to such practices. In 1786, however, the Founding Fathers could never have possibly imagined these technological advances and just how intrusive these searches could become.

In more recent times, the Supreme Court has considered the use of highly technical devices by law enforcement officers to investigate crimes. A central theme of these cases appears to be that if a criminal investigation is directed at a home, the courts are more likely to require law enforcement officers to obtain a search warrant than if it occurs in a more public area. This remains true even if investigators employ highly sophisticated technology, often not available to the general public.

For example, an early case that involved a high technology investigation by law enforcement agents occurred in *Dow Chemical Company v. United States*, 476 U.S. 227 (1986). Here, the United States Environmental Protection Agency (EPA) hired a commercial aerial photographer to take high-tech photos of a 2,000-acre chemical manufacturing facility, after the company had refused to allow an EPA inspection of the plant. Dow then challenged the Agency's right to take such technical photographs without a search warrant. The U.S. Supreme Court rejected this argument. Chief Justice Warren Burger stated:

It may well be, as the government concedes, that surveillance of private property by using highly sophisticated surveillance equipment not generally available to the public, such as satellite technology, might be constitutionally proscribed absent a warrant. But the photographs here are not so revealing of intimate details as to raise constitutional concerns. . . . The mere fact that human vision is enhanced somewhat, at least to the degree here, does not give rise to constitutional problems. (238)

In a dissenting opinion, Justice Louis Powell asserted that under the majority's analysis, "the existence of an asserted privacy interest apparently will be decided solely by reference to the manner of surveillance used to [intrude] on that interest. Such an inquiry will not protect Fourth Amendment rights, but rather *permit their gradual decay as technology advances*" (239) [emphasis added]. As Justice Powell predicted, highly sophisticated technological devices are being used currently by law enforcement agents in public places without search warrants. The courts have generally upheld these searches, despite their implications for personal privacy. For example, if a police cruiser's video camera surveys the license plate numbers of all automobiles in a particular place, does it compromise the personal privacy interests of all vehicle occupants in the area? Moreover, where is the information stored and how long is it kept by law enforcement agencies? Are these simply modern high technology manifestations of governmental dragnet searches, or "fishing expeditions," that the Founding Fathers would have clearly despised? Such searches are not targeted at homes, so the courts would be likely to uphold the practice under *Dow Chemical*. Unfortunately, Justice Powell's statement about decaying constitutional protections seems eerily prophetic as surveillance technology has continued to advance.

Some of the same privacy interests are implicated in cases involving police body-mounted cameras. Should police officers be required to record all encounters with citizens, or should they retain the discretion to turn them on and off at will? What should be done with the recordings that are not used in a criminal case? Should they be erased immediately, or stored in a law enforcement database for possible later use? Although the use of body cameras does appear to have significant potential for improving law enforcement encounters with the public, privacy concerns must be addressed.

ACLU Senior Policy Analyst Jay Stanley supports the use of police body cameras, subject to certain limitations. Stanley recommends that law enforcement agencies develop appropriate policies to insure that police officers cannot "edit on the fly," or choose which encounters to record with limitless discretion. He believes that if the police are free to turn the cameras on and off at their discretion, the cameras' "role in providing a check and balance against police power will shrink and they will no longer become a net benefit." Moreover, Stanley asserts that it is imperative that any law enforcement deployment of body cameras be accompanied by good privacy policies so that the "benefits of the technology are not outweighed by invasions of privacy." Further, the ACLU asserts that the data produced by these cameras should be retained no longer than necessary for the purpose for which it was collected. Thus, most recordings should be deleted quickly.

The Harvard Law Review has assembled a list of potential problems with the use of police body cameras. First, there are reasons to be skeptical that video footage will lead to more just outcomes in excessive force cases.

In addition, the widespread adoption of such a pervasive, indiscriminate technology may have unintended negative consequences. For example, officers may circumvent the technology, or even erase footage prior to its review, to insulate the police from oversight. Moreover, there are pressing concerns about public access to the recordings, as well as significant privacy issues that must be addressed, including the long-term digital storage of these encounters.

As you read the articles presented in this section, consider whether you believe that requiring the police to wear body cameras and record their encounters with citizens is a positive development for American law enforcement. Is it likely to improve the overall performance of police officers and lead to heightened professionalism? Or is it, to paraphrase Justice Powell, another step down the slippery slope of decaying constitutional protections in criminal cases?

YES ⬎

Jay Stanley

Police Body-Mounted Cameras: With Right Policies in Place, a Win for All

Since we published the first version of this policy white paper in October 2013, interest in police body cameras has exploded. The August 2014 shooting of Michael Brown in Ferguson, Missouri and the subsequent protests focused new public attention on the problem of police violence—and on the possibility that body cameras might be part of the solution. The following December, a grand jury's decision not to indict an officer in the videotaped choke hold death of Eric Garner in New York City further intensified discussion of the technology.

With so much attention being paid to body cameras, we have received a lot of thoughtful feedback on our policy recommendations. Overall, considering how early in the discussion we issued our paper, we believe our recommendations have held up remarkably well. But in this revision of the paper we have seen fit to refine our recommendations in some areas, such as when police should record. And of course, the intersection of technology and human behavior being highly complex and unpredictable, we will continue to watch how the technology plays out in the real world, and will most likely continue to update this paper.

"On-officer recording systems" (also called "body cams" or "cop cams") are small, pager-sized cameras that clip on to an officer's uniform or are worn as a headset, and record audio and video of the officer's interactions with the public. Recent surveys suggest that about 25% of the nation's 17,000 police agencies were using them, with fully 80% of agencies evaluating the technology.

Much interest in the technology stems from a growing recognition that the United States has a real problem with police violence. In 2011, police killed six people in Australia, two in England, six in Germany and, according to an FBI count, 404 in the United States. And that FBI number counted only "justifiable homicides," and was comprised of *voluntarily submitted* data from just 750 of 17,000 law enforcement agencies. Attempts by journalists to compile more complete data by collating local news reports have resulted in estimates as high as 1,000 police killings per year in the United States. Fully a quarter of the deaths involved a white officer killing a black person.

The ACLU's Interest

Although we at the ACLU generally take a dim view of the proliferation of surveillance cameras in American life, police on-body cameras are different because of their potential to serve as a check against the abuse of power by police officers. Historically, there was no documentary evidence of most encounters between police officers and the public, and due to the volatile nature of those encounters, this often resulted in radically divergent accounts of incidents. Cameras have the potential to be a win-win, helping protect the public against police misconduct, and at the same time helping protect police against false accusations of abuse.

We're against pervasive government surveillance, but when cameras primarily serve the function of allowing public monitoring of the government instead of the other way around, we generally support their use. While we have opposed government video surveillance of public places, for example, we have supported the installation of video cameras on police car dashboards, in prisons, and during interrogations.

At the same time, body cameras have more of a potential to invade privacy than those deployments. Police officers enter people's homes and encounter bystanders, suspects, and victims in a wide variety of sometimes stressful and extreme situations.

For the ACLU, the challenge of on-officer cameras is the tension between their potential to invade privacy and their strong benefit in promoting police accountability. Overall, we think they can be a win-win—but *only* if they are deployed within a framework of strong policies to ensure they protect the public without becoming yet another system for routine surveillance *of* the public, and maintain public confidence in the integrity of those privacy protections. Without such a framework, their accountability benefits would not exceed their privacy risks.

On-officer cameras are a significant technology that implicates important, if sometimes conflicting, values. We will have to watch carefully to see how they are deployed and what their effects are over time, but in this paper we outline our current thinking about and recommendations for the technology. These recommendations are subject to change.

Control Over Recordings

Perhaps most importantly, policies and technology must be designed to ensure that police cannot "edit on the fly"—i.e., choose which encounters to record with limitless discretion. If police are free to turn the cameras on and off as they please, the cameras' role in providing a check and balance against police power will shrink and they will no longer become a net benefit.

The primary question is how that should be implemented.

Purely from an accountability perspective, the ideal policy for body-worn cameras would be for continuous recording throughout a police officer's shift, eliminating any possibility that an officer could evade the recording of abuses committed on duty.

The problem is that continuous recording raises many thorny privacy issues, for the public as well as for officers. For example, as the Police Executive Research Forum (PERF) pointed out in their September 2014 report on body cameras, crime victims (especially victims of rape, abuse, and other sensitive crimes), as well as witnesses who are concerned about retaliation if seen cooperating with police, may have very good reasons for not wanting police to record their interactions. We agree, and support body camera policies designed to offer special privacy protections for these individuals.

Continuous recording would also mean a lot of mass surveillance of citizens' ordinary activities. That would be less problematic in a typical automobile-centered town where officers rarely leave their cars except to engage in enforcement and investigation, but in a place like New York City it would mean unleashing 30,000 camera-equipped officers on the public streets, where an officer on a busy sidewalk might encounter thousands of people an hour. That's a lot of surveillance. That would be true of many denser urban neighborhoods—and of course, the most heavily policed neighborhoods,

poor and minority areas, would be the most surveilled in this way.

Continuous recording would also impinge on police officers when they are sitting in a station house or patrol car shooting the breeze—getting to know each other as humans, discussing precinct politics, etc. We have some sympathy for police on this; continuous recording might feel as stressful and oppressive in those situations as it would for any employee subject to constant recording by their supervisor. True, police officers with their extraordinary powers are not regular employees, and in theory officers' privacy, like citizens', could be protected by appropriate policies (as outlined below) that ensure that 99% of video would be deleted in relatively short order without ever being reviewed. But on a psychological level, such assurances are rarely enough. There is also the danger that the technology would be misused by police supervisors against whistleblowers or union activists—for example, by scrutinizing video records to find minor violations to use against an officer.

On the other hand, if the cameras do not record continuously, that would place them under officer control, which allows them to be manipulated by some officers, undermining their core purpose of detecting police misconduct. Indeed, this is precisely what we are seeing happening in many cases.

The balance that needs to be struck is to ensure that officers can't manipulate the video record, while also placing reasonable limits on recording in order to protect privacy.

One possibility is that some form of effective automated trigger could be developed that would allow for minimization of recording while capturing any fraught encounters—based, for example, on detection of raised voices, types of movement, etc. With dashcams, the devices are often configured to record whenever a car's siren or lights are activated, which provides a rough and somewhat (though not entirely) non-discretionary measure of when a police officer is engaged in an encounter that is likely to be a problem. That policy is not applicable to body cams, however, since there is no equivalent to flashing lights. And it's not clear that any artificial intelligence system in the foreseeable future will be smart enough to reliably detect encounters that should be recorded. In any case, it is not an option with today's technology.

Another possibility is that police discretion be minimized by requiring the recording of all encounters with the public. That would allow police to have the cameras off when talking amongst themselves, sitting in a squad care, etc., but through that bright-line rule still allow officers no discretion, and thus no opportunity to circumvent the oversight provided by cameras.

An all-public-encounters policy is what we called for in the first version of this white paper, but (as we first explained here), we have refined that position. The problem is that such a policy does not address the issues mentioned above with witnesses and victims, and greatly intensifies the privacy issues surrounding the cameras, especially in those states where open-records laws do not protect the privacy of routine video footage.

If a police department is to place its cameras under officer control, then it becomes vitally important that it put in place tightly effective means of limiting officers' ability to choose which encounters to record. Policies should require that an officer activate his or her camera *when responding to a call for service or at the initiation of any other law enforcement or investigative encounter between a police officer and a member of the public*. That would include stops, frisks, searches, arrests, consensual interviews and searches, enforcement actions of all kinds. This should cover any encounter that becomes in any way hostile or confrontational.

If officers are to have control over recording, it is important not only that clear policies be set, but also that they have some teeth. In too many places (Albuquerque, Denver, and other cities) officer compliance with body camera recording and video-handling rules has been terrible. Indeed, researchers report that compliance rates with body camera policies are as low as 30%.

When a police officer assigned to wear a body camera fails to record or otherwise interferes with camera video, three responses should result:

1. Direct disciplinary action against the individual officer.
2. The adoption of rebuttable evidentiary presumptions in favor of criminal defendants who claim exculpatory evidence was not captured or was destroyed.
3. The adoption of rebuttable evidentiary presumptions on behalf of civil plaintiffs suing the government, police department and/or officers for damages based on police misconduct. The presumptions should be rebuttable by other, contrary evidence or by proof of exigent circumstances that made compliance impossible.

Evidentiary presumptions against a defendant-officer in a criminal proceeding should not be sought, as they are insufficient for meeting the burden of proof in a criminal case and might lead to false convictions.

Limiting the Threat to Privacy from Cop Cams

The great promise of police body cameras is their oversight potential. But equally important are the privacy interests and fair trial rights of individuals who are recorded. Ideally there would be a way to minimize data collection to only what was reasonably needed, but there's currently no technological way to do so.

Police body cameras mean that many instances of entirely innocent behavior (on the part of both officers and the public) will be recorded. Perhaps most troubling is that some recordings will be made inside people's homes, whenever police enter—including in instances of consensual entry (e.g., responding to a burglary call, voluntarily participating in an investigation) and such things as domestic violence calls. In the case of dashcams, we have also seen video of particular incidents released for no important public reason, and instead serving only to embarrass individuals. Examples have included DUI stops of celebrities and ordinary individuals whose troubled and/or intoxicated behavior has been widely circulated and now immortalized online. The potential for such merely embarrassing and titillating releases of video is significantly increased by body cams.

Therefore it is vital that any deployment of these cameras be accompanied by good privacy policies so that the benefits of the technology are not outweighed by invasions of privacy. The core elements of such a policy follow.

Notice to Citizens

Most privacy protections will have to come from restrictions on subsequent retention and use of the recordings. There are, however, a few things that can be done at the point of recording.

1. Body cameras should generally be limited to uniformed police officers and marked vehicles, so people know what to expect. Exceptions should be made for non-uniformed officers involved in SWAT raids or in other planned enforcement actions or uses of force.
2. Officers should be required, wherever practicable, to notify people that they are being recorded (similar to existing law for dashcams in some states such as Washington). One possibility departments might consider is for officers to wear an easily visible pin or sticker saying "lapel camera in operation" or words to that effect. Cameras might also have blinking red lights when they record, as is standard on most other cameras.

3. It is especially important that the cameras not be used to surreptitiously gather intelligence information based on First Amendment protected speech, associations, or religion. (If the preceding policies are adopted, this highly problematic use would not be possible.)

Recording in the Home

Because of the uniquely intrusive nature of police recordings made inside private homes, officers should be required to provide clear notice of a camera when entering a home, except in circumstances such as an emergency or a raid. And departments should adopt a policy under which officers ask residents whether they wish for a camera to be turned off before they enter a home in non-exigent circumstances. (Citizen requests for cameras to be turned off must themselves be recorded to document such requests.) Cameras should never be turned off in SWAT raids and similar police actions.

Retention

Data should be retained no longer than necessary for the purpose for which it was collected. For the vast majority of police encounters with the public, there is no reason to preserve video evidence, and those recordings therefore should be deleted relatively quickly.

1. Retention periods should be measured in weeks not years, and video should be deleted after that period unless a recording has been flagged. Once a recording has been flagged, it would then switch to a longer retention schedule (such as the three-year period currently in effect in Washington State).
2. These policies should be posted online on the department's website, so that people who have encounters with police know how long they have to file a complaint or request access to footage.
3. Flagging should occur automatically for any incident:
   - involving a use of force;
   - that leads to detention or arrest; or
   - where either a formal or informal complaint has been registered.
4. Any subject of a recording should be able to flag a recording, even if not filing a complaint or opening an investigation.
5. The police department (including internal investigations and supervisors) and third parties should also be able to flag an incident if they have some basis to believe police misconduct has occurred or

have reasonable suspicion that the video contains evidence of a crime. We do not want the police or gadflies to be able to routinely flag all recordings in order to circumvent the retention limit.
6. If any useful evidence is obtained during an authorized use of a recording (see below), the recording would then be retained in the same manner as any other evidence gathered during an investigation.
7. Back-end systems to manage video data must be configured to retain the data, delete it after the retention period expires, prevent deletion by individual officers, and provide an unimpeachable audit trail to protect chain of custody, just as with any evidence.

Use of Recordings

The ACLU supports the use of cop cams for the purpose of police accountability and oversight. It's vital that this technology not become a backdoor for any kind of systematic surveillance or tracking of the public. Since the records will be made, police departments need to be subject to strong rules around how they are used. The use of recordings should be allowed only in internal and external investigations of misconduct, and where the police have reasonable suspicion that a recording contains evidence of a crime. Otherwise, there is no reason that stored footage should even be reviewed by a human being before its retention period ends and it is permanently deleted. Nor should such footage be subject to face recognition searches or other analytics.

Subject Access

People recorded by cop cams should have access to, and the right to make copies of, those recordings, for however long the government maintains copies of them. That should also apply to disclosure to a third party if the subject consents, or to criminal defense lawyers seeking relevant evidence.

Public Disclosure

When should the public have access to cop cam videos held by the authorities? Public disclosure of government records can be a tricky issue pitting two important values against each other: the need for government oversight and openness, and privacy. Those values must be carefully balanced by policymakers. One way to do that is to attempt to minimize invasiveness when possible:

- Public disclosure of any recording should be allowed with the consent of the subjects, as discussed above.
- Redaction of video records should be used when feasible—blurring or blacking out of portions of video and/or distortion of audio to obscure the identity of subjects. If recordings are redacted, they should be discloseable.
- Unredacted, unflagged recordings should not be publicly disclosed without consent of the subject. These are recordings where there is no indication of police misconduct or evidence of a crime, so the public oversight value is low. States may need to examine how such a policy interacts with their state open records laws.
- Flagged recordings are those for which there is the highest likelihood of misconduct, and thus the ones where public oversight is most needed. Redaction of disclosed recordings is preferred, but when that is not feasible, unredacted flagged recordings should be publicly discloseable, because in such cases the need for oversight generally outweighs the privacy interests at stake.

Good Technological Controls

It is important that close attention be paid to the systems that handle the video data generated by these cameras.

- Systems should be architected to ensure that segments of video cannot be destroyed. A recent case in Maryland illustrates the problem: surveillance video of an incident in which officers were accused of beating a student disappeared (the incident was also filmed by a bystander). An officer or department that has engaged in abuse or other wrongdoing will have a strong incentive to destroy evidence of that wrongdoing, so technology systems should be designed to prevent any tampering with such video.
- In addition, all access to video records should be automatically recorded with immutable audit logs.
- Systems should ensure that data retention and destruction schedules are properly maintained.
- It is also important for systems be architected to ensure that video is only accessed when permitted according to the policies we've described above, and that rogue copies cannot be made. Officers should not be able to, for example, pass around video of a drunk city council member, or video generated by an officer responding to a call in a topless bar, or video of a citizen providing information on a local street gang.
- If video is held by a cloud service or other third party, it should be encrypted end-to-end so that the service provider cannot access the video.

It is vital that public confidence in the integrity of body camera privacy protections be maintained. We don't want crime victims to be afraid to call for help because of fears that video of their officer interactions will become public or reach the wrong party. Confidence can only be created if good policies are put in place and backed up by good technology.

As the devices are adopted by police forces around the nation, studies should be done to measure their impact. Only very limited studies have been done so far. Are domestic violence victims hesitating to call the police for help by the prospect of having a camera-wearing police officer in their home, or are they otherwise affected? Are privacy abuses of the technology happening, and if so what kind and how often?

Although fitting police forces with cameras will generate an enormous amount of video footage and raises many tricky issues, if the recording, retention, access, use, and technology policies that we outline above are followed, very little of that footage will ever be viewed or retained, and at the same time those cameras will provide an important protection against police abuse. We will be monitoring the impact of cameras closely, and if good policies and practices do not become standard, or the technology has negative side effects we have failed to anticipate, we will have to reevaluate our position on police body cameras.

Use of Body Cameras in Different Contexts

Body cameras are not justified for use by government officials who do not have the authority to conduct searches and make arrests, such as parking enforcement officers, building inspectors, teachers, or other non-law enforcement personnel. Police officers have the authority, in specific circumstances, to shoot to kill, to use brutal force, and to arrest people—and all too often, abuse those powers. The strong oversight function that body cameras promise to play with regards to police officers makes that deployment of the technology a unique one. For other officials, the use of body cameras does not strike the right balance between the oversight function of these cameras and their potential intrusiveness.

Jay Stanley is a Senior Policy Analyst with the American Civil Liberties Union's (ACLU) Speech, Privacy and Technology Project, where he researches, writes, and speaks about technology-related privacy and civil liberties issues and their future. He is the editor of the ACLU's "Free Future" blog and has authored and coauthored a variety of influential reports on privacy and technology topics.

Harvard Law Review

→ **NO**

Considering Police Body Cameras

A.

One evening in early December 2014, thousands of people gathered on the historic Boston Common, not to view the annual Christmas-tree lighting, but to add their voices to a growing movement.[1] They carried with them signs inscribed with the mantras of that movement—phrases like "Hands Up, Don't Shoot" and "Black Lives Matter"—and they joined together to call for justice, for police accountability, and for the nation to address the structural forces that permit white police officers to kill a black person at least every eighty-four hours.[2] These displays of solidarity, inspired by earlier protests in Ferguson, Missouri, spread across the country: from Oakland[3] to Chicago[4] to New York City,[5] citizens took to the streets to demand reform from their government.

This widespread initiative—said to evoke the civil rights movement[6]—began largely in response to a Missouri grand jury's decision not to indict police officer Darren Wilson for any crime related to his fatal shooting of Michael Brown, a black teenager who was unarmed when shot.[7] A little over a week later, the failure of a Staten Island grand jury to indict NYPD Officer Daniel Pantaleo for his fatal use of a choke hold on Eric Garner, yet another unarmed black man, further catalyzed the movement—particularly because this deadly encounter was captured on film by nearby onlookers.[8]

The outrage over Officer Pantaleo's nonindictment presents an interesting challenge for reformers. Prior to the grand jury's decision, both protestors and politicians were calling for police departments across the country to outfit their officers with body cameras.[9] The hope was that video recordings of police-civilian interactions would deter officer misconduct and eliminate the ambiguity present in cases like Michael Brown's, making it easier to punish officers' use of excessive force.[10] This initiative gained "overwhelming support from every stakeholder in the controversy—the public, the White House, federal legislators, police officials, [and] police unions."[11] Indeed, on December 1, 2014—two days prior to the grand jury decision in Garner's case—President Obama announced

$263 million in federal funding to allow law enforcement agencies "to purchase body-worn cameras and improve training."[12] The American Civil Liberties Union (ACLU) also repeatedly voiced its support for widespread adoption of this new technology, heralding body cameras as "a win-win" as long as civilian privacy remained properly protected.[13]

This widespread galvanization over body cameras[14] exemplifies the human tendency, in times of tragedy, to latch on to the most readily available solution to a complex problem. But as the outcome of Garner's case demonstrates, even when high-quality, graphic footage is available, officers may still not be indicted, let alone convicted.[15] Moreover, body cameras are a powerful—and indiscriminate—technology. Their proliferation over the next decade will inevitably change the nature of policing in unexpected ways, quite possibly to the detriment of the citizens the cameras are intended to protect.[16] So although video footage has the potential to move citizens as it did in the Garner case,[17] proper implementation of this new policing tool requires careful consideration of current policy proposals, rather than the rapid, reactionary adoptions currently taking place nationwide.[18] Their adoption should also not be used as an excuse to stifle continued conversation about the root causes of police violence and fractured community relations, as body cameras alone will never be the hoped-for cure-all . . .

B.

1. "It's not real."[19] On August 5, five days before Michael Brown's death, John Crawford III entered the local Walmart with his girlfriend.[20] He was there to buy ingredients to make s'mores at a cookout with his family later that day.[21] But instead of leaving with graham crackers, he was taken from the store in an ambulance—fatally shot by police officers in an aisle.[22] Crawford was twenty-two years old.[23]

The Beavercreek Walmart in Ohio, the site of Crawford's shooting, has over two hundred video cameras.[24] These cameras show Crawford on his cell phone, walking through the store. He then picks up an unloaded pellet gun, a product stocked on the Walmart shelves.[25] At the same time, Ronald Ritchie—another patron—dials the police, reporting a black man walking around with a gun in the store.[26] (Ritchie relayed this observation even though Ohio is an open-carry state.[27]) Ritchie originally claimed that Crawford was pointing the toy gun at people, though he later recanted that statement.[28] Officers responded to the scene with their guns drawn. The surveillance footage then shows them confronting Crawford and firing shots at him as he scrambles to retreat.[29] Despite the fact that Crawford was holding a toy gun, that Ritchie recanted his earlier statement, and that the surveillance footage documented the entire police encounter (including officers firing while the toy gun was on the ground), a grand jury declined to indict either officer involved.[30] Crawford's case thus became the third case in five years in which a Greene County, Ohio, grand jury failed to indict officers who had fatally shot civilians.[31]

2. Notwithstanding the potential benefits of body cameras discussed in section B, Crawford's death provides one reason to be skeptical that video footage will necessarily lead to more just outcomes in excessive-force cases. And as several critics have cautioned, the adoption of such a pervasive, indiscriminate technology may have unintended negative consequences.[32] Because questions remain about whether body cameras will in fact increase police transparency and accountability, this section examines several potential drawbacks to body-camera proposals. These drawbacks should be given careful consideration to ensure that camera policies accomplish their intended objectives.

(a) Locus of Control.—So far, this Chapter has primarily included examples of police-civilian interactions that were filmed by citizens rather than by the police. The widespread circulation of these videos has been instrumental in shedding light on issues of police misconduct.[33] In theory, body cameras offer this benefit on an unprecedented scale: unlike citizens, who will not always be present or who may choose not to record, a police force outfitted with body cameras could potentially document every officer-citizen encounter. But once the locus of control shifts to the officers, the very organization meant to be held accountable will be able to prevent these videos from being created in the first instance or shared after the fact.

For instance, only two days after Michael Brown was killed, a New Orleans police officer shot "[an] unarmed black man while trying to take him into custody." The victim, Armand Bennet, spent four days in the intensive care unit and needed staples to treat the wound on his forehead.[34] The officer had been wearing a body camera, but she had "apparently shut off her camera prior to the encounter."[35] Though the officer claimed she had turned the camera off just prior to the end of her shift, the shooting took place at 1:15 a.m., and her shift ended at 2:00 a.m.[36] Although New Orleans police recently adopted body cameras in an effort to build trust between law enforcement and the public,[37] this sort of incident demonstrates how officers can still circumvent the technology to insulate themselves from oversight.[38] Even an officer's *willful* refusal to record is not a fireable offense in New Orleans.[39] And if the treatment of dashboard-camera footage is any indication, some officers will also erase footage prior to its review—an action likely to go unnoticed or unpunished by supervisors.[40]

Even for properly recorded and stored footage, pressing concerns about public access remain. Many police departments currently do not allow private individuals or the media to access footage,[41] and the open-records laws in most states make it possible for departments to deny access indefinitely. While body-camera footage should constitute a public record under disclosure laws, most states have disclosure exemptions for records involved in a law enforcement investigation.[42] The definition of an "investigation" is malleable, and courts may be particularly inclined to defer to officers when it comes to matters of public safety. Some courts have ruled that law enforcement video footage does not fall under the exemption for criminal investigatory records;[43] however, this type of litigation is in its early stages, and in many states the public (including individuals featured on the tapes) may remain unable to access the footage.[44] Although wholesale public access would likely prove undesirable, efforts by officers to thwart the goals of a body-camera regime do raise the question of *who* stands to benefit most from this technology.[45] Some departments, for example, allow officers to review video footage before making a statement on the record about an incident. As one police chief explained:

> If you make a statement that you used force because you thought a suspect had a gun but the video later shows that it was actually a cell phone, it looks like you were lying. . . . An officer should be given the chance to make a statement using all of the evidence available; otherwise, it looks like we are just trying to catch an officer in a lie.[46]

This asymmetric access to the footage is therefore problematic as it allows officers to adapt their testimony in order to bolster their credibility while civilian witnesses cannot do the same.

(b) Privacy.—Privacy is a counterpoint to access: increasing transparency necessarily means more people will view body-camera footage, which will frequently feature civilians who may not want the recordings of themselves shared. This type of access raises the issue of whether officers must affirmatively warn all citizens that they are being recorded. The ACLU, for one, has called for notice to citizens "wherever practicable," potentially in the form of "an easily visible pin or sticker saying 'lapel camera in operation' or words to that effect."[47] But questions remain, especially about the appropriateness of "police recordings made inside private homes" given the footage's "uniquely intrusive nature."[48] Officers' ability to review tapes, slow them down, and enhance images means that a recorded search of a home or a vehicle can lead to the discovery of evidence that would otherwise have gone unnoticed.

Beyond initial police-citizen encounters, the long-term digital storage of those interactions, especially intimate interactions (such as recordings of domestic disputes[49]), also raises privacy concerns. It is unclear whether filmed individuals will have a right to request that the footage be deleted or not be shared with the public.[50] Footage taken inside the home could, for instance, be requested by other citizens (like neighbors), even though the privacy implications of these sorts of requests remain largely unexplored. Contextual policies thus need to be developed about when cameras should stop rolling—for example, during interviews of sexual assault victims—and when footage should cease to be stored. Without further guidance on these issues, civilians' privacy may be violated or, equally problematic, police may raise privacy concerns as an excuse to curtail public oversight.

(c) Costs and Storage.—As more departments acquire body cameras, and as officers' cameras roll each day, police departments will inevitably amass a colossal amount of footage, much of it likely irrelevant to any disputes over police-civilian interactions. While the start-up cost of outfitting a force with body cameras is not trivial for cashstrapped departments, the costs of storing and transmitting this data can be particularly staggering: some departments have already spent hundreds of thousands or even millions of dollars managing their data.[51] However, these costs may be offset by savings on litigation, if cameras do in fact lead to fewer complaints and more efficient resolution of police misconduct cases.[52]

Still, this price tag leaves open the question of who exactly will bear the costs of this new technology—especially when politicians are wary of raising taxes while the country recovers from the Great Recession.[53] In New Jersey, one proposed legislative answer has been to increase fines on certain defendants to finance the state's body-camera program: in particular, individuals convicted of DUIs and sex offenses would pay higher penalties. This type of defendant-funded policing initiative raises concerns about profit motives in the criminal justice system. It also demonstrates that even though a broad coalition of support has formed around body cameras, it will likely be the most vulnerable populations (and those most likely to be negatively affected by this technology, given the disproportionate police presence in lowincome, minority neighborhoods) that are forced to foot the bill. If that is the case, it may fairly be asked whether body cameras are indeed a necessity or whether politicians are committed to such reform efforts only when it doesn't cost them political capital. Reformers should be cognizant of the regressive effects this type of funding scheme would have, and should search for other means of financing the body-camera initiative.

(d) Surveillance State.—In a post-9/11 world, the addition of yet another form of government surveillance should not go unexamined: recent technological advances have allowed the state to move beyond the use of traditional electronic surveillance devices—like wiretaps and bugs—toward more pervasive surveillance techniques.[54] From the Snowden leaks[55] to reports of police drone use,[56] citizens are more conscious than ever of being watched by their government.[57] Moreover, "mission creep" on the part of camera manufacturers has already begun: at least one city has made plans to outfit its parking attendants with body cameras, and some advocates have called for expanding cameras into other arenas, like the classroom.

So although police body cameras have the potential to benefit citizens and officers alike, they nevertheless represent another substantial step toward a surveillance state. Police departments in recent decades have become increasingly militarized,[58] complete with intelligence departments, devices that mimic cell phone towers, and facial recognition software. Facial recognition software in particular may pose a threat to civilian privacy when coupled with body cameras:

> [T]he increasing effectiveness of facial recognition software, even in consumer products like Facebook, means that simply recording an image of a person (in a private or public space) can lead to further identification. . . . Officer-mounted

wearable cameras, paired with facial recognition, could easily become much like the current crop of automated license readers, constantly reading thousands of faces (license plates), interpreting identity (plate number), and cross-checking this information against national and local crime databases in real-time.[59]

While not necessarily "inimical to individual liberty," this rapid expansion of police oversight may do less to empower civilians to "watch their watchers," and more to enable the government to effectively track, detain, and arrest individuals.[60] Indeed, many policing initiatives that have been adopted in the name of "protecting" civilians have later been used against them.[61] Past experiences should inform present debates over national adoption of body cameras, and proponents should be particularly careful to consider the long-term ramifications of normalizing this technology.

(e) The "Objectivity" of Video Evidence.—A final, fundamental concern regarding body cameras goes to the heart of their functionality: the reliability of the video footage they produce. This footage is, undoubtedly, the main advantage of the cameras in that it allows for ex post review of officer conduct in the field. But the perceived "objectivity" of video evidence also creates a danger of overreliance.[62] "Video purports to be an objective, unbiased, transparent observer of events that evenhandedly reproduces reality for the viewer," and "[f]rom an evidentiary standpoint, video evidence often will be overwhelming proof at trial."[63] Even with body cameras rolling at all times, though, the picture may not capture either "what happened outside the camera's view or the causation for actions shown . . . depend[ing] on 'the camera's perspective (angles) and breadth of view (wide shots and focus).'"[64] Perspective may have an outsized influence on a factfinder's impression of the video: for instance, mock juries shown a first-person interrogation tape without the officer on screen are "significantly less likely to find an interrogation coercive, and more likely to believe in the truth and accuracy of the confession," than are jurors who are shown the identical interrogation but from a wider angle that includes the officer.[65] This sort of distortion is especially concerning given that body-camera footage will always be filmed from the perspective of the officer, making it easier for a jury to credit this perspective.

Beyond the technological limitations of these cameras, an empirical study conducted by Professor Dan Kahan illustrates that even video footage thought to be unambiguous[66] is susceptible to multiple interpretations depending on the "cultural outlook[]" of the individual viewing the tape.[67] These sorts of implicit biases may subtly affect how viewers—in their living room or in the courtroom—process the story told by body-camera footage. This phenomenon may also allow for the unconscious incorporation of implicit biases when determining whether an officer's actions were "reasonable" under the circumstances for purposes of an indictment or conviction.

Given that body-camera footage (with all its fallibilities) will inevitably be used as an effective tool for the state in prosecuting defendants caught on film, it again must be asked *who* in fact benefits most from the adoption of this technology if officers are not also held accountable even when captured on tape. Because video evidence will likely prove singularly powerful in these sorts of excessive force cases, careful consideration must be given to how this type of evidence can be manipulated or distorted—both intentionally and unintentionally—in a manner that systematically favors the officers. . . .

Notes

1. Travis Andersen et al., *Thousands Protest Eric Garner Case in Downtown Boston*, Bos. Globe (Dec. 4, 2014).

2. *See* Kevin Johnson et al., *Local Police Involved in 400 Killings per Year*, USA Today (Aug. 15, 2014, 9:41 AM) (finding that white police officers killed black people an average of two times per week based on self-reported statistics).

3. *See, e.g.,* Jessica Guynn, *Berkeley Protesters March for Fourth Night, Briefly Block Freeway*, USA TODAY (Dec. 11, 2014, 8:28 AM) (detailing protests of over 1500 individuals and noting that 223 protestors had already been arrested).

4. *See, e.g.,* Associated Press, *Ferguson Decision Brings Protests to Lake Shore Drive*, Crain's Chi. Bus. (Nov. 24, 2014).

5. *See, e.g.,* Rocco Parascandola, *Eric Garner Case Protesters Block Traffic in Staten Island Near Verrazano-Narrows Bridge*, N.Y. Daily News (Dec. 8, 2014, 10:37 AM).

6. *See* Randy Kennedy & Jennifer Schuessler, *Ferguson Images Evoke Civil Rights Era and Changing Visual Perceptions*, N.Y. Times, Aug. 15, 2014 (noting that, despite "formal similarities" between images, depictions of the police "could not have been more different," as "[t]oday's riot police officers [are] wearing military-style camouflage and carrying military-style rifles, their heads and faces obscured by black helmets and gas masks as they [stand] in front of an armored vehicle"); Dani McClain, *The Civil Rights Movement Came Out of a Moment Like This One*, The Nation (Dec. 4, 2014, 5:47 PM).

7. *See* Eyder Peralta & Bill Chappell, *Ferguson Jury: No Charges for Officer in Michael Brown's Death*, NPR: THE TWO-WAY (Nov. 24, 2014, 3:37 PM).

8. *See* Aaron Blake, *Why Eric Garner Is the Turning Point Ferguson Never Was*, WASH. POST: THE FIX (Dec. 8, 2014).

9. *See, e.g., Michael Brown's Family in Atlanta to Begin Campaign for Police Body Cameras*, WSB-TV (Sept. 21, 2014, 9:38 PM).

10. *See* Michael McAuliff, *Police Body Cameras Seen as a Fix for Ferguson-Style Killings*, HUFFINGTON POST (Nov. 25, 2014, 7:59 PM) ("Civil liberties advocates argue that video records prevent cops from abusing their authority, while law enforcement groups note that a person cannot falsely accuse an officer if their encounter is recorded.").

11. Howard M. Wasserman, *Moral Panics and Body Cameras*, WASH. U. L. REV. COMMENTARIES, Nov. 18, 2014, at 2.

12. Sink, *supra* note 10. This money "would be used by the federal government to match up to 50 percent spending by state and local police departments on body-worn cameras and storage for the equipment. The White House estimate[d] that aspect of the program, which would cost $75 million, would help fund the purchase of 50,000 body-worn cameras." *Id.*

13. Jay Stanley, *Police Body-Mounted Cameras: With Right Policies in Place, a Win for All*, ACLU (Oct. 9, 2013), *see also* Jay Stanley, *Accountability vs. Privacy: The ACLU's Recommendations on Police Body Cameras*, ACLU (Oct. 9, 2013, 11:00 AM).

14. A recent survey revealed that 77% of Americans would feel safer if officers were equipped with body cameras, and 74% felt that officers "should be required to wear body cameras." Tammy Payne, *Arrest of OKC Officer Highlights Benefits of Body Cameras*, NEWS 9 (Aug. 22, 2014, 8:14 AM).

15. For footage of Garner's death, see *'I Can't Breathe': Eric Garner Put in Chokehold by NYPD Officer—Video*, THE GUARDIAN (Dec. 4, 2014, 2:46 PM). This lack of accountability occurred despite the deadly use of a chokehold, Goodman & Baker, *supra* note 9, a maneuver banned by the NYPD since 1993. Tierney Sneed, *Tale of the Tape: When Police Brutality Is Caught on Camera*, U.S. NEWS & WORLD REP. (Aug. 7, 2014, 2:30 PM) (discussing the chokehold ban, but adding that the department has still received over 1000 allegations of chokeholds between 2009 and 2013). The ban "specifically [does]

not distinguish between various types of holds, but rather ban[s] them categorically." Ian Fisher, *Kelly Bans Choke Holds by Officers*, N.Y. TIMES, Nov. 24, 1993.

16. Historically, many reforms undertaken for the professed purpose of "protecting" civilians have ultimately ended up empowering police officers. For example, the stop-and-frisk programs, ostensibly implemented to deter violence in high-crime neighborhoods, have enabled officers to stop and search a grossly disproportionate number of minorities without any proven efficacy. *See, e.g.,* Ray Rivera, *Pockets of City See Higher Use of Force During Police Stops*, N.Y. TIMES (Aug. 15, 2012) (reporting that NYPD officers made 680,000 stops in 2011, over 80% of which involved stopping a black or Latino individual, and finding that "police used some level of physical force in more than one in five stops across the city . . . [y]et the high level of force seldom translated into arrests"); Donald Braman, *Stop-and-Frisk Didn't Make New York Safer*, THE ATLANTIC (Mar. 26, 2014, 3:26 PM) ("There's no good evidence that the invasive policing strategy brought down crime.").

17. Indeed, it is unlikely that the grassroots movement formed in response to Brown's and Garner's deaths would have become nearly as widespread or bipartisan without such footage. *See* Blake, *supra* note 9 (citing a study finding that 60% of Americans disagree with the grand jury outcome in Garner's case, as compared to 36% of Americans disagreeing with the outcome in Brown's case, and arguing that the disparity is due to the existence of video footage of the Garner incident, which significantly lessened the "debate about the particulars of precisely what happened").

18. As Professor José Gabilondo has observed, times of "moral panic" often arise out of "an incident or pattern [that] catalyzes preexisting social anxiety [from which] an ad hoc issues movement is born. The media fans the flames through sensationalist and reductionist news stories. . . . Usually, a hasty legal reform results from the panic. Driven as it is by irrationality, the reforms usually miss the point of the original problem and suffer from disproportionality." José Gabilondo, *Financial Moral Panic! Sarbanes-Oxley, Financier Folk Devils, and Off-Balance-Sheet Arrangements*, 36 SETON HALL L. REV. 781, 792 (2006); *see also* Wasserman, *supra* note 12, at 4.

19. Last words of John Crawford III before being shot and killed by police officers in an Ohio Walmart for carrying an unloaded toy gun. Nisha Chittal, *Cops Shoot and Kill Man Holding Toy Gun in Wal-Mart,* MSNBC (Aug. 13, 2014, 8:06 PM).

20. Jon Swaine, *Doubts Cast on Witness's Account of Black Man Killed by Police in Walmart,* THE GUARDIAN (Sept. 7, 2014, 10:37 AM).

21. *Id.*

22. *Id.*

23. *Id.* Crawford was not the only casualty that day: "[F]ellow shopper Angela Williams, a 37- year-old nursing home worker reported to have suffered from a heart condition, was in cardiac arrest after collapsing trying to flee the melee. She died later that evening in hospital." *Id.* She and Crawford left behind four and two children, respectively. *Id.*; Jill Drury, *Mom Died at Walmart, Trying to Save Kids After Shooting,* WDTN.COM (Aug. 21, 2014, 3:20 PM).

24. Beairshelle Edmé & Jill Drury, *Police Release Dispatch Audio, Video of Walmart Shooting,* WDTN.COM (Aug. 21, 2014, 6:57 PM).

25. Swaine, *supra* note 63.

26. *Id.*

27. *See* Charles C.W. Cooke, Op-Ed., *Do Black People Have Equal Gun Rights?,* N.Y. TIMES, Oct. 26, 2014.

28. *See* Swaine, *supra* note 63. To view a video synching Ritchie's 911 call to the video footage of Crawford, which makes evident the discrepancies between the two, see Jon Swaine, *'It Was a Crank Call': Family Seeks Action Against 911 Caller in Walmart Shooting,* THE GUARDIAN (Sept. 26, 2014, 4:02 PM).

29. To view this footage, see Elahe Izadi, *Ohio Wal-Mart Surveillance Video Shows Police Shooting and Killing John Crawford III,* WASH. POST (Sept. 25, 2014).

30. Joe Coscarelli, *No Charges Against Ohio Police in John Crawford III Walmart Shooting, Despite Damning Security Video,* N.Y. MAG. (Sept. 24, 2014, 2:57 PM).

31. *See id.* Another recent Ohio case involved Tamir Rice—a twelve-year-old African American boy—who was shot to death by Ohio police after someone called the police to report that Rice was "waving what looked like a gun in a park near [Rice's] home. Within seconds of arriving, a police officer shot [Rice], but [Rice's] gun turned out to be a toy used to fire plastic pellets." Richard A. Oppel, Jr., *Police Shooting of Tamir Rice Is Ruled a Homicide,* N.Y. TIMES (Dec. 12, 2014).

32. *See, e.g.,* AJ Vicens, *Putting Body Cameras on Cops Is Hardly a Cure-All for Abuses,* MOTHER JONES (Aug. 21, 2014, 12:03 PM).

33. Perhaps the most famous example of citizen surveillance was George Holliday's filming of the brutal beating of Rodney King by several Los Angeles police officers in the early 1990s. *See* John Carman, *The Story Behind the King Videotape,* ST. PETERSBURG TIMES, May 10, 1992, at 3A. After Holliday shared his tape with the local news, the story was picked up—playing nationwide on repeat, *id.,* and sparking one of the most significant controversies in modern American race relations.

34. *Id.*

35. *Id.*

36. *Id.*

37. *See* Martin Kaste, *Can Cop-Worn Cameras Restore Faith in New Orleans Police?,* NPR (May 22, 2014, 5:38 PM).

38. This would not be the first time that technology has been oversold as a panacea for policing problems: after the Rodney King beating in Los Angeles, the LAPD required officers to wear voice recorders that would "switch on automatically when their cruiser sirens [were] activated." Elise Hu, *Using Technology to Counter Police Mistrust Is Complicated,* NPR (Sept. 2, 2014, 12:10 PM), (quoting Sean Bonner, *Body Cameras and Law Enforcement,* SBDC (Aug. 31, 2014, 11:02 AM).

39. Martin Kaste, *Even Police Body Cameras Can Lose Sight of the Truth,* NPR (Aug. 23, 2014, 11:41 AM). This lack of accountability is deeply problematic: a recent report found that "[w]hen New Orleans police officers exert force in the field, most of those interactions still are not being recorded despite new department protocols to activate body-worn cameras. . . ." Ken Daley, *Cameras Not on Most of the Time When NOPD Uses Force, Monitor Finds,* TIMES-PICAYUNE (Sept. 4, 2014, 10:05 PM).

40. *See* Robinson Meyer, *Seen It All Before: 10 Predictions About Police Body Cameras,* THE ATLANTIC (Dec. 5, 2014, 7:15 AM).

41. *See, e.g.,* Liam Dillon, *Police Body Camera Videos Will Stay Private—At Least for Now,* VOICE SAN DIEGO (Mar. 19, 2014).

42. *See, e.g.,* IND. CODE § 5-14-3-4(b)(1) (2014) (exempting "[i]nvestigatory records of law enforcement agencies"); MASS. GEN. LAWS ch.

4, § 7, cl.26(f) (2014) (exempting "investigatory materials necessarily compiled out of the public view by law enforcement or other investigatory officials the disclosure of which materials would probably so prejudice the possibility of effective law enforcement that such disclosure would not be in the public interest"); W. Va. Code § 29B-1-4(a)(4) (2014) (same for law enforcement records).

43. *See, e.g.,* Paff v. Ocean Cnty. Prosecutor's Office, No. OCN-L-1645-14, 2014 WL 5139407 (N.J. Super. Ct. Law Div. Oct. 2, 2014) (dashboard cameras); Paff v. Ocean Cnty. Prosecutor's Office, No. OCN-L-1645-14, 2014 WL 3886839 (N.J. Super. Ct. Law Div. July 31, 2014) (same). In the *Paff* cases, a New Jersey Superior Court judge ruled (over the government's objection) both that dashboard-camera footage is a public record, and that such footage is not covered by the public records laws' exemption for criminal investigatory records. The judge reasoned that "OPRA's criminal investigatory records exception does not render otherwise public government records confidential because they document some aspect of a crime." *Paff,* 2014 WL 3886839, at *4.

44. *See, e.g.,* Dillon, *supra* note 86.

45. Given that police and prosecutors can use the footage in court to prosecute individuals caught committing crimes on camera, *see* Int'l Ass'n Chiefs Police, *supra* note 57, at 21, those most likely to be disadvantaged by the footage are low-income, minority individuals because of the heavy police presence in their neighborhoods.

46. PERF Report, *supra* note 55, at 29 (quoting Topeka Police Chief Ron Miller).

47. Stanley, *Police Body-Mounted Cameras, supra* note 14.

48. *Id.*

49. Despite the highly personal nature of these encounters, police departments are in fact eager to use body cameras to resolve domestic violence cases: some commentators believe that the cameras will allow courts to see "just how bad it was that night" and will allow battered women to avoid facing their partners in court after a violent incident. *See Push for Body Cameras in Domestic Violence Cases,* ABC News 4 (Sept. 18, 2014, 6:57 PM).

50. For example, under the court's rulings in *Paff,* any member of the public likely can request access to footage from an officer's body camera, which may intrude upon the privacy of the taped individual. *See supra* note 88; *see also Video: Washington Agencies Overwhelmed by Records Requests May Drop Body Cams,* Police (Nov. 11, 2014).

51. PERF Report, *supra* note 55, at 32 (describing the data storage costs as "crippling" for some departments and noting that the New Orleans Police Department expects to spend $1.2 million over five years on its body-camera program, with most expenditures going toward data storage).

52. Litigating citizen complaints has proven immensely expensive: for instance, the Oakland Police Department spent a total of $13,149,000 in fiscal year 2010–2011 on legal costs for officer misconduct, Ali Winston, *Police-Related Legal Costs Spike in Oakland,* E. Bay Express (June 27, 2012), Chicago Police Department spent $84.6 million in 2013 for misconduct settlements, judgments, and legal fees, Andy Shaw, *City Pays Heavy Price for Police Brutality,* Chi. Sun Times (Apr. 14, 2014, 2:23 AM).

53. *See* U.S. Dep't of Justice, The Impact of the Economic Downturn on American Police Agencies 13 (2011) (estimating that between 12,000 and 15,000 police officers were laid off as a result of recent budget cuts).

54. *See* Christopher Slobogin, Privacy At Risk, at ii (2007) (discussing "the [government's] use of sophisticated technology to observe our daily activities," as "[o]ur wanderings, our work, and our play can now be monitored not only through binoculars and other types of telescopic lenses but also with night scopes, tracking mechanisms, satellite cameras, and devices that detect heat and images through walls," and our transactional data can be accessed "via snoopware, commercial data brokers, and ordinary Internet searches").

55. In June 2013, Edward Snowden, a former CIA technician, leaked classified documents detailing the National Security Agency's (NSA) daily collection of phone records from millions of cell phone customers. *See* Glenn Greenwald, *NSA Collecting Phone Records of Millions of Verizon Customers Daily,* The Guardian (Jun. 6, 2013, 6:05 AM). The NSA and the Obama Administration have both faced rampant criticism for these infringements on civilian privacy, since further leaks revealed the NSA's attempts to "circumvent widely used web encryption technologies," frequent requests for data from large tech companies such as Google and Facebook, and daily collection of millions of text messages from around

the world. Lorenzo Franceschi-Bicchierai, *The 10 Biggest Revelations from Edward Snowden's Leaks,* Mashable (Jun. 5, 2014, 2:47 PM), http://mashable.com/2014/06/05/edward-snowden-revelations [http://perma.cc/96F8-Y38H].

56. *See, e.g.,* Phil Willon & Melanie Mason, *Governor Vetoes Bill that Would Have Limited Police Use of Drones,* L.A. Times (Sept. 28, 2014, 7:09 PM), (discussing California Governor Jerry Brown's veto of a bill that would have required law enforcement agencies to obtain warrants before using drones for surveillance of citizens); *see also* Jennifer O'Brien, Comment, *Warrantless Government Drone Surveillance: A Challenge to the Fourth Amendment,* 30 J. Marshall J. Info. Tech. & Privacy L. 155, 165–66 (2013) (noting that President Obama signed into law the FAA Modernization and Reform Act of 2012, which "expressly directs the FAA to permit law enforcement operation of unmanned aircraft that weigh less than 4.4 pounds under specified restrictions").

57. Indeed, the media, the public, and even some politicians have vocalized ardent criticisms of the government's ever-expanding surveillance apparatus. *See, e.g.,* Spencer Ackerman & Paul Lewis, *NSA Surveillance Challenged in Court as Criticism Grows over US Data Program,* The Guardian (Jun. 11, 2013, 5:44 PM).

58. *See generally* Radley Balko, Rise of the Warrior Cop (2013).

59. Bryce Clayton Newell, *Crossing Lenses: Policing's New Visibility and the Role of "Smartphone Journalism" as a Form of Freedom-Preserving Reciprocal Surveillance,* 2014 U. Ill. J.L. Tech. & Pol'y 59, 90. With the advancement of technology, it may also become possible to review years of stored body-camera footage using facial recognition software, looking for "cold" hits.

60. *See id.* Given the number of primarily low-income, minority individuals who have outstanding warrants for unpaid fines or other minor offenses, *see supra* ch. I, pp. 1727–29, this combination of body cameras and facial recognition software may prove especially insidious.

61. For example, wiretapping laws were originally written to ensure that law enforcement respected "the privacy rights of individuals." Travis S. Triano, Note, *Who Watches the Watchmen? Big Brother's Use of Wiretap Statutes to Place Citizens in Timeout,* 34 Cardozo L. Rev

389, 391–96 (2012). But since their inception, these statutes have instead been used to arrest and prosecute citizens for alleged violations of their states' wiretapping statutes, including for filming the police. *See id.* at 396; *see also infra* section D.

62. *See* Howard M. Wasserman, *Orwell's Vision: Video and the Future of Civil Rights Enforcement,* 68 MD. L. Rev. 600, 620 (2009) ("The certainty that video purports to provide . . . is more myth than reality."); *cf.* Susan Sontag, On Photography 5–6 (1977) ("A photograph passes for incontrovertible proof that a given thing happened. . . . Whatever the limitations (through amateurism) or pretentions (through artistry) of the individual photographer, a photograph—any photograph—seems to have a more innocent, and therefore more accurate, relation to visible reality than do other mimetic objects.").

63. Wasserman, *supra* note 114, at 619.

64. *Id.* at 620 (quoting Jessica Silbey, *Cross-Examining Film,* 8 U. MD. L.J. Race Religion Gender & Class 17, 29 (2008)). It is likely that the "source of a recording also might affect viewer perception," as more or less legitimacy may be given to footage provided by the police, as opposed to the press, bystanders, or the civilian involved in the encounter. *Id.* at 640.

65. Jennifer L. Mnookin, *Can a Jury Believe What It Sees?,* N.Y. Times, July 14, 2014.

66. In particular, the Supreme Court relied on the video of a purportedly high-speed chase in *Scott v. Harris,* 550 U.S. 372 (2007), to find that a police officer was justified in using potentially deadly force in response.

67. Dan Kahan et al., *Whose Eyes Are You Going to Believe? Scott v. Harris and the Perils of Cognitive Illiberalism,* 122 Harv. L. Rev. 837, 903 (2009). Identity-defining factors such as race, age, socioeconomic status, education, cultural orientation, and party affiliation all affected the viewer's interpretation of the video. *Id.* at 867–70.

The **Harvard Law Review** is a student-run organization whose primary purpose is to publish a journal of legal scholarship. The organization is independent of Harvard Law School. Student editors make all editorial and organizational decisions.

EXPLORING THE ISSUE

Should the Police Be Required to Wear Body Cameras?

Critical Thinking and Reflection

1. Why did the Founding Fathers include the Fourth Amendment in the Constitution's Bill of Rights?
2. What is the current legal status of the use of high technology surveillance by government agents?
3. What is the significance of the Supreme Court's decisions in *Dow Chemical Corporation v. United States?*
4. What are several arguments for and against requiring police officers to wear body cameras?
5. What are the privacy implications of requiring the police to wear body cameras?
6. What is the significance of the Supreme Court's decision in *Tennessee v. Garner* (1985)?
7. What is the significance of the "Rialto Study" on the use of body cameras by the police?

Is There Common Ground?

Should the police be required to wear body cameras? The authors of the YES and NO selections in this issue provide different answers to these questions. Jay Stanley contends that police officers' use of body cams may have an overall positive impact on law enforcement policy in the United States. The Harvard Law Review lists several different problems associated with the use of these devices. In any case, it seems clear that increased public demands for law enforcement officer accountability may require police departments to embrace this new technology in coming years. Several recent cases serve to underscore the highly significant role that this technology is likely to play.

In 2014, a *USA Today* newspaper article observed that "Local Police are involved in 400 killings per year." During that same year, police officers in Ferguson, Missouri, shot and killed Michael Brown, which led to several days of rioting in the community and demands for increased police accountability. Shortly thereafter, a citizen's cellphone recording was used as evidence in a New York City case involving Eric Garner, who was accused of a minor crime and placed in a choke hold by police officers; Garner later died from the injuries he received. A grand jury declined to indict the officers involved.

If videotapes of the Ferguson case had been available, would the police officers involved have been indicted and charged with a crime? It is difficult to tell. Moreover, just how much force would be police officers in these cases have been justified in using? Were the police justified in using a choke hold in the Garner case, a violation of their department's policy? U.S. Supreme Court

precedents appear to provide some guidance. First, when the police restrain the freedom of someone to walk away, they have "seized" that person, which implicates the Fourth Amendment. Second, there is no question that apprehending someone by use of deadly force is a "seizure" subject to the reasonableness requirement of the Fourth Amendment.

In *Tennessee v. Garner,* 471 U.S. 1 (1985) (unrelated to the Erik Garner "choke hold" case in 2014) the Supreme Court considered the issue of police use of deadly force to stop a fleeing felon. Memphis police officers were dispatched to investigate a possible burglary. When they arrived on scene, the officers saw a woman standing on her porch and gesturing toward an adjacent house. One officer heard a door slam and saw a suspect run across the backyard. The officer saw no sign of a weapon and believed the suspect was not armed, but he was attempting to escape by climbing a 6-feet-high chain link fence. The officer called out "police, halt" and moved toward the suspect. Convinced that if Garner had made it over the fence he would escape, the officer shot him. The bullet hit Garner in the back of the head and he later died on the operating table. Ten dollars and a purse taken from the house were later found on his body.

In using deadly force to prevent the escape, the police officer was acting under the authority of a Tennessee law that permitted the use of deadly force to stop a fleeing burglary suspect. A grand jury refused to indict the officer. The Supreme Court held that a reviewing court must examine the totality of the circumstances that support a particular sort of search or seizure. Justice Byron White asserted:

The use of deadly force to prevent the escape of all felony suspects, whatever, the circumstances is constitutionally unreasonable. It is not better that all suspects die than that they escape. Where the suspect poses no immediate threat to the officer or to others, the harm resulting from failing to apprehend him does not justify the use of deadly force to do so. It is no doubt unfortunate when a suspect who is in sight escapes, but the fact that the police arrive a little late or are a little slower afoot does not always justify killing the suspect. A police officer may not seize an unarmed, nondangerous suspect by shooting him dead. The Tennessee statute is unconstitutional insofar as it authorizes the use of deadly force against such fleeing suspects. (11)

It seems plausible that under this standard the amount of force used in the Erik Garner "choke hold" case may have been unreasonable. Erik Garner was suspected of committing a minor misdemeanor offense. Was it really worth using potentially deadly force to take him into custody for such a crime?

Another example is provided by the Harvard Law Review. Marcus Jeter was charged in 2012 with "eluding police, resisting arrest and aggravated assault on a police officer." (8). Much of the incident was videotaped by a dashboard camera in the police cruiser. Jeter asserted that the officers had used excessive force while arresting him and that he had not acted violently. Following an internal police department investigation that had concluded that "the officers did nothing wrong," Jeter's attorney discovered evidence that a second police cruiser, with a second video recorder, had been on the scene that night. The videotape was allegedly never viewed by the prosecutor's office, though it had been in the possession of the police department since 2012. In the second video, the police car is seen "swerving across oncoming traffic and running into the front of Jeter's SUV, causing him to hit his head on the steering wheel." (9). The video also showed Jeter with his hands in the air, sitting passively in the driver's seat as officers approached the car. One officer pointed a pistol at the window and another had a shotgun. The video then showed an officer using a nightstick to smash the driver's side window. He then pulled Jeter from the car and threw him on the ground. While beating Jeter, the officer yelled "stop resisting" and "stop trying to take my f—gun." The video indicated that Jeter was neither resisting nor capable of reaching for the officer's gun. As Jeter was dragged out of the car his face was smashed into the cement and another officer took a swing at his head.

As a result of the discovery of the second videotape, the prosecutors dropped all charges against Jeter. The

officers were indicted: one retired after pleading guilty to tampering, and two were arraigned on charges of official misconduct, tampering with public records, and false swearing. (10). If it had not been for the video recording, Jeter may well have spent several years in prison and the police would not have been held accountable. (Id.).

As this case illustrates, video recordings can be an effective measure to ensure just outcomes in criminal cases. Moreover, these devices may help to professionalize the delivery of police services and enhance accountability. In any case, it seems that police body cams are a practice that is here to stay and should be embraced by modern law enforcement agencies. This may well be a net positive development for both law enforcement officers and suspects in criminal proceedings: To paraphrase the late William O. Douglas, the longest serving U.S. Supreme Court Justice in history, "sunshine can be the best disinfectant."

Moreover, the available empirical evidence appears to suggest that police who wear body cameras use force much less often than those who do not. In a research project that has become known as the "Rialto Study," the authors concluded that shifts without cameras had twice as many use of force incidents as those with cameras, and "the rate of use of force incidents per 1000 contacts was reduced by 2.5 times." (Harvard Law Review, 13, citing Barak Ariel & Tony Farrar, Police Foundation, "Self-Awareness to Being Watched and Socially-Desirable Behavior: A Field Experiment on the Effect of Body-Worn Cameras on Police Use of Force," 8 (2013).

Additional Resources

Police Executive Research Forum (PERF), "Implementing a Body-Worn Camera Program," 25 (2014).

Connie Fossi-Garcia and Dan Lieberman, "Investigation of 5 Cities Finds Body Cameras Usually Help Police," *Fusion* (December 7, 2014).

Thomas J. Hickey, Christopher Capsambelis, and Anthony LaRose, "Constitutional Issues in the Use of Video Surveillance in Public Places," *Criminal Law Bulletin* (vol. 39, no. 5, September–October 2003).

A.J. Vicens, "Putting Body Cameras on Cops Is Hardly a Cure-All for Abuses," *Mother Jones* (August 21, 2014).

Robinson Meyer, "Seen It All Before: 10 Predictions About Police Body Cameras," *The Atlantic* (December 5, 2014).

Internet References . . .

National Institute of Justice, *A Primer on Body-Worn Cameras for Law Enforcement* (NIJ, 2012); PoliceOne Staff, "Poll Results: Cops Speak Out About Body Cameras."

www.policeone.com

U.S. Dept. of Justice, "Police Use of Excessive Force: A Conciliation Handbook for the Police and the Community," 2002.

www.justice.gov/archive

The Stanford Justice Advocacy Project.

https://law.stanford.edu/stanford-justice-advocacy-project/

Three Strikes Organization, "15 Years of 'Three Strikes,' 1994 to 2008 and Still Working."

www.threestrikes.org/pdf/

Selected, Edited, and with Issue Framing Material by:
Thomas J. Hickey, *State University of New York at Cobleskill*

ISSUE

Should Apple Be Forced to Assist the Government's Efforts to Crack Cell Phones Needed for Criminal Investigations?

YES: **William J. Bratton and John J. Miller,** "Seeking iPhone Data, Through the Front Door," *The New York Times* (2016)

NO: **Kim Z. Dale,** "Apple Shouldn't Unlock the San Bernardino Shooter's iPhone for the FBI," *ChicagoNow* (2016)

Learning Outcomes

After reading this issue, you will be able to:

- Discuss the government's arguments that Apple, Inc., should be required to assist them in cracking an iPhone's encryption in the "San Bernardino Massacre" case.
- Discuss Kim Z. Dale's arguments that it should not be required to help the government to crack the suspects' iPhone's encryption in the "San Bernardino Massacre" case.
- Discuss the holding of the U.S. Magistrate Court in *In re Order Requiring Apple, Inc., to Assist in the Execution of a Search Warrant Issued by this Court.*
- Discuss the "All Writs Act" (AWA).
- Discuss why Judge Orenstein ruled that allowing the AWA to require Apple to help to crack the encryption on the iPhone used by the suspects in the "San Bernardino Massacre" would violate the "separation of powers" principle.
- Discuss why some people might argue that technological advances "are not always a wonderful thing."

ISSUE SUMMARY

YES: New York City Police Commissioner William J. Bratton and Deputy Commissioner for Counterterrorism and Intelligence John J. Miller assert that Apple has a responsibility to assist the government with encryption whenever it has a warrant supported by probable cause for a cell phone search and that the company should comply with lawful court orders.

NO: Blogger Kim Z. Dale believes that Apple should not be forced to help the government to unlock an iPhone in a criminal investigation, even in a case as compelling as the one involving the San Bernardino shooter. She further contends that unlocking that iPhone would be "opening a Pandora's box," with serious implications for personal privacy and government accountability.

Technological advances often seem like a wonderful thing. They can make life easier and more convenient, enhance communication, and make the world seem like a much smaller place. One of the more dramatic changes in our methods of communication in recent years has been the development and nearly ubiquitous adoption of the cellular telephone. Please take a moment to check your pockets, purse, or backpack as you sit in your classroom today. Based on recent studies, it is very likely that you have a cellular telephone, which is also likely to be a "smart phone." (An unscientific survey of my classes revealed recently that more than 94 percent of the students had these devices.) Thus, as products of the "information age," people have virtually unlimited access to the Internet, which we can use to answer almost any question we wish to ask. Such information access is unprecedented in world history. Most people feel that the ready availability of quick access to information is a highly positive development. For example, it is wonderful when a physician can almost immediately access proper drug dosage information for a sick patient. Likewise, it is great to be able to answer legal questions quickly and efficiently by tapping a few buttons on your cell phone. But, does such convenience come at a price? Can the same devices that improve our access to information be used by the government to severely limit personal privacy? The answer to this question is almost certainly a resounding "yes."

For example, are you aware that your cell phone can be used to track your movements and document the places you have been? Even though a cell phone's tracking feature can be turned off, unless you take affirmative steps to protect your privacy, it occurs automatically on most phones. (For information on how to turn this feature off, a quick Internet search will provide instructions.) Should the police be given access to such information if they are investigating whether you have committed a crime? Should they be required to obtain a search warrant if they want access to your cell phone records? Moreover, should you be required to provide them with assistance, such as password information, if they wish to search your phone? Moreover, if you are unwilling to assist the government in gaining access to your phone, should a corporation like Apple be forced to provide the assistance?

In the very recent case that is the focus of this issue, the U.S. government sought to force Apple, Inc., to help them to crack the encryption protecting its iPhone products. As of February, 2016, Apple had identified nine similar requests filed in federal courts across the country in which it had been ordered to help the government bypass the password security of a total of 12 different devices. In each case Apple had objected. At the time of the instant case, none of the other cases had been finally resolved, and Apple had not yet provided the requested assistance in any of them.

In *In re Order Requiring Apple, Inc. to Assist in the Execution of a Search Warrant Issued by this Court,* 15-MC-1902 (JO), dated February 29, 2016, the issue of whether Apple could be compelled to assist the government finally came to a head. U.S. Magistrate Judge James Orenstein first considered the government's argument that Apple should be

compelled to assist help them to decrypt a cellular telephone believed to have been used in the "San Bernardino Massacre," a case involving an act of domestic terrorism in which 14 people were shot to death at a Christmas party in a county office building. The suspects in this case, a husband and wife who were later killed in a shootout with the police, were believed to have used an iPhone to contact others who may have been involved in the incident. The government relied on a Colonial-era statute called "The All Writs Act," (AWA) (28 U.S.C. Section 1651(a)) which, it argued, authorized the federal courts to issue an order to a company such as Apple to assist in a criminal investigation. According to Judge Orenstein:

> The plain text of the statute thus confers on all federal courts the authority to issue orders where three requirements are satisfied:
>
> 1. Issuance of the writ must be "in aid of" the issuing court's jurisdiction;
> 2. The type of writ requested must be "necessary or appropriate" to provide such aid to the issuing court's jurisdiction; and
> 3. The issuance of the writ must be "agreeable to the usages and principles of the law." (11)

Judge Orenstein next asserted that if an application by the government under the AWA meets all of these requirements, a court "may" issue the requested writ in the exercise of its discretion—but it is not required to do so. He concluded, however, that in the circumstances of this case, the government's application did not fully satisfy the AWA's statutory requirements because "the extraordinary relief it seeks cannot be considered 'agreeable to the usages and principles of law." Stated Judge Orenstein: "In arguing to the contrary, the government posits a reading [of the law] so expansive—and in particular, in such tension with the doctrine of separation of powers—as to cast doubt on the AWA's constitutionality if adopted." (12). Therefore, the judge concluded:

> Ultimately, the question to be answered in this matter, and in others across the country, is not whether the government should be able to force Apple to help it unlock a specific device; it is instead whether the All Writs Act resolves the issue and many other like it yet to come. . . . I conclude that it does not. The government's motion is denied. (50)

What Judge Orenstein means when he discusses the "separation of powers" doctrine is that if the courts were to issue such orders under the AWA, they would infringe on the authority and prerogatives of the U.S. Congress, which is given the power to pass laws in Article I of the U.S. Constitution. As the Judge cogently observed: "How best to balance [the interests of society, businesses, and individuals] is a matter of critical importance to our society, and the need for an answer becomes more pressing daily, as the tide to technological advance flows ever further past the boundaries of what was seen possible even a few decades ago." (49). He continued: "[T]hat debate . . . must take place among legislators who are equipped to consider the technological and cultural realities of a world their predecessors could not begin to conceive." (Id.).

In a nutshell, this case presents the issue of the rights of criminal terrorists versus society's interest in investigating such cases? The government's decision to go forward with their effort to secure Apple's help to crack into the suspects' cell phone in a case involving Islamic terrorists who had murdered numerous people on American soil was no accident. There could hardly be a more compelling set of circumstances favoring the government's position. Moreover, it is possible that a higher federal court could overturn this ruling at a later date. Under these circumstances, do you agree with Judge Orenstein's ruling? The authors of the YES and NO selections in this issue would be likely to provide contrasting answers to this question.

Blogger and author Kim Z. Dale contends that Apple is right to refuse to comply with the court order holding that it must help the government to crack the iPhone in this case. She further asserts that "what is at stake is too valuable to lose." She asserts: "The FBI is asking Apple to develop a weakened version of the iPhone operating system that would exploit a security flaw in that phone and make it easier for the FBI to access the data on that phone. The problem is that once this weakened version of the operating [system] exists, it exists. Apple and the FBI could try to protect it, but there are too many cases of systems being hacked or technology being misused to guarantee this would not be used to access more iPhones and for reasons far less acceptable than fighting terrorism." New York City Police Commissioner William J. Bratton and Deputy Commissioner for Counterterrorism and Intelligence John J. Miller, in contrast, assert that Apple has a responsibility to assist the government with encryption whenever it has a search warrant supported by probable cause for a cell phone and that the company should comply with all court orders to that effect.

As you read the articles, try to determine who has the more compelling arguments. Moreover, consider whether Apple's refusal to assist in decrypting its products is consistent with the principle of "social utility"—the idea that social policy should reflect the greatest good for the greatest number of people.

YES ⤹

William J. Bratton and John J. Miller

Seeking iPhone Data, Through the Front Door

The government and Apple have chosen interesting ground on which to contest the limits of government access to data on mobile devices. The case involves an F.B.I. request for Apple's assistance in opening a phone once carried by Syed Rizwan Farook, who with his wife was responsible for the terrorist attack in San Bernardino, Calif., that left 14 dead and 22 wounded.

On one level, this should be comfortable space for the government. First, the phone is owned by the County of San Bernardino, which issued it to Mr. Farook, an employee of its health department. The county, as Apple's customer, has no problem having its phone opened. Second, Mr. Farook and his wife were killed in a gun battle with the police early last December. Under the law, dead people have no privacy rights.

But Apple is making a stand because the government wants it to create something against its will: code that would disable a feature that erases all content after 10 failed password attempts. Tim Cook, Apple's chief executive, has said that if this happens, the floodgates will open to similar law enforcement requests, putting customers' data at risk. And not just in the United States: Apple supporters have raised concerns that other countries, particularly China and Russia, are likely to follow suit.

Mr. Cook's position is hyperbolic, in our view. But beyond the legal case, there is an ethics issue unfolding here.

Until 17 months ago, Apple held the key that could override protections and open phones. Apple used this "master key" to comply with court orders in drug, kidnapping, murder, and terrorism cases. There was no documented instance of this code getting out to hackers or to the government. So what was the problem Apple was trying to fix when it abruptly announced, in September 2014, that with its new iOS 8, "Apple will not perform iOS data extractions in response to government search warrants"?

Some believe that allegations by Edward J. Snowden of mass surveillance of phone and Internet communications by the National Security Agency stoked fears among Apple's customers that the government was spying on them. Perhaps an iPhone that even Apple couldn't unlock might allay such fears, while also helping sales by offering more privacy and security.

But Mr. Snowden claimed that the N.S.A. was capturing some Americans' Internet traffic from overseas, not that the agency was hacking into smartphones. Moreover, Apple's position on privacy seems at odds with its own strategy of encouraging customers to pay to store personal data on iCloud, which is also vulnerable to hackers.

Apple partisans also argue that the company is trying to protect privacy in places like China, where governments could demand access to phones belonging to dissidents. But Apple could refuse those requests, or have China make them through the State Department, a means of insulating itself from unreasonable demands. That is often how the United States asks for assistance from overseas corporations in investigations.

Apple and privacy advocates have framed this debate as the government wanting to "create a back door" into people's devices. But the Constitution protects people from unreasonable search and seizure. And for more than 200 years, the standard has been for law enforcement to obtain a warrant signed by a judge, based on probable cause.

What the government is actually requesting here is that Apple restore a key that was available until late 2014. Complying with constitutionally legal court orders is not "creating a back door"; in a democracy, that is a front door.

WILLIAM J. BRATTON is the current New York City police commissioner. He served previously as Boston's police chief, as well as chief of the Los Angeles Police Department. Bratton is widely associated with helping to develop the doctrine of "zero tolerance" and the "broken windows" theory of policing. He currently also serves as an advisor to the British government on policing issues.

JOHN J. MILLER serves presently as the deputy commissioner of intelligence and counterterrorism of the New York Police Department. He was the former associate deputy director for analytic transformation and technology. Prior to his service with the NYPD, Miller was the assistant director of public affairs for the Federal Bureau of Investigation (FBI). He had formerly served as an ABC News reporter and as a senior correspondent for CBS News.

Kim Z. Dale   **NO**

Apple Shouldn't Unlock the San Bernardino Shooter's iPhone for the FBI

By now you have likely heard that the FBI wants Apple to unlock the iPhone that belonged to one of the San Bernardino shooters (who is now dead). Apple has refused to unlock the iPhone, and I fully support them. This debate is far bigger than one act of terrorism or even the group that orchestrated that terrorism. This case has broad implications about security and privacy that should not be taken as lightly as many media accounts have been presenting them.

This Is Not Just About One iPhone

It isn't like the FBI is asking Tim Cook to press a magical button at Apple headquarters that would instantly unlock this the San Bernardino shooter's iPhone. The FBI is asking Apple to develop a weakened version of the iPhone operating system that would exploit a security flaw in that phone version and make it easier for the FBI to access the data on the phone.

The problem is that once this weakened version of the operating exists, it exists. Apple and the FBI could try to protect it, but there are too many cases of systems being hacked or technology being misused to guarantee this would not be used to access more iPhones and for reasons far less acceptable than fighting terrorism.

As Apple CEO Tim Cook wrote in "A Message to Our Customers," [https://www.apple.com/customer-letter/?utm_content =bufferda64e&utm_medium=social&utm_source=twitter .com&utm_campaign=buffer]

> The government suggests this tool could only be used once, on one phone. But that's simply not true. Once created, the technique could be used over and over again, on any number of devices. In the physical world, it would be the equivalent of a master key, capable of opening hundreds of millions of locks—from restaurants and banks to

stores and homes. No reasonable person would find that acceptable.

This Is Not Just About iPhones

Technology companies have been fighting for years against government demands for backdoors to encryption software. Now the government is emboldened by a case that focuses on a known terrorist instead of an abstraction. If Apple is forced to create a backdoor in a version of its operating system, it is likely that other companies will be forced to put backdoors in their systems as well.

As Bruce Schneier wrote in his *Washington Post* article "Why you should side with Apple, not the FBI, in the San Bernardino iPhone Case." [https://www.washingtonpost .com/posteverything/wp/2016/02/18/why-you-should-side-with -apple-not-the-fbi-in-the-san-bernardino-iphone-case/?hpid=hp _no-name_opinion-card-d%3Ahomepage%2Fstory]

> Either everyone gets security or no one does. Either everyone gets access or no one does. The current case is about a single iPhone 5c, but the precedent it sets will apply to all smartphones, computers, cars and everything the Internet of Things promises. The danger is that the court's demands will pave the way to the FBI forcing Apple and others to reduce the security levels of their smart phones and computers, as well as the security of cars, medical devices, homes, and everything else that will soon be computerized.

Privacy Is Important

All those pieces of technology that could have their security weakened and put data privacy at risk are things that a lot of people and organizations (even the FBI!) depend on. Encryption backdoors would hurt governments, corporations, and individuals.

Dale, Kim Z., "Apple Shouldn't Unlock the San Berndardino Shooter's iPhone" *Chicago Now: Listing Beyond Forty*, February 28, 2016. Used by permission of the author.

Of course, the go-to argument in such situations tends to be "people (or organizations or companies) with nothing to hide don't have anything to worry about." The problem is even good people and good organizations have things to hide.

Below are my "Five reasons you should care about privacy," which I copied, with only slight modifications, from a post I wrote about the NSA [http://www.chicagonow.com/listing-beyond-forty/2013/06/5-reasons-to-care-about-privacy-issues/] after Edward Snowden leaked his documents about their privacy invasive programs. The same reasons also apply to why you should not support security backdoors, such as what Apple is being asked to create.

1. You probably aren't as open as you think you are

Maybe you don't care if the government knows what phone numbers you dial or what your emails say. There are probably still limitations to what you are comfortable sharing with certain audiences.

- Would you put social security number and credit card information on a public website?
- Would you show your current spouse or partner correspondence you had with your ex?
- Do you want your children to see you have sex? What about your neighbor? Or your boss?

When people say they don't care about privacy they mean they don't care about a specific privacy issue. Most people still close the bathroom door when they poop.

2. Standards change

What society deems acceptable changes over time. For decades it was perfectly reasonable to be a member of the Communist Party in the United States, but in the 1950s McCarthyism and the "red scare" meant that even a casual history with that party could get you in trouble. A detail about you that seems innocent today could make you a target for harassment, discrimination, or worse in the future.

3. Trust has limitations

By allowing a government or corporation to access your information you are trusting that their intentions are honorable. Maybe you are comfortable with that, but you are also trusting that all of their employees' intentions are honorable. You are also trusting that all of their third party contractors' employees are honorable. This can be thousands of people.

4. Security has limitations

Maybe you truly do trust all the people given access to your data. What about the people who aren't granted access? If there is a collection of data about you it is vulnerable to hacking or other security breaches. Security issues can rapidly become privacy issues.

5. Some people do have things to hide

Maybe you don't have anything to hide, but others do. I'm not just talking about criminals and terrorists. Whistle-blowers, undercover cops, workers at shelters for abused women, and many others rely on secrecy to do good. Surveillance technology puts these people at risk.

As Tim Cook stated in the above-mentioned letter:

> Compromising the security of our personal information can ultimately put our personal safety at risk. That is why encryption has become so important to all of us.

I strongly support Apple's position and hope they prevail in this fight. If, however, Apple is forced to create a weakened iOS to help unlock that iPhone, I hope that whatever the FBI finds on it is tremendously valuable in fighting terrorism, bringing down ISIS, stopping world hunger, curing cancer, etc. Unlocking that iPhone is opening Pandora's box, so whatever is on it damn well better be worth the demons it unleashes.

KIM Z. DALE is a writer and blogger. She describes herself as a "McSweeney's girl in a Buzzfeed world." She is also a playwright with a master's degree in information security. She has two children and states that she has "too many ideas." She further states that she is a "Big Apple born Steel Town girl" living in the Windy City and loving it.

EXPLORING THE ISSUE

Should Apple Be Forced to Assist the Government's Efforts to Crack Cell Phones Needed for Criminal Investigations?

Critical Thinking and Reflection

1. Is technological development and progress always a positive development for society?
2. Should the police be able to gain access to your cell phone records if you are a suspect in a criminal case? Should they be required to obtain a search warrant?
3. Do you agree or disagree with Judge Orenstein's decision in *In re Order Requiring Apple, Inc., to Assist in the Execution of a Search Warrant Issued by this Court*?
4. What was the legal basis for Judge Orenstein's ruling that the All Writs Act (AWA) did not require Apple, Inc., to assist the government in decrypting an iPhone owned by a suspect in the San Bernardino massacre?
5. Did Apple's refusal to assist the government in decrypting its product under these circumstances comply with the principle of social utility?

Is There Common Ground?

The compelling question posed in this issue exists at the forefront of emerging U.S. Constitutional Law doctrine. Issue 17, which examined the use of police body cameras, observed that our historic conceptions of privacy may not have kept pace with the rapid advancements in technology. Likewise, Judge Orenstein's ruling in the case discussed in this issue took note of this phenomenon when he stated that the U.S. law had to keep pace "as the tide of technological advance flows ever farther past the boundaries of what seemed possible even a few decades ago." What, then, is the possible solution to this dilemma? Perhaps earlier U.S. Supreme Court precedents suggest a resolution.

In *Rakas v. Illinois*, 439 U.S. 128 (1979) the Supreme Court held that "[T]he capacity to claim the protection of the Fourth Amendment depends not upon a property right in the invaded place but upon whether the person who claims the protection of the Amendment has a legitimate expectation of privacy in the invaded place." (131). As the Court's decision in *Katz v. United States*, 389 U.S. 347 (1967) indicated: "No less than an individual in a business office, in a friend's apartment, or in a taxicab, a person in a telephone booth may rely on the protection of the Fourth Amendment." (352). *Rakas* and *Katz*, then, indicate that individual privacy interests

are the linchpin of Fourth Amendment protection. Do you believe that it is reasonable to argue that individual privacy interests do not allow the government to search cell phone records, or permit them to compel the cooperation of those with technical skills to crack the encryption on these devices?

In any case, technological advances, such as those discussed in this issue, will continue at a rapid pace. We can only hope that our Constitution will be interpreted by U.S. courts in a way that will guarantee personal privacy and ensure government compliance with due process of law.

Additional Resources

Wayne R. LaFave, *Search and Seizure: A Treatise on the Fourth Amendment*, 5th Ed. (Thompson West, 2016).

Eve Primus, Jerold Israel, Orin S. Kerr, Wayne R. LaFave, and Yale Kamisar, *Modern Criminal Procedure: Cases, Comments, and Questions*, 13th Ed. (West Academic, 2012).

Thomas J. Hickey and Rolando V. del Carmen, "The Evolution of Standing in Search and Seizure Cases," *Criminal Law Bulletin* (vol. 27, no. 2, March/April, 1991).

Internet References . . .

Glenn Greenwald and Jenna McLaughlin, "Apple Wins Major Court Victory Against FBI in a Case Similar to San Bernardino." *The Intercept*, May 16, 2016.

https://theintercept.com

Timothy B. Lee, *Vox*, "Apple's Battle with the FBI over iPhone Security, Explained." February 17, 2016.

https://vox.com/2016

The L.A. Times Editorial Board, "Government Agencies Shouldn't Get Keys to Unlock Our Encrypted Devices." *Editorial*. February 24, 2016.

www.latimes.com/opinion/editorials/

Unit 5

The U.S. Supreme Court, Crime, and the Justice System

*T*he three branches of the U.S. governmental system have a tremendous impact on the operations of our state and federal justice systems. The executive branch, which includes our law enforcement agencies, is given the responsibility to execute and apply the laws in Article I of the U.S. Constitution. The legislative branch has Article II authority to develop and change laws as our society evolves. The courts have Article III jurisdiction to interpret the laws and ensure that they conform to constitutional requisites. This section focuses primarily on the U.S. Supreme Court's role in our governmental system. Cutting-edge issues are considered such as whether sentencing a juvenile to a mandatory term of life in prison without the possibility of parole, whether the Second Amendment protects the right to possess a firearm, whether it should be lawful for the police to conduct jailhouse strip searches of persons arrested for minor offenses, and whether an imprisoned convict who claims actual innocence should have a constitutional right to access a state's evidence for DNA testing. These issues exist at the forefront of U.S. constitutional law and will have a great impact on evolving conceptions of "justice" in the modern era.

Does Sentencing a Juvenile to Life in Prison Without the Possibility of Parole Constitute Cruel and Unusual Punishment? by Hickey

275

Selected, Edited, and with Issue Framing Material by:
Thomas J. Hickey, *State University of New York at Cobleskill*

ISSUE

Does Sentencing a Juvenile to a Mandatory Term of Life in Prison Without the Possibility of Parole Constitute Cruel and Unusual Punishment?

YES: Elena Kagan, from "Majority Opinion," *Miller v. Alabama*, U.S. Supreme Court (2012)

NO: John Roberts, from "Dissenting Opinion," *Miller v. Alabama*, U.S. Supreme Court (2012)

Learning Outcomes

After reading this issue, you will be able to:

- Present arguments for and against sentencing a juvenile to a mandatory term of life in prison without the possibility of parole constitutes cruel and unusual punishment.
- Discuss whether there should be a fundamental difference between how we sentence adult offenders and the penalties that are assigned to juvenile criminals.
- Discuss the four major historical goals of U.S. sentencing policy.
- Discuss whether you believe that sentencing a juvenile to a mandatory life term without the possibility of parole "forswears the rehabilitative ideal" and demonstrates an "irrevocable judgment about an offenders value and place in society."
- Discuss the Eighth Amendment's Cruel and Unusual Punishment Clause.
- Discuss four factors that a court will use to assess whether a penalty constitutes cruel and unusual punishment.
- Discuss whether mandatory life imprisonment laws for juveniles who commit serious crimes satisfy the "social utility" principle.
- Discuss how the financial costs of incarcerating criminals may influence the debate about sentencing a juvenile to a mandatory term of life in prison without the possibility of parole.
- Discuss why *Montgomery v. Louisiana* (2016) is an important qualification of *Miller v. Alabama*.

ISSUE SUMMARY

YES: U.S. Supreme Court Associate Justice Elena Kagan asserts that imprisoning offenders for life without the possibility of parole for crimes committed when they were juveniles violates the Eighth Amendment's Cruel and Unusual Punishment Clause.

NO: U.S. Supreme Court Chief Justice John Roberts argues, in contrast, that the determination of appropriate punishments for crimes should be left to the legislative branches of government.

I can recall rather clearly as a child raised in a some-what traditional religious environment being told that a sign posted above the gates of hell commanded: "You who enter here, abandon all hope." While some might argue that U.S. prison systems are a far cry from the "gates of hell," a mandatory sentence of life in prison without the possibility of parole certainly presents some interesting similarities. In fact, someone who has received this most severe sentence may well come to think that they should "abandon all hope" and resign themselves to a lifetime behind bars. But, is such a severe mandatory sentence war-ranted for juvenile offenders who commit heinous crimes, however? Should there be a fundamental difference between how we sentence adult offenders and the penal-ties that are assigned to juvenile criminals? The answer to these questions will almost certainly depend on what objectives our penal system is meant to serve.

From a historical perspective, U.S. sentencing poli-cies have largely been geared toward satisfying four essential and sometimes inconsistent goals: Retribution, incapacitation, deterrence, and rehabilitation. As Justice Kagan cogently observed in her majority opinion in *Miller v. Alabama,* the key to understanding *retribution* is an offender's "blameworthiness." A strong case can be made that a juvenile offender, who is less mature and lacks the experiences of an adult criminal, is morally less "blameworthy." In addition, it is possible that an even more compelling case can be made for this proposition if an individual juvenile has a personal history of men-tal illness, has suffered from physical or mental abuse, is addicted to drugs or alcohol, has grown up in extreme poverty, or whose personal circumstances reveal that they had little chance to succeed to begin with. Thus, it can be argued plausibly that the retribution rationale would not be well-served by sentencing a juvenile to a mandatory prison term of life without parole because the individual is often not as "blameworthy" as an adult offender.

The second goal of sentencing policy in the United States is *incapacitation.* Justice Kagan considered this objective in her majority opinion as well. Stated Kagan: "[i]ncapacitation could not support [a] life without parole" sentence for juveniles because "Deciding that a 'juvenile offender forever will be a danger to society' would require 'making a judgment that he is incorrigible'—but 'incorri-gibility is inconsistent with youth.'" In other words, there is a measure of hope that a juvenile offender will "turn his life around," whereas a more-hardened adult criminal would be less likely to do so.

The third traditional goal of U.S. sentencing policy is *deterrence.* This concept posits that offenders will consider the threat of punishment and make a rational decision to avoid criminal behavior. As Justice Kagan suggests, this rationale is not supported by imposing mandatory life prison terms on juvenile offenders because many of the same characteristics that make them less responsible for crimes than adults—their immaturity, recklessness, and impulsiveness make them less likely to consider the potential consequences of their actions.

In an effort to illustrate this contention, permit me to suggest a short in-class assignment. Spread your seats out so that you are situated in such a way that no one can see what you are writing. Everyone take out a sheet of paper, but please do not write your name on it. This exer-cise is intended to be COMPLETELY ANONYMOUS and your instructor will destroy all papers before you leave the room. The assignment: Take five minutes to list all of the crimes that you know that you have committed as a juvenile (the instructor should leave the room while the assignment is being completed.) When you are finished, please bring your folded paper to the front of the room and shuffle all papers. When the five minute time limit is over, the instructor should return to the room and read the papers aloud. After he/she has read the papers, they should be destroyed. I think you will be amazed at the results. As a college professor for 30 years, I have used this exercise in many different undergraduate classes. I can honestly say that the traditional college students who have enrolled in my classes have self-reported commit-ting almost every crime you can imagine. These include rape, robbery, burglary, forgery, auto theft, larceny, child abuse, drug abuse, drug manufacturing, and drug trafficking.

Although this exercise involved a decidedly unscien-tific survey, it does tell us some interesting things about deterrence and juveniles. First, I would be willing to bet that many students revealed that they had committed serious felonies in the past. Apparently, as juveniles they were not deterred by the prospect of serious punishments for the crimes they committed. Could this be because they thought they would never be caught committing their various offenses? Moreover, at a minimum this exercise would seem to add considerable support to Justice Kagan's observation that juveniles are more likely than adults to be immature, reckless, and impetuous.

The final goal underlying U.S. sentencing poli-cies is *rehabilitation,* which may be defined as providing offenders with experiences that will permit them to once again become productive members of society. As Justice Kagan observed, sentencing a juvenile to a mandatory life term without the possibility of parole "forswears alto-gether the rehabilitative ideal." Moreover, it demonstrates an "'irrevocable judgment about [an offender's] value and place in society,' at odds with a child's capacity for change." Thus, it would seem that the imposition of a mandatory life sentence without the possibility of parole for juvenile offenders does not satisfy any of the historical goals of sentencing policy in the United States, with the possible exception of incapacitation. Even if this sentencing practice fails to satisfy these objectives, however, does it constitute a violation of the U.S. Constitution's Eighth Amendment Cruel and Unusual Punishment Clause?

The U.S. Supreme Court has considered the issue of precisely what constitutes "cruel and unusual punishment" on many different occasions. Several important propositions emerge from these decisions. As former renown Supreme Court Justice Thurgood Marshall has observed: "The primary concern of the drafters [of the Eighth Amendment's Cruel and Unusual Punishment Clause] was to proscribe 'tortures and other barbarous methods of punishment.'" He further stated that it does more than that, however. It also embodies "broad and idealistic concepts of dignity, civilized standards, humanity and decency." (*Estelle v. Gamble*, 429 U.S. 97 (1976)). An analysis of the Supreme Court's Eighth Amendment precedents interpreting the Cruel and Unusual Punishment Clause identifies at least four factors that they will use to determine if a penalty is unconstitutional.

First, a punishment will be held unconstitutional if it inflicts *unnecessary and wanton pain*. For example, whipping a convicted offender would be held to violate the Eighth Amendment. Second, a penalty will be held unconstitutional if it is *unacceptable in society,* or, to paraphrase Justice Marshall, it violates human dignity, civilized standards, humanity and decency. One should note that this argument is being made presently by opponents of capital punishment and based on recent Court decisions it seems possible that the death penalty will be outlawed in the United States in the not too distant future. Third, a punishment violates the Eighth Amendment if it is *disproportionate* to the offense for which it was imposed. For example, sentencing someone to a long prison term for possession of one marijuana joint is likely to constitute cruel and unusual punishment. Finally, a punishment may violate the Clause if it is imposed in a *racially discriminatory* manner. For example, if a state imposed the death penalty only on African-American defendants convicted of murder, it would clearly violate the Eighth Amendment.

Does sentencing a juvenile to a mandatory term of life in prison without the possibility of parole constitute cruel and unusual punishment? The authors of the opinions in this issue have very different views on this controversy. Justice Elena Kagan, author of the Majority Opinion of the Court, states:

> [A] judge or jury must have the opportunity to consider mitigating circumstances before imposing the harshest possible penalty for juveniles. By requiring that all children convicted of homicide receive lifetime incarceration without the possibility of parole, regardless of their age and age-related characteristics and the nature of their crimes, the mandatory sentencing schemes before us violate this principle of proportionality, and so the Eighth Amendment's ban on cruel and unusual punishment.

Chief Justice John Roberts, however, disagrees. In a Dissenting Opinion joined by Justices Scalia, Thomas, and Alito, he asserts:

> The parties agree that nearly 2,500 prisoners are presently serving life sentences without the possibility of parole for murders they committed before the age of 18. The Court accepts that over 2,000 of those prisoners received that sentence because it was mandated by a legislature. And it recognizes that the Federal Government and most States impose such mandatory sentences. Put simply, if a 17-year-old is convicted of deliberately murdering an innocent victim, it is not 'unusual' for the murderer to receive a mandatory sentence of life without parole. That reality should preclude finding that mandatory life imprisonment for juvenile killers violates the Eighth Amendment.

If you were a member of the Supreme Court, would you be more likely to join Justice Kagan's majority opinion, or Chief Justice Roberts's dissenting opinion? After reading the excerpted opinions try to decide which is the more persuasive. Moreover, consider once again the principle of social utility: Does imposing a mandatory life sentence on someone for a crime committed when he/she was a juvenile, satisfy the mandate that social policies should represent the greatest good for the greatest number of people?

YES ↵

Majority Opinion, *Miller v. Alabama*

Justice KAGAN delivered the opinion of the Court.

The two 14-year-old offenders in these cases were convicted of murder and sentenced to life imprisonment without the possibility of parole. In neither case did the sentencing authority have any discretion to impose a different punishment. State law mandated that each juvenile die in prison even if a judge or jury would have thought that his youth and its attendant characteristics, along with the nature of his crime, made a lesser sentence (for example, life *with* the possibility of parole) more appropriate. Such a scheme prevents those meting out punishment from considering a juvenile's "lessened culpability" and greater "capacity for change," *Graham v. Florida.* 560 U.S. __, __, __, 130 S.Ct. 2011, 2026–2027, 2029–2030, 176 L.Ed.2d 825 (2010). and runs afoul of our cases' requirement of individualized sentencing for defendants facing the most serious penalties. We therefore hold that mandatory life without parole for those under the age of 18 at the time of their crimes violates the Eighth Amendment's prohibition on "cruel and unusual punishments."

I

A

In November 1999, petitioner Kuntrell Jackson, then 14 years old, and two other boys decided to rob a video store. En route to the store, Jackson learned that one of the boys, Derrick Shields, was carrying a sawed-off shotgun in his coat sleeve. Jackson decided to stay outside when the two other boys entered the store. Inside, Shields pointed the gun at the store clerk, Laurie Troup, and demanded that she "give up the money." *Jackson v. State.* 359 Ark. 87. 89. 194 S.W.3d 757. 759 (2004) (internal quotation marks omitted). Troup refused. A few moments later, Jackson went into the store to find Shields continuing to demand money. At trial, the parties disputed whether Jackson warned Troup that "[w]e ain't playin'," or instead told his friends, "I thought you all was playin'." *Id.*, at 91, 194 S.W.3d, at 760 (internal quotation marks omitted).

When Troup threatened to call the police, Shields shot and killed her. The three boys fled empty-handed. See *id.*, at 89–92, 194 S.W.3d, at 758–760.

Arkansas law gives prosecutors discretion to charge 14-year-olds as adults when they are alleged to have committed certain serious offenses. See Ark.Code Ann. § 9-27-318(c)(2) (1998). The prosecutor here exercised that authority by charging Jackson with capital felony murder and aggravated robbery. Jackson moved to transfer the case to juvenile court, but after considering the alleged facts of the crime, a psychiatrist's examination, and Jackson's juvenile arrest history (shoplifting and several incidents of car theft), the trial court denied the motion, and an appellate court affirmed. . . . A jury later convicted Jackson of both crimes. Noting that "in view of [the] verdict, there's only one possible punishment," the judge sentenced Jackson to life without parole. . . . ("A defendant convicted of capital murder or treason shall be sentenced to death or life imprisonment without parole").[1] Jackson did not challenge the sentence on appeal, and the Arkansas Supreme Court affirmed the convictions. . . .

Following *Roper v. Simmons*, 543 U.S. 551, 125 S.Ct. 1183, 161 L.Ed.2d 1 (2005), in which this Court invalidated the death penalty for all juvenile offenders under the age of 18, Jackson filed a state petition for habeas corpus. He argued, based on *Roper's* reasoning, that a mandatory sentence of life without parole for a 14-year-old also violates the Eighth Amendment. The circuit court rejected that argument and granted the State's motion to dismiss. See Jackson App. 72–76. While that ruling was on appeal, this Court held in *Graham v. Florida* that life without parole violates the Eighth Amendment when imposed on juvenile nonhomicide offenders. After the parties filed briefs addressing that decision, the Arkansas Supreme Court affirmed the dismissal of Jackson's petition. . . . The majority found that *Roper* and *Graham* were "narrowly tailored" to their contexts: "death-penalty cases involving a juvenile and life-imprisonment-without-parole cases for nonhomicide offenses involving a juvenile." *Id.*, at 5, __ S.W.3d, at __. Two justices dissented. They noted that Jackson was not the shooter and that "any evidence of intent to kill was severely lacking." *Id.*, at 10, __ S.W.3d, at __ (Danielson, J., dissenting). And they argued that Jackson's mandatory sentence ran afoul of *Graham's* admonition that "'[a]n offender's age is relevant to the Eighth Amendment, and criminal procedure laws that fail to take defendants' youthfulness into account at all would be flawed.'" *Id.*, at 10–11, __ S.W.3d, at __ (quoting *Graham*, 560 U.S., at __, 130 S.Ct., at 2031).[2]

B

Like Jackson, petitioner Evan Miller was 14 years old at the time of his crime. Miller had by then been in and out of foster care because his mother suffered from alcoholism and drug addiction and his stepfather abused him. Miller, too, regularly used drugs and alcohol; and he had attempted suicide four times, the first when he was six years old. See *E.J.M. v. State*, 928 So.2d 1077, 1081 (Ala.Crim.App. 2004) (Cobb, J., concurring in result); App. in No. 10-9646, pp. 26–28 (hereinafter Miller App.).

One night in 2003, Miller was at home with a friend, Colby Smith, when a neighbor, Cole Cannon, came to make a drug deal with Miller's mother. See 6 Record in No. 10-9646, p. 1004. The two boys followed Cannon back to his trailer, where all three smoked marijuana and played drinking games. When Cannon passed out, Miller stole his wallet, splitting about $300 with Smith. Miller then tried to put the wallet back in Cannon's pocket, but Cannon awoke and grabbed Miller by the throat. Smith hit Cannon with a nearby baseball bat, and once released, Miller grabbed the bat and repeatedly struck Cannon with it. Miller placed a sheet over Cannon's head, told him "'I am God, I've come to take your life,'" and delivered one more blow. *Miller v. State*, 63 So.3d 676, 689 (Aia.Crim. App.2010). The boys then retreated to Miller's trailer, but soon decided to return to Cannon's to cover up evidence of their crime. Once there, they lit two fires. Cannon eventually died from his injuries and smoke inhalation. See *id.*, at 683–685, 689.

Alabama law required that Miller initially be charged as a juvenile, but allowed the District Attorney to seek removal of the case to adult court. . . . The D.A. did so, and the juvenile court agreed to the transfer after a hearing. Citing the nature of the crime, Miller's "mental maturity," and his prior juvenile offenses (truancy and "criminal mischief"), the Alabama Court of Criminal Appeals affirmed. . . .[3] The State accordingly charged Miller as an adult with murder in the course of arson. That crime (like capital murder in Arkansas) carries a mandatory minimum punishment of life without parole. . . .

Relying in significant part on testimony from Smith, who had pleaded to a lesser offense, a jury found Miller guilty. He was therefore sentenced to life without the possibility of parole. The Alabama Court of Criminal Appeals affirmed, ruling that life without parole was "not overly harsh when compared to the crime" and that the mandatory nature of the sentencing scheme was permissible under the Eighth Amendment. 63 So.3d. at 690; see *id.*, at 686-691. The Alabama Supreme Court denied review. . . .

II

The Eighth Amendment's prohibition of cruel and unusual punishment "guarantees individuals the right not to be subjected to excessive sanctions." *Roper*, 543 U.S., at 560, 125 S.Ct. 1183. That right, we have explained, "flows from the basic 'precept of justice that punishment for crime should be graduated and proportioned'" to both the offender and the offense. *Ibid.* (quoting *Weems v. United States*, 217 U.S. 349, 367, 30 S.Ct. 544, 54 L.Ed. 793 (1910)). As we noted the last time we considered life-without-parole sentences imposed on juveniles, "[t]he concept of proportionality is central to the Eighth Amendment." *Graham*, 560 U.S., at __, 130 S.Ct., at 2021. And we view that concept less through a historical prism than according to "'the evolving standards of decency that mark the progress of a maturing society.'" *Estelle v. Gamble*, 429 U.S. 97, 102, 97 S.Ct. 285, 50 L.Ed.2d 251 (1976) (quoting *Trop v. Dulles*, 356 U.S. 86, 101, 78 S.Ct. 590, 2 L.Ed.2d 630 (1958) (plurality opinion)).

The cases before us implicate two strands of precedent reflecting our concern with proportionate punishment. The first has adopted categorical bans on sentencing practices based on mismatches between the culpability of a class of offenders and the severity of a penalty. See *Graham*, 560 U.S., at __, 130 S.Ct., at 2022–2023 (listing cases). So, for example, we have held that imposing the death penalty for nonhomicide crimes against individuals, or imposing it on mentally retarded defendants, violates the Eighth Amendment. See *Kennedy v. Louisiana*. 554 U.S. 407, 128 S.Ct. 2641, 171 L.Ed.2d 525 (2008); *Atkins v. Virginia*, 536 U.S. 304, 122 S.Ct. 2242, 153 L.Ed.2d 335 (2002). Several of the cases in this group have specially focused on juvenile offenders, because of their lesser culpability. Thus, *Roper* held that the Eighth Amendment bars capital punishment for children, and *Graham* concluded that the Amendment also prohibits a sentence of life without the possibility of parole for a child who committed a nonhomicide offense. *Graham* further likened life without parole for juveniles to the death penalty itself, thereby evoking a second line of our precedents. In those cases, we have prohibited mandatory imposition of capital punishment, requiring that sentencing authorities consider the characteristics of a defendant and the details of his offense before sentencing him to death. See _Woodson v. North Carolina_, 428 U.S. 280, 96 S.Ct. 2978, 49 L.Ed.2d 944 (1976) (plurality opinion); _Lockett v. Ohio_, 438 U.S. 586, 98 S.Ct. 2954, 57 L.Ed.2d 973 (1978). Here, the confluence of these two lines of precedent leads to the conclusion that mandatory life-without-parole sentences for juveniles violate the Eighth Amendment.[4]

To start with the first set of cases: _Roper_ and _Graham_ establish that children are constitutionally different from adults for purposes of sentencing. Because juveniles have diminished culpability and greater prospects for reform, we explained, "they are less deserving of the most severe punishments." _Graham_, 560 U.S., at __, 130 S.Ct., at 2026. Those cases relied on three significant gaps between juveniles and adults. First, children have a "'lack of maturity and an underdeveloped sense of responsibility,'" leading to recklessness, impulsivity, and heedless risk-taking. _Roper_, 543 U.S., at 569, 125 S.Ct. 1183. Second, children "are more vulnerable . . . to negative influences and outside pressures," including from their family and peers; they have limited "contro[l] over their own environment" and lack the ability to extricate themselves from horrific, crime-producing settings. _Ibid._ And third, a child's character is not as "well formed" as an adult's; his traits are "less fixed" and his actions less likely to be "evidence of irretrievabl[e] deprav[ity]." _Id._, at 570, 125 S.Ct. 1183.

Our decisions rested not only on common sense—on what "any parent knows"—but on science and social science as well. _Id._, at 569, 125 S.Ct. 1183. In _Roper_, we cited studies showing that "'[o]nly a relatively small proportion of adolescents'" who engage in illegal activity "'develop entrenched patterns of problem behavior.'" _Id._, at 570, 125 S.Ct. 1183 (quoting Steinberg & Scott, Less Guilty by Reason of Adolescence: Developmental Immaturity, Diminished Responsibility, and the Juvenile Death Penalty, 58 Am. Psychologist 1009, 1014 (2003)). And in _Graham_, we noted that "developments in psychology and brain science continue to show fundamental differences between juvenile and adult minds"—for example, in "parts of the brain involved in behavior control." 560 U.S., at __, 130 S.Ct., at 2026.[5] We reasoned that those findings—of transient rashness, proclivity for risk, and inability to assess consequences—both lessened a child's "moral culpability" and enhanced the prospect that, as the years go by and neurological development occurs, his "'deficiencies

will be reformed.'" _Id._, at __, 130 S.Ct., at 2027 (quoting _Roper_, 543 U.S., at 570, 125 S.Ct. 1183).

Roper and _Graham_ emphasized that the distinctive attributes of youth diminish the penological justifications for imposing the harshest sentences on juvenile offenders, even when they commit terrible crimes. Because "'[t]he heart of the retribution rationale'" relates to an offender's blameworthiness, "'the case for retribution is not as strong with a minor as with an adult.'" _Graham_, 560 U.S., at __, 130 S.Ct., at 2028 (quoting _Tison v. Arizona_, 481 U.S. 137, 149, 107 S.Ct. 1676, 95 L.Ed.2d 127 (1987); _Roper_, 543 U.S., at 571, 125 S.Ct. 1183). Nor can deterrence do the work in this context, because "'the same characteristics that render juveniles less culpable than adults'"—their immaturity, recklessness, and impetuosity—make them less likely to consider potential punishment. _Graham_, 560 U.S., at __, 130 S.Ct. at 2028 (quoting _Roper_, 543 U.S., at 571, 125 S.Ct. 1183). Similarly, incapacitation could not support the life-without-parole sentence in _Graham_: Deciding that a "juvenile offender forever will be a danger to society" would require "mak[ing] a judgment that [he] is incorrigible"—but "'incorrigibility is inconsistent with youth.'" 560 U.S., at __, 130 S.Ct., at 2029 (quoting _Workman v. Commonwealth_, 429 S.W.2d 374, 378 (Ky.App. 1968)). And for the same reason, rehabilitation could not justify that sentence. Life without parole "forswears altogether the rehabilitative ideal." _Graham_, 560 U.S., at __, 130 S.Ct., at 2030. It reflects "an irrevocable judgment about [an offender's] value and place in society," at odds with a child's capacity for change. _Ibid._

Graham concluded from this analysis that life-without-parole sentences, like capital punishment, may violate the Eighth Amendment when imposed on children. To be sure, _Graham's_ flat ban on life without parole applied only to nonhomicide crimes, and the Court took care to distinguish those offenses from murder, based on both moral culpability and consequential harm. See _id._, at __, 130 S.Ct., at 2027. But none of what it said about children—about their distinctive (and transitory) mental traits and environmental vulnerabilities—is crime-specific. Those features are evident in the same way, and to the same degree, when (as in both cases here) a botched robbery turns into a killing. So _Graham's_ reasoning implicates any life-without-parole sentence imposed on a juvenile, even as its categorical bar relates only to nonhomicide offenses.

Most fundamentally, _Graham_ insists that youth matters in determining the appropriateness of a lifetime of incarceration without the possibility of parole. In the circumstances there, juvenile status precluded a life-without-parole sentence, even though an adult could receive it for a similar crime. And in other contexts as well, the characteristics of youth, and the way they weaken rationales for punishment, can render a life-without-parole sentence disproportionate. Cf. *id.*, at __, 130 S.Ct., at 2028–2032 (generally doubting the penological justifications for imposing life without parole on juveniles). "An offender's age," we made clear in *Graham*, "is relevant to the Eighth Amendment," and so "criminal procedure laws that fail to take defendants' youthfulness into account at all would be flawed." *Id.*, at __, 130 S.Ct., at 2031. THE CHIEF JUSTICE, concurring in the judgment, made a similar point. Although rejecting a categorical bar on life-without-parole sentences for juveniles, he acknowledged "*Roper's* conclusion that juveniles are typically less culpable than adults," and accordingly wrote that "an offender's juvenile status can play a central role" in considering a sentence's proportionality. *Id.*, at __, 130 S.Ct., at 2039; see *id.*, at __, 130 S.Ct., at 2042 (*Graham's* "youth is one factor, among others, that should be considered in deciding whether his punishment was unconstitutionally excessive").[6]

But the mandatory penalty schemes at issue here prevent the sentencer from taking account of these central considerations. By removing youth from the balance—by subjecting a juvenile to the same life-without-parole sentence applicable to an adult—these laws prohibit a sentencing authority from assessing whether the law's harshest term of imprisonment proportionately punishes a juvenile offender. That contravenes *Graham's* (and also *Roper's*) foundational principle: that imposition of a State's most severe penalties on juvenile offenders cannot proceed as though they were not children.

And *Graham* makes plain these mandatory schemes' defects in another way: by likening life-without-parole sentences imposed on juveniles to the death penalty itself. Life-without-parole terms, the Court wrote, "share some characteristics with death sentences that are shared by no other sentences." 560 U.S., at __, 130 S.Ct., at 2027. Imprisoning an offender until he dies alters the remainder of his life "by a forfeiture that is irrevocable." *Ibid.* (citing *Solem v. Helm, 463 U.S. 277, 300–301, 103 S.Ct. 3001. 77 L.Ed.2d 637 (1983)*). And this lengthiest possible incarceration is an "especially harsh punishment for a juvenile," because he will almost inevitably serve "more years and a greater percentage of his life in prison than an adult offender." *Graham*, 560 U.S., at __, 130 S.Ct., at 2028. The penalty when imposed on a teenager, as compared with an older person, is therefore "the same . . . in name only." *Id.*, at __, 130 S.Ct., at 2028. All of that suggested a distinctive set of legal rules: In part because we viewed this ultimate penalty for juveniles as akin to the death penalty, we treated it similarly to that most severe punishment. We imposed

a categorical ban on the sentence's use, in a way unprecedented for a term of imprisonment. See *id.*, at __, 130 S.Ct., at 2022; *id.*, at __, 130 S.Ct., at 2046 (THOMAS, J., dissenting) ("For the first time in its history, the Court declares an entire class of offenders immune from a noncapital sentence using the categorical approach it previously reserved for death penalty cases alone"). And the bar we adopted mirrored a proscription first established in the death penalty context—that the punishment cannot be imposed for any nonhomicide crimes against individuals. See *Kennedy, 554 U.S. 407, 128 S.Ct. 2641, 171 L.Ed.2d 525; Coker v. Georgia, 433 U.S. 584, 97 S.Ct. 2861, 53 L.Ed.2d 982 (1977)*.

That correspondence—*Graham's* "[t]reat[ment] [of] juvenile life sentences as analogous to capital punishment," 560 U.S., at __, 130 S.Ct., at 2038–2039 (ROBERTS, C.J., concurring in judgment)—makes relevant here a second line of our precedents, demanding individualized sentencing when imposing the death penalty. In *Woodson, 428 U.S. 280. 96 S.Ct. 2978, 49 L.Ed.2d 944*, we held that a statute mandating a death sentence for first-degree murder violated the Eighth Amendment. We thought the mandatory scheme flawed because it gave no significance to "the character and record of the individual offender or the circumstances" of the offense, and "exclud[ed] from consideration . . . the possibility of compassionate or mitigating factors." *Id.*, at 304, 96 S.Ct. 2978. Subsequent decisions have elaborated on the requirement that capital defendants have an opportunity to advance, and the judge or jury a chance to assess, any mitigating factors, so that the death penalty is reserved only for the most culpable defendants committing the most serious offenses. See, *e.g.*, *Sumner v. Shuman, 483 U.S. 66, 74–76. 107 S.Ct. 2716, 97 L.Ed.2d 56 (1987); Eddings v. Oklahoma, 455 U.S. 104, 110–112, 102 S.Ct. 869, 71 L.Ed.2d 1 (1982); Lockett, 438 U.S., at 597–609. 98 S.Ct. 2954 (plurality opinion)*.

Of special pertinence here, we insisted in these rulings that a sentencer have the ability to consider the "mitigating qualities of youth." *Johnson v. Texas, 509 U.S. 350, 367, 113 S.Ct. 2658, 125 L.Ed.2d 290 (1993)*. Everything we said in *Roper* and *Graham* about that stage of life also appears in these decisions. As we observed, "youth is more than a chronological fact." *Eddings, 455 U.S., at 115, 102 S.Ct. 869*. It is a time of immaturity, irresponsibility, "impetuousness [,]and recklessness." *Johnson, 509 U.S., at 368, 113 S.Ct. 2658*. It is a moment and "condition of life when a person may be most susceptible to influence and to psychological damage." *Eddings, 455 U.S., at 115, 102 S.Ct. 869*. And its "signature qualities" are all "transient." *Johnson, 509 U.S., at 368, 113 S.Ct. 2658. Eddings* is especially on point. There, a 16-year-old shot a police officer point-blank and killed him. We invalidated his death sentence because the judge did not consider evidence of his neglectful and violent family background (including his mother's drug abuse and his father's physical abuse) and his emotional disturbance. We found that evidence "particularly relevant"—more so than it would have been in the case of an adult offender. 455 U.S., at 115, 102 S.Ct. 869. We held: "[J]ust as the chronological age of a minor is itself a relevant mitigating factor of great weight, so must the background and mental and emotional development of a youthful defendant be duly considered" in assessing his culpability. Id., at 116, 102 S.Ct. 869.

In light of Graham's reasoning, these decisions too show the flaws of imposing mandatory life-without-parole sentences on juvenile homicide offenders. Such mandatory penalties, by their nature, preclude a sentencer from taking account of an offender's age and the wealth of characteristics and circumstances attendant to it. Under these schemes, every juvenile will receive the same sentence as every other—the 17-year-old and the 14-year-old, the shooter and the accomplice, the child from a stable household and the child from a chaotic and abusive one. And still worse, each juvenile (including these two 14-year-olds) will receive the same sentence as the vast majority of adults committing similar homicide offenses— but really, as Graham noted, a greater sentence than those adults will serve.[7] In meting out the death penalty, the elision of all these differences would be strictly forbidden. And once again, Graham indicates that a similar rule should apply when a juvenile confronts a sentence of life (and death) in prison.

So Graham and Roper and our individualized sentencing cases alike teach that in imposing a State's harshest penalties, a sentencer misses too much if he treats every child as an adult. To recap: Mandatory life without parole for a juvenile precludes consideration of his chronological age and its hallmark features—among them, immaturity, impetuosity, and failure to appreciate risks and consequences. It prevents taking into account the family and home environment that surrounds him—and from which he cannot usually extricate himself—no matter how brutal or dysfunctional. It neglects the circumstances of the homicide offense, including the extent of his participation in the conduct and the way familial and peer pressures may have affected him. Indeed, it ignores that he might have been charged and convicted of a lesser offense if not for incompetencies associated with youth—for example, his inability to deal with police officers or prosecutors (including on a plea agreement) or his incapacity to assist his own attorneys. See, e.g., Graham, 560 U.S., at __, 130 S.Ct., at 2032 ("[T]he features that distinguish

juveniles from adults also put them at a significant disadvantage in criminal proceedings"); J.D.B. v. North Carolina, 564 U.S. __, __, 131 S.Ct. 2394, 2400–2401, 180 L.Ed.2d 310 (2011) (discussing children's responses to interrogation). And finally, this mandatory punishment disregards the possibility of rehabilitation even when the circumstances most suggest it.

Both cases before us illustrate the problem. Take Jackson's first. As noted earlier, Jackson did not fire the bullet that killed Laurie Troup; nor did the State argue that he intended her death. Jackson's conviction was instead based on an aiding-and-abetting theory; and the appellate court affirmed the verdict only because the jury could have believed that when Jackson entered the store, he warned Troup that "[w]e ain't playin'," rather than told his friends that "I thought you all was playin'." See 359 Ark., at 90–92, 194 S.W.3d. at 759–760; supra, at 2461. To be sure, Jackson learned on the way to the video store that his friend Shields was carrying a gun, but his age could well have affected his calculation of the risk that posed, as well as his willingness to walk away at that point. All these circumstances go to Jackson's culpability for the offense. See Graham, 560 U.S., at __, 130 S.Ct., at 2027 ("[W]hen compared to an adult murderer, a juvenile offender who did not kill or intend to kill has a twice diminished moral culpability"). And so too does Jackson's family background and immersion in violence: Both his mother and his grandmother had previously shot other individuals. See Record in No. 10-9647, pp. 80–82. At the least, a sentencer should look at such facts before depriving a 14-year-old of any prospect of release from prison.

That is true also in Miller's case. No one can doubt that he and Smith committed a vicious murder. But they did it when high on drugs and alcohol consumed with the adult victim. And if ever a pathological background might have contributed to a 14-year-old's commission of a crime, it is here. Miller's stepfather physically abused him; his alcoholic and drug-addicted mother neglected him; he had been in and out of foster care as a result; and he had tried to kill himself four times, the first when he should have been in kindergarten. See 928 So.2d, at 1081 (Cobb, J., concurring in result); Miller App. 26–28; supra, at 2461–2462. Nonetheless, Miller's past criminal history was limited—two instances of truancy and one of "second-degree criminal mischief." No. CR-03-0915, at 6 (unpublished memorandum). That Miller deserved severe punishment for killing Cole Cannon is beyond question. But once again, a sentencer needed to examine all these circumstances before concluding that life without any possibility of parole was the appropriate penalty.

We therefore hold that the Eighth Amendment forbids a sentencing scheme that mandates life in prison without possibility of parole for juvenile offenders. Cf. *Graham*, 560 U.S., at __, 130 S.Ct., at 2030 ("A State is not required to guarantee eventual freedom," but must provide "some meaningful opportunity to obtain release based on demonstrated maturity and rehabilitation"). By making youth (and all that accompanies it) irrelevant to imposition of that harshest prison sentence, such a scheme poses too great a risk of disproportionate punishment. Because that holding is sufficient to decide these cases, we do not consider Jackson's and Miller's alternative argument that the Eighth Amendment requires a categorical bar on life without parole for juveniles, or at least for those 14 and younger. But given all we have said in *Roper*, *Graham*, and this decision about children's diminished culpability and heightened capacity for change, we think appropriate occasions for sentencing juveniles to this harshest possible penalty will be uncommon. That is especially so because of the great difficulty we noted in *Roper* and *Graham* of distinguishing at this early age between "the juvenile offender whose crime reflects unfortunate yet transient immaturity, and the rare juvenile offender whose crime reflects irreparable corruption." *Roper*, 543 U.S., at 573, 125 S.Ct. 1183; *Graham*, 560 U.S., at __, 130 S.Ct., at 2026–2027. Although we do not foreclose a sentencer's ability to make that judgment in homicide cases, we require it to take into account how children are different, and how those differences counsel against irrevocably sentencing them to a lifetime in prison.[8]

Ill

Alabama and Arkansas offer two kinds of arguments against requiring individualized consideration before sentencing a juvenile to life imprisonment without possibility of parole. The States (along with the dissents) first contend that the rule we adopt conflicts with aspects of our Eighth Amendment caselaw. And they next assert that the rule is unnecessary because individualized circumstances come into play in deciding whether to try a juvenile offender as an adult. We think the States are wrong on both counts.

A

The States (along with Justice THOMAS) first claim that *Harmelin v. Michigan*, 501 U.S. 957, 111 S.Ct. 2680, 115 L.Ed.2d 836 (1991), precludes our holding. The defendant in *Harmelin* was sentenced to a mandatory life-without-parole term for possessing more than 650 grams of cocaine. The Court upheld that penalty, reasoning that "a sentence which is not otherwise cruel and unusual" does not "becom[e] so simply because it is 'mandatory.'" *Id.*, at 995, 111 S.Ct. 2680. We recognized that a different rule, requiring individualized sentencing, applied in the death penalty context. But we refused to extend that command to noncapital cases "because of the qualitative difference between death and all other penalties." *Ibid.*; see *id.*, at 1006, 111 S.Ct. 2680 (KENNEDY, J., concurring in part and concurring in judgment). According to Alabama, invalidating the mandatory imposition of life-without-parole terms on juveniles "would effectively overrule *Harmelin*." Brief for Respondent in No. 10-9646, p. 59 (hereinafter Alabama Brief); see Arkansas Brief 39.

We think that argument myopic. *Harmelin* had nothing to do with children and did not purport to apply its holding to the sentencing of juvenile offenders. We have by now held on multiple occasions that a sentencing rule permissible for adults may not be so for children. Capital punishment, our decisions hold, generally comports with the Eighth Amendment—except it cannot be imposed on children. See *Roper*, 543 U.S. 551, 125 S.Ct. 1183, 161 L.Ed.2d 1; *Thompson*, 487 U.S. 815, 108 S.Ct. 2687, 101 L.Ed.2d 702. So too, life without parole is permissible for nonhomicide offenses—except, once again, for children. See *Graham*, 560 U.S., at __, 130 S.Ct., at 2030. Nor are these sentencing decisions an oddity in the law. To the contrary, "'[o]ur history is replete with laws and judicial recognition' that children cannot be viewed simply as miniature adults." *J.D.B.*, 564 U.S., at __, 131 S.Ct., at 2404 (quoting *Eddings*, 455 U.S., at 115-116, 102 S.Ct. 869, citing examples from criminal, property, contract, and tort law). So if (as *Harmelin* recognized) "death is different," children are different too. Indeed, it is the odd legal rule that does *not* have some form of exception for children. In that context, it is no surprise that the law relating to society's harshest punishments recognizes such a distinction. Cf. *Graham*, 560 U.S., at __, 130 S.Ct., at 2040 (ROBERTS, C.J., concurring in judgment) ("*Graham*'s age places him in a significantly different category from the defendan[t] in . . . *Harmelin*"). Our ruling thus neither overrules nor undermines nor conflicts with *Harmelin*.

Alabama and Arkansas (along with THE CHIEF JUSTICE and Justice ALITO) next contend that because many States impose mandatory life-without-parole sentences on juveniles, we may not hold the practice unconstitutional. In considering categorical bars to the death penalty and life without parole, we ask as part of the analysis whether "'objective indicia of society's standards, as expressed in legislative enactments and state practice,'" show a "national consensus" against a sentence for a particular class of offenders. *Graham*, 560 U.S., at __, 130 S.Ct., at 2022 (quoting *Roper, 543 U.S., at 563, 125 S.Ct. 1183*). By our count, 29 jurisdictions (28 States and the Federal Government) make a life-without-parole term mandatory for some juveniles convicted of murder in adult court.[9] The States argue that this number precludes our holding.

We do not agree; indeed, we think the States' argument on this score *weaker* than the one we rejected in *Graham*. For starters, the cases here are different from the typical one in which we have tallied legislative enactments. Our decision does not categorically bar a penalty for a class of offenders or type of crime—as, for example, we did in *Roper* or *Graham*. Instead, it mandates only that a sentencer follow a certain process—considering an offender's youth and attendant characteristics—before imposing a particular penalty. And in so requiring, our decision flows straightforwardly from our precedents: specifically, the principle of *Roper*, *Graham*, and our individualized sentencing cases that youth matters for purposes of meting out the law's most serious punishments. When both of those circumstances have obtained in the past, we have not scrutinized or relied in the same way on legislative enactments. See, *e.g.*, *Sumner v. Shuman, 483 U.S. 66, 107 S.Ct. 2716, 97 L.Ed.2d 56* (relying on *Woodson's* logic to prohibit the mandatory death penalty for murderers already serving life without parole); *Lockett, 438 U.S., at 602–608, 98 S.Ct. 2954 (plurality opinion)* (applying *Woodson* to require that judges and juries consider all mitigating evidence); *Eddings, 455 U.S., at 110–117, 102 S.Ct. 869* (similar). We see no difference here.

In any event, the "objective indicia" that the States offer do not distinguish these cases from others holding that a sentencing practice violates the Eighth Amendment. In *Graham*, we prohibited life-without-parole terms for juveniles committing nonhomicide offenses even though 39 jurisdictions permitted that sentence. See 560 U.S., at __, 130 S.Ct., at 2023. That is 10 *more* than impose life without parole on juveniles on a mandatory basis.[10] And in *Atkins*, *Roper*, and *Thompson*, we similarly banned the death penalty in circumstances in which "less than half" of the "States that permit[ted] capital punishment (for whom the issue exist[ed])" had previously chosen to do so. *Atkins, 536 U.S., at 342, 122 S.Ct. 2242 (SCALIA, J., dissenting)* (emphasis deleted); see *Id.*, at 313–315, *122 S.Ct. 2242* (majority opinion); *Roper, 543 U.S., at 564–565, 125 S.Ct. 1183; Thompson, 487 U.S., at 826–827, 108 S.Ct. 2687 (plurality opinion)*. So we are breaking no new ground in these cases.[11]

Graham and *Thompson* provide special guidance, because they considered the same kind of statutes we do and explained why simply counting them would present a distorted view. Most jurisdictions authorized the death penalty or life without parole for juveniles only through the combination of two independent statutory provisions. One allowed the transfer of certain juvenile offenders to adult court, while another (often in a far-removed part of the code) set out the penalties for any and all individuals tried there. We reasoned that in those circumstances, it was impossible to say whether a legislature had endorsed a given penalty for children (or would do so if presented with the choice). In *Thompson*, we found that the statutes "t[old] us that the States consider 15-year-olds to be old enough to be tried in criminal court for serious crimes (or too old to be dealt with effectively in juvenile court), but t[old] us nothing about the judgment these States have made regarding the appropriate punishment for such youthful offenders." 487 U.S., at 826, n. 24, 108 S.Ct. 2687 (plurality opinion) (emphasis deleted); see also *Id.*, at 850, 108 S.Ct. 2687 (O'Connor. J., concurring in judgment); *Roper, 543 U.S., at 596*. n., 125 S.Ct. 1183 (O'Connor. J., dissenting). And *Graham* echoed that reasoning: Although the confluence of state laws "ma[de] life without parole possible for some juvenile nonhomicide offenders," it did not "justify a judgment" that many States actually "intended to subject such offenders" to those sentences. 560 U.S., at __, 130 S.Ct., at 2025.[12]

All that is just as true here. Almost all jurisdictions allow some juveniles to be tried in adult court for some kinds of homicide. See Dept. of Justice, H. Snyder & M. Sickmund, Juvenile Offenders and Victims: 2006 National Report 110–114 (hereinafter 2006 National Report). But most States do not have separate penalty provisions for those juvenile offenders. Of the 29 jurisdictions mandating life without parole for children, more than half do so by virtue of generally applicable penalty provisions, imposing the sentence without regard to age.[13] And indeed, some of those States set no minimum age for who may be transferred to adult court in the first instance, thus applying life-without-parole mandates to children of any age—be it 17 or 14 or 10 or 6.[14] As in *Graham*, we think that "underscores that the statutory eligibility of a juvenile offender for life without parole does not indicate that the penalty has been endorsed throuh deliberate, express, and full legislative consideration." 560 U.S., at __, 130 S.Ct., at 2026. That Alabama and Arkansas can count to 29 by including these possibly (or probably) inadvertent legislative outcomes does not preclude our determination that mandatory life without parole for juveniles violates the Eighth Amendment.

Does Sentencing a Juvenile to Life in Prison Without the Possibility of Parole Constitute Cruel and Unusual Punishment? by Hickey

285

B

Nor does the presence of discretion in some jurisdictions' transfer statutes aid the States here. Alabama and Arkansas initially ignore that many States use mandatory transfer systems: A juvenile of a certain age who has committed a specified offense will be tried in adult court, regardless of any individualized circumstances. Of the 29 relevant jurisdictions, about half place at least some juvenile homicide offenders in adult court automatically, with no apparent opportunity to seek transfer to juvenile court.[15] Moreover, several States at times lodge this decision exclusively in the hands of prosecutors, again with no statutory mechanism for judicial reevaluation.[16] And those "prosecutorial discretion laws are usually silent regarding standards, protocols, or appropriate considerations for decisionmaking." Dept of Justice, Office of Juvenile Justice and Delinquency Prevention, P. Griffin, S. Addie, B. Adams, & K. Firestine, Trying Juveniles as Adults: An Analysis of State Transfer Laws and Reporting 5 (2011). . . .

IV

Graham, *Roper*, and our individualized sentencing decisions make clear that a judge or jury must have the opportunity to consider mitigating circumstances before imposing the harshest possible penalty for juveniles. By requiring that all children convicted of homicide receive lifetime incarceration without possibility of parole, regardless of their age and age-related characteristics and the nature of their crimes, the mandatory sentencing schemes before us violate this principle of proportionality, and so the Eighth Amendment's ban on cruel and unusual punishment. We accordingly reverse the judgments of the Arkansas Supreme Court and Alabama Court of Criminal Appeals and remand the cases for further proceedings not inconsistent with this opinion.

It is so ordered. . . .

U.S. Supreme Court Associate Justice **Elena Kagan** received an A.B. degree from Princeton University in 1981, an MPhil from Oxford in 1983, and a J.D. from Harvard Law School in 1986. She clerked for Judge Abner Mikva of the U.S. Court of Appeals (D.C. Cir.) and later for the late Supreme Court Associate Justice Thurgood Marshall. After briefly practicing law, she became a law professor, first at the University of Chicago and later at the Harvard Law School. She also served for four years as Associate Counsel to President Bill Clinton and later as Deputy Assistant to the President for Domestic Policy. Between 2003 and 2009 she served as the Dean of the Harvard Law School. In 2009, President Obama nominated her to be the Solicitor General of the United States and a year later he nominated her as an Associate Justice of the U.S. Supreme Court.

U.S. Supreme Court

Dissenting Opinion, *Miller v. Alabama*

Chief Justice ROBERTS, with whom Justice SCALIA, Justice THOMAS, and Justice ALITO join, dissenting.

Determining the appropriate sentence for a teenager convicted of murder presents grave and challenging questions of morality and social policy. Our role, however, is to apply the law, not to answer such questions. The pertinent law here is the Eighth Amendment to the Constitution, which prohibits "cruel and unusual punishments." Today, the Court invokes that Amendment to ban a punishment that the Court does not itself characterize as unusual, and that could not plausibly be described as such. I therefore dissent.

The parties agree that nearly 2,500 prisoners are presently serving life sentences without the possibility of parole for murders they committed before the age of 18. Brief for Petitioner in No. 10-9647, p. 62, n. 80 (Jackson Brief); Brief for Respondent is No. 10-9646, p. 30 (Alabama Brief). The Court accepts that over 2,000 of those prisoners received that sentence because it was mandated by a legislature. *Ante,* at 2471-2472, n. 10. And it recognizes that the Federal Government and most States impose such mandatory sentences. *Ante,* at 2470-2471. Put simply, if a 17-year-old is convicted of deliberately murdering an innocent victim, it is not "unusual" for the murderer to receive a mandatory sentence of life without parole. That reality should preclude finding that mandatory life imprisonment for juvenile killers violates the Eighth Amendment.

Our precedent supports this conclusion. When determining whether a punishment is cruel and unusual, this Court typically begins with "'objective indicia of society's standards, as expressed in legislative enactments and state practice.'" *Graham v. Florida,* 560 U.S. __, __, 130 S.Ct. 2011, 2022, 176 L.Ed.2d 825 (2010); see also, *e.g., Kennedy v. Louisiana,* 554 U.S. 407, 422, 128 S.Ct. 2641, 171 L.Ed.2d 525 (2008); *Roper v. Simmons,* 543 U.S. 551, 564, 125 S.Ct. 1183, 161 L.Ed.2d 1 (2005). We look to these "objective indicia" to ensure that we are not simply following our own subjective values or beliefs. *Gregg v. Georgia,* 428 U.S. 153,

173, 96 S.Ct. 2909, 49 L.Ed.2d 859 (1976) (joint opinion of Stewart, Powell, and Stevens, JJ.). Such tangible evidence of societal standards enables us to determine whether there is a "consensus against" a given sentencing practice. *Graham, supra,* at __, 130 S.Ct., at 2022-2023. If there is, the punishment may be regarded as "unusual." But when, as here, most States formally require and frequently impose the punishment in question, there is no objective basis for that conclusion.

Our Eighth Amendment cases have also said that we should take guidance from "evolving standards of decency that mark the progress of a maturing society." *Ante,* at 2463 (quoting *Estelle v. Gamble,* 429 U.S. 97, 102, 97 S.Ct. 285, 50 L.Ed.2d 251 (1976); internal quotation marks omitted). Mercy toward the guilty can be a form of decency, and a maturing society may abandon harsh punishments that it comes to view as unnecessary or unjust. But decency is not the same as leniency. A decent society protects the innocent from violence. A mature society may determine that this requires removing those guilty of the most heinous murders from its midst, both as protection for its other members and as a concrete expression of its standards of decency. As judges we have no basis for deciding that progress toward greater decency can move only in the direction of easing sanctions on the guilty.

In this case, there is little doubt about the direction of society's evolution: For most of the 20th century, American sentencing practices emphasized rehabilitation of the offender and the availability of parole. But by the 1980's, outcry against repeat offenders, broad disaffection with the rehabilitative model, and other factors led many legislatures to reduce or eliminate the possibility of parole, imposing longer sentences in order to punish criminals and prevent them from committing more crimes. See, *e.g.,* Alschuler, The Changing Purposes of Criminal Punishment, 70 U. Chi. L.Rev.n 1, 1-13 (2003); see generally Crime and Public Policy (J. Wilson & J. Petersilia eds. 2011). Statutes establishing life without parole sentences in particular became more common in the past quarter century. See *Baze v. Rees,* 553, U.S. 35, 78, and n. 10,

128 S.Ct. 1520, 170 L.Ed.2d 420 (2008) (Stevens, J., concurring in judgment). And the parties agree that most States have changed their laws relatively recently to expose teenage murderers to mandatory life without parole. Jackson Brief 54-55; Alabama Brief 4-5.

The Court attempts to avoid the import of the fact that so many jurisdictions have embraced the sentencing practice at issue by comparing this case to the Court's prior Eighth Amendment cases. The Court notes that *Graham* found a punishment authorized in 39 jurisdictions unconstitutional, whereas the punishment it bans today is mandated in 10 fewer. *Ante*, at 2471. But *Graham* went to considerable lengths to show that although theoretically allowed in many States, the sentence at issue in that case was "exceedingly rare" in practice. 560 U.S., at __, 130 S.Ct., at 2026. The Court explained that only 123 prisoners in the entire Nation were serving life without parole for nonhomicide crimes committed as juveniles, with more than half in a single State. It contrasted that with statistics showing nearly 400,000 juveniles were arrested for serious nonhomicide offenses in a single year. Based on the sentence's rarity despite the many opportunities to impose it, *Graham* concluded that there was a national consensus against life without parole for juvenile nonhomicide crimes. *Id.*, at __, 130 S.Ct., at 2024-2026.

Here the number of mandatory life without parole sentences for juvenile murderers, relative to the number of juveniles arrested for murder, is over 5,000 times higher than the corresponding number in *Graham*. There is thus nothing in this case like the evidence of national consensus in *Graham*.[1]

The Court disregards these numbers, claiming that the prevalence of the sentence in question results from the number of statutes requiring its imposition. *Ante*, at 2471-2472, n. 10. True enough. The sentence at issue is statutorily mandated life without parole. Such a sentence can only result from statutes requiring its imposition. In *Graham* the Court relied on the low number of actual sentences to explain why the high number of statutes allowing such sentences was not dispositive. Here, the Court excuses the high number of actual sentences by citing the high number of statutes imposing it. To say that a sentence may be considered unusual *because* so many legislatures approve it stands precedent on its head.[2]

The Court also advances another reason for discounting the laws enacted by Congress and most state legislatures. Some of the jurisdictions that impose mandatory life without parole on juvenile murderers do so as a result of two statutes: one providing that juveniles charged with serious crimes may be tried as adults, and another generally mandating that those convicted of murder be imprisoned for life. According to the Court, our cases suggest that where the sentence results from the interaction of two such statutes, the legislature can be considered to have imposed the resulting sentences "inadvertent[ly]." *Ante*, at 2472-2474. The Court relies on *Graham* and *Thompson v. Oklahoma*, 487 U.S. 815, 826, n. 24. 108 S.Ct. 2687, 101 L.Ed.2d 702 (1988) (plurality opinion), for the proposition that these laws are therefore not valid evidence of society's views on the punishment at issue.

It is a fair question whether this Court should ever assume a legislature is so ignorant of its own laws that it does not understand that two of them interact with each other, especially on an issue of such importance as the one before us. But in *Graham* and *Thompson* it was at least plausible as a practical matter. In *Graham*, the extreme rarity with which the sentence in question was imposed could suggest that legislatures did not really intend the inevitable result of the laws they passed. See 560 U.S., at __, 130 S.Ct., at 2025-2026. In *Thompson*, the sentencing practice was even rarer—only 20 defendants had received it in the last century. 487 U.S., at 832, 108 S.Ct. 2687 (plurality opinion). Perhaps under those facts it could be argued that the legislature was not fully aware that a teenager could receive the particular sentence in question. But here the widespread and recent imposition of the sentence makes it implausible to characterize this sentencing practice as a collateral consequence of legislative ignorance.[3]

Nor do we display our usual respect for elected officials by asserting that legislators have *accidentally* required 2,000 teenagers to spend the rest of their lives in jail. This is particularly true given that our well-publicized decision in *Graham* alerted legislatures to the possibility that teenagers were subject to life with parole only because of legislative inadvertence. I am aware of no effort in the wake of *Graham* to correct any supposed legislative oversight. Indeed, in amending its laws in response to *Graham* one legislature made especially clear that it *does* intend juveniles who commit first-degree murder to receive mandatory life without parole. See Iowa Code Ann. § 902.1 (West Cum. Supp. 2012).

In the end, the Court does not actually conclude that mandatory life sentences for juvenile murderers are unusual. It instead claims that precedent "leads to" today's decision, primarily relying on *Graham* and *Roper*. *Ante*, at 2464. Petitioners argue that the reasoning of those cases "compels" finding in their favor. Jackson Brief 34. The Court is apparently unwilling to go so far, asserting only that precedent points in that direction. But today's decision invalidates the laws of dozens of legislatures and Congress. This Court is not easily led to such a result. See, *e.g.*, *United States v. Harris*, 106 U.S. 629, 635, 1 S.Ct.

601, 27 L.Ed. 290 (1883) (courts must presume an Act of Congress is constitutional "unless the lack of constitutional authority . . . is clearly demonstrated"). Because the Court does not rely on the Eighth Amendment's text or objective evidence of society's standards, its analysis of precedent alone must bear the "heavy burden [that] rests on those who would attack the judgment of the representatives of the people." *Gregg*, 428 U.S., at 175, 96 S.Ct. 2909. If the Court is unwilling to say that precedent compels today's decision, perhaps it should reconsider that decision.

In any event, the Court's holding does not follow from *Roper* and *Graham*. Those cases undoubtedly stand for the proposition that teenagers are less mature, less responsible, and less fixed in their ways than adults—not that a Supreme Court case was needed to establish that. What they do not stand for, and do not even suggest, is that legislators—who also know that teenagers are different from adults—may not require life without parole for juveniles who commit the worst types of murder.

That *Graham* does not imply today's result could not be clearer. In barring life without parole for juvenile nonhomicide offenders, *Graham* stated that "[t]here is a line 'between homicide and other serious violent offenses against the individual.'" 560 U.S., at __, 130 S.Ct., at 2027 (quoting *Kennedy*, 554 U.S., at 438, 128 S.Ct. 2641). The whole point of drawing a line between one issue and another is to say that they are different and should be treated differently. In other words, the two are in different categories. Which *Graham* also said: "defendants who do not kill, intend to kill, or foresee that life will be taken are *categorically* less deserving of the most serious forms of punishment than are murderers." 560 U.S., at __, 130 S.Ct., at 2027 (emphasis added). Of course, to be especially clear that what is said about one issue does not apply to another, one could say that the two issues cannot be compared. *Graham* said that too: "Serious nonhomicide crimes . . . cannot be compared to murder." *Ibid.* (internal quotation marks omitted). A case that expressly puts an issue in a different category from its own subject, draws a line between the two, and states that the two should not be compared, cannot fairly be said to control that issue.

Roper provides even less support for the Court's holding. In that case, the Court held that the death penalty could not be imposed for offenses committed by juveniles, no matter how serious their crimes. In doing so, *Roper* also set itself in a different category than this case, by expressly invoking "special" Eighth Amendment analysis for death penalty cases. 543 U.S., at 568-569, 125 S.Ct. 1183. But more importantly, *Roper* reasoned that the death penalty was not needed to deter juvenile murderers in part because "life imprisonment without the possibility of parole" was available. *Id.*, at 572, 125 S.Ct. 1183. In a classic bait and switch, the Court now tells state legislatures that—*Roper's* promise notwithstanding—they do not have power to guarantee that once someone commits a heinous murder, he will never do so again. It would be enough if today's decision proved Justice SCALIA's prescience in writing that *Roper's* "reassurance . . . gives little comfort." *Id.*, at 623, 125 S.Ct. 1183 (dissenting opinion). To claim that *Roper* actually "leads to" revoking its own reassurance surely goes too far.

Today's decision does not offer *Roper* and *Graham's* false promises of restraint. Indeed, the Court's opinion suggests that it is merely a way station on the path to further judicial displacement of the legislative role in prescribing appropriate punishment for crime. The Court's analysis focuses on the mandatory nature of the sentences in this case. See *ante*, at 2466-2469. But then—although doing so is entirely unnecessary to the rule it announces—the Court states that even when a life without parole sentence is not mandatory, "we think appropriate occasions for sentencing juveniles to this harshest possible penalty will be uncommon." *Ante*, at 2469. Today's holding may be limited to mandatory sentences, but the Court has already announced that discretionary life without parole for juveniles should be "uncommon"—or, to use a common synonym, "unusual."

Indeed, the Court's gratuitous prediction appears to be nothing other than an invitation to overturn life without parole sentences imposed by juries and trial judges. If that invitation is widely accepted and such sentences for juvenile offenders do in fact become "uncommon," the Court will have bootstrapped its way to declaring that the Eighth Amendment absolutely prohibits them.

This process has no discernible end point—or at least none consistent with our Nation's legal traditions. *Roper* and *Graham* attempted to limit their reasoning to the circumstances they addressed—*Roper* to the death penalty, and *Graham* to nonhomicide crimes. Having cast aside those limits, the Court cannot now offer a credible substitute, and does not even try. After all, the Court tells us, "none of what [*Graham*] said about children . . . is crime-specific." *Ante*, at 2465. The principle behind today's decision seems to be only that because juveniles are different from adults, they must be sentenced differently. See *ante*, at 2467-2469. There is no clear reason that principle would not bar all mandatory sentences for juveniles, or any juvenile sentence as harsh as what a similarly situated adult would receive. Unless confined, the only stopping point for the Court's analysis would be never permitting juvenile offenders to be tried as adults. Learning that an Amendment that bars only "unusual" punishments requires the abolition of this uniformly established practice would be startling indeed.

It is a great tragedy when a juvenile commits murder—most of all for the innocent victims. But also for the murderer, whose life has gone so wrong so early. And for society as well, which has lost one or more of its members to deliberate violence, and must harshly punish another. In recent years, our society has moved toward requiring that the murderer, his age notwithstanding, be imprisoned for the remainder of his life. Members of this Court may disagree with that choice. Perhaps science and policy suggest society should show greater mercy to young killers, giving them a greater chance to reform themselves at the risk that they will kill again. See *ante*, at 2464-2466. But that is not our decision to make. Neither the text of the Constitution nor our precedent prohibits legislatures from requiring that juvenile murderers be sentenced to life without parole. I respectfully dissent. . . .

U.S. Supreme Court Chief Justice **John Roberts** received an A.B. and J.D. degrees from Harvard. He served as a law clerk to Judge Henry J. Friendly of the U.S. Court of Appeals (2nd Cir.), and later as a clerk to U.S. Supreme Chief Justice William H. Rehnquist. He later became a Special Assistant to the Attorney General, U.S. Department of Justice, Associate Counsel to President Ronald Reagan, and Principal Deputy Solicitor General, U.S. Department of Justice, from 1989 to 1993. He later practiced law in Washington, D.C. He was appointed to the U.S. Court of Appeals (D.C. Cir.) and was later nominated by George W. Bush to be the Chief Justice of the U.S. Supreme Court.

EXPLORING THE ISSUE

Does Sentencing a Juvenile to a Mandatory Term of Life in Prison Without the Possibility of Parole Constitute Cruel and Unusual Punishment?

Critical Thinking and Reflection

1. What, in your opinion, constitutes cruel and unusual punishment?
2. Should "incapacitation," or "rehabilitation" be the ultimate goal of punishing offenders?
3. If a punishment is applied in a racially discriminatory manner, should it held to be a cruel and unusual punishment?
4. What do you think about the late Justice Thurgood Marshall's assertion that the Eighth Amendment's Cruel and Unusual Punishment Clause "embodies 'broad and idealistic concepts of dignity, civilized standards, humanity, and decency'?"
5. Does sentencing a juvenile to a mandatory term of life in prison without the possibility of parole comply with the principle of social utility?
6. What is the importance of the U.S. Supreme Court's decision in *Montgomery v. Louisiana* 2016?

Is There Common Ground?

The question posed in this issue is a challenging one. On one hand, it may seem reasonable to imprison an offender who has committed a heinous crime such as murder to a life term without the possibility of parole. On the other hand, it may be draconian and perhaps even unenlightened to impose this penalty, except in the most extreme cases. To illustrate, consider the facts of the case presented in this chapter, *Miller v. Alabama*, in which the Supreme Court consolidated two cases that presented similar issues. In each of the cases, a 14-year-old was convicted of murder and sentenced to a mandatory term of life imprisonment without the possibility of parole. In the first case, Jackson, the juvenile offender, accompanied two other boys to a video store to commit a robbery; on the way to the store, he learned that one of the boys was carrying a sawed-off shotgun. Jackson stayed outside the store for most of the robbery, but after he entered, one of his companions shot and killed the store clerk. Arkansas charged Jackson as an adult with capital felony murder and aggravated robbery, and a jury convicted him of both crimes. The court imposed a statutorily mandated sentence of life without the possibility of parole.

Did Jackson's case warrant such a severe sentence? Jackson was convicted under a longstanding criminal law doctrine called the *felony-murder rule*. According to this principle, a participant in a felony criminal enterprise that results in a victim's death is guilty of murder. Jackson was a more or less passive participant in this crime—he did not pull the trigger and there was no evidence that he had planned to kill anyone. Under Arkansas' felony-murder rule, however, he was just as culpable as the actual shooter.

Under these circumstances, does this sentence make sense? Assuming that Jackson's life expectancy is approximately 75 years, the sentence imposed would result in his confinement for 61 years. The Preface to this volume considered the astronomical costs of incarceration in our state and federal prison systems. According to a 2012 report by the Vera Institute of Justice, the State of Alabama spends $462.5 million per year on its prison system. That comes to $17,285.00 per inmate and that figure falls on the lower end of the scale in the United States. Jackson had no previous criminal record of violent crimes; he committed no violent act in this case. Assuming, however, that Jackson spends 61 years in the Alabama prison system the state will spend more than $1 million for his confinement. At a time of shrinking state budgets, cutbacks in school spending, social welfare programs, and other important social priorities, does spending this money to confine one individual conform to the principle of social utility? Moreover, does it make "moral sense" to confine someone in prison for 61 years who has committed no violent act?

In an important 2016 clarification of *Miller v. Alabama*, the U.S. Supreme Court ruled in *Montgomery v. Louisiana*, 136 S.Ct. 718 (2016) that *Miller* is to be applied by the states *retroactively*. This means that all cases that occurred before *Miller* was decided in which juveniles had been sentenced under a mandatory life without parole sentencing statute had to provide the incarcerated individual with a new hearing "where youth and its attendant characteristics are considered." According to the Court, states may remedy a *Miller* problem by permitting these offenders to be considered for parole. If, as Chief Justice Roberts observed in his dissenting opinion, there are approximately 2500 individuals confined in U.S. prisons who were sentenced to mandatory life without parole terms under these laws, *Montgomery* is a highly significant case.

Perhaps the best common ground in cases such as this, however, is what Justice Kagan suggested in her Majority Opinion in *Miller*: Justice systems should abandon mandatory sentencing schemes and require consideration of a juvenile defendant's individual circumstances prior to imposing sentences. Such a policy would have the potential to mitigate overly harsh punishment and better satisfy the principle of social utility.

Additional Resources

Arthur W. Campbell, *Law of Sentencing*, 3rd (Clark Boardman Callahan, 2015).

Joseph A. Melusky and Keith A. Pesto, *Cruel and Unusual Punishment* (ABC-Clio, Inc., 2013).

Kristen O'Donnell Tubb, *Freedom from Cruel and Unusual Punishment* (Gale Group, 2005).

Internet References . . .

The Campaign for the Fair Sentencing of Youth, *"Miller v. Alabama."*

www.fairsentencingofyouth.org

Equal Justice Institute (EJI), "U.S. Supreme Court Rules *Miller v. Alabama* is Retroactive." January 25, 2016.

www.eji.org/node/1209

Scott Hecinger, "Another Bite at the Graham Cracker: The Supreme Court's Surprising Revisiting of Juvenile Life Without Parole in *Miller v. Alabama*," *Georgetown Law Journal Online.*

www.georgetownlawjournal.org

Selected, Edited, and with Issue Framing Material by:
Thomas J. Hickey, *State University of New York at Cobleskill*

ISSUE

Does the Second Amendment to the U.S. Constitution Protect the Right to Possess a Firearm?

YES: Antonin E. Scalia, from "Majority Opinion," *District of Columbia v. Heller*, U.S. Supreme Court (2008)

NO: John Paul Stevens, from "Dissenting Opinion," *District of Columbia v. Heller*, U.S. Supreme Court (2008)

Learning Outcomes

After reading this issue, you will be able to:

- Discuss whether the text of the Second Amendment is clear and explicit.
- Discuss whether the Second Amendment provides an individual right to bear arms, or if the right applies only to a citizen militia.
- Discuss the Supreme Court's decision in *United States v. Miller* (1939).
- Discuss the limitations that states and cities may place on firearms ownership after *District of Columbia v. Heller* (2008).
- Discuss the impact of the Supreme Court's decision in *McDonald v. City of Chicago* (2010) on the right to own firearms.

ISSUE SUMMARY

YES: Justice Antonin E. Scalia, writing for the U.S. Supreme Court in *District of Columbia v. Heller* (2008), held that a District of Columbia law making it a crime to carry an unregistered handgun and prohibiting the registration of handguns, but that authorizes the police chief to issue one-year licenses, and requires residents to keep lawfully owned handguns unloaded and dissembled or bound by a trigger lock or similar device, violates the Second Amendment.

NO: Justice John Stevens, dissenting in *District of Columbia v. Heller* (2008), asserted that neither the text of the Second Amendment nor the arguments advanced by its proponents evidenced the slightest interest in limiting any legislature's authority to regulate private civilian uses of firearms. Moreover, there is no indication that the Framers intended to enshrine the common-law right of self-defense in the constitution.

The Right to Bear Arms may well be one of the more controversial issues in this volume. Proponents of such a right, including powerful lobbying interests such as the National Rifle Association (NRA), believe that the right to bear arms is a fundamental one. Firearms ownership should be an individual right guaranteed by the Second Amendment to the U.S. Constitution. Opponents of an individual right to bear arms contend that the Second Amendment refers to the right of a citizen militia to possess guns and that states and the U.S. federal government may justifiably regulate the ownership of firearms. This controversy is further exacerbated by the text of the Second Amendment, which on its face is not entirely clear:

> A well regulated Militia, being necessary to the security of a free State, the right of the people to keep and bear Arms, shall not be infringed.

Does the wording of this amendment imply that only persons who are part of a "well regulated Militia" have a right to keep and bear arms? Or, does it imply that the "people" have a "right to keep and bear Arms," independent of their association with a militia? These are questions that have challenged U.S. courts throughout U.S. history.

In *United States v. Emerson*, 270 F.3d 203 (5th Cir. 2001), the U.S. Court of Appeals identified three different basic interpretations of the Second Amendment. First, the "Second Amendment does not apply to individuals; rather, it merely recognizes the right of a state to arm its militia."

Advocates of another model of the Second Amendment assert that it recognizes some limited individual rights. "However, this supposedly 'individual' right to bear arms can only be exercised by members of a functioning, organized state militia who bear the arms while and as a part of actively participating in the organized militia's activities." It applies only if the U.S. federal or state governments fail to provide the firearms necessary for such militia service. The Court also asserted that the only such organized and actively functioning militia is the National Guard. Moreover, "under this model, the Second Amendment poses no obstacle to the wholesale disarmament of the American people." This perspective on the Second Amendment is often termed "the collective rights model."

A third model emphasizes that the Second Amendment provides a right for individuals to keep and bear arms. This view has received considerable academic endorsement, "especially in the last two decades." The U.S. Court of Appeals agreed with this perspective and held that the Second Amendment to the U.S. Constitution guarantees individuals the right to keep and bear arms.

The U.S. Court of Appeals for the Ninth Circuit has a different view of the Second Amendment, however. *Silveira v. Lockyear*, 312 F.3d 1052 (9th Cir. 2002), presented a challenge to California's gun control laws that placed restrictions on the possession, use, and transfer of semiautomatic weapons, often called "assault weapons." The plaintiff asserted, among other things, that the Second Amendment conferred an individual right to own and possess firearms. The U.S. Court of Appeals held, however, that "[t]he Amendment protects the people's right to maintain an effective state militia, and does not establish an individual right to own or possess firearms for personal or other use."

Both of the decisions cited above considered an important but somewhat cryptic Supreme Court precedent interpreting the Second Amendment. In *United States v. Miller*, 307 U.S. 174 (1939), the defendant was charged with possessing and transporting in interstate commerce a sawed-off shotgun with a barrel less than 18 inches long,

without having registered it and without having in his possession a stamp-affixed written order for it, as required by the National Firearms Act. At his trial in the U.S. District Court, Western District of Arkansas, the defendant alleged that the statute was an unconstitutional violation of the Tenth Amendment because it usurped states' "police power." The defendant further argued that the statute violated the Second Amendment to the U.S. Constitution. The U.S. District Court agreed and held that the National Firearms Act violated the Second Amendment.

On appeal, Justice James C. McReynolds, writing for the U.S. Supreme Court, quickly dismissed the defendant's Tenth Amendment claim. The defendant's Second Amendment claim was somewhat more compelling; however, Justice McReynolds held:

> In the absence of any evidence tending to show that possession or use of a "shotgun having a barrel of less than eighteen inches in length" at this time has some reasonable relationship to the preservation or efficiency of a well regulated militia, we cannot say that the Second Amendment guarantees the right to keep and bear such an instrument.

Justice McReynolds also presented a detailed historical analysis of what the Framers of the Second Amendment considered a "militia" to be. He stated that the militia in colonial America comprised "all males physically capable of acting in concert for the common defense." Further, when these individuals were called for service they "were expected to appear bearing arms supplied by themselves and of the kind in common use at that time." Therefore, the Court held that because the Second Amendment did not protect an individual's right to own firearms, the National Firearms Act was a lawful exercise of Congressional authority.

In 2008, the U.S. Supreme Court considered the case excerpted in this section, *District of Columbia v. Heller*, 554 U.S. 570 (2008). In *Heller*, the Court was asked to reconsider *United States v. Miller*'s holding that the Second Amendment did not protect an individual's right to own firearms. The facts that gave rise to *Heller* are as follows: The District of Columbia had passed a law making it a crime to carry an unregistered handgun and prohibiting the registration of handguns, but that authorized the police chief to issue one-year licenses, and required residents to keep lawfully owned handguns unloaded and dissembled or bound by a trigger lock or similar device. Heller, a D.C. special policeman, applied to register a handgun he wished to keep at home, but the city denied his application. He then filed suit in U.S. District Court to prevent the city from enforcing the ban on handgun registration, the licensing requirement insofar as it prohibits carrying an unlicensed firearm in the home, and the trigger-lock requirement insofar as it prohibits the use of functional firearms in the home. The District Court dismissed the suit, but the U.S. Court of Appeals (D.C. Cir.) reversed, holding that the Second Amendment protects an individual's right to possess firearms and that the city's total ban on handguns, as well as its requirement that firearms in the home be kept non-functional even when needed for self-defense, violated that right.

The U.S. Supreme Court granted certiorari and held that the Second Amendment protects an individual right to possess a firearm unconnected with service in a militia, and to use that weapon for traditionally lawful purposes, such as self-defense. Accordingly, Justice Antonin Scalia, writing for a five-to-four majority, concluded:

> We are aware of the problem of handgun violence in this country, and we take seriously the concerns raised by the many amici who believe that prohibition of handgun ownership is the solution. The Constitution leaves the District of Columbia a variety of tools for combating that problem, including some measures regulating handguns. But the enshrinement of constitutional rights necessarily takes certain policy choices off the table. These include the absolute prohibition of handguns held and used for self-defense in the home. . . . It is not the role of this Court to pronounce the Second Amendment extinct.

In a compelling dissenting opinion, Justice John Stevens took issue with the majority's conclusion. Stated Justice Stevens:

> The court properly disclaims any interest in evaluating the wisdom of the specific policy choice challenged in this case, but it fails to pay heed to a far more important policy choice—the choice made by the Framers themselves. The Court would have us believe that over 200 years ago, the Framers made a choice to limit the tools available to elected officials wishing to regulate civilian uses of weapons, and to authorize this Court to use the common-law process of case-by-case judicial lawmaking to define the contours of acceptable gun control policy. Absent compelling evidence that is nowhere to be found in the Court's opinion, I could not possibly conclude that the Framers made such a choice.

Who presents the more compelling view of the rights guaranteed by the Second Amendment, Justice Scalia or Justice Stevens? If you agree with Justice Scalia, what, if any limitations, would you allow society to place on firearms ownership? Moreover, as you read the excerpts from the opinions in this important case, consider whether society should be able to limit other aspects of firearms ownership, such as the possession of Teflon-coated bullets, which can penetrate the bulletproof vests worn by many police officers.

YES ↵

Antonin E. Scalia

Majority Opinion, *District of Columbia v. Heller*

Justice Scalia delivered the opinion of the Court.

We consider whether a District of Columbia prohibition on the possession of usable handguns in the home violates the Second Amendment to the Constitution.

I

The District of Columbia generally prohibits the possession of handguns. It is a crime to carry an unregistered firearm, and the registration of handguns is prohibited. See D. C. Code §§7-2501.01(12), 7-2502.01(a), 7-2502.02(a)(4) (2001). Wholly apart from that prohibition, no person may carry a handgun without a license, but the chief of police may issue licenses for 1-year periods. See §§22-4504(a), 22-4506. District of Columbia law also requires residents to keep their lawfully owned firearms, such as registered long guns, "unloaded and dissembled or bound by a trigger lock or similar device" unless they are located in a place of business or are being used for lawful recreational activities. See §7-2507.02.

Respondent Dick Heller is a D.C. special police officer authorized to carry a handgun while on duty at the Federal Judicial Center. He applied for a registration certificate for a handgun that he wished to keep at home, but the District refused. He thereafter filed a lawsuit in the Federal District Court for the District of Columbia seeking, on Second Amendment grounds, to enjoin the city from enforcing the bar on the registration of handguns, the licensing requirement insofar as it prohibits the carrying of a firearm in the home without a license, and the trigger-lock requirement insofar as it prohibits the use of "functional firearms within the home." App. 59a. The District Court dismissed respondent's complaint, see *Parker v. District of Columbia*, 311 F. Supp. 2d 103, 109 (2004). The Court of Appeals for the District of Columbia Circuit, construing his complaint as seeking the right to render a firearm operable and carry it about his home in that condition only when necessary for self-defense, reversed, see *Parker v.*

District of Columbia, 478 F. 3d 370, 401 (2007). It held that the Second Amendment protects an individual right to possess firearms and that the city's total ban on handguns, as well as its requirement that firearms in the home be kept nonfunctional even when necessary for self-defense, violated that right. See *id.*, at 395, 399–401. The Court of Appeals directed the District Court to enter summary judgment for respondent.

We granted certiorari. 552 U.S. ___ (2007).

II

We turn first to the meaning of the Second Amendment.

A

The Second Amendment provides: "A well regulated Militia, being necessary to the security of a free State, the right of the people to keep and bear Arms, shall not be infringed." In interpreting this text, we are guided by the principle that "[t]he Constitution was written to be understood by the voters; its words and phrases were used in their normal and ordinary as distinguished from technical meaning." *United States v. Sprague*, 282 U. S. 716, 731 (1931); see also *Gibbons v. Ogden*, 9 Wheat. 1, 188 (1824). Normal meaning may of course include an idiomatic meaning, but it excludes secret or technical meanings that would not have been known to ordinary citizens in the founding generation.

The two sides in this case have set out very different interpretations of the Amendment. Petitioners and today's dissenting Justices believe that it protects only the right to possess and carry a firearm in connection with militia service. See Brief for Petitioners 11-12; *post,* at 1 (Stevens, J., dissenting). Respondent argues that it protects an individual right to possess a firearm unconnected with service in a militia, and to use that arm for traditionally lawful purposes, such as self-defense within the home. See Brief for Respondent 2-4.

Scalia, Antonin E. Supreme Court of the United States, June 26, 2008.

The Second Amendment is naturally divided into two parts: its prefatory clause and its operative clause. The former does not limit the latter grammatically, but rather announces a purpose. The Amendment could be rephrased, "Because a well regulated Militia is necessary to the security of a free State, the right of the people to keep and bear Arms shall not be infringed." See J. Tiffany, A Treatise on Government and Constitutional Law §585, p. 394 (1867); Brief for Professors of Linguistics and English as *Amici Curiae* 3 (hereinafter Linguists' Brief). Although this structure of the Second Amendment is unique in our Constitution, other legal documents of the founding era, particularly individual-rights provisions of state constitutions, commonly included a prefatory statement of purpose. See generally Volokh, The Commonplace Second Amendment, 73 N. Y. U. L. Rev. 793, 814–821 (1998).

Logic demands that there be a link between the stated purpose and the command. The Second Amendment would be nonsensical if it read, "A well regulated Militia, being necessary to the security of a free State, the right of the people to petition for redress of grievances shall not be infringed." That requirement of logical connection may cause a prefatory clause to resolve an ambiguity in the operative clause ("The separation of church and state being an important objective, the teachings of canons shall have no place in our jurisprudence." The preface makes clear that the operative clause refers not to canons of interpretation but to clergymen.) But apart from that clarifying function, a prefatory clause does not limit or expand the scope of the operative clause. See F. Dwarris, A General Treatise on Statutes, 268–269 (P. Potter ed. 1871) (hereinafter Dwarris); T. Sedgwick, The Interpretation and Construction of Statutory and Constitutional Law, 42–45 (2d ed. 1874). "It is nothing unusual in acts . . . for the enacting part to go beyond the preamble; the remedy often extends beyond the particular act or mischief which first suggested the necessity of the law." J. Bishop, Commentaries on Written Laws and Their Interpretation §51, p. 49 (1882) (quoting *Rex v. Marks*, 3 East, 157, 165 (K. B. 1802)). Therefore, while we will begin our textual analysis with the operative clause, we will return to the prefatory clause to ensure that our reading of the operative clause is consistent with the announced purpose.

1. Operative Clause.

a. "Right of the People." The first salient feature of the operative clause is that it codifies a "right of the people." The unamended Constitution and the Bill of Rights use the phrase "right of the people" two other times, in the First Amendment's Assembly-and-Petition Clause and in the Fourth Amendment's Search-and-Seizure Clause. The Ninth Amendment uses very similar terminology ("The enumeration in the Constitution, of certain rights, shall not be construed to deny or disparage others retained by the people"). All three of these instances unambiguously refer to individual rights, not "collective" rights, or rights that may be exercised only through participation in some corporate body.

Three provisions of the Constitution refer to "the people" in a context other than "rights"—the famous preamble ("We the people"), §2 of Article I (providing that "the people" will choose members of the House), and the Tenth Amendment (providing that those powers not given the Federal Government remain with "the States" or "the people"). Those provisions arguably refer to "the people" acting collectively—but they deal with the exercise or reservation of powers, not rights. Nowhere else in the Constitution does a "right" attributed to "the people" refer to anything other than an individual right.

What is more, in all six other provisions of the Constitution that mention "the people," the term unambiguously refers to all members of the political community, not an unspecified subset. As we said in *United States v. Verdugo-Urquidez*, 494 U. S. 259, 265 (1990):

> "'[T]he people' seems to have been a term of art employed in select parts of the Constitution. . . . [Its uses] sugges[t] that 'the people' protected by the Fourth Amendment, and by the First and Second Amendments, and to whom rights and powers are reserved in the Ninth and Tenth Amendments, refers to a class of persons who are part of a national community or who have otherwise developed sufficient connection with this country to be considered part of that community."

This contrasts markedly with the phrase "the militia" in the prefatory clause. As we will describe below, the "militia" in colonial America consisted of a subset of "the people"—those who were male, able bodied, and within a certain age range. Reading the Second Amendment as protecting only the right to "keep and bear Arms" in an organized militia therefore fits poorly with the operative clause's description of the holder of that right as "the people."

We start therefore with a strong presumption that the Second Amendment right is exercised individually and belongs to all Americans.

b. "Keep and bear Arms." We move now from the holder of the right— "the people"—to the substance of the right: "to keep and bear Arms."

Before addressing the verbs "keep" and "bear," we interpret their object: "Arms." The 18th-century meaning is no different from the meaning today. The 1773 edition of Samuel Johnson's dictionary defined "arms" as "weapons of offence, or armour of defence." 1 *Dictionary of the English Language* 107 (4th ed.) (hereinafter Johnson). Timothy Cunningham's important 1771 legal dictionary defined "arms" as "any thing that a man wears for his defence, or takes into his hands, or useth in wrath to cast at or strike another." 1 *A New and Complete Law Dictionary* (1771); see also N. Webster, American Dictionary of the English Language (1828) (reprinted 1989) (hereinafter Webster) (similar).

The term was applied, then as now, to weapons that were not specifically designed for military use and were not employed in a military capacity. For instance, Cunningham's legal dictionary gave as an example of usage: "Servants and labourers shall use bows and arrows on *Sundays,* &c. and not bear other arms." See also, e.g., An Act for the trial of Negroes, 1797 Del. Laws ch. XLIII, §6, p. 104, in *First Laws of the state of Delaware* 102, 104 (J. Cushing ed. 1981 (pt. 1)); see generally *State v. Duke,* 42 Tex. 455, 458 (1874) (citing decisions of state courts construing "arms"). Although one founding-era thesaurus limited "arms" (as opposed to "weapons") to "instruments of offence *generally* made use of in war," even that source stated that all firearms constituted "arms." 1 J. Trusler, The Distinction Between Words Esteemed Synonymous in the English Language 37 (1794) (emphasis added).

Some have made the argument, bordering on the frivolous, that only those arms in existence in the 18th century are protected by the Second Amendment. We do not interpret constitutional rights that way. Just as the First Amendment protects modern forms of communications, e.g., *Reno v. American Civil Liberties Union,* 521 U. S. 844, 849 (1997), and the Fourth Amendment applies to modern forms of search, e.g., *Kyllo v. United States,* 533 U. S. 27, 35–36 (2001), the Second Amendment extends, prima facie, to all instruments that constitute bearable arms, even those that were not in existence at the time of the founding.

We turn to the phrases "keep arms" and "bear arms." Johnson defined "keep" as, most relevantly, "[t]o retain; not to lose," and "[t]o have in custody." Johnson 1095. Webster defined it as "[t]o hold; to retain in one's power or possession." No party has apprised us of an idiomatic meaning of "keep Arms." Thus, the most natural reading of "keep Arms" in the Second Amendment is to "have weapons."

The phrase "keep arms" was not prevalent in the written documents of the founding period that we have found, but there are a few examples, all of which favor viewing the right to "keep Arms" as an individual right unconnected with militia service. William Blackstone, for example, wrote that Catholics convicted of not attending service in the Church of England suffered certain penalties, one of which was that they were not permitted to "keep arms in their houses." 4 Commentaries on the Laws of England 55 (1769) (hereinafter Blackstone); see also 1 W. & M., c. 15, §4, in 3 Eng. Stat. at Large 422 (1689) ("[N]o Papist . . . shall or may have or keep in his House . . . any Arms . . ."); 1 Hawkins, Treatise on the Pleas of the Crown 26 (1771) (similar). Petitioners point to militia laws of the founding period that required militia members to "keep" arms in connection with militia service, and they conclude from this that the phrase "keep Arms" has a militia-related connotation. See Brief for Petitioners 16-17 (citing laws of Delaware, New Jersey, and Virginia). This is rather like saying that, since there are many statutes that authorize aggrieved employees to "file complaints" with federal agencies, the phrase "file complaints" has an employment-related connotation. "Keep arms" was simply a common way of referring to possessing arms, for militiamen and everyone else.

At the time of the founding, as now, to "bear" meant to "carry." See Johnson 161; Webster; T. Sheridan, A Complete Dictionary of the English Language (1796); 2 Oxford English Dictionary 20 (2d ed. 1989) (hereinafter Oxford). When used with "arms," however, the term has a meaning that refers to carrying for a particular purpose—confrontation. In *Muscarello v. United States,* 524 U. S. 125 (1998), in the course of analyzing the meaning of "carries a firearm" in a federal criminal statute, Justice Ginsburg wrote that "[s]urely a most familiar meaning is, as the Constitution's Second Amendment . . . indicate[s]: 'wear, bear, or carry . . . upon the person or in the clothing or in a pocket, for the purpose . . . of being armed and ready for offensive or defensive action in a case of conflict with another person.'" *Id.,* at 143 (dissenting opinion) (quoting *Black's Law Dictionary* 214 (6th ed. 1998)). We think that Justice Ginsburg accurately captured the natural meaning of "bear arms." Although the phrase implies that the carrying of the weapon is for the purpose of "offensive or defensive action," it in no way connotes participation in a structured military organization. . . .

c. Meaning of the Operative Clause. Putting all of these textual elements together, we find that they guarantee the individual right to possess and carry weapons in case of confrontation. This meaning is strongly confirmed by the historical background of the Second Amendment. We look to this because it has always been widely understood that the Second Amendment, like the First and Fourth Amendments, codified a *pre-existing* right. The very text of the Second Amendment implicitly recognizes the pre-existence of the right and declares only that it "shall not be infringed." As we said in *United States v. Cruikshank,* 92 U. S. 542, 553 (1876), "[t]his is not a right granted by the Constitution. Neither is it in any manner dependent upon that instrument for its existence. The Second amendment declares that it shall not be infringed. . . ."

There seems to us no doubt, on the basis of both text and history, that the Second Amendment conferred an individual right to keep and bear arms. Of course the right was not unlimited, just as the First Amendment's right of free speech was not, see, e.g., *United States v. Williams,* 553 U.S.___ (2008). Thus, we do not read the Second Amendment to protect the right of citizens to carry arms for *any sort* of confrontation, just as we do not read the First Amendment to protect the right of citizens to speak for *any purpose.* Before turning to limitations upon the individual right, however, we must determine whether the prefatory clause of the Second Amendment comports with our interpretation of the operative clause.

2. Prefatory Clause.

The prefatory clause reads: "A well regulated Militia, being necessary to the security of a free State. . . ."

a. "Well-Regulated Militia." In *United States v. Miller,* 307 U. S. 174, 179 (1939), we explained that "the Militia comprised all males physically capable of acting in concert for the common defense." That definition comports with founding-era sources. See, e.g., Webster ("The militia of a country are the able bodied men organized into companies, regiments and brigades . . . and required by law to attend military exercises on certain days only, but at other times left to pursue their usual occupations"); *The Federalist* No. 46, pp. 329, 334 (B. Wright ed. 1961) (J. Madison) ("near half a million of citizens with arms in their hands"); Letter to Destutt de Tracy (Jan. 26, 1811), in *The Portable Thomas Jefferson* 520, 524 (M. Peterson ed. 1975) ("[T]he militia of the State, that is to say, of every man in it able to bear arms").

Petitioners take a seemingly narrower view of the militia, stating that "[m]ilitias are the state- and congressionally-regulated military forces described in the Militia Clauses (art. I, §8, cls. 15-16)." Brief for Petitioners 12. Although we agree with petitioners' interpretive assumption that "militia" means the same thing in Article I and the Second Amendment, we believe that petitioners identify the wrong thing, namely, the organized militia. Unlike armies and navies, which Congress is given the power to create ("to raise . . . Armies"; "to provide . . . a Navy," Art. I, §8, cls. 12-13), the militia is assumed by Article I already to be *in existence.* Congress is given the power to "provide for calling forth the militia," §8, cl. 15; and the power

not to create, but to "organiz[e]" it—and not to organize "a" militia, which is what one would expect if the militia were to be a federal creation, but to organize "the" militia, connoting a body already in existence, *ibid.,* cl. 16. This is fully consistent with the ordinary definition of the militia as all able-bodied men. From that pool, Congress has plenary power to organize the units that will make up an effective fighting force. That is what Congress did in the first militia Act, which specified that "each and every free able-bodied white male citizen of the respective states, resident therein, who is or shall be of the age of eighteen years, and under the age of forty-five years (except as is herein after excepted) shall severally and respectively be enrolled in the militia." Act of May 8, 1792, 1 Stat. 271. To be sure, Congress need not conscript every able-bodied man into the militia, because nothing in Article I suggests that in exercising its power to organize, discipline, and arm the militia, Congress must focus upon the entire body. Although the militia consists of all able-bodied men, the federally organized militia may consist of a subset of them.

Finally, the adjective "well-regulated" implies nothing more than the imposition of proper discipline and training. See Johnson 1619 ("Regulate": "To adjust by rule or method"); Rawle 121–122; cf. Va. Declaration of Rights §13 (1776), in 7 Thorpe 3812, 3814 (referring to "a well-regulated militia, composed of the body of the people, trained to arms").

b. "Security of a Free State." The phrase "security of a free state" meant "security of a free polity," not security of each of the several States as the dissent below argued, see 478 F. 3d, at 405, and n. 10. Joseph Story wrote in his treatise on the Constitution that "the word 'state' is used in various senses [and in] its most enlarged sense, it means the people composing a particular nation or community." 1 Story §208; see also 3 *id.,* §1890 (in reference to the Second Amendment's prefatory clause: "The militia is the natural defence of a free country"). It is true that the term "State" elsewhere in the Constitution refers to individual States, but the phrase "security of a free state" and close variations seem to have been terms of art in 18th-century political discourse, meaning a "free country" or free polity. See Volokh, "Necessary to the Security of a Free State," 83 *Notre Dame L. Rev.* 1, 5 (2007); see, e.g., 4 Blackstone 151 (1769); Brutus Essay III (Nov. 15, 1787), in *The Essential Antifederalist* 251, 253 (W. Allen & G. Lloyd eds., 2d ed. 2002). Moreover, the other instances of "state" in the Constitution are typically accompanied by modifiers making clear that the reference is to the several States—"each state," "several states," "any state," "that state," "particular states," "one state," "no state." And the presence of the term "foreign state" in Article I and Article III shows that the word "state" did not have a single meaning in the Constitution.

There are many reasons why the militia was thought to be "necessary to the security of a free state." See 3 Story §1890. First, of course, it is useful in repelling invasions and suppressing insurrections. Second, it renders large standing armies unnecessary—an argument that Alexander Hamilton made in favor of federal control over the militia. The Federalist No. 29, pp. 226, 227 (B. Wright ed. 1961) (A. Hamilton). Third, when the able-bodied men of a nation are trained in arms and organized, they are better able to resist tyranny.

3. Relationship between Prefatory Clause and Operative Clause

We reach the question, then: Does the preface fit with an operative clause that creates an individual right to keep and bear arms? It fits perfectly, once one knows the history that the founding generation knew and that we have described above. That history showed that the way tyrants had eliminated a militia consisting of all the able-bodied men was not by banning the militia but simply by taking away the people's arms, enabling a select militia or standing army to suppress political opponents. This is what had occurred in England that prompted codification of the right to have arms in the English Bill of Rights. . . .

It is therefore entirely sensible that the Second Amendment's prefatory clause announces the purpose for which the right was codified: to prevent elimination of the militia. The prefatory clause does not suggest that preserving the militia was the only reason Americans valued the ancient right; most undoubtedly thought it even more important for self-defense and hunting. But the threat that the new Federal Government would destroy the citizens' militia by taking away their arms was the reason that right—unlike some other English rights—was codified in a written Constitution. Justice Breyer's assertion that individual self-defense is merely a "subsidiary interest" of the right to keep and bear arms, see *post*, at 36, is profoundly mistaken. He bases that assertion solely upon the prologue—but that can only show that self-defense had little to do with the right's *codification*; it was the *central component* of the right itself.

Besides ignoring the historical reality that the Second Amendment was not intended to lay down a "novel principl[e]" but rather codified a right "inherited from our English ancestors," *Robertson v. Baldwin,* 165 U. S. 275, 281 (1897), petitioners' interpretation does not even achieve the narrower purpose that prompted codification of the right. If, as they believe, the Second Amendment right is

no more than the right to keep and use weapons as a member of an organized militia, see *Brief for Petitioners* 8—if, that is, the *organized* militia is the sole institutional beneficiary of the Second Amendment's guarantee—it does not assure the existence of a "citizens' militia" as a safeguard against tyranny. For Congress retains plenary authority to organize the militia, which must include the authority to say who will belong to the organized force. That is why the first Militia Act's requirement that only whites enroll caused States to amend their militia laws to exclude free blacks. See Siegel, The Federal Government's Power to Enact Color-Conscious Laws, 92 *Nw. U. L. Rev.* 477, 521 (1998). Thus, if petitioners are correct, the Second Amendment protects citizens' right to use a gun in an organization from which Congress has plenary authority to exclude them. It guarantees a select militia of the sort the Stuart kings found useful, but not the people's militia that was the concern of the founding generation.

B

Our interpretation is confirmed by analogous arms-bearing rights in state constitutions that preceded and immediately followed adoption of the Second Amendment. Four States adopted analogues to the Federal Second Amendment in the period between independence and the ratification of the Bill of Rights. Two of them— Pennsylvania and Vermont—clearly adopted individual rights unconnected to militia service. Pennsylvania's Declaration of Rights of 1776 said: "That the people have a right to bear arms *for the defence of themselves,* and the state. . . ." §XIII, in 5 Thorpe 3082, 3083 (emphasis added). In 1777, Vermont adopted the identical provision, except for inconsequential differences in punctuation and capitalization. See Vt. Const., ch. 1, §15, in 6 *id.,* at 3741. . . .

We therefore believe that the most likely reading of all four of these pre-Second Amendment state constitutional provisions is that they secured an individual right to bear arms for defensive purposes. Other States did not include rights to bear arms in their pre-1789 constitutions—although in Virginia a Second Amendment analogue was proposed (unsuccessfully) by Thomas Jefferson. (It read: "No freeman shall ever be debarred the use of arms [within his own lands or tenements]." 1 The Papers of Thomas Jefferson 344 (J. Boyd ed. 1950)). . . .

The historical narrative that petitioners must endorse would thus treat the Federal Second Amendment as an odd outlier, protecting a right unknown in state constitutions or at English common law, based on little more than an overreading of the prefatory clause.

C

Justice Stevens relies on the drafting history of the Second Amendment—the various proposals in the state conventions and the debates in Congress. It is dubious to rely on such history to interpret a text that was widely understood to codify a pre-existing right, rather than to fashion a new one. But even assuming that this legislative history is relevant, Justice Stevens flatly misreads the historical record. . . .

D

1. Post-ratification Commentary

[I]mportant founding-era legal scholars interpreted the Second Amendment in published writings. All three understood it to protect an individual right unconnected with militia service. . . .

We have found only one early 19th-century commentator who clearly conditioned the right to keep and bear arms upon service in the militia—and he recognized that the prevailing view was to the contrary. "The provision of the constitution, declaring the right of the people to keep and bear arms, Etc. was probably intended to apply to the right of the people to bear arms for such [militia-related] purposes only, and not to prevent congress or the legislatures of the different states from enacting laws to prevent the citizens from always going armed. A different construction however has been given to it." B. Oliver, The Rights of an American Citizen 177 (1832). . . .

4. Post-Civil War Commentators

Every late 19th-century legal scholar that we have read interpreted the Second Amendment to secure an individual right unconnected with militia service. The most famous was the judge and professor Thomas Cooley, who wrote a massively popular 1868 Treatise on Constitutional Limitations. Concerning the Second Amendment it said:

> "Among the other defences to personal liberty should be mentioned the right of the people to keep and bear arms. . . . The alternative to a standing army is 'a well-regulated militia,' but this cannot exist unless the people are trained to bearing arms. How far it is in the power of the legislature to regulate this right, we shall not undertake to say, as happily there has been very little occasion to discuss that subject by the courts." *Id.,* at 350. . . .
>
> "[The purpose of the Second Amendment is] to secure a well-armed militia. . . . But a militia would be useless unless the citizens were enabled to exercise themselves in the use of warlike

weapons. To preserve this privilege, and to secure to the people the ability to oppose themselves in military force against the usurpations of government, as well as against enemies from without, that government is forbidden by any law or proceeding to invade or destroy the right to keep and bear arms. . . . The clause is analogous to the one securing the freedom of speech and of the press. Freedom, not license, is secured; the fair use, not the libellous abuse, is protected." J. Pomeroy, An Introduction to the Constitutional Law of the United States 152–153 (1868) (hereinafter Pomeroy). . . .

> "The right to bear arms has always been the distinctive privilege of freemen. Aside from any necessity of self-protection to the person, it represents among all nations power coupled with the exercise of a certain jurisdiction. . . . [I]t was not necessary that the right to bear arms should be granted in the Constitution, for it had always existed." J. Ordronaux, Constitutional Legislation in the United States 241–242 (1891).

E

We now ask whether any of our precedents forecloses the conclusions we have reached about the meaning of the Second Amendment. . . .

Justice Stevens places overwhelming reliance upon this Court's decision in *United States v. Miller,* 307 U. S. 174 (1939). "[H]undreds of judges," we are told, "have relied on the view of the amendment we endorsed there," *post,* at 2, and "[e]ven if the textual and historical arguments on both side of the issue were evenly balanced, respect for the well-settled views of all of our predecessors on this Court, and for the rule of law itself . . . would prevent most jurists from endorsing such a dramatic upheaval in the law," *post,* at 4. And what is, according to Justice Stevens, the holding of *Miller* that demands such obeisance? That the Second Amendment "protects the right to keep and bear arms for certain military purposes, but that it does not curtail the legislature's power to regulate the nonmilitary use and ownership of weapons." *Post,* at 2.

Nothing so clearly demonstrates the weakness of Justice Stevens' case. *Miller* did not hold that and cannot possibly be read to have held that. The judgment in the case upheld against a Second Amendment challenge two men's federal convictions for transporting an unregistered short-barreled shotgun in interstate commerce, in violation of the National Firearms Act, 48 Stat. 1236. It is entirely clear that the Court's basis for saying that the Second Amendment did not apply was *not* that the defendants were "bear[ing] arms" not "for . . . military purposes" but for "nonmilitary use," *post,* at 2. Rather, it was that the *type of weapon at issue* was not eligible for Second Amendment protection: "In the absence of any evidence tending to show that the possession or use of a [short-barreled shotgun] at this time has some reasonable relationship to the preservation or efficiency of a well regulated militia, we cannot say that the Second Amendment guarantees the right to keep and bear *such an instrument.*" 307 U. S., at 178 (emphasis added). "Certainly," the Court continued, "it is not within judicial notice that this weapon is any part of the ordinary military equipment or that its use could contribute to the common defense." *Ibid.* Beyond that, the opinion provided no explanation of the content of the right.

This holding is not only consistent with, but positively suggests, that the Second Amendment confers an individual right to keep and bear arms (though only arms that "have some reasonable relationship to the preservation or efficiency of a well regulated militia"). Had the Court believed that the Second Amendment protects only those serving in the militia, it would have been odd to examine the character of the weapon rather than simply note that the two crooks were not militiamen. Justice Stevens can say again and again that *Miller* did "not turn on the difference between muskets and sawed-off shotguns, it turned, rather, on the basic difference between the military and nonmilitary use and possession of guns," *post,* at 42–43, but the words of the opinion prove otherwise. The most Justice Stevens can plausibly claim for *Miller* is that it declined to decide the nature of the Second Amendment right, despite the Solicitor General's argument (made in the alternative) that the right was collective, see Brief for United States, O. T. 1938, No. 696, pp. 4–5. *Miller* stands only for the proposition that the Second Amendment right, whatever its nature, extends only to certain types of weapons. . . .

We may as well consider at this point (for we will have to consider eventually) *what* types of weapons *Miller* permits. Read in isolation, *Miller*'s phrase "part of ordinary military equipment" could mean that only those weapons useful in warfare are protected. That would be a startling reading of the opinion, since it would mean that the National Firearms Act's restrictions on machineguns (not challenged in *Miller)* might be unconstitutional, machineguns being useful in warfare in 1939. We think that *Miller*'s "ordinary military equipment" language must be read in tandem with what comes after: "[O]rdinarily when called for [militia] service [able-bodied] men were expected to appear bearing arms supplied by themselves and of the kind in common use at the time." 307 U. S., at 179. The traditional militia was formed from a pool of

men bringing arms "in common use at the time" for lawful purposes like self-defense. "In the colonial and revolutionary war era, [small-arms] weapons used by militiamen and weapons used in defense of person and home were one and the same." *State v. Kessler,* 289 Ore. 359, 368, 614 P. 2d 94, 98 (1980) (citing G. Neumann, Swords and Blades of the American Revolution 6–15, 252–254 (1973)). Indeed, that is precisely the way in which the Second Amendment's operative clause furthers the purpose announced in its preface. We therefore read *Miller* to say only that the Second Amendment does not protect those weapons not typically possessed by law-abiding citizens for lawful purposes, such as short-barreled shotguns. That accords with the historical understanding of the scope of the right, see Part III, infra.

We conclude that nothing in our precedents forecloses our adoption of the original understanding of the Second Amendment. It should be unsurprising that such a significant matter has been for so long judicially unresolved. For most of our history, the Bill of Rights was not thought applicable to the States, and the Federal Government did not significantly regulate the possession of firearms by law-abiding citizens. Other provisions of the Bill of Rights have similarly remained unilluminated for lengthy periods. This Court first held a law to violate the First Amendment's guarantee of freedom of speech in 1931, almost 150 years after the Amendment was ratified, see Near *v. Minnesota ex rel. Olson,* 283 U.S. 697 (1931), and it was not until after World War II that we held a law invalid under the Establishment Clause, see *Illinois ex rel. McCollum v. Board of Ed. of School Dist. No. 71, Champaign Cty.,* 333 U. S. 203 (1948). Even a question as basic as the scope of proscribable libel was not addressed by this Court until 1964, nearly two centuries after the founding. See *New York Times Co. v. Sullivan,* 376 U. S. 254 (1964). It is demonstrably not true that, as Justice Stevens claims, *post,* at 41–42, "for most of our history, the invalidity of Second-Amendment-based objections to firearms regulations has been well settled and uncontroversial." For most of our history the question did not present itself.

III

Like most rights, the right secured by the Second Amendment is not unlimited. From Blackstone through the 19th-century cases, commentators and courts routinely explained that the right was not a right to keep and carry any weapon whatsoever in any manner whatsoever and for whatever purpose. See, e.g., *Sheldon,* in 5 Blume 346; Rawle 123; Pomeroy 152–153; Abbott 333. For example, the majority of the 19th-century courts to consider the question held that prohibitions on carrying concealed weapons were lawful under the Second Amendment or state analogues. See, e.g., *State v. Chandler*, 5 La. Ann., at 489–490; *Nunn v. State*, 1 Ga., at 251; see generally 2 Kent *340, n. 2; The American Students' Blackstone 84, n. 11 (G. Chase ed. 1884). Although we do not undertake an exhaustive historical analysis today of the full scope of the Second Amendment, nothing in our opinion should be taken to cast doubt on longstanding prohibitions on the possession of firearms by felons and the mentally ill, or laws forbidding the carrying of firearms in sensitive places such as schools and government buildings, or laws imposing conditions and qualifications on the commercial sale of arms.

We also recognize another important limitation on the right to keep and carry arms. *Miller* said, as we have explained, that the sorts of weapons protected were those "in common use at the time." 307 U.S., at 179. We think that limitation is fairly supported by the historical tradition of prohibiting the carrying of "dangerous and unusual weapons." . . .

IV

We turn finally to the law at issue here. As we have said, the law totally bans handgun possession in the home. It also requires that any lawful firearm in the home be disassembled or bound by a trigger lock at all times, rendering it inoperable.

As the quotations earlier in this opinion demonstrate, the inherent right of self-defense has been central to the Second Amendment right. The handgun ban amounts to a prohibition of an entire class of "arms" that is overwhelmingly chosen by American society for that lawful purpose. The prohibition extends, moreover, to the home, where the need for defense of self, family, and property is most acute. Under any of the standards of scrutiny that we have applied to enumerated constitutional rights, banning from the home "the most preferred firearm in the nation to 'keep' and use for protection of one's home and family," 478 F. 3d, at 400, would fail constitutional muster.

Few laws in the history of our Nation have come close to the severe restriction of the District's handgun ban. And some of those few have been struck down. In *Nunn v. State*, the Georgia Supreme Court struck down a prohibition on carrying pistols openly (even though it upheld a prohibition on carrying concealed weapons). See 1 Ga., at 251. In *Andrews v. State*, the Tennessee Supreme Court likewise held that a statute that forbade openly carrying a pistol

"publicly or privately, without regard to time or place, or circumstances," 50 Tenn., at 187, violated the state constitutional provision (which the court equated with the Second Amendment). That was so even though the statute did not restrict the carrying of long guns. *Ibid*. See also *State v. Reid*, 1 Ala. 612, 616–617 (1840) ("A statute which, under the pretence of regulating, amounts to a destruction of the right, or which requires arms to be so borne as to render them wholly useless for the purpose of defence, would be clearly unconstitutional").

It is no answer to say, as petitioners do, that it is permissible to ban the possession of handguns so long as the possession of other firearms (i.e., long guns) is allowed. It is enough to note, as we have observed, that the American people have considered the handgun to be the quintessential self-defense weapon. There are many reasons that a citizen may prefer a handgun for home defense: It is easier to store in a location that is readily accessible in an emergency; it cannot easily be redirected or wrestled away by an attacker; it is easier to use for those without the upper-body strength to lift and aim a long gun; it can be pointed at a burglar with one hand while the other hand dials the police. Whatever the reason, handguns are the most popular weapon chosen by Americans for self-defense in the home, and a complete prohibition of their use is invalid.

We must also address the District's requirement (as applied to respondent's handgun) that firearms in the home be rendered and kept inoperable at all times. This makes it impossible for citizens to use them for the core lawful purpose of self-defense and is hence unconstitutional. The District argues that we should interpret this element of the statute to contain an exception for self-defense. See *Brief for Petitioners* 56–57. But we think that is precluded by the unequivocal text, and by the presence of certain other enumerated exceptions: "Except for law enforcement personnel . . ., each registrant shall keep any firearm in his possession unloaded and disassembled or bound by a trigger lock or similar device unless such firearm is kept at his place of business, or while being used for lawful recreational purposes within the District of Columbia." D. C. Code §7-2507.02. The nonexistence of a self-defense exception is also suggested by the D. C. Court of Appeals' statement that the statute forbids residents to use firearms to stop intruders, see *McIntosh v. Washington*, 395 A. 2d 744, 755–756 (1978). . . .

In sum, we hold that the District's ban on handgun possession in the home violates the Second Amendment, as does its prohibition against rendering any lawful firearm in the home operable for the purpose of immediate self-defense. Assuming that Heller is not disqualified from the exercise of Second Amendment rights, the District must permit him to register his handgun and must issue him a license to carry it in the home.

*   *   *

We are aware of the problem of handgun violence in this country, and we take seriously the concerns raised by the many *amici* who believe that prohibition of handgun ownership is a solution. The Constitution leaves the District of Columbia a variety of tools for combating that problem, including some measures regulating handguns, see *supra,* at 54–55, and n. 26. But the enshrinement of constitutional rights necessarily takes certain policy choices off the table. These include the absolute prohibition of handguns held and used for self-defense in the home. Undoubtedly some think that the Second Amendment is outmoded in a society where our standing army is the pride of our Nation, where well-trained police forces provide personal security, and where gun violence is a serious problem. That is perhaps debatable, but what is not debatable is that it is not the role of this Court to pronounce the Second Amendment extinct.

We affirm the judgment of the Court of Appeals.

It is so ordered.

ANTONIN E. SCALIA is an associate justice of the U.S. Supreme Court. He taught law at the University of Virginia, the American Enterprise Institute, Georgetown University, and the University of Chicago before being nominated to the U.S. Court of Appeals by President Ronald Reagan in 1982. He served in that capacity until he was nominated by Reagan to the Supreme Court in 1986.

John Paul Stevens → **NO**

Dissenting Opinion, *District of Columbia v. Heller*

Supreme Court of the United States District of Columbia, *et al.*, Petitioners *v.* Dick Anthony Heller

Justice Stevens, **with whom** Justice Souter, Justice Ginsburg, **and** Justice Breyer **join, dissenting.**

The question presented by this case is not whether the Second Amendment protects a "collective right" or an "individual right." Surely it protects a right that can be enforced by individuals. But a conclusion that the Second Amendment protects an individual right does not tell us anything about the scope of that right.

Guns are used to hunt, for self-defense, to commit crimes, for sporting activities, and to perform military duties. The Second Amendment plainly does not protect the right to use a gun to rob a bank; it is equally clear that it *does* encompass the right to use weapons for certain military purposes. Whether it also protects the right to possess and use guns for nonmilitary purposes like hunting and personal self-defense is the question presented by this case. The text of the Amendment, its history, and our decision in *United States v. Miller*, 307 U. S. 174 (1939), provide a clear answer to that question.

The Second Amendment was adopted to protect the right of the people of each of the several States to maintain a well-regulated militia. It was a response to concerns raised during the ratification of the Constitution that the power of Congress to disarm the state militias and create a national standing army posed an intolerable threat to the sovereignty of the several States. Neither the text of the Amendment nor the arguments advanced by its proponents evidenced the slightest interest in limiting any legislature's authority to regulate private civilian uses of firearms. Specifically, there is no indication that the Framers of the Amendment intended to enshrine the common-law right of self-defense in the Constitution.

In 1934, Congress enacted the National Firearms Act, the first major federal firearms law. Upholding a conviction under that Act, this Court held that, "[i]n the absence of any evidence tending to show that possession or use of a 'shotgun having a barrel of less than eighteen inches in length' at this time has some reasonable relationship to the preservation or efficiency of a well regulated militia, we cannot say that the Second Amendment guarantees the right to keep and bear such an instrument." *Miller*, 307 U.S., at 178. The view of the Amendment we took in *Miller*—that it protects the right to keep and bear arms for certain military purposes, but that it does not curtail the Legislature's power to regulate the nonmilitary use and ownership of weapons—is both the most natural reading of the Amendment's text and the interpretation most faithful to the history of its adoption.

Since our decision in *Miller,* hundreds of judges have relied on the view of the Amendment we endorsed there; we ourselves affirmed it in 1980. See *Lewis v. United States,* 445 U.S. 55, n. 8 (1980). No new evidence has surfaced since 1980 supporting the view that the Amendment was intended to curtail the power of Congress to regulate civilian use or misuse of weapons. Indeed, a review of the drafting history of the Amendment demonstrates that its Framers *rejected* proposals that would have broadened its coverage to include such uses.

The opinion the Court announces today fails to identify any new evidence supporting the view that the Amendment was intended to limit the power of Congress to regulate civilian uses of weapons. Unable to point to any such evidence, the Court stakes its holding on a strained and unpersuasive reading of the Amendment's text; significantly different provisions in the 1689 English Bill of Rights, and in various 19th-century State Constitutions; postenactment commentary that was available to the Court when it decided *Miller;* and, ultimately, a feeble attempt to distinguish *Miller* that places more emphasis on the Court's decisional process than on the reasoning in the opinion itself.

Even if the textual and historical arguments on both sides of the issue were evenly balanced, respect for the well-settled views of all of our predecessors on this Court,

Stevens, John P. Supreme Court of the United States, June 26, 2008.

and for the rule of law itself, see *Mitchell v. W. T. Grant Co.,* 416 U. S. 600, 636 (1974) (Stewart, J., dissenting), would prevent most jurists from endorsing such a dramatic upheaval in the law. As Justice Cardozo observed years ago, the "labor of judges would be increased almost to the breaking point if every past decision could be reopened in every case, and one could not lay one's own course of bricks on the secure foundation of the courses laid by others who had gone before him." The Nature of the Judicial Process 149 (1921).

In this dissent I shall first explain why our decision in *Miller* was faithful to the text of the Second Amendment and the purposes revealed in its drafting history. I shall then comment on the postratification history of the Amendment, which makes abundantly clear that the Amendment should not be interpreted as limiting the authority of Congress to regulate the use or possession of firearms for purely civilian purposes.

I

The text of the Second Amendment is brief. It provides: "A well regulated Militia, being necessary to the security of a free State, the right of the people to keep and bear Arms, shall not be infringed."

Three portions of that text merit special focus: the introductory language defining the Amendment's purpose, the class of persons encompassed within its reach, and the unitary nature of the right that it protects.

"A well regulated Militia, being necessary to the security of a free State"

The preamble to the Second Amendment makes three important points. It identifies the preservation of the militia as the Amendment's purpose; it explains that the militia is necessary to the security of a free State; and it recognizes that the militia must be "well regulated." In all three respects it is comparable to provisions in several State Declarations of Rights that were adopted roughly contemporaneously with the Declaration of Independence. Those state provisions highlight the importance members of the founding generation attached to the maintenance of state militias; they also underscore the profound fear shared by many in that era of the dangers posed by standing armies. While the need for state militias has not been a matter of significant public interest for almost two centuries, that fact should not obscure the contemporary concerns that animated the Framers. . . .

"The right of the people."

. . . The Court overlooks the significance of the way the Framers used the phrase "the people" in these constitutional provisions. In the First Amendment, no words define the class of individuals entitled to speak, to publish, or to worship; in that Amendment it is only the right peaceably to assemble, and to petition the Government for a redress of grievances, that is described as a right of "the people." These rights contemplate collective action. While the right peaceably to assemble protects the individual rights of those persons participating in the assembly, its concern is with action engaged in by members of a group, rather than any single individual. Likewise, although the act of petitioning the Government is a right that can be exercised by individuals, it is primarily collective in nature. For if they are to be effective, petitions must involve groups of individuals acting in concert.

Similarly, the words "the people" in the Second Amendment refer back to the object announced in the Amendment's preamble. They remind us that it is the collective action of individuals having a duty to serve in the militia that the text directly protects and, perhaps more importantly, that the ultimate purpose of the Amendment was to protect the States' share of the divided sovereignty created by the Constitution. . . .

"To keep and bear Arms"

Although the Court's discussion of these words treats them as two "phrases"—as if they read "to keep" and "to bear"—they describe a unitary right: to possess arms if needed for military purposes and to use them in conjunction with military activities.

As a threshold matter, it is worth pausing to note an oddity in the Court's interpretation of "to keep and bear arms." Unlike the Court of Appeals, the Court does not read that phrase to create a right to possess arms for "lawful, private purposes." *Parker v. District of Columbia,* 478 F. 3d 370, 382 (CADC 2007). Instead, the Court limits the Amendment's protection to the right "to possess and carry weapons in case of confrontation." *Ante,* at 19. No party or *amicus* urged this interpretation; the Court appears to have fashioned it out of whole cloth. But although this novel limitation lacks support in the text of the Amendment, the Amendment's text *does* justify a different limitation: the "right to keep and bear arms" protects only a right to possess and use firearms in connection with service in a state-organized militia.

The term "bear arms" is a familiar idiom; when used unadorned by any additional words, its meaning is "to serve as a soldier, do military service, fight." 1 *Oxford English Dictionary* 634 (2d ed. 1989). It is derived from the Latin *arma ferre,* which, translated literally, means "to bear *[ferre]* war equipment *[arma]*." Brief for Professors of Linguistics and English as *Amici Curiae* 19. One 18th-century dictionary defined "arms" as "weapons of offence, or armour of defence," 1 S. Johnson, *A Dictionary of the English Language* (1755), and another contemporaneous source explained that "[b]y *arms,* we understand those instruments of offence generally made use of in war; such as firearms, swords, & c. By *weapons,* we more particularly mean instruments of other kinds (exclusive of fire-arms), made use of as offensive, on special occasions." 1 J. Trusler, The Distinction Between Words Esteemed Synonymous in the English Language 37 (1794). Had the Framers wished to expand the meaning of the phrase "bear arms" to encompass civilian possession and use, they could have done so by the addition of phrases such as "for the defense of themselves," as was done in the Pennsylvania and Vermont Declarations of Rights. The *unmodified* use of "bear arms," by contrast, refers most naturally to a military purpose, as evidenced by its use in literally dozens of contemporary texts. The absence of any reference to civilian uses of weapons tailors the text of the Amendment to the purpose identified in its preamble. But when discussing these words, the Court simply ignores the preamble. . . .

This reading is confirmed by the fact that the clause protects only one right, rather than two. It does not describe a right "to keep arms" and a separate right "to bear arms." Rather, the single right that it does describe is both a duty and a right to have arms available and ready for military service, and to use them for military purposes when necessary. Different language surely would have been used to protect nonmilitary use and possession of weapons from regulation if such an intent had played any role in the drafting of the Amendment.

*   *   *

When each word in the text is given full effect, the Amendment is most naturally read to secure to the people a right to use and possess arms in conjunction with service in a well-regulated militia. So far as appears, no more than that was contemplated by its drafters or is encompassed within its terms. Even if the meaning of the text were genuinely susceptible to more than one interpretation, the burden would remain on those advocating a departure from the purpose identified in the preamble and from settled law to come forward with persuasive new arguments or evidence. The textual analysis offered by respondent and embraced by the Court falls far short of sustaining that heavy burden. And the Court's emphatic reliance on the claim "that

the Second Amendment . . . codified a *pre-existing* right," *ante,* at 19, is of course beside the point because the right to keep and bear arms for service in a state militia was also a pre-existing right.

Indeed, not a word in the constitutional text even arguably supports the Court's overwrought and novel description of the Second Amendment as "elevat[ing] above all other interests" "the right of law-abiding, responsible citizens to use arms in defense of hearth and home." *Ante,* at 63.

II

The proper allocation of military power in the new Nation was an issue of central concern for the Framers. The compromises they ultimately reached, reflected in Article I's Militia Clauses and the Second Amendment, represent quintessential examples of the Framers' "splitting the atom of sovereignty." . . .

Madison, charged with the task of assembling the proposals for amendments sent by the ratifying States, was the principal draftsman of the Second Amendment. He had before him, or at the very least would have been aware of, all of these proposed formulations. In addition, Madison had been a member, some years earlier, of the committee tasked with drafting the Virginia Declaration of Rights. That committee considered a proposal by Thomas Jefferson that would have included within the Virginia Declaration the following language: "No freeman shall ever be debarred the use of arms [within his own lands or tenements]." 1 Papers of Thomas Jefferson 363 (J. Boyd ed. 1950). . . .

With all of these sources upon which to draw, it is strikingly significant that Madison's first draft omitted any mention of nonmilitary use or possession of weapons. Rather, his original draft repeated the essence of the two proposed amendments sent by Virginia, combining the substance of the two provisions succinctly into one, which read: "The right of the people to keep and bear arms shall not be infringed; a well armed, and well regulated militia being the best security of a free country; but no person religiously scrupulous of bearing arms, shall be compelled to render military service in person." Cogan 169.

Madison's decision to model the Second Amendment on the distinctly military Virginia proposal is therefore revealing, since it is clear that he considered and rejected formulations that would have unambiguously protected civilian uses of firearms. When Madison prepared his first draft, and when that draft was debated and modified, it is reasonable to assume that all participants in the drafting process were fully aware of the other formulations that would have protected civilian use and possession of weapons and that their choice to craft the Amendment as they did represented a rejection of those alternative formulations.

Madison's initial inclusion of an exemption for conscientious objectors sheds revelatory light on the purpose of the Amendment. It confirms an intent to describe a duty as well as a right, and it unequivocally identifies the military character of both. The objections voiced to the conscientious-objector clause only confirm the central meaning of the text. Although records of the debate in the Senate, which is where the conscientious-objector clause was removed, do not survive, the arguments raised in the House illuminate the perceived problems with the clause: Specifically, there was concern that Congress "can declare who are those religiously scrupulous, and prevent them from bearing arms." The ultimate removal of the clause, therefore, only serves to confirm the purpose of the Amendment—to protect against congressional disarmament, by whatever means, of the States' militias. . . .

The history of the adoption of the Amendment thus describes an overriding concern about the potential threat to state sovereignty that a federal standing army would pose, and a desire to protect the States' militias as the means by which to guard against that danger. But state militias could not effectively check the prospect of a federal standing army so long as Congress retained the power to disarm them, and so a guarantee against such disarmament was needed. As we explained in *Miller:* "With obvious purpose to assure the continuation and render possible the effectiveness of such forces the declaration and guarantee of the Second Amendment were made. It must be interpreted and applied with that end in view." 307 U.S., at 178. The evidence plainly refutes the claim that the Amendment was motivated by the Framers' fears that Congress might act to regulate any civilian uses of weapons. And even if the historical record were genuinely ambiguous, the burden would remain on the parties advocating a change in the law to introduce facts or arguments "newly ascertained," *Vasquez,* 474 U.S., at 266; the Court is unable to identify any such facts or arguments.

III

Although it gives short shrift to the drafting history of the Second Amendment, the Court dwells at length on four other sources: the 17th-century English Bill of Rights; Blackstone's Commentaries on the Laws of England; post-enactment commentary on the Second Amendment; and post-Civil War legislative history. All of these sources shed only indirect light on the question before us, and in any event offer little support for the Court's conclusion. . . .

Thus, for most of our history, the invalidity of Second-Amendment-based objections to firearms regulations has been well settled and uncontroversial. Indeed, the Second Amendment was not even mentioned in either full House of Congress during the legislative proceedings that led to the passage of the 1934 Act. Yet enforcement of that law produced the judicial decision that confirmed the status of the Amendment as limited in reach to military usage. After reviewing many of the same sources that are discussed at greater length by the Court today, the *Miller* Court unanimously concluded that the Second Amendment did not apply to the possession of a firearm that did not have "some reasonable relationship to the preservation or efficiency of a well regulated militia." 307 U.S., at 178.

The key to that decision did not, as the Court belatedly suggests, *ante,* at 49–51, turn on the difference between muskets and sawed-off shotguns; it turned, rather, on the basic difference between the military and nonmilitary use and possession of guns. Indeed, if the Second Amendment were not limited in its coverage to military uses of weapons, why should the Court in *Miller* have suggested that some weapons but not others were eligible for Second Amendment protection? If use for self-defense were the relevant standard, why did the Court not inquire into the suitability of a particular weapon for self-defense purposes? . . .

The Court is simply wrong when it intones that *Miller* contained *"not a word"* about the Amendment's history. *Ante,* at 52. The Court plainly looked to history to construe the term "Militia," and, on the best reading of *Miller,* the entire guarantee of the Second Amendment. After noting the original Constitution's grant of power to Congres and to the States over the militia, the Court explained:

> "With obvious purpose to assure the continuation and render possible the effectiveness of such forces the declaration and guarantee of the Second Amendment were made. It must be interpreted and applied with that end in view."
>
> "The Militia which the States were expected to maintain and train is set in contrast with Troops which they were forbidden to keep without the consent of Congress. The sentiment of the time strongly disfavored standing armies; the common view was that adequate defense of country and laws could be secured through the Militia—civilians primarily, soldiers on occasion."
>
> "The signification attributed to the term Militia appears from the debates in the Convention,

the history and legislation of Colonies and States, and the writings of approved commentators." *Miller*, 307 U.S., at 178–179.

The majority cannot seriously believe that the *Miller* Court did not consider any relevant evidence; the majority simply does not approve of the conclusion the *Miller* Court reached on that evidence. Standing alone, that is insufficient reason to disregard a unanimous opinion of this Court, upon which substantial reliance has been placed by legislators and citizens for nearly 70 years.

V

The Court concludes its opinion by declaring that it is not the proper role of this Court to change the meaning of rights "enshrine[d]" in the Constitution. *Ante,* at 64. But the right the Court announces was not "enshrined" in the Second Amendment by the Framers; it is the product of today's law-changing decision. The majority's exegesis has utterly failed to establish that as a matter of text or history, "the right of law-abiding, responsible citizens to use arms in defense of hearth and home" is "elevate[d] above all other interests" by the Second Amendment. *Ante,* at 64.

Until today, it has been understood that legislatures may regulate the civilian use and misuse of firearms so long as they do not interfere with the preservation of a well-regulated militia. The Court's announcement of a new constitutional right to own and use firearms for private purposes upsets that settled understanding, but leaves for future cases the formidable task of defining the scope of permissible regulations. Today judicial craftsmen have confidently asserted that a policy choice that denies a "law-abiding, responsible citize[n]" the right to keep and use weapons in the home for self-defense is "off the table." *Ante,* at 64. Given the presumption that most citizens are law abiding, and the reality that the need to defend oneself may suddenly arise in a host of locations outside the home, I fear that the District's policy choice may well be just the first of an unknown number of dominoes to be knocked off the table.

I do not know whether today's decision will increase the labor of federal judges to the "breaking point" envisioned by Justice Cardozo, but it will surely give rise to a far more active judicial role in making vitally important national policy decisions than was envisioned at any time in the 18th, 19th, or 20th centuries.

The Court properly disclaims any interest in evaluating the wisdom of the specific policy choice challenged in this case, but it fails to pay heed to a far more important policy choice—the choice made by the Framers themselves. The Court would have us believe that over 200 years ago, the Framers made a choice to limit the tools available to elected officials wishing to regulate civilian uses of weapons, and to authorize this Court to use the common-law process of case-by-case judicial lawmaking to define the contours of acceptable gun control policy. Absent compelling evidence that is nowhere to be found in the Court's opinion, I could not possibly conclude that the Framers made such a choice.

For these reasons, I respectfully dissent.

John Paul Stevens is an associate justice of the U.S. Supreme Court. He worked in law firms in Chicago, Illinois, for 20 years before being nominated by President Richard Nixon to the U.S. Court of Appeals in 1970. He served in that capacity until he was nominated to the Supreme Court by President Gerald Ford in 1975.

EXPLORING THE ISSUE

Does the Second Amendment to the U.S. Constitution Protect the Right to Possess a Firearm?

Critical Thinking and Reflection

1. Does the Second Amendment provide an individual right to bear arms, or does the right only apply to a citizen militia?
2. What is the significance of the Supreme Court's decision in *United States v. Miller* (1939)?

Is There Common Ground?

This issue presents one of the more controversial debates considered in this volume. Many Americans love guns. In fact, recent studies have indicated that there are more than 200,000,000 guns owned privately in the United States. That is almost one gun for every 1.5 Americans. What explains this fascination with guns?

Some persons believe that America has a "gun culture." The image of the United States as a frontier nation with a history of gun usage for the self-defense, the acquisition of food, and as a part of the cultural heritage of the Wild West is a compelling one. America's love affair with guns has come at a substantial cost, however.

Professor Franklin E. Zimring asserts that while guns are used in only about 4 percent of all crimes, and only about 20 percent of all violent crimes, they are involved in almost 70 percent of all criminal homicides. States Zimring: "If the problem is lethal violence, the market share for firearms is 70 percent. Guns alone account for twice as many criminal deaths as all other means of killing combined." (Zimring, *Firearms, Violence, and the Potential Impact of Firearms Control* (2004, p. 34)). In response to the question "Can gun control work?" Professor Zimring states:

The answer to this general question is a highly qualified 'yes, but.' If and to the extent that regulation reduces the use of loaded guns in crimes it will save American lives. But reducing the share of violence with guns is not an easy task to achieve in urban environments with large inventories of available handguns. Most gun control efforts do not make measurable impacts on gun use, particularly low budget symbolic legislation. If

Congress when creating what it called a 'gun-free school zone' by legislation did reduce firearms violence, the result would be on a par with that of the miracle of loaves and fishes. But New York City's effort to tightly enforce one of the nation's most restrictive handgun laws did apparently have a substantial payoff in reduced shootings that saved many lives.

Professor Lance K. Stell responds, however:

Strict gun control, by effect if not intent, institutionalizes the natural predatory advantages of larger, stronger, violence-prone persons or gangs of such persons, and yet its proponents incur no liability to offset resulting risks. . . .

Prohibiting competent, adult, non-felons to possess 'equalizers' also has distributional wealth effects not only between criminals and the law-abiding, but also among the law-abiding. Strict gun control disproportionately increases the risks of violent victimization for less well-off law-abiding citizens who cannot take advantage of the privileged connections to officials that wealthier citizens take for granted.

As you can see, the gun control debate is not an easy one. Is it better to restrict the number of guns in the population, or to arm everyone in the interests of having a "fair fight"? These are difficult questions that seem unable to produce little compromise among even very rational proponents of the different viewpoints.

Moreover, the gun control debate appears to be raging within the U.S. Supreme Court as well. The Court's five-to-four decision in *District of Columbia v. Heller* appears to reflect the cultural divide in the nation as a whole.

It seems important to recognize, however, that *Heller* does not appear to have opened the floodgates to unrestricted private firearms ownership. Justice Scalia stated, "[W]e do not read the Second Amendment to protect the right of citizens to carry arms for any sort of confrontation just as we do not read the First Amendment to protect the right of citizens to speak for any purpose." He continued:

[T]he right [to bear arms is] not a right to keep and carry any weapon whatsoever in any manner whatsoever and for whatever purpose... [N]othing in our opinion should be taken to cast doubt on longstanding prohibitions on the possession of firearms by felons and the mentally ill, or laws forbidding the carrying of firearms in sensitive places such as schools and government building, or laws imposing conditions and qualification on the commercial sale of firearms.

Therefore, it appears that *Heller* will not mean that Americans will witness persons sauntering down Main Street with high-powered assault rifles, such as AK-47s, sawed-off shotguns, or fully automatic weapons, anytime soon. Stated Justice Scalia in *Heller*, "[W]e therefore read *Miller* to say only that the Second Amendment does not protect those weapons not typically possessed by law-abiding citizens for lawful purposes, such as short-barreled shotguns." Moreover, it seems to indicate as well that governments will continue to be able to impose meaningful "time, place, and manner," restrictions on firearms possession. For example, laws prohibiting firearms possession in places such as bars and taverns, where alcohol is sold, are likely to continue to be upheld by U.S. Courts. However, now that the Supreme Court has recognized an individual right to possess firearms under the Second Amendment, where do we go from here?

Another case was decided recently by the U.S. Supreme Court that may have further implications for the development of a Constitutional Right to Bear Arms. In 2010, *McDonald v. City of Chicago*, 561 U.S. ___ (2010), presented a challenge to the city of Chicago's gun control law. Specifically, the plaintiff challenged the following aspects of the city's law: (1) its prohibition on the registration of handguns; (2) its requirement for gun registration before they can be purchased by Chicago residents; (3) the city's requirement for the reregistration of guns on an annual basis, along with the payment of an annual fee; and (4) the city's declaration that if the registration lapses on any gun, it may never be registered again.

An important distinction between *District of Columbia v. Heller* and *McDonald v. City of Chicago* is that the former case involved a federal jurisdiction, the District of Columbia, whereas the latter one originated in the state of Illinois. The distinction is crucial because the *Heller* Court's recognition of an individual right to bear arms under the Second Amendment had not yet been applied to the state and local governments, which were free to continue to maintain restrictive firearms laws.

In *McDonald*, however, the plaintiff argued that the Second Amendment's Right to Bear Arms should be applied to the states, or "incorporated," through the Due Process Clause of the Fourteenth Amendment. Essentially, the plaintiff argued that the right to bear arms is "implicit in the concept of ordered liberty," and is thus a "fundamental" right that the states, or municipalities, may not deny. Writing for the Court, Justice Samuel Alito agreed. He stated that the Fourteenth Amendment's Due Process Clause guaranteed the right of individuals to keep and bear arms for self-defense because the Constitution's Framers believed that those rights were "necessary to the Nation's system of ordered liberty." Thus, states and municipalities across the United States may not prohibit firearms possession for self-defense within their jurisdictions.

Additional Resources

The issues discussed in this section present a great many challenging questions. Additional resources to pursue further study in this area include Kathleen M. Sullivan and Gerald Gunther, *Constitutional Law* (Foundation Press, 15th ed., 2004); Laurence H. Tribe, *American Constitutional Law* (Foundation Press, 2nd ed., 1988); Alpheus Thomas Mason and Donald Grier Stephenson, Jr., *American Con-stitutional Law* (Pearson Prentice Hall, 14th ed., 2005; 15th ed., 2009); Bernard Schwartz, *A History of the Supreme Court* (Oxford University Press, 1993); Kermit L. Hall, Paul Finkelman, and James Ely, Jr., *American Legal History: Cases and Materials* (Oxford University Press, 3rd ed., 2005); Kermit L. Hall, *The Oxford Companion to the Supreme Court of the United States* (Oxford University Press, 1992); Walter F. Murphy, James E. Flemming, Sotirios A. Barber, and Stephen Macedo, *American Constitutional Interpretation* (Foundation Press, 3rd ed., 2003); David M. O'Brien, *Constitutional Law and Politics: Struggles for Power and Government Accountability* (W.W. Norton & Company, 6th ed., 2005); Craig R. Ducat, *Constitutional Interpretation* (Wadsworth, 9th ed., 2009); John H. Garvey, T. Alexander Aleinikoff, and Daniel A. Farber, *Modern Constitutional Theory: A Reader* (Thompson West, 5th ed., 2004). See also: Cramer and Olson, "What Did 'Bear Arms' Mean in the Second Amendment?" *Georgetown Journal of Law & Public Policy* (vol. 6, 2008, p. 511); Cramer, Johnson, and Mocsary, "This Right Is Not Allowed by Governments

That Are Afraid of the People: The Public Meaning of the Second Amendment," *George Mason Law Review* (vol. 17, 2010, p. 823); Henigan, "The Second Amendment and the Right to Bear Arms After *D.C. v. Heller:* The Heller Paradox," *UCLA Law Review* (vol. 823, 2009, p. 1171); Zimring, "Firearms, Violence, and the Potential Impact of Firearms Control," *Journal of Law Medicine & Ethics* (vol. 32, 2004, p. 1); Stell, "The Production of Criminal Violence in America: Is Strict Gun Control the Solution?" *Journal of Law Medicine & Ethics* (vol. 32, 2004, p. 1); Tushnet, "*Heller* and the New Originalism," *Ohio State Law Journal* (vol. 69, 2008, p. 609).

Internet References . . .

National Rifle Association

http://home.nra.org/

Second Amendment Foundation

www.saf.org/

Selected, Edited, and with Issue Framing Material by:
Thomas J. Hickey, *State University of New York at Cobleskill*

ISSUE

Should It Be Lawful for the Police to Conduct JailHouse Strip Searches of Persons Arrested for Minor Offenses?

Yes: Anthony M. Kennedy, from "Majority Opinion," *Florence v. Board of Chosen Freeholders of County of Burlington,* U.S. Supreme Court (2012)

No: Stephen Breyer, from "Dissenting Opinion," *Florence v. Board of Chosen Freeholder of County of Burlington,* U.S. Supreme Court (2012)

Learning Outcomes

After reading this issue, you will be able to:

- Discuss why jailhouse strip searches pose such serious personal privacy concerns.
- Discuss whether there should be a different strip search rule for pretrial detainees as opposed to convicted offenders.
- Discuss whether jailhouse safety and security justifies strip searches of those arrested for minor offenses.
- Discuss the decisions of the U.S. Supreme Court in *Bell v. Wolfish, Hudson v. Palmer,* and *Atwater v. Lago Vista.*
- Discuss whether law enforcement officials should be required to have at least a "reasonable suspicion" that a crime is being committed, or that an arrested individual poses a danger before conducting a strip search.

ISSUE SUMMARY

Yes: U.S. Supreme Court Associate Justice Anthony M. Kennedy asserts that police officers and correctional officials must be permitted to develop reasonable search policies to detect and deter the possession of contraband within their facilities. Moreover, exempting people arrested for minor offenses from such searches may put the police at greater risk and result in more contraband being brought into jails.

No: Associate Justice Stephen Breyer, in contrast, believes that because strip searches involve close observation of the private areas of the body, they constitute a serious invasion of personal privacy and may not be justified in cases involving minor offenses.

Personal privacy is a fundamental value of most Americans. The topic considered in this section is strip searches of those arrested for crimes and taken to jail. It would be hard to imagine any practice that would violate an American conception of personal privacy more than a strip search during which one's clothing is removed and private bodily areas examined to determine if they conceal weapons or possible contraband. People may have a tendency to believe that strip searches are directed by law enforcement agents only against "serious bad guys," who commit heinous crimes. As the Supreme Court's recent decision in *Florence v. Board of Chosen Freeholders of County of Burlington,* 566 U.S. ___ (2012), illustrates, however, that is not always the case.

For example, several months ago, in a case that mirrors *Florence*, one of my former clients was stopped by the police for a nonserious traffic violation, a broken taillight lens. The same individual had been stopped by the police and ticketed for speeding a few months earlier. She had pled guilty by mail to the speeding charge, sent in the requisite fine of approximately $160.00, and thought nothing more about the incident. That is, until she was stopped for the broken taillight. After examining her driver's license and auto registration, the officer told her that an arrest warrant had been issued due to her nonpayment of the earlier speeding ticket. (The clerk of the court who had accepted the guilty plea had neglected to record the $160.00 payment.)

This individual was placed under arrest and transported to the county jail by the police officer. Fortunately, this incident occurred during normal weekday business hours, and the officer involved used common sense and checked quickly with the court that had issued the arrest warrant about my former client's contention that she had paid the earlier speeding fine. Within a few minutes, the officer was able to verify that she was telling the truth and discharged her from the county jail.

What would have happened, however, if the same incident had occurred on a weekend, or a holiday? In that case, it is highly probable that the officer would not have been able to contact court personnel who could verify the clerical recording error. In these circumstances, it is very likely that my client would have been placed in jail until she could "make bail," or until the police could contact the court that issued the arrest warrant to ascertain that there had been an error.

Under the U.S. Supreme Court's ruling in *Florence v. Board of Chosen Freeholders of County of Burlington*, 566 U.S. ___ (2012), it would appear that the police and/or correctional officials at the jail would have been justified in conducting a full strip search of my client. Such a search is highly intrusive and would involve the removal of all clothing and a visual inspection of highly personal areas and body cavities. One should note, however, at the time of my client's arrest most police and corrections agencies would have had a policy in place that requires that a person of the same gender as the arrested individual actually conduct the strip search.

Prior to *Florence*, many law enforcement agencies had strip search policies that provided for this type of invasive search procedure only in specified serious cases. For example, if an individual was being charged with a serious crime, possession of illegal drugs, or whenever officers had a reasonable suspicion to believe that the alleged offender could possess a weapon or illegal contraband. After *Florence*, law enforcement agencies appear to be free to adopt a blanket rule that permits anyone who is arrested for a crime to be strip searched if they are going to be held in a local jail. While most reasonable persons would be likely to support such a rule for *convicted* offenders being taken to prison, or those serving their sentence in a local jail, it is significant that the Supreme Court held that even those who had not yet been convicted of any offense could be subjected to this type of intrusive search.

The U.S. Supreme Court's rationale for permitting strip searches and body-cavity inspections of those who had been charged with a crime and taken to jail, but who had not yet been convicted, was first developed in *Bell v. Wolfish*, 441 U.S. 520 (1979). In that case, *pretrial detainees* in a newly constructed jail, the Metropolitan Correctional Center in Washington, D.C., challenged several of the jail's policies in federal court. One of the challenged policies required a strip search and body-cavity inspection of all persons awaiting trial at the jail. The Supreme Court held that because the Fourth Amendment prohibits only "unreasonable searches," the jail's practices were subject to a "reasonableness test," which "is not capable of precise definition or mechanical application." The Court observed: "In each case, it requires a balancing of the need for the particular search against the invasion of personal rights that the search entails." Chief Justice Rehnquist continued:

> We do not underestimate the degree to which these searches may invade the personal privacy of inmates. Nor do we doubt . . . that, on occasion, a security guard may conduct the search in an abusive fashion. Such abuse cannot be condoned. The searches must be conducted in a reasonable manner . . . But here we deal with the question whether visual body cavity inspections can *ever* be conducted on less than probable cause. Balancing the significant and legitimate security interests of the institution against the privacy interests of the inmates, we conclude that they can. (441 U.S. 520, 560).

The Supreme Court's decision in *Florence v. Board of Chosen Freeholders of County of Burlington*, expanded the principle laid down in *Bell v. Wolfish*. In *Florence*, an individual was arrested during a traffic stop by a police officer who had checked a statewide computer database and found a warrant for the motorist's arrest for failing to appear at a hearing to enforce a fine. Like my unfortunate client discussed previously, he was initially detained at a county jail, but released once it was determined that he had paid the fine. At the jail, the unfortunate motorist, like all detainees, had to shower with a delousing agent and was checked for scars, marks, gang tattoos, and contraband as he undressed. He also had to open his mouth, lift his tongue, hold out his arms, turn around, and lift his genitals.

The arrested motorist filed a federal Civil Rights lawsuit under 42 U.S.C. Section 1983 against the government entities that ran the jails and the officers who conducted the searches, arguing that persons arrested for minor offenses cannot be subjected to invasive searches unless jail official have reason to suspect concealment of weapons, drugs, or other contraband. The U.S. District Court agreed, but the Third Circuit U.S. Court of Appeals reversed. The U.S. Supreme Court granted certiorari and in a five to four decision affirmed the decision of the Court of Appeals.

Justice Kennedy, writing for the Court, stated that "correctional officials must be permitted to devise reasonable search policies to detect and deter the possession of contraband in their facilities." Moreover, stated Kennedy, "[t]he danger of [new detainees] introducing lice or contagious infections . . . is well-documented . . . [and] it may be difficult to identify and treat these problems until detainees remove their clothes for a visual inspection." Justice Kennedy also rejected the motorist's argument that those detained for nonserious offenses should not be subjected to invasive searches unless there is reasonable suspicion to believe that he or she possesses contraband or may be concealing a weapon. Stated Kennedy: "[T]he seriousness of an offense is a poor predictor of who has contraband and it would be difficult in practice to determine whether individuals fall within the proposed exemption. People detained for minor offenses can turn out to be the most devious and dangerous criminals."

Justice Stephen Breyer, dissenting, took issue with the majority's opinion. Justice Breyer stated:

> In my view, a search of an individual arrested for a minor offense that does not involve drugs or violence—say a traffic offense, a regulatory offense, an essentially civil matter, or any other such misdemeanor—is an 'unreasonable search' forbidden by the Fourth Amendment, unless prison authorities have reasonable suspicion to believe that the individual possesses drugs or other contraband.

At first glance do you agree with Justice Kennedy, or Justice Breyer? Do you think that a "reasonable suspicion" requirement for conducting a strip and body-cavity search of a person being admitted to a jail would be a practical standard? The authors of the opinions presented in this section have very different perspectives on this issue.

YES ↵

Anthony M. Kennedy

Majority Opinion

Correctional officials have a legitimate interest, indeed a responsibility, to ensure that jails are not made less secure by reason of what new detainees may carry in on their bodies. Facility personnel, other inmates, and the new detainee himself or herself may be in danger if these threats are introduced into the jail population. This case presents the question of what rules, or limitations, the Constitution imposes on searches of arrested persons who are to be held in jail while their cases are being processed. The term "jail" is used here in a broad sense to include prisons and other detention facilities. The specific measures being challenged will be described in more detail; but, in broad terms, the controversy concerns whether every detainee who will be admitted to the general population may be required to undergo a close visual inspection while undressed.

The case turns in part on the extent to which this Court has sufficient expertise and information in the record to mandate, under the Constitution, the specific restrictions and limitations sought by those who challenge the visual search procedures at issue. In addressing this type of constitutional claim courts must defer to the judgment of correctional officials unless the record contains substantial evidence showing their policies are an unnecessary or unjustified response to problems of jail security. That necessary showing has not been made in this case.

I

In 1998, seven years before the incidents at issue, petitioner Albert Florence was arrested after fleeing from police officers in Essex County, New Jersey. He was charged with obstruction of justice and use of a deadly weapon. Petitioner entered a plea of guilty to two lesser offenses and was sentenced to pay a fine in monthly installments. In 2003, after he fell behind on his payments and failed to appear at an enforcement hearing, a bench warrant was issued for his arrest. He paid the outstanding balance less

than a week later; but, for some unexplained reason, the warrant remained in a statewide computer database.

Two years later, in Burlington County, New Jersey, petitioner and his wife were stopped in their automobile by a state trooper. Based on the outstanding warrant in the computer system, the officer arrested petitioner and took him to the Burlington County Detention Center. He was held there for six days and then was transferred to the Essex County Correctional Facility. It is not the arrest or confinement but the search process at each jail that gives rise to the claims before the Court.

Burlington County jail procedures required every arrestee to shower with a delousing agent. Officers would check arrestees for scars, marks, gang tattoos, and contraband as they disrobed. Petitioner claims he was also instructed to open his mouth, lift his tongue, hold out his arms, turn around, and lift his genitals. (It is not clear whether this last step was part of the normal practice.) Petitioner shared a cell with at least one other person and interacted with other inmates following his admission to the jail.

The Essex County Correctional Facility, where petitioner was taken after six days, is the largest county jail in New Jersey. It admits more than 25,000 inmates each year and houses about 1,000 gang members at any given time. When petitioner was transferred there, all arriving detainees passed through a metal detector and waited in a group holding cell for a more thorough search. When they left the holding cell, they were instructed to remove their clothing while an officer looked for body markings, wounds, and contraband. Apparently without touching the detainees, an officer looked at their ears, nose, mouth, hair, scalp, fingers, hands, arms, armpits, and other body openings. This policy applied regardless of the circumstances of the arrest, the suspected offense, or the detainee's behavior, demeanor, or criminal history. Petitioner alleges he was required to lift his genitals, turn around, and cough in a squatting position as part of the process. After a mandatory shower, during which his clothes were inspected, petitioner was admitted to the facility. He was

Kennedy, Anthony M. From United States Supreme Court, 2012.

released the next day, when the charges against him were dismissed.

Petitioner sued the governmental entities that operated the jails, one of the wardens, and certain other defendants. The suit was commenced in the United States District Court for the District of New Jersey. Seeking relief under 42 U. S. C. § 1983 for violations of his Fourth and Fourteenth Amendment rights, petitioner maintained that persons arrested for a minor offense could not be required to remove their clothing and expose the most private areas of their bodies to close visual inspection as a routine part of the intake the process. Rather, he contented officials could conduct this kind of search only if they had reason to suspect to particular inmate of concealing a weapon, drugs, or other contraband. . . .

After discovery, the court granted petitioner's motion for summary judgment on the unlawful search claim. It concluded that any policy of "strip searching" nonindictable offenders without reasonable suspicion violated the Fourth Amendment. A divided panel of the United States Court of Appeals for the Third Circuit reversed, holding that the procedures described by the District Court struck a reasonable balance between inmate privacy and the security needs of the two jails. The case proceeds on the understanding that the officers searched detainees prior to their admission to the general population, as the Court of Appeals seems to have assumed. Petitioner has not argued this factual premise is incorrect.

The opinions in earlier proceedings, the briefs on file, and some cases of this Court refer to a "strip search." The term is imprecise. It may refer simply to the instruction to remove clothing while an officer observes from a distance of, say, five feet or more; it may mean a visual inspection from a closer, more uncomfortable distance; it may include directing detainees to shake their heads or to run their hands through their hair to dislodge what might be hidden there; or it may involve instructions to raise arms, to display foot insteps, to expose the back of the ears, to move or spread the buttocks or genital areas, or to cough in a squatting position. In the instant case, the term does not include any touching of unclothed areas by the inspecting officer. There are no allegations that the detainees here were touched in any way as part of the searches.

The Federal Courts of Appeals have come to differing conclusions as to whether the Fourth Amendment requires correctional officials to exempt some detainees who will be admitted to a jail's general population from the searches here at issue. This Court granted certiorari to address the question. 563 U. S. — (2011).

II

The difficulties of operating a detention center must not be underestimated by the courts. Jail (in the stricter sense of the term, excluding prison facilities) admit more than 13 million inmates a year. The largest facilities process hundreds of people every day; smaller jails may be crowded on weekend nights, after a large police operation, or because of detainees arriving from other jurisdictions. Maintaining safety and order at these institutions requires the expertise of correctional officials, who must have substantial discretion to devise reasonable solutions to the problems they face. The Court has confirmed the importance of deference to correctional officials and explained that a regulation impinging on an inmate's constitutional rights must be upheld "if it is reasonably related to legitimate penological interests."

. . .

The Court's opinion in *Bell* v. *Wolfish*, 441 U. S. 520 (1979), is the starting point for understanding how this framework applies to Fourth Amendment challenges. That case addressed a rule requiring pretrial detainees in any correctional facility run by the Federal Bureau of Prisons "to expose their body cavities for visual inspection as a part of a strip search conducted after every contact visit with a person from outside the institution." Inmates at the federal Metropolitan Correctional Center in New York City argued there was no security justification for these searches. Officers searched guests before they entered the visiting room, and the inmates were under constant surveillance during the visit. There had been but one instance in which an inmate attempted to sneak contraband back into the facility. The Court nonetheless upheld the search policy. It deferred to the judgment of correctional officials that the inspections served not only to discover but also to deter the smuggling of weapons, drugs, and other prohibited items inside. The Court explained that there is no mechanical way to determine whether intrusions on an inmate's privacy are reasonable. The need for a particular search must be balanced against the resulting invasion of personal rights.

Policies designed to keep contraband out of jails and prisons have been upheld in cases decided since *Bell*. In *Block* v. *Rutherford*, 468 U. S. 576 (1984), for example, the Court concluded that the Los Angeles County Jail could ban all contact visits because of the threat they posed:

> "They open the institution to the introduction of drugs, weapons, and other contraband. Visitors can easily conceal guns, knives, drugs, or other

contraband in countless ways and pass them to an inmate unnoticed by even the most vigilant observers. And these items can readily be slipped from the clothing of an innocent child, or transferred by other visitors permitted close contact with inmates."

There were "many justifications" for imposing a general ban rather than trying to carve out exceptions for certain detainees. Among other problems, it would be "a difficult if not impossible task" to identify "inmates who have propensities for violence, escape, or drug smuggling." This was made "even more difficult by the brevity of detention and the constantly changing nature of the inmate population."

The Court has also recognized that deterring the possession of contraband depends in part on the ability to conduct searches without predictable exceptions. In *Hudson* v. *Palmer*, 468 U. S. 517 (1984), it addressed the question of whether prison officials could perform random searches of inmate lockers and cells even without reason to suspect a particular individual of concealing a prohibited item. The Court upheld the constitutionality of the practice, recognizing that "[f]or one to advocate that prison searches must be conducted only pursuant to an enunciated general policy or when suspicion is directed at a particular inmate is to ignore the realities of prison operation." Inmates would adapt to any pattern or loopholes they discovered in the search protocol and then undermine the security of the institution.

These cases establish that correctional officials must be permitted to devise reasonable search policies to detect and deter the possession of contraband in their facilities. ("[Maintaining institutional security and preserving internal order and discipline are essential goals that may require limitation or retraction of retained constitutional rights of both convicted prisoners and pretrial detainees"). The task of determining whether a policy is reasonably related to legitimate security interests is "peculiarly within the province and professional expertise of corrections officials." This Court has repeated the admonition that, "in the absence of substantial evidence in the record to indicate that the officials have exaggerated their response to these considerations courts should ordinarily defer to their expert judgment in such matters."

In many jails officials seek to improve security by requiring some kind of strip search of everyone who is to be detained. These procedures have been used in different places throughout the country, from Cranston, Rhode Island, to Sapulpa, Oklahoma, to Idaho Falls, Idaho.

Persons arrested for minor offenses may be among the detainees processed at these facilities. This is, in part, a consequence of the exercise of state authority that was the subject of *Atwater* v. *Lago Vista,* 532 U. S. 318 (2001). *Atwater* addressed the perhaps more fundamental question of who may be deprived of liberty and taken to jail in the first place. The case involved a woman who was arrested after a police officer noticed neither she nor her children were wearing their seatbelts. The arrestee argued the Fourth Amendment prohibited her custodial arrest without a warrant when an offense could not result in jail time and there was no compelling need for immediate detention. The Court held that a Fourth Amendment restriction on this power would put officers in an "almost impossible spot." Their ability to arrest a suspect would depend in some cases on the precise weight of drugs in his pocket, whether he was a repeat offender, and the scope of what counted as a compelling need to detain someone. The Court rejected the proposition that the Fourth Amendment barred custodial arrests in a set of these cases as a matter of constitutional law. It ruled, based on established principles, that officers may make an arrest based upon probable cause to believe the person has committed a criminal offense in their presence. The Court stated that "a responsible Fourth Amendment balance is not well served by standards requiring sensitive, case-by-case determinations of government need, lest every discretionary judgment in the field be converted into an occasion for constitutional review."

Atwater did not address whether the Constitution imposes special restrictions on the searches of offenders suspected of committing minor offenses once they are taken to jail. Some Federal Courts of Appeals have held that corrections officials may not conduct a strip search of these detainees, even if no touching is involved, absent reasonable suspicion of concealed contraband. . . .

III

The question here is whether undoubted security imperatives involved in jail supervision override the assertion that some detainees must be exempt from the more invasive search procedures at issue absent reasonable suspicion of a concealed weapon or other contraband. The Court has held that deference must be given to the officials in charge of the jail unless there is "substantial evidence" demonstrating their response to the situation is exaggerated. Petitioner has not met this standard, and the record provides full justifications for the procedures used.

A

Correctional officials have a significant interest in conducting a thorough search as a standard part of the intake process. The admission of inmates creates numerous risks for facility staff, for the existing detainee population, and for a new detainee himself or herself. The danger of introducing lice or contagious infections, for example, is well documented. The Federal Bureau of Prisons recommends that staff screen new detainees for these conditions. Persons just arrested may have wounds or other injuries requiring immediate medical attention. It may be difficult to identify and treat these problems until detainees remove their clothes for a visual inspection.

Jails and prisons also face grave threats posed by the increasing number of gang members who go through the intake process. The groups recruit new members by force, engage in assaults against staff, and give other inmates a reason to arm themselves. Fights among feuding gangs can be deadly, and the officers who must maintain order are put in harm's way. These considerations provide a reasonable basis to justify a visual inspection for certain tattoos and other signs of gang affiliation as part of the intake process. The identification and isolation of gang members before they are admitted protects everyone in the facility.

Detecting contraband concealed by new detainees, furthermore, is a most serious responsibility. Weapons, drugs, and alcohol all disrupt the safe operation of a jail. Correctional officers have had to confront arrestees concealing knives, scissors, razor blades, glass shards, and other prohibited items on their person, including in their body cavities. . . . They have also found crack, heroin, and marijuana. The use of drugs can embolden inmates in aggression toward officers or each other; and, even apart from their use, the trade in these substances can lead to violent confrontations.

There are many other kinds of contraband. The textbook definition of the term covers any unauthorized item. . . . Contraband obviously includes drugs or weapons, but it can also be money, cigarettes, or even some types of clothing. Everyday items can undermine security if introduced into a detention facility:

> "Lighters and matches are fire and arson risks or potential weapons. Cell phones are used to orchestrate violence and criminality both within and without jailhouse walls. Pills and medications enhance suicide risks. Chewing gum can block locking devices; hair pins can open handcuffs; wigs can conceal drugs and weapons."

Something as simple as an overlooked pen can pose a significant danger. Inmates commit more than 10,000 assaults on correctional staff every year and many more among themselves.

Contraband creates additional problems because scarce items, including currency, have value in a jail's culture and underground economy. Correctional officials inform us "[t]he competition . . . for such goods begets violence, extortion, and disorder." Gangs exacerbate the problem. They "orchestrate thefts, commit assaults, and approach inmates in packs to take the contraband from the weak." This puts the entire facility, including detainees being held for a brief term for a minor offense, at risk. Gangs do coerce inmates who have access to the outside world, such as people serving their time on the weekends, to sneak things into the jail. . . . These inmates, who might be thought to pose the least risk, have been caught smuggling prohibited items into jail. Concealing contraband often takes little time and effort. It might be done as an officer approaches a suspect's car or during a brief commotion in a group holding cell. Something small might be tucked or taped under an armpit, behind an ear, between the buttocks, in the instep of a foot, or inside the mouth or some other body cavity.

It is not surprising that correctional officials have sought to perform thorough searches at intake for disease, gang affiliation, and contraband. Jails are often crowded, unsanitary, and dangerous places. There is a substantial interest in preventing any new inmate, either of his own will or as a result of coercion, from putting all who live or work at these institutions at even greater risk when he is admitted to the general population.

B

Petitioner acknowledges that correctional officials must be allowed to conduct an effective search during the intake process and that this will require at least some detainees to lift their genitals or cough in a squatting position. These procedures, similar to the ones upheld in *Bell*, are designed to uncover contraband that can go undetected by a patdown, metal detector, and other less invasive searches. Petitioner maintains there is little benefit to conducting these more invasive steps on a new detainee who has not been arrested for a serious crime or for any offense involving a weapon or drugs. In his view these detainees should be exempt from this process unless they give officers a particular reason to suspect them of hiding contraband. It is reasonable, however, for correctional officials to conclude this standard would be unworkable. The record provides evidence that the seriousness of an offense is a poor predictor of who has contraband and that it would be difficult in practice to determine whether individual detainees fall within the proposed exemption.

1

People detained for minor offenses can turn out to be the most devious and dangerous criminals. Hours after the Oklahoma City bombing, Timothy McVeigh was stopped by a state trooper who noticed he was driving without a license plate. Police stopped serial killer Joel Rifkin for the same reason. One of the terrorists involved in the September 11 attacks was stopped and ticketed for speeding just two days before hijacking Flight 93. Reasonable correctional officials could conclude these uncertainties mean they must conduct the same thorough search of everyone who will be admitted to their facilities.

Experience shows that people arrested for minor offenses have tried to smuggle prohibited items into jail, sometimes by using their rectal cavities or genitals for the concealment. They may have some of the same incentives as a serious criminal to hide contraband. A detainee might risk carrying cash, cigarettes, or a penknife to survive in jail. Others may make a quick decision to hide unlawful substances to avoid getting in more trouble at the time of their arrest. This record has concrete examples. Officers at the Atlantic County Correctional Facility, for example, discovered that a man arrested for driving under the influence had "2 dime bags of weed, 1 pack of rolling papers, 20 matches, and 5 sleeping pills" taped under his scrotum. A person booked on a misdemeanor charge of disorderly conduct in Washington State managed to hide a lighter, tobacco, tattoo needles, and other prohibited items in his rectal cavity. San Francisco officials have discovered contraband hidden in body cavities of people arrested for trespassing, public nuisance, and shoplifting. There have been similar incidents at jails throughout the country.

Even if people arrested for a minor offense do not themselves wish to introduce contraband into a jail, they may be coerced into doing so by others. . . . This could happen any time detainees are held in the same area, including in a van on the way to the station or in the holding cell of the jail. If, for example, a person arrested and detained for unpaid traffic citations is not subject to the same search as others, this will be well known to other detainees with jail experience. A hardened criminal or gang member can, in just a few minutes, approach the person and coerce him into hiding the fruits of a crime, a weapon, or some other

contraband. As an expert in this case explained, "the interaction and mingling between misdemeanants and felons will only increase the amount of contraband in the facility if the jail can only conduct admission searches on felons." Exempting people arrested for minor offenses from a standard search protocol thus may put them at greater risk and result in more contraband being brought into the detention facility. This is a substantial reason not to mandate the exception petitioner seeks as a matter of constitutional law.

2

It also may be difficult, as a practical matter, to classify inmates by their current and prior offenses before the intake search. Jails can be even more dangerous than prisons because officials there know so little about the people they admit at the outset. An arrestee may be carrying a false ID or lie about his identity. The officers who conduct an initial search often do not have access to criminal history records. . . . Petitioner's rap sheet is an example. It did not reflect his previous arrest for possession of a deadly weapon. In the absence of reliable information it would be illogical to require officers to assume the arrestees in front of them do not pose a risk of smuggling something into the facility.

The laborious administration of prisons would become less effective, and likely less fair and evenhanded, were the practical problems inevitable from the rules suggested by petitioner to be imposed as a constitutional mandate. Even if they had accurate information about a detainee's current and prior arrests, officers, under petitioner's proposed regime, would encounter serious implementation difficulties. They would be required, in a few minutes, to determine whether any of the underlying offenses [was] serious enough to authorize the more invasive search protocol. Other possible classifications based on characteristics of individual detainees also might prove to be unworkable or even give rise to charges of discriminatory application. Most officers would not be well equipped to make any of these legal determinations during the pressures of the intake process. ("[T]he Court's approach will necessitate a case-by-case evaluation of the seriousness of particular crimes, a difficult task for which officers and courts are poorly equipped"). To avoid liability, officers might be inclined not to conduct a thorough search in any close case, thus creating unnecessary risk for the entire jail population. . . .

Individual jurisdictions can of course choose "to impose more restrictive safeguards through statutes limiting warrantless arrests for minor offenders."

. . . Officers who interact with those suspected of violating the law have an "essential interest in readily administrable rules. The officials in charge of the jails in this case urge the Court to reject any complicated constitutional scheme requiring them to conduct less thorough inspections of some detainees based on their behavior, suspected offense, criminal history, and other factors. They offer significant reasons why the Constitution must not prevent them from conducting the same search on any suspected offender who will be admitted to the general population in their facilities. The restrictions suggested by petitioner would limit the intrusion on the privacy of some detainees but at the risk of increased danger to everyone in the facility, including the less serious offenders themselves.

IV

This case does not require the Court to rule on the types of searches that would be reasonable in instances where, for example, a detainee will be held without assignment to the general jail population and without substantial contact with other detainees. . . . The accommodations provided in these situations may diminish the need to conduct some aspects of the searches at issue . . . The circumstances before the Court, however, do not present the opportunity to consider a narrow exception [that] might restrict whether an arrestee whose detention has not yet been reviewed by a magistrate or other judicial officer, and who can be held in available facilities removed from the general population, may be subjected to the types of searches at issue here.

Petitioner's *amici* raise concerns about instances of officers engaging in intentional humiliation and other abusive practices. ("[I]ntentional harassment of even the most hardened criminals cannot be tolerated by a civilized society"). There also may be legitimate concerns about the invasiveness of searches that involve the touching of detainees. These issues are not implicated on the facts of this case, however, and it is unnecessary to consider them here.

V

Even assuming all the facts in favor of petitioner, the search procedures at the Burlington County Detention Center and the Essex County Correctional Facility struck a reasonable balance between inmate privacy and the needs of the institutions. The Fourth and Fourteenth Amendments do not require adoption of the framework of rules petitioner proposes.

The judgment of the Court of Appeals for the Third Circuit is affirmed.

It is so ordered.

Anthony M. Kennedy is an associate justice of the U.S. Supreme Court. He received his LLB from Harvard Law School in 1961 and worked for law firms in San Francisco and Sacramento, California, until he was nominated by President Gerald Ford to the U.S. Court of Appeals for the Ninth Circuit in 1975. He was nominated by President Ronald Reagan to the Supreme Court in 1988.

Should It Be Lawful for the Police to Conduct JailHouse Strip Searches of Persons Arrested for Minor Offenses? by Hickey

321

Stephen Breyer

 **NO**

Dissenting Opinion

The petition for certiorari asks us to decide "[w]hether the Fourth Amendment permits a . . . suspicionless strip search of every individual arrested for any minor offense . . . ." This question is phrased more broadly than what is at issue. The case is limited to strip searches of those arrestees entering a jail's general population. And the kind of strip search in question involves more than undressing and taking a shower (even if guards monitor the shower area for threatened disorder). Rather, the searches here involve close observation of the private areas of a person's body and for that reason constitute a far more serious invasion of that person's privacy.

The visually invasive kind of strip search at issue here is not unique. A similar practice is well described in *Dodge* v. *County of Orange*, 282 F. Supp. 2d 41 (SONY 2003). In that New York case, the "strip search" (as described in a relevant prison manual) involved:

> "a visual inspection of the inmate's naked body. This should include the inmate opening his mouth and moving his tongue up and down and from side to side, removing any dentures, running his hands through his hair, allowing his ears to be visually examined, lifting his arms to expose his arm pits, lifting his feet to examine the sole, spreading and/or lifting his testicles to expose the area behind them and bending over and/or spreading the cheeks of his buttocks to expose his anus. For females, the procedures are similar except females must in addition, squat to expose the vagina."

Because the *Dodge* court obtained considerable empirical information about the need for such a search in respect to minor offenders, and because the searches alleged in this case do not differ significantly, I shall use the succinct *Dodge* description as a template for the kind of strip search to which the Question Presented refers. . . .

In my view, such a search of an individual arrested for a minor offense that does not involve drugs or violence—say a traffic offense, a regulatory offense, an essentially civil matter, or any other such misdemeanor—is an "unreasonable searc[h]" forbidden by the Fourth Amendment, unless prison authorities have reasonable suspicion to believe that the individual possesses drugs or other contraband. And I dissent from the Court's contrary determination.

I

Those confined in prison retain basic constitutional rights. *Bell* v. *Wolfish*, 441 U. S. 520, 545 (1979). . . . The constitutional right at issue here is the Fourth Amendment right to be free of "unreasonable searches and seizures." And, as the Court notes, the applicable standard is the Fourth Amendment balancing inquiry announced regarding prison inmates in *Bell* v. *Wolfish, supra.* The Court said:

> "The test of reasonableness under the Fourth Amendment is not capable of precise definition or mechanical application. In each case it requires a balancing of the need for the particular search against the invasion of personal rights that the search entails. Courts must consider the scope of the particular intrusion, the manner in which it is conducted, the justification for initiating it, and the place in which it is conducted."

I have described in general terms, the place, scope and manner of "the particular intrusion." I now explain why I believe that the "invasion of personal rights" here is very serious and lacks need or justification—at least as to the category of minor offenders at issue.

II

A strip search that involves a stranger peering without consent at a naked individual, and in particular at the most private portions of that person's body, is a serious invasion of privacy. We have recently said, in respect to a schoolchild (and a less intrusive search), that the "meaning of such a search, and the degradation its subject may reasonably feel, place a search that intrusive in a category

Breyer, Stephen. Supreme Court of the United States 2012.

of its own demanding its own specific suspicions." The Courts of Appeals have more directly described the privacy interests at stake, writing, for example, that practices similar to those at issue here are "demeaning, dehumanizing, undignified, humiliating, terrifying, unpleasant, embarrassing, [and] repulsive, signifying degradation and submission." ("[A]ll courts" have recognized the "severe if not gross interference with a person's privacy" that accompany visual body cavity searches). Even when carried out in a respectful manner, and even absent any physical touching, such searches are inherently harmful, humiliating, and degrading. And the harm to privacy interests would seem particularly acute where the person searched may well have no expectation of being subject to such a search, say, because she had simply received a traffic ticket for failing to buckle a seatbelt, because he had not previously paid a civil fine, or because she had been arrested for a minor trespass.

In *Atwater* v. *Logo Vista*, 532 U. S. 318, 323–324 (2001), for example, police arrested a mother driving with her two children because their seat belts were not buckled. This Court held that the Constitution did not forbid an arrest for a minor seatbelt offense. But, in doing so, it pointed out that the woman was held for only an hour (before being taken to a magistrate and released on bond) and that the search—she had to remove her shoes, jewelry, and the contents of her pockets,—was not "'unusually harmful to [her] privacy or . . . physical interests.'" Would this Court have upheld the arrest had the magistrate not been immediately available, had the police housed her overnight in the jail, and had they subjected her to a search of the kind at issue here?

The petitioner, Albert W. Florence, states that his present arrest grew out of an (erroneous) report that he had failed to pay a minor civil fine previously assessed because he had hindered a prosecution (by fleeing police officers in his automobile). He alleges that he was held for six days in jail before being taken to a magistrate and that he was subjected to two strip searches of the kind in question.

Amicus briefs present other instances in which individuals arrested for minor offenses have been subjected to the humiliations of a visual strip search. They include a nun, a Sister of Divine Providence for 50 years, who was arrested for trespassing during an antiwar demonstration. They include women who were strip-searched during periods of lactation or menstruation. . . . They include victims of sexual violence. . . . They include individuals detained for such infractions as driving with a noisy muffler, driving with an inoperable headlight, failing to use a turn signal, or riding a bicycle without an audible bell. . . . They include persons who perhaps should never have been placed in the general jail population in the first place. . . .

I need not go on. I doubt that we seriously disagree about the nature of the strip search or about the serious affront to human dignity and to individual privacy that it presents. The basic question before us is whether such a search is nonetheless justified when an individual arrested for a minor offense is involuntarily placed in the general jail or prison population.

III

The majority, like the respondents, argues that strip searches are needed (1) to detect injuries or diseases, such as lice, that might spread in confinement, (2) to identify gang tattoos, which might reflect a need for special housing to avoid violence, and (3) to detect contraband, including drugs, guns, knives, and even pens or chewing gum, which might prove harmful or dangerous in prison. In evaluating this argument, I, like the majority, recognize: that managing a jail or prison is an "inordinately difficult undertaking," that prison regulations that interfere with important constitutional interests are generally valid as long as they are "reasonably related to legitimate penological interests," that finding injuries and preventing the spread of disease, minimizing the threat of gang violence, and detecting contraband are "legitimate penological interests," and that we normally defer to the expertise of jail and prison administrators in such matters.

Nonetheless, the "particular" invasion of interests must be "reasonably related" to the justifying "penological interest" and the need must not be "exaggerated." It is at this point that I must part company with the majority. I have found no convincing reason indicating that, in the absence of reasonable suspicion, involuntary strip searches of those arrested for minor offenses are necessary in order to further the penal interests mentioned. And there are strong reasons to believe they are not justified.

The lack of justification is fairly obvious with respect to the first two penological interests advanced. The searches already employed at Essex and Burlington include: (a) pat-frisking all inmates; (b) making inmates go through metal detectors (including the Body Orifice Screening System (BOSS) chair used at Essex County Correctional Facility that identifies metal hidden within the body); (c) making inmates shower and use particular delousing agents or bathing supplies; and (d) searching inmates' clothing. In addition, petitioner concedes that detainees could be lawfully subject to being viewed in their undergarments by jail officers or during showering (for security purposes). ("Showering in the presence of officers is not something that requires reasonable suspicion"). No one here has offered any reason, example, or empirical evidence suggesting the inadequacy of such practices for detecting injuries, diseases, or tattoos. In particular, there is no connection between the genital lift and the "squat and cough" that Florence was allegedly subjected to and health or gang concerns.

The lack of justification for such a strip search is less obvious but no less real in respect to the third interest, namely that of detecting contraband. The information demonstrating the lack of justification is of three kinds. First, there are empirically based conclusions reached in specific cases. The New York Federal District Court, to which I have referred, conducted a study of 23,000 persons admitted to the Orange County correctional facility between 1999 and 2003. These 23,000 persons underwent a strip search of the kind described. Of these 23,000 persons, the court wrote, "the County encountered three incidents of drugs recovered from an inmate's anal cavity and two incidents of drugs falling from an inmate's underwear during the course of a strip search." The court added that in four of these five instances there may have been "reasonable suspicion" to search, leaving only one instance in 23,000 in which the strip search policy "arguably" detected additional contraband. The study is imperfect, for search standards changed during the time it was conducted. But the large number of inmates, the small number of "incidents," and the District Court's own conclusions make the study probative though not conclusive.

Similarly, in *Shain v. Ellison*, 273 F. 3d 56, 60 (CA2 2001), the court received data produced by the county jail showing that authorities conducted body-cavity strip searches, similar to those at issue here, of 75,000 new inmates over a period of five years. In 16 instances the searches led to the discovery of contraband. The record further showed that 13 of these 16 pieces of contraband would have been detected in a patdown or a search of shoes and outer-clothing. In the three instances in which contraband was found on the detainee's body or in a body cavity, there was a drug or felony history that would have justified a strip search on individualized reasonable suspicion.

Second, there is the plethora of recommendations of professional bodies, such as correctional associations, that have studied and thoughtfully considered the matter. The American Correctional Association (ACA)—an association that informs our view of "what is obtainable and what is acceptable in corrections philosophy,"—has promulgated a standard that forbids suspicionless strip searches. And it has done so after consultation with the American

Jail Association, National Sheriffs Association, National Institute of Corrections of the Department of Justice, and Federal Bureau of Prisons. A standard desk reference for general information about sound correctional practices advises against suspicionless strip searches.

Moreover, many correctional facilities apply a reasonable suspicion standard before strip searching inmates entering the general jail population, including the U.S. Marshals Service, the Immigration and Customs Service, and the Bureau of Indian Affairs. The Federal Bureau of Prisons (BOP) itself forbids suspicionless strip searches for minor offenders, though it houses separately (and does not admit to the general jail population) a person who does not consent to such a search.

Third, there is general experience in areas where the law has forbidden here-relevant suspicionless searches. Laws in at least 10 States prohibit suspicionless strip searches. . . .

At the same time at least seven Courts of Appeals have considered the question and have required reasonable suspicion that an arrestee is concealing weapons or contraband before a strip search of one arrested for a minor offense can take place. Respondents have not presented convincing grounds to believe that administration of these legal standards has increased the smuggling of contraband into prison.

Indeed, neither the majority's opinion nor the briefs set forth any clear example of an instance in which contraband was smuggled into the general jail population during intake that could not have been discovered if the jail was employing a reasonable suspicion standard. The majority does cite general examples from Atlantic County and Washington State where contraband has been recovered in correctional facilities from inmates arrested for driving under the influence and disorderly conduct. Similarly, the majority refers to information, provided by San Francisco jail authorities, stating that they have found handcuff keys, syringes, crack pipes, drugs, and knives during body-cavity searches, including during searches of minor offenders, including a man arrested for illegally lodging (drugs), and a woman arrested for prostitution and public nuisance ("bindles of crack cocaine"). And associated statistics indicate that the policy of conducting visual cavity searches of *all* those admitted to the general population in San Francisco may account for the discovery of contraband in approximately 15 instances per year.

But neither San Francisco nor the respondents tell us *whether reasonable suspicion was present or absent* in *any* of the 15 instances. Nor is there any showing by the majority that the few unclear examples of contraband recovered in Atlantic County, Washington State, or anywhere else could not have been discovered through a policy that required reasonable suspicion for strip searches. And without some such indication, I am left without an example of any instance in which contraband was found on an individual through an inspection of their private parts or body cavities which could not have been found under a policy requiring reasonable suspicion. Hence, at a minimum these examples, including San Francisco's statistics, do not provide a significant counterweight to those presented in *Dodge* and *Shain*.

Nor do I find the majority's lack of examples surprising. After all, those arrested for minor offenses are often stopped and arrested unexpectedly. And they consequently will have had little opportunity to hide things in their body cavities. Thus, the widespread advocacy by prison experts and the widespread application in many States and federal circuits of "reasonable suspicion" requirements indicates an ability to apply such standards in practice without unduly interfering with the legitimate penal interest in preventing the smuggling of contraband.

The majority is left with the word of prison officials in support of its contrary proposition. And though that word is important, it cannot be sufficient.

The majority also relies upon *Bell,* 441 U. S. 520, itself. In that case, the Court considered a prison policy requiring a strip search of *all* detainees after "contact visits" with unimprisoned visitors. The Court found that policy justified. Contrary to the majority's suggestion, that case does not provide precedent for the proposition that the word of prison officials (accompanied by a "single instance" of empirical example) is sufficient to support a strip search policy. The majority correctly points out that there was but "one instance" in which the policy had led to the discovery of an effort to smuggle contraband. But the Court understood that the prison had been open only four months. And the Court was also presented with other examples where inmates attempted to smuggle contraband during contact visits. . . .

The *Bell* Court had no occasion to focus upon those arrested for minor crimes, prior to a judicial officer's determination that they should be committed to prison.

I share JUSTICE ALITO's intuition that the calculus may be different in such cases, given that "[m]ost of those arrested for minor offenses are not dangerous, and most are released from custody prior to or at the time of their initial appearance before a magistrate." As he notes, this case does not address, and "reserves judgment on," whether it is always reasonable "to strip search an arrestee before the arrestee's detention has been reviewed by a judicial officer." In my view, it is highly questionable that officials would be justified, for instance, in admitting to the dangerous world of the general jail population and subjecting to a strip search someone with no criminal background arrested for jaywalking or another similarly minor crime. Indeed, that consideration likely underlies why the Federal Government and many States segregate such individuals even when admitted to jail, and several jurisdictions provide that such individuals be released without detention in the ordinary case.

In an appropriate case, therefore, it remains open for the Court to consider whether it would be reasonable to admit an arrestee for a minor offense to the general jail population, and to subject her to the "humiliation of a strip search," prior to any review by a judicial officer.

. . .

For the reasons set forth, I cannot find justification for the strip search policy at issue here—a policy that would subject those arrested for minor offenses to serious invasions of their personal privacy. I consequently dissent.

STEPHEN BREYER is an associate justice of the U.S. Supreme Court. He received an AB from Stanford University, a BA from Magdalen College, Oxford, and an LLB from Harvard Law School. He served as a law clerk to Justice Arthur Goldberg of the Supreme Court of the United States during the 1964 term. Prior to being appointed as a judge of the United States Court of Appeals for the First Circuit, he was a professor at Harvard Law School. From 1990 to 1994, he served as chief judge for the First Circuit Court of Appeals. President Clinton nominated him as an associate Justice of the Supreme Court in 1994.

Should It Be Lawful for the Police to Conduct JailHouse Strip Searches of Persons Arrested for Minor Offenses? by Hickey

325

EXPLORING THE ISSUE

Should It Be Lawful for the Police to Conduct JailHouse Strip Searches of Persons Arrested for Minor Offenses?

Critical Thinking and Reflection

1. When is it appropriate for enforcement officials to perform a strip search?
2. Are strip searches a reasonable tool needed to maintain order and security?

Is There Common Ground?

This is a challenging issue. On one hand, as Associate Justice Kennedy asserts, police officers and correctional officials must be accorded some latitude to develop jailhouse policies that will ensure the safety of inmates and the staff. Moreover, the presence of contraband and illegal substances inside correctional facilities are a real and significant problem. As the Supreme Court observed in *Bell v. Wolfish*, the need to maintain order and security will clearly justify some intrusion on the individual Fourth Amendment rights of those individuals confined within these institutions. The question is: How far should this principle extend?

In *Florence, Bell v. Wolfish*, and many other Fourth Amendment cases over the last half-century, the Supreme Court has often utilized a "balancing test," to weigh the various interests at stake. Although a detailed treatment of this very interesting subject is beyond the scope of the present initiative, such a test most often balances an individual's privacy rights under the Fourth Amendment against a purported governmental interest in restricting those rights for some compelling reason.

For example, in the well-known case of *Michigan v. Sitz*, 496 U.S. 444 (1990), the Supreme Court, using "balancing" methodology, sanctioned the use of sobriety checkpoints designed to catch intoxicated drivers, even though there was no reasonable suspicion or probable cause to believe that persons stopped at those checkpoints were operating under the influence of alcohol. They reached this conclusion by balancing the relatively "minor" intrusion on individual privacy of motorists traveling on public highways who are stopped at these checkpoints with the compelling public/governmental interest in combatting

drunken driving. Cast in this manner, is it surprising that the individual privacy interest was sacrificed to the public interest in stopping driving while intoxicated (DWI) on our nation's highways?

Cases such as *Sitz*, however, have led some legal scholars to conclude that the Supreme Court's use of "balancing" analysis is designed to arrive at a preordained conclusion in Fourth Amendment cases: That individual privacy interests must give way to more important government interests in virtually all cases involving issues such as motor vehicle stops, jailhouse searches, searches for evidence of crimes or contraband (especially in illegal drug cases), and various other practices implicating privacy rights. In fact, some years ago, Professor Silas Wasserstrom, an expert in Fourth Amendment law, who had conducted a detailed analysis of these issues, wrote an article titled "The Incredible Shrinking Fourth Amendment," which implied that the Supreme Court's balancing methodology was simply a form of *conservative judicial activism* designed to narrow the scope of individual rights in Fourth Amendment cases.

Regardless of one's position on whether "balancing methodology" is a legitimate form of legal analysis, it is clear that the Supreme Court has narrowed the scope of individual Fourth Amendment rights in recent years. Is it a good thing that the Supreme Court in various Fourth Amendment cases has made it easier for law enforcement officers to apprehend those who have committed crimes? To paraphrase the renowned Supreme Court Justice Benjamin Cardozo, "Should the criminal go free because the constable has blundered?" Or, is it preferable to require police officers to comply with the constraints imposed by due process and individual privacy rights, even if it means that a factually guilty person must be set free? These are difficult questions.

The Supreme Court's decision in *Florence* signals that a majority of the present Supreme Court is likely to tilt the Fourth Amendment balancing test toward the side of governmental interests in the administration of justice, rather than vindicating individual privacy rights. Whether or not this is seen as a positive development is likely to depend on one's personal values and political orientation

Justice Anthony Kennedy, writing the majority in *Florence*, clearly adopted a position that favored governmental interests in the administration of justice. Stated Justice Kennedy:

> Detecting contraband concealed by new detainees . . . is a most serious responsibility. Weapons, drugs, and alcohol all disrupt the safe operation of a jail. Correctional officers have had to confront arrestees concealing knives, scissors, razorblades, glass shards, and other prohibited items on their person, including in their body cavities.

Justice Breyer and the dissenting justices in contrast, would have struck the Fourth Amendment balance in favor of the individual privacy interests of those who stand accused of nonserious crimes. According to Justice Breyer:

> [S]uch a search of an individual arrested for a minor offense that does not involve drugs or violence—say a traffic offense, a regulatory offense, an essentially civil matter, or any other such misdemeanor—is an "unreasonable search" forbidden by the Fourth Amendment, unless prison authorities have reasonable suspicion to believe that the individual possesses drugs or other contraband.

After reading the case excerpts presented in this section, do you agree with Justice Kennedy's Majority opinion, or Justice Breyer and the dissenting justices?

Additional Resources

Whatever your opinion is in this case, additional reading in this area is readily available. See Kathleen M. Sullivan and Gerald Gunther, *Constitutional Law* (Foundation Press, 15th ed., 2004); Laurence H. Tribe, *American Constitutional Law* (Foundation Press, 2nd ed., 1988); Rolando V. del Carmen, *Criminal Procedure: Law and Practice* (Academic Press, 8th ed., 2009); Thomas J. Hickey, *Criminal Procedure* (McGraw Hill, 2001); Yale A. Kamisar, Wayne R. LaFave, Jerold H. Israel et al., *Modern Criminal Procedure* (West Publishing Co., 12th ed., 2008);. See also: Wasserstrom, "The Incredible Shrinking Fourth Amendment," 21 *American Criminal Law Review.* (1984); Akhil Reed Amar, "Fourth Amendment First Principles," 107 *Harvard Law Review* 4 (1994); Ivan Eland, "Bush's War and the State of Civil Liberties," 14 *Mediterranean Quarterly* 4 (2003); Larson, "Women, the Criminal Justice System, and Incarceration: Processes of Power, Silence and Resistance," 20 *NWSA Journal* 2 (2008).

Internet References . . .

New York Times

www.nytimes.com/2012/04/03/us/justices
-approve-strip-searches-for-any-offense
.html?pagewanted=all&_r=0

Selected, Edited, and with Issue Framing Material by:
Thomas J. Hickey, *State University of New York at Cobleskill*

ISSUE

Does an Imprisoned Convict Who Claims Innocence Have a Constitutional Right to Access the State's Evidence for DNA Testing?

YES: John Paul Stevens, from "Dissenting Opinion," *District Attorney's Office v. Osborne,* U.S. Supreme Court (2009)

NO: John Roberts, from "Majority Opinion," *District Attorney's Office v. Osborne,* U.S. Supreme Court (2009)

Learning Outcomes

After reading this issue, you will be able to:

- Discuss the findings of the "Innocence Project" with respect to wrongful convictions.
- Discuss several potential uses of DNA evidence.
- Discuss why DNA is such powerful evidence.
- Discuss whether or not a state's refusal to provide a convicted offender with evidence for DNA testing is "shocking to the conscience" and contrary to American notions of justice.
- Discuss whether convicted offenders should have a constitutional right to conduct DNA tests on evidence presented at their trials, or whether state laws provide sufficient protection for these individuals.

ISSUE SUMMARY

YES: Justice John Stevens, in a dissenting opinion in *District Attorney's Office for the Third Judicial District v. Osborne* (2009), contends that a fundamental responsibility to ensure that "justice" has been served requires a state to provide a defendant with postconviction access to DNA evidence. Because it could conclusively establish whether an accused had committed the crime in the first place, this right should be protected by the Fourteenth Amendment's Due Process Clause.

NO: Chief Justice John Roberts, writing for the majority opinion in *District Attorney's Office for the Third Judicial District v. Osborne* (2009), held that the U.S. Constitution's Due Process Clause provides no right to postconviction access to DNA evidence because it would take the development of rules and procedures in criminal cases out of the hands of state legislatures and courts.

The U.S. Constitution requires that in criminal prosecutions, a defendant's guilt must be proven "beyond a reasonable doubt." In practical terms, this means that the prosecution must demonstrate that the accused has committed the charged offense and that there is unlikely to be a plausible alternative explanation. Moreover, in *In re*

Winship, 397 U.S. 358 (1970), the Supreme Court held that the prosecution is required to present evidence to prove each element of the charged crime beyond a reasonable doubt.

One of the more compelling types of evidence that is sometimes produced in either criminal or civil cases involves the use of DNA sequencing.

DNA evidence may be used in a number of different ways. The Human Genome Project lists several examples:

- To identify potential suspects whose DNA may match evidence left at crime scenes.
- To exonerate persons wrongly accused of crimes.
- To identify crime and catastrophe victims.
- To establish paternity and other family relationships.
- To identify endangered and protected species as an aid to wildlife officials (could be used for prosecuting poachers).
- To detect bacteria and other organisms that may pollute air, water, soil, and food.
- To match organ donors with recipients in transplant programs (www.gneomics.energy.gov).

According to the Human Genome Project, scientists seeking to identify a particular individual will scan 13 different DNA regions, termed *loci*, which vary from person to person and can be used to create someone's unique DNA profile. States scientist Daniel Drell:

> DNA identification can be quite effective if used intelligently. . . . [Y]ou can look for matches (based on sequence or on numbers of small repeating units of DNA sequence) at many different locations on a person's genome; one or two (even three) aren't enough to be confident that the suspect is the right one, but thirteen sites are used. A match at all thirteen is rare enough that you (or a prosecutor or a jury) can be very confident ('beyond a reasonable doubt') that the right person is accused.
>
> —(www.genomics.energy.gov)

Therefore, because there is virtually no chance that two persons will have identical DNA profiles, it becomes very powerful evidence in cases where the identity of a perpetrator is an issue.

In addition, an important federal law, the DNA Identification Act of 1994, mandated the development of a national DNA data bank administered by the Federal Bureau of Investigation (42 U.S.C. Section 14135a). The acronym for this database is CODIS, the Combined DNA Index System, which uses two different indices to produce leads when biological evidence is recovered from a crime scene. The Convicted Offender Index contains DNA profiles of felony sex offenders as well as other violent criminals. The Forensic Index contains DNA profiles found from crime scene evidence. Federal, state, and local law enforcement officers take DNA samples from biological evidence left at crime scenes that have no suspect and compare it to DNA samples in the CODIS systems. If a match is found, the CODIS database can be used to identify the perpetrator (*Id.*).

All 50 states authorize the collection and analysis of DNA samples from convicted state offenders and enter the profiles into CODIS. Several states also authorize the collection of DNA samples from all individuals they arrest (Federal Register, vol. 73, no. 238/Wednesday, December 10, 2008).

For example, the state of California mandates DNA collection from persons in the following circumstances:

a. Any person (adult or juvenile) who is newly convicted/adjudicated of a felony offense, or who is newly convicted/adjudicated of a misdemeanor or infraction offense but has a prior felony of record; . . .

b. Any person (adult or juvenile) currently in custody or on probation, parole, or any other supervised release after conviction for any felony offense; . . .

c. Any person (adult or juvenile) currently on probation or any other supervised release for any offense with a prior felony . . . of record. (Cal. Pen. Code, Sections 295, 296, 296.1)

Currently, California has collected approximately 1,337,105 offender profiles and 33,673 forensic samples, and has 12,777 *investigations aided*, which is the primary measuring criterion used to assess the effectiveness of CODIS (www.fbi.gov/about-us/lab/codis/ndis-statistics).

To illustrate just how comprehensive the CODIS national database has become, as of March, 2011, the National DNA Index (NDIS) contained more than 9,535,059 offender profiles and 366,762 forensic profiles. It has produced more than 141,000 "hits" assisting in more than 135,000 investigations.

As scholars and commentators from across the political spectrum have observed, one of the most compelling uses of DNA evidence is to exonerate persons who have been wrongly convicted. Once someone has been convicted of a crime, however, should they have a federal constitutional right to have DNA evidence reevaluated if it was not available during their original trial? Or, should the states be free to develop their own protections for those who may have been wrongly convicted?

In formulating your response to these questions, it is important to keep in mind that these cases involve a request for *postconviction* relief by a defendant who has already had a full and fair trial in a state court. One of the principal modes of challenging a conviction after an offender has exhausted his or her appeals in state courts is termed a *habeas corpus lawsuit,* a civil proceeding in federal court, which asserts that a prisoner is being held unlawfully due to an error in the state proceedings (42 U.S.C. Section 1983). Although a comprehensive discussion of these issues is beyond the scope of this initiative, it is safe to say that the U.S. Congress and the federal courts have seemed determined in recent years to stem the tide of federal habeas corpus lawsuits filed by state prison inmates. So, once a defendant has exhausted his or her appeals in state court, should the U.S. Supreme Court recognize a special constitutional right for postconviction review of DNA evidence, due to its exceptional ability to ensure that "justice has been served" by exonerating the wrongly accused?

The questions presented above are compelling ones. Justice John Stevens, dissenting in *District Attorney's Office v. Osborne*, 557 U.S. ____ (2009), asserts that the U.S. Constitution should recognize such a right. Stevens summarizes the issues posed in this case as follows:

> The State of Alaska possesses physical evidence that, if tested, will conclusively establish whether [Osborne] committed rape and attempted murder. If he did, justice has been served by his conviction and sentence. If not, Osborne has needlessly spent decades behind bars while the true culprit has not been brought to justice. The DNA test Osborne seeks is a simple one, its cost modest, and its results uniquely precise. Yet for reasons the State has been unable or unwilling to articulate, it refuses to allow Osborne to test the evidence at his own expense and to thereby ascertain the truth once and for all.

Justice Stevens's opinion also emphasizes that a criminal conviction does not eliminate the constitutional liberty interests of convicted persons, "including the fundamental liberty of freedom from [wrongful] physical restraint." Justice Stevens concludes that "there is no reason to deny access to the evidence and there are many reasons to provide it, not least of which is a fundamental concern in ensuring that justice has been done in this case."

Chief Justice John Roberts disagrees, however. He states that Osborne has proposed "the recognition of a freestanding and far-reaching constitutional right of access to [DNA] evidence." Justice Roberts believes that such an "approach would take the development of rules and procedures in this area out of the hands of legislatures and state courts shaping policy in a focused manner and turn it over to federal courts applying the broad parameters of the Due Process Clause."

Who presents the more compelling argument: Justice Stevens or Chief Justice Roberts? Despite the fact that the states have a strong interest in the administration of their own justice systems, do you believe that the unique accuracy of DNA evidence and its potential for acquitting the wrongly convicted justify the development of a special federal constitutional right designed to vindicate these interests? Consider Chief Justice Roberts's assertion that the justice system "like any human endeavor, cannot be perfect." Should properly collected and analyzed DNA evidence constitute an exception to that rule? Finally, would you agree with the famous and authoritative British jurist William Blackstone's assertion that it is "better that ten guilty persons escape than one innocent suffer?" (William Blackstone, *Commentaries* [vol. 4, p. 358]). Do you believe that the majority opinion in *District Attorney's Office v. Osborne* is consistent with Blackstone's famous aphorism?

YES ↵

John Paul Stevens

Dissenting Opinion, *District Attorney's Office v. Osborne*

Justice Stevens, with whom Justice Ginsburg and Justice Breyer join, and with whom Justice Souter joins as to Part I, dissenting.

The State of Alaska possesses physical evidence that, if tested, will conclusively establish whether respondent William Osborne committed rape and attempted murder. If he did, justice has been served by his conviction and sentence. If not, Osborne has needlessly spent decades behind bars while the true culprit has not been brought to justice. The DNA test Osborne seeks is a simple one, its cost modest, and its results uniquely precise. Yet for reasons the State has been unable or unwilling to articulate, it refuses to allow Osborne to test the evidence at his own expense and to thereby ascertain the truth once and for all.

On two equally problematic grounds, the Court today blesses the State's arbitrary denial of the evidence Osborne seeks. First, while acknowledging that Osborne may have a due process right to access the evidence under Alaska's postconviction procedures, the Court concludes that Osborne has not yet availed himself of all possible avenues for relief in state court. As both a legal and factual matter, that conclusion is highly suspect. More troubling still, based on a fundamental mischaracterization of the right to liberty that Osborne seeks to vindicate, the Court refuses to acknowledge "in the circumstances of this case" any right to access the evidence that is grounded in the Due Process Clause itself. Because I am convinced that Osborne has a constitutional right of access to the evidence he wishes to test and that, on the facts of this case, he has made a sufficient showing of entitlement to that evidence, I would affirm the decision of the Court of Appeals.

I

The Fourteenth Amendment provides that "[n]o State shall . . . deprive any person of life, liberty, or property, without due process of law." §1. Our cases have frequently recognized that protected liberty interests may arise "from the Constitution itself, by reason of guarantees implicit in the word 'liberty,' . . . or it may arise from an expectation or interest created by state laws or policies." . . . Osborne contends that he possesses a right to access DNA evidence arising from both these sources.

Osborne first anchors his due process right in Alaska Stat. §12.72.010(4) (2008). Under that provision, a person who has been "convicted of, or sentenced for, a crime may institute a proceeding for post-conviction relief if the person claims... that there exists evidence of material facts, not previously presented and heard by the court, that requires vacation of the conviction or sentence in the interest of justice." . . . Osborne asserts that exculpatory DNA test results obtained using state-of-the-art Short Tandem Repeat (STR) and Mitochondrial (mtDNA) analysis would qualify as newly discovered evidence entitling him to relief under the state statute. The problem is that the newly discovered evidence he wishes to present cannot be generated unless he is first able to access the State's evidence—something he cannot do without the State's consent or a court order.

Although States are under no obligation to provide mechanisms for postconviction relief, when they choose to do so, the procedures they employ must comport with the demands of the Due Process Clause . . . by providing litigants with fair opportunity to assert their state-created rights. Osborne contends that by denying him an opportunity to access the physical evidence, the State has denied him meaningful access to state postconviction relief, thereby violating his right to due process.

Although the majority readily agrees that Osborne has a protected liberty interest in demonstrating his innocence with new evidence under Alaska Stat. §12.72.010(4) . . . it rejects the Ninth Circuit's conclusion that Osborne is constitutionally entitled to access the State's evidence. The Court concludes that the adequacy of the process afforded to Osborne must be assessed under the standard set forth . . . Under that standard, Alaska's

Stevens, John P. Supreme Court of the United States, 129 S.Ct 2308, June 19, 2009.

procedures for bringing a claim under §12.72.010(4) will not be found to violate due process unless they "'offen[d] some principle of justice so rooted in the traditions and conscience of our people as to be ranked as fundamental,' or 'transgres[s] any recognized principle of fundamental fairness in operation.'" . . . After conducting a cursory review of the relevant statutory text, the Court concludes that Alaska's procedures are constitutional on their face.

While I agree that the statute is not facially deficient, the state courts' application of §12.72.010(4) raises serious questions whether the State's procedures are fundamentally unfair in their operation. As an initial matter, it is not clear that Alaskan courts ordinarily permit litigants to utilize the state postconviction statute to obtain new evidence in the form of DNA tests. . . .

Of even greater concern is the manner in which the state courts applied §12.72.010(4) to the facts of this case. In determining that Osborne was not entitled to relief under the postconviction statute, the Alaska Court of Appeals concluded that the DNA testing Osborne wished to obtain could not qualify as "newly discovered" because it was available at the time of trial. . . . In his arguments before the state trial court and his briefs to the Alaska Court of Appeals, however, Osborne had plainly requested STR DNA testing, a form of DNA testing not yet in use at the time of his trial. . . . The state appellate court's conclusion that the requested testing had been available at the time of trial was therefore clearly erroneous. Given these facts, the majority's assertion that Osborne "attempt[ed] to sidestep state process" by failing "to use the process provided to him by the State" is unwarranted. . . .

The same holds true with respect to the majority's suggestion that the Alaska Constitution might provide additional protections to Osborne above and beyond those afforded under afforded under §12.72.010(4). In Osborne's state postconviction proceedings, the Alaska Court of Appeals held out the possibility that even when evidence does not meet the requirements of §12.72.010(4), the State Constitution might offer relief to a defendant who is able to make certain threshold showings. . . . On remand from that decision, however, the state trial court denied Osborne relief on the ground that he failed to show that (1) his conviction rested primarily on eyewitness identification; (2) there was a demonstrable doubt concerning his identity as the perpetrator; and (3) scientific testing would like be conclusive on this issue. . . .

Osborne made full use of available state procedures in his efforts to secure access to evidence for DNA testing so that he might avail himself of the postconviction relief afforded by the State of Alaska. He was rebuffed at every turn. The manner in which the Alaska courts applied state

law in this case leaves me in grave doubt about the adequacy of the procedural protections afforded to litigants under Alaska Stat. §12.72.010(4), and provides strong reason to doubt the majority's flippant assertion that if Osborne were "simply [to] see[k] the DNA through the State's discovery procedures, he might well get it." . . . However, even if the Court were correct in its assumption that Osborne might be given the evidence he seeks were he to present his claim in state court a second time, there should be no need for him to do so.

II

Wholly apart from his state-created interest in obtaining postconviction relief under Alaska Stat. §12.72.010(4), Osborne asserts a right to access the State's evidence that derives from the Due Process Clause itself. Whether framed as a "substantive liberty interest . . . protected through a procedural due process right" to have evidence made available for testing, or as a substantive due process right to be free of arbitrary government action, . . . the result is the same: On the record now before us, Osborne has established his entitlement to test the State's evidence.

The liberty protected by the Due Process Clause is not a creation of the Bill of Rights. Indeed, our Nation has long recognized that the liberty safeguarded by the Constitution has far deeper roots. See Declaration of Independence ¶2 (holding it self-evident that "all men are . . . endowed by their Creator with certain unalienable Rights," among which are "Life, Liberty, and the pursuit of Happiness.") . . . The "most elemental" of the liberties protected by the Due Process Clause is "the interest in being free from physical detention by one's own government." . . .

Although a valid criminal conviction justifies punitive detention, it does not entirely eliminate the liberty interests of convicted persons. For while a prisoner's "rights may be diminished by the needs and exigencies of the institutional environment[, [. . . [t]here is no iron curtain drawn between the Constitution and the prisons of this country." . . . Our cases have recognized protected interests in a variety of postconviction contexts, extending substantive constitutional protections to state prisoners on the premise that the Due Process Clause of the Fourteenth Amendment requires States to respect certain fundamental liberties in the postconviction context. . . . It is therefore far too late in the day to question the basic proposition that convicted persons such as Osborne retain a constitutionally protected measure of interest in liberty, including the fundamental liberty of freedom from physical restraint.

Recognition of this right draws strength from the fact that 46 States and the Federal Government have passed statutes providing access to evidence for DNA testing, and 3 additional states (including Alaska) provide similar access through court-made rules alone, . . . These legislative developments are consistent with recent trends in legal ethics recognizing that prosecutors are obliged to disclose all forms of exculpatory evidence that come into their possession following conviction. . . . The fact that nearly all the States have now recognized some postconviction right to DNA evidence makes it more, not less, appropriate to recognize a limited federal right to such evidence in cases where litigants are unfairly barred from obtaining relief in state court.

Insofar as it is process Osborne seeks, he is surely entitled to less than "the full panoply of rights," that would be due [10] a criminal defendant prior to conviction. . . . That does not mean, however, that our pretrial due process cases have no relevance in the postconviction context. In *Brady* v. *Maryland,* 373 U.S. 83, 87 (1963), we held that the State violates due process when it suppresses "evidence favorable to an accused" that is "material either to guilt or to punishment, irrespective of the good faith or bad faith of the prosecution." Although *Brady* does not directly provide for a postconviction right to such evidence, the concerns with fundamental fairness that motivated our decision in that case are equally present when convicted persons such as Osborne seek access to dispositive DNA evidence following conviction.

Recent scientific advances in DNA analysis have made "it literally possible to confirm guilt or innocence beyond any question whatsoever, at least in some categories of cases." . . . As the Court recognizes today, the powerful new evidence that modern DNA testing can provide is "unlike anything known before." . . . Discussing these important forensic developments in his often-cited opinion in Harvey, Judge Luttig explained that although "no one would contend that fairness, in the constitutional sense, requires a post-conviction right of access or a right to disclosure anything approaching in scope that which is required pretrial," in cases "where the government holds previously produced forensic evidence, the testing of which concededly could prove beyond any doubt that the defendant did not commit the crime for which he was convicted, the very same principle of elemental fairness that dictates pre-trial production of all potentially exculpatory evidence dictates post-trial production of this infinitely narrower category of evidence." . . . It does so "out of recognition of the same systemic interests in fairness and ultimate truth." . . .

If the right Osborne seeks to vindicate is framed as purely substantive, the proper result is no less clear. "The touchstone of due process is protection of the individual against arbitrary action of government.". . . When government action is so lacking in justification that it "can properly be characterized as arbitrary, or conscience shocking, in a constitutional sense," . . . violates the Due Process Clause. In my view, the State's refusal to provide Osborne with access to evidence for DNA testing qualifies as arbitrary.

Throughout the course of state and federal litigation, the State has failed to provide any concrete reason for denying Osborne the DNA testing he seeks, and none is apparent. Because Osborne has offered to pay for the tests, cost is not a factor. And as the State now concedes, there is no reason to doubt that such testing would provide conclusive confirmation of Osborne's guilt or revelation of his innocence. In the courts below, the State refused to provide an explanation for its refusal to permit testing of the evidence, . . . and in this Court, its explanation has been, at best, unclear. Insofar as the State has articulated any reason at all, it appears to be a generalized interest in protecting the finality of the judgment of conviction from any possible future attacks. . . .

While we have long recognized that States have an interest in securing the finality of their judgments, . . . finality is not a stand-alone value that trumps a State's overriding interest in ensuring that justice is done in its courts and secured to its citizens. Indeed, when absolute proof of innocence is readily at hand, a State should not shrink from the possibility that error may have occurred. Rather, our system of justice is strengthened by "recogniz[ing] the need for, and imperative of, a safety valve in those rare instances where objective proof that the convicted actually did not commit the offense later becomes available through the progress of science.". . . DNA evidence has led to an extraordinary series of exonerations, not only in cases where the trial evidence was weak, but also in cases where the convicted parties confessed their guilt and where the trial evidence against them appeared overwhelming. The examples provided by amici of the power of DNA testing serve to convince me that the fact of conviction is not sufficient to justify a State's refusal to perform a test that will conclusively establish innocence or guilt.

This conclusion draws strength from the powerful state interests that offset the State's purported interest in finality *per se.* When a person is convicted for a crime he did not commit, the true culprit escapes punishment. DNA testing may lead to his identification. . . . Crime victims, the law enforcement profession, and society at large share a strong interest in identifying and apprehending the actual perpetrators of vicious crimes, such as the rape and attempted murder that gave rise to this case.

The arbitrariness of the State's conduct is highlighted by comparison to the private interests it denies. It seems to me obvious that if a wrongly convicted person were to produce proof of his actual innocence, no state interest would be sufficient to justify his continued punitive detention. If such proof can be readily obtained without imposing a significant burden on the State, a refusal to provide access to such evidence is wholly unjustified.

In sum, an individual's interest in his physical liberty is one of constitutional significance. That interest would be vindicated by providing postconviction access to DNA evidence, as would the State's interest in ensuring that it punishes the true perpetrator of a crime. In this case, the State has suggested no countervailing interest that justifies its refusal to allow Osborne to test the evidence in its possession and has not provided any other nonarbitrary explanation for its conduct. Consequently, I am left to conclude that the State's failure to provide Osborne access to the evidence constitutes arbitrary action that offends basic principles of due process. . . .

III

. . . Before our decision in *Powell* v. *Alabama*, 287 U. S. 45 (1932), state law alone governed the manner in which counsel was appointed for indigent defendants. "Efforts to impose a minimum federal standard for the right to counsel in state courts routinely met the same refrain: 'in the face of these widely varying state procedures', this Court refused to impose the dictates of 'due process' onto the states and 'hold invalid all procedure not reaching that standard." . . . When at last this Court

recognized the Sixth Amendment right to counsel for all indigent criminal defendants in *Gideon* v. *Wainwright*, 372 U. S. 335 (1963), our decision did not impede the ability of States to tailor their appointment processes to local needs, nor did it unnecessarily interfere with their sovereignty. It did, however, ensure that criminal defendants were provided with the counsel to which they were constitutionally entitled. In the same way, a decision to recognize a limited right of postconviction access to DNA testing would not prevent the States from creating procedures by which litigants request and obtain such access; it would merely ensure that States do so in a manner that is nonarbitrary. . . .

IV

Osborne has demonstrated a constitutionally protected right to due process which the State of Alaska thus far has not vindicated and which this Court is both empowered and obliged to safeguard. On the record before us, there is no reason to deny access to the evidence and there are many reasons to provide it, not least of which is a fundamental concern in ensuring that justice has been done in this case. I would affirm the judgment of the Court of Appeals, and respectfully dissent from the Court's refusal to do so.

JOHN PAUL STEVENS is an associate justice of the U.S. Supreme Court. He worked in law firms in Chicago, Illinois, for 20 years before being nominated by President Richard Nixon to the U.S. Court of Appeals in 1970. He served in that capacity until he was nominated to the Supreme Court by President Gerald Ford in 1975.

John Roberts

Majority Opinion, *District Attorney's Office v. Osborne*

Chief Justice Roberts delivered the opinion of the Court.

DNA testing has an unparalleled ability both to exonerate the wrongly convicted and to identify the guilty. It has the potential to significantly improve both the criminal justice system and police investigative practices. The Federal Government and the States have recognized this, and have developed special approaches to ensure that this evidentiary tool can be effectively incorporated into established criminal procedure—usually but not always through legislation.

Against this prompt and considered response, the respondent, William Osborne, proposes a different approach: the recognition of a freestanding and far-reaching constitutional right of access to this new type of evidence. The nature of what he seeks is confirmed by his decision to file this lawsuit in federal court under 42 U. S. C. §1983, not within the state criminal justice system. This approach would take the development of rules and procedures in this area out of the hands of legislatures and state courts shaping policy in a focused manner and turn it over to federal courts applying the broad parameters of the Due Process Clause. There is no reason to constitutionalize the issue in this way. Because the decision below would do just that, we reverse.

I

A

This lawsuit arose out of a violent crime committed 16 years ago, which has resulted in a long string of litigation in the state and federal courts. On the evening of March 22, 1993, two men driving through Anchorage, Alaska, solicited sex from a female prostitute, K. G. She agreed to perform fellatio on both men for $100 and got in their car. The three spent some time looking for a place to stop and ended up in a deserted area near Earthquake Park. When K. G. demanded payment in advance, the two men pulled out a gun and forced her to perform fellatio on the driver while the passenger penetrated her vaginally, using a blue condom she had brought. The passenger then ordered K. G. out of the car and told her to lie face-down in the snow. Fearing for her life, she refused, and the two men choked her and beat her with the gun. When K. G. tried to flee, the passenger beat her with a wooden axe handle and shot her in the head while she lay on the ground. They kicked some snow on top of her and left her for dead. 521 F. 3d 1118, 1122 (CA9 2008) (case below); *Osborne* v. *State,* 163 P. 3d 973, 975–976 (Alaska App. 2007) (*Osborne II*); App. 27, 42–44.

K. G. did not die; the bullet had only grazed her head. Once the two men left, she found her way back to the road, and flagged down a passing car to take her home. Ultimately, she received medical care and spoke to the police. At the scene of the crime, the police recovered a spent shell casing, the axe handle, some of K. G.'s clothing stained with blood, and the blue condom. . . .

Six days later, two military police officers at Fort Richardson pulled over Dexter Jackson for flashing his headlights at another vehicle. In his car they discovered a gun (which matched the shell casing), as well as several items K. G. had been carrying the night of the attack. . . . The car also matched the description K. G. had given to the police. Jackson admitted that he had been the driver during the rape and assault, and told the police that William Osborne had been his passenger. . . . Other evidence also implicated Osborne. K. G. picked out his photograph (with some uncertainty) and at trial she identified Osborne as her attacker. Other witnesses testified that shortly before the crime, Osborne had called Jackson from an arcade, and then driven off with him. An axe handle similar to the one at the scene of the crime was found in Osborne's room on the military base where he lived.

The State also performed DQ Alpha testing on sperm found in the blue condom. DQ Alpha testing is a relatively inexact form of DNA testing that can clear some wrongly accused individuals, but generally cannot narrow the perpetrator down to less than 5% of the

Roberts, John. Supreme Court of the United States, 129 S.Ct 2308, June 18, 2009.

population. . . . The semen found on the condom had a genotype that matched a blood sample taken from Osborne, but not ones from Jackson, K. G., or a third suspect named James Hunter. Osborne is black, and approximately 16% of black individuals have such a genotype. App. 117–119. In other words, the testing ruled out Jackson and Hunter as possible sources of the semen, and also ruled out over 80% of other black individuals. The State also examined some pubic hairs found at the scene of the crime, which were not susceptible to DQ Alpha testing, but which state witnesses attested to be similar to Osborne's. . . .

B

Osborne and Jackson were convicted by an Alaska jury of kidnaping, assault, and sexual assault. They were acquitted of an additional count of sexual assault and of attempted murder. Finding it "'nearly miraculous'" that K. G. had survived, the trial judge sentenced Osborne to 26 years in prison, with 5 suspended. *Id.,* at 128a. His conviction and sentence were affirmed on appeal. *Id.,* at 113a–130a.

Osborne then sought postconviction relief in Alaska state court. He claimed that he had asked his attorney, Sidney Billingslea, to seek more discriminating restriction-fragment-length-polymorphism (RFLP) DNA testing during trial, and argued that she was constitutionally ineffective for not doing so. Billingslea testified that after investigation, she had concluded that further testing would do more harm than good. She planned to mount a defense of mistaken identity, and thought that the imprecision of the DQ Alpha test gave her "Very good numbers in a mistaken identity, cross-racial identification case, where the victim was in the dark and had bad eyesight'. "

Osborne I, 110 P. 3d, at 990. Because she believed Osborne was guilty, "'insisting on a more advanced . . . DNA test would have served to prove that Osborne committed the alleged crimes.'" *Ibid.* The Alaska Court of Appeals concluded that Billingslea's decision had been strategic and rejected Osborne's claim. *Id.,* at 991–992.

In this proceeding, Osborne also sought the DNA testing that Billingslea had failed to perform, relying on an Alaska postconviction statute, Alaska Stat. §12.72 (2008), and the State and Federal Constitutions. In two decisions, the Alaska Court of Appeals concluded that Osborne had no right to the RFLP test. According to the court, §12.72 "apparently" did not apply to DNA testing that had been available at trial.[1] *Osborne I,* 110 P. 3d, at 992–993. The court found no basis in our precedents for recognizing a federal constitutional right to DNA evidence. *Id.,* at 993. After a remand for further findings, the Alaska Court of Appeals concluded that Osborne could not claim a state

constitutional right either, because the other evidence of his guilt was too strong and RFLP testing was not likely to be conclusive. *Osborne II,* 163 P. 3d, at 979–981. Two of the three judges wrote separately to say that "[i]f Osborne could show that he were in fact innocent, it would be unconscionable to punish him," and that doing so might violate the Alaska Constitution. *Id.,* at 984–985 (Mannheimer, J., concurring).

The court relied heavily on the fact that Osborne had confessed to some of his crimes in a 2004 application for parole—in which it is a crime to lie. *Id.,* at 978–979, 981 (majority opinion) (citing Alaska Stat. §11.56.210 (2002)). In this statement, Osborne acknowledged forcing K. G. to have sex at gunpoint, as well as beating her and covering her with snow. *Id.,* at 977–978, n. 11. He repeated this confession before the parole board. Despite this acceptance of responsibility, the board did not grant him discretionary parole. App. to Pet. for Cert. 8a. In 2007, he was released on mandatory parole, but he has since been rearrested for another offense, and the State has petitioned to revoke this parole. Brief for Petitioners 7, n. 3.

Meanwhile, Osborne had also been active in federal court, suing state officials under 42 U. S. C. §1983. He claimed that the Due Process Clause and other constitutional provisions gave him a constitutional right to access the DNA evidence for what is known as short-tandemrepeat (STR) testing (at his own expense). App. 24. This form of testing is more discriminating than the DQ Alpha or RFLP methods available at the time of Osborne's trial. The District Court first dismissed the claim under *Heck* v. *Humphrey,* 512 U. S. 477 (1994), holding it "inescapable" that Osborne sought to "set the stage" for an attack on his conviction, and therefore "must proceed through a writ of habeas corpus." App. 207 (internal quotation marks omitted). The United States Court of Appeals for the Ninth Circuit reversed, concluding that §1983 was the proper vehicle for Osborne's claims, while "express[ing] no opinion as to whether Osborne ha[d] been deprived of a federally protected right." 423 F. 3d, at 1056. . . .

We granted certiorari to decide whether Osborne's claims could be pursued using §1983, and whether he has a right under the Due Process Clause to obtain postconviction access to the State's evidence for DNA testing. . . . We now reverse on the latter ground.

II

Modern DNA testing can provide powerful new evidence unlike anything known before. Since its first use in criminal investigations in the mid-1980s, there have been several major advances in DNA technology, culminating in STR technology. It is now often possible to determine whether a biological tissue matches a suspect with near certainty. While of course many criminal trials proceed without any forensic and scientific testing at all, there is no technology comparable to DNA testing for matching tissues when such evidence is at issue. Postconviction DNA Testing 1–2; Future of Forensic DNA Testing 13-14. DNA testing has exonerated wrongly convicted people, and has confirmed the convictions of many others.

At the same time, DNA testing alone does not always resolve a case. Where there is enough other incriminating evidence and an explanation for the DNA result, science alone cannot prove a prisoner innocent. See *House v. Bell*, 547 U. S. 518, 540–548 (2006). The availability of technologies not available at trial cannot mean that every criminal conviction, or even every criminal conviction involving biological evidence, is suddenly in doubt. The dilemma is how to harness DNA's power to prove innocence without unnecessarily overthrowing the established system of criminal justice.

That task belongs primarily to the legislature. "[T]he States are currently engaged in serious, thoughtful examinations," *Washington* v. *Glucksberg*, 521 U. S. 702, 719 (1997), of how to ensure the fair and effective use of this testing within the existing criminal justice framework. Forty-six States have already enacted statutes dealing specifically with access to DNA evidence. . . . The Federal Government has also passed the Innocence Protection Act of 2004, §411, 118 Stat. 2278, codified in part at 18 U. S. C. §3600, which allows federal prisoners to move for court-ordered DNA testing under certain specified conditions. That Act also grants money to States that enact comparable statutes . . . and as a consequence has served as a model for some state legislation. At oral argument, Osborne agreed that the federal statute is a model for how States ought to handle the issue. . . .

These laws recognize the value of DNA evidence but also the need for certain conditions on access to the State's evidence. A requirement of demonstrating materiality is common, . . . but it is not the only one. The federal statute, for example, requires a sworn statement that the applicant is innocent. . . . This requirement is replicated in several state statutes. . . . States also impose a range of diligence requirements. Several require the requested testing to "have been technologically impossible at trial." . . . Others deny testing to those who declined testing at trial for tactical reasons. . . .

Alaska is one of a handful of States yet to enact legislation specifically addressing the issue of evidence requested for DNA testing. But that does not mean that such evidence is unavailable for those seeking to prove their innocence. Instead, Alaska courts are addressing how to apply existing laws for discovery and postconviction relief to this novel technology. . . . The same is true with respect to other States that do not have DNA-specific statutes. . . .

First, access to evidence is available under Alaska law for those who seek to subject it to newly available DNA testing that will prove them to be actually innocent. Under the State's general postconviction relief statute, a prisoner may challenge his conviction when "there exists evidence of material facts, not previously presented and heard by the court, that requires vacation of the conviction or sentence in the interest of justice." . . . Such a claim is exempt from otherwise applicable time limits if "newly discovered evidence," pursued with due diligence, "establishes by clear and convincing evidence that the applicant is innocent." . . .

Both parties agree that under these provisions of [Alaska Law] "a defendant is entitled to post-conviction relief if the defendant presents newly discovered evidence that establishes by clear and convincing evidence that the defendant is innocent." . . . If such a claim is brought, state law permits general discovery. . . . Alaska courts have explained that these procedures are available to request DNA evidence for newly available testing to establish actual innocence. . . .

In addition to this statutory procedure, the Alaska Court of Appeals has invoked a widely accepted three-part test to govern additional rights to DNA access under the State Constitution. . . . Drawing on the experience with DNA evidence of State Supreme Courts around the country, the Court of Appeals explained that it was "reluctant to hold that Alaska law offers no remedy to defendants who could prove their factual innocence." . . . It was "prepared to hold, however, that a defendant who seeks post-conviction DNA testing . . . must show (1) that the conviction rested primarily on eyewitness identification evidence, (2) that there was a demonstrable doubt concerning the defendant's identification as the perpetrator, and (3) that scientific testing would likely be conclusive on this issue." . . . Thus, the Alaska courts have suggested that even those who do not get discovery under the State's criminal rules have available to them a safety valve under the State Constitution.

This is the background against which the Federal Court of Appeals ordered the State to turn over the DNA evidence in its possession, and it is our starting point in analyzing Osborne's constitutional claims. . . .

IV

A

"No State shall . . . deprive any person of life, liberty, or property, without due process of law." U. S. Const., Amdt. 14, §1; accord Amdt. 5. This Clause imposes procedural limitations on a State's power to take away protected entitlements. . . . Osborne argues that access to the State's evidence is a "process" needed to vindicate his right to prove himself innocent and get out of jail. Process is not an end in itself, so a necessary premise of this argument is that he has an entitlement (what our precedents call a "liberty interest") to prove his innocence even after a fair trial has proved otherwise. We must first examine this asserted liberty interest to determine what process (if any) is due. . . .

In identifying his potential liberty interest, Osborne first attempts to rely on the Governor's constitutional authority to "grant pardons, commutations, and reprieves." Alaska Const., Art. Ill, §21. That claim can be readily disposed of. We have held that noncapital defendants do not have a liberty interest in traditional state executive clemency, to which no particular claimant is *entitled* as a matter of state law. . . . Osborne therefore cannot challenge the constitutionality of any procedures available to vindicate an interest in state clemency.

Osborne does, however, have a liberty interest in demonstrating his innocence with new evidence under state law. As explained, Alaska law provides that those who use "newly discovered evidence" to "establis[h] by clear and convincing evidence that [they are] innocent" may obtain "vacation of [their] conviction or sentence in the interest of justice." . . . This "state-created right can, in some circumstances, beget yet other rights to procedures essential to the realization of the parent right." . . .

The Court of Appeals went too far, however, in concluding that the Due Process Clause requires that certain familiar preconviction trial rights be extended to protect Osborne's postconviction liberty interest. . . .

A criminal defendant proved guilty after a fair trial does not have the same liberty interests as a free man. At trial, the defendant is presumed innocent and may demand that the government prove its case beyond reasonable doubt. But "[o]nce a defendant has been afforded a fair trial and convicted of the offense for which he was charged, the presumption of innocence disappears." . . . "Given a valid conviction, the criminal defendant has been constitutionally deprived of his liberty." . . .

The State accordingly has more flexibility in deciding what procedures are needed in the context of postconviction relief. "[W]hen a State chooses to offer help to those seeking relief from convictions," due process does not "dictat[e] the exact form such assistance must assume." . . . Osborne's right to due process is not parallel to a trial right, but rather must be analyzed in light of the fact that he has already been found guilty at a fair trial, and has only a limited interest in postconviction relief. . . .

Instead, the question is whether consideration of Osborne's claim within the framework of the State's procedures for postconviction relief "offends some principle of justice so rooted in the traditions and conscience of our people as to be ranked as fundamental," or "transgresses any recognized principle of fundamental fairness in operation." . . . Federal courts may upset a State's postconviction relief procedures only if they are fundamentally inadequate to vindicate the substantive rights provided.

We see nothing inadequate about the procedures Alaska has provided to vindicate its state right to postconviction relief in general, and nothing inadequate about how those procedures apply to those who seek access to DNA evidence. Alaska provides a substantive right to be released on a sufficiently compelling showing of new evidence that establishes innocence. It exempts such claims from otherwise applicable time limits. The State provides for discovery in postconviction proceedings, and has—through judicial decision—specified that this discovery procedure is available to those seeking access to DNA evidence. . . . These procedures are not without limits. The evidence must indeed be newly available to qualify under Alaska's statute, must have been diligently pursued, and must also be sufficiently material. These procedures are similar to those provided for DNA evidence by federal law and the law of other States, . . . and they are not inconsistent with the "traditions and conscience of our people" or with "any recognized principle of fundamental fairness." . . .

And there is more. While the Alaska courts have not had occasion to conclusively decide the question, the Alaska Court of Appeals has suggested that the State Constitution provides an additional right of access to DNA. In expressing its "reluctan[ce] to hold that Alaska law offers no remedy" to those who belatedly seek DNA testing, and in invoking the three-part test used by other state courts, the court indicated that in an appropriate case the State Constitution may provide a failsafe even for those who cannot satisfy the statutory requirements under general postconviction procedures. . . .

To the degree there is some uncertainty in the details of Alaska's newly developing procedures for obtaining postconviction access to DNA, we can hardly fault the State for that. Osborne has brought this §1983 action without ever using these procedures in filing a state or federal habeas claim relying on actual innocence. In other words, he has not tried to use the process provided to him by the State or attempted to vindicate the liberty interest that is now the centerpiece of his claim. When Osborne *did* request DNA testing in state court, he sought RFLP testing that had been available at trial, not the STR testing he now seeks, and the state court relied on that fact in denying him testing under Alaska law. . . .

His attempt to sidestep state process through a new federal lawsuit puts Osborne in a very awkward position. If he simply seeks the DNA through the State's discovery procedures, he might well get it. If he does not, it may be for a perfectly adequate reason, just as the federal statute and all state statutes impose conditions and limits on access to DNA evidence. It is difficult to criticize the State's procedures when Osborne has not invoked them. This is not to say that Osborne must exhaust state-law remedies. . . . But it is Osborne's burden to demonstrate the inadequacy of the state-law procedures available to him in state postconviction relief. . . . These procedures are adequate on their face, and without trying them, Osborne can hardly complain that they do not work in practice.

As a fallback, Osborne also obliquely relies on an asserted federal constitutional right to be released upon proof of "actual innocence." Whether such a federal right exists is an open question. We have struggled with it over the years, in some cases assuming, *arguendo*, that it exists while also noting the difficult questions such a right would pose and the high standard any claimant would have to meet. . . . In this case too we can assume without deciding that such a claim exists, because even if so there is no due process problem. . . .

B

The Court of Appeals below relied only on procedural due process, but Osborne seeks to defend the judgment on the basis of substantive due process as well. He asks that we recognize a freestanding right to DNA evidence untethered from the liberty interests he hopes to vindicate with it. We reject the invitation and conclude, in the circumstances of this case, that there is no such substantive due process right. "As a general matter, the Court has always been reluctant to expand the concept of substantive due process because guideposts for responsible decisionmaking in this unchartered area are scarce and open-ended." . . . Osborne seeks access to state evidence so that he can apply new DNA-testing technology that might prove him innocent. There is no long history of such a right, and "[t]he mere novelty of such a claim is reason enough to doubt that 'substantive due process' sustains it." . . .

And there are further reasons to doubt. The elected governments of the States are actively confronting the challenges DNA technology poses to our criminal justice systems and our traditional notions of finality, as well as the opportunities it affords. To suddenly constitutionalize this area would short-circuit what looks to be a prompt and considered legislative response. . . . In the past decade, 44 States and the Federal Government have followed suit, reflecting the increased availability of DNA testing. As noted, Alaska itself is considering such legislation. . . . "By extending constitutional protection to an asserted right or liberty interest, we, to a great extent, place the matter outside the arena of public debate and legislative action. We must therefore exercise the utmost care whenever we are asked to break new ground in this field." . . . "[J]udicial imposition of a categorical remedy . . . might pretermit other responsible solutions being considered in Congress and state legislatures." . . . If we extended substantive due process to this area, we would cast these statutes into constitutional doubt and be forced to take over the issue of DNA access ourselves. We are reluctant to enlist the Federal Judiciary in creating a new constitutional code of rules for handling DNA.

Establishing a freestanding right to access DNA evidence for testing would force us to act as policymakers, and our substantive-due-process rulemaking authority would not only have to cover the right of access but a myriad of other issues. We would soon have to decide if there is a constitutional obligation to preserve forensic evidence that might later be tested. . . . If so, for how long? Would it be different for different types of evidence? Would the State also have some obligation to gather such evidence in the first place? How much, and when? No doubt there would be a miscellany of other minor directives. . . .

In this case, the evidence has already been gathered and preserved, but if we extend substantive due process to this area, these questions would be before us in short order, and it is hard to imagine what tools federal courts would use to answer them. At the end of the day, there is no reason to suppose that their answers to these questions would be any better than those of state courts and legislatures, and good reason to suspect the opposite. . . .

*   *   *

DNA evidence will undoubtedly lead to changes in the criminal justice system. It has done so already. The question is whether further change will primarily be made by legislative revision and judicial interpretation of the existing system, or whether the Federal Judiciary must leap ahead—revising (or even discarding) the system by creating a new constitutional right and taking over responsibility for refining it.

Federal courts should not presume that state criminal procedures will be inadequate to deal with technological change. The criminal justice system has historically accommodated new types of evidence, and is a time-tested means of carrying out society's interest in convicting the guilty while respecting individual rights. That system, like any human endeavor, cannot be perfect. DNA evidence shows that it has not been. But there is no basis for Osborne's approach of assuming that because DNA has shown that these procedures are not flawless, DNA evidence must be treated as categorically outside the process, rather than within it. That is precisely what

his §1983 suit seeks to do, and that is the contention we reject.

The judgment of the Court of Appeals is reversed, and the case is remanded for further proceedings consistent with this opinion.

It is so ordered.

Note

1. It is not clear whether the Alaska Court of Appeals was correct that Osborne sought *only* forms of DNA testing that had been available at trial, compare *Osborne I, supra*, at 992, 995, with 521 F. 3d 1118, 1123, n. 2 (CA9 2008), but it resolved the case on that basis.

JOHN ROBERTS is the current chief justice of the U.S. Supreme Court. He received an AB from Harvard College in 1976 and a JD from Harvard Law School in 1979. He served as a law clerk for former U.S. Supreme Court Chief Justice William H. Rehnquist during the 1980 term and in various other legal capacities until his appointment to the U.S. Court of Appeals for the District of Columbia Circuit in 2003. President George W. Bush nominated him as chief justice in 2005.

EXPLORING THE ISSUE

Does an Imprisoned Convict Who Claims Innocence Have a Constitutional Right to Access the State's Evidence for DNA Testing?

Critical Thinking and Reflection

1. What is the significance of the "Innocence Project" with respect to wrongful convictions?
2. Should convicted offenders have a constitutional right to conduct DNA tests on evidence presented at their trials, or do state laws provide sufficient protection for these individuals? Explain your answer.

Is There Common Ground?

This is a difficult issue. On one hand, Chief Justice Roberts contends that the states play an important role in the formation of justice system policy that the federal courts should respect. Conversely, it is difficult to imagine how our justice system can live with the realization that innocent persons may be confined for crimes they did not commit, when it is relatively simple to prove the matter conclusively with DNA evidence. It is also important to note that DNA evidence, as compelling as it may be in various cases, may not be infallible. Perhaps the most celebrated case in recent years that has used DNA evidence was the O. J. Simpson murder trial. It appears as though the Simpson jury concluded that the DNA evidence in that case carried little or no weight due to improper collection methods and sloppy laboratory analysis of the evidence.

One factor that may influence the debate about the use of DNA evidence is the extent to which DNA evidence has already been used to exonerate innocent persons who have been incarcerated. The "Innocence Project" is an organization that has worked tirelessly to free wrongfully convicted persons since its founding in 1992 at Yeshiva University by Barry C. Sheck and Peter Neufeld. The nonprofit clinic's stated mission is to "exonerate wrongfully convicted people through DNA testing and [to] reform the criminal justice system to prevent future injustice." Most of the project's clients are indigent and have exhausted all of the traditional legal avenues for relief. The project emphasizes that DNA evidence has "provided scientific proof that our system convicts and sentences innocent people—and that wrongful convictions are not isolated or rare events."

To this point, the Innocence Project has determined the following:

- Seventeen people had been sentenced to death before DNA proved their innocence and led to their release.
- The average sentence served by those who have been exonerated by DNA evidence has been 13 years.
- About 70 percent of those exonerated by DNA testing are members of minority groups.
- In almost 40 percent of DNA exoneration cases, the actual perpetrator has been identified by DNA testing.
- Exonerations have won in 34 states and Washington, D.C. (www.innocenceproject.org)

Thus, it is clear that while the U.S. justice system often does an effective job of balancing important social interests in attaining justice for the victims of crime and the individual rights of suspected criminals, it sometimes makes mistakes. Given this fact and the unprecedented ability of DNA evidence to conclusively establish a person's guilt or innocence, the question then becomes, "What approach should the justice system take in these cases?"

If you agree with Chief Justice John Roberts's assertion that the "task of establishing rules to harness DNA's power to prove innocence without unnecessarily overthrowing the established criminal justice system belongs primarily to the [state] legislature[s]," do you think that the cause of "justice" has been served by the majority's holding in Osborne? Further, do you agree with Chief Justice Roberts's statement that "[t]he elected governments of the

Does an Imprisoned Convict Who Claims Innocence Have a Constitutional Right to Access the State's Evidence for DNA Testing? by Hickey

341

States are actively confronting the challenges DNA technology poses to our criminal justice systems and our traditional notions of finality, as well as the opportunities it affords. To suddenly constitutionalize this area would short-circuit what looks to be a prompt and considered legislative response." Would the Supreme Court's intervention in this area force the Court to "act as policymakers," or is it more important to ensure that justice has been done and free those who are wrongfully accused? As Justice Stevens's opinion emphasizes, do you feel that Osborne "demonstrated a constitutionally protected right to due process that the State of Alaska thus far has not vindicated and which this Court is both empowered and obliged to safeguard"?

Additional Resources

These are contentious issues. Fortunately, there are numerous additional resources to consult for further discussion of these important matters, including Kathleen M. Sullivan and Gerald Gunther, *Constitutional Law* (Foundation Press, 15th ed., 2004); Laurence H. Tribe, *American Constitutional Law* (Foundation Press, 2nd ed., 1988); Simon J. Walsh, *Forensic DNA Evidence Interpretation* (CBC Press, 2004); Ron C. Michaelis, *A Litigator's Guide to DNA: From the Laboratory to the Courtroom* (Academic Press, 2008); John M. Butler, *Forensic DNA Typing: Biology, Technology and Genetics of STR Markers* (Academic Press, 2005); Jay D. Aronson, *Genetic Awareness: Science, Law, and Controversy* (Rutgers University Press, 2007); and David H. Kaye, *The Double Helix and the Law of Evidence* (Harvard University Press, 2010). See also Millard, "*District Attorney's Office for the Third Judicial District v. Osborne*: Leaving Prisoners' Access to DNA Evidence in Limbo?" *Maryland Law Review* (vol. 69, 2010, p. 4); Comment, "Due Process—Postconviction Access to DNA Evidence," *Harvard Law Review* (vol. 123, 2009, p. 222); Cooley, "Advancing DNA Technology and Evolving Standards of Decency," *Charleston Law Review* (vol. 4, 2009, p. 582); Hoeffel, "The Roberts Court's Failed Innocence Project," *Chicago Kent Law Review* (2010); Roach, "The Role of Innocence Commissions: Discovery, Systematic Reform, or Both?" *Chicago Kent Law Review* (2010); and Thornton, "A Second Comment on *Skinner v. Switzer*," *American Criminal Law Review* (2010).

Internet References . . .

Reason

http://reason.com/archives/2009/03/02/does-the
-constitution-grant-a

The Innocence Project

www.innocenceproject.org/Content/The
_Constitutional_Right_to_DNA_Testing_Resources
_in_the_Osborne_Case.php